THE ROUGH GUIDE TO

Cambodia

This fifth edition updated by

Emma Boyle and Gavin Thomas

ROUGH
GUIDES

roughguides.com

Contents

Introduction to
Cambodia

Cambodia is a small country with a big history. Now a modest player on the world stage, this was once the seat of one of Asia's most magnificent early civilizations, the mighty Khmer empire of Angkor, whose legendary temples continue to provide a touchstone of national identity – as well as attracting millions of visitors every year. Away from the temples, much of the country remains refreshingly untouristed and, in many places, largely unexplored.

Cambodia's sleepy **towns** and cities are a delight, with their faded colonial architecture and old-fashioned charm, while in the countryside a host of memorable **landscapes** await, from the mighty Mekong River and great Tonle Sap lake to the remote forested highlands of Rattanakiri, Mondulkiri and the Cardamom Mountains. Down south, in complete contrast, the coast serves up a beguiling cocktail of party-lifestyle hedonism, idyllic beaches and magical islands.

Much of Cambodia's appeal derives from its slightly anachronistic, faintly time-warped character. Compared to the far more populous and economically developed countries of Thailand and Vietnam that hem it in on either side, Cambodia remains an essentially **rural** society, and something of a regional backwater. The country's provincial hinterlands appear to have changed little in generations, offering a refreshing throwback to an older and simpler era (from the outside at least), with beautiful stilted wooden houses set amid a patchwork of rice paddies and sugar palms. And although living standards for most of the population are basic in the extreme, Cambodians as a whole remain among Asia's most friendly and welcoming people.

It's perhaps this warmth and hospitality which most impresses many visitors to Cambodia – and which is all the more astonishing given the country's tragic recent past. For many, Cambodia remains synonymous with the bloody excesses of the murderous **Khmer Rouge** regime, whose delusional leaders succeeded in killing or causing the deaths of perhaps two million or more of their fellow citizens – around twenty percent of the population. Not until 1998 were the Khmer Rouge driven from their final strongholds,

ABOVE WEAVING NEAR BANLUNG; ROYAL PALACE, PHNOM PENH

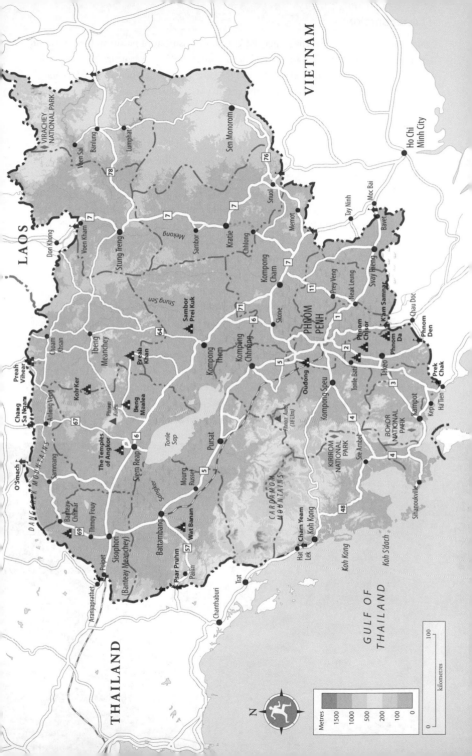

and even now many of their former cadres occupy positions of power and responsibility, not least premier Hun Sen, the nation's leader since 1985. Unsurprisingly, emotional scars from this period run deep and through every layer of Cambodian society – the memory of a nightmare from which the country is only slowly and painfully awakening.

Where to go

Dubbed the "Pearl of Asia" during its colonial heydey, **Phnom Penh** remains one of Southeast Asia's most engaging capitals: big enough (and with sufficient anarchic traffic and urban edge) to get the pulse racing, but still retaining a distinct small-town charm, its tree-lined streets fringed with ramshackle old French-colonial buildings and dotted with rustic temples and bustling markets. The heart of the city is the beautiful riverfront, backdropped by the magnificent Royal Palace and Silver Pagoda's colourful stupas, while the nearby National Museum showcases a stunning collection of ancient Khmer art. Further afield, the contrastingly sombre Toul Sleng Genocide Museum provides harrowing reminders of the country's tragic recent past.

The main reason that most people come to Cambodia, however, is to visit the world-famous **temples of Angkor**. Dozens of magnificent monuments dot the countryside here, rising out of the enveloping forest like the archetypal lost-in-the-jungle ancient ruins of every Hollywood filmmaker's wildest dreams. Top of most visitors' lists are the unforgettable **Angkor Wat**, with its five soaring corncob towers; the surreal **Bayon**, plastered with hundreds of superhuman faces; and the jungle temple of **Ta Prohm**, its crumbling ruins clamped in the grip of giant kapok trees. It's also well worth heading further afield to escape the crowds and visit other Angkorian monuments, including beautiful **Banteay Srei**, covered in an

Author picks

Our intrepid authors spent months researching this latest edition of the *Rough Guide to Cambodia*, travelling ceaselessly in their attempts to unearth the best the country has to offer. Here are a few of their personal favourite experiences.

Running amok The national dish, *amok* (see p.30) offers a quintessential taste of Cambodia. Although no two recipes are the same, the best *amoks* are soothingly mild, with intense lemongrass flavours, seasoned with coconut and galangal and a hint of spice. Try one at *Smile* (see p.214), *Angkor Palm* (see p.150) or *Frizz* (see p.85).

Shopping for kramas Hunting for *kramas* (see p.40) is a great way to explore Cambodia's markets. Kompong Cham market (see p.212), the Angkor Night Market in Siem Reap (see p.154) and Phnom Penh's Russian Market (see p.90) offer fertile *krama*-hunting territory – or visit Phnom Srok (see p.128) to see them being produced.

Lesser-known temples Some of the finest temples are, paradoxically, relatively free from crowds. The magnificent Pre Rup (see p.182) and Bakong (see p.187) see only a fraction of the visitors who overrun Angkor Wat and the Bayon. And for a real Indiana Jones experience, head for the remote temples of Banteay Chhmar (see p.128) and Preah Khan (Kompong Thom) (see p.194).

Taking to the water Lakes and rivers are writ large on the map of Cambodia. Be sure to see the Tonle Sap floating villages (see p.109, p.112 & p.158), go dolphin-watching or kayaking on the Mekong (see p.219 & p.221), or relax on a sunset river cruise in Kampot (see p.270) and Phnom Penh (see p.61).

Desert island paradise It doesn't take much effort to find your own strip of pure white sand on one of Cambodia's idyllic islands. Scene-stealers include Long Set Beach on Koh Rong (see p.259), Lazy Beach on Koh Rong Samloem (see p.260) and Koh Totang's pretty shores (see p.262).

> Our author recommendations don't end here. We've flagged up our favourite places – a perfectly sited hotel, an atmospheric café, a special restaurant – throughout the Guide, highlighted with the ★ symbol.

LEFT MARKET, BATTAMBANG **RIGHT FROM TOP** KOH RONG SAMLOEM; CHICKEN *AMOK*; PREAH KHAN TEMPLE

FACT FILE

• Cambodia is about one and a half times the **size** of England – roughly the same area as the US state of Oklahoma.

• Cambodia's population is just over **15 million**, of which ninety percent is Khmer. The remainder consists of ethnic Chinese and Vietnamese (together around 6 percent), the Cham (2.5 percent) and the chunchiet (1 percent).

• **Theravada Buddhism** is practised by 96 percent of the population, alongside some animism and ancestor worship; the Cham are Muslim.

• Cambodia is a **constitutional monarchy**, with an elected government comprising two houses of parliament, the National Assembly and the Senate.

• Average **annual income** is just $944 per capita, making Cambodia the third poorest country in Asia (after Nepal and Bangladesh – and compared to a per capital income of $5480 in neighbouring Thailand). Average life expectancy, though improving, is just 63 years.

• Cambodia has one of the world's highest rates of **deforestation**, the fifth highest globally, according to recent figures. Primary rainforest cover fell from over 70 percent in 1970 to just 3.1 percent in 2007.

• Cambodia has changed its **name** more frequently than almost any other country in the world. Within the past half-century it's been known variously as the Khmer Republic (1970–75), Democratic Kampuchea (under the Khmer Rouge, 1976–79) and the People's Republic of Kampuchea (1979–89). It's now officially called the Kingdom of Cambodia.

• The **Cambodian flag** is embellished with an image of Angkor Wat – the only national flag in the world with a picture of a building on it.

extravagent flourish of carvings; the jungle-smothered ruins of **Beng Mealea**; the sprawling city-temple complex of **Koh Ker**; and, especially, the magnificent **Preah Vihear**, dramatically situated on top of a mountain above the Thai border. Gateway to the temples is vibrant **Siem Reap** – Cambodia's principal tourist town, but retaining plenty of idiosyncratic charm, and well worth a visit in its own right. From Siem Reap, looping around the great **Tonle Sap lake** – an attraction in itself, home to dozens of remarkable floating villages – brings you to **Battambang**, one of the country's most engaging cities.

Cambodia's **east** retains something of a frontier atmosphere, with the majestic Mekong River bounding one side of the region and the remote highlands of Rattanakiri and Mondulkiri to the west. All routes into the region pass through the atmospheric colonial-era Mekong-side town of **Kompong Cham**, beyond which the road continues north along the river to **Kratie** with a similarly languid riverside ambience and a small population of rare Irrawaddy dolphins just upstream. Getting out to the remote northeastern provincial capitals of **Banlung** and **Sen Monorom** takes more time and effort but is worth it for a sight of Cambodia's remote forested uplands which (despite rampant logging) remain home to abundant wildlife and the nation's ever-diminishing indigenous chunchiet communities.

A world away in scenery and atmosphere from pretty much everywhere else in the country, Cambodia's rapidly developing **coast** offers an increasingly upbeat and hedonistic taste of tropical beach life. The biggest and busiest town here is **Sihanoukville**, looking increasingly like a miniature slice of Thailand, with beaches and bars aplenty. Just offshore lies a string of more tranquil (though also rapidly developing) islands, while just outside Sihanoukville are the idyllic bays, beaches and

RIGHT BANTEAY SREI

mangrove forests of the lush **Ream National Park**. Quieter coastal destinations include attractive **Kampot**, with its mixed French and Chinese influences, and the beguiling resort of **Kep**, with a minuscule beach and atmosphere of faded gentility. Backdropping the heavily touristed coast, the contrastingly remote and difficult-to-reach **Cardamom Mountains**, best accessed from the southwestern province of **Koh Kong**, provide unspoilt upland scenery and pockets of remarkable biodiversity.

When to go

Cambodia is warm all year round, though there are several distinct seasons. There is little rain between November and May, the so-called **dry season**, which itself divides into two distinct phases. The **cool season** (Nov–Feb) is the peak time for tourism – mild enough to explore the temples in comfort but warm enough to sunbathe by the coast. Humidity and temperatures rise slightly during the **hot season** (March–May), with Phnom Penh and Battambang seeing peak daytime temperatures of 33–35°C. This is an excellent time to hit the coast, although Angkor is usually bakingly hot. Visiting during the **rainy season** (roughly June–Oct) can present certain practical challenges, but it is also a fascinating time to see the country as it transforms into a waterlogged expanse of tropical green under the daily monsoon deluges (fortunately, the rains falls mainly in the afternoon; mornings are generally dry). Getting around (particularly in September and October) isn't always easy: dirt roads turn to mud and flooding is commonplace. Not surprisingly it's also the quietest time for tourism (even Angkor is relatively quiet) and the countryside is at its lushest.

18

things not to miss

It's not possible to see everything that Cambodia has to offer in one trip – and we don't suggest you try. What follows is a selective and subjective taste of the country's highlights: natural attractions and cultural treasures, serene beaches and vibrant towns, and – of course – the finest of the temples at Angkor and elsewhere. Each highlight has a page reference to take you straight into the Guide, where you can find out more. Coloured numbers refer to chapters in the Guide section.

1

ROYAL PALACE AND SILVER PAGODA
Page 61

The extravagant Royal Palace and Silver Pagoda, in the heart of Phnom Penh, are home to fabulous murals and a treasure-trove of Khmer sculpture.

KAMPOT
Page 267

Blissfully unhurried southern backwater with a plethora of idyllic guesthouses and restaurants beside the Kampot River.

BANTEAY SREI
Page 188

One of the smallest but most perfect of all Angkor's temples, constructed from delicate rose-pink sandstone and covered in a positive riot of intricate carvings.

ANGKOR WAT
Page 165

This unforgettable temple, crowned with soaring towers and embellished with intricate bas-reliefs, represents the zenith of Khmer architecture.

5 OTRES BEACH
Page 249

Sihanoukville's furthest flung beach is mellower (and prettier) than its sandy in-town siblings; perfect for a few days of idle beachcombing.

10

6 IRRAWADDY DOLPHINS
Page 219
These rare mammals live in small groups along a stretch of the Mekong in the northeast.

7 TOUL SLENG AND CHOEUNG EK
Pages 71 & 99
Harrowing monuments to Cambodia's grisly past during the Khmer Rouge's murderous rule.

8 ANGKOR THOM
Page 171
Angkor's greatest walled city, entered through magnificent gateways and housing some of the country's finest monuments, including the haunting Bayon.

9 KHMER ART
Pages 67 & 142
Some of the country's most stunning art, including ancient statues, are on display in Phnom Penh's National Museum and the Angkor National Museum in Siem Reap.

10 APSARA
Page 154
Khmer classical dance at its most elegantly stylized, with beautifully costumed performers evoking the legendary apsaras of Hindu mythology.

11 TONLE SAP LAKE
Page 156
The watery heart of rural Cambodia, this miniature inland sea is dotted with dozens of traditional floating and stilted villages, many inhabited by the country's ethnic Vietnamese.

CHI PHAT
Page 267
A village community project in the southern Cardamoms offering homestays, birdwatching, mountain biking and trekking.

 WILDLIFE AND BIRDWATCHING
Pages 159, 231 & 238
Walking with the elephants in Mondulkiri, gibbon-spotting in Rattanakiri, birdwatching around the Tonle Sap – Cambodia offers a wealth of natural attractions.

 CAMBODIAN CUISINE
Page 26
Cambodia's cuisine offers plenty of surprises – and there are numerous courses available to help you unravel the secrets of Khmer cooking.

 PSAR TOUL TOM POUNG
Page 90
Wonderful Phnom Penh city market, packed with vibrant silks and curios.

REAM NATIONAL PARK
Page 261
Abundant wildlife, secluded beaches and bays, and the beautiful mangrove-fringed Prek Touek Sap River.

 TREKKING IN RATTANAKIRI
Page 231
Trek into the forested highlands of Rattanakiri, home to tall trees, rare wildlife and the indigenous chunchiet.

PREAH VIHEAR
Page 196
Magnificent Angkor temple on a mountaintop near the Thai border.

Itineraries

Cambodia is a small country by Asian standards, but you'll still need at least a month to really see everything it has to offer. The rapidly improving road network means that it has never been easier to explore, making many formerly remote destinations much more accessible. That said, getting from A to B can still be time-consuming, and the country is best taken at a leisurely pace.

THE GRAND TOUR

Two weeks suffice to get a taste of the best that Cambodia has to offer, from the great temples of Angkor to the hedonistic beaches of the south.

❶ Phnom Penh Acclimatize in the vibrant but endearingly small-scale capital. **See p.50**

❷ Kratie Head to the engagingly somnolent French-colonial town of Kratie for a taste of riverside life next to the magical Mekong, with rare Irrawaddy dolphins, floating villages, river islands and flooded forests aplenty. **See p.216**

❸ Siem Reap and Angkor Settle down to a few days (or more) in lively Siem Reap, exploring the magnificent Angkor temples and the floating villages of the Tonle Sap. **See p.134**

❹ Preah Vihear and further flung temples Venture out to the stunning mountaintop temple of Preah Vihear, perhaps with a side-trip to the jungle temple of Beng Mealea and the vast ruined citadel of Koh Ker. **See p.196**

❺ Battambang Colonial riverside town with laidback nightlife and the quaint bamboo railway. **See p.114**

❻ Sihanoukville and the islands Venture south to Cambodia's coastal party town, a good base for some lovely offshore islands. **See p.247**

❼ Kep's offshore islands Use Kep as a jump-off point for sleepy Rabbit Island (Koh Tonsay), among others. **See p.278**

❽ Kampot Chill out in this pretty, laidback riverside town, a good base for the picturesque surrounding province. **See p.267**

WILD CAMBODIA

Cambodia boasts an outstanding array of natural attractions, from the great Mekong River to remote upland forests.

❶ Kratie Go dolphin-spotting at nearby Kampie, then take to a kayak or bike to explore the marvellous river islands, flooded forests and floating villages of the Mekong. **See p.216**

❷ Banlung Trek into the forests of Viracheay National Park and explore the waterfalls and volcanic lake of Yeak Laom. **See p.228**

❸ Sen Monorom Walk with elephants at the Elephant Valley Project and go birdwatching or gibbon-spotting in the pristine tracts of forest surrounding Sen Monorom. **See p.236**

❹ Beng Mealea Visit the jungle-smothered ruins of Beng Mealea temple – looking much as it must have done when the first Western explorers stumbled upon it a century ago. **See p.191**

❺ Phnom Kulen Discover where the great Angkorian empire began at the remote mountain shrine of Phnom Kulen. **See p.191**

ABOVE RABBIT ISLAND

◑ Tonle Sap Take the ferry from Siem Reap to Battambang across the great Tonle Sap lake, which during the rains becomes the largest freshwater lake in Southeast Asia. **See p.156**

➐ Chi Phat Head to this village in the southern Cardamoms for organized hikes through upland forests to waterfalls and ancient sites. **See p.267**

➑ Ream Spy shore birds and dolphins as you explore the lush mangroves and beaches of this beautiful national park by boat. **See p.261**

UNDISCOVERED CAMBODIA

There might be some two million visitors a year clambering over the ruins of Angkor, but much of Cambodia remains undiscovered.

➊ Stung Treng Rewarding, little-visited stretch of the Cambodian Mekong, complete with dolphins, flooded forests, ancient ruins and spectacular waterfalls. **See p.222**

➋ Tbeng Meanchey Take the new cross-country highway through Cambodia's northern backcountry to the remote provincial capital of Tbeng Meanchey. **See p.195**

➌ Anlong Veng Notorious for its associations with the infamous Pol Pot, the modern boomtown of Anlong Veng provides a fascinatingly bizarre mixture of Khmer Rouge history and contemporary casino chic. **See p.199**

➍ Banteay Chhmar For a truly authentic lost-in-the-jungle temple experience, ride the bumpy road from Sisophon to the vast temple complex of Banteay Chhmar, buried in the forests of Cambodia's far northwest. **See p.128**

➎ Kompong Chhnang For an alternative to the increasingly touristed floating villages of Siem Reap, make for the floating villages just outside Kompong Chhnang. **See p.109**

➏ Angkor Borei Stuffed with statues, ceramics and photographs of the excavations, Angkor Borei's fascinating museum makes the trip to the remains of this Funan-era city highly worthwhile. **See p.280**

➐ Koh S'dach archipelago These picturesque islands offer a truly authentic taste of coastal Cambodia. **See p.262**

➑ Koh Kong: the Areng Valley The biodiverse Areng Valley, deep in the Cardamoms, is home to the endangered Siamese crocodile and prime territory for trekking, kayaking and mountain biking. It's accessible on tours from Koh Kong but you'll need at least four days – better still a week – to do it justice. **See p.265**

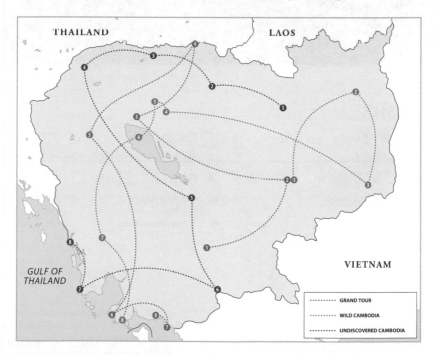

NEGOTIATING A CAMBODIAN ROAD

Basics

Getting there

There are no direct flights to Cambodia from Europe, North America, Australasia or South Africa, so if you plan to fly into the country you'll need to get a connecting flight from elsewhere in Southeast or East Asia.

There are direct flights to **Phnom Penh** from an increasing number of cities in the region including Kuala Lumpur, Singapore, Seoul, Bangkok, Vientiane, Ho Chi Minh City, and several cities in China (including frequent connections with Hong Kong). Alternatively, it's also possible to fly direct to **Siem Reap** from Singapore, Bangkok, Ho Chi Minh City, Kuala Lumpur and a number of other Asian destinations.

Flights from the UK and Ireland

There are plenty of daily flights, many nonstop, from **London Heathrow** to Southeast Asian cities, with some airlines offering connections to Phnom Penh. Flight times vary depending on routing. The most direct route is via Bangkok (around 11–12hr from London, plus another 1hr on to Phnom Penh), followed by Kuala Lumpur and Ho Chi Minh City (Saigon). There are also a growing number of connections via the Gulf, although these will entail at least two stops. From **Ireland**, it's a matter of either getting a cheap connection to London Heathrow or flying to Cambodia via a different European (or possibly Gulf) hub.

Thai Airways (Ⓦthaiairways.com), Singapore Airlines (Ⓦsingaporeair.com) and Malaysia Airlines (Ⓦmalaysia-airlines.com) offer some of the most competitive fares to Cambodia, with return fares to Phnom Penh starting at around £650.

Flights from the US and Canada

Flying from the **east coast** of North America to Cambodia it's quickest to travel via Europe. Conversely, from the **west coast** it may well be quicker and cheaper to fly westward via an Asian city such as Seoul or Taipei (the latter has direct connections to Phnom Penh on EVA Air; Ⓦevaair .com). There are daily flights from New York and Los Angeles to Bangkok, Hong Kong, Kuala Lumpur and Singapore, all of which have onward connections to Phnom Penh. Fares from both the east and west coasts to Phnom Penh start from around US$1500. **From Canada**, low-season return fares from Toronto to Phnom Penh start at around Can$2000, and Can$1500 return from Vancouver.

Flights from Australia, New Zealand and South Africa

There's a wide selection of flights from **Australia and New Zealand** to Bangkok, Kuala Lumpur, Singapore and Ho Chi Minh City, with onward connections to Phnom Penh and Siem Reap. Return fares from Australia to Phnom Penh start at around Aus$1000; from Auckland, Christchurch and Wellington flights start from roughly NZ$2000.

Travelling from **South Africa** to Cambodia via an Asian hub city, fares start at around ZAR12,000 return.

Round-The-World flights

If Cambodia is only one stop on a longer journey, you might want to consider buying a **Round-The-World (RTW)** ticket. Cambodia can be added to itineraries offered by airline consortium Star Alliance (Ⓦstaralliance.com) for example. Bangkok or Singapore are more common ports of call for many RTW tickets; from the UK, figure on around £1000 plus taxes for an RTW ticket including either of these destinations.

Getting there from neighbouring countries

There are numerous land borders into Cambodia open to foreigners from neighbouring Thailand, Vietnam and Laos. **Visas** at all are issued on arrival (see p.48).

A BETTER KIND OF TRAVEL

At Rough Guides we are passionately committed to travel. We believe it helps us understand the world we live in and the people we share it with – and of course tourism is vital to many developing economies. But the scale of modern tourism has also damaged some places irreparably, and climate change is accelerated by most forms of transport, especially flying. All Rough Guides' flights are carbon-offset, and every year we donate money to a variety of environmental charities.

From Thailand

There are currently six border crossings between Cambodia and **Thailand** open to foreigners. All are open daily (7am–8pm) with visas being issued on arrival at all points; although **e-visas** (see p.48) are currently only accepted at Poipet and Koh Kong.

Far and away the most popular of the six crossings is the mildly infamous crossing at **Poipet**, on the main highway between Bangkok and Siem Reap (see p.130). The Trat/**Koh Kong** crossing further south (see p.264) is good for Sihanoukville and Phnom Penh. There are two further crossings in the east at Ban Pakard/**Pailin (Psar Pruhm)**, an hour by road to Battambang, and at Ban Leam/**Daun Lem** (although this crossing is basically a casino development in the middle of nowhere, and of zero practical use unless you're on a visa run from Bangkok). Finally, there are two remote and little-used (by foreigners at least) crossing points in northern Cambodia at Surin/**O'Smach**, and Chong Sa Ngam/**Anlong Veng** – both 150km north of Siem Reap (2hr by taxi). These are not busy crossing points though, so your transport options on the Cambodian side will be limited.

From Vietnam

There are currently seven border crossings open to foreigners travelling overland from **Vietnam** (daily 7am–5pm); Cambodian visas are issued on arrival at all points, although heading into Vietnam you'll need to have acquired a visa in advance. The busiest crossing is at Moc Bai/**Bavet** (see p.103), 200km southeast of Phnom Penh on the main road to Ho Chi Minh City. Also popular is the crossing at Chau Doc/**K'am Samnar** (see p.103) on the Bassac River. There are two further border crossings in the south at Tinh Bien/**Phnom Den** near Takeo, and at Hat Tien/**Prek Chak** east of Kep, plus three little-used crossings in eastern Cambodia (see p.211) at Xa Mat/**Trapeang Phlong** east of Kompong Cham; Loc Ninh/**Trapeang Sre**, southeast of Snuol, and Le Tanh/**O Yadow**, east of Banlung.

From Laos

There's just one border crossing with **Laos**, at Nong Nok Khiene/**Trapeang Kriel** (see p.224) in the far north of Cambodia, 57km beyond Stung Treng. The border is open daily (7am–5pm) and both Cambodian and Lao visas are available on arrival.

Tour operators

If you want to avoid the hassle of making your own arrangements you might consider travelling with a specialist tour operator. However, although Cambodia is well covered, many tour companies still include it only as part of a visit to another Southeast Asian country. Tour prices start at around £500 for land-only options; those that include international flights tend to be £1200 to £1500, while choosing luxury accommodation and specialist activities, such as golfing, can set you back more than £4000.

Agents and operators

AGENTS

North South Travel UK ☎ 01245 608 291, ⓦ northsouthtravel .co.uk. Friendly, competitive travel agency, offering discounted fares worldwide. Profits are used to support projects in the developing world, especially the promotion of sustainable tourism.

STA Travel UK ☎ 0333 321 0099, US ☎ 1800 781 4040, Australia ☎ 134 782, New Zealand ☎ 0800 474 400, South Africa ☎ 0861 781 781, ⓦ statravel.co.uk. Worldwide specialists in independent travel; also student IDs, travel insurance, car rental, rail passes, and more. Good discounts for students and under-26s.

Trailfinders UK ☎ 0207 368 1200, Ireland ☎ 021 464 8800, ⓦ trailfinders.com. One of the best-informed and most efficient agents for independent travellers.

Travel CUTS Canada ☎ 1800 667 2887, ⓦ travelcuts.com. Canadian youth and student travel firm.

USIT Ireland ☎ 01 602 1906, ⓦ usit.ie. Ireland's main student and youth travel specialists.

SPECIALIST TOUR OPERATORS

Adventure Center US ☎ 1 800 228 8747, ⓦ adventurecenter .com. Wide range of competitively priced Cambodia tours.

Audley Travel UK ☎ 01993 838000, ⓦ audleytravel.com. Off-the-peg or customized tours, plus an interesting choice of escorted group tours.

Cambodia Community Based Ecotourism Network ⓦ ccben .org. Cambodian organization offering homestays and visits to ecotourism sites throughout the country.

Exotissimo Travel Cambodia SSN Center no. 66, Norodom Blvd, Phnom Penh ☎ 023 218 948, ⓦ cambodia.exotissimo.com. Long-standing operator offering a range of soft adventure tours and visiting places other tour companies don't usually reach.

Explore! UK ☎ 0843 634 5321, US ☎ 1 800 715 1746, Canada ☎ 1 888 216 3401, Australia ☎ 1300 439 756, New Zealand ☎ 0800 269 263, ⓦ explore.co.uk. Small-group operator offering a good selection of tours including soft adventure trips.

Gecko's UK ☎ 0808 274 5981, ⓦ geckosadventures.com. Grassroots trips using local guides with plenty of competitively priced tours starting at less than £500 for twelve days.

Geographic Expeditions US ☎ 1 800 777 8183, ⓦ geoex.com. Luxury customized and small-group tours including Angkor jaunts alongside more off-the-beaten-track offerings including Cardamom Mountains village homestays.

Intrepid Travel UK ☎ 0808 274 5111, US ☎ 1 510 285 0604, Australia ☎ 1300 364 512, ⓦ intrepidtravel.com. Southeast Asia specialist with an impressive choice of Cambodia offerings and an emphasis on low-impact tourism.

Khiri Travel B-Ray Tower, 166 Norodom Blvd, Tonle Bassac, Phnom Penh ☎ 023 215 970, ⓦ khiri.com. Indochina specialists offering many unique Cambodian experiences including visits to the Kep crab market and elephant trekking in Mondulkiri.

Noble Caledonia UK ☎ 020 7752 0000, ⓦ noble-caledonia .co.uk. Pricey boat tours boarding in the Vietnamese Delta, cruising the Mekong to Phnom Penh and Kompong Cham, exploring the Tonle Sap and finally disembarking at Siem Reap for the temples of Angkor.

Peregrine UK & Republic of Ireland ☎ 0808 274 5438, ⓦ peregrineadventures.com. Reasonably priced Southeast Asian tours, mostly combining Cambodia with a neighbouring country – one interesting option is the Saigon to Angkor Cycle. Pedalling through Cambodia may be challenging, but you'll get fit and see plenty of local life along the way.

Responsibletravel.com UK ☎ 01273 823 700, ⓦ responsibletravel.com. Online travel agent with an extensive range of Cambodia tours from different companies, all with an ethical emphasis.

See Cambodia Differently ☎ 0208 150 5150, ⓦ seecambodiadifferently.com. Cambodian specialists offering moderately priced group and customized tours, including an excellent selection of wildlife-themed trips.

Silk Steps UK ☎ 01278 722460, ⓦ silksteps.co.uk. Bespoke, reasonably priced tours to Cambodia with suggested itineraries to help you build your own trip.

Trans Indus UK ☎ 0208 566 3739, ⓦ transindus.co.uk. Leading Asia specialists with a choice of private and group tours including fine Mekong river cruises and a wider-than-average range of destinations.

Travel Indochina UK ☎ 01865 268 940, ⓦ travelindochina.co.uk. Affordable group tours lasting from five to eighteen days – the Highlights of Cambodia tour offers a handy and affordable introduction to the country in just seven days.

Urban Adventures ☎ 0788 570 8828, ⓦ urbanadventures.com. Part of the Intrepid travel group, offering a number of well-guided city tours from Phnom Penh and Siem Reap.

Getting around

Getting around Cambodia is all part of the adventure. Massive improvements to the national highway network in the past few years have made getting around the country much easier than it once was, with many formerly dirt roads now surfaced and new highways built. Even so, getting from A to B remains time-consuming: roads are still narrow and bumpy, while regular wet-season inundations play havoc with transport (and often wash away large sections of tarmac in their wake).

Note that travel can be difficult over **public holidays**, especially the Khmer New Year (see p.38). On New Year's Eve everyone heads for their home village and all available transport heads out of town – even more packed than usual. Phnom Penh in particular becomes very quiet, with hardly a moto or tuk-tuk available, and the few that remain make a killing by doubling their fares.

By plane

Cambodia Angkor Air (ⓦ cambodiaangkorair.com) is the nearest thing Cambodia currently has to a national airline and operates the country's only domestic flights, with services between Phnom Penh, Siem Reap and Sihanoukville (around $70 return), from Siem Reap to Ho Chi Minh City, and also from Phnom Penh to Hanoi, Saigon and Bangkok. Note that from Phnom Penh and Siem Reap there's a $6 departure tax for domestic flights.

By bus

Buses (*laan tom*) are the cheapest – and also usually the most convenient and comfortable – way to get around Cambodia, connecting all major cities and towns (although some smaller places aren't yet on the bus network, and others – Banlung, Sen Monorom and Pailin, for example – have only one or two services a day). Many services start in Phnom Penh, meaning that you'll most likely have to go through the capital if travelling from one side of the country to the other.

All buses are **privately run**, operated by a growing number of companies. Phnom Penh Sorya is the biggest; others include Rith Mony, GST, Paramount Angkor and Capitol Tours, while other companies such as Giant Ibis and Mekong Express operate luxury express buses on the most popular routes.

Buses generally arrive and depart from their respective **company offices**. Unfortunately, this means there are no bus stations or suchlike in which to get centralized information about timetables and fares. Some guesthouses or tour operators can provide this information; otherwise you'll have to visit all the individual offices. To guarantee a seat, buy your **ticket** the day before; no standing passengers are allowed, so if all the seats have been sold you'll have to wait for the next bus with space.

Fares are very reasonable, starting from just $4 from Phnom Penh to Sihanoukville and $6 to Siem Reap, and are generally much of a muchness on all but the most-travelled routes. All buses are reasonably comfortable, while on popular routes you'll

TOP 5 JOURNEYS

The bamboo railway, Battambang
See p.116

Boat trips on the Tonle Sap See p.157

Cycling around the Angkor temples
See p.190

Kayaking along the Mekong See p.221

Safaris by boat in Ream National Park
See p.262

find more expensive deluxe coaches (Giant Ibis is one of the main operators) with modern vehicles, free snacks and even on-board wi-fi.

By minibus

Minibuses, which leave from local transport stops, provide the main alternative to buses, at a similar price. These generally serve the same routes as buses, and also go to smaller destinations not served by bus. They also tend to be slightly faster. On the downside, most usually get absolutely packed and can be horribly uncomfortable, especially for taller travellers (there's little legroom at the best of times, unlike on the buses, which are relatively luxurious in comparison).

There are also a few **"luxury minibus"** services on the main intercity and international routes (Mekong Express's "limousine bus" services, for example), although these get mixed reviews, and you can never be entirely certain of what you're getting until it's possibly too late.

By shared taxi and pick-up

Shared taxis are the third main option when it comes to travelling by road. These are generally slightly more expensive but also somewhat faster than buses and minibuses, although the driving can often be hair-raising, especially if you're sat in the front. They also serve local destinations off the bus and minibus network. On the downside, like minibuses they get absurdly packed: three people on the front passenger seat is the norm (with the driver sharing his seat as well), and four in the back. You can pay double the standard fare to have the whole front seat to yourself, and you can hire the entire taxi for around five or six times the individual fare. Shared taxis usually leave from the local transport stop. There are no fixed schedules, although most run in the morning, leaving when (very) full.

Pick-up trucks cover some of the country's most off-the-beaten-track routes, and also roads that are impassable by buses and minibuses, although they're gradually becoming obsolete thanks to the improving network. Seats in the cab – four in the rear, two in the front – cost roughly the same as in a shared taxi; and, as in taxis, you can pay for an extra seat if you want more comfort. Sitting on the **back of a pick-up** is the cheapest way to get around, costing around half the price of seats inside, though you'll have to sit on (or fit around) the goods being transported, and you risk being bounced around with nothing much to grab hold of. Take plenty of water and a sense of humour, and dust-proof your face by wrapping it in a scarf or *krama*.

By boat

For years, Cambodia's appalling roads meant travelling **by boat** was the principal means of getting between Phnom Penh and Siem Reap, but these days it's easier and quicker to travel by road. Even so, boats (seating about thirty people) still run daily between Phnom Penh (see p.77) and Siem Reap (see p.144), as well as Siem Reap and Battambang (see p.118). The trip to or from Phnom Penh isn't particularly scenic, as the Tonle Sap lake is so vast it's more like being at sea. The trip to or from Battambang is more interesting, combining a trip across the Tonle Sap with a journey down the Sangker River. Neither journey is particularly comfortable: space and movement are restricted, and a cushion, plenty of water, food and a hat will make things more bearable. Be aware that in rough weather the Tonle Sap can whip up some fierce waves.

Boats run daily south along the Mekong between Phnom Penh and the Vietnamese border at **Chau Doc** – this can be arranged via local guesthouses. From **Sihanoukville** in the south regular ferries and fast catamarans depart a few times a day to Koh Rong, with a few continuing on to the neighbouring island of Koh Rong Samloem.

By train

Cambodia's colonial-era **railway network** formerly consisted of two lines, one connecting Phnom Penh with Battambang and Poipet, and the other linking the capital with Kampot and Sihanoukville. The tracks were largely destroyed during the Khmer Rouge period, however, and there have been no passenger services since 2009. In the same year, a major railway renovation programme was launched with Australian assistance. The line south to Sihanoukville was reopened to freight services in 2012, although the project subsequently hit major (possibly terminal) delays, and it seems unlikely that any passenger services will be launched for the next two or three years – possibly a lot longer. In the meantime the only way of getting on the rails is to take a ride on Battambang's quirky **"bamboo railway"** (see p.116).

By car

It's virtually impossible to rent a **self-drive car** in Cambodia, and even if you do, driving yourself entails numerous headaches. **Problems** include finding appropriate documentation (your driving licence from home may or may not be considered sufficient – some companies will ask for a Cambodian driving licence, for which you'll need to take a driving test) haphazard driving by other road users; and insufficient insurance – any loss or damage to the vehicle is your responsibility.

The lack of designated car parks is another real problem. Whenever you park you should get someone to look after the vehicle; in town you'll usually find a parking attendant near markets and restaurants who will keep an eye on the vehicle for 1000 riel. It's normal to park as directed and leave the handbrake disengaged so that the car can be pushed out of the way to let other cars in or out. To prevent theft and damage when leaving the vehicle overnight, you'll need to look for a hotel with parking or find a local with off-road space where they'll let you park for a few dollars. Given all this, it's far less hassle, and probably cheaper, to hire a **car and driver** (see p.25).

By motorbike or bicycle

Both **cycling** and renting a **motorbike** are popular ways to explore Cambodia, though even with the improved road conditions, poor driving by other motorists makes it safer to travel only in daylight hours. Whether you ride a motorbike or bicycle, it's worth wearing sunglasses, long trousers and a long-sleeved shirt to protect you not only from the sun but also from the grit and gravel thrown up on the dusty roads.

When heading off into the countryside, remember that Cambodia (in spite of clearance programmes) has a huge problem with **land mines**, and no matter how tempting it may be to go cross-country, stick to well-used tracks and paths.

Motorbike rental

You can rent an **off-road 250cc bike** from a number of companies, particularly in Phnom Penh (see p.79), although you'll have to leave your passport as security. Check the condition of the bike before heading off on a long trip – if it breaks down, it's your responsibility to get it repaired or returned to the owner. Away from the main highways take advice on local road conditions, as often even relatively short distances can take a long time. Motorcycle **helmets** are compulsory (for the driver only) and you risk being stopped by the police and issued with a spot fine ($5) if you're not wearing one. Note that road checks are particularly prevalent just before holidays and the weekend.

Motorbike theft, in Sihanoukville and the south in particular, is a real issue. The bike's **security** is your responsibility, so look to rent from a company that provides installed wheel locks and always make sure you leave it somewhere secure when you stop – at night guesthouses will often bring it inside for you.

Foreigners cannot rent motorbikes in **Siem Reap**. Originally safety was given as the reason for the ban, but it's more likely to be a protectionist move to keep the moto "mafias" in business. In other towns it's easiest to use the **110cc run-arounds** available for rent from guesthouses and hire shops; rates are around $5–8 per day.

Cycling

Cycling in Cambodia can be a rewarding experience – the Mekong Discovery Trail (see p.218), for example, positively invites you to explore on two wheels. Bicycles are available for rent at many guesthouses and rental shops in towns for around $1.50–3 per day, although what you get **varies** considerably from swish mountain bikes to sturdy but gearless affairs.

The main **hazard** is the heavy traffic on the highways – it's essential to note that all motorized traffic takes precedence over bicycles, and you may find you have to veer onto the verge to get out of the way of speeding cars and trucks. You'd be advised to try to get to your destination by late afternoon since many Cambodian vehicles travel without lights and so won't see you as darkness falls.

City and town transport

When travelling around Cambodian towns and cities you will most likely use either a *romorque*,

ADDRESSES

Finding your way around towns in Cambodia is generally easy as most of them are laid out on a **grid plan**. Nearly all towns have street signs; usually a few main streets have names, with the majority being numbered. Despite that, most Cambodians have little idea of street numbers, so to locate a specific address you're best off heading for a nearby landmark and asking from there.

generally known as a **tuk-tuk** (a passenger carriage pulled by a motorbike) or a **moto** or motorbike taxi (a small motorbike-cum-moped with a space in front of the driver for baggage). In Phnom Penh you'll also find **cyclos**, Cambodia's version of the bicycle rickshaw, though these are less and less common. When travelling by any of these forms of transport, it's important to always **agree the fare beforehand**. In Phnom Penh you'll rarely pay less than $2 for a tuk-tuk (motos and cyclos are cheaper), but elsewhere a short journey around town by moto or tuk-tuk will typically cost $1, or $2 for longer journeys.

Motos and tuk-tuks are also useful for short **tours** and trips out of many towns (especially around the temples of Angkor, where tuk-tuks are the most commonly used form of transport) – we've given estimated costs throughout the Guide. Fares for longer hire periods will vary depending on what sort of mileage you'll be doing and the state of the roads you'll be travelling along.

City taxis are available in Phnom Penh and Siem Reap.

Motos

Motorbike taxis, or **motos**, are the staple means of travelling short (and sometimes long) distances in Cambodia, although riding on the back of a moto in the middle of anarchic traffic isn't everybody's idea of fun – and bag-snatchings do occur (see p.36) – so you may feel safer taking a tuk-tuk or taxi. Moto drivers tend to congregate around transport stops, major local landmarks and road junctions within towns, and they may well offer their services as you walk down the street.

If you have **bags**, the driver will squeeze them into the space between his knees and the handlebars – moto drivers are adept at balancing baggage, from rice sacks to backpacks, between their legs while negotiating chaotic traffic. Passengers ride pillion behind the driver – Cambodians typically squeeze on as many passengers as possible (three is common), although it's best not to follow their example and to stick to just one passenger per bike (in Siem Reap, motos are

forbidden from taking more than one foreigner at a time). Although you'll see Cambodian women sitting side-saddle, it's safer if you sit astride and, if necessary, hang onto the driver.

Motos can be taken on quite long trips **out of town** – indeed it's the only way to get to some places, although it's not particularly comfortable. You'll probably have to pay for fuel in addition to the day hire. In the provinces drivers are sometimes irrationally fearful of bandits and can be reluctant to travel in remote areas late in the day, so bear their concerns in mind when planning your excursions.

Tuk-tuks

Pricier than motos, **tuk-tuks** were introduced to Cambodia in 2001, when police in Siem Reap banned foreigners riding three-up on a moto. They have since caught on in a big way and are now found in most provincial towns. Pulled by a motorbike, these covered passenger cabs seat up to four people and, with their drop-down side-curtains, have the advantage of affording some protection against the sun and rain. The motorbikes that pull them, however, are the same ones used as motos, and so are woefully underpowered, which makes for a slow trip, especially if you've got three or four people on board – even with just one or two passengers they can struggle to go much faster than your average bicycle.

Cyclos

A dying breed, found only in Phnom Penh, and decreasingly so there, the **cyclo** (pronounced *see-klo*, from the French – *cyclopousse*) is much slower than a moto or tuk-tuk. They are good for leisurely rides and views of the street but more or less useless for longer journeys or if you want to get anywhere in a hurry. Cyclos take one passenger (or two at a squash) in a seat at the front, with the driver perched on a seat behind over the rear wheel.

City taxis

Both Phnom Penh and Siem Reap have **city taxis** (as opposed to shared taxis). These don't tout for fares on the streets but instead congregate outside major hotels or, in the capital, on the riverfront. In Phnom Penh you can order one by phone (see p.79); fares are around $4–8 per journey.

In other towns you'll need to find a **car and driver**. These can be hired for both short hops around town and long journeys (expect to pay around $40 per day for running around town, or $40–80 for an out-of-town trip, depending on how far you plan to travel).

Organized tours

If you're short on time, or simply don't want to do it yourself, then you might consider an **organized tour**, which can get you around the country to the major sights with minimum effort. An increasing number of travel agencies and tour operators in Phnom Penh (see p.77) and Siem Reap (see p.145) arrange individual tours offering a convenient if relatively expensive way of seeing the country – allow upwards of $120 per person per day, excluding food.

Accommodation

Finding accommodation is seldom a problem. Phnom Penh, Siem Reap and Sihanoukville all have plenty of accommodation in all categories, and even smaller towns usually have a reasonable choice of guesthouses and a couple of modest hotels.

In most towns **touts** meet incoming transport and will take you free of charge to their favourite establishment; if you don't like it, feel free to go elsewhere. Sometimes tuk-tuk and moto drivers get a dollar or so in commission for dropping you off at a particular guesthouse – this premium may be added to your room rate. In Sihanoukville some drivers may resist taking you to a guesthouse of your choice, asserting that it has closed or is full of prostitutes or some such excuse in the hope of being able to take you to a place that pays them commission. Mostly, however, they're just keen to introduce themselves and to secure work driving or guiding you for the duration of your stay. If you've

TOP 5 BOUTIQUE HOTELS

The 252, Phnom Penh See p.81
Knai Bang Chatt, Kep See p.276
The Pavilion, Phnom Penh See p.82
Sala Lodges, Siem Reap See p.148
Terres Rouges Lodge, Banlung See p.231

booked accommodation in advance, some hotels and guesthouses will send someone to pick you up from the bus, boat or plane for no extra charge.

Note that **camping** in Cambodia is technically illegal and also potentially dangerous due to the risk of land mines.

Budget accommodation

Budget accommodation in Cambodia is generally excellent value, available in a range of guesthouses and hotels (note that many places which call themselves guesthouses are actually more like small hotels). Most places are functional concrete boxes, rather lacking in character, although a few livelier establishments geared towards Western backpackers can be found in the major tourist centres. Sihanoukville and the islands have a plethora of bungalow resorts; these are very simple timber affairs (usually with shutters rather than glass windows) perhaps with a fan (although this is rare on the islands), that can cost as little as $5 for a simple room.

Most budget rooms **cost** in the region of $7 a night (slightly more in Phnom Penh and Siem Reap) and are usually clean and tidy with cotton sheet(s), basic toiletries and towels, a TV and ceiling fan, and sometimes with optional air conditioning for an extra $5 or so a night. A lot of budget guesthouses and hotels also have fancier rooms with air conditioning for around $15 a night. Virtually all except the very cheapest budget rooms come with en-suite **bathroom** with Western-style toilet and sometimes hot water as well. **Wi-fi** is now available in the vast majority of places, although **mosquito nets** are only rarely provided – bring your own.

A few places also have **dorm beds**, typically costing around $3–10 per night, and there are a

Accommodation **prices** throughout the Guide are based on the cost of the cheapest **double room** or **dorm bed** available at each particular establishment in high season (Nov–Feb). Prices tend to fall during the rainy season (June–Oct), particularly at more upmarket places, where rates can drop by up to a third.

VILLAGE HOMESTAYS

An increasing number of off-the-beaten-track destinations in Cambodia are now organizing **village homestays**, offering visitors the chance to experience traditional rural life at first hand. Homestays typically provide simple but comfortable accommodation in a local house, with traditional Khmer meals included. Homestays are usually sold as part of integrated tour packages, often including transport along with various activities that might include walking or cycling tours, wildlife spotting or the chance to explore the culture of your host village and interact with the locals. Rewarding homestays include those at the Mekong villages of Koh Pdao and Koh Preah (see box, p.220); at the Dei Ey Forest Experience near Sen Monorom (p.239); at the magnificient Banteay Chhmar temple (p.130); and at Chi Phat in the southern Cardamom Mountains (p.267).

---

couple of hostels in Siem Reap. On the islands a number of establishments offer hammocks for a few dollars, and tents ($6–25), the most expensive of which are crafted into spacious "rooms".

Note that you might also be able to bargain down your room rate if you're going to be staying in one guesthouse/hotel for a few nights or longer, especially in more downmarket places.

Mid-range and luxury

Mid-range (roughly $25–75 per night) and luxury ($75 and upwards per night) accommodation is found only in major towns and tourist hotspots. **Mid-range** accommodation ranges from smart business-style hotels to lower-end boutique hotels and resorts. Facilities are often not significantly different from those in more expensive rooms in budget hotels and guesthouses (with a/c, hot water, minibar and perhaps tea- and coffee-making facilities), although rooms are likely to be more comfortably and stylishly furnished, and you'll probably also get a pool plus in-house restaurant and perhaps other facilities including a gym or spa. Breakfast may also be included in the price.

Luxury accommodation is widely available in Phnom Penh, Siem Reap, Battambang, Sihanoukville and Kep, with even a few places elsewhere. It's worth making a reservation if you want to stay somewhere particular, and you should always check online for special deals. Accommodation in this price bracket ranges from international five-star chain hotels through to chic boutique hotels and idyllic resorts constructed in traditional Khmer style. Many top-end establishments offer memorable style and luxury at far lower prices than you might pay in other Asian countries, although rates at the very best places still commonly run into hundreds of dollars per night.

At more expensive places be sure to check whether **government tax and service** are included in the rack rate, as these can add as much as twenty percent onto the bill.

Food and drink

Many Cambodian dishes are variations on food from other Asian countries, especially China, on which Khmer cuisine draws heavily. Cambodian food isn't particularly spicy, although it's often delicately flavoured with herbs such as lemongrass and coriander.

Food is traditionally cooked in a single pot or wok over a charcoal stove; although gas burners are being introduced in the cities, many people prize the smoky flavour that food acquires when it's cooked over charcoal. A lot of dishes are fried in palm oil and aren't drained before serving, so can be quite greasy; if you're **vegetarian** it's worth being aware that the pan is seldom washed out between cooking the meat and vegetable dishes.

As in many countries where rice is the staple food, the most common way to refer to eating in Cambodia is **nyam bai**, literally "eat rice".

Where to eat

The cheapest food in Cambodia (around $0.50–1.50) is available from **street hawkers**, who ply the streets with their handcarts or baskets dangling from a shoulder pole loaded up with offerings ranging from fried noodles and baguettes, which you can enjoy from as little as $0.50, through to fresh fruit and ice cream. The country's **markets** are another good source of cheap food, open both day and night (though often in separate locations) and with stalls selling a variety of dishes and desserts at prices only slightly higher than those charged by street hawkers. Each stall usually has its own speciality, and you can order from any stall in the market irrespective of where you're sitting. When you've finished, you pay the stall closest to you for the whole lot and they'll sort out the money among themselves.

Noodle shops and cheap restaurants can be found all over town centres and are especially plentiful around markets and transport stops. **Noodle shops** (*haang geautieuv*) open around 5.30am for the breakfast trade, serving various noodle soups, along with dumplings and rice porridge in the larger establishments. By 9/10am they turn into **coffee shops**, serving hot and cold coffee and tea, as well as soft drinks and fresh coconuts, until they close at around 4/5pm.

Cheap restaurants (*haang bai*) are recognizable by a row of pots set out on a table out front, containing the day's food – not dissimilar to Cambodian home cooking. To find out what's on offer, lift the lids and peer inside; the dishes you have chosen will be served to you in separate bowls along with a plate of rice. Food in these places is not only pretty decent but also invariably good value at around $1–1.50 per portion – similar in price to eating at a market stall – inclusive of rice and iced tea, a jug of which is kept replenished at the table.

Tourist restaurants across the country serve up a generic range of international cuisine – pizzas, pasta, burgers, salads, sandwiches and simple grilled meat and fish dishes, all executed with varying levels of authenticity and success. Phnom Penh and Siem Reap also have a decent range of more upmarket restaurants specializing in French, Italian, Indian, Thai, Japanese and other leading international cuisines. At the other end of the scale, eating possibilities in smaller towns and **rural areas** can be quite restricted, and in the evenings you may be hard pushed to find anything more than a bowl of instant noodles.

Khmers tend to eat early by Western standards. In the provinces, especially, don't expect to find anywhere open after 9pm, and some places close even earlier.

In general, there's no need to **book in advance**, even to eat at expensive restaurants – although we've given telephone numbers throughout the Guide, so you could choose to call ahead during busy periods for popular spots.

What to eat

Many Cambodian dishes are variations on **Chinese** equivalents and are **stir-fried** in a wok to order. Just

MARKET DELICACIES

Cambodians eat just about everything, including **insects**. In the markets you'll see big trays of grasshoppers, beetles and crickets, usually fried, sold by the bag and eaten like sweets; **snails** are also a popular market-stall snack. **Spiders** are a speciality of Skuon (see box, p.28), while fried **snakes** are also a common sight, as are tiny sparrows (*jarb jeyan*), and other small **birds**, deep-fried and served whole, complete with tiny shrivelled head and claws. **Frogs**, meanwhile, are commonly used in stir-fries both in local markets and upmarket restaurants.

about any combination of ingredients can be ordered: chicken, pork or frogs' legs might be stir-fried with ginger, spring onions and garlic; prawn or chicken with basil leaves. Rice or noodles can themselves be stir-fried with chopped pork, beef, crab or vegetables, with an egg scrambled in or fried and served on top. Stir-fried sweet-and-sour dishes are also available, usually made with fish or pork – though you can ask for a vegetarian version – and flavoured with a combination of ingredients including pineapple, onion and either green or red tomatoes.

Stews and curries are often available at market stalls and cheap restaurants. Cambodian **stews** are usually based on a light stock (with beef or fish), complemented by bitter gourd or field melon; it's not unusual for them to contain hard-boiled eggs. **Curries**, usually made with beef, are only mildly spicy and generally quite dry.

Smoky, **charcoal-grilled** chicken and fish are available everywhere from roadside stalls to restaurants: fish is served with a dip of grated green mango, chilli, garlic and fish sauce; chicken with salad garnish and a sweet chilli sauce.

Khmer cuisine features two kinds of soup: **somlar**, freshly prepared to order and cooked quickly, and **sop**, based on a stock that has been simmering for a while. One of the commonest soups on restaurant menus is *somlar jerooet*, a clear soup made from either chicken or fish and cooked with coconut, lemongrass and chives.

Breakfast

For **breakfast**, Cambodians often eat rice with either fried chicken or fried pork, served with sliced cucumber and pickled vegetables, and a side bowl of clear soup. Also popular in

SPIDERVILLE

Most visitors to Cambodia pass through the nondescript little town of **Skuon** at some point in their travels. Located at the junction of NR6 and NR7 between Phnom Penh, Siem Reap and Kompong Cham, it's one of the most important crossroads towns in Cambodia. What it's really famous for, however, is its **edible spiders** – more precisely, a type of Asian tarantula, around 5cm across, known locally as *ah pieng* and considered something of a delicacy when deep-fried with a hint of salt and garlic. According to local gourmands they taste a bit like crunchy fried prawns and are best tackled as though eating a crab: pull off the legs and you can suck the flesh which comes away with them, though be wary of the body, as it can be unappetizingly slushy and bitter. Spiders also crop up around the country **pickled in wine**, a tonic especially favoured by pregnant women.

Quite how the practice of eating spiders began is something of a mystery. One theory suggests that it dates from the starvation years of Khmer Rouge rule, when desperate villagers began foraging for eight-legged snacks in the jungles of Kompong Thom province. Nowadays you'll likely see platters piled high with spiders at restaurants in and around Skuon – a lot of buses stop here for a comfort break – giving you the chance to see, and perhaps even try, this unusual delicacy.

the mornings is **geautieuv sop**, rice noodles in a clear broth with chicken, pork or beef pieces; you might wish to decline the other ingredients, namely sliced-up intestines or gizzard and a chunk of congealed blood, which the Khmers slurp with relish, as it's said to make you strong. A dish of bean sprouts and a slice of lime will be provided on the side, which you can add to taste.

In the tourist centres **Western breakfasts** are available in guesthouses, hotels, cafés and restaurants catering for tourists and expats. In the provinces it's usually difficult to find anything other than Khmer food first thing in the morning.

Snacks

Cambodian **snack foods** are legion, the range varying with the time of day. Eaten with breakfast or as an afternoon snack, available from street vendors and at restaurants, **noam bpaow** are steamed dumplings, originating from Chinese cuisine, made from white dough filled with a mix of minced pork, turnip, egg and chives. There's a second, less common version, smaller and sweeter and filled with a green mung-bean paste.

In the afternoon and evening, crusty **baguettes**, filled with your choice of pâté or sardines and pickled vegetables, can be bought from street hawkers for around 2000 riel.

Bany chaev are savoury wok-fried pancakes commonly available at market stalls; they're made from rice flour flecked with chives and coloured vivid yellow using turmeric. Filled with fried minced pork, onion, prawns and bean sprouts, they're eaten by wrapping pieces of the pancake in a lettuce leaf

and dipping them in a fish sauce mixed with garlic, lemon and crushed peanuts.

Steamed or grilled eggs are incredibly popular and are available everywhere, most commonly from street hawkers, night markets and at transport stops – where you'll often get a choice of eggs, with bite-sized quails' eggs easy to find. The black "thousand-year eggs" that you see at markets and food stalls are duck eggs that have been stored in jars of salt until the shells turn black; by that time the whites and the yolks have turned into a jelly, not dissimilar in texture to soft-boiled eggs. They are eaten with rice or *borbor* (see opposite), a soupçon of egg being taken with each spoonful of rice.

Often found at night markets or served up with beer is **pong dteer gowne**, literally ducks' eggs with duckling. Said to give strength and good health, it really does contain an unhatched duckling, boiled and served with herbs and a sauce of salt, pepper and lemon juice – not too bad if you don't look too closely at what you're eating.

Cooked bananas are also widely eaten as snacks, seasoned with salt and grilled over charcoal braziers, or wok-fried in a batter containing sesame seeds, which are at their most delicious when they're piping hot. Both are available in the markets, as are **noam ensaum jayk**, sweet sticky-rice parcels in different shapes, such as pyramids or rolls, containing a piece of banana and wrapped in banana leaves.

Among the more unusual snacks is the much-prized **grolan**, bamboo tubes containing a delicious mix of sticky rice, coconut milk and black beans, cooked over charcoal and sold bundled together by hawkers (usually in the provinces). The woody outer layer of the bamboo is removed after cooking, leaving a thin shell that you peel down to get at the contents. Seasonally available are **chook**, the cone-shaped, green seeds of the lotus flower, sold in bundles of three or five heads; to eat, pop the seeds out from the green rubbery pod, peel off their outer skins and consume the insides, which taste a bit like garden peas.

Accompaniments

No Cambodian meal is complete without a variety of accompaniments. One of the most prized of these is **prohok**, a salted, fermented fish paste that looks like a pinkish pâté and has an incredibly strong anchovy-like taste. A dollop is served on a plate with raw vegetables, *gee* (see p.31) and edible flowers; it's eaten either by adding a tiny amount to the accompanying vegetables or by taking a morsel with a spoonful of rice. *Prohok* isn't usually found on the menus of classy restaurants but is always available at market stalls and in Cambodian homes.

Though it's less pungent than *prohok*, **fish sauce** is still pretty smelly. Used as a dip with every type of food, it's made from both salt- and freshwater fish, which are layered with salt in large vats; as the fish ferments the juice is extracted from the bottom and bottled.

Other accompaniments include **dips** of chilli sauce and soy sauce – to which you can add chopped chillies and garlic – which are either left in pots on the table or served in individual saucers.

Rice and noodles

Besides boiled rice, Cambodians enjoy rice cooked up as a porridge called **borbor**, usually available at market stalls, night markets and in some cheap restaurants, either as breakfast or an evening dish. *Borbor* can either be left unseasoned and used as a base to which you add your own ingredients – dried fish, pickles, salted egg or fried vegetables – or cooked in stock, with pieces of chicken, fish or pork and bean sprouts added before serving. Shredded ginger, a squeeze of lime and spicy soya-bean paste from pots at the table can also be added to taste.

White rice-flour noodles, **geautiev** (pronounced *"goy teal"*), are available in different shapes and sizes – in fine threads for noodle soup, or wide and thick for use in **nom bany jowk**. The latter is sold by female street vendors from baskets dangling on shoulder poles and consists of noodles served cold with a lukewarm curry sauce over the top. Yellow egg noodles – **mee** – made from wheat flour are used in soups and stir-fries. Freshly made *mee* – called *mee kilo* because it's sold by weight – are available in the major towns, though elsewhere people make do with instant noodles imported in packets from Thailand and Vietnam. **Loat chat**, a hollow noodle similar to macaroni, is fried up by hawkers using hand-carts equipped with charcoal burners.

Meat

Meat is comparatively expensive and is invariably cut into small pieces and mixed with plenty of vegetables. **Pork** is commonly available, attested to by the number of pigs wandering around even the smallest village, but **beef** is more difficult to obtain as cows are prized as work animals and not necessarily killed for food. The best beef is available in large towns; elsewhere it's often tough and chewy (in Western restaurants it is generally imported).

Not so much a soup as a meal in itself, **sop chhnang day** is a bit like a fondue: a clay pot of hot stock and meatballs is brought to the table and placed on a small burner in the middle. Once the soup is boiling you add a selection of ingredients to the pot according to taste, choosing from side plates featuring slices of raw beef (or venison), often mixed with raw egg prior to cooking; sprigs of herbs; various vegetables; yellow and white noodles; tofu; dried sheets of soya bean (which looks a bit like chicken skin); and mushrooms. Both the stock and the dishes are replenished as long as you keep on eating, and at the end of the meal the bill is calculated according to the number of side plates on the table. Restaurants specializing in *sop chhnang day* often display a sign outside depicting a steaming pan over a burner.

Another Cambodian favourite is **sait gow ang**, beef grilled over a small charcoal burner at the table. Nibbled with pickled vegetables and fresh herbs, it tends to be eaten as an evening snack to accompany drinking. Similar in style but more of a meal is **chhnang phnom pleung**, "volcano pot", so named because the burner is said to resemble a

---

TOP 5 FINE DINING

Chanrey Tree, Siem Reap See p.150
Cuisine Wat Damnak, Siem Reap See p.152
Jaan Bai, Battambang See p.119
Malis, Phnom Penh See p.85
Tepui, Phnom Penh See p.83

volcano in appearance; the beef (venison is also used) comes to the table ready sliced, with a raw egg stirred into the meat before cooking. It's accompanied by side dishes of raw vegetables such as green tomatoes, capsicum and salad greens. Once you've grilled the meat and vegetables to your taste, they're wrapped in a salad leaf and dipped in a sauce before being eaten.

Typically found at cheap restaurants, **kaar** is a stew usually made with pig's trotters and green cabbage (it can also be made with fish or bamboo shoots) and eaten with unseasoned rice porridge (*borbor*). Pork is the usual ingredient in **spring rolls** (though Vietnamese restaurants especially may do a vegetarian version as an appetizer); they're either steamed or fried and then rolled up in a lettuce leaf with sliced cucumber, bean sprouts and herbs, and eaten dipped in a sweet chilli sauce.

Chicken and duck

Chicken and duck in Cambodia often have a high bone-to-flesh ratio; except in tourist restaurants, the whole carcass is chopped up, which means you have to pick out the bones from each mouthful. Worth looking out for is **baked chicken** (*sait mowan dot*), cooked in a metal pot in a wood-fired oven and really tasty. It's usually prepared to order, so there is quite a wait involved. Also worth trying is the refreshing **somlar ngam ngouw**, a clear lemon broth flavoured with pickled limes and herbs.

Fish

Fish is plentiful and the main source of protein for most Cambodians. Near the Tonle Sap lake there's a particularly good choice of **freshwater** varieties, and **sea fish** is plentiful along the coast, though inland it's only readily available in the specialist (and inevitably expensive) restaurants of Phnom Penh.

Fish is served up in all manner of ways – grilled, fried, in soups and stews. Popular in tourist areas is **amok**, a mild Cambodian-style fish curry (chicken is also used); the fish is mixed with coconut milk and seasonings and baked wrapped in banana leaves (or sometimes cooked in the shell of a young coconut).

Dried fish is a particular favourite. Much prized for sun-drying are large freshwater fish from the Tonle Sap, which are sliced lengthwise like kippers and grilled over charcoal, to be eaten with rice. When fish is cheap you'll see people drying their own in baskets outside their houses.

Vegetables

Cambodia's markets offer up a wide range of vegetables, some of which will be unfamiliar, all delivered fresh daily. Regrettably, you won't come across many of these on restaurant menus, though one unusual vegetable you will find in restaurants is **morning glory** (*trokooen*), a water plant with a thick, hollow stem and elongated heart-shaped leaves, which are carefully removed prior to cooking; it's often served stir-fried with garlic and oyster sauce, and tastes a bit like spinach.

Fried mixed vegetables are ubiquitous in Khmer restaurants, the constituents varying according to what's available (in some establishments you may be able to choose from a selection). Green tomatoes, crisp and refreshing, are often added to this and other dishes; red ones are only available in limited quantities for special recipes. For a decent selection of vegetable dishes, though, you'll need to try the Chinese restaurants. At street stalls and in the markets you'll find *noam gachiey*, best described as chive burgers. Made from rice flour,

---

VEGETARIANS AND VEGANS

Although strict Cambodian Buddhists do have a vegetarian meal once every two weeks on offering days, Cambodians in general can't understand why anyone who can afford meat or fish would not want to eat it.

The best way to get a **vegetarian dish** is to ask for your order to be cooked without meat (*ot dak sait*) or fish (*ot dak trei*); in principle, most stir-fries and soups can be done this way. You might be told that the dish is "not delicious" without meat, and the waiter may also come back a couple of times just to check he's got it straight. However, to be sure that prawns, chicken, duck or even intestines aren't substituted, or that a meat stock or fish sauce isn't used, you'll need to specify a whole list of things to avoid. **Vegans** will need to make sure that no eggs are included (*ot yoh pong mowan*) as these are widely used, but should have few problems avoiding dairy products, which are unlikely to be found outside Western restaurants.

In tourist centres one or two vegetarian restaurants have opened, while restaurants catering for foreigners will also have more choice and a better idea of what being a vegetarian means.

chives and herbs, they're steamed or fried, and dished up with either a sweet sauce (based on fish sauce) or soy sauce.

Gee is the generic Cambodian term for all manner of herbs, used in cooking, served up by the plateful to be eaten on the side, or taken medicinally. You'll probably only recognize a few, such as mint and coriander; others include various types of water grass, vines and young tree leaves.

Pickles made with brine are frequently served in Cambodia as an appetizer or a side dish, and as a filling for baguettes. There are many variations, made from combinations of cabbage, cucumber, ginger, turnip, bamboo shoots, onions and bean sprouts, often sculpted into shapes for extra visual appeal. **Green mango salad** (*chruok svay*), made from shredded green mango, dried shrimp and fish paste topped with crushed peanut, is served up in restaurants, to be eaten as a starter or snack.

Desserts and sweets

Specialist stalls, opening around lunchtime in the markets or in the late afternoon and evening along the street, serve Cambodian **desserts** in a vast range of colours and textures. Small custards, jellies and sticky-rice confections are displayed in large flat trays and cut or shaped into bite-sized pieces to be served in bowls, topped with grated ice and a slug of condensed milk; mixes of dried and crystallized fruits, beans and nuts are also on offer, served with ice and syrup. Other desserts include sweet sticky rice mixed with corn kernels, mung beans or lotus seed, poached pumpkin with syrup, and palm fruit with syrup, all of which are served up from large bowls by market stalls.

Khmer restaurants seldom serve desserts other than fresh fruit, though recently a few upmarket places are starting to offer them along with imported ice creams. Towns generally have a bakery or two producing a variety of **cakes**, many of which are approximations of familiar Western goodies. Market stalls in all towns sell small, freshly baked sponge cakes.

Fruit

Colourful **fruit** stalls can be found everywhere in Cambodia, and the selection is enormous – stall-holders will always let you try before you buy if you don't know what you're looking at. Imported apples, pears and grapes are also available, though comparatively expensive.

Bananas come in several varieties, some of which are seldom seen in the West; they're grown just about everywhere, and are sold in huge quantities – cheaply, at around 1000 riel a bunch – for snacking, cooking and as offerings for the pagoda. Commonest are *jayk oumvong*, which is slender and stays green when ripe; *jayk numvar*, a medium-sized, plump, yellow banana, said to cool the body; and the finger-sized, very sweet *jayk pong mowan*, said to be warming, which is a little pricier than the other kinds. Relatively rare are the large, dry and fibrous red or green bananas, generally used for cooking.

The **durian** (*tooren*) is a rugby-ball-sized fruit with a hard, spiky exterior. Much sought after by Khmers, it's an acquired taste for most Westerners thanks to its fetid smell (often compared to that of a blocked drain). Inside are several segments, each containing two or three stones surrounded by pale yellow, creamy textured flesh, which can be quite addictive once you've got over the odour.

Longans (*meeyan*) have a long season and are often sold still on the twig. The cherry-sized fruit have a hard brown skin; the flesh inside is similar to that of lychees in texture and flavour. Bright green and prickly skinned, **soursops** (*tee-ab barang*) are pure white inside and have a tart but sweet taste. Hard, round and a bit like a bright-green cricket ball, **guavas** (*troubike*) have a crunchy, dry texture a bit like a hard pear. The flat brown pods of **tamarind** (*umpbel*) are simple to eat: split open the pods and discard the fibrous thread inside, then suck off the rich brown tangy flesh, minding the hard seeds. The most picturesque of Khmer fruits, though, has to be the rosy pink **dragon fruit** (*pelai sroegar ne-yak*), grown on a climbing cactus-like vine. Inside its waxy skin, the moist, pure-white flesh is dotted with black seeds and has quite a subtle taste, verging on bland.

Drinks

Bottled water is found everywhere, as Cambodian **tap water** isn't considered safe to drink. Be aware that the ice that is invariably added to cold drinks (unless you request otherwise) may not be hygienic except in Western restaurants.

Tea and coffee

Cambodians drink plenty of **green tea**, which is readily available in coffee shops and from market stalls; it's normally served free of charge with food in restaurants. If you like your tea strong, try *dtai grolab*, made by putting water and a mass of tea

SUGAR PALMS

Crowned with distinctive mops of spiky leaves, **sugar palms** are of great importance to the rural Cambodian economy, with every part of the tree being put to good use. The sweet **juice** extracted from the palm's flower-bearing stalk is either drunk fresh or fermented to produce **palm beer**, traditionally sold by hawkers, although nowadays also available in tourist centres and local supermarkets. **Palm sugar**, much used in Khmer cooking, is made by thickening the juice in a cauldron and then pouring it into cylindrical tubes to set, after which it resembles grainy honey-coloured fudge. Palm **fruits**, slightly larger than a cricket ball, have a tough, fibrous black coating containing juicy, delicately flavoured kernels, which are translucent white and have the consistency of jelly; they're eaten either fresh or with syrup as a dessert.

Further sugar-palm products include the **leaves**, traditionally used as a form of paper and still used in thatch and to make wall panels, woven matting, baskets, fans and even packaging. The **root** of the tree is used in traditional medicine as a cure for stomachache and other ailments. Perhaps because the trees furnish so many other products, they are seldom cut for their **wood**, which is extremely durable. However, palm-wood souvenirs can be found in Phnom Penh and Siem Reap, easily identifiable by their distinctive light-and-dark striped grain, and palm-wood furniture has become fashionable in some of the country's boutique hotels.

leaves into a small glass, placing a saucer on top, and turning the whole thing upside down to brew. When it's dark enough, the tea is decanted into another cup and plenty of sugar added, but no milk. **Lemon tea** (*dtai gdouw kroit chhmar*), made with Chinese red-dust tea and lemon juice, is refreshing both hot and iced, and is generally served with a hefty dose of sugar. **Black tea**, sold locally under the Lipton brand, is served in hotels, guesthouses and restaurants that cater to foreigners.

Noodle shops, coffee shops and restaurants serve **coffee** from early morning to late afternoon, but in the evenings it can be difficult to find except at restaurants geared up for foreigners. The beans are generally imported from Laos and Vietnam – although domestically produced coffee from Rattanakiri and Mondulkiri can be found in some places. Beans are traditionally roasted with butter and sugar, plus various other ingredients that might include anything from rum to pork fat, giving the beverage a strange, sometimes faintly chocolatey aroma – something of an acquired taste. Black coffee (*kafei kmaow*) will often be served with sugar unless you specify otherwise and is often served (and generally tastes better) **iced** (*kafei kmaow tuk kork*). Cambodians often have their coffee or tea iced, even for breakfast; if you want yours hot, ask for it to be served without ice (*ot dak tuk kork*).

Note that if you order white coffee (*kafei tuk duh gow*), it sometimes comes with a slug of condensed milk already in the glass, so don't stir it all in if you don't like your drink too sweet. Most of the milk (*tuk duh*) available is either sterilized, canned or sweetened condensed.

Soft drinks

For a drink on the hoof, iced **sugar-cane juice** (*tuk umpow*) is very refreshing and not actually that sweet. It's sold everywhere from yellow carts equipped with a mangle through which the peeled canes are passed, sometimes with a piece of orange added for extra taste. Equally refreshing is the juice of a **green coconut** (*tuk dhowng*): the top is hacked off and you drink the juice before getting it cut in half so you can eat the soft, jelly-like flesh.

Fruit shakes (*tuk krolok*) are an important part of an evening's consumption: juice stalls, recognizable by their fruit displays and blenders, set up in towns all over the country from the late afternoon. You can order a mixture of fruits to be juiced or just one or two; coconut milk, sugar syrup, condensed milk and shaved ice are also added, as is a raw egg (unless you specify otherwise – *ot yoh pong mowan*).

When not added to coffee or tea, **milk** (*tuk duh*) is sometimes drunk iced, perhaps with a bright red or green cordial added. Freshly made **soya milk** (*tuk sun dike*) is sold in the morning by street vendors; the green version is sweetened and thicker than the unsweetened white. Soya milk is also available canned, as is **winter-melon tea**, a juice made from the field melon that has a distinctive sweet, almost earthy taste.

Alcohol

Besides nightclubs and bars, most restaurants and night-market stalls serve **beer** (*sraa bier*). Cambodia's national beer is Angkor, brewed by an Australian/Cambodian joint venture in Sihanoukville; it's available in cans, large bottles and sometimes on draught, prices varying from around $1 for a glass of draught beer to around $2–2.50 for a large bottle. Tiger, VB, Beer Lao and ABC Stout are also readily available, and there are many more local brews. Even if already chilled, beer is often drunk with ice.

Spirits are generally only found in larger restaurants, nightclubs and Western bars. Imported wines are available in smarter restaurants and Western-oriented places, and can be bought in supermarkets and minimarkets. When not downing beer, Cambodians themselves usually prefer to stick to local, medicinal **rice wines**, which are available at stalls and shops where glasses of the stuff are ladled from large jars containing various plant or animal parts. Though quite sweet, they're strong and barely palatable, but cheap. Another local brew is **sugar-palm beer**, sold and brewed straight from the bamboo tubes in which the juice is collected. It's quite refreshing, and readily available in villages and from vendors in the towns; it's also now available in tourist-oriented shops in nicely labelled bottles.

Health

Health care in Cambodia is poor. Even the best hospitals have inadequate facilities, low standards of cleanliness and appalling patient care, and should be used only in a dire emergency. For anything serious, if you are able to travel then get to Bangkok. Should you have no option but to go to a Cambodian hospital, try to get a Khmer-speaker to accompany you.

In Phnom Penh a couple of private Western-oriented **clinics** offer slightly better care than the hospitals, at a higher cost. If you get ill outside Phnom Penh or Siem Reap, self-diagnosis and treatment is often better than visiting a clinic. Wherever you seek medical attention, you will be expected to pay upfront for treatment, medication and food.

Although every town has a number of **pharmacies** (typically daily 7am–8pm) stocking an extensive range of medications, the staff aren't required to have a dispensing qualification, so you may want to check the product sheets (and even expiry dates) before you buy. Fake medicines abound and there's no easy way to determine if what you're buying is the real thing. Whenever possible buy only in Phnom Penh (see p.92) or Siem Reap (see p.156), which have a couple of reputable

pharmacies employing qualified personnel who can help with diagnosis and remedies for simple health problems.

Consider getting a pre-trip **dental check-up** if you're travelling for an extended period, as the only places to get reliable dental treatment in Cambodia are in Phnom Penh and Siem Reap. If you wear **glasses**, it's worth taking along a copy of your prescription (or a spare pair of glasses); you can get replacements made quite cheaply in Phnom Penh and Siem Reap.

Vaccinations and immunizations

It's worth checking before you leave that you are up to date with **routine** immunizations, such as tetanus and diphtheria. For Cambodia, you should consider immunizing yourself against hepatitis A, tuberculosis and typhoid; inoculations against hepatitis B, rabies and Japanese encephalitis are recommended if you are going to be at a particular risk (for example if you're working in a remote area). You'll need to produce proof that you've been vaccinated against yellow fever in the event of arriving from an infected area (West and Central Africa, or South America).

It is as well to consult your doctor or travel clinic as early as possible since it can take anything up to eight weeks to complete a full course of immunizations. All inoculations should be recorded on an **international travel vaccination card**, which is worth carrying with you in case you get sick.

Hepatitis

Hepatitis A, a viral infection of the liver, can be contracted from contaminated food and water – shellfish sold by hawkers and untreated water are particular risks in Cambodia – or by contact with an infected person. Symptoms include dark-coloured urine, aches and pains, nausea, general malaise and tiredness, with jaundice following after a few days. A blood test is needed for diagnosis, and rest, plenty of nonalcoholic fluids and a high-carbohydrate diet are recommended for convalescence. A single shot of immunoglobulin offers short-term protection against hepatitis A.

Far more serious is **hepatitis B**, passed via contaminated body fluids; it can be contracted through non-sterile needles (including those used in tattooing and acupuncture), sexual contact or from a blood transfusion that hasn't been properly screened. Symptoms include nonspecific abdominal pain, vomiting, loss of appetite, dark-coloured urine and jaundice. Immunization may be recommended if you are staying in Asia for longer than six months. If you think you have contracted hepatitis B, it's especially important to seek medical attention.

A **combined vaccine** is available offering ten years' protection against hepatitis A and five years' against hepatitis B; your doctor will be able to advise on its suitability.

Tuberculosis, rabies and tetanus

Tuberculosis, contracted from droplets coughed up by infected persons, is widespread in Cambodia and is a major cause of death in young children. You may have been inoculated against the disease in childhood, but if you're unsure, consider a skin (Heaf) test, which will determine if you already have immunity.

Rabies is contracted from the bite or saliva of an infected animal. Vaccinations are recommended if you're going to be spending a long time in rural areas; but even if you've been vaccinated, if you are bitten (or licked on an open wound) you will need to get two booster injections as quickly as possible, preferably within 24 to 48 hours.

Tetanus, a bacterial infection that causes muscular cramps and spasms, comes from spores in the earth and can enter the blood circulatory system through wounds and grazes. If left untreated it can cause breathing problems and sometimes death. It's worth checking if you've been vaccinated against tetanus in the last ten years and getting a booster if necessary.

Typhoid and cholera

Typhoid and cholera, bacterial infections that affect the digestive system, are spread by contam-inated food and water, and outbreaks are thus usually associated with particularly unsanitary conditions.

Symptoms of **typhoid** include tiredness, dull headaches and spasmodic fevers, with spots appearing on the abdomen after about a week. Vaccination is suggested if you plan to stay in rural areas of Cambodia, but it doesn't confer complete immunity, so it remains important to maintain good standards of hygiene.

Sudden, watery diarrhoea and rapid dehydration are among the symptoms of **cholera**, and medical advice is essential to treat the infection with antibi-otics. Vaccination is no longer recommended for cholera due to its poor efficacy. From time to time there are outbreaks of cholera in Cambodia that are well publicized in the media.

General precautions

Cambodia is a hot and humid country, and **dehydration** is a potential problem, its onset indicated by headaches, dizziness, nausea and dark urine. **Cuts** and raw blisters can rapidly become infected and should be promptly treated by cleaning and disinfecting the wound and then applying an air-permeable dressing.

Bites and stings

Insects are legion in Cambodia and are at their worst around November, at the start of the dry season, when there are stagnant pockets of water left from the rains. Even during the hot season (March–May) they come out in the evenings, swarming around light bulbs and warm flesh – they're annoying rather than harmful, with the exception of mosquitoes (see opposite).

On the coast, **sand flies** appear in the late afternoon and evening, delivering nasty bites that don't erupt until a few hours later, when they become incredibly red and itchy. Once you scratch, the bites become even more inflamed and can take up to a month to recede, leaving behind nasty scars. These little blighters have a limited range and mostly attack victims on the sand; if you're on or near the beach, it's probably best to use an insect repellent.

Sun and heat

Even when the sky is overcast the Cambodian sun is fierce, and you should take precautions against sunburn and heat stroke wherever you are. Cover up, use a high-protection-factor **sunscreen**, wear a hat and drink plenty of fluids throughout the day.

Hygiene and stomach complaints

Though catering facilities at many restaurants and food stalls can appear basic, the **food** you'll be served is usually absolutely fresh; all ingredients are bought daily and are mostly cooked to order. A good rule of thumb when selecting a place to eat is to pick one that is popular with local people, as the Khmers are fussy about their food and seldom give a place a second chance if they've found the food isn't fresh. Food from street hawkers is usually fine if it's cooked in front of you. Tap water isn't drinkable, but bottled water is available everywhere – stick to that and be cautious with ice, which is often cut up in the street from large blocks and handled by several people before it gets to your glass (though in Western restaurants it will probably come from an ice-maker).

Stomach complaints

The most common travellers' ailment is **upset tummy**. Travellers' **diarrhoea** often occurs in the early days of a trip as a result of a simple change in diet, though stomach cramps and vomiting may mean it's food poisoning. If symptoms persist for more than a couple of days, seek medical help as you may need antibiotics to clear up the problem.

Most diarrhoea is short-lived and can be handled by drinking plenty of fluids and avoiding rich or spicy food. Activated charcoal tablets help by absorbing the bad bugs in your gut and usually speed recovery; they're sold across the counter at pharmacies, but it's worth bringing some with you from home. It's often a good idea to rest up for a day or two if your schedule allows. In the event of persistent diarrhoea or vomiting, it's worth taking **oral rehydration salts**, available at most pharmacies (or make your own from half a teaspoon of salt and eight teaspoons of sugar per litre of bottled water).

Unless you're going on a long journey, avoid taking Imodium and Lomotil. These bung you up by stopping gut movements and can extend the problem by preventing your body expelling the bugs that gave rise to the diarrhoea in the first place.

Dysentery and giardiasis

If there is blood or mucus in your faeces and you experience severe stomach cramps, you may have dysentery, which requires immediate medical attention. There are two forms of the disease, the more serious of which is **amoebic dysentery**. Even though the symptoms may well recede over a few days, the amoebae will remain in the gut and can go on to attack the liver; treatment with an antibiotic, metronidazole (Flagyl) is thus essential. Equally unpleasant is **bacillary dysentery**, also treated with antibiotics.

Giardiasis is caused by protozoa usually found in streams and rivers. Symptoms, typically watery diarrhoea and bad-smelling wind, appear around two weeks after the organism has entered the system and can last for up to two weeks. Giardiasis can be diagnosed from microscope analysis of stool samples, and is treated with metronidazole.

Mosquito-borne diseases

Given the prevalence in Cambodia of serious diseases spread by mosquitoes, including multi-resistant **malaria**, it is important to **avoid being bitten**. Mosquito nets often aren't provided in guesthouses and hotels, so it's worth bringing your own.

Wearing long trousers, socks and a long-sleeved top will reduce the chances of being bitten. **Insect repellents** containing DEET are the most effective, although you may want to consider a natural alternative such as those based on citronella.

Malaria

Malaria is prevalent year-round and throughout the country – with the exception of Phnom Penh, Siem Reap and the area immediately around the Tonle Sap lake. More than 40,000 cases were reported in 2013, and almost 70,000 in 2012.

Malaria is contracted from the night-biting female *anopheles* mosquito, which injects a parasite into the bloodstream. Chills, fevers and sweating ensue after an incubation period of around twelve days, often along with aching joints, a cough and vomiting, and the symptoms repeat after a couple of days. In Cambodia the dangerous **falciparum** strain of the disease predominates; if untreated, it can be fatal.

Before you travel, it is important to take advice on a suitable **prophylaxis** regime, as a course of antimalarial medication needs to be started in advance of arriving in a risk area. **Malarone** (atovaquone/proguanil) and **doxycycline** are the two most frequently prescribed antimalarials for Cambodia. **Mefloquine** (aka Larium) is also sometimes recommended, but has the drawback of well-publicized side effects and may not be effective in western and northern provinces close to the Thai border thanks to the presence of mefloquine-resistant malaria in these areas. Note that taking antimalarials doesn't guarantee that you won't contract the disease, a fact that reinforces the need to avoid being bitten.

Emergency treatment for falciparum malaria is 600mg of quinine sulphate, taken three times a day for three days, followed by a single dose of three Fansidar tablets once the quinine course is completed. These tablets are available over the counter at pharmacies throughout Cambodia, but if you suspect malaria you should still see a doctor for a diagnostic blood test.

Dengue fever

Outbreaks of **dengue fever** occur annually in Cambodia with 37 deaths reported in 2009. Spread by the day-biting female *aedes* mosquito, this is a viral disease that takes about a week to develop following a bite. It resembles a bad case of flu; symptoms include high fever, aches and pains, headache and backache. After a couple of days a red rash appears on the torso, gradually spreading to the limbs. There may also be abnormal bleeding, which requires medical attention.

No vaccine is available at the time of writing, and there is no effective treatment, although paracetamol can be taken to relieve the symptoms (*not* aspirin, which can increase the potential for bleeding); you should also drink plenty of fluids and get lots of rest. Although the symptoms should improve after five or six days, lethargy and depression can last for a month or more – consult a doctor if symptoms persist. Anyone who has previously contracted dengue fever is at particular risk if they subsequently contract a different virus strain, which can result in **dengue haemorrhagic fever**. In this condition the usual symptoms of dengue fever are accompanied by abdominal pain and vomiting; immediate medical help should be sought, as it can be fatal.

Japanese encephalitis

Japanese encephalitis is a serious viral disease carried by night-biting mosquitoes that breed in the rice fields. The risk is highest between May and October. It's worth considering vaccination if you're going to be in rural areas of Cambodia for an extended time or are visiting during the high-risk period. Symptoms, which appear five to fifteen days after being bitten, include headaches, a stiff neck, flu-like aches and chills; there's no specific treatment, but it's wise to seek medical advice and take paracetamol or aspirin to ease the symptoms.

Sexually transmitted diseases

Cambodia has one of Asia's highest levels of **HIV/AIDS** infection, much of it the result of the country's burgeoning sex trade. An estimated 0.7 percent of the adult population aged 15–49 carries the disease, although rates are slowly falling from a high of 2 percent at the beginning of the millennium thanks to vigorous intervention by health services. **Syphilis** and **gonorrhoea** are also rife. **Condoms** are widely available, although it's best to stick to Western brands wherever possible.

MEDICAL RESOURCES

Canadian Society for International Health ☎ 613 241 5785, Ⓦ csih.org. Extensive list of travel health centres.

CDC ☎ 1800 232 6348, Ⓦ cdc.gov/travel. Official US government travel health site.
Hospital for Tropical Diseases Travel Clinic UK Ⓦ scotmas.com.
International Society for Travel Medicine US ☎ 1404 373 8282, Ⓦ istm.org. A full list of travel health clinics.
MASTA (Medical Advisory Service for Travellers Abroad) UK Ⓦ masta-travel-health.com for the nearest clinic.
Tropical Medical Bureau Ireland ☎ 1850 487 674, Ⓦ tmb.ie.
The Travel Doctor – TMVC ☎ 1300 658 844, Ⓦ traveldoctor.com.au. Lists travel clinics in Australia, New Zealand and South Africa.

Crime and personal safety

Despite its turbulent recent history, Cambodia is now a generally safe country in which to travel. It's important to be mindful, however, of the fact that Cambodia is one of the most heavily mined countries in the world, and also has significant quantities of unexploded ordnance (UXO) lying around. In the countryside you must stick to well-trodden paths.

Crime

Mines and ordnance apart, there is still a culture of **guns** in Cambodia, and there have been incidents of armed robbery against locals and tourists alike. Gun crime is a regular occurrence in Phnom Penh (although considerably less common elsewhere in the country), usually reaching a peak at festival times, most notably Khmer New Year. Don't be paranoid, but, equally, be aware that a small but significant number of visitors continue to be mugged at gunpoint (and occasionally shot), even in busy and touristed areas. Given this, it's a very good idea to keep all valuables well out of sight. If you are unfortunate enough to find yourself being robbed, on no account resist – the consequences if you do so could possibly be fatal. It's also worth making sure that all bags are hidden between your legs if travelling by moto – snatch-and-grab robberies have also been reported, with victims occasionally being pulled off the back of motos by the straps of their bags during attempted grabs. All incidents should be reported to the **police** as soon as possible – you'll need a signed, dated report from them to claim on your travel insurance – and, if you lose your passport, to your

CHILDREN AT RISK

Cambodia has an unfortunate reputation as a destination for paedophiles, and child sex tourism has grown here as a result of crackdowns on child prostitution in other Southeast Asian countries.

The Ministry of the Interior (National Police) asks that anyone witnessing child prostitution in Cambodia immediately report it to the police on their national **"child-wise" hotline** (☎023 997919). ChildSafe also has a 24-hour national hotline to report children at risk (☎012 311112, ⊚childsafe-cambodia.org). You could also consider contacting **ECPAT** (End Child Prostitution, Abuse and Trafficking, ⊚ecpat.net).

embassy as well. In Phnom Penh, Siem Reap and Sihanoukville, English-speaking **tourist police** will help, but in the provinces you'll have to deal with the local police, who are unlikely to have more than a smattering of English, so if possible take a Khmer-speaker with you.

Though the vast majority of Cambodian police will do their best to help in an emergency, a small minority are not averse to trying to elicit money from foreigners. If you're riding a motorbike or driving a motor vehicle, they may well deem that you've committed an offence. You can argue the "fine" down to a few dollars and may as well pay up, although if you can stand the hassle and don't mind wasting a lot more time you may feel it worth reporting such incidents to the police commissioner.

Road accidents usually attract vast crowds of curious onlookers, and if any damage to property or injury to a person or domestic animal has occurred, then you'll have to stay at the scene until the police arrive. It's the driver's responsibility to come to a financial arrangement with the other parties involved. In spite of their general amiability, it's not unknown for locals to try to coerce foreigners into coughing up money, even if they are the innocent party or merely a passenger.

Drugs

As you'd expect given its proximity to some of the world's major drug-producing regions, drugs both soft and hard are common in Cambodia. **Marijuana** is widely available, especially around the southern beaches, and you'll be approached by peddlers on a fairly regular basis in all major tourist spots. Possession is of course illegal, and although prosecutions are rare, purchasing and consuming dope always carries a risk of falling foul of the police – and most likely having to pay some sort of backhander in order to avoid having charges pressed. **Hard drugs** including opium, cocaine and

so on are also available. Needless to say the authorities take a much dimmer view of these than of dope, and possession may well earn you a term in the nearest Cambodian prison – and, given the suspect quality of a lot of the drugs sold on the street, could even be fatal. There have been cases of travellers dying after buying what they believed to be cocaine but which turned out to be pure heroin.

Note that in the case of any medical complications the nearest properly equipped hospital is in Bangkok.

Land mines and unexploded ordnance

The UN estimates that between four and six million **land mines** were laid in Cambodia between 1979 and 1991, but no one really knows. The Vietnamese and the government laid them as protection against Khmer Rouge guerrillas, who in turn laid them to intimidate local populations; neither side recorded the locations of the minefields. To date more than two thousand minefields have been identified (usually through members of the local population being blown up), and new locations are regularly being reported. Several organizations are actively working at de-mining the countryside, and at last the number of casualties is decreasing; but given the scale of the problem, it will be many years before the mines are cleared completely (see p.297). The **border area with Thailand** between Koh Kong and Preah Vihear is particularly dangerous. In rural areas, take care not to leave well-used paths and never take short-cuts across rice fields without a local guide. Areas known to be badly contaminated are signed with a red skull and the words "Beware Mines".

As if this problem weren't enough, in the 1970s the United States dropped more than half a million tonnes of **bombs** on Cambodia. This began as part of a secret and illicit plan to expose the Ho Chi Minh Trail used by communist North

Vietnamese troops, and ended up in a massive countrywide bombing campaign to support the pro-American Lon Nol government against the Khmer Rouge. **Unexploded ordnance** (UXO), or explosive remnants of war (ERW), remains a risk in rural areas, with the southeast, centre and northeast of the country particularly affected; in the countryside it's foolish to pick up or kick any unidentified metal objects.

The media

Much of Cambodia's media is sponsored by the country's political parties, and though the prime minister has declared his support for press freedom, the media continues to be subject to the government's whims.

Newspapers and magazines

Cambodia has around seven daily **Khmer-language newspapers**. The two main dailies are *Rasmei Kampuchea* (*Light of Cambodia*) and *Koh Santepheap*, both of which are pro-government.

Cambodia's two **English-language newspapers** – the *Cambodia Daily* (🔊 cambodiadaily.com; published daily except Sun) and the *Phnom Penh Post* (🔊 phnompenhpost.com; Mon–Fri) – can be found at newsstands in larger cities. It's also worth looking out for the several English-language **magazines**. *Asia Life* (🔊 asialifemagazine.com; free from cafés and restaurants) is the *Time Out* of Phnom Penh with a host of articles related to new things happening in the city. *Bayon Pearnik* (🔊 bayonpearnik.com), a free satirical monthly, available in Western restaurants and bars in Phnom Penh, includes travel features and news of bar and club launches.

Television and radio

Cambodia's seven **Khmer TV stations** broadcast a mix of political coverage, game shows, concerts, cartoons, sport – kick-boxing is a huge favourite – and Thai soaps dubbed into Khmer. The state broadcaster, TVK, is owned by the ruling CPP, who also have influence with most of the other channels. Guesthouses and hotels usually offer **cable** and, increasingly, **satellite TV** stations, enabling you to watch a vast selection of foreign channels, typically including BBC World, CNN, CNBC, HBO, National Geographic and Star Sport.

Among the many **Khmer radio stations**, just a couple carry English programmes. The principal local station favoured by foreigners is Love FM on **97.5 FM**, featuring a mix of Western pop, news stories and phone-ins.

Festivals and events

Cambodians are always celebrating a festival of some sort, heading out to the pagoda with family and friends or taking off for the provinces; unsurprisingly, festivals are the busiest times for shopping and travelling. For details of public holidays, consult the "Travel essentials" (see p.44).

The most significant **festival** of the year is **Bonn Chaul Chhnam** (Khmer New Year; April 13 or 14), when families get together, homes are spring-cleaned and people flock to the temples with elaborate offerings. **Bonn Pchum Ben** (late Sept), or "Ancestors' Day", is another key date on the festive calendar. Families make offerings to their ancestors in the fifteen days leading up to it, and celebrations take place in temples on the day itself.

Marking the start of the planting season in May, the ceremony of **Bonn Chroat Preah Nongkoal** (Royal Ploughing Ceremony), held at Lean Preah Sre park in Phnom Penh, combines animism, Buddhism and plenty of pomp. It begins with chanting monks asking the earth spirits for permission to plough. Then ceremonial furrows are drawn, rice is scattered and offerings are made to the divinities. The most important part of the ceremony, however, is what the Royal Bulls choose when offered rice, grain, grass, water and wine. Rice or grain augur well; water signifies rain; grass is a sign that crops will be devastated by insects; and wine, that there will be drought.

Though it has been cancelled for the last few years, the **Bonn Om Toeuk** (early Nov) water festival has traditionally been celebrated when the current of the Tonle Sap River, which swells so much during the rainy season that it actually pushes water upstream, reverses and flows back into the Mekong. The centre of festivities is Phnom Penh's riverbank, where everyone gathers to watch boat racing, an illuminated boat parade and fireworks.

Buddhist **offering days** (exact dates vary according to the lunar calendar) are also colourful occasions: stalls do a roaring trade in bunches of flowers that are taken to temples and used to decorate shrines at home. Lotus buds – the traditional offering flower to the Buddha – are artistically folded to expose their pale-pink inner petals, while jasmine buds are threaded onto sticks and strings as fragrant tokens.

Culture and etiquette

These days the handshake has become quite common in Cambodia, and is used between Cambodian men or when Cambodian men greet foreigners; generally, however, women still greet foreigners using the traditional Cambodian form of greeting, the sompeyar.

The **sompeyar** is a gesture of politeness and a sign of respect. Typically, it is performed with hands placed palms together, fingers pointing up, in front of the body at chest level, and the head is inclined slightly forward as if about to bow. When greeting monks, however, the hands should be placed in front of the face, and when paying respects to Buddha (or the king), the hands are put in front of the forehead. The *sompeyar* is always used towards those older than yourself, and is taught to children at an early age.

Cambodians are reserved people and find **public displays of affection** offensive; people in the provinces are particularly conservative. Holding hands or linking arms in public, though quite a common sign of friendship between two men or two women, is considered unacceptable if it involves a member of the opposite sex; even married couples won't touch each other in public. Traditionally, Cambodian women would not have gone out drinking or have been seen with a man who was not her fiancé or husband. Times are changing, however, and a more cosmopolitan attitude is gaining ground in the towns, where you'll see groups of girls and boys out together.

Everywhere in Cambodia, travellers will gain more respect if they are **well dressed**. Cambodians themselves dress modestly, men usually wearing long trousers and a shirt. Many women wear blouses rather than T-shirts, and *sampots* (sarongs) or knee-length skirts, but many also wear trousers or jeans, and younger girls in larger cities can

increasingly be seen in the kind of short skirts and strappy tops favoured by their Western counterparts. Even so, as a general rule it's best to avoid skimpy clothes and shorts unless you're at the beach.

When **visiting temples** it's important to wear clothes that keep your shoulders and legs covered. Hats should be removed when passing through the temple gate and shoes taken off before you go into any of the buildings (shoes are also removed before entering a Cambodian home). If you sit down on the floor inside a shrine, avoid pointing the soles of your feet towards any Buddha images (in fact, you should observe the same rule towards people generally, in any location). **Monks** are not allowed to touch women, so women should take care when walking near monks, and avoid sitting next to them on public transport.

Cambodians are often intrigued at the **appearance of foreigners**, and it is not considered rude to stare quite intently at visitors. Local people may also giggle at men with earrings – in Cambodia boys are given an earring in the belief it will help an undescended testicle. It's worth bearing in mind that **displaying anger** won't get you far, as the Khmers simply find this embarrassing.

Shopping

Cambodia has a wide range of souvenirs – colourful cotton and silk fabrics, wood and stone carvings, lacquerware, jewellery and much more. Local handicrafts have also been given a boost thanks to various local and NGO schemes set up to give Cambodia's large disabled population and other disadvantaged members of society a new source of income by training them in various traditional crafts.

Local **markets** are often the best place to hunt for collectibles. In the capital, Psar Toul Tom Poung (Russian Market) is the acknowledged place to buy souvenirs, and there are also several excellent markets in Siem Reap. In both towns you'll also find plenty of specialist **shops**, galleries and hotel boutiques – usually more expensive, though quality is generally significantly higher.

As a general rule, when shopping for souvenirs it's a good idea to buy it when you see it. Something unusual you chance upon in the provinces may not be available elsewhere.

BARGAINING

Prices are fixed in shops and malls, but you're expected to **bargain** in markets and when buying from hawkers. Bargaining is seen as an amicable game and social exchange. The seller usually starts at a moderately inflated price: for cheapish items, with a starting price below $10, expect to be able to knock around a third off; with pricier items you might be lucky to get a reduction of ten percent. To keep a sense of perspective while bargaining, it's worth remembering that on items like a T-shirt or *krama*, the vendor's margin is often as little as a thousand riel.

Textiles

The ubiquitous chequered scarf, the **krama**, worn by all Cambodians, is arguably the country's most popular tourist souvenir, and there are plenty to buy in markets everywhere. Many *krama*s are woven from mixed synthetic threads; although the cloth feels soft, a *krama* of this sort is hot to wear and doesn't dry very well if you want to use it as a towel. The very best *krama*s come from Kompong Cham and Phnom Sarok and are made from cotton (*umbok*). Those from Kompong Cham are often to be had from female peddlers in the markets – a large one costs around $3.

Though cotton *krama*s feel stiff and thin at first, a few good scrubs in cold water will soften them up and increase the density of texture. They last for years and actually improve with wear, making a cool, dust-proof and absorbent fabric.

Silk

The weaving of **silk** in Cambodia can be traced back to the Angkor era, when the Khmer started to imitate imported cloth from India. Weaving skills learned over generations were lost with the Khmer Rouge, but the 1990s saw a resurgence of silk weaving in many Cambodian villages (the thread is usually imported from Vietnam, though a few Cambodian villages have again started to keep their own silkworms). Most of the cloth is produced to order for the dealers and silk-sellers of Phnom Penh, so if you visit a village where silk is woven, don't be surprised if they haven't any fabric for sale. Unpatterned silk is sometimes available by the metre in dark and pastel colours, and modern designs are also becoming available.

Silk is produced in fixed widths – nearly always 800mm – and sold in two lengths: a **kabun** (3.6m), sufficient for a long straight skirt and short-sleeved top; and a **sampot** (half a *kabun*), which is enough for a long skirt. A *sampot* starts at around $15–20, but you can easily pay double this, depending on quality and design. Sometimes the silk will have been washed, which makes it softer in both texture and hue – and slightly more expensive. **Silk scarves** are inexpensive (around $5–6) and readily available. They come in a range of colours and are usually pre-washed, with the ends finished in hand-tied knots.

There are several different styles of fabric, with villages specializing in particular types of weaving. **Hol** is a time-honoured cloth decorated with small patterns symbolizing flowers, butterflies and diamonds, and traditionally produced with threads of five basic colours – yellow, red, black, green and blue (modern variations use pastel shades). The vibrant, shimmering hues change depending on the direction from which they are viewed. **Parmoong** is a lustrous ceremonial fabric, made by weaving a motif or border of gold or silver thread onto plain silk. Some *parmoong* is woven exclusively for men in checks or stripes of cream, green or red, to be worn in sarongs. Traditional wall-hangings, **pedan**, come in classical designs often featuring stylized temples and animals such as elephants and lions; they're inexpensive ($5–10) and easily transportable.

Wood and stone carvings

Wood and stone carvings are available in a wide range of sizes, from small heads of Jayavarman VII, costing just a couple of dollars, to almost life-sized dancing apsaras costing hundreds of dollars. In Phnom Penh you'll find a good selection along Street 178 near the National Museum, or in Psar Toul Tom Poung, though the fact that they're mass-produced means that they lack a certain finesse; to find something really fine you're better off at the workshop of the Artisans d'Angkor in Siem Reap (see p.141) or a traditional stone-carving village such as Santok (see p.205).

Antiques and curios

Antiques and **curios** can be found at specialist stalls in and around Psar Toul Tom Poung in Phnom Penh, and at the Siem Reap Night Market. Look out for the partitioned **wooden boxes** used to store betel-chewing equipment, as well as elegant silver boxes for the betel nuts, phials for the leaves and paste, and cutters – a bit like small shears – for slicing the nuts. There are plenty of **religious artefacts** available too, from wooden Buddha images and other carvings to brass bowls and offering plates.

You may occasionally find antiquated traditional **musical instruments**, such as the *chapei*, a stringed instrument with a long neck and a round sound-box; and the *chhing*, in which the two small brass plates, similar to castanets in appearance, are played by being brushed against each other.

Compasses used in the ancient Chinese art of feng shui can be bought for just a few dollars; they indicate compass directions related to the five elements – wood, fire, earth, metal and water. You might also be able to search out **opium weights**, used to weigh out the drug and often formed in the shape of small human figures or animals.

Cambodia's ancient temples have suffered massively from looting, and although it's unlikely that you'll be offered ancient figurines (most of the trade goes to Bangkok or Singapore), many other stolen artefacts – such as chunchiet funerary statues from Rattanakiri – are finding their way onto the market. To export anything purporting to be an antique you'll need the correct paperwork, so check the dealer can provide this before agreeing a deal. Also be aware that Cambodians are expert at artificially ageing their wares and be sure that you want the item for its own sake rather than because of its alleged antiquity.

Woven baskets, rattan and bamboo

A versatile fibre, **rattan** is used to produce furniture as well as household items such as baskets, bowls and place mats. In Rattanakiri you can find **khapa**, deep, conical rattan-and-bamboo baskets fitted with shoulder straps so that they can be worn on the back; they cost around $10 and are still used by the chunchiet to carry produce to market. Everyday items made from rattan and bamboo and available in the markets can also make interesting souvenirs, including noodle ladles and nested baskets; the latter

are used to measure out portions of rice but are also useful back home for storing fruit and vegetables.

Silver and gold

Most **silverware** in Cambodia is sold in Phnom Penh and produced in villages nearby, particularly Kompong Luong. The price will give you an indication of whether an item is solid silver or silver-plated copper – a few dollars for the silver-plated items; more than double that for a comparable item in solid silver. Small silver or silver-plated boxes in the shape of fruits or animals make terrific, inexpensive gifts. Considerably more expensive are ceremonial plates and offering bowls, usually made of solid silver and intricately decorated with leaf motifs. Silver necklaces, bracelets and earrings, mostly imported from Indonesia, are sold only for the tourist market (Khmers don't rate the metal for jewellery) and go for just a few dollars in the markets; modern silver designer jewellery is also available in the NGO-run shops and boutiques of Phnom Penh and Siem Reap.

There's nothing sentimental or romantic about the Khmer obsession with **gold jewellery**. This is considered a means of investment and explains the hundreds of gold dealers in and around markets all over the country, where it's not unusual to see local people negotiating to trade in their jewellery for more expensive pieces. Gold is good value and items can be made up quickly and quite cheaply to your own design, and even set with gems from Pailin and Rattanakiri.

Travel essentials

Climate

Cambodia remains consistently hot year-round – seasons are defined principally by rainfall rather than temperature (see box, p.42). The **dry season** runs from November to May, subdivided into the so-called **cool season** (Nov–Feb), the peak tourist period, and the slightly warmer and more humid **hot season** (March–May). The **rainy season** (roughly June–Oct) is when the country receives most of its annual rainfall, although occasional downpours can occur at pretty much any time of year.

Costs

Cambodia is one of the cheapest Asian countries to visit, and although prices are starting to creep up, the country still offers outstanding value.

TOP 5 MARKETS
Angkor Night Market, Siem Reap
See p.154
Banlung market See p.228
Central Market, Phnom Penh See p.75
Psar Chas, Siem Reap See p.154
Russian Market, Phnom Penh See p.90

AVERAGE MAXIMUM DAILY TEMPERATURES (°C) AND AVERAGE MONTHLY RAINFALL (MM)												
	Jan	Feb	Mar	Apr	May	Jun	Jul	Aug	Sep	Oct	Nov	Dec
PHNOM PENH												
°C	31	32	34	35	34	33	32	32	31	30	30	30
Rainfall (mm)	10	10	45	80	120	150	165	160	215	240	135	55

Good budget **rooms** are available for around $7 in most parts of the country (slightly more in Phnom Penh and Siem Reap). **Eating** is also cheap. A meal at a local market or Khmer restaurant can be had for $2 or even less, while main courses in tourist restaurants start from as little as $2 (although upscale places can cost considerably more). A small bottle of mineral water costs just 1000 riel, while draught beer usually sells for $1 a glass. **Transport** is similarly inexpensive – $1 per hour of travel suffices as a rough rule of thumb, although you'll pay a bit more on certain routes or when travelling with more upmarket bus companies. **Entrance fees** are also generally modest – tickets to visit the temples at Angkor are excellent value, although a few museums and other sights are disproportionately expensive.

Transport and **tours** are the two things most likely to blow your budget. Hiring a car and driver to explore remote temples like Banteay Chhmar, Koh Ker, Preah Khan (Kompong Thom) and Preah Vihear can easily set you back something in the region of $60–100 per day. Tours are also pricey. Visiting the temples of Angkor by tuk-tuk is relatively inexpensive, but more unusual tours – personalized itineraries around the Mekong Trail, trekking in Rattanakiri, birdwatching and boat trips, quad-biking, horseriding, and so on – will generally set you back at least $60 a day, and often much more.

All of which means that staying in budget guesthouses, eating at local restaurants and markets and travelling on public transport you could conceivably get by on as little as $10 per person a day if travelling in a couple and cutting out all extras. Eating in tourist restaurants, indulging in a few beers and taking the occasional tour by tuk-tuk will push this up to $15–20 a day. For $50 a day you can live comfortably, staying in nice hotels and eating well, while $100 a day allows you to stay in luxurious accommodation – although it's also possible to spend a lot more than this.

A **sales tax** (comprising a ten percent government tax and ten percent service) is often charged in mid-range hotels. Always check in advance. Tax is also sometimes added to food at restaurants – in which case this should be clearly stated on the menu.

Electricity

The electrical supply is 220 volts AC, 50Hz. Most Cambodian sockets take two-pin, round-pronged plugs (although you'll also find some which take two-pin, flat-pronged plugs). The electricity supply is pretty reliable, although power cuts are not unknown and some places (particularly island resorts in the south) may rely on solar power.

Gay and lesbian Cambodia

Gay and lesbian travellers shouldn't experience any problems when travelling in Cambodia – homosexuality is not illegal, although neither is it recognized and talked about. It's acceptable for two men or two women to link hands or arms in public, which would be unacceptable for straight couples. Cambodians find overt displays of affection offensive, however, so it's as well to be discreet. Be that as it may, there's an emerging **gay scene** (Ⓦ cambodia-gay.com) with gay-friendly establishments in Phnom Penh, Siem Reap (which has the country's only male-exclusive resort, the *Men's Resort and Spa*; Ⓦ mens-resort.com) and Sihanoukville.

Insurance

Before travelling to Cambodia you'd do well to take out an insurance policy to cover against theft, loss of personal items and documentation, illness and injury. However, before you pay for a new policy, it's worth checking whether you are already covered: some all-risks home insurance policies may cover your possessions when overseas, and many private medical schemes include cover when abroad –

ROUGH GUIDES TRAVEL INSURANCE

Rough Guides has teamed up with WorldNomads.com to offer great **travel insurance deals**. Policies are available to residents of more than 150 countries, with cover for a wide range of adventure sports, 24hr emergency assistance, high levels of medical and evacuation cover and a stream of travel safety information. Roughguides.com users can take advantage of their policies online 24/7, from anywhere in the world – even if you're already travelling. And since plans often change when you're on the road, you can extend your policy and even claim online. Roughguides.com users who buy travel insurance with WorldNomads.com can also leave a positive footprint and donate to a community development project. For more information, go to ⓦroughguides.com/travel-insurance.

check that they cover Cambodia. Students will often find that their student health coverage extends during the vacations and for one term beyond the date of last enrolment.

A typical **travel insurance policy** usually provides cover for the loss of baggage, tickets and – up to a certain limit – cash or cheques, as well as cancellation or curtailment of your journey. Most of them exclude so-called "dangerous" activities unless an extra premium is paid: in Cambodia this can mean scuba diving, riding a motorbike and trekking.

Internet

Getting online in Cambodia is relatively easy. Almost all hotels and guesthouses now offer **free wi-fi** (as do many restaurants and bars), while most towns of any size boast at least one internet café. Rates are generally cheap (2000–4000 riel/hr), although connections may be slow.

Laundry

You can get laundry done practically everywhere, at hotels and guesthouses or at private laundries in all towns – look for the signs in English. Prices are pretty uniform, at 500–1000 riel per item or $1–2 per kilogram. In Phnom Penh and Siem Reap there are a number of places with driers, giving a speedy turnaround (3hr).

Mail

Mail to Europe, Australasia and North America takes between five and ten days. Stamps for **postcards** cost around 3000 riel to Europe/North America.

Airmail parcels to Europe and North America cost more than $20 per kilo, so if you're heading to Thailand it's worth waiting until you get there, where postage is cheaper. You'll be charged 3000 riel for the obligatory customs form, detailing the

contents and their value, but it isn't necessary to leave the package open for checking. Post offices also sell cardboard boxes for mailing items.

Poste restante mail can be received at the main post offices in Phnom Penh, Sihanoukville and Siem Reap, for 500 riel per item. When collecting mail, bring your passport as proof of identity and ask them to check under both your first name and your family name.

Maps

Most maps of Cambodia are horribly inaccurate and/or out of date. Far and away the best is Reise Know-How's *Kambodscha* map (that's "Cambodia" in German), beautifully drawn on un-rippable water-proof paper, and as detailed and up-to-date as you could hope, given Cambodia's ever-developing road network.

Money

Cambodia uses a **dual-currency system**, with local currency, the riel, used alongside (and interchange-ably with) the US dollar, converted at the rate of 4000 riel to US$1 (an exchange rate which has remained stable for several years now). **Riel notes** (there are no riel coins, nor is US coinage used in Cambodia) are available in denominations of 100, 500, 1000, 2000, 5000, 10,000, 20,000, 50,000 and 100,000. You can **pay** for most things – and will receive change – either in dollars, in riel, or even in a mixture of the two; there's no need to change dollars into riel. Larger sums are usually quoted in dollars and smaller amounts in riel (although sometimes, as in menus, prices are quoted in both currencies).

Things get a bit more confused near the Thai border, where Thai **baht** are generally preferred to riel, or at Bavet, the Vietnamese border crossing, where you may be quoted prices in Vietnamese **dong**. If you don't have baht you can generally pay

> ### MONEY ON ARRIVAL
> There are ATMs at both Phnom Penh and Siem Reap international airports and in the border areas at Poipet, Bavet and Koh Kong, so you can get US$ cash as soon as you **arrive in Cambodia**. Note also that unless you have obtained a **Cambodian visa** in advance, you'll need $20 in cash to buy one on arrival.

in US dollars or riel, though you might end up paying fractionally more.

Bargaining

Prices at upmarket hotels, shops, food stalls, cafés and restaurants are fixed, as are fares for flights, bus journeys and boat trips. However, when shopping in markets, taking motos, tuk-tuks or cyclos, **bargaining** is expected. Prices in more downmarket hotels can often be negotiated as well, especially if you're going to be staying for a few nights or longer.

Accessing your money

All large (and an increasing number of smaller) Cambodian towns now have **ATMs** accepting foreign cards and dispensing US dollars. The two main networks are those belonging to **Canadia Bank** (which accept both Visa and MasterCard) and **Acleda Bank** (pronounced *A-See-Lay-Dah*, which accept Visa only). Canadia Bank ATMs won't charge you a commission fee to withdraw money – although you'll still be charged by your card issuer back home – while Acleda and other banks generally charge $4–5 on top of whatever fees are levied by your card provider.

An increasing number of places accept **credit cards**, typically mid- and upper-range hotels and Western-oriented restaurants and shops in bigger towns and cities. You may be charged a surcharge (around five percent) if paying by card, however.

Most banks also change **travellers' cheques**, usually for a two-percent commission; travellers' cheques in currencies other than dollars are sometimes viewed with suspicion and may be rejected. You can also get **cash advances** on Visa and MasterCard at some banks and exchange bureaux (including the Canadia, ANZ and Acleda banks – although the last accepts Visa only). It's also possible to have money **wired from home**. The Acleda Bank handles Western Union transfers, while the Canadia Bank is the agent for Moneygram. Fees, needless to say, can be steep.

While there's no need to change dollars into riel, if you need to **change currency** you can head to a bank – there will be one or two **money-changers** around most markets in the country. Thai baht, pounds sterling and euros are all widely accepted for exchange, although other currencies may not be, especially outside larger cities and tourist centres. Check your money carefully before leaving and feel free to reject any notes in particularly dire condition, especially larger-denomination dollar bills with tears or blemishes.

Banking hours are generally Monday to Friday 8.30am to 3.30pm (often also Sat 8.30–11.30am).

Opening hours and public holidays

Key **tourist sights**, such as the National Museum, the Royal Palace, Silver Pagoda and Toul Sleng Genocide Museum in Phnom Penh, are open every day including most public holidays. The temples at Angkor, Tonle Bati and Sambor Prei Kuk and the country's national parks are open daily from dawn to dusk. **Markets** open daily from around 6am until 5pm, **shops** between 7am and 7pm (or until 9/10pm in tourist areas). The main **post office** in Phnom Penh is open from 7.30am to 5pm Monday to Friday, 7.30am to 11am on Saturday. In the provinces, post office hours tend to be 8am to 11am and 2pm to 5.30pm (earlier on Saturday), with some, in Siem Reap, for example, open on Sunday. **Banks** tend to open Monday to Friday from 8.30am to 3.30pm, and sometimes on Saturday as well, between 8.30am and 11.30am.

Public holidays

Dates for Buddhist religious **holidays** are variable, changing each year with the lunar calendar. Any public holidays that fall on a Saturday or Sunday are taken the following Monday.

Note that public holidays are often "stretched" by a day or so, particularly at Khmer New Year, Bonn Pchum Ben and for the Water Festival.

CALENDAR OF PUBLIC HOLIDAYS

January 1 International New Year's Day
January 7 Victory Day, celebrating the liberation of Phnom Penh from the Khmer Rouge in 1979
February (variable) Meak Mochea, celebrating Buddhist teachings and precepts
March 8 International Women's Day
April 13/14 (variable) Bonn Chaul Chhnam (Khmer New Year)
April/May (variable) Visaka Bochea, celebrating the birth, enlightenment and passing into nirvana of the Buddha

May 1 Labour Day
May (variable) Bonn Chroat Preah Nongkoal, the "Royal Ploughing Ceremony"
May 13–15 (variable) King Sihamoni's Birthday
June 1 International Children's Day
June 18 Her Majesty the Queen Mother's Birthday
September 24 Constitution Day
Late September/early October (variable) Bonn Pchum Ben, "Ancestors' Day"
October 15 King Father's Commemoration Day, celebrating the memory of Norodom Sihanouk
October 23 Anniversary of the Paris Peace Accords
October 29–November 1 (variable) King's Coronation Day
November 9 Independence Day
Early November Bonn Om Toeuk, "Water Festival"
December 10 UN Human Rights Day

Outdoor activities

Cambodia's vast potential for **outdoor and adventure activities** is slowly being tapped, with myriad tour operators offering an ever-expanding spread of one-day trips and more extended tours. The main appeal of most outdoor activities is the chance to get off the beaten track and out into the countryside for a glimpse of the time-forgotten lifestyles of rural Cambodia, with numerous trekking opportunities, along with trips by bike, kayak and boat.

Trekking, ranging from one-day to week-long hikes, is the major draw in the upland forests of eastern Cambodia. Banlung is the main trekking centre, while there are also a growing range of hiking opportunities at Sen Monorom, including the chance to walk through the forest with elephants at the innovative Elephant Valley Project (see p.238). Hiking trips around Siem Reap can be arranged through Hidden Cambodia and Terre Cambodge (see p.145). In the south, you can hike into the southern Cardamoms from the community-based ecotourism project Chi Phat (see p.267) – they arrange trekking and cycling trips that last

from just a morning to a few days. The Wild KK Project in Koh Kong (see p.265) offers multi-day adventures into the Areng Valley (deep in the Cardamoms), including hiking, cycling and kayaking.

Cycling tours are another popular option, ideally suited to Cambodia's predominantly flat terrain and extensive network of relatively traffic-free rural backroads. Tours are run by Camouflage, Terre Cambodge and Hidden Cambodia in Siem Reap (see p.145), Grasshopper Adventures in Phnom Penh (see p.78) and Siem Reap (see p.14), Soksabike in Battambang (see p.118) and the Wild KK Project in the south (see p.265). There are also many cycling possibilities around the Mekong Trail (see p.218), with tours run by Xplore Asia in Stung Treng (see p.226), who can also arrange trekking, cycling and fishing trips. The country's rough backcountry dirt tracks are also a magnet for **off-road motorbike** enthusiasts; Hidden Cambodia (see p.145) in Siem Reap organizes a range of group dirt-biking tours. **Quad-biking** excursions can also be arranged in Siem Reap through Quad Adventures Cambodia (see p.145) and in Kampot through Quad Cambodia Kampot (see p.270).

Cambodia's majestic lakes and rivers are another major draw. **Kayaking** trips are run by Sorya Kayaking Adventures in Kratie (see p.221), Green Orange Kayak in Battambang (see p.118), Indo Chine EX in Siem Reap and Xplore Asia (see p.226) in Stung Treng. There are also plenty of **boat trips** on the Mekong available at Kompong Cham, Kratie and Stung Treng; around the various floating villages on the Tonle Sap at Siem Reap, Kompong Chhnang and Pursat; and around Ream National Park, Koh S'dach and the islands near Kep in the south. There are also plenty of **watersports** and snorkelling/island-hopping trips available from Sihanoukville, plus **diving** at Sihanoukville and Koh S'dach (see p.252).

Elephant rides remain popular in Banlung, Sen Monorom and around the temples of Angkor, while

---

SEY

Walk around any Cambodian town towards dusk and you'll see groups of young men stood in circles in parks, on pavements, or any other available space playing the uniquely Cambodian game of **sey**. The aim of the game is simple, with a kind of large, heavily weighted shuttlecock being kicked from player to player around the circle, the goal being to keep the shuttlecock in the air for as long as possible. It's a kind of collaborative keepy-uppy rather than a competitive sport, although players typically attempt to outdo one another in the flamboyance of their footwork. Simple side-footed kicks keep the shuttlecock moving; cheeky backheels gain extra marks for artistic merit; and for maximum kudos players attempt spectacular behind-the-back overhead kicks, before the shuttlecock falls to the ground, and the game begins again.

horseriding excursions are available through The Happy Ranch in Siem Reap (see p.145). There's some outstanding **birdwatching** around the Tonle Sap lake at the Prek Toal Biosphere Reserve and at Ang Trapaeng Thmor Crane Sanctuary between Siem Reap and Sisophon. Visits can be most easily arranged through tour operators in Siem Reap such as Osmose tours and the excellent, albeit pricey, Sam Veasna Centre (see p.145).

There are **balloon**, **helicopter** and **microlight** flights above the temples of Angkor, while real adrenaline junkies should make for Flight of the Gibbon in Siem Reap (p.145), offering tree-top **ziplining** adventures through the forest canopy or **rock climbing** in Kampot (p.270).

Phones

If you are going to be spending long in Cambodia or making a lot of calls it's well worth buying a local **Sim card**, which will get you rates for both domestic and international calls far below what you're likely to pay using your home provider (although obviously you'll need to make sure that your handset is unlocked first – or buy one locally that is). Sim cards can be bought for a few dollars at most mobile phone shops; you'll need to show your passport as proof of identity. International calls can cost as little as US$0.25 per minute, while domestic calls will cost about 300–500 riel per minute.

Cambodia's three main **mobile phone service providers** are Cellcard/Mobitel (W mobitel.com.kh), Smart (W smart.com.kh), and Metfone (W metfone .com.kh), all of which offer reliable countrywide

---

CALLING HOME FROM CAMBODIA

There is no international directory enquiries service in Cambodia.
To Australia ☎ 001 or ☎ 007 + 61+ city code without the initial zero
To New Zealand ☎ 001 or ☎ 007 + 64 + city code without the initial zero
To the Republic of Ireland ☎ 001 or ☎ 007 + 353 + city code without the initial zero
To South Africa ☎ 001 or ☎ 007 + 27 + city code without the initial zero
To the UK ☎ 001 or ☎ 007 + 44 + area code without the initial zero
To the US and Canada ☎ 001 or ☎ 007 + 1 + city code without the initial zero

---

coverage, with Cellcard/Mobitel perhaps being the best. A pre-paid mobile broadband account costs around $30 per month, although given the universal availability of wi-fi, it's unlikely to be worth the money unless you're spending a lot of time in very out of the way places.

If you want to use your home mobile phone, you'll need to check with your phone service provider whether it will work abroad, and what the call charges are to use it in Cambodia. Most mobiles in the UK, Australia and New Zealand use GSM, which works well in Southeast Asia, but a North American cellphone is unlikely to work unless it's a tri-band phone.

You can make **domestic** and **international phone calls** at the post offices and telecom offices in most towns. These services are invariably run by the government telecommunications network, Camintel (W camintel.com).

Many internet cafés also allow you to make calls via **Skype**; better places have headphones with a microphone so that you can talk in reasonable privacy.

For **domestic calls** only, the cut-price **glass-sided booths** found in all major towns are a cheap option at around 500 riel per minute, payable to the attendant. The booths vary in their coverage of Cambodia's various networks: accessible numbers will be written on the side of the booths.

To **call Cambodia from abroad**, dial your international access code, followed by ☎ 855, then the local area code (minus the initial 0), then the number.

Photography

Cambodians generally love being photographed – although it is common courtesy to ask first; they also take a lot of photos themselves and may well ask you to stand in theirs. It's best to avoid taking photographs of anything with a military connotation, just in case. You can get your digital shots transferred to CD or printed at most photographic shops in Phnom Penh and Siem Reap, although the quality of the prints may not be as good as you'd get at home.

Time

Cambodia is 7hr ahead of GMT; 12hr ahead of New York and Montréal; 15hr ahead of Los Angeles and Vancouver; 1hr behind Perth; 4hr behind Sydney and 5hr behind Auckland; 5hr ahead of South Africa. There is no daylight saving time.

CAMBODIA ONLINE

GENERAL INFORMATION

Beauty and Darkness Ⓦ mekong.net/cambodia. Documents the dark side of Cambodia's recent history, and contains a photo gallery and biographies of some of those who survived the Khmer Rouge atrocities; also some travelogues.

Cambodia Daily Ⓦ cambodiadaily.com. Selected features and supplements from recent editions of the newspaper.

Cambodian Information Centre Ⓦ cambodia.org. Varied site offering information on everything from clubs and organizations to the legal system and even e-cards.

Cambodia Tribunal Monitor Ⓦ cambodiatribunal.org. Up-to-the-minute information on the Genocide Tribunal.

Go Cambodia Ⓦ gocambodia.com. Easy to navigate, general-purpose site featuring articles on all aspects of Cambodian life – from sport to music to women's rights and recipes – with links to other sites.

Phnom Penh Post Ⓦ phnompenhpost.com. Key articles from the daily English-language newspaper.

Royal Government of Cambodia Ⓦ cambodia.gov.kh. Official website of the Cambodian government, with profiles of the king, premier, information about the senate and constitution, and links to ministry and department pages.

TRAVEL AND TOURISM

Andy Brouwer Ⓦ andybrouwer.co.uk. This Cambodiaphile's site is full of travelogues, interviews with eminent Cambodian experts and links to associated sites.

Bayon Pearnik Ⓦ bayonpearnik.com. Online version of the free satirical magazine.

Cambodian Ministry of Tourism Ⓦ mot.gov.kh. Features the country's highlights, province by province, plus information on

accommodation, history and Khmer culture.

Canby Publications Ⓦ canbypublications.com. Convenient online extracts from Cambodian city guides.

Tales of Asia Ⓦ talesofasia.com. In-depth look at Cambodia by long-term Siem Reap resident, Gordon Sharpless, with plenty of tales and practical information on the vagaries of the country.

Tipping

Tipping is not generally expected, but a few hundred riel extra for a meal or a tuk-tuk or moto ride is always appreciated.

Toilets

Apart from in places that are used to catering for foreigners, squat toilets are the rule. In general there are no public toilets apart from a few places set up by enterprising individuals that you can use for a few hundred riel. It is fine to ask to use the loo at restaurants, even if you're not eating there, although you may sometimes wish you hadn't as they are often unsavoury. At transport stops there are almost always toilets out at the back, but you'll need to bring your own toilet paper, sold in the markets and worth carrying with you. Sometimes you may have to do as the locals do and take to the bushes – but remember there is still a risk of mines, so don't stray off well-trodden paths.

Tourist information

There are **tourist offices** in many larger towns, but most are chronically underfunded, totally lacking in English-speaking staff, and often closed even when they should be open. The best source of local infor-

mation on the ground is likely to be your hotel or guesthouse, or a local tour operator or travel agent. There are no Cambodian tourist offices abroad, and Cambodian embassies aren't equipped to handle tourist enquiries; there is some useful information online, however.

Travellers with disabilities

Cambodia has the unhappy distinction of having one of the world's highest proportions of disabled people per capita (around 1 in 250 people) – due to land mines and the incidence of polio and other wasting diseases. That said, there is no special provision for the disabled, so travellers with disabilities will need to be especially self-reliant. Stock up on any medication, get any essential equipment serviced and take a selection of spares and accoutrements. Ask about hotel facilities when booking, as lifts are still not as common in Cambodia as you might hope.

Getting around temples can be a problem, as even at relatively lowly pagodas there are flights of steps and entrance kerbs to negotiate. The temples at Angkor are particularly difficult, with steps up most entrance pavilions and the central sanctuaries. However, negotiating at least the most accessible parts of the temples is possible with assistance, while some tour operators may also be able to

---

SIX FUN THINGS FOR KIDS

Ballooning above Angkor See p.174
The bamboo railway See p.116
**Biking, horseriding and quad-biking in
Siem Reap** See p.145
A trip to the circus See p.118 & p.153
**Elephant rides at Angkor and Sen
Monorom** See p.170, p.176 & p.273
Kayaking in Kratie See p.221

---

arrange customized visits including all required
assistance – try Cambodia specialists About Asia
(Ⓦ aboutasiatravel.com).

Travelling with children

Travelling through Cambodia with children in tow is
not for the nervous or over-protective parent,
although many families find it a rewarding experience, especially with slightly older kids. Cambodians love children, although they do have a habit
of greeting them with an affectionate pinch, which
can be disconcerting – the protectiveness of the
West is nonexistent and there are no special facilities or particular concessions made for kids. On
public transport, children travel free if they share
your seat; otherwise expect to pay the adult fare. It's
worth considering hiring a car and driver – not only
will this mean you can stop when you want for food
and comfort breaks, but it'll be more comfortable –
although note that child car seats are not available.
Some **hotels** have family rooms, while extra beds
can usually be arranged. Note that under-11's are
admitted free to the Angkor Archaeological Park
(passport required as proof, or they'll be charged
the adult fee).

If you're travelling with a baby or toddler, you'll be
able to buy disposable nappies, formula milk and
tins or jars of baby food at supermarkets and minimarkets in the major cities, but elsewhere you need
to take your own supplies.

Visas

Visas for Cambodia are required by everyone
other than nationals of Laos, Malaysia, the Philippines, Singapore, Vietnam, Thailand and
Indonesia. Visas are issued on arrival for $20 at
Phnom Penh and Siem Reap international
airports, at Sihanoukville port, at all overland
crossings from Thailand and Vietnam, and at Voen
Kham from Laos.

A single-entry **tourist visa** obtained on arrival
($20; one passport photograph required, or pay a
small surcharge – usually a dollar or two – to have
your passport photo scanned) is valid for thirty
days, including the day of issue, and can be
extended once only, for one month. Note that at
the Thai border Cambodian officials may ask for an
bit more than the official fee (see p.264) – having an
e-visa (see below) avoids this hassle. You can also
buy a **business visa** ($25; one passport photo) on
arrival. Like the tourist visa this is valid for thirty
days, but can be extended in a variety of ways
(ranging from one-month single-entry extension,
three months' single-entry, six months' multiple-
entry and twelve months' multiple-entry; costs
range from $42 to $270). Multiple entries are only
available on a business visa.

Single-entry, thirty-day tourist **e-visas** are available
online at Ⓦ evisa.mfaic.gov.kh for $20 plus a $5
processing charge, although they are only supported
if you enter through the airports at Phnom Penh or
Siem Reap, or overland at Koh Kong, Bavet and
Poipet. They must be used within three months of
the date of issue. They're mainly useful if you're
entering via Poipet and wish to avoid the traditional
hassles associated with that crossing (see p.130).

Tourist and business visas can only be **extended**
in Phnom Penh at the Department for Immigration
(Mon–Fri 8–11am & 2–4pm; ☎017 812763,
Ⓦimmigration.gov.kh) 8km out of the centre
opposite the airport at 332 Russian Blvd. Given the
serious amounts of red tape involved and the
inconvenient location of the office, however, it's far
preferable to use one of the **visa-extension
services** offered by travel agents and guesthouses
in town, who will do all the running around for a
commission of around $5–10. If you **overstay** your
visa you'll be charged $5 per day. There is no
departure tax.

CAMBODIAN EMBASSIES AND CONSULATES

Australia & New Zealand Ⓦ embassyofcambodia.org.nz/au.htm.
Canada c/o Embassy of Canada, 15th Floor, Abdulrahim Place, 990
Rama IV Rd, Bangrak, Bangkok 10500, Thailand (☎ 066 2646 4300,
✉ bngkk@international.gc.ca).
Laos Thadeua Rd, KM2 Vientiane, BP 34 (☎ 02 131 4950,
✉ recamlao@laotel.com).
South Africa c/o Embassy of South Africa, 12th A Floor, M Thai
Tower, All Seasons Place, 87 Wireless Rd, Lumpini, Pathumwan,
Bangkok (☎ 066 2659 2900, Ⓦ dirco.gov.za/Bangkok).
Thailand 518/4 Pracha Uthit Rd (Soi Ramkamhaeng 39),
Wangtonglang, Bangkok 10310 (☎ 957 5851, ✉ recbkk@cscoms
.com).

BEER GIRLS AND TAXI GIRLS

Cambodia's **beer girls**, mostly working in local restaurants and bars, will approach you almost before you've sat down. Each representing a brand of beer, they rely on commissions based on the amount they manage to sell, and will keep opening bottles or cans and topping up your glass, hoping to get you to drink more. You don't pay them for the beer, as the cost is calculated at the end by counting up the empties. Although it is not part of the deal, some beer girls may drink and chat with men to up their consumption, but that's as far as it goes. In some Western establishments, beer girls may also help serve food.

Although things are more relaxed than they used to be, "decent" Cambodian women tend neither go to bars nor drink alcohol, so, while beer girls are somewhat looked down upon, the **taxi girls** who frequent the karaoke parlours and nightclubs are beyond the pale. Usually from very poor families, they have a role akin to that of hostess, dance partner and sometimes call girl rolled into one. If you invite them to join you at your table or dance with you, the charge will be added to your bill at the end of the evening, as will the cost of their drinks.

The **abuse** that taxi girls receive is a serious issue, and a number of NGOs in Cambodia – Ⓦ daughtersofcambodia.org, for example – have been set up to offer women alternative incomes in the form of spa and beautician training, handicrafts and the like.

UK & Ireland Ⓦ cambodianembassy.org.uk.
US Ⓦ embassyofcambodia.org.
Vietnam 71A Tran Hung Dao St, Hanoi (Ⓣ 04 942 4788,
Ⓔ camemb.vnm@mfa.gov.kh); 41 Phung Khac Khoan, Ho Chi Minh City (Ⓣ 08 829 2751, Ⓔ camcg.hcm@mfa.gov.kh).

Volunteering

There are plenty of opportunities to do **voluntary work** in Cambodia – although in many cases you will actually have to pay to do it. The UK charity Voluntary Service Overseas (Ⓦ vso.org.uk) and Australian Volunteers International (Ⓦ australianvolunteers.com) both recruit volunteers to work on projects in Cambodia, paid at local rates. Frontier (Ⓦ frontier.ac.uk) has projects teaching English or helping with wildlife conservation, while Coral Cay Conservation (Ⓦ coralcay.org) has an ongoing project on Koh Rong (cheaper if you have diving experience). When you're in Cambodia keep your eye out in cafés and bars where organizations post their projects and ask for volunteers. The services of teachers, doctors and vets will be much appreciated even if it's only for a day or so.

Women travellers

Travelling around Cambodia shouldn't pose any problems for foreign women. All the same, it's as well to dress modestly and to avoid overfamiliarity, which can be misconstrued, particularly after men have had a few beers. If someone does overstep the mark, a firm "no" will normally suffice to ward them off. A good ruse used by Khmer women is to subtly put yourself in a position of superiority, by referring to yourself as the older sister (*bpong serey*) or aunt (*ming*) or by addressing the man as nephew (*kmaoy bprohs*). If this doesn't work, then kick up a huge fuss so that everyone in the vicinity knows that you're being harassed, which should shame the man into backing off.

Phnom Penh and around

WAT PHNOM BAS-RELIEF, PHNOM PENH

1

Phnom Penh and around

"A city of white buildings, where spires of gold and stupas of stone rocket out of the greenery into the vivid blue sky." Such was American visitor Robert Casey's description of Phnom Penh in 1929, in which he also noted the shady, wide streets and pretty parks. The image bears a remarkable resemblance to the Phnom Penh of today, and life then seems to have been much as it is now, the open-fronted shops and shophouses bustling with haggling traders, and roadsides teeming with food vendors and colourful, busy markets. The capital of Cambodia and the heart of government is a captivating city of great charm and vitality, crisscrossed by broad tree-lined boulevards and dotted with old colonial villas. Situated in a virtually flat area at the confluence of the Tonle Sap, Bassac and Mekong rivers, the compact city hasn't yet been overwhelmed by the towering high-rise developments that blight neighbouring Southeast Asian capitals, although the construction of newer, higher, and more modern buildings is certainly gaining pace.

Such is the city's enterprise and energy that it's difficult to believe that a generation ago it was forcibly evacuated and left to ruin by the **Khmer Rouge**. Inevitably, and in spite of many improvements, some of the scars are still evident: side roads are pot-holed and strewn with rubble, some of the elegant villas are ruined beyond repair, and when it rains the antiquated drainage system backs up, flooding the roads.

It is testimony to the unflappable good nature and stoicism of the city's inhabitants that, despite past adversity, they remain upbeat. Many people do two jobs to get by, keeping government offices ticking over for a few hours each day and then moonlighting as moto drivers or tutors; furthermore, the Cambodian belief in **education** is particularly strong here, and anyone who can afford to sends their children to supplementary classes outside school hours. This dynamism constantly attracts people from the provinces – newcomers soon discover, though, that it's tougher being poor in the city than in the country, and are often forced to rent tiny rooms in one of the many **shanties** on the city's outskirts, ripped off for the privilege by affluent landlords.

Most of the city's **sights** are located between the Tonle Sap River and Monivong Boulevard, in an area bordered by Sihanouk Boulevard in the south and Wat Phnom in the north. For tourists and locals alike, the lively **riverfront** – a wide promenade that runs beside the Tonle Sap for nearly 2km – is the city's focal point. In the

NATIONAL MUSEUM, PHNOM PENH

Highlights

❶ Mekong boat trips Cruise the river as the sun sinks behind the Royal Palace. **See p.61**

❷ Royal Palace The soaring golden spires of the ceremonial Throne Room are Phnom Penh's most memorable sight. **See p.61**

❸ Silver Pagoda Home to a sacred emerald Buddha and a vast mural. **See p.64**

❹ National Museum A superb collection of sculpture from Cambodia's temples. **See p.67**

❺ Toul Sleng Genocide Museum Former torture chamber, now a grim museum to Khmer Rouge atrocities. **See p.71**

❻ Wat Phnom See the city from a different angle from the summit-top temple of Wat Phnom. **See p.72**

❼ Cyclo rides Enjoy an unhurried spin through the old French quarter. **See p.79**

❽ Psar Toul Tom Poung (Russian Market) Bargain for fine silks, antiques and curios at Phnom Penh's most enjoyable market. **See p.90**

❾ Choeung Ek The macabre killing fields, marked with a memorial containing thousands of human skulls. **See p.99**

HIGHLIGHTS ARE MARKED ON THE MAPS ON P.54 & PP.58–59

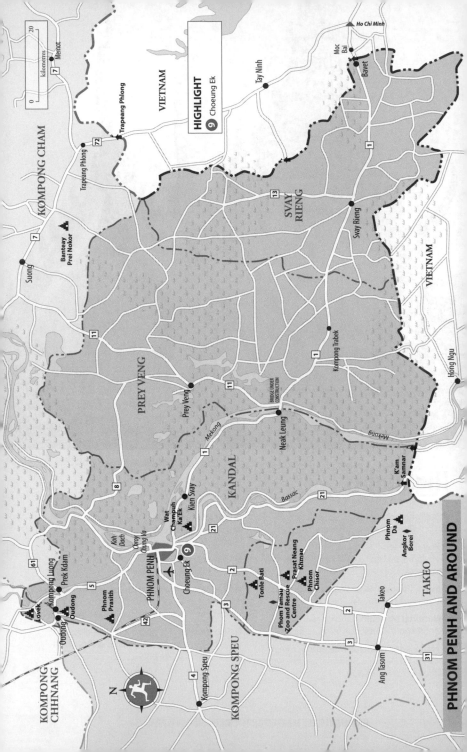

evenings, residents come here to take the air, snack on hawker food and enjoy the impromptu waterside entertainment; the strip also shows the city at its most cosmopolitan, lined with Western restaurants, cafés and bars. Three key tourist sights lie close by. Arguably the most impressive of the city's attractions is the elegant complex housing the **Royal Palace** and **Silver Pagoda** that dominate the southern riverfront. The palace's distinctive four-faced spire towers above the pitched golden roofs of its Throne Hall, while the adjacent Silver Pagoda is home to a stunning collection of Buddha statues. A block north of the palace is the **National Museum**, a dramatic, hybrid building set in leafy surroundings housing a fabulous collection of ancient Khmer sculpture dating back to as early as the sixth century. Also near the river are **Wat Ounalom** – one of five pagodas founded during Phnom Penh's first spell as the capital, whose austere grey stupa houses the ashes of many prominent Khmers – and bustling hilltop **Wat Phnom**, one of the city's prime pleasure spots, whose foundation is said to predate that of the city. The old French administrative area, often referred to as the **French quarter**, surrounds the hill on which Wat Phnom sits, boasting many fine **colonial buildings**, some restored, while to the southwest the daffodil-yellow Art Deco **Central Market** sits close to the city's business district. To the south of the city, the jam-packed **Russian Market** is a popular souvenir-sourcing spot while another much-visited sight, though for completely different reasons, is the **Toul Sleng Genocide Museum**: a one-time school that became a centre for the torture of men, women and children who fell foul of the Pol Pot regime.

Many visitors stay just a couple of days in Phnom Penh before hopping on to Siem Reap and Angkor, Sihanoukville and the southern beaches or to the Vietnamese border crossings at Bavet and Chau Doc. There are, however, plenty of reasons to linger. The capital has the best **shopping** in the country, with a vast selection of souvenirs and crafts, and an excellent range of **cuisines** in its many restaurants. There are also several rewarding **day-trips** from the capital out into the surrounding countryside.

Brief history

Cambodian legend – passed down through so many generations that the Khmers regard it as fact – has it that in 1372 a wealthy widow, **Daun Penh** (Grandmother Penh), was strolling along the Chrap Chheam River (now the Tonle Sap) when she came across the hollow trunk of a koki tree washed up on the banks. Inside it she discovered five Buddha statues, four cast in bronze and one carved in stone. As a mark of respect, she created a sanctuary for the statues on the top of a low mound, which became known as **Phnom Penh**, literally the hill of Penh; in due course, the hill gave its name to the city that grew up around it.

The founding of the city

Phnom Penh began its first stint as a **capital** in 1432, when King **Ponhea Yat** fled south from Angkor and the invading Siamese. He set up a royal palace, increased the height of Daun Penh's hill and founded five **monasteries** – Wat Botum, Wat Koh, Wat Langka, Wat Ounalom and Wat Phnom – all of which survive today. When Ponhea Yat died, his sons variously took succession, but for reasons that remain unclear, in the sixteenth century the court had moved out to Lovek, and later Oudong, and Phnom Penh reverted to being a fishing village.

Little is known of the subsequent three hundred years in Phnom Penh, though records left by missionaries indicate that by the seventeenth century a multicultural community of Asian and European traders had grown up along the banks of the Tonle Sap, and that Phnom Penh, with easy access by river to the ocean, had developed into a prosperous **port**. Gold, silk and incense were traded along with hides, bones, ivory and horn from elephants, rhinoceros and buffalo. Phnom Penh's prosperity declined in the later part of the century, when the Vietnamese invaded the Mekong delta and cut off

1

SAFETY IN PHNOM PENH

While Phnom Penh is no longer the Wild West town it once was, **robberies** are not unknown, and there have been instances of bags being snatched from tourists walking around key tourist areas including the riverfront and Central Market. Moto passengers, too, are increasingly becoming the target of bag-snatchers, so you should also exercise a bit of caution when taking **motos** at night. It's certainly not worth being paranoid, but taking a tuk-tuk at night may be safer (although bags have been known to be snatched from tuk-tuks too); keep your bag well out of sight of passing motorbikes.

Phnom Penh's access to the sea. The eighteenth century was a period of **dynastic squabbles** between pro-Thai and pro-Vietnamese factions of the royal family, and in 1770, Phnom Penh was actually burnt down by the Siamese, who proceeded to install a new king and take control of the country.

As the nineteenth century dawned, the Vietnamese assumed suzerainty over Cambodia. In 1812 Phnom Penh became the capital once again, though the court retreated to Oudong twice over the next fifty years amid continuing power-struggles between the Thais and Vietnamese.

Phnom Penh under the French

In 1863, King Norodom (great-great-grandfather of the current king, Norodom Sihamoni), fearful of another Vietnamese invasion, signed a treaty for Cambodia to become a **French protectorate**. At the behest of the French, he uprooted the court from Oudong and the role of capital returned decisively to Phnom Penh, a place which the recently arrived French described as "an unsophisticated settlement made up of a string of thatched huts clustered along a single muddy track, the riverbanks crowded with the houseboats of fisher-folk". In fact, an estimate of its population at the time put it at around 25,000. Despite Phnom Penh regaining its access to the sea (the Mekong delta was now under French control) it remained very much an outpost, with the French far more concerned with the development of Saigon.

In 1889, a new Senior Resident, **Hyun de Verneville**, was appointed to the protectorate. Wanting to make Phnom Penh a place fit to be the French administrative centre in Cambodia, he created a chic colonial town. By 1900, roads had been laid out on a grid plan, a law court, public works and telegraph offices set up, and banks and schools built. A **French quarter** grew up in the area north of Wat Phnom, where imposing villas were built for the city's French administrators and traders; Wat Phnom itself gained landscaped gardens and a zoo.

Towards independence

In the 1920s and 1930s, Phnom Penh grew prosperous. The road network was extended, facilitated by the infilling of drainage canals; the Mekong was dredged, making the city accessible to seagoing vessels; parks were created and communications improved. In 1932, the city's **train station** was built and the railway line linking the capital to Battambang was completed. Foreign travellers were lured to Cambodia by exotic tales of hidden cities in the jungle.

The country's first **secondary school**, Lycée Sisowath, opened in Phnom Penh in 1936, and slowly an educated elite developed, laying the foundations for later political changes. During **World War II**, the occupying Japanese allowed the French to continue running things and their impact on the city was relatively benign; in October 1941, after the Japanese had arrived, the coronation of Norodom Sihanouk went ahead pretty much as normal in Phnom Penh.

With **independence** from the French in 1954, Phnom Penh at last became a true seat of government and an educated middle class began to gain prominence; café society began to blossom, cinemas and theatres thrived, and motorbikes and cars took to the boulevards. In the mid-1960s a national sports venue, the Olympic Stadium, was built and world celebrities began to visit.

The civil war and the Khmer Rouge

The period of optimism was short-lived. Phnom Penh started to feel the effects of the Vietnam War in the late 1960s, when refugees began to flee the heavily bombed border areas for the capital. The **civil war** of the early 1970s turned this exodus into a flood. **Lon Nol**'s forces fought a losing battle against the **Khmer Rouge** and, as the city came under siege, food became scarce despite US efforts to fly in supplies.

On **April 17, 1975**, the Khmer Rouge entered Phnom Penh. At first they were welcomed as harbingers of peace, but within hours the soldiers had ordered the population out of the capital. Reassurances that it was "just for a few days" were soon discredited, and as the people – the elderly, infirm and the dying among them – left laden with armfuls of possessions, the Khmer Rouge set about destroying the city. Buildings were ransacked, roofs blown off; even the National Bank was blown up. For three years, eight months and twenty days Phnom Penh was a ghost town.

Vietnamese and UN control

With the **Vietnamese entry** into Phnom Penh on January 7, 1979, both returnees and new settlers began to arrive – although many former inhabitants either could not or would not return, having lost everything and everyone. Those arriving in the city took up residence in the vacant buildings, and to this day many still live in these same properties. During the Vietnamese era, the capital remained impoverished and decrepit, with much of the incoming aid from the Soviet Union and India finding its way into the pockets of senior officials. By 1987, Vietnamese interest was waning, and by 1989 they had **withdrawn** from Cambodia.

The UN subsequently took charge, and by 1992 the country was flooded with highly paid **UNTAC** forces. The atmosphere in Phnom Penh became surreal: its infrastructure was still in tatters, electricity and water were spasmodic, telecommunications nonexistent and evening curfews in force, but the city boomed as hotels, restaurants and bars sprang up to keep the troops entertained. Many Phnom Penh residents got rich quick on the back of this – supplying prostitutes and drugs played a part – and the capital gained a reputation for being a free-rolling, lawless city, one which it is still trying to lay to rest.

Modern Phnom Penh

The city of today is slowly **repairing** the dereliction caused nearly three decades ago; roads are much improved, electricity is reliable and many of the charming colonial buildings are being restored. Alongside, an increasing number of skyscrapers, high-rise apartment blocks and shopping malls are steadily peppering the horizon, particularly along Monivong and Sihanouk boulevards. With tourism firmly in its sights, the municipal government has set out elaborate plans to continue smartening up the city, ranging from dictating the colour in which buildings will be painted – creamy yellow

---

PHNOM PENH ORIENTATION

The city of Phnom Penh roughly extends from the **Chroy Chung Va Bridge** in the north to **Yothapol Khemarak Pholimin** in the south. The area around the yellow-domed **Psar Thmei** (literally New Market, although it's popularly known as the Central Market) where you'll find most banks, is loosely regarded as the **centre**.

There are two major north–south routes, **Norodom** and **Monivong** boulevards (and to a lesser extent, the easterly **Sothearos Boulevard** that snakes north towards **Sisowath Quay**), both intersected by the two great arcs of **Sihanouk/Nehru** and **Mao Tse Toung** boulevards, which act as ring roads; together, these four thoroughfares cut the city into segments and can be useful points of reference for specifying locations to taxi, tuk-tuk and moto drivers.

1

PHNOM PENH

Mekong

Choy Chung Va Peninsula

Tonle Sap

Docks

FRENCH QUARTER

Sokha Hotel (under construction)

Wat Sampeuv Trleak Temple

Chatomuk Theatre

Boat Terminal (Tourist Docks)

PsarChas

Wat Ounalom

National Museum

Royal Palace

Silver Pagoda

Ucare

SISOWATH QUAY

Wat Phnom

Tied Gun Monument

Transport for Mandulkiri

British Embassy

French Embassy

Calmette Hospital

Acleda Bank

Raffles Hotel Le Royal

Train Station

National Library/ Bibliothèque Nationale

Pharmacie de la Gare

Ucare

Psar Thmei (Central Market)

You Nam Supermarket

Psar Orussey

Psar Depot

Royal Rattanak Hospital

Psar Tuolkok (Tuolkok Market)

University

SEE 'CENTRAL PHNOM PENH' MAP FOR DETAIL

SOTHEAROS (3)

SOTHEAROS (3)

MONIVONG

NORODOM

PASTEUR (51)

CONFEDERATION DE LA RUSSIE (POCHENTONG BOULEVARD)

TCHECOSLOVAQUIE

AWAHARLAL NEHRU (215)

KAMPUCHEA KROM (128)

KIM IL SUNG (289)

YUGOSLAVIE

MAO TSE TOUNG

PENN NOUTH 289

CONFEDERATION DE LA RUSSIE

N

▲ National Highway 6 & Koh Dach

▼ Kingdom Breweries, Oudong, Lovek, Phnom Brasat & National Highway 5

▼ Phnom Penh Water Park, National Highway 4 & Airport

■ ACCOMMODATION

Cambodiana	3
Fairyland Hotel	4
Lazy Gecko	2
Narin 1	5
Okay	1
Sunday	7
TAT	6
TATTOO	8
Terrace on 95	9

● EATING

Alma Cafe	8
Café Yeji	7
Khmer-Thai Restaurant	5
K'nyay	2
The Lost Room	3
Shiva Shakti	6
Tepui	1
Topaz	4

◆ SHOPPING

Bayon Supermarket	2
Nyemo	8
Peace Handicrafts	9
Psar BKK	7
Psar Olympic	4
Psar Orussey	3
Psar Toul Tom Poung (Russian Market)	6
Rajana	10
Tabitha-Cambodia	5
Thai Huot	1
Tooit Tooit	8
Watthan Artisans Cambodia	6

■ NIGHTLIFE

The Doors	1

National Highway 1 & Bavet

Takeo, Tonle Batt, Phnom Chisor & National Highway 2

Wat Jum Pos Ka-Aik

Choeung Ek

HIGHLIGHTS

1 Mekong boat trips
2 Royal Palace
3 Silver Pagoda
4 National Museum
5 Toul Sleng Genocide Museum
6 Wat Phnom
7 Cyclo rides
8 Psar Toul Tom Poung (Russian Market)

– to evicting squatters and makeshift shops from areas designated for development. Boeng Kak Lake, for example, once a popular backpacker area, is now all but filled in and deserted to make way for a vast private development. On the eastern end of Sihanouk Boulevard, **Hun Sen Park** and **Naga World** – a sprawling casino and hotel complex heavily invested in by Cambodia's Prime Minister, Hun Sen – dominates the waterfront. It remains to be seen how many other changes this dynamic city will face, but for now at least, the feeling is broadly optimistic.

The riverfront

Sisowath Quay, hugging the river for nearly 4km from the Chroy Chung Va Bridge to Chatomuk Theatre, is the heart of the tourist scene in Phnom Penh, with a **weekend night market** and a plethora of Western **bars and restaurants** close to the Royal Palace and National Museum. From Street 106, midway along, the quay forms a broad promenade extending almost 2km south.

Every autumn, the river thrums with crowds flocking to the boat races and festivities of **Bonn Om Toeuk** (see below). For the rest of the year, the riverfront is fairly quiet by day, when it's a pleasant place to walk, and gets busier in the late afternoon when the locals come out to **dah'leng** – a term that means anything from a short stroll to an all-day trip out of town. At about 5pm, the pavements around the public garden by the Royal Palace turn into a huge picnic ground as mats are spread out, food and drink vendors appear and impromptu entertainment begins.

Preah Ang Dong Kar shrine

Home to a statue of a four-armed Buddha, the small **Preah Ang Dong Kar shrine**, opposite the Royal Palace, draws big crowds. The story goes that many years ago a crocodile-shaped flag appeared in the river and on Buddhist holidays it would miraculously appear on a flagpole. Now, the spirit of the flag, Preah Ang Dong Kar, has a permanent home here and people make offerings asking for wealth and happiness – at the same time helping the nearby flower and incense vendors to make a living.

Wat Ounalom

Sothearos Blvd, between streets 172 and 156 • Daily 6am–6pm

The rather sombre concrete chedi that fronts Sisowath Quay belies the fact that **Wat Ounalom** is one of Phnom Penh's oldest and most important pagodas, dating all the

---

THE BONN OM TOEUK TRAGEDY

The most important festival in the Cambodian calendar, **Bonn Om Toeuk** (known as the Water Festival), attracts more than two million visitors to the capital from the provinces each year to celebrate the reversing of the flow of the Tonle Sap River (variable, late Oct to mid-Nov). Many come to support their teams during the three days of boat racing, but most are happy to soak up the atmosphere with their families, eat copiously from the myriad street vendors and scoop up bargains from the sellers who lay their wares out along the riverfront. After dark the town remains just as animated, with free concerts and fireworks.

The sheer volume of people weaving a fragile dance along the riverfront is a spectacle in itself. Given the volatile mixture of millions of exuberant people and zero crowd control, it was almost inevitable that at some point something would go wrong. During the extravagant closing ceremony of the 2010 celebrations panic broke out as the several-thousand-strong crowd poured onto a narrow footbridge, causing a stampede in which 351 died. The following year's festival was cancelled as a mark of respect.

MEKONG CRUISES

Boats and their captains can be hired for a late afternoon **cruise** on the Mekong (around $10/hr, depending on the number of passengers; look out for the signs at the north end of the promenade), where you can sup a beer (bring your own) and watch the sun set behind the Royal Palace. Try friendly **Crocodile Cruises** (☎012 981559, �🌐crocodilecruise.com; sunset tour $10/person for 90min, Silk Island $25/3hr 30min, private hire $25/hr), which offers free pick-ups and a little more style (and comfort) than other boats; theirs are fitted with cushioned armchairs and loungers.

way back to the reign of Ponhea Yat in the fifteenth century – though there's little evidence now of its age. In the early 1970s, more than five hundred monks lived at the pagoda, which also housed the library of the Institut Bouddhique, subsequently destroyed, along with many of the buildings, by the Khmer Rouge.

The pagoda gets its name from its role as repository for an *ounalom*, a hair from the **Buddha's eyebrow**, contained in the large chedi behind the vihara; you can gain access if you ask at the small bookshop near the entrance. Within the chedi are four sanctuaries, the most revered being the one facing east, where there's a fine bronze Buddha. The monks use the **vihara**, which dates from 1952, in the early morning, after which time visitors can enter. Unusually, it's built on three floors, and houses a commemorative statue of Samdech Huot Tat, the venerable fourth patriarch of Cambodian Buddhism, who was murdered by the Khmer Rouge. Despite its unappealing exterior, the dark-grey chedi is worth a quick look for its **crypt**, in which hundreds of small cubicles hold the funerary urns of Cambodian notables, most of which are adorned with bright plastic flowers and a photograph of the deceased.

Royal Palace and Silver Pagoda

The **Royal Palace** and **Silver Pagoda** are Phnom Penh's most iconic buildings, their roofs adorned with soaring golden nagas and spires that glint enticingly against the sky. Built in traditional Khmer style, the crenellated wall that encases this complex of royal buildings, manicured gardens and relic-stuffed temples is painted pale yellow and white, the two colours representing respectively the Buddhist and Hindu faiths. Nothing now exists of King Ponhea Yat's palace, built here in 1434, and very little remains of the wooden palace of King Norodom – the great-great-grandfather of the current king, who moved his capital here from

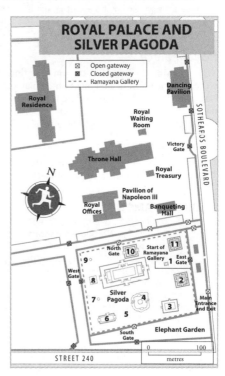

ROYAL PALACE AND SILVER PAGODA

- ⊠ Open gateway
- ⊠ Closed gateway
- --- Ramayana Gallery

STREET 240

1 Equestrian Statue of King Norodom
2 Chedi of King Ang Duong
3 Buddha's Footprint
4 Phnom Kailassa
5 Chedi of Kantha Bopha
6 Royal Pavilion
7 Chedi of King Norodom Suramarit
8 Scale model of Angkor Wat
9 Bell Tower
10 Mondap
11 Chedi of King Norodom

1

Oudong in 1863. Indeed, the current Royal Palace, official residence of **King Sihamoni**, dates back less than a hundred years, with most of the buildings having been reconstructed in concrete in the early twentieth century. Even so, the complex is well worth a visit for its classic Khmer architecture, its ornate gilding and its tranquil French-style landscaped gardens. The Silver Pagoda – ringed by a mythological muralled wall – is a particular highlight for its elaborate silver-tiled floor and priceless Buddha statues.

ESSENTIALS

Location The entrance to the complex is on Sothearos Blvd, between streets 240 & 184.

Opening hours Daily 8–11am & 2–5pm; to do the complex justice you'll need at least 2hr, but note that the staff start to close up 30min before the actual closing time.

Entry fee $6.50 or 25,000 riel, inclusive of camera fee.

Route From the palace entrance you're routed in an anticlockwise direction, visiting first the royal buildings and finally the Silver Pagoda.

Restrictions The royal residence itself is always closed to the public. On occasions, the Throne Hall is closed for royal receptions and when the king has a meeting with his ministers.

Dress code You must dress appropriately to be admitted: knees and elbows must be covered, and you are not allowed to wear hats or carry a (full-size) backpack.

Guides English-speaking guides can be hired by the ticket office for a whopping $10, but they provide a wealth of information, not just on the palace and pagoda, but also Buddhist and Khmer culture.

Photography Not permitted inside the Throne Hall or the Silver Pagoda.

Eating and drinking There are a couple of pricey refreshment stalls.

Shopping A shop on the site sells expensive silk, postcards and silver pieces.

Royal Palace

When visiting the **Royal Palace**, you may find that one or two of the royal buildings are either cordoned off or no longer on display (at the time of writing the **Pavilion of Napoleon III** was the latest to close for refurbishments, with an inconclusive opening date). There's still plenty to see, but if there's something you're particularly interested in then make sure to check with the guides at the entrance for the latest on any closures.

The Victory Gate

Entering the pristine outer gardens dotted with topiary trees takes you towards the **Victory Gate**, which opens onto Sothearos Boulevard and faces the entrance steps to the

---

KING SIHAMONI

Dancer, teacher, artistic director and United Nations representative, **Norodom Sihamoni** (born 1953) – son of the late **Norodom Sihanouk** and his seventh wife Monineath, and his name made up from the first four letters of each of their names – was elected to be Cambodia's king by the Throne Council in October 2004 on the surprise abdication of his father. Most of Sihamoni's life was spent outside Cambodia: from the age of 9 he was educated in Prague where he learned dance, music and theatre; he later studied cinematography in Korea.

In fact, other than his early childhood, the three years he spent **imprisoned** with his family in Phnom Penh during the Khmer Rouge years was the longest he spent in the country until becoming king. On the arrival of the Vietnamese, the royal family went into **exile** and for a year Sihamoni acted as private secretary to his father, but from 1980 he was in Paris (where he spent the next twenty years) as a professor of classical dance. From 1992, Sihamoni was Cambodia's permanent representative at the United Nations, and in 1993 he became its **UNESCO ambassador** – resigning both positions on becoming king. Sharing his father's love of cinema, Sihamoni was also director general of a production company, Khemara Pictures, and has a couple of ballet films to his credit. The king is a bachelor and keeps a lower profile than his late father. As yet he hasn't done anything to excite the media, though he is seen around the country and seems well regarded by his subjects.

Throne Hall. This was traditionally only used by the king and queen, though it's now used to admit visiting dignitaries. Just to the north of the gate, the **Moonlight Pavilion** (Preah Tineang Chan Chhaya) was built for twilight performances of classical Cambodian dance, as a dais for the king to address the crowds and as a venue for state and royal banquets.

The Throne Hall

The present **Throne Hall** (Preah Tineang Tevea Vinicchay) was inaugurated by King Bat Sisowath in 1919 as a faithful reproduction of Norodom's wooden palace, demolished in 1915. As befits a building used for coronations and ceremonies, it's the most impressive building in the royal compound, topped by a much-photographed four-faced tower. The roof has seven tiers (counted from the lowest level up to the base of the spire) tiled in orange, sapphire and green, representing, respectively, prosperity, nature and freedom. Golden nagas at the corners of each level protect against evil spirits.

The hall's broad entrance staircase, its banisters formed by seven-headed nagas, leads up to a colonnaded veranda, each column of which is topped by a garuda with wings outstretched, appearing to support the overhanging roof. Peering into the **Throne Room** from the east door, you'll find a ceiling painted with finely detailed scenes from the *Reamker* (see box, p.65) in muted colours, and walls stencilled with pastel leaf motifs and images of celestial beings, hands together in *sompeyar*. Down the centre of the hall runs a 35m-long, deep-pile carpet, its pattern and colours matching the surrounding tiles flanked by rows of gilt standard **lamps**, the lampshades supported by ceremonial nagas. The north and south entrance doors are protected by large mirrors, which are believed to deflect bad spirits. Unfortunately, since access to the throne room is forbidden it is almost impossible to get a proper view of the two elaborate golden **coronation thrones** ahead. They occupy a dais in the centre of the hall, above which a nine-tiered white and gold parasol, symbolizing peacefulness, heaven and ambition, is suspended; two large garudas guard the thrones from their position on the ceiling.

At the rear of the hall is an area where the king holds audiences with visiting VIPs and where the busts of six royal ancestors are displayed. **Anterooms** off the hall are used for different purposes: there are separate bedrooms for the king and the queen, to be used during the seven nights after the coronation, during which the royal couple have to sleep apart; another room serves as the king's prayer room; the last room is used to store the king's ashes after his death, while his chedi is being built.

The Royal Waiting Room

The imposing **Royal Waiting Room** (Hor Samranphirum), to the north of the Throne Room, is used on coronation days, when king and queen mount ceremonial elephants from the platform attached to the east side of the building for the coronation procession. A room at ground level serves to store the royal musical instruments and coronation paraphernalia. The pavilion is currently home to a collection of artefacts gifted to the monarch by foreign heads of state.

The Royal Treasury

Just south of the Throne Hall is the **Royal Treasury** (Hor Samritvimean), also known as the 'Bronze Palace', which houses regalia vital to the coronation ceremony, including the Great Crown of Victory, the Sacred Sword and the Victory Spear.

The Pavilion of Napoleon III

The incongruous grey cast-iron building with a domed clock tower and observation gallery is the **Pavilion of Napoleon III**, used by Empress Eugénie during the inauguration of the Suez Canal in 1869. Presented to King Norodom by Napoleon III in 1876, the pavilion was re-erected here and now serves as a museum of **royal memorabilia**, although it was closed for refurbishment at the time of writing. Downstairs, glass cases

1

contain a collection of royal silver and china tableware. There's also an anteroom housing paintings on subjects ranging from Venetian canals to Chinese landscapes, and a room glinting with gleaming medals. At the top of the stairs, the austerity of the building is relieved by a collection of silk costumes elaborately embroidered in gold thread; these were made by Queen Kossomak, the present king's grandmother, for the Royal Ballet. Royal portraits upstairs include pictures of the former King Sihanouk as a dashing young man.

Preah Tineang Phochani

The rather plain building to the east of the Napoleon pavilion is **Preah Tineang Phochani**, a classical dance hall often used to host royal receptions and meetings. Adjacent is the royal complex's south gate; passing through it, you cross the alleyway to enter the courtyard of the Silver Pagoda by its north gate.

Silver Pagoda

Constructed in 1962 by former King Sihanouk to replace the wooden pagoda built by his grandfather in 1902, the **Silver Pagoda** is so named because of its 5329 silver floor tiles, each around 20cm square and weighing more than 1kg. It's also known as **Wat Preah Keo Morokot**, the Pagoda of the Emerald Buddha, after the green Baccarat crystal **Buddha** within. The pagoda itself is clearly influenced by Bangkok's Wat Phra Kaeo, also home to a precious crystal Buddha to which the one in Phnom Penh bears an uncanny resemblance. Although more than half its contents were stolen during the Khmer Rouge years, the pagoda itself survived pretty much unscathed, and was used to demonstrate to the few international visitors that the regime was caring for Cambodia's cultural history. A rich collection of artefacts and **Buddha images** remains, making the pagoda more a museum than place of worship.

The pagoda

The vihara is approached by a stairway of specially imported Italian grey marble. On the veranda you'll need to leave your **shoes** in the racks. The silver tiles at the entrance are almost entirely covered with a rather tatty protective carpet, though a roped-off section close to the entrance affords glimpses of their delicately hand-engraved leaf motifs. Atop a five-tiered dais in the centre of the pagoda is the **Emerald Buddha**, seated in meditation. Some sources say this is a modern reproduction, though others date it from the seventeenth century; whatever the case, at just 50cm in height it's put in the shade by the magnificence of the images surrounding it. One of the most dazzling is the life-sized **solid gold Buddha** at ground level, in the centre of the dais; produced in Phnom Penh in 1907 for King Sisowath, it weighs 90kg and is encrusted with 2086 diamonds and precious stones taken from royal jewellery. To its left, a silver seated Buddha is perched on top of a display case, while to the right is a case containing some delightful gold **statuettes** depicting key events from the Buddha's life. The tiny, highly detailed representations show him taking his first steps as a child on seven lotus pads, meditating under a bodhi tree and reclining on reaching nirvana.

Tucked away behind the dais is a serene life-sized standing Buddha from Burma, the elegance of its aged, cream marble not diminished by the brash red of the wooden pedestal. A haphazard, though interesting, collection of Buddhas and other artefacts lines the back wall. The weighty gilded-wood **ceremonial litter**, over two metres long, and complete with throne, was used to transport the king on coronation day and required twelve men to carry it.

Display cases containing a diverse collection of objects line the pagoda walls, which include daggers, cigarette cases, headdresses and masks used for performances of the *Reamker* by the Royal Ballet. Sadly, recent years have seen many of the most impressive and precious exhibits replaced by a motley selection of frankly not very exciting items.

It's not known if they are away for restoration or have been removed permanently. Before leaving, check out the unusual **stained-glass windows**: one shows Hanuman (see below) astride a winged tiger.

The courtyard

Quiet and verdant, the pagoda courtyard is full of monuments. Just east of the Silver Pagoda you'll see the monument of a **horseman**. Now bearing a head of Norodom, it began life as an equestrian statue of Napoleon III, a typically megalomaniac gift from the French emperor. To either side of the statue are heavily embellished twin **chedi** – Norodom's to the north, Ang Duong's to the south (the latter also has a chedi at Oudong). In the east corner of the compound, a small plain pavilion contains a huge **footprint of the Buddha** (Buddhapada), a representation of the Buddha dating from the time before images were permitted to be made. There are also ancient manuscripts written on palm leaves, rare survivors of Cambodia's humid climate. Another stylized Buddha's footprint, this one a gift from Sri Lanka, can be found nearby in the pavilion atop the artificial hill, **Phnom Mondap**.

Southwest of Phnom Mondap lies the open-sided chedi of the daughter of King Norodom Sihanouk, Kantha Bopha, who died as an infant in 1952 of leukaemia and whose name has been given to children's hospitals in both Phnom Penh and Siem Reap. Behind the Silver Pagoda is a **scale model** of Angkor Wat – incongruous amid the religious and funerary relics. In the west corner of the compound is a **bell tower**, the pealing of whose bell used to signal the opening and closing of the gates to the compound. By the north gate is the **Mondap**, once housing palm-leaf texts, though now it houses a statue of Nandin, the bull ridden by Shiva.

THE RAMAYANA

The famous Hindu epic poem, the **Ramayana**, addresses the moral themes of good versus evil, duty, suffering and karma through the story of **Rama**, the seventh avatar of **Vishnu** (see p.302). A popular theme in Cambodian art and culture, its many episodes are depicted in temple carvings, pagoda art, classical dance and shadow puppetry. A simplified Cambodian version, the **Reamker**, also exists, more often portrayed in dance than in visual art.

At the outset of the story, ten-headed, twenty-armed **Ravana**, king of the *rakasa* demons, is terrorizing the world. As only a human can kill him, Vishnu agrees to appear on earth in human form to re-establish peace, and is duly born as Rama, one of the sons of Emperor Dasaratha. In due course, a sage teaches Rama mystical skills which come in handy in defeating the demons that crop up in the tale and in stringing Shiva's bow, by which feat Rama wins the hand of a princess, **Sita**.

The emperor plans to name Rama as his heir, but the mother of one of Rama's half-brothers tricks her husband into **banishing** Rama to the forest; he is accompanied there by Sita and another of his half-brothers, the loyal **Lakshmana**. After Rama cuts off the ears and nose of a witch who attacks Sita, Ravana gets his revenge by luring Rama away using a demon disguised as a golden deer; Lakshmana is despatched to find Rama, whereupon Ravana abducts Sita and takes her to his island kingdom of **Lanka**. While Rama enlists the help of Sugriva, the monkey king, Sita's whereabouts are discovered by **Hanuman**, son of the wind god. Rama and the monkey army rush to Lanka, where a mighty battle ensues; ultimately Rama looses the golden arrow of Brahma at Ravana who, pierced in the heart, dies ignominiously.

Although the tale as told in Cambodia often ends here, there are two standard denouements. In one, Sita steps into fire and emerges unscathed, proving she has not been defiled by Ravana, after which the couple return home to a joyous welcome and Rama is crowned king. In the alternative, sad, ending, Sita is exiled back to the forest, where she gives birth to twins. When they are 12, the twins are taken to court and Rama is persuaded that he is really their father. He begs forgiveness from Sita and she calls on Mother Earth to bear witness to her good faith. In a moment she is swallowed up by the earth, leaving Rama to mourn on earth for 11,000 years, until he is recalled by death to Brahma.

1

CENTRAL PHNOM PENH

Raffles
Hotel
Le Royal

National Library/
Bibliothèque
Nationale

Wat Phnom

US Embassy

Boat Terminal
(Tourist Docks)

Giant Ibis
Psar Reatrey
(Night Market)

Virak Buntham

Tropical & Travellers
Medical Clinic

NCDP

Psar
Chas

Canadia
Bank

ANZ
Bank

Foreign
Trade Bank
of Cambodia

Ucare

★ Transport Stop

The Flicks 2

Psar Thmei
(Central
Market)

Ucare

Psar
Kandal

KAMPUCHEA KROM

Vicious Cycles/
Grasshopper
Adventures

Wat
Ounalom

Sorya Bus
Station

Sorya
Shopping
Centre

Golden Sorya
Shopping
Centre

Seeing
Hands

Bodia Spa/
Ucare

Little
Bikes

Reyum
Gallery

Asasax Art

Mittapheap
Travel & Tours

Romeet

National
Museum

Royal
Palace

Preah Ang
Dong Kar
Shrine

Wat Ko

Psar
Orussey

RED CROSS ST

French
Cultural
Centre

Silver
Pagoda

Lucky
Lucky
Motorbikes

JOSEPH BROZ TITO
YOUGOSLAVIE

AEA International
SOS Clinic

KU Travel &
Tours

Cambodian-Vietnamese
Friendship Monument

Wat
Botum

Wat
Botum
Park

Phnom Penh
Tower

Diethelm
Travel

Canadian
Embassy

Naga Medical
Centre

Naga Medical

Ucare

ANZ
Bank

Independence
Monument

SURAMARIT

SIHANOUK BOULEVARD

Amret Spa

Wat
Langka

SIHANOUK BOULEVARD

Psar
Kabkoh

Lucky
Supermarket

Sayana
Rumdul
Spa

Meta
House

Azladee Spa

NataRaj Yoga

Cambodian
Living Arts

0   200
metres

ACCOMMODATION

11 Happy Backpackers	6
The 252	17
Anise	19
Billabong	12
Blue Lime	13
Bougainvillier	7
Camory Backpackers	3
Capitol 1	14
Dara Raeng Sey	4
Fancy Guest House	8
FCC Phnom Penh	10
Goldie Boutique	21
Lone Star Saloon	9
Mad Monkey	25
Manor House	18
Mini Banana	23
One Up Banana Hotel	24
Pacific	11
Paragon	5
The Patio	22
The Pavilion	16
The Quay	7
Raffles Hotel Le Royal	1
River 108	2
Top Banana	20
White Mansion	15
You Khin	26

NIGHTLIFE

L'Absinthe	11	Dodo Rhum House	13	Equinox	16	Metro	4	Score!	17
Aussie XL	18	Dusk Till Dawn	10	FCC	7	Le Moon	6	Sharky's	3
Bar Sito	14	Eclipse Sky Bar	15	Fish Bar	2	Pontoon	9	
Blue Chilli	12	Elephant Bar	1	Heart of Darkness	8	Rainbow Bar	5	

The Ramayana mural

Around the courtyard runs a fabulous 642m-long **mural**. Telling the epic tale of the *Ramayana* in minute detail, the mythical scenes were painted in vibrant colours by forty artisans working in 1903–04. The gallery cover has not protected the panels from water damage and despite a partial restoration in 1985, more work will be needed to preserve what remains. Running **clockwise**, from the east entrance gate, the depiction begins with the **birth of Rama** and covers his marriage to **Sita**, her abduction and her rescue by the **monkey army**. Two of the most delightful scenes, both in good condition, show the monkey army setting out for Lanka (south gallery) and crossing to the island (north gallery).

Outside the south gate

Leaving the courtyard by the south gate, there is a jumble of buildings and a small garden where **elephants** were tied up when not at work: look out for the elephant-shaped boxes and a pavilion of howdahs and cow carts. Another building houses an exhibition related to the coronation of King Sihamoni.

National Museum

Street 13, cnr street 178, north of the Royal Palace • Daily 8am–5pm, last admission 4.30pm • $5, camera/video (courtyard only) $1/$3; English-speaking guides can be hired at the entrance ($6)

Cambodia's impressive dark-red sandstone **National Museum** houses a rich collection of sculpture, relics and artefacts dating from prehistoric times to the present. The collection had to be abandoned in 1975 when the city was emptied by the Khmer Rouge; it was subsequently looted and the museum's director murdered. By 1979, when the population returned, the roof had collapsed and the galleries and courtyard gone to ruin – for a time the museum had to battle to protect its exhibits from the guano produced by the millions of **bats** that had colonized the roof; these were finally driven out in 2002.

The museum opened in 1918, and, designed by the French archeologist, George Groslier, comprises four linked **galleries** that form a rectangle around a leafy courtyard, its roof topped with protective nagas. **Entrance** to the museum is via the central flight of steps leading to the East Gallery. The massive wooden doors here, dating from 1918, and each weighing over a tonne, have carvings reminiscent of those at Banteay Srei (see p.188). The four galleries are arranged broadly chronologically, going clockwise from the southeast corner; allow yourself at least an hour for the visit.

East Gallery

The most striking piece in the **East Gallery** is a massive sandstone **garuda** – more than 2m tall, its wings outstretched – which dates from the tenth-century Koh Ker period. Displays in this collection comprise mainly sculpture, including an interesting combination of Buddhist and Hindu images; some from the fifteenth to seventeenth centuries are of gilded copper and lacquer. The case to the left, closest to the gallery entrance,

1

houses a fine statuette of Shiva and Uma on Nandin, while another contains an intricate Buddha atop a naga, framed within a separate arcature; just beyond is a miscellaneous collection of hands and feet from long-disintegrated statues.

The gallery also has a number of bronze artefacts, some dating back to the Funan period (first to sixth century). These include an assortment of elaborate candleholders, heavy elephant bells, religious water vessels and the paraphernalia for **betel-nut** preparation, including betel-nut containers in the shape of peacocks.

The far corner chamber has an interesting collection of **wooden Buddha statues** in various states of gentle decay, all post-Angkor and showing signs of the gilt paints with which they were once decorated.

South Gallery

The gracious head and shoulders of a vast, hollow reclining **Shiva**, with two of his four arms remaining, takes pride of place in the southeast corner of the museum. Beyond, in the **South Gallery**, a small but intricate collection of **Sanskrit inscriptions** on stones dating back to the fifth and sixth centuries are on display, many from the southern province of Takeo, supporting evidence of the region's political and religious importance during the pre-Angkor period.

Pre-Angkor

Further into the South Gallery, the focus is still on the **pre-Angkor** period (pre-ninth century), with slim, shapely sixth-century Buddhas in relaxed postures, their hair piled on top of their heads in tight ringlets. These early sculptors, though dextrous – the carved garments give an impression of the contours of the bodies underneath – had yet to master carving in the round, so the statues are carved in **high relief**, with stone remaining between the legs and arms.

Occupying pride of place is a 3m-tall, eight-armed image of **Vishnu** dating from the Phnom Da era (sixth century). The figure wears a plain, pleated loincloth low at the front and pulled up between the legs; the hands variously hold a flame, a conch and a thunderbolt, all symbols of Vishnu. A stone arc supports the figure, but in a step towards carving in the round, the stone has been chipped away between the arc and the limbs. Close by, on the south wall, is a sixth-century high relief of **Krishna**, standing left arm aloft, holding up Mount Govardhara.

Tucked under the roof in the central courtyard is a fine and varied collection of **linga** in excellent condition, while a series of voluptuous female statues of Durga and female divinities, wearing elegantly draped *sampots*, line the wall.

Angkor period

A ninth-century, Kulen-style **Vishnu** in the portico of the South Gallery marks the shift to the more formal **Angkor period** (ninth to thirteenth centuries) – notice how the sculptors stabilized the statue's bulk, carving the right leg slightly forward of the body and supporting the arms with a staff and sword. The late ninth-century **Preah Ko period** is characterized by comely figures, epitomized by the shapely statue of Queen Rajendradevi in the west corner of the central section of the South Gallery.

Passing between a pair of delicately carved sandstone columns, you enter the west section of the South Gallery and move into the **Bakheng period** (late ninth to early tenth century), exemplified by a 2m-tall Shiva from Phnom Krom.

During the **Koh Ker period** (early to mid-tenth century) sculpture became more dynamic, as illustrated by the athletic torsos of two wrestlers entwined in a throw (in the courtyard window). It's worth stepping outside here to see some of the original heads from the divinities of the causeway to Angkor Thom, and also an unusual ablutions bowl made from polished schist, the spout in the shape of a buffalo head.

This section also contains some particularly fine statues from the tenth-century temple of **Banteay Srei**, regarded by many scholars as one of the high points of Khmer art. On a central plinth, a smiling **Shiva** and his (sadly headless) wife Uma face the south. He is unadorned save for a carved necklace, but in situ they would both have been draped with precious jewellery. On the wall a striking pediment from Banteay Srei illustrates a scene from the *Mahabharata*, the Hindu epic of two warring families, showing two cousins, Bhima and Duryodhana, in mortal combat.

West Gallery

Dating from the late tenth century on, the sculpture in the **West Gallery** is more formal than in earlier periods. An elegant example of a graceful female statue of the eleventh-century **Baphuon period** is the slender, small-breasted Lakshmi, consort of Vishnu; her *sampot* dips at the front to reveal her navel and rises above the waist at the back. By this time, Buddhism was gaining influence, illustrated here by the Baphuon-era seated Buddhas, some showing a faint smile and sheltered by the seven-headed naga.

The **Angkor period** is lightly represented, freestanding sculptures having been largely replaced by the mighty bas-reliefs carved in situ at the temples. One of the few noteworthy examples, by the west wall, is a pediment from the west entrance of Angkor Wat, depicting part of the *Jataka*, the stories describing the previous incarnations of the Buddha.

Towards the far end of the gallery is the museum's most famous statue, the image of **Jayavarman VII**, from the **Bayon period** (late twelfth and early thirteenth centuries). Sitting cross-legged in meditation, the king is portrayed as a clean-shaven, slightly rotund middle-aged man, the expression peaceful. The head may well be familiar – it's much reproduced as a tourist souvenir. The Buddhist theme resumes in the Bayon-period exhibits at the north end of the gallery, where a thirteenth-century pediment from Prah Palilay shows a seated Buddha in the earth-witnessing *mudra*.

North Gallery

Leaving the stone statuary behind, you skip forward a few centuries to the miscellany of the **North Gallery**. By far the most impressive exhibit here is the cabin of a nineteenth-century **royal boat**, made of elaborately carved koki wood. Inside, the floorboards are smooth and polished, while leaves, flowers and dragons decorate the exterior; the cabin would have been lavishly furnished, ensuring that the king could travel in relative comfort.

The massive funerary **urn** in the centre of the gallery, nearly 3m tall and made of wood, silver and copper overlaid with gilt, was used for the ashes of King Sisowath in 1927 and again for those of King Norodom Suramarit, the grandfather of the present king, in 1960.

Not to be missed, just outside under the eaves behind the refreshment stand, is a magnificent **wall panel**, one of a pair looted from Banteay Chhmar temple in 1998 by the military personnel who were supposed to be guarding it. The blocks were cut out from the enclosing wall using machinery, loaded onto lorries and smuggled across the Thai border en route for sale in Bangkok, but were seized by Thai police on the way. Both were returned to Cambodia in 2000. Another panel reassembled here depicts a larger-than-life, multi-armed image of Lokesvara.

Wat Botum Park and around

South of the Royal Palace complex, flanking Sothearos Boulevard, the peaceful **Wat Botum Park** gets its name from the adjacent temple. Within the park is a golden stupa commemorating the sixteen people killed outside the old National Assembly (corner of Street 240 and Sothearos Blvd) building on March 30, 1997, when

1

grenades were thrown into a rally led by the Sam Rainsy party. Further south, the **Cambodian-Vietnamese Friendship Monument** – massive sandstone figures of a Khmer woman holding a baby, flanked by two armed Vietnamese liberation soldiers – commemorates the Vietnamese liberation of Phnom Penh from the Khmer Rouge in January 1979.

The park is a lovely place to stroll just before sunset, when a handful of trainers set up boom boxes and Cambodians pay 1000 riel to join them in a rigorously choreographed, unofficial **aerobics** class. You will see others taking a gentler, but equally serious, approach to exercise by walking determined laps around the park.

Wat Botum

Sothearos Blvd

Wat Botum is one of the five original monasteries founded by Ponhea Yat in 1442 (see p.55). Situated west of the Wat Botum Park, the present structure was built by King Sisowath Monivong and dates from 1937; fortunately, it escaped damage by the Khmer Rouge. The grounds are crammed with elaborate and picturesque chedis – notably the tall white gold-tipped Buddha's Relic Pagoda – many of which hold the ashes of rich politicians and important monks; enormous, gaudy statues of giants, lions and tigers pepper the grounds.

Hun Sen Park complex

Hun Sen Park, now home to **Naga World**, a gaudy casino, hotel and restaurant complex, lies east of Sotheraos Boulevard, and spills into adjacent **Koh Pich**, or Diamond. Once a quaint offshore farming village, the area now hosts a children's park, ornamental gardens, a golf course, a water park and a vast exhibition centre. It was on the footbridge linking Diamond Island to the mainland that the **stampede** occurred during the water festival in November 2010 (see box, p.60). Opposite Naga World is **Dreamworld**, Cambodia's biggest amusement park, while to the south lies the **Buddhist Institute** and the enormous **National Assembly** building. This stretch of road is particularly popular with the city's rich boys who come here to road-race their powerful SUVs in full sight of the police on guard at the Assembly building.

Independence Monument

Intersection of Sihanouk and Norodom blvds

Sitting amid an elongated strip of grassy park stretching west from Hun Sen Park and Naga World, the **Independence Monument** (aka Victory Monument) was built to commemorate independence from the French in 1953 but now also serves as a cenotaph to the country's war dead. The distinctive, dark-red sandstone tower, completed in 1958, is reminiscent of an Angkorian sanctuary tower, its multitiered roofs embellished with more than a hundred nagas. At night it makes a dramatic sight when the fountains are floodlit in red, blue and white, the primary colours of the national flag.

SPIRIT HOUSES

The alleys around Wat Prayuvong, around 300m south of the Independence Monument, are the city's centre for the manufacture of **spirit houses** (see p.305) and religious statuary – you can't miss the brightly painted displays on the roadside. Although everything is now made in concrete, the artistry remains elaborate and the variety is fascinating; a number of artists here also do religious paintings, some on an impressive scale.

Wat Langka

Cnr Sihanouk Blvd & Street 51 • Public meditation classes are held four times a week (see p.78)

Sprawling **Wat Langka**, one of the five pagodas founded in the city by Ponhea Yat in 1442, gets its name from its historic ties with monks in Sri Lanka. The pagoda vies with Wat Ounalom for importance, and many of the monks here are highly regarded teachers. Within the vihara scenes from the Buddha's life feature an idiosyncratic local touch – one shows Angkor Wat, while another depicts tourists climbing Wat Phnom.

Toul Sleng Genocide Museum

Entrance off Street 113 • Daily 7.30am–5.30pm; Bophana docudrama screened at 10am & 3pm • $2; English-speaking guide $6 • A short moto ride from the centre

Originally the Toul Svay High School, from 1975 to 1979 the disturbing **Toul Sleng Genocide Museum** was the notorious Khmer Rouge prison known as **S-21**, through whose gates more than thirteen thousand people (up to twenty thousand according to some estimates) passed to their deaths. S-21 was an interrogation centre designed for the educated and elite: doctors, teachers, military personnel and government officials. The regime was indiscriminate in its choice of victims; even babies and children were among those detained, and subsequently slaughtered, to eliminate the possibility of them one day seeking to avenge their parents' deaths.

Beyond the gates, still surrounded by high walls and ringed by barbed wire, an eerie silence descends on the complex of four buildings, juxtaposing harshly against the palm and frangipani trees in the former school playground. Up to 1500 prisoners were housed here at any time, either confined in tiny cells or chained to the floor or each other in the former classrooms.

Block A

The southernmost block, **Block A** (to the left of the ticket booth), comprises three floors of cells that still contain **iron bedsteads** and the shackles used to chain the prisoners to the beds. Chilling, grainy photos in each room depict the unrecognizable corpse of the bed's final inhabitant.

Block B

Walking across the garden past school gym apparatus used by the Khmer Rouge as a grotesque torture device, you come to **Block B**. On the ground floor you can see hundreds of black-and-white **photographs** of the victims, their eyes expressing a variety of emotions, from fear through defiance to emptiness. Each one holds a number; the Khmer Rouge were meticulous in documenting their prisoners and sometimes photographed victims following torture (also on display). The guides can tell you stories of some of the photographed victims.

Block C

The terrace and upper-storey **balconies** of **Block C** are still enclosed with the barbed-wire mesh that prevented the prisoners attempting escape or jumping to a premature death. The partition cells on each floor, of wood or brick, are so small that there is hardly room to lie down. When the Vietnamese army entered the prison in January 1979, they found just seven prisoners alive; the corpses of fourteen prisoners who had died shortly before were discovered in the cells and buried in graves in the courtyard. Although the majority murdered here were Cambodian, including scores of Khmer

Rouge cadres detained by the paranoid regime, foreigners, both Western and Asian, were also interrogated and tortured.

Block D

Things get no easier emotionally as you progress into **Block D**. Here methods of **torture** are outlined, some of them unflinchingly depicted in paintings by the artist Van Nath, one of the survivors. Prominent is a **water chamber** where prisoners were systematically held under water until they confessed. Worth reading are the sombre extracts in the exhibition area from forced "confessions", and the exchanges of letters between the cadres, who continued to victimize prisoners until their declarations conformed to the guards' own version of the truth. Newer exhibitions detail the ongoing criminal tribunals against the surviving Khmer Rouge leaders, the faces in many of the pictures so covered in graffiti that they now sit behind glass.

Upstairs in the same block, in the Documentation Centre of Cambodia, an hour-long made-for-television docudrama is screened twice daily: *Bophana*, by Rithy Panh, traces the tangled, tragic romance between two Cambodians caught up with the Khmer Rouge.

The French quarter

During the colonial era, **Wat Phnom** was at the heart of the **French quarter**, its leafy boulevards graced by several delightful **colonial buildings**, including the main post office, the National Library, *Raffles Hotel Le Royal* and the rather grand train station. Many of these survive today and the area is worth exploring to get a taste of their historic grandeur.

Wat Phnom

Northern end of Norodom Blvd • Daily 7am–6pm • Foreigners $1

In the northeast of the city, set back just a few hundred metres from the riverfront, the imposing white chedi of **Wat Phnom** sits atop the hill that gave the city its name. This is one of the principal pleasure-spots for the inhabitants of Phnom Penh, drawing the crowds especially at weekends and on public holidays. Before climbing the hill (which is just 27m high), you can either buy your **ticket** from the payment booth or a roving guard will inevitably approach you for cash once you reach the top. The nicest way up the hill is by the **naga staircase** on the east side, passing bronze friezes (depicting scenes of battle) and dancing apsaras (reproductions of bas-reliefs at Angkor Wat) on the way.

The sanctuary on the summit has been rebuilt many times, most recently in 1926, and nothing remains of the original structures. The surrounding **gardens** were originally landscaped in the late nineteenth century by the French, who also installed a zoo (of which nothing remains) and the clock on the south side of the hill, restored for the Millennium, with a dial that glows in fluorescent colours at dusk.

The vihara

Inside the **vihara** (remove shoes before entering) is a sitting Buddha, visible through the haze of burning incense, encircled by wall paintings evoking depictions of the *Jataka* stories. A constant stream of Khmer pass through the pagoda, paying their respects and trying to discover their fortunes by holding a palm-leaf book above their head and, without looking, inserting a small pointer between the pages; the page contains the prediction, although sometimes it takes three attempts to get an acceptable fortune.

Behind the vihara is a small shrine to **Daun Penh**, the woman credited with founding the sanctuary here (see p.55); the shrine contains her genial image, much revered. The large white chedi contains the ashes of King Ponhea Yat.

Preah Chao shrine

On the north side of the hill just below the summit is a busy shrine to **Preah Chao**, a Tao goddess whom people come to ask for good luck, health or success with their business; her helpers, Thien Ly Than (who can see for 1000 miles) and Thuan Phong Nhi (who can hear sounds 1000 miles away), stand close by. Judging by the elaborate **offerings** on the altar, it seems that many requests are granted – it's not unusual to see whole cooked chickens, surrounded by their cooked innards and unlaid eggs offered on plates. Resident **monkeys** frequently steal the offerings; feeding them is said to be a good way of acquiring merit for the next life, as is releasing the tiny birds that hawkers sell from cages all around the hill – you may spot a Cambodian buying up an entire cage – although it is rumoured that the birds are trained to fly back to their cages once released.

The post office

Street 13, cnr Street 102, one block east of Wat Phnom • Mon–Fri 7.30am–5pm, Sat 7.30–11am

Phnom Penh's main **post office** is housed in a fine colonial building east of Wat Phnom. Dating from the early twentieth century, it occupies one side of a colonial square just off the river which in pre-Khmer Rouge years bustled with cafés and restaurants; an attempt is being made to resurrect the area, but there's a way to go yet. The post office itself was restored in 2001; an old photograph of the interior hangs on the wall inside, the counters shown still recognizable today.

The National Library (Bibliothèque Nationale)

Street 92, between Wat Phnom and Raffles Le Royal • Mon–Fri 8–11am & 2–5pm

Set well back from the road, the **National Library** is a fine colonial building dating from 1924. During Pol Pot's regime, the books were either destroyed or tossed out onto the pavement, and the building was turned into a stable. In the 1980s, the Vietnamese filled up the shelves with their own books, though barely a decade later these were bound with string and sold by the kilo. It's now the French who are helping to gradually restock the library's eclectic collection (with Francophone titles). A room off the ground-floor reading room contains a collection of rare, century-old palm-leaf manuscripts, the colour of parchment.

Raffles Hotel Le Royal

Western end of Street 92

The **Raffles Hotel Le Royal**, established in 1929 and set in lush tropical gardens, is a fabulous blend of colonial, Khmer and Art Deco styles. Even if you're not staying (see p.81), you should take a look at the grand teak staircase and the vintage photos in the *Writers' Bar*, head to the *Elephant Bar* for cocktails (see p.87) or simply drop into the conservatory, a delightful spot to take morning coffee or afternoon tea.

The train station

Western end of Street 106

The **train station** occupies a commanding position facing the grassy avenue that runs between streets 106 and 108 to the river. Built in the early 1930s, it has an impressive Art Deco facade, but there's little activity here other than the freight

> **HORROR IN THE EMBASSY**
>
> Screened by high white walls, the **French Embassy** sits on the western side of Monivong Boulevard, just south of the traffic island. In April 1975, eight hundred foreigners and six hundred Cambodians took refuge here from the Khmer Rouge, whereupon they were held hostage and denied diplomatic privileges. Eventually, foreigners and Cambodian women married to foreign men were released and escorted to the airport. Cambodian men married to foreign women had to remain, never to be seen again.

trains running to and from Kampot. The unmistakeable blue chedi in front of the station, **Preah Sakyamoni**, used to contain a relic of the Buddha (it was removed to the more tranquil Oudong in 2002, from where it was stolen in 2013), while behind the station, an old 1929 steam train has been restored and put on permanent display.

Traditional healers work in front of the station, treating patients either by "coining" (scraping the flesh of arms, back or chest with a copper disc to raise the blood vessels) or "cupping", the alternative therapy championed in the West by Gwyneth Paltrow, where a heated glass jar is applied to the skin, causing raised red circles of flesh. Headaches, cold and flu symptoms, general aches and pains – indeed, just about any ailment – are claimed to be treatable by these methods.

Psar Thmei (Central Market)

Daily 7am–5pm

Edged on four sides by busy traffic-clogged streets, the much-photographed **Psar Thmei**, or **Central Market**, was designed by the French in 1937 and hailed at the time as Asia's largest. The original Art Deco design, highlighted by the enormous central dome and unusual cruciform shape, has made it a central, if unlikely, landmark. Reopened in 2011 after extensive renovations, its atmospheric central hall is laid out with stalls selling jewellery, spectacles and watches while its four enormous wings house low-grade electronics, household items, clothing and fabrics along with fresh produce, souvenirs and flowers. It is a smelly and eye-opening experience to stroll around the food stalls here, where every type of meat, fish, fruit and vegetable is on display. It's a good place for a cheap feed, too; fringing the market to the south are **food stands** selling local dishes for a few thousand riel.

Chroy Chung Va Bridge and around

As you travel north towards the **Chroy Chung Va (Japanese) Bridge**, the city becomes less attractive, albeit interesting for its history. The bridge, spanning the Tonle Sap, was blown up in 1973 either by (depending on who you believe) Lon Nol forces attempting to hold off the Khmer Rouge from entering the city, or by the advancing Khmer Rouge forces. Known from then on as *spean bak*, "broken bridge", it is now often referred to as *chuowa chuoul hauwy*, "not broken anymore". To others it is the "Japanese Bridge", as it was rebuilt with funds from Japan in 1993.

The traffic island at the northern end of Monivong Boulevard, just before the bridge, contains the curious **Tied Gun Monument**. In 1999, the government, concerned about the proliferation of firearms, seized all the guns it could lay its hands on and, amid great political fanfare, had them crushed. The remains were melted down and a sculpture of a **revolver** with a knot tied in its barrel was cast. However, cynics say that only the broken guns were smashed and that the good ones were handed out to the police and military.

1

KINGDOM BREWERIES

Cambodian beer might not be world famous but a brewery tour offers a fun diversion from Phnom Penh's more conventional sights. **Kingdom Breweries**, 1748 NR5, 200m north of the Chroy Chung Va Bridge (tours Mon–Sat 1–7pm by arrangement; $6; ☎023 430 1802, ⓦkingdombreweries.com), was established in 2009 as a boutique label. The 45-minute tour gives you an insight into the brewing process – interesting if you've never witnessed this sort of thing before – and includes a tasting at the end. The beer's not bad either!

ARRIVAL AND DEPARTURE PHNOM PENH

If you're travelling to Phnom Penh by **road** or **boat**, you'll most likely arrive at one of several terminals that lie within 1.5km of Psar Thmei. **Flights** arrive 8km west of town. Wherever and whenever you arrive, there are always tuk-tuks or motos available. Most towns and cities in Cambodia can be reached directly from Phnom Penh. **Siem Reap** is particularly easy to get to, served by a daily boat up the Tonle Sap, plentiful road transport along NR6 and regular, if expensive, flights.

BY PLANE

Pochentong International Airport The compact airport is 9km west of the city on NR4, a 30–60min drive from the centre, depending upon the traffic. Facilities in the international arrivals hall include several 24hr ATMs, money exchange, phones, luggage storage, a post office (daily 8am–6pm), a tourist information desk (see p.77) and an efficient tuk-tuk and taxi booth operating a fixed-price ($7 tuk-tuk; $9 taxi) service to the city. Motos are not allowed to hang around the terminal, but there are always plenty waiting on the main road, about 200m across the car park; the fare into town is $3–5.

Airlines Bangkok Airways, 61 Street 214 (☎023 966556, ⓦbangkokair.com); Cambodia Angkor Air, 206 Preah Norodom Blvd (☎023 666 6786, ⓦcambodiaangkorair .com); China Southern Airlines, 53 Monivong Blvd (☎023 430877, ⓦcs-air.com); Dragon Air, A4–A5 Regency Square, 168 Monireth Blvd (☎023 424300, ⓦdragonair.com); EVA Air, Suite 11, 79 Street 205 (☎023 219911, ⓦevaair .com); Jet Star Asia Airlines, 333B Monivong Blvd (☎023 220909, ⓦjetstaraisa.com); Lao Airlines, 58C Sihanouk Blvd (☎023 222956, ⓦlaoairlines.com); Malaysia Airlines, 35–37 Street 214 (☎023 426688, ⓦmalaysiaairlines.com); Qatar Airways, *Intercontinental Phnom Penh*, 296 Mao Tse Toung Blvd (☎023 424013, ⓦqatar.airways.com); SilkAir, Suite 2–4a, Street 217 (☎023 988629, ⓦsilkair.com); Thai Airways, 298 Mao Tse Toung Blvd (☎023 214359, ⓦthaiair .com); Vietnam Airlines, 41 Street 214 (☎023 215998, ⓦvietnamairlines.com).

Destinations: international Bangkok (7 daily; 1hr 10min); Doha via Ho Chi Minh (daily; 10hr 30min); Hanoi (4 weekly; 1hr 45min); Ho Chi Minh City (4–5 daily; 45min); Hong Kong (1–2 daily; 2hr 25min); Kuala Lumpur (4 daily; 1hr 50min); Shanghai (daily; 3hr 40min); Siem Reap (5–6 daily; 45min); Singapore (4 daily; 2hr); Taipei (1–2 daily; 3hr 15min); Vientiane (1–2 daily; 1hr 20min).

Destinations: domestic Domestic carriers in Cambodia come and go with alarming frequency and schedules change regularly, so it's best to check with a travel agent for the latest timetable. At the time of writing, Cambodia Angkor Air was the only domestic carrier operating (expensive) services to Siem Reap.

BY BUS

Bus companies There is no central bus station. Buses depart from their own offices or depots, many of which are in the vicinity of Psar Thmei or near the night market (and Street 104) at the northern end of Sisowath Quay. In addition, an increasing number offer free pick-up from city-centre hotels and guesthouses. Phnom Penh Sorya (southwest of Psar Thmei) has the largest depot in the city and serves all provincial towns, using smaller twenty- to thirty-seat coaches for the more distant or less popular destinations, including Kompong Chhnang, Kompong Cham, Kompong Speu, Neak Leung, Oudong, Tonle Bati and Takeo. They also run daily a/c coaches to Bangkok, Vientiane and Ho Chi Minh City. Giant Ibis and Mekong Express offer the most comfortable services to Siem Reap, Battambang, Sihanoukville, Kampot and HCMC. Virak Buntham's night buses (some with flat beds) travel to Siem Reap, Sihanoukville, Battambang and Bangkok via Poi Pet. Most operators schedule long-distance departures for the morning, although those for the most popular destinations, including Siem Reap and Sihanoukville, leave throughout the day. As at all bus stations and depots, it's a good idea to keep a close eye on your bags, whichever company you travel with.

To HCMC Journeys to HCMC, which is still often referred to as Saigon, can be made without joining a new bus across the border, and any official dealings are done with the assistance of the bus operators (although you still have to get your visa at least 24 hours in advance from your guesthouse).

To Bangkok Getting to Bangkok from Phnom Penh involves a change of vehicle after crossing the border (whereas from Siem Reap you can now take a direct bus).

To Laos If you're not heading direct to Vientiane check if your ticket is just to the border or through to Don Det, 4000 Islands.

Destinations Bangkok, Thailand (3 daily; 12–13hr); Battambang (10–12 daily; 6hr); Bavet (10 daily; 3hr 30min); Ho Chi Minh City (14 daily; around 6hr); Kampot (10 daily; 4–5hr); Kep (10 daily; 4–5 hr); Kompong Cham (10 daily; 2hr); Kampong Chhnang (10 daily; 3hr); Koh Kong (3 daily; 6–7hr); Kompong Speu (9 daily; 1hr 30min); Kratie (4 daily; 7hr); Mondulkiri (daily; 8–9hr); Neak Leung (10 daily; 2hr); Oudong (10 daily; 1hr); Poipet (8 daily; 8hr); Pursat (8 daily; 4hr); Rattanakiri (2 daily; 10hr); Sen Monorom (daily; 7hr); Siem Reap (hourly; 6–7hr); Sihanoukville (hourly; 4–5hr); Sisophon (12 daily; 7hr); Stung Treng (3 daily; 8hr); Takeo (5 daily; 2hr 30min); Vientiane (daily; 24hr); Voen Kham, for Laos (daily; 8–10hr).

BY SHARED TAXI AND MINIBUS

Since there are now decent buses from Phnom Penh to all but the most remote locations in Cambodia, shared transport options, in particular minibuses, are less popular nowadays, at least for foreign travellers, and often used only as a last resort. However, it's worth knowing that dramatic improvements in the roads mean that shared taxis and minibuses now run to Kratie, Stung Treng, Rattanakiri and Mondulkiri.

Transport stops For destinations north of the city, including Kompong Thom, Siem Reap, Kompong Cham, Battambang, Sisophon and Poipet, shared taxis and minibuses use the transport stop (and the streets around it) 100m northwest of Psar Thmei. For Kampot, Kep, Sihanoukville or Takeo you can pick up a shared vehicle from Psar Damkor on Mao Tse Toung Blvd in the southwest of the city, while transport to Sre Ambel and Koh Kong set off from a bit nearer the centre, at Psar Depot on Nehru Blvd. Destinations southeast of Phnom Penh, Neak Leung (for Prey Veng and the boat to Chau Doc in Vietnam), Svay Rieng and the border town of Bavet (commonly called Moc Bai after the town on the Vietnamese side of the border) are served by transport leaving from both Psar Olympic and Psar Chbar Ampov, the latter across the Monivong Bridge. Transport stops are inundated with moto and tuk-tuk drivers, although they often won't speak much English so it's useful to carry a map. If you're going a long way, it's worth getting to your preferred transport stop by 6am or 7am. Later, when fewer people travel, you can have a long wait while the drivers gather up enough customers to make the trip worthwhile. For destinations closer to town you'll easily be able to get a shared taxi until mid-afternoon – after that, departures become less frequent. Note that the frequencies listed below are rough estimates – there are no fixed schedules.

Destinations Banlung (several daily; at least 10hr); Battambang (10 daily; 6hr); Bavet (15 daily; 3hr); Kampot (8 daily; 3hr); Koh Kong (several daily; 6hr); Kompong Cham (15 daily; 2hr 30min); Kompong Chhnang (2 daily; 2hr 30min); Kompong Thom (8 daily; 3hr); Neak Leung (15 daily; 1hr 30min); Pailin (6 daily; 6hr); Poipet (5 daily; 8hr); Pursat (5 daily; 4hr); Sen Monorom (several daily; at least 8hr); Siem Reap (hourly; 6–8hr); Sihanoukville (6 daily; 3hr 30min); Sisophon (6 daily; 7hr); Svay Rieng (6 daily; 2hr 30min); Takeo (10 daily; 2hr 30min).

BY BOAT

Since travelling by bus has become cheaper and faster, taking the boat to Siem Reap is no longer a popular option, and there's just one service a day. A handful of express boats also depart daily for Chau Doc in Vietnam. Guesthouse touts meet boats arriving in Phnom Penh, and there are plenty of tuk-tuk and moto drivers on hand; a moto ride into the centre will cost you about 4000 riel. Note that there are no longer boat services to Battambang, Kompong Cham or Kratie.

Departures Boats for Siem Reap (foreigners' fare $35), and Chau Doc ($25–33), leave from the passenger boat terminal (also known as the Tourist Docks) on the river near the main post office and Street 104. Companies take it in turns to depart for Siem Reap at 7am daily. Seating is reserved; you can buy your ticket in advance from most hostels and guesthouses and at the docks, where you can also purchase them on the morning of departure. Of the operators, both Delta Adventure (Ⓦ deltaadventuretours .com) and Blue Cruiser (Ⓦ bluecruiser.com) have offices along the riverfront.

Destinations Chau Doc (3 daily; 5hr); Siem Reap (1 daily; 5hr).

INFORMATION

Tourist information At the airport's international arrivals hall (Mon–Fri 8am–4pm). There is also a tourist information office near the Chatomak Theatre, although it is not very useful and mainly touts city tours.

Visitor guides and listings Phnom Penh Visitors Guide is a free quarterly English-language booklet with details of places to stay, restaurants and sights, a map and a bit of history. You'll find copies in most guesthouses, restaurants and Western cafés; extracts are available online at Ⓦ canbypublications.com. For film screenings, theatre performances and other entertainment, the Cambodia Daily has a "What's On" section on Fri, with classified ads for restaurants and bars on Tues and Thurs; the daily Phnom Penh Post is another useful source of information. Asia Life (Ⓦ asialifecambodia.com), a free glossy "What's On" guide to Phnom Penh, is published monthly; it has features and useful accounts of new openings and exhibitions. Online, Ⓦ talesofasia.com takes a refreshingly opinionated look at the local tourist scene.

Travel agents The following well-established firms employ English-speaking staff and act as both travel agents and domestic tour operators: KU Travel & Tours, 77 Street

1

240 (☎023 723456, ⓦkucambodia.com), and Mittapheap, 262 Monivong Blvd (☎023 218585, ⓦmittapheap.com).

For local day-trips, Mango Cambodia (☎023 998657, ⓦmangocambodia.com) gets great reviews.

TOURS

Culinary tours Ducky, a passionate foodie, offers excellent local food experiences on trips ranging from 1hr breakfast market tours ($15) through to roving dinners ($70) where you'll eat each course in a different restaurant (ⓦurbanforage.co).

Cycling tours Grasshopper Adventures at Vicious Cycles, 23Eo Street 144 (☎012 462165, ⓦgrasshopperadventures .com) organizes excellent half-day guided tours of Koh Dach's quiet backwaters ($33) and one-day trips for experienced riders up to Oudong ($75) on quality mountain bikes. They also offer a five-day trip from Phnom Penh to Sihanoukville visiting Kep, Kampot and

Ream National Park ($1250 including accommodation). **Cyclo tours** Khmer Architecture Tours run a cyclo tour around the key post-1953 architectural sights on the second and last Sun of each month (ⓦka-tours.org; 2–3hr; $15). You can also download a self-guided walking map of the sights from their website.

Quad biking Blazing Saddles (☎012 676381) offer guided self-drive ATV tours to the Killing Fields and neighbouring villages (daily 7.30am & 12.30pm; $25) as well as a sunset tour (daily 4pm; $25) and a full day visiting the Killing Fields, Tonle Bati and the Phnom Tamao Wildlife Sanctuary (on demand 7am; $110).

ACTIVITIES

Cookery courses Learn to prepare traditional Khmer food at Cambodia Cooking Class; book through *Frizz* restaurant, 67 Street 240 (☎012 524801, ⓦcambodia-cooking-class .com; half-full day $14/$23).

Massages and spas Many massage parlours double as brothels, but there are now a number of reputable private spas where you can get a massage, aromatherapy, body scrubs and other treatments. Amret Spa, 3 Street 57 (☎023 997994; 9am–10pm), and Aziadée, 16A Street 282 (☎023 996921; 9am–9pm), both have jacuzzis and offer a range of treatments. Slightly more expensive are the blissful massages, facials, wraps and beauty treatments on offer at Bodia Spa, cnr Street 178 & Sothearos Blvd (☎023 226119; 10am–11pm), while Sayana Rumdul, 1 Street 282 (☎023 727158; 10am–10pm), offers waxing, steam rooms and all styles of massage. Seeing Hands, set up with the help of an NGO which works with the blind in Cambodia, offer anma, Thai and shiatsu massage and reflexology; they're at

6 Street 178, just around the corner from the *FCC* (☎012 234519; 8am–10pm; $8/hr), and at 12 Street 13, opposite the post office (☎012 680934; same times and price).

Meditation and yoga One-hour silent meditation sessions are held at Wat Langka (Mon, Thurs & Sat 6pm, Sun 8.30am; free), supervised by English-speaking monks. Some wats have more yoga-orientated meditation classes, and NataRaj Yoga, 52 Street 302 (☎012 250817), has yoga and Pilates classes for $9/session.

Running The Hash House Harriers meet on Sun at 2.15pm outside the train station at Monivong Blvd and Street 106 (ⓦp2h3.com).

Swimming The *Blue Lime*, *Cambodiana*, *Circa 51*, *Patio* and *252* hotels have pools open to non-residents for around $5–7/visit; the fee is sometimes redeemable against food and drink. The Phnom Penh Water Park on the airport road has water slides and swimming pools (daily 9am–6pm; $3).

GETTING AROUND

Although it's possible to see many of Phnom Penh's sights on foot, the heat and humidity, allied with the city's traffic and dust, don't make **walking** a particularly pleasant experience. Pedestrians *never* have the right of way in Cambodia, and Phnom Penh is a place to exercise 360-degree vision, even at traffic lights and the striped, so-called pedestrian crossings. **Motos**, **tuk-tuks** and to a lesser extent **cyclos** are the workhorses of local transport, readily available all over town, picking you up from the kerb and dropping you outside your destination.

BY MOTO

Fares Around $1–2 per trip, more if you're travelling out of the centre, in the rain, or after dark, when you might pay $3–4. It may be safer to take a tuk-tuk at night.

Drivers Some moto drivers speak a little English, especially those who hang out around the riverfront and other places where foreigners congregate. Elsewhere, you'll find English-speaking drivers few and far between, so it's useful to learn some landmarks, such as markets and monuments, and have a map handy.

BY TUK-TUK

A fairly recent introduction to the capital, but now integral, tuk-tuks are more comfortable than motos, especially when two or more people are travelling together, or in the rain, as they have roll-down side-curtains. Don't expect a speedy trip though; tuk-tuks are powered by titchy motorbikes and progress can be painfully slow, particularly if there are a few people and their bags aboard.

Fares Journeys around town cost $2–4 or about $15 for a half-day.

PHNOM PENH ADDRESSES

Thanks to the French, who laid out the city on a **grid system**, Phnom Penh is remarkably easy to navigate. The **major streets** all have little-used official names, which have been changed periodically to honour particular regimes or sponsoring countries; the current names have been around since the mid-1990s. The rest of the streets are **numbered** and generally pretty easy to find. North–south streets have the odd numbers, with the low numbers nearest the river; even-numbered streets run east–west, with the low numbers in the north of the city. Signage is improving, and areas of town are even acquiring district names that are posted above the road.

Individual **buildings** are numbered, but are almost without exception difficult to locate, as the numbering doesn't run consecutively, with the same number often being used more than once on the same street – Street 76, for example, boasted three no. 25s on the last count. Cruising until you spot your destination may be the only option unless you can call ahead for directions.

BY CYCLO

Unique to the capital and increasingly rare, cyclos provide a leisurely way to get around, although they do cost slightly more than motos. To find one, head to the Cyclo Centre Phnom Penh, an NGO set up to help cyclo drivers, offering showers, medical care and education at 9 Street 158, not far from Sorya Mall (Mon–Fri 8–11am & 1–5pm, Sat 1–5pm; ☎ 023 991178). Starting your ride from here is a good way to support the drivers, who rank among the poorest people in the capital. You can also take city tours by cyclo (see p.78).

BY TAXI

Taxis don't cruise for fares, although a few enterprising drivers meet incoming boats along the riverfront. They can be hired at any of the major hotels, or by calling a recommended firm; expect to pay $4–5 for a single daytime journey within the city, or $6–8 at night. Most vehicles are unmarked, but a few now use a meter system and thus have illuminated signs on their roofs.

Day hire Taxis for hire by the day can often be found lined up on the east side of Monivong Blvd, near the intersection with Kampuchea Krom; the going rate is $25–35/day around the city, and $40–70/day out of town, depending where you're going.

Taxi firms Bailey's (☎ 012 890000) offers reliable 24hr service, as does Taxi Vantha (☎ 023 993433 or ☎ 012 855000, ☎ taxivantha.com), which is also available for long-distance trips. Global (☎ 011 311888) and Choice (☎ 023 888023) taxis have metered cars.

BY CAR OR MOTORBIKE

Due to the chaotic driving, the shameless speed traps and the police checks, the vast majority of visitors to Phnom Penh find hiring a ride better than driving, although motorbikes are a great way of exploring the surrounding countryside. If you do intend to drive yourself or rent a motorcycle you should be aware that, even compared to the impatient standards of Cambodian driving, the people of Phnom Penh take the biscuit. It's best not to insist on claiming your right of way or to be too heavy on the horn – incidents of road rage here can be violent. More an annoyance than a danger are the policemen who stop foreigners and blatantly demand a $5 "fine" (ie bribe), usually with the phrase "beer money". It's unlikely you'll get away without paying, so it's easier to simply pay up rather than bravely protesting your innocence; you can usually bargain them down to a dollar or two.

Car rental firms Most travellers rent a car with driver; however, if you want to go it alone try The Car Rental Co, 49 Street 592 (☎ 012 950950), which has a selection of self-drive vehicles.

Motorbike rental firms Western-run Little Bikes, 223 Street 13, near *Friends* restaurant (☎ 023 991570; daily 9am–6pm), has 100cc city runabouts for $5/day or high-quality trail bikes (up to 650cc) from $15/day, all with wheel locks. They offer 24/7 support and organize tours, too. Lucky! Lucky!, 413 Monivong Blvd (☎ 012 212788), has been going for years, and charges $7/day for a 110cc moped and $12/day for a 250cc off-road bike, with discounts on rentals of a week or longer. Helmets are provided, but no insurance.

ACCOMMODATION

Phnom Penh has an increasing number of guesthouses and hotels catering for all pockets and tastes, from basic rooms to opulent colonial-era suites, and no matter when you arrive, you should have no difficulty **finding a room** – though the very cheapest places fill quickly. If you intend to stay for more than a couple of nights, it's worth asking for a **discount** at guesthouses and mid-range places. With deluxe accommodation you'll often get a better deal by booking online or taking a package. Free **wi-fi** is generally offered in all but the most expensive hotels.

1

ESSENTIALS

Budget hotels The former backpacker area around Boeng Kak lake has now all but disappeared along with the water. Most of the budget accommodation is now in little clusters to the south of Psar Orussey, and on Street 258 and Street 172 in the centre of town. There are also several cheap places with coveted locations either right on or near the riverfront.

Mid-range hotels Recent years have seen increased competition in the mid-range bracket, with plenty of options along Monivong Blvd and in Boeng Keng Kang (known as BKK), the area broadly around Street 278, near the NGO residential area. Along with the trendy Street 240, BKK is one of the hottest locations in town, with cosmopolitan restaurants, cafés, spas and boutiques springing up all around.

Deluxe hotels Phnom Penh has some wonderful upmarket options, many of them proving excellent value, with the pride of place going to *Raffles Hotel Le Royal*.

Serviced apartments If you are staying for a month or more, you could consider one of the serviced apartments offered by several hotels. Comprising bedroom, sitting room, bathroom and kitchenette, these go for around $800–1000/month.

THE RIVERFRONT

Bougainvillier 272C Sisowath Quay ☎ 023 220528, ⓦ bougainvillierhotel.com; map p.66. This hotel has a terrific location and well-appointed, spacious rooms with Cambodian textiles and furnishings in muted tones (the newest ones are in the next-door building). Also boasts a fine French restaurant. Wi-fi and breakfast included. Monthly rates available, too. **$70**

Cambodiana 313 Sisowath Quay ☎ 023 426288, ⓦ hotelcambodiana.com.kh; map pp.58–59. Set by the river, the colossal *Cambodiana* hasn't quite accepted that its days as the city's premier hotel have long gone. Rooms are large and comfy enough, the views are great and the casino gives the hotel a raffish air, while amenities include Asian and Western restaurants, bars, bakery, spa, gym, tennis courts, swimming pool and grounds running down to the river. However, you'll find far more charm and style for your money elsewhere. **$180**

★**Camory Backpackers** 167 Sisowath Quay ☎ 012 664567, ⓦ camoryhostelandrestaurant.com; map p.66. With a top location right on the waterfront, three squeaky clean a/c dorms and friendly, caring staff, this small hostel is a cut above; the big front dorm comes with a deep river-facing balcony and all beds have reading lamps. There's also a good restaurant and bar, and breakfast is included in the rate. Book ahead. **$12**

FCC Phnom Penh (Formerly known as the Foreign Correspondents Club of Cambodia) 363 Sisowath Quay ☎ 023 992284, ⓦ fcccambodia.com; map p.66. Booking

is essential to secure one of the seven en-suite rooms (all named after Angkorian temples) at this legendary establishment. Comfortable, modern accommodation is equipped to satisfy the needs of the visiting journo crowd, with writing desk, high-speed wi-fi and cable TV. Breakfast included. **$75**

Lazy Gecko 1 Street 258 ☎ 017 912935 or ☎ 012 619924, ⓔ lazygeckocafe@gmail.com; map pp.58–59. Aussie-run guesthouse that stands out along this backpacker street for its great-value rooms with fans (a/c a few dollars more), decent beds, cool café and cocktail bar, board games and popular quiz night. Fan **$7**

Okay 38 Street 258 ☎ 012 300804, ⓦ okay-guesthouse .com; map pp.58–59. This long-standing backpacker favourite has a good range of cheap rooms, the more expensive with a/c, some a little faded, and a busy restaurant where travellers congregate to use the free wi-fi, watch films and swap stories. They can arrange visa extensions, onward travel and laundry service. Fan **$5**

Paragon 219B Sisowath Quay ☎ 023 222607, ⓔ info_paragonhotel@yahoo.com; map p.66. It's a no-frills place, but for the price and location a real bargain, and they've recently installed a lift. Rooms (all a/c) are plain but spotless – a river view and private balcony can be had for just $38. **$18**

★**The Quay** Sisowath Quay ☎ 023 224894, ⓦ thequayhotel.com; map p.66. This luxurious hotel – soft cushions and plush carpets, cutting-edge design – has an excellent restaurant, *Chow*, as well as roof terrace with jacuzzi; perfect for happy-hour drinks overlooking the river. Staff are delightful. **$90**

River 108 2 Street 108 ☎ 023 218785, ⓦ river108.com; map p.66. A luxurious Art Deco-styled boutique hotel, in shades of muted silver and gold with tinkling fountains, just a stone's throw from the water. **$85**

AROUND THE NATIONAL MUSEUM AND ROYAL PALACE

★**Blue Lime** 42 Street 19Z (off Street 19) ☎ 023 222260, ⓦ bluelime.asia; map p.66. This boutique hotel, tucked away down a little alley behind the National Museum, has the understated, contemporary style and service ethos to rival anything in Paris or New York. An exclusive haven from the bustle of town, the rooms are minimalist and fresh, with all mod cons, and some have their own private plunge-pool and terrace. The day-beds around the main pool itself are the perfect place to unwind, and the restaurant serves Western food. Breakfast included. **$45**

Lone Star Saloon 30 Street 23 ☎ 012 577860, ⓦ lonestarcambodia.com; map p.66. Friendly, American-owned guesthouse just around the corner from buzzy Street 172, with four surprisingly large a/c rooms; even the "small" room is sizeable. Huge portions of Texan-style food is served downstairs. **$25**

AROUND PSAR THMEI (CENTRAL MARKET) AND TOWARDS THE RIVERFRONT

11 Happy Backpackers 87–89 Street 136 ☎088 777 7421, ⓦ11happy.asia; map p.66. Big, friendly place with a mix of no-bunk, a/c dorms and simple en-suite fan and a/c rooms (some without windows) plus a brilliant leafy rooftop restaurant-bar with pool table, hammocks and lots of nooks for hiding away. Next to The Flicks cinema. Dorms $5; doubles (fan) $12

Dara Raeng Sey Cnr streets 118 & 13 ☎023 427469, ⓦdarareangsay.com; map p.66. Functional rooms, with TV, in a rambling corner building conveniently located for both the riverfront and the French quarter. Staff are friendly and helpful, and can help organize day-trips and onward travel. Fan $15; a/c $20

Fancy Guest House 169B Street 15 ☎023 211829, ⓦthefancyguesthouse.com; map p.66. In a great location near the riverfront, this family-run hotel ticks all the boxes, with sparkling rooms with a/c and hot showers. The cheapest have no windows, the more expensive have balconies. $18

AROUND WAT PHNOM

★**Raffles Hotel Le Royal** Street 92, off Monivong Blvd ☎023 981888, ⓦraffles.com; map p.66. Dating from 1929, this impressive Art Deco hotel, set in lovely gardens, was restored in 1997 to its original understated elegance, and still offers every modern convenience. Engravings of old Cambodia grace the corridors, and the luxurious guest rooms are individually decorated with specially commissioned prints and Cambodian artefacts. There's a choice of restaurants and bars plus a patisserie, shop, spa and pool. Taking a cocktail at happy hour (daily 4–9pm; half-price) in the *Elephant Bar* is a must. $240

BETWEEN PSAR THMEI (CENTRAL MARKET) AND THE OLYMPIC STADIUM

Billabong 5 Street 158 ☎023 223703, ⓦthebillabong hotel.com; map p.66. An unassuming small hotel with a range of comfortable, en-suite a/c rooms (all with TV), including quad-share family rooms, helpful management and a nice pool. $50

Capitol 1 14 Street 182 ☎12 548409 or ☎023 214104 for buses, ⓦcapitolkh.com; map p.66. The original Phnom Penh backpackers' guesthouse, which also runs its own buses to popular destinations including Bangkok and Ho Chi Minh. Travellers' cheques are accepted and changed, and there's an in-house ATM. Rooms have no frills, though some have a/c and hot water. The restaurant serves inexpensive food, mostly stir-fries. Fan $5; a/c $10

Fairyland Hotel 99 Street 141 ☎023 214510, ⓔfairylandhotel@yahoo.com; map pp.58–59. A sparkling guesthouse built in a marble-floored tower with immaculate a/c rooms and a lift – definitely more hotel

than budget guesthouse (and pretty good value), if a little soulless. Free wi-fi. $15

Narin 1 50 Street 125 ☎023 991955 or ☎099 881133, ⓦnaringuesthouse.com; map pp.58–59. One of Phnom Penh's earliest guesthouses, this old wooden house has decent, cosy rooms (some with a/c and hot water), friendly English-speaking staff, cheap food in a balcony restaurant and traveller services. Fan $7

Pacific 234 Monivong Blvd ☎023 218592, ⓦpacifichotel.com.kh; map p.66. The fifty or so a/c rooms here are large, bright and nicely furnished, with sturdy Cambodian wood furniture, minibars and TVs. Service is excellent. Breakfast included. $28

Sunday 97 Street 141 ☎023 211623, ⓦsundayguesthouse.hostel.com; map pp.58–59. Welcoming guesthouse on a quiet street with comfortable rooms, a small restaurant, breezy terrace and a friendly atmosphere. Internet access and traveller services, including minibuses to Choeng Ek. $8

★**TAT** 52 Street 125 ☎012 921211, ⓦtattooguest house.com; map pp.58–59. This cheerful family-run guesthouse is an old favourite with brightly decorated rooms (optional a/c for a few dollars extra) and good furniture, internet access, a communal TV and video, and a rooftop restaurant serving decent Cambodian and Chinese food. Sister guesthouse *TATTOO*, to the south, is a decent and similarly priced alternative when *TAT* is fully booked. Fan $8

BOENG KENG KANG AND AROUND THE INDEPENDENCE MONUMENT

★**The 252** 19 Street 252 ☎023 633 1252, ⓦthe-252 .com; map p.66. French-run, this superb boutique hotel stands out for its stylish well-appointed rooms, some with fab balconies, helpful smiling staff and lovely 13m pool with lounging pavilions. The food and cocktails are pretty good, too. $50

Anise 2C Street 278, off Street 57 ☎023 222522, ⓦanisehotel.kh; map p.66. A very popular, well-run mid-range hotel with eighteen stylishly decorated rooms (some in a new wing across the street), all with a/c, minibar, flatscreen TV and safety box. The best have balconies and there are a few with kitchenettes ($60). Its bakery produces fresh croissants, while the restaurant serves delicious Southeast Asian cuisine; the *Terrace Café* is a relaxed place for a coffee or cocktail. $47

Goldie Boutique 6 Street 57, between streets 282 & 278 ☎023 996670, ⓦgoldieguesthouse.com; map p.66. The a/c rooms in this little hotel are well equipped and brightly decorated, with free wi-fi, and some have a sweet balcony. The management can help with all travel queries. $20

★**Mad Monkey** 26 Street 302 ☎023 987091, ⓦphnompenhhostels.com; map p.66. This well-run hostel isn't the cheapest but the a/c dorms have big, cosy

1

beds, and there are a few single rooms and nice upmarket en-suite a/c doubles in a new "villa" next door. Great food and a lively bar, and they can sort you out with bus tickets, book local tours and assist with visas. Dorms $7; doubles $14

Manor House 21 Street 262 ☎017 802922, ⓦmanorhousecambodia.com; map p.66. A relaxed, gay-friendly villa-style guesthouse – once the home of a Japanese diplomat – with a leafy garden and swimming pool. Spacious rooms have capacious bathrooms, cable TV, DVD player, safe, minibar and some of the original owner's furniture. Breakfast is included, as is wi-fi. Over-18s only. $50

One Up Banana Hotel Z9-132 Street 51 ☎023 211344, ⓦ1uphotelcambodia.com; map p.66. A secure, well-organized hotel with tidy a/c rooms with writing desks, kitchenettes, kettles, TVs, minibars, hairdryers and safes. The upper rooms are a bit quieter. Long-term rates available. $39

The Patio 134z, Street 51 ☎023 997900, ⓦpatio -hotel.com; map p.66. Hidden down a side street, the a/c rooms here are chic and colourful, if a tad overpriced, and the more expensive have balconies. The rooftop infinity pool is fabulous, with some of the best views in town (non-guests $7). $90

The Pavilion 227 Street 19, behind Wat Botum ☎023 222280, ⓦthepavilion.asia; map p.66. Boutique guesthouse in two impeccably converted colonial mansions. Rooms (all a/c) are beautifully presented but vary; the garden bungalows are tiny, while some come with private pools. With a swimming pool (guests and members only, no kids allowed), sunbeds, verdant gardens, wi-fi and a restaurant, bar and small spa, it's almost too hard to leave. Advance reservations required by email only. $50

Top Banana Cnr streets 51 & 278 ☎012 885572, ⓦtopbanana.biz; map p.66. Two floors of a/c dorms and simple budget rooms with a/c or fan in a prime location. Hot showers, communal TV and DVDs; laundry; onward

transport and tours (although a little pricey); plus a top-notch balcony restaurant and bar (almost) overlooking Wat Langka that hosts impromptu parties most nights. The *Mini Banana*, their new, much smaller and less party-orientated sister guesthouse (same price range), is just two blocks south along Street 51. Dorms $6; fan doubles $10; a/c doubles $18

White Mansion 26 Street 240 ☎023 555 0955, ⓦhotelphnompenh-whitemansion.com; map p.66. An impressive family-friendly hotel in a purpose-built Cambodian villa that gets rave reviews for its big, opulent rooms and helpful staff. There's also a nice little lap pool tucked on to one side of the building. $130

SOUTH OF THE CENTRE

★**Terrace on 95** 43 Street 95 ☎023 996143, ⓦtheterraceon95.com; map pp.58–59. Formerly the *Boddhi Tree del Gusto*, this graceful, out-of-the-way guesthouse offers beautifully decorated rooms in a traditional 1930s Khmer wooden house. Replete with French colonial atmosphere, rooms are adorned with vibrant Rajasthani block-printed fabrics and colourful art. It is also home to the good veggie-friendly *K'jnay Restaurant* and is next to The Flicks cinema. $50

You Khin 13A Street 830 ☎023 224843, ⓦyoukhinhouse.com; map p.66. This charming guesthouse is closely linked to the neighbouring school and allows the pupils to use the pool during the week. Despite this it is a lovely, serene spot just a few blocks from the action. Seven smart a/c rooms off an airy central staircase, each one tastefully decorated and with enclosed shower cubicles (as opposed to the usual wet rooms) and a small relaxation area. The intimate restaurant includes a collection of guitars for guests to strum on. On the first floor is a beauty spa and above a library with TV and pool table. Very calm and welcoming. $38

EATING

Phnom Penh has a vast range of places to eat, from cheap noodle shops and market stalls to sophisticated, pricey Western places. In addition many guesthouses have small, if usually undistinguished, restaurants, and on the whole, the food in the city is reasonable. The bustling **riverfront and Sisowath Quay** are lined with cafés, restaurants and bars serving cuisine from all over the world; the attractive location means that the cheapest single-course meals go for $4–5, and the myriad vendors and beggars can get a little wearing. For a cheaper choice of backpacker-friendly restaurants and bars, head to nearby neon-lit

---

EATING WITH A CONSCIENCE

Several cafés and restaurants in Phnom Penh either train the underprivileged in the hospitality trade or donate profits to help those in need. Expect to pay around $10–12 for a starter and main course.

Le Café (Mith Samlanh) See p.86.
Café Yejj See p.86.
Friends (Mith Samlanh) See p.84.

Le Lotus Blanc See p.85.
Romdeng See p.85.
Sugar 'n Spice Café See p.86.

Street 172, or a little more upmarket (but much more laidback than the riverfront), **Boeng Keng Kang** – broadly Street 278 from streets 51 to 63, but extending to the area around 294 – packed with swish cafés, refined but reasonably priced restaurants and bars. A further clutch of classy cafés and gastro-spots are found on **Street 240** between streets 7 and 19.

ESSENTIALS

Prices You can easily eat for well below $5 if you stick to market stalls, unfussy Cambodian restaurants and some of the Indian and Chinese places. In backpacker guesthouses you'll be able to eat for around $4, but once you venture into tourist-centred and Western-oriented establishments, prices rise and you'll be looking at around $4–7 for a simple main course. In slightly plusher places, and those with a prestigious location, expect to pay upwards of $6–10 for a main, maybe slightly more. The most expensive places to eat are in the restaurants of the premier hotels and in a few independent establishments (many of them French), where you could easily pay $15–20 and above for a main course (especially if it involves imported meat), with extra for vegetables and accompaniments.

Markets The markets are great places to fill up on traditional Khmer dishes: try the Central Market (see p.75) and Psar Kabkoh, a few blocks southeast of Independence Monument, where dozens of sellers cook into the early evening.

Street food Stalls and roadside vendors sell simple takeaway noodle and rice dishes for roughly 4000 riel, while fresh baguettes and rolls are sold in the markets in the morning and are available all day around the city from hawkers with handcarts.

Self-catering and picnics It's easy to buy fresh produce and tinned goods from the markets; to buy Western provisions such as cheese, yoghurt, chocolate and brown bread, you'll have to go to one of the supermarkets (see p.91). Fresh fruit can be bought from markets and at the specialist stalls on Monivong Blvd south of Sihanouk, and on Sihanouk Blvd itself southwest of the Olympic Stadium.

RESTAURANTS

Street 136, west of Psar Thmei, is home to a cluster of inexpensive – and roaringly popular – Chinese places, and for a slap-up meal, several of the deluxe hotels have excellent Chinese restaurants. There are also plenty of Indian, Pakistani and Bangladeshi restaurants, which are especially popular with the expat community, and a staggering variety of Western establishments – you could eat something different every night for a week, from pizza and pasta to grilled steaks, pork belly and crunchy salads. For fine dining on imported meat and wine, there are some noteworthy French restaurants as well as some fancy fusion places – expensive by Cambodian terms, but they charge a fraction of what you would pay in the West. Near Psar Kabkoh, south of Independence Monument, are a few barbecue restaurants beloved of the Khmers. Most Cambodians come here to take away, but you can eat in at small plastic stools. For *sop chhnang day*, where you cook

meat and vegetables in a pot of stock at your table, there are plenty of establishments on Monivong and Sihanouk blvds.

THE RIVERFRONT AREA

Bopha Phnom Penh (Titanic) Sisowath Quay, just south of the Tourist Docks ☎023 427209, ⊛bopha -phnompenh.com; map p.66. A huge, decadent restaurant and lounge bar with an open front looking over the Tonle Sap. Gilt furnishings, wide wicker chairs and ornamental water features abound, and the food is perfectly good (fish fillet papillote $9.75), but the main draw is the nightly apsara performance between 7 and 9pm. Daily 6am–10pm.

Chi Cha 27 Street 110, near Psar Chas ☎023 220442; map p.66. Excellent, budget Bangladeshi-owned restaurant in a seedy part of town: opt for the good-value *thali* (set meal) for $4.50. Daily 7am–10pm.

Happy Herb Pizza 345 Sisowath Quay ☎097 994 3225, ⊛happyherbpizza.com; map p.66. This long-running place still serves up a decent pizza (and good vegetarian choices). Pizzas start at $4.50 and can be made "happy" – with a marijuana-infused butter baste – for $1 more. Also tasty pasta, plus omelettes, pork chops and steak for a moderate price. Call for free delivery. Daily 8am–11pm.

Khmer Borane 99 Sisowath Quay ☎092 290092, ⊛borane.net; map p.66. In a prime riverfront spot, this unpretentious restaurant serves up great Khmer food (the fish *amok* is superb). Staff are attentive, prices economical. Daily 11am–11pm.

Pop Café da Giorgio 371 Sisowath Quay, near the FCC ☎012 562892; map p.66. This tiny Italian restaurant is where the expats come to eat authentic pasta (from $6), pizza (from $8) and gnocchi ($7.50). What it lacks in size, it more than makes up for in atmosphere and the quality of its food. Daily 11.30am–2pm & 6–9.30pm.

River Crown 1 Street 178 ☎023 555 2599; map p.66. Second-floor restaurant with views of the river and the *FCC*. Staff are attentive and the food well priced (burgers from $5.50, chicken fettuccini $6.50). It's also a good spot for a sunset drink, with a 4.30–7.30pm happy hour on draft beer and cocktails. Daily 9am–11pm.

★**Tepui** Sisowath Quay ☎023 991514, ⊛chinesehouse.asia; map pp.58–59. Dining at this atmospheric French-quarter villa, known as the Chinese House (see p.89), is a must. The Mediterranean- and South American-influenced menu is a treat; options include veggie *empanadas* with pesto ($6), pepper-crusted Brazilian beef tenderloin ($19) and a black-ink seafood

1

paella for two ($28). Fine wines and sambuca. Mon–Sat 6–10.30pm.

AROUND THE NATIONAL MUSEUM AND ROYAL PALACE

Alley Cat Café 43 Street 19Z ☎012 306845, ⓦalleycatcafe.biz; map p.66. This rocking restaurant-bar dishes up enormous breakfasts and Mexican dishes, with nightly specials including Tues and Sat ribs ($6 for a half-kilo) and burgers on Thurs. A great place to hang out for a few happy-hour beers. Daily 10am–10pm.

Chat 'N Chew 54 Street 172 ☎012 865191; map p.66. One of the better restaurants lining Street 172, with friendly staff, a nice streetside terrace and a menu of home-cooked Western and Asian dishes that includes a tasty fish *amok* ($4) as well as, unusually, a beef Wellington ($10). Daily 7am–midnight.

★**Friends (Mith Samlanh)** 215 Street 13, near the National Museum ☎012 802072, ⓦfriends-restaurant.org; map p.66. Run by the street children's NGO Mith Samlanh, training street youths in the restaurant and catering trade, this restaurant is famous for its tapas, Western and Asian snacks, shakes, iced coffees and cocktails. The spicy braised pork *quesadillas* ($6.50) are good, as is the Burmese chicken curry ($5.75). Fri–Sun & Wed 11am–9pm, Tues & Thurs 11am–1pm & 5–9pm.

Le Wok 33 Street 178 ☎098 821857; map p.66. Chic French fusion restaurant connected with the Silk & Pepper boutique next door. Delicious dishes such as sautéed chicken with ginger and honey ($7.50), reasonably priced set-lunch menus (two courses $9) and impeccable service. Daily 8am–10pm.

AROUND PSAR THMEI (CENTRAL MARKET) AND TOWARDS THE RIVERFRONT

East India Curry 9 Street 114 ☎023 992007, ⓦeastindiacurry.com; map p.66. Extensive range of moderately priced dishes, all enticingly presented on banana leaves; try the chicken pepper fry ($8). Excellent veggie options include a generous *thali* ($7). Daily 11am–2.30pm & 5–10pm.

★**Mamak's** 17 Street 114 ☎012 777990; map p.66. Since opening in 1992, this inexpensive halal Malaysian restaurant has become a Phnom Penh institution. *Roti chanai*, a paper-thin bread cooked on a griddle and eaten with curry sauce ($1), is a popular breakfast dish, washed down with *teh tarek*, a sweet, milky red tea, or *teh thomada*, the same but without the sweet milk. Other dishes include spicy fish steaks, crispy fried chicken, plenty of vegetable dishes and a tasty *nasi lemak* ($3.50). Daily 7am–9pm.

La Marmite 80 Street 108 ☎012 391746; map p.66. Sweet little corner bistro not far from the night market, with a fine, mostly French menu (beef bordelaise $8.50,

burgundy snails $6.50), wine list and the best *crème brûlée* in town. Daily 11am–2pm & 6–10pm.

Restaurant 26 Cnr streets 13 & 136; map p.66. Come here for a filling *bai sach chrouk* (pork and rice 5000 riel) breakfast; its early hours make it a good place to fuel up before catching a morning bus. Daily 4am–6.30pm.

Sam Doo 56–58 Kampuchea Krom Blvd ☎023 218773; map p.66. The a/c scarlet-hued surroundings of this popular Chinese restaurant are a welcome respite from the busy market; standouts include the juicy Sichuan pepper shrimps ($6.50), roast duck ($6) and renowned *dim sum* (from $1.80). Daily 7am–2am.

AROUND WAT PHNOM

Beirut 117 Sisowath Quay, near the night market ☎023 720111; map p.66. A homely place with a lip-smacking Lebanese menu of charcoaled meats, *meshwi* (skewered) kebabs, hot/cold meze platters ($4), beef *shawarmas* ($3) and tasty baklava ($1). It's close to the Giant Ibis and Virath Buntham bus offices, a convenient option for takeaway if you're heading off on a long journey. Daily 10am–11pm.

Van's 5 Place de la Poste, Street 102 ☎023 722067, ⓦvans-restaurant.com; map p.66. In a beautiful, restored colonial property opposite the post office, this is Phnom Penh's best French cuisine (with a price tag to match). Service has the kind of flair you'd expect in Paris, and the food is traditional, rich and extravagant – see the fois gras and wagyu beef menus, for example. Roasted rack of lamb is $30; the two-course business lunch is good value at $10. Daily 11.30am–2.30pm & 5–10.30pm.

La Volpaia Place de la Poste, 20–22 Street 13 ☎023 992739, ⓦlavolpaia.com; map p.66. Opposite the post office and *Van's*, this no-frills family Italian keeps it simple and delicious, and boasts a great French and Italian wine list to accompany the pasta and pizza dishes (risotto al funghi $8). Mon–Fri noon–2.30pm & 5.30–10pm, Sat & Sun noon–10.30pm.

SOUTH OF PSAR THMEI (CENTRAL MARKET)

Beef Soup Restaurant Favour Hotel, 429 Monivong Blvd ☎023 219336; map p.66. Locals reckon this is the best place in town for *sop chhnang day*. The beef version is the house speciality – you'll pay around $10/person for a serving of thinly sliced meat, several plates of vegetables, including mushrooms and tofu, noodles and a bubbling pot of stock. The waitresses will help you with the protocol, or just copy the locals. Daily 4.30–10pm.

Mama's 10 Street 111; map p.66. Set between *Capitol* and *Narin* guesthouses, *Mama's* has become a bit of an institution – the expansive Cambodian landlady dishes up cheap traditional Khmer and French food from a picture menu. Great place for breakfast before the early bus. Daily 7am–3pm & 5–9pm.

Nouveau Pho de Paris 258 Monivong Blvd ☎023 723076; map p.66. An enduring favourite, this popular Chinese, Cambodian and Vietnamese restaurant serves huge steaming bowls of tasty *pho* (lotus root and chicken soup $4.50), spring rolls with chilli and peanut dipping sauce, succulent crispy duck and the like (around $4–6 each) from a picture menu. Daily 7am–midnight.

★**Romdeng** 74 Street 174, near Monivong Blvd ☎092 219565, ⓦromdeng-restaurant.org; map p.66. This nonprofit training school for former street youths (organized by the Mith Samlanh NGO) serves excellent Cambodian food in a colonial villa with pool. Try the lotus root salad with chicken ($6.50) or the crispy fried tarantulas ($4) if you dare. Mon–Sat 11am–9.30pm.

Royal India 21 Street 111 ☎023 692 2205; map p.66. This simple, friendly restaurant dishes up consistently good and reasonably priced Indian food. The comprehensive menu includes chicken and mutton curries, *thalis*, fresh samosas, naan and good, sweet *lassis*; the butter chicken is recommended ($5). Daily 10am–10pm.

BOENG KENG KANG AND AROUND

INDEPENDENCE MONUMENT

Chinese Noodle House 553 Monivong Blvd ☎012 937805; map p.66. This tiny place is always, justifiably, packed – the fresh pulled noodles, made at the front of the restaurant, sunk into soups or fried, are delicious, as are the speciality pork-and-chive dumplings ($1.50). Daily 7am–9pm.

Ebony Tree 29 Street 29 ☎012 581291; map p.66. A charming little restaurant in a laidback alfresco garden, serving a selection of well-priced dishes (chicken in white wine with Kampot pepper, $6.50), plus lots of veggie specials, juices ($2) and cocktails (two-for-one 4–8pm). A small boutique sells handmade clothes and accessories near the entrance. Mon–Sat 11am–11pm.

Frizz 67 Street 240 ☎023 220953, ⓦfrizz-restaurant .com; map p.66. The menu at this small but excellent, moderately priced restaurant helpfully includes an accurate English translation of Cambodian dishes. Try the Khmer barbecue, fish *amok* or *chhnang phnom pleung* ("volcano pot") – a table-top charcoal brazier, on which you can cook your own meat and vegetables ($5.75). They also offer cookery courses (see p.78). Daily 10am–10pm.

Le Lotus Blanc 152 Street 51 ☎017 602251; map p.66. This vocational training restaurant, run by the charity Pour un Sourire d'Enfant, serves an extensive range of French and Asian dishes for around $6.50, and has a good all-you-can-eat lunchtime salad-and-soup buffet ($5). Profits support the children from the Stung Meanchey rubbish dump. Daily 7–10am, noon–2pm & 6–9pm.

Magnolia 55 Street 51 ☎012 529977; map p.66. Served with style at this breezy courtyard restaurant, the mouthwatering menu of Vietnamese and Thai delicacies

offers real value for money. The $6 *tom yam* soup is excellent and will feed two with rice. Breakfast *pho ha noi* costs $3 – a bargain. Daily 6am–10pm.

★**Malis** 136 Norodom Blvd ☎023 221022, ⓦmalis -restaurant.com; map p.66. A trendy, upmarket Cambodian restaurant with stylish modern building and tables around a raised pond in the courtyard. Popular with wealthier Khmers and the city's expat business and NGO workers, it serves traditional and modern Khmer food, such as scallops cooked in banana blossom. It's not cheap though; a breakfast of *geautieuv sop* (rice noodles in a clear broth with meat) and coffee will set you back around $5 (until 11am), while dinner dishes start at $8 and rise steadily. Daily 6am–10pm.

Piccola Italia de Luigi 36 Eo Street 308 ☎017 323273; map p.66. A teeny Sicilian-owned pizzeria – the closely packed tables spill onto the street – serving the city's biggest and, arguably, best pizzas. The thin-crust pizzas are big enough for two (Italian sausage $7.75). Tues–Sun 11.30am–2pm & 5.30–10pm.

★**La P'tite France** 38 Street 306 ☎016 642630; map p.66. A quaint, hard-to-find Parisian-style bistro with an intimate ambience. The chef, Didier, is proud of his entirely home-made menu, boasting beautifully prepared French classics (stewed beef cheek $11) and fabulous desserts (*crème brûlée* $5.50). Daily 11am–10pm.

Sovanna Street 21; map p.66. This authentic Cambodian BBQ restaurant is beloved by Khmers for its charcoaled meats and ice-cold beers. Barbecued dishes come with a zesty dipping sauce that you mix yourself and raw veggies; you might want to order a fried rice, too. Options include grilled spicy frog (11,500 riel), grilled chicken breast (10,500 riel) or fried beef with ant eggs (17,000 riel). Daily 4–11pm.

Tamarind 31 Street 240 ☎012 830139; map p.66. This breezy three-storey restaurant done up in the colours and tiles of North Africa serves excellent tagines (fish lemon tagine $8) and a mouthwatering selection of tapas, Lebanese meze ($5.75) and small Asian dishes. The *baklava* with rum-and-raisin ice cream is heaven. Try and get a table on the upper terrace and enjoy a cocktail looking over the street. Daily 9am–midnight.

The Vegetarian 158 Street 19 ☎012 905766; map p.66. This veggie restaurant with a pretty garden terrace serves super-cheap food; all mains are less than $3. Juices cost from $1.75 and the creamy lotus root with cashew nut curry will set you back just $2.50. Avoid the fried dishes, though, as they can be a little greasy. Daily 10.30am–8.30pm.

Yakitori Jidaiya 17 Street 278 ☎023 630 2254; map p.66. Staff shout "*sama sama!*" (welcome) as you enter this Japanese BBQ restaurant that serves up sticky *kushi yaki* skewers, a particularly good *teppanyaki* beef fillet ($6) and *yakitori don* (chicken rice; $4). Daily 11.30am–2pm & 5–11pm.

1

SOUTH OF THE CENTRE

★Alma Café Cnr streets 123 & 454 ☎092 424903, ⓦfacebook.com/almacambodia; map pp.58–59. Charming, authentic Mexican place near the Russian Market. *Huevos rancheros* ($4) is offered for breakfast and daily changing lunch menus (posted nightly on their Facebook page) include handmade corn tortillas with beans and tender pork or baked chicken with home-made guacamole, washed down with bottomless cups of Mexican tea ($5). A real find. Wed–Mon 7am–2pm.

Café Yejj 170 Street 450, near the Russian Market ☎092 600750, ⓦcafeyejj.com; map pp.58–59. The café-bar helps women at risk by providing them with training and support. Serves filter coffee (free refills), Western bistro-style food (spaghetti zucchini $5), paninis and wraps. The rooftop bar is open from 4pm, with happy hour until 9pm (25 percent discount). Daily 8am–9pm.

Khmer-Thai Restaurant 26 Street 135, near Wat Toul Tom Poung ☎012 321616; map pp.58–59. Somewhat out of the way, this classy restaurant doesn't advertise, but is still packed every night by locals in the know. Inexpensive Khmer and Thai food is served efficiently and in good-sized portions; try the tasty pickled cabbage with pork $4. Daily 11am–2pm & 4.30–9pm.

K'nyay 43 Street 95, at Terrace on 95 ☎093 665225; map pp.58–59. This place does one of the best sweet potato, pumpkin and coconut curries ($5) in the city – almost the entire menu is dedicated to delicious vegan and vegetarian dishes. Tues–Fri noon–9pm, Sat & Sun 7am–9pm.

★The Lost Room 43 Street 21 ☎078 700001; map pp.58–59. This exposed brick bistro with small back bar is home to some of the city's best fusion food. Dishes, designed for sharing, include a moreish crispy pork belly in dark ale ($8), a Moroccan spiced crispy duck ($9) and pear and blue cheese parcels ($5.50). Book ahead, and ask them to send a tuk-tuk to pick you up; it's tricky to find. Daily 5–10pm.

Shiva Shakti 17 Street 63 ☎012 813817; map pp.58–59. Classical Indian-Moghul cuisine in an upmarket setting, with specialities including tender kebabs and tandoori dishes. Expect to pay upwards of $8 for a single dish with rice and chapati or naan bread. Tues–Sun 11.30am–2pm & 5.30–10.30pm.

Topaz 182 Norodom Blvd, next to Wat Than ☎023 221622, ⓦtopaz-restaurant.com; map pp.58–59. Arguably the best French food in town, served in a startlingly modern building, with fine wines and exceptional succulent steaks; although you can fork out up to $70 for a top-of-the-range steak, most mains are under $30. Expensive, but worth it. Daily 11.30am–2pm & 6–10.30pm.

CAFÉS AND COFFEE SHOPS

Though Phnom Penh's busy café society of the 1950s and 1960s vanished during the war, there has been a massive revival recently, with many places attached to galleries, shops or internet centres and new ones opening every week. Note that *Browns* is the country's very own (and very upmarket) chain of coffee shops.

ARTillery 13B Street 278 ☎078 985530, ⓦartillerycafe.com; map p.66. A creative little café that's hands-down the best place for healthy, organic, vegan, gluten- and sugar-free food. Try the hummus heaven sandwich ($4), super foods salad ($5) or the vitamin vitalizer power juice ($2.50). They have a second, larger, sister café on Street 240 ½. Mon 7.30am–5pm, Tues–Sun 7.30am–5.30pm.

Le Café (Mith Samlanh) Street 184, in the grounds of the French Cultural Centre ☎092 471791; map p.66. Serving sandwiches, French/Khmer daily specials and tasty crêpes, organized by the street children's NGO Mith Samlanh. Dishes from 10,000 riel. Mon–Sat 7am–5pm.

Café Fresco 361 Sisowath Quay, under the FCC; map p.66. Whether you want a croissant, mid-morning coffee, smoothie or lunchtime sandwich (including a choice of breads) you'll be satisfied here. Not the cheapest place in town, but given the quality and the location you're unlikely to be disappointed. Daily 7am–8pm.

Delishop (Comme à la Maison) 13 Street 57 ☎023 360801; map p.66. Adored by expats and visitors alike, this café is set off the road in a quiet garden and does a roaring trade in fresh bread and pastries (coffee éclair $2.50). Perfect for coffee and a croissant while you read the paper. Daily 6am–9pm.

★Feel Good Café 79 Street 136 ☎017 497538; map p.66. This might be the only café in the city to roast, grind and brew their coffee (flat white $2.50) on site, and the smell of roasting beans entices you through the front door. On the menu are wraps, sandwiches, burgers and bagels. Upstairs is a spa and gallery. Daily 8am–8pm.

Java 56 Sihanouk Blvd, east of Independence Monument ☎023 987420, ⓦjavacafeandgallery.com; map p.66. As well as full breakfasts and Italian coffees, this café-gallery does light meals and a delightful range of home-made bagels, muffins and desserts, including a wicked white-chocolate cheesecake ($2.75). The bakery at the back has delicious pastries to take away. Daily 7am–10pm.

★The Shop 39 Street 240 ☎092 955963, ⓦtheshop-cambodia.com; map p.66. More London than Phnom Penh, not only does *The Shop* offer a fantastic café atmosphere, but has great deli sandwiches and pastries (from $0.75) and coffee too. Daily 6.30am–7pm.

Sugar 'n Spice Café 65 Street 178 ☎077 657678, ⓦdaughtersofcambodia.com; map p.66. This first-floor café is run by Daughters of Cambodia, an NGO offering sex workers and victims of trafficking support and employment. Snack on delicious chocolate brownies, perhaps, or opt for a healthy mango, cucumber and avocado salad ($4.50). Mon–Sat 9am–6pm.

DRINKING AND NIGHTLIFE

When it comes to **drinking**, foreign visitors and expats in Phnom Penh have three types of option: the seedy, smoky girlie bars that proliferate off Sisowath Quay and along Street 51; sophisticated, trendy cocktail bars, either with a river view or in a prime location along trendy Street 240 and **BKK** (see p.80); and lower-key hangouts, often with live music, that may double up as pick-up joints but have an easygoing attitude. Most bars and restaurants promote daily **happy hours** from late afternoon to well after sunset (although many start much earlier) when you can sink 50c glasses of draft beer, $1.50 G&Ts or $2 cocktails. Otherwise, Phnom Penh's nightlife is geared to Khmer men and revolves around girlie bars, karaoke, dance halls and local discos. Under the strobe lights, you'll hear a deafening mix of Thai, Filipino and Western pop as well as traditional Khmer music and songs. Ask locals for the most popular spots of the moment; **nightclubs** usually don't get going until 10pm and beer girls (see box, p.49) are usually on hand to pour the drinks. Keep your wits about you and don't get too drunk or obnoxious; there is sometimes a thuggish element in places frequented by the rich, bored sons of the Cambodian nouveau riche. Step on their feet while dancing or stare at their female companions and you may have a real incident on your hands. Phnom Penh has an emerging **gay scene**, with a few great venues and more popping up every year.

BARS AND PUBS
THE RIVERFRONT AREA

FCC 277 Sisowath Quay ☎ 023 210142, ⓦ fcccambodia .com; map p.66. Possibly the most atmospheric bar-cum-restaurant in the region (imagine a Southeast Asian version of the bar in *Casablanca*). The balmy air, whirring ceiling fans and spacious armchairs invite you to spend a hot afternoon getting slowly smashed. Relatively pricey; the drinks are worth it (happy hour 5–7pm) but the food, however, is not. Daily 6.30am–midnight.

Fish Bar Cnr Sisowath Quay & Street 108 ☎ 023 222685; map p.66. Cool cocktail bar popular with both wealthy Khmers and expats, with a good international wine list and fantastic fish and chips ($8.60). Happy hour 3–8pm and live music Wed–Sat from 7pm. Daily 7am–11pm.

Metro Cnr Sisowath Quay & Street 148 ☎ 023 222275; map p.66. A smart, Western, a/c cocktail bar (lychee martini $5.20), with a no-smoking policy before 10pm. Cool ambience, stylish bar staff and delicious, minimalist food attract wealthy Khmers and expats. Daily 9.30am–1am.

Le Moon Amanjaya Pancam Hotel, 1 St 154 ☎ 023 219579; map p.66. A swanky rooftop bar with comfy sofas and enviable views of the river, Wat Ounalom and the glinting spires of the palace. The excellent cocktail list (from $5) is complemented by nibbles such as salmon blinis. Daily 5pm–1am.

AROUND THE NATIONAL MUSEUM AND ROYAL PALACE

Bar Sito 3 Street 240½ (opposite Public House) ☎ 077 555447; map p.66. A small, seductive speakeasy located up an easy-to-miss alleyway just off Street 240 that serves amazing cocktails in low-lit a/c surroundings, including a moreish lychee *caipiroska* ($5). Daily 5pm–midnight.

Blue Chilli 36 Street 178 ☎ 012 566353; map p.66. Expect extravagant decor and handsome barmen at this all-welcoming gay bar near the National Museum. Artistic, and very funny, drag shows on Fri and Sat nights (11pm). Daily 6pm–late.

★Dodo Rhum House 42 Street 178 ☎ 012 549373; map p.66. A brilliant bar that makes its own flavoured rum (varieties include chocolate, passion fruit, ginger or peanut, for $2.50 a shot) and traditional Ti punch along with French food and snacks, open late for an easy-going crowd. Daily 5pm–late.

AROUND PSAR THMEI (CENTRAL MARKET) AND TOWARDS THE RIVERFRONT

L'Absinthe 216 Street 51 ☎ 097 285 3217; map p.66. Some of the sixteen varieties of European-imported absinthes on offer at this upscale bar are 85 percent proof. Let owner Thibault show you the proper way to appreciate this fiery brew. Daily 4pm–1am.

Dusk Till Dawn 46–48 Street 172 ☎ 017 839546; map p.66. An upbeat rooftop Kenyan-owned reggae bar doling out plenty of rum and cokes and fruit punches high above Street 51's throbbing nightclub district. A really go place to start or end your night. Daily 5pm–6am.

Rainbow Bar 134 Street 136 ☎ 098 712332; map p.66. Friendly, with a mix of indoor and outdoor space, this glitter-, tinsel- and sequin-adorned gay bar hosts karaoke nights on Mon, $2 cocktail nights on Tues and nightly drag shows at 10pm. Daily 7pm–midnight.

AROUND WAT PHNOM

Elephant Bar Raffles Hotel Le Royal, Street 92 ☎ 023 981888, ⓦ raffles.com; map p.66. Splash out on a cocktail and soak up the 1930s elegance, with ambience and service to match, plus live music from the resident pianist. Two-for-one happy hour 4–9pm. Mon–Fri 2pm–midnight, Sat & Sun noon–midnight.

SOUTH OF PSAR THMEI (CENTRAL MARKET) AND TOWARDS THE OLYMPIC STADIUM

Eclipse Sky Bar Phnom Penh Tower, Monivong Blvd ☎ 023 964171; map p.66. This upscale open-air rooftop bar isn't cheap but is easily the best place for sunset cocktails (from $5; 30 percent discount 5–7pm) and dazzling 360-degree panoramas of the city, river and distant hills. Daily 5pm–2am.

BOENG KENG KANG AND AROUND
INDEPENDENCE MONUMENT

Aussie XL 205A Street 51 (near Street 288) ☎ 023 301001, ⓦ aussiexl.com; map p.66. Popular spot near Street 278 whose cheap drinks and food (including home-made pies, burgers, spit-roasted pork and wood-fired pizza) attract a lively mix of backpackers, travellers and expats. Also shows Aussie sports matches. Daily 9am–11pm.

Score! 5 Street 282 ☎ 023 221357, ⓦ scorekh.com; map p.66. Cavernous sports bar with a 5m x 5m screen, a handful of slate pool tables and loungers, plus Converse sneaker-clad staff and Western food (including a mean weekend lunchtime roast). Sun–Thurs 8am–midnight, Fri & Sat 8am–2am.

LIVE MUSIC AND NIGHTCLUBS
THE RIVERFRONT/WAT PHNOM AREA

★**The Doors** Cnr streets 47 & 84 ☎ 023 986114, ⓦ doorspp.com; map pp.58–59. This awesome new urban venue hosts a diverse variety of musical acts ranging from classical Spanish guitarists, opera singers and pianists to international DJs and local funk bands. Decor is distinctive, with the murals of street artist Sheryo adorning the walls. Drinks are brilliantly inventive – "toast and berries" (a gin-based cocktail) is served in a jam jar with a broken eggshell containing fresh bread and jam ($5) clipped to the edge. Their Spanish tapas are excellent too. Daily 11am–midnight.

AROUND PSAR THMEI (CENTRAL MARKET) AND TOWARDS THE RIVERFRONT

Heart of Darkness 26 Street 51 ☎ 077 837777, ⓦ heartofdarknessclub.com.kh; map p.66. This gothy place was *the* hipster hangout in Phnom Penh a decade ago; these days it's the haunt of affluent young Khmers and becomes progressively more seedy as the night goes on, with fights frequently breaking out. Daily 9pm–5am.

Pontoon Cnr streets 178 & 51 ☎ 016 779966, ⓦ pontoonclub.com; map p.66. This famed nightspot started out on the river before finding its feet in the clubbing district of Street 51. While it's still the preserve of local and international DJs, spinning house, hip-hop and commercial tunes, its over-the-top drag and cabaret shows (Thurs; free entry and two-for-one drinks until 11.30pm) and regular comedy club nights make it a pioneer in the city's nightlife. Around $8 cover after 11.30pm at weekends. Sun–Thurs 9pm–4am, Fri & Sat 9pm–5am.

Sharky's 126 Street 130 ☎ 023 211825, ⓦ sharkycambodia.com; map p.66. Cambodia's longest-running rock-and-roll bar and low-key pick-up spot is a great, lively hangout and serves decent Mexican, Thai and American food. Daily drink specials from 5pm. Daily 5pm–2am.

BOENG KENG KANG AND AROUND
INDEPENDENCE MONUMENT

★**Equinox** 3A Street 278, just off Street 51 ☎ 023 676 7593, ⓦ equinox-cambodia.com; map p.66. This bar-restaurant in the heart of BKK is one of the hottest nightspots in town, an impressive small art gallery that hosts an eclectic line-up of live acts several nights a week. Daily 8am–1am.

ENTERTAINMENT AND ARTS

After being virtually obliterated by the Khmer Rouge, Cambodia's **artistic and cultural traditions** are gradually seeing a revival, thanks largely to the few performers and instructors who survived the regime. See the *Phnom Penh Post* and Friday's *Cambodia Daily* for full details of what's on. The city is also showing interest in cinema – after the years of repression 2010 saw the launch of the first annual **Cambodian International Film Festival** (ⓦ cambodia-iff.com), with screenings of 120 films from thirty countries at theatres and outdoor arenas throughout the city. Now in its fourth year (and held annually in December), the festival is going strong. **Galleries**, meanwhile, hosting changing exhibitions of art and sculpture, proliferate; check the magazine *Asia Life* to find out what is coming up.

ARTS AND CULTURE

Cambodian Living Arts ⓦ cambodianlivingarts.org. The CLA aims to revive and encourage the practice of traditional cultural expression in communities across Cambodia by hosting living arts classes and supporting performing arts productions at the National Museum (7pm; Oct–March).

Chaktomuk Theatre On the riverfront near the Cambodiana ☎ 023 725119. From time to time this eye-catching building hosts performances of classical dance and shadow puppetry.

Kickboxing Reproduced on the bas-reliefs of Angkor Wat, the ancient tradition of kickboxing is now enjoying a revival. Bouts start with loud music and much posturing by the contestants – though watching the animated antics of the crowd, for whom betting on the fight is the main attraction, can be as fascinating as the fights. Ask at your hotel or guesthouse for details of forthcoming bouts, which are advertised in the Khmer press.

Meta House German Cultural Centre, 37 Sothearos Blvd ⓦ meta-house.com. Interesting and relevant Cambodian documentaries (4pm; free) and films (7pm; $2, includes a soft drink or beer) are screened daily at Meta House, a fantastic multimedia centre that also hosts exhibitions, workshops, visual poetry and musical events including jazz, DJs and live bands at weekends. Tues–Sun 10am–10pm.

Sovanna Phum Cnr streets 99 & 484 ⓦshadow -puppets.org. Cultural shows at a performing arts society a little way out of town, with performances of classical and folk dance, and shadow puppetry at 7.30pm on Fri and Sat nights ($10).

CINEMA

The Flicks 1 & 2 Street 95 (next to Terrace on 95) & Street 136 (next to Number 11 Backpackers) ⓦtheflicks-cambodia.com. These intimate volunteer-run community movie houses show a weekly changing selection of Western, art-house and Cambodian films nightly (cover charge $3.50 for the day). *The Killing Fields* is screened daily at 10.30am at The Flicks 2 and occasionally on Sun nights. You can reserve your ticket online.

Institut Français 218 Street 184 ⓦinstitutfrancais -cambodge.com. Regular free screenings of French films, usually subtitled in English, shown during the week at 6.30pm.

Platinum Multiplex Sorya Mall, Street 63, near Psar Thmei ⓦplatinumcineplex.com.kh. Three screens, including one in 3D; movies are shown throughout the day, with start times from 9am to 9pm.

GALLERIES

Asasax Art Cnr streets 178 & 13 (opposite the park in front of the National Museum). Displays work by local modern artists and sells attractive prints. Daily 8am–7.30pm.

Chinese House 45 Sisowath Quay ⓦchinesehouse .asia. Permanent and temporary exhibitions by Asian artists in a beautifully restored colonial villa in the heart of the French quarter.

Reyum 47 Street 178, near the National Museum ⓦreyum.org. In conjunction with the Institute of Arts and Culture, Reyum puts on varied exhibitions of work by Cambodian students.

Romeet 34E Street 178 ⓦromeet.com. Established by Battambang-based NGO Phare Ponleu Selpak (PPS) in 2011 as a platform for the work of artists graduating from the Visual Art School. Focuses on Cambodian contemporary art. Tues–Sat 10am–noon & 2–6pm, Sun 2–6pm.

SHOPPING

Phnom Penh is the best place to shop in Cambodia, with **traditional markets** selling everything from beautiful **silk** *sampots* – the word for both the traditional Khmer skirt and a sufficient length of fabric to make one – which a **tailor** can then make up into garments of your own design, to myriad hand-crafted wooden, stone and silver trinkets. Contemporary woodcarvings and marble statues make bulky souvenirs, but are so evocative of Cambodia that it's hard not to pick up one or two. You will also see hundreds of intricate (usually low-grade) silver pots in the shape of animals on sale, which tuck more neatly into backpack or suitcase. **Jewellery** is sold in abundance too, gold and silver, set with stones and gems in all imaginable designs and colours, and there are wonderful **antiques and curios**, both originals and replicas of old wooden pagoda statues and a huge assortment of decorative boxes and trunks. **Haggling** is an essential part of market shopping, with prices starting ludicrously high – check around a few stalls before buying, as they will often sell identical pieces.

MARKETS

Psar BKK South of streets 380; map pp.58–59. Very few visitors venture to this market, which is a shame as it's one of the cleanest in the city. The fresh food stalls are particularly appealing and the main *ban hoi* (rice noodle salad; 5000 riel) vendor has been cooking this same breakfast dish here for some 25 years. Uniquely, Psar BKK also has a few stalls selling vintage clothes and bags from across Asia. Daily 7am–5pm.

Psar Chas Cnr Street 13 & Ang Duong; map p.66. Otherwise known as the Old Market, and located at the southern end of the French quarter, this is one of the city's more traditional markets. Although it's not the cleanest it's easy to get to, and its fruit and vegetable stalls are particularly photogenic. Daily 8am–6pm.

Psar Kabkoh Street 9, south of Sihanouk Blvd; map p.66. A small market geared around fresh produce, with a number of good food vendors. Daily 7am–6pm.

Psar Kandal Street 13, near Wat Ounalom; map p.66. A genuine and easily accessible low-slung market close to the riverfront, where you can browse the usual displays of clothing, jewellery, electronics, fruit, meat and vegetables and get a cheap meal at one of the noodle vendors. Daily 7am–6pm.

Psar Olympic Off Street 199 southwest of the Olympic Stadium; map pp.58–59. A top spot for fabrics, visited by people from all over the country who buy wholesale here for resale. Daily 7.30am–5pm.

Psar Orussey Street 182; map pp.58–59. Vendors from all over Cambodia, selling just about anything from dried fish to TVs, trade at this sprawling place with two floors and a mezzanine. The stalls are crammed together and it can be confusing, but the merchandise is a good bit cheaper than elsewhere. The adjacent Street 166 is big on traditional Khmer medicine shops, where leaves, tree bark and various animal parts, usually boiled in

1

water or soaked in wine, are sold as tonics. Daily 7am–5pm.

Psar Reatrey Along the riverfront between streets 106 and 108; map p.66. A night market, popular mainly with local youngsters, selling clothes, such as the ubiquitous *krama*, mobile phones and a good range of souvenirs, art and curios. It's a good place to go native and enjoy a meal on the mats laid out by street hawkers at the western end as the sun goes down. Fri–Sun 5.30–11.30pm.

Psar Thmei See p.75.

Psar Toul Tom Poung Cnr streets 163 & 444; map pp.58–59. Also known as the "Russian Market" because all its goods used to come from Russia, one of the few countries to provide aid to Cambodia during the Vietnamese occupation. The collapse of the USSR put paid to cheap imports, but ramshackle and tremendous, this market retains its reputation as *the* place to buy textiles, antiques and silver – not to mention motorbike parts. At the south end of the market you'll find stalls selling bootleg DVDs, fake designer bags, silver jewellery, Chinese-style furniture, photocopied books, handicrafts and piles of multicoloured silks; book sellers colonize the west, and the north is taken over with hardware stalls, a small food quarter and mechanics workshops. It is charming in its dilapidation, though a high fire risk with narrow exit routes – it's also meltingly hot. Daily 8am–5pm.

SHOPPING WITH A CONSCIENCE

Numerous NGOs, other organizations and some private individuals have shops and outlets that directly help street children, women at risk and/or the disabled and other disadvantaged groups.

Cambodian Craft (Aka Chamber of Professional and Micro-Enterprises of Cambodia) South side of Wat Phnom traffic circle, just off Norodom Blvd; map p.66. This co-operative provides training and support to rural villagers. Their Phnom Penh premises, housed in a beautiful 70-year-old traditional building, hosts regular exhibitions and occasional artisan demonstrations. It's well stocked with quality silverware, baskets, ceramics and textiles. Daily 9am–5pm.

Daughters of Cambodia 65 Street 178; map p.66. This little boutique, selling interesting jewellery and accessories, doubles up as a spa and boutique and occasionally hosts temporary exhibitions. The shop is run by women who have been rescued from the sex trafficking industry, and profits go towards saving other victims. You can sponsor a girl and or donate directly to the foundation. Mon–Sat 9am–6pm.

Friends 'N Stuff 215 Street 13; map p.66. A branch of the *Friends* family (see p.84), the shop sells clothes, bags, jewellery and secondhand books, and has a nail salon. Tues–Sat 10am–7pm, Sun 9am–2pm.

Mekong Quilts 47–49 Street 240; map p.66. Brightly coloured quilts, cushions and throws in every pattern imaginable, made by impoverished women from the provinces who receive the profits of their work. Mekong Plus, the NGO behind the outlet, provides scholarships and promotes health initiatives in remote villages of the Svay Rieng province. Daily 9am–7pm.

NCDP (National Centre of Disabled Persons) Compound of the Ministry for Women's Affairs, 3 Norodom Blvd; map p.66. A retail outlet for quality products made by disabled (primarily land-mine-disabled) people throughout the country. Especially good silk bags, purses and hanging mobiles. Daily 8am–6pm.

Nyemo Stall 14, Russian Market (south side); map pp.58–59. Unique soft furnishings, accessories, bags and toys, with profits helping to train and support vulnerable women. Daily 8am–5pm.

Peace Handicrafts 39C Street 155; map pp.58–59. Land-mine- and polio-disabled people produce carefully crafted silk items for sale in their co-operative shop. Mon–Sat 7.30am–6pm.

Rajana Cnr streets 450 & 155; map pp.58–59. Sales of silk and bamboo crafts and jewellery help to support the NGOs' Fair Trade training programmes. Mon–Sat 7am–6pm, Sun 10.30am–6pm.

Rehab Craft 1 Street 278; map p.66. Women with disabilities and victims of land mines sell a variety of high-quality silver, wood and stone items here, as well as silk scarves and attractive leather goods. Daily 10am–9pm.

Tabitha-Cambodia Cnr streets 51 & 360; map pp.58–59. Noprofit NGO-run place selling silks made into garments and soft furnishings, cards, packed coffee and more. It operates by training disadvantaged women to sew. They then work from home and Tabitha buys their output. Daily 9am–8pm.

Tooït Tooït Stall 312, Russian Market (west side, main aisle); map pp.58–59. Supporting parents so that their children can go to school, selling such items as shopping bags, beads and toys made from recycled materials including newspapers, plastic bags and rice sacks. Daily 8am–5pm.

Watthan Artisans Cambodia (WAC) Wat Than, 180 Norodom Blvd; map pp.58–59. A co-operative of disabled artisans who produce a range of handicrafts: silk scarves, home furnishings, woodcarvings and basketwork, for example. Daily 9am–5pm.

SHOPS AND MALLS

There is a growing number of classy boutiques selling clothes, jewellery and soft furnishings, particularly in BKK (see p.80) and swanky Street 240. Sihanouk Blvd, near Lucky Supermarket, has several designer stores, including Lacoste, and a branch of the high-street store Mango.

BOOKSHOPS

Bohr's Books 47 Street 172 (near Wat Ounalom); map p.66. New and used titles, and a decent selection of Cambodia-and Southeast Asia-related guides. Also at 3 Sisowath Quay. Daily 8am–8pm.

D's Books 79 Street 240; map p.66. An excellent place to stock up on secondhand books (both fiction and non-fiction) in many languages. Also at 12 Street 178 (near the FCC). Daily 9am–9pm.

Monument Books 111 Norodom Blvd (near Street 240); map p.66. English-language fiction and nonfiction in a full range of subjects including Cambodia and Southeast Asia, children's books, travel, cookery, art and design. There's another branch in the airport. Daily 7am–8.30pm.

BOUTIQUES

Bliss 29 Street 240; map p.66. Well-known boutique specializing in stylish women's resort wear; their breezy lightweight cottons are perfect for the beach. Also a kid's collection and homewares. Daily 9am–9pm.

Kabas Boutique 18 Street 282; map p.66. Clothing in Cambodian fabrics for men and women with an on-site tailor who can adjust clothes to fit with a two-day turnaround. Also silk accessories and cushions. Mon–Sat 9am–7pm, Sun 9am–3pm.

Trunkh Cnr Sothearos Blvd & Street 294; map p.66. Cool new concept store selling loungewear, Khmer-influenced homewares, screen-printed tea towels, artwork and vintage-style signs. Tues–Sun 10am–7pm.

MALLS

Golden Sorya Shopping Centre Street 51; map p.66. Aiming at the middle to lower end of the market, this low-rise mall sells clothes and electrical goods and has a couple of mini-marts. Hours vary.

Sorya Shopping Centre 11–13 Street 63; map p.66. This eight-storey monolith south of the Central Market feels more like a department store; here you'll find fashion, sportswear, electrical equipment and a Lucky supermarket. There's also a food hall, cinema and roller rink. Daily 8am–8.30pm.

SOUVENIRS

Art Steel 87 Street 240; map p.66. Little shop on fashionable Street 240 selling wrought-iron furnishings and accessories including rather cute, hand-painted pressed-steel geckos for mounting on the wall (or ceiling). Daily 7am–8pm.

"Art Street" Street 178; map p.66. Dozens of small warehouses selling an array of paintings and small sculptures created for the tourist market. Generally daily 9am–6pm.

Artisans Angkor 12 Eo Street 13, in front of the post office ☎023 992409, ⊚artisansangkor.com; map p.66. Two-storey boutique selling Cambodian fine arts and crafts – including silks, cushions and statues – produced in Siem Reap. Daily 9am–6pm.

Le Lezard Bleu 61 Street 240; map p.66 ☎012 928005. A boutique gallery focusing on contemporary art and design, including paintings and little brass Buddhas. Mon–Sat 8am–7pm, Sun 8am–5pm.

SUPERMARKETS

Bayon Supermarket 33–34 Street 114; map pp.58–59. A good selection of canned produce, cereals and other dry goods, as well as chilled items and cheese. Daily 8am–9pm.

Lucky 160 Sihanouk Blvd near cnr of Monivong; map p.66. Good for toiletries and imported deli items such as meats, fruits and cheeses. Also branches in the Sorya Mall, the Sovanna Mall and the Olympic City Mall. Daily 8am–9pm.

Thai Huot 99–105 Monivong Blvd & 6 Street 592; map pp.58–59. European deli foods, herbs and fresh bread. Daily 7.30am–8.30pm.

DIRECTORY

Dentists International SOS Medical & Dental Clinic, 161 Street 51 (☎023 216911), has English-speaking staff. European Dental Clinic, 160A Norodom Blvd (Mon–Fri 8am–1pm & 2–7pm, Sat 8am–1pm; ☎023 211363, emergency ☎012 854408), has French, Thai and Khmer dentists.

Doctors English is spoken at the excellent but expensive International SOS Medical & Dental Clinic, 161 Street 51 (Mon–Fri 8am–5.30pm, Sat 8am–noon; ☎023 216911, ⊚internationalsos.com); Naga Medical Centre, 11 Street 254 (24hr; ☎023 211300, ⊚nagaclinic.com); Tropical and Travellers Medical Clinic, near Wat Phnom at 88 Street 108 (Mon–Fri 8.30am–noon & 2pm–5pm, Sat 8.30am–noon; ☎023 306802, ⊚travellersmedicalclinic.com).

Embassies and consulates Australia, 16B National Assembly (☎023 213470, ⊚cambodia.embassy.gov.au); Canada, 9 Street 254 (⊚phnompenh.gc.ca); UK, 27–29 Street 75 (☎023 427124, ⊚ukincambodia.fco.gov.uk); France, 1 Monivong Blvd (☎023 430020); Laos, 15–17 Mao Tse Toung Blvd (☎023 983632); Thailand, 196 Norodom Blvd (☎023 726306, ⊚thaiembassy.org /phnompenh); US, cnr streets 96 & 51 (☎023 728000,

1

ⓦ cambodia.usembassy.gov); Vietnam, 436 Monivong Blvd (ⓣ 023 726274, ⓦ vietnamembassy-cambodia.org/en).

Emergencies Ambulance ⓣ 119 (from an 023 phone) or ⓣ 023 217764; fire ⓣ 118 (from an 023 phone) or ⓣ 023 786693; police ⓣ 117 (from an 023 phone) or ⓣ 023 366841 or ⓣ 012 722067); hotline for the police to report child exploitation (national and in Phnom Penh) ⓣ 023 720555 – English is spoken on all these numbers.

Hospitals Royal Rattanak Hospital, 11 Street 592 (ⓣ 012 365555, ⓦ royalrattanakhospital.com), south of the Tuolkok Market; or try Calmette, north end of Monivong Blvd (ⓣ 023 426948).

Internet There are internet cafés all over town. Rates are typically around $1/hr.

Money Acleda Bank, 61 Monivong Blvd and 28 Mao Tse Toung Blvd; ANZ Royal, cnr Street 114 (Kramoun Sar) with branches around town; Canadia Bank, 315 Monivong Blvd; Foreign Trade Bank of Cambodia (FTB), 3 Street 114 (Kramoun Sar). There are 24hr ATMs at the Acleda, ANZ and Cambodian Asia (branches around town) banks but they charge $4 handling fee for international cards. At the time of writing, Canadia Bank had the only ATM that didn't charge a handling fee. Western Union has branches all over town where you can exchange travellers' cheques, receive/make money transfers and get money on Visa and MasterCard (US$ only). Exchange booths around town display their rates for dollars into riel; some of the best rates are to be had at Psar Thmei.

Opticians Opticians cluster along Sihanouk Blvd near Lucky Supermarket, and in general offer a speedy, good service. Modern Optics, 181 Norodom Blvd, has a good reputation (ⓣ 078 787876), or try I Care Optical, 166–170 Norodom Blvd (ⓣ 023 991148).

Pharmacies Pharmacie de la Gare, cnr Monivong and Pochentong blvds (Mon–Sat 7am–7pm, Sun 7am–5pm), has English-speaking pharmacists and a good selection of Western drugs; they accept credit cards. Ucare has a handful of branches with English-speaking pharmacists (all daily 8am–11pm): cnr Sothearos Blvd and Street 178 (ⓣ 023 222499); cnr Sihanouk Blvd and Street 55 (ⓣ 023 224099); cnr Norodom Blvd and Street 136 (ⓣ 023 224299); and 207–209 Sisowath Quay (ⓣ 023 223499).

Photography and film There are outlets all over town, with some of the better ones (where you'll find items such as digital memory cards) on Monivong Blvd, near Psar Thmei.

Post The main post office, on Street 13, between streets 98 and 102 (Mon–Fri 7.30am–5pm, Sat 7.30–11am), provides the full range of services, including parcel post, fax, telephones and poste restante. There's a booth where you can buy aerogrammes, postcards, envelopes, writing paper and stamps. EMS in the same building (ⓣ 023 427428) offers an efficient and cost-effective courier service. Alternatively, try TNT, 28 Monivong Blvd (ⓣ 023 430922); DHL, 353 Street 110 (ⓣ 023 427726); UPS, Hong Kong Centre (ⓣ 023 023 219213); or Fedex, 71 Street 242 (ⓣ 023 216712).

Visa extensions At the Department for Immigration opposite the airport (see p.76). Almost all hotels and guesthouses can arrange extensions for $5–10 commission.

Around Phnom Penh

Just a short journey from Phnom Penh brings you to a landscape of rice paddies and sugar palms, scattered with small villages and isolated pagodas. The **Chroy Chung Va peninsula**, the tip of land facing the city centre at the confluence of the Tonle Sap and Mekong rivers, is home to a collection of villages and feels very removed from the bustle of central Phnom Penh; its western side, facing the Royal Palace, is being transformed into a riverside park. The southernmost tip is now the property of the *Sokha Resort* group whose newest concrete monolith is rapidly growing. A short way further northeast, reached by a short ferry trip from Phnom Penh, lies **Koh Dach**, a lush green island in the Mekong, whose inhabitants weave silk and grow a wide variety of produce on the fertile alluvial soil. **Wat Champuk Ka-Ek**, east of town off NR1, has a remarkable collection of ten thousand Buddhas and can be tied in with a trip to **Kien Svay**, a popular riverside village about 15km from the city. **Phnom Brasat**, some 27km northwest of town off NR5, is home to a kitsch collection of pagodas, while further north rise the distinctive hills of the old capital **Oudong**, dotted with the chedi of various kings; you might want to combine a trip here with a visit to the scant remains of nearby **Lovek**, its predecessor as capital.

A short moto-ride southwest of the city, the killing fields and memorial at **Choeung Ek** make a logical, if macabre, progression from a visit to the Toul Sleng Genocide Museum. Also south of the city, off NR2, the compact Angkorian temple of **Tonle Bati** enjoys a riverside location, and is a good place for a picnic and a swim. Further south,

1

there are spectacular views from the ancient hilltop temple of **Phnom Chisor**. Both sites could be combined as a day-trip, along with **Phnom Tamau**, Cambodia's only state-run zoo and wildlife rescue centre.

Chroy Chung Va peninsula

At the confluence of the Tonle Sap and Mekong rivers, facing Phnom Penh city centre • Once across the Chroy Chung Va Bridge, take the first right, which heads right around the headland (moto $2)

The 3km spit of land that makes up the **Chroy Chung Va peninsula** was once a farming area – controversially, however, the Phnom Penh cleared out the villagers from the western side and turned it into a riverside park, facing the promenade on the city side. It's a good spot to watch the sunset over the city, sipping a coconut at one of the refreshment stalls, and if you make your way northeast along the banks of the Mekong you'll pass through several friendly villages inhabited by the **Cham**, Cambodia's Muslim minority.

Koh Dach

Some 6km from Phnom Penh • Ferries run regularly throughout the day, departing when full (moto and driver 1500 riel, foot passengers 1000 riel) from jetties signposted off NR6 across Chroy Chung Va – alternatively, guesthouses organize group tours (from $10/person) and private cruises run from the tourist dock ($20/hr)

Set in the middle of the Mekong 6km from Phnom Penh is the quiet island of **Koh Dach**. Primarily an agricultural community (peanuts are an important cash crop), the 10km-long island is home to a number of stilt-house villages, and you'll see a good cross-section of rural life as you meander along its leafy tracks. The island is noted for its **weaving** of *sampots*, and in the dry season looms clack away beneath the houses, producing colourful reams of cotton and silk. As soon as you arrive you'll be invited into a home to watch the weavers in action, before being encouraged to browse and buy. As the river level falls after the rainy season, a wide sandy **beach** is exposed at the northern end of Koh Dach, where food stalls and picnic huts serve traditional dishes and tasty fried chicken.

Wat Champuh Ka'Ek

12km east of Phnom Penh, off NR1 • After the Monivong Bridge take the first right (Street 369) along the Bassac River – the pagoda is on the left after 7km (a moto should cost no more than $5 return)

The ten thousand Buddha statues at **Wat Champuh Ka'Ek**, fashioned in just about every possible shape, size and material, were donated by wealthy patrons, from whose gifts the pagoda derives its conspicuous affluence. The monks here are much respected and well connected – it's not unusual to find them performing elaborate ceremonies for dignitaries and well-heeled Cambodians who wish to gain merit in the next life or to receive blessings in this one.

The pagoda is entered through an avenue lined with devas (gods) on one side and asuras (demons) on the other, a favourite Cambodian theme; the Buddhas are arrayed in air-conditioned splendour in the modern-looking **hall** across the compound, ranged in floor-to-ceiling tiers and illustrating every one of the forty *mudras* along the way. One of the most sublime images – a life-size standing bronze Buddha – is at the centre of the display towards the front. The hands are held out in front of the body, palms facing out with fingers pointed up in *abhaya mudra*, the position of giving protection; a diamond is embedded in the centre of each palm.

If the **vihara** is open, it's worth putting your head inside to see the unusually decorated walls – by Cambodian standards these are stark, painted pale yellow and stencilled with golden Buddha images. A small white stupa nearby, in front of the bathing pool, contains skulls and bones found in the pagoda grounds of people murdered by the Khmer Rouge.

Kien Svay and around

Optimistically hailed by some locals as "the new Kep", **KIEN SVAY** (or Koki Beach, as it's also known), 15km southeast of Phnom Penh, is really more of a muddy riverbank. That said, it positively throngs at weekends with people venturing out from Phnom Penh to picnic at the rows of stilt-huts on the banks of the Mekong. Hawkers and food stalls sell all kinds of food, which you can eat while lazing around your hut (rented for around 5000 for a few hours). The village is particularly noted for its crispy **fried bugs** – different sorts of beetle, cricket, silkworm and a variety of pupas – while small boats ply the river with fish and lobsters for sale, cooking your chosen specimen for you on their on-board braziers.

The villages around Kien Svay are well known for their **weaving**, traditionally done by the women, though more men are joining in; silk and mixed-thread scarves and *kramas* are produced here for the markets in Phnom Penh.

ARRIVAL AND DEPARTURE	**KIEN SVAY**

By moto or tuk-tuk Stay on NR1 until, 14km after the Monivong Bridge, you pass the *L'Imprevu* resort; the turning for the beach is 1km beyond, to the left (north), through an ornate portico that looks like a pagoda gateway lined with food vendors. Expect to pay around $6 for a return moto, or $12 by tuk-tuk.

By bus You could take a direct bus from Psar Thmei to Kien Svay or a service to Psar Koki, the town market, followed by a moto for the remaining 0.5km ride to the beach.

Phnom Prasith

24km northwest of Phnom Penh • Take NR5 north for 11km to Prek Pneuv Market, then take a left onto an unsealed road and continue for 13km to the site (a moto should cost $8–12 return, tuk-tuk $15–20)

The complex of pagodas at **Phnom Prasith**, spread over a distance of about 5km, originally comprised just two hilltop sites (the "East Hill" and the "West Hill"), but now sprawls over four locations. The monks and nuns here hope to develop the site to Angkorian proportions; the seemingly never-ending programme of construction includes a futuristic glass domed edifice. As the building of new sanctuaries is seen as gaining particular merit, it's not unusual for wealthy patrons to make sizeable financial contributions.

Wat Phnom Reap

The most popular of the four sites is **Wat Phnom Reap**, reached through a Bayon-style gateway of enormous faces flanked by elephants. The track is lined with asuras and devas tugging on two nagas, there to protect the city's wealth in an impressive attempt at re-creating the southern gate of Angkor Thom in Siem Reap. Dominating the compound is the amazing carmine-red concrete reproduction of Angkor Wat, **Prasat Mahar Nokor Vitmean Sooer**; it was completed in 1998, after just two years' work. A colonnaded gallery runs around the outside, sheltering elaborately decorated walls; apsaras nestle in niches, while bas-reliefs illustrate scenes from the life of Buddha and commemorate the construction of the temple by depicting the people who donated either money or labour.

In the same complex, the entrance to **Prasat Pik Vongkot Boreay Brom Mlop** is guarded by two imposing statues of Hanuman, each standing on one leg with sword raised. Inside, an enormous seated Buddha dominates the hall; behind it and curling around it, a cheerful mural of the bodhi tree is dotted with birds and animals.

East Hill Buddha

A few kilometres up the road beyond Wat Phnom Reap, on the first hill you come to, is the **East Hill Buddha**, a much-restored, 15m-long reclining Buddha carved out of the hillside. It's reputedly quite ancient and may conceivably be the only surviving part of the sixth-century pre-Angkorian ruins known to have been here.

1

PREAH VESSANDAA

A popular theme at Cambodian pagodas is the tale of Preah Vessandaa – one of the previous **incarnations of the Buddha** – which is often told in tableaux, the figures usually life-sized and garishly coloured. According to the story, an old man, Chuchuk, was given a young woman, Amita, to be his wife in repayment of a debt. The couple were unable to have children, and Amita was snubbed by the other women. Knowing of King Vessandaa's generosity, Amita persuaded her husband to ask Vessandaa for two of his children. When depicted in temples, the story, usually told in a series of ten or so scenes, tells of Chuchuk's adventures on the way to the palace. One scene at Phnom Prasith shows Chuchuk dangling in a tree where he has been chased by the hunter Chetabut and his dogs; to escape, the old man lies that he is one of the king's messengers. As Chuchuk approaches the palace, the king's children run off, only to be discovered hiding under lily pads by the king, who grants them to the old man. After getting lost on his way home, Chuchuk ends up in the kingdom of the children's grandfather, who pays a ransom to buy them back. As told in Cambodia, the story ends when Chuchuk spends the money on a feast at which he gorges himself to death – a graphic injunction against the vice of gluttony.

Steps lead up to the summit and vihara, where a series of **tableaux** illustrate scenes from the story of Preah Vessandaa (see box above). Bizarrely, Cambodia's gun culture pervades even here; in a painting of Angkor Wat, a man – presumably the benefactor – proudly displays his pistol holster.

Kompong Luong

Heading north out of the capital, NR5 follows the Tonle Sap River most of the way to Oudong, passing Cham villages and new mosques (most mosques having been destroyed – and Cham religious leaders murdered – by the Khmer Rouge). This area is important for the production of **prohok** (fermented fish paste), and in January and February the air is pungent with the odour of drying fish. Just beyond the new bridge at Prek K'dam, around 33km from Phnom Penh, is the village of **KOMPONG LUONG**. Once the royal port for Oudong, the village has for centuries been famous for its **silverwork**, and several generations of silversmiths still work together here to craft cups, bowls and all manner of small boxes in animal and fruit designs, shaping and decorating them by hand. Visitors are welcome to watch and buy, though there's not much difference in price from the markets of Phnom Penh.

Oudong and around

Oudong, 37km northwest of Phnom Penh, was the capital of Cambodia for 248 years, playing host to the crowning of several monarchs, including Norodom, great-great-grandfather of the current king. However, in 1866, King Norodom was persuaded by the French to relocate the capital from here to the more strategically positioned Phnom Penh; the court, totalling more than ten thousand people, moved en masse and Oudong was abandoned. The old wooden city has long since rotted away, but the **site**, with shrines and chedi scattered across two **hills**, remains important to pilgrims and has been designated a tourist spot. Food stalls are in abundance as are the ubiquitous hammock-strung stilted huts beloved of the Cambodians who pile in here on weekends and national holidays.

Phnom Preah Reach Troap

Visible from afar, the chedi on top of **Phnom Preah Reach Troap**, the larger of the two hills at Oudong, are something of a landmark. Approaching from NR5, you'll arrive at the foot of this hill – otherwise known as the Hill of Royal Fortune, as the royal treasure was hidden here during the war with the Siamese in the sixteenth century.

As you approach, before ascending the staircase, you'll pass a small building on the left that contains human remains collected from a Khmer Rouge execution site nearby.

The new chedi

After a steep slog up 509 steps you arrive at a gleaming marble terrace, behind which, and framed by the Buddhist and Cambodian flags, the spire of the modern grey, 42m-high **chedi** dominates the skyline. From here, the panoramic vistas across flooded rice fields, villages pricked by sugar palms and the Tonle Sap are stunning. A short staircase leads up to the base of the chedi, adorned with nagas, elephants and lions. As you wander around this upper terrace, views of the western plains are revealed; just to the northwest lies the sparkling, modern golden temple of the modern Vipassana Dhura Buddhist Centre complex (see p.98). Built in 2002 to safeguard a sacred golden urn thought to contain the ashes of three small bones of the Buddha (which were originally interred in Phnom Penh), the chedi was broken into in 2013. Thieves stole the urn, along with other sacred relics, causing widespread outrage; at the time of writing the investigation was ongoing.

Damrei Sam Poan

South from the new chedi is a trio of funerary reliquaries. The oldest of these, **Damrei Sam Poan**, was built in 1623 by Preah Bat Chey Cheta for the ashes of his uncle and predecessor, King Soriyopor. Surrounded by charmingly decayed elephant statues, the chedi is badly overgrown and the inner brick is starting to crumble. Until recently it had the tallest spire on the hill.

Tray Troeng

Beyond Damrei Sam Poan is the crumbling **Tray Troeng**, built in 1891 by King Norodom for the ashes of his father, King Ang Duong (though there's some dispute as to whether the ashes are really here or in the Silver Pagoda in Phnom Penh). Some of the glazed ceramic flowers that once covered this distinctive chedi can still be seen, but since local children used to sell them to tourists when they "fell off", they've now been replaced with modern alternatives.

Chet Dey Mak Prohm

As you wander down the pathway to the southeast of Tray Troeng, you come across a fourth notable structure, known as **Chet Dey Mak Prohm**, and easily recognized by the four faces that cap its spire. The pale-yellow chedi contains the ashes of King Sisowath Monivong (r. 1927–41).

Preah Ko and Preah Neak

Several of the older shrines southeast of Chet Dey Mak Prohm are worth seeking out. These include **Preah Ko**, featuring a particularly appealing statue of Nandin, the sacred mount of Shiva. Worshippers pour water over the bull's head, rendering the water holy, to then be taken home. Nearby, **Preah Neak** contains a Buddha seated on a coiled naga, its multiple heads curved over to afford him protection.

Preah Atharas

Just before you hit the hill's southeastern staircase, a huge pagoda comes into view. The once ruined columns and rotten roof beams of **Preah Atharas** (*atharas* being an ancient unit of measure equal to eighteen cubits) have been replaced and restoration work is ongoing. This pagoda was built by the Chinese in the thirteenth century to seal the cave – so legend has it – of a mythical sea monster, which had to be contained to stop the Chinese losing their dominance over the Khmer. The vihara was heavily damaged during fighting between Lon Nol and Khmer Rouge and received further attacks from the Khmer Rouge post-1975. For many years only a shoulder and part of the right side of the 11m-high seated Buddha remained; it has now been resplendently restored.

1

Oudong's smaller hill

A separate stairway flanked by nagas leads up Oudong's **smaller hill**, 100m beyond the foot of the southeastern staircase of Phnom Preah Reach Troap. At the top is a small, damaged mosque, **Vihara Ta Sann**, and the ruins of a large reclining Buddha whose giant feet are all that can be seen rearing up from the pink bougainvillea. Just beyond is a stark, ageing chedi dating back to 1567 and built by King Bat Boromintho Reachea – for whom, no one seems to know.

Vipassana Dhura Buddhist Centre

At the foot of Phnom Preah Reach Troap, the expansive **Vipassana Dhura Buddhist Centre** complex is worth a quick visit to marvel at its imposing jade Buddha and beautifully painted walls. Another vast reclining Buddha can be seen in the smaller shrine southeast of the complex, and in the centre of the large basin to the north stands a golden statue of **Preah Neang Kong Hing**, goddess of the Earth who draws water from the end of her long plaited hair. In a small pavilion next to the temple lies the glass-encased remains of an orange-robed mummified monk, the most venerable Sam Bunthoem, who was shot in Wat Langka in 2003 by assailants angry at his encouragement of monks to vote in the National Assembly elections.

ARRIVAL AND DEPARTURE   OUDONG

By bus Oudong can be reached by taking the Kompong Chhnang bus from Phnom Penh; let the driver know where you're going and get off at the orange archway (around 37km from the capital). From here, take one of the waiting motos for the final 3km ($1–2).

By tuk-tuk With a tuk-tuk – for around $25 – you could take in several rural villages en route to Oudong; for a few dollars more you could combine Oudong with visits to Phnom Brasat or Lovek.

By bicycle You can cycle to Oudong on a guided trip with Grasshopper Adventures (see p.78).

Lovek

54km northwest of Phnom Penh • By moto, head north from Oudong on NR5 in the direction of Kompong Chhnang; after 12km take the turning at the small blue sign on the right for Traleng Keng Pagoda site – beyond the concrete portico flanked by golden lions, the village stretches along a 5km straight track, before it bends at a right angle towards the shrines (you could get as far as the main road turning on the Phnom Penh–Kompong Chhnang bus, but you'll need to clearly state your intentions to the driver)

Little is known about **LOVEK**, the capital of Cambodia during the reign of King Ang Chan in the sixteenth century. It was captured by the Siamese in the latter part of the century, and the name has been passed down through a well-known local legend (see box below) as much as anything else. Today a sparse village stretches across the site, consisting of a few houses, a school and two fine **shrines** at the farthest reaches: the larger Wat Preah Kaew (Pagoda of the Emerald Buddha) and Wat Preah Ko (Pagoda of the Sacred Cow) a little further beyond. In both wats, every bit of wall is painted with

---

THE LEGEND OF LOVEK

When Lovek was capital, it was said to house two statues of **Preah Ko** and **Preah Kaew** that contained sacred texts, written in gold, recording "all the knowledge and wisdom in the world". During one of the periodic conflicts between the Thai and Khmer, the Thai army was encamped outside Lovek, which it had repeatedly failed to capture, and was about to make its seasonal retreat in advance of the rains. The story goes that the Thai fired a cannon loaded with silver coins into the bamboo thickets that afforded the city some natural protection. During the rainy season, the Khmer gradually cleared the bamboo in their search for the coins, such that the Thai were easily able to capture the city in the following dry season. Removing the statues to Ayutthaya, the Thai were able to read the sacred texts and so became more knowledgeable than the Khmer. The legend has it that the statues are still hidden in Bangkok and that when they are returned to Cambodia the country will once again have ascendancy over Thailand.

1

colourful murals of the legend. To the south of Wat Preah Ko is a 2m-high, smiling, green-marble Buddha surrounded by bowls of water that worshippers use to bathe him.

Choeung Ek

12km southwest of Phnom Penh • Daily 7am–5.30pm • $3; audioguide $3 • Easily accessible by moto and tuk-tuk, or on excursions run by various Phnom Penh guesthouses (some of which also include side-trips to Tonle Bati); you could even cycle there if you're prepared to brave the traffic (and dust) – to drive here, find Monireth Blvd and follow it south, forking left at the large petrol station, from where it's about 5km to Choeung Ek

Just 12km from Phnom Penh is the notorious site of **Choeung Ek**, where prisoners from Toul Sleng were brought for execution. As graphically portrayed in the film *The Killing Fields*, certain sites around the country – this is the best known – became places of **mass murder**, where the Khmer Rouge disposed of its enemies: men, women and children – even babies – who had allegedly betrayed the state. Early on, the victims were shot; later, to save on valuable bullets, they were bludgeoned or stabbed to death, and babies killed by being savagely thrown against trees, as loud music blared in the background. As fuel became scarce, victims were dragged out of the city and killed en route, their bodies dumped in the rice paddies closer to town.

Set amid peaceful fields and pleasant countryside, in what was once a Chinese burial ground, the **Choeung Ek Memorial** now contains the remains of 8985 bodies exhumed here in 1980, when 86 of the burial pits were excavated. Anecdotal estimates suggest that more than 17,000 people may have been slaughtered here, and a further 43 mass graves under the lake at the site remain untouched; there are no plans for these to be investigated since as yet there is nowhere sufficient to house the remains to Buddhist standards. Inside the memorial, a gleaming glass-fronted chedi, skulls and bones are piled on shelves, seventeen tiers high, arranged by age and gender, their tattered clothes below.

An excellent **audioguide** leads you circuitously around the site, stopping at various key points and finishing up at the memorial stupa. It includes harrowing commentary from victims and a former Khmer Rouge guard. Make sure to wander around the eerily beautiful lake.

Before you leave, drop into the museum, where you can cool off in the air-conditioned "theatre" by watching a dated but informative short video. A raw and emotional declaration close by states, "We are absolutely determined no [sic] to let this genocidal regime to reoccur in Kampuchea".

Tonle Bati

35km south of Phnom Pehn, off NR2 • Daily 7am–5pm • $3, picnic hut rental 5000 riel/day • Take the Takeo bus: buy your ticket directly from the bus operator for the best price, and get off by the Sokimex petrol station – where there's a large hoarding showing the temple – and take a moto the final 2.5km to the temple (1000 riel); alternatively, you can do the return journey from the capital by moto ($8–10) and tuk-tuk ($15–20)

Peaceful **Tonle Bati** is set on the banks of the Bati River in a well-tended grove of coconut and mango trees, where you can swim and picnic as well as seeing the two small but appealing **temples**. You will be met immediately by a gaggle of young girls selling flowers, who will most likely follow you around until you leave, even if you're adamant about not buying.

Some 300m northwest of the temples are dozens of **picnic huts** built on stilts over the river, rentable by the day. The owners provide floor mats and cushions, plus a tray of drinks and snacks, and even inflated inner tubes for swimming. Food's on offer too, but it's pricey so you might want to bring your own provisions.

Ta Prohm

The first temple you come to on entering the site is the larger of the two, **Ta Prohm**. Constructed by Jayavarman VII – creator of the magnificent Angkor Thom – on the

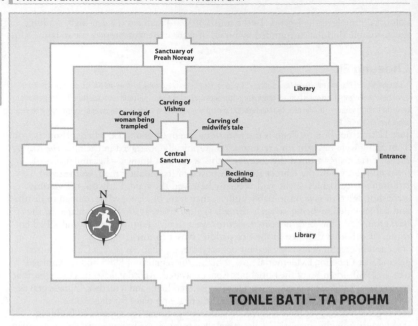

TONLE BATI – TA PROHM

site of a sixth-century shrine, it's dedicated to the Hindu god Shiva (though Jayavarman eventually adopted Theravada Buddhism). The main entrance is from the east along a short laterite causeway, edged by flowers and shrubs; piled up to the side at the entrance are broken chunks of masonry, some elaborately carved with scenes from the Churning of the Ocean of Milk (see p.169) or the *Ramayana* (see box, p.65).

The sanctuaries

At the centre of the inner enclosure are the temple's five **sanctuaries**, its antechambers built in a cruciform shape, with shrines to the cardinal directions. Above the entrance, a carved stone image of a reclining Buddha has been colourfully coated in paint. The **main sanctuary**, of sandstone, contains an upright Buddha image, while the antechambers house damaged stone linga. Another image of Buddha, over the north arm of the cruciform, has been superimposed with a carving of a six-armed Vishnu, a change probably made when the Angkorian kingdom reverted to Hinduism after the death of Jayavarman VII.

Well-preserved **carvings** decorate the outside of the sanctuary and several tell unusual tales. High up on the northeast corner is a scene of two women and a kneeling man: one woman carries a basket on her head, containing the afterbirth from her recent confinement; the midwife, shown standing, was not given sufficient respect during the birth and has condemned the new mother to carry the basket for the rest of her life; her husband is shown begging for forgiveness. The corresponding spot on the northwest corner shows a king sitting next to his wife, who is said to have been unfaithful; below she is put to death by being trampled by a horse.

The north gopura

The north gopura once contained a statue of **Preah Noreay**, a Hindu deity who is said to bestow fertility upon childless women; although the statue is still undergoing restoration at the National Museum (minus his feet which are still in the gopura), women continue to arrive here to seek his help.

LEGENDS OF YEAH PEAU

Various legends surround the **Yeah Peau temple**. One tells how King Preah Ket Mealea fell in love with a young girl named Peau, who gave birth to his son, whom she named Prohm. The king returned to his court but left behind a ring and sacred dagger so that in years to come Prohm would be able to prove his regal descent. Prohm duly went to his father's court and stayed many years, presumably forgetting his mother, for when he finally returned home he fell in love with her, refusing to believe her when she said he was her son. To resolve the matter, it was agreed that Peau and Prohm would each build a temple; if he finished first she would marry him, and if she finished first he would acknowledge her as his mother. The contest took place at night with the women helping Peau and the men assisting Prohm. In the middle of the night, the women raised a lighted candle into the sky. The men, thinking this was the morning star, settled down to sleep in the belief that they could not be beaten, leaving the women to carry on working and complete their temple first. (This rivalry between women and men is a common theme in Cambodian pagodas, cropping up many times in different guises.)

Yeah Peau

Some 100m north of Ta Prohm in the grounds of the modern Wat Tonle Bati, lies the single, sandstone twelfth-century temple of **Yeah Peau**. Wat Tonle Bati was badly damaged by the Khmer Rouge and some pieces of gnarled metal behind the main Buddha are all that is left of the original headless statue. Beside the Buddha is a statue of Peau, while outside in the courtyard are five large seated Buddhas, each with their hands in a different *mudra*.

Phnom Chisor

65km south of Phnom Penh, off NR2 • Daily 7am–5pm • Foreigners $2 (pay at the summit) • The Takeo bus from Phnom Penh stops along the main road, where enterprising moto drivers are on hand to take you the final 2km for around $1; alternatively, take an excursion with one of the capital's travel agents or guesthouses

Originally known as Suryadri ("Sun Mountain"), **Phnom Chisor** was built early in the eleventh century by Suryavarman I and was once a site of some significance, housing one of four sacred linga installed by the king in temples at the boundaries of his kingdom. A hot and tiring flight of 412 steps ascends the hill from the south, though there is a shady pavilion two thirds up, and refreshment-sellers at the top and bottom. There's a modern pagoda at the summit and a burgeoning number of sanctuaries scattered about.

The **villages** east of Phnom Chisor weave very fine traditional *hol*, a patterned silk **sampot** traditionally worn during ceremonies. It's worth buying a piece if you can find someone with a finished length, although this isn't easy as most is produced to order. UNESCO is helping the weavers here relearn the use of natural dyes, a skill that was lost during the Pol Pot years.

Prasat Preah Ko Preah Kaew

One of the more interesting pagodas at Phnom Chisor, **Prasat Preah Ko Preah Kaew** (turn right at the top of the staircase when you reach the summit) contains images of the cow and small boy from which it gets its name. According to one legend, also repeated at the Preah Ko shrine in Lovek, a pregnant woman climbed a mango tree to eat some fruit, despite being warned not to, and fell; the shock induced labour, and from her womb emerged a baby boy and a cow.

Prasat Boran

At the far, northern, end of the hill, the ancient temple of **Prasat Boran** still retains some well-preserved carved sandstone lintels. The temple was built opening to the east,

1

from which side you get a stunning view across the plains to Angkor Borei. From the eastern doorway, the old entrance road leads straight to the foot of the hill and still retains its two gatehouses. In the entrance, two stone **basins** are filled with water, which is ladled out for blessings using a couple of large seashells. The *achars* say the basins used to fill naturally – presumably from a spring – but after a US bomb came through the roof of the central sanctuary in the 1970s (thankfully it didn't explode) this stopped; the roof remains covered with corrugated iron. The very fine internal doors to the central sanctuary are decorated with images of Shiva standing on the back of a pig – although no one knows why.

Cave shrine
A path leads around the hill to the east to a small **cave shrine**, really more a collection of rocks, but containing enough room for two or three people to squeeze inside the crevice. There's sometimes an *achar* here dispensing blessings for a consideration. He might also sell you one of his handkerchiefs decorated with holy symbols for protection and prosperity.

Phnom Tamau Zoo and Rescue Centre
50km south of Phnom Penh, off NR2 • Daily 8.30am–4.30pm • Foreigners $5, car 2000 riel, motorbike 1000 riel • The Takeo bus from Phnom Penh passes the turning, but as the site stretches over several kilometres it is best visited with your own transport (look out for the signposts and archway 10km beyond Tonle Bati, from where it's a further 5km up the side road to the zoo entrance) – or contact Betelnut Tours (🕸 betelnuttours.com) for full-day trips from the Lazy Gecko guesthouse (Tues–Sun 9.45am; $40) or Free the Bears (🕸 freethebears.org.au), who operate a Bear Keeper for the Day programme ($70 for one person, $65 each for two)

The **Phnom Tamau Zoo and Rescue Centre** is more of a safari park, set in an area of regenerating scrub forest between Tonle Bati and Phnom Chisor. Most animals here were rescued from desperate situations: some as they were being taken out of the country to satisfy demand for exotic foods and medicine in China and Thailand, others from markets where they were kept in tiny cages as pets or destined for restaurant tables. Although many of the animals still have far from adequate facilities, the team of dedicated keepers do their best with limited finances. With an annual feeding bill alone of more than $100,000, the centre relies on private donations and sponsorship, so your entrance fee is going to a good cause.

One of the star attractions are the **tigers**, which by day prowl around a purpose-built deluxe enclosure; at night they are secured indoors and protected by armed keepers – poachers are still a cause for concern and a dead tiger can net thousands of dollars. Other highlights include **Malayan sun bears** and **black bears** (129 at the last count) and there are other indigenous species – elephants, pileated gibbons, Siamese crocodiles, macaques, pangolins and various wild cats and fairly tame cranes, among others.

Elderly **beggars** line the road on the way to the zoo from the main road. Having no one to care for them, they walk daily from their villages to ask for alms, so you may wish to take a bundle of small notes.

Neak Leung
The dusty transit town of **NEAK LEUNG** is the jumping-off point for Vietnam: its ferries form a crucial link between Phnom Penh and the border at **Bavet**, while boats set off down the Mekong for the alternative crossing at **Chau Doc**. With so many buses now travelling between Phnom Penh and HCMC direct there's little need, if any, to make a stop en route.

Divided by the Mekong, Neak Leung still lacks a bridge (although one is being constructed), and is consequently congested with vehicles revving up in semi-orderly queues to board the ferries that crisscross the Mekong. Beyond the river NR1 travels southeast through the sleepy provincial town of Svay Rieng and eventually, Bavet, toward the Vietnamese border. Neak Leung is known for its river lobster (*bong kong*), served in the **restaurants** close by the east-bank ferry terminal. The town's other culinary speciality is sparrow; you'll see plucked birds strung up and ready for cooking.

ARRIVAL AND DEPARTURE

NEAK LEUNG

By bus The bus from Phnom Penh arrives at the west bank; the town's restaurants and market are all on the east bank. Ferry tickets (300 riel) can be bought at the ticket office by the traffic barrier at the end of the road, or while boarding. Note that during public holidays the queues for the ferry can be horrendous.

Destinations Bavet (10 daily; 2hr); Phnom Penh (10 daily; 2hr); Svay Rieng (every 30min; 1hr).

By shared taxi or minibus Shared taxis depart from the transport stop on the western side of the river.

Destinations Bavet (10 daily; 1hr 30min); Phnom Penh (10 daily; 1hr 30min); Svay Rieng (10 daily; 1hr).

TO VIETNAM

K'am Samnar: Chau Doc border crossing Many people heading for Chau Doc in Vietnam go on organized trips from Phnom Penh (try *Capitol* guesthouse; $10), in which case your guide will arrange transfers between the various different forms of transport. You will need to organize your visa separately, though this can often be done via your guesthouse, too. If you're going about it independently, it's possible to take an express boat ($25–35) from Phnom Penh to Chau Doc direct. You could also make the journey by bus, though this is a little trickier – catch a bus to Neak Leung and get off on the west bank, from where it is a 350m walk south along the road adjacent to the riverfront to the pier. Scheduled ferries

leave for K'am Samnar (10,000 riel; 2hr) or you could charter a speedboat ($55; 1hr); the boat leaves from behind a blue-roofed warehouse that isn't signposted (if you reach the bridge you've gone too far). The various immigration and customs buildings at the border post (daily 7am–8pm) are quite scattered, so you'll need to rent a moto (about 4000 riel). After entering Vietnam at Vinh Xuong, you need to take a *xe om* (moto in Vietnamese; about $5) to get to Chau Doc, a journey of less than an hour. From the central market at Chau Doc, you can hop aboard a minibus bound for HCMC ($3).

Bavet: Moc Bai border crossing For direct services between Phnom Penh and HCMC (and vice versa), you no longer have to change buses at the Moc Bai border crossing (daily 7am–8pm); the bus operator will handle everything, although as with all crossings into Vietnam you will need to get your visa beforehand in Phnom Penh. If you're going it alone and haven't booked through transport to HCMC, jump on a bus to Bavet and once you've crossed the border, take a motorbike taxi or minibus the 10km from Moc Bai to Go Dau, where you can get direct onward transport to HCMC – from the border, the journey should take less than 2hr. If you're coming into Cambodia from Moi Bac, you can jump in a shared taxi from Bavet to Phnom Penh (around $5) or take a private ride for $50. If you get stuck, you could stay in one of Bavet's many casinos.

Battambang and the northwest

FLOATING VILLAGE LIFE, TONLE SAP LAKE

Battambang and the northwest

2

Strike north from Phnom Penh along NR5, west of the Tonle Sap, and you'll be following the route along which the Khmer Rouge retreated from Phnom Penh in 1979, ahead of the liberating Vietnamese forces. This is also the route that the invading Thai armies used in the opposite direction, as they repeatedly headed south to sack and pillage. Much of the northwest still shows clear Thai influence – not surprising, given that the area has been under Thai control for much of its modern history, and was only finally returned to Cambodia in 1946. These days the road is a busy corridor linking the capital to the Thai border and a trade route along which rice is transported from the sparsely populated but fertile plains to the more populous south.

The first two towns of any size along NR5 out of Phnom Penh are Kompong Chhnang and Pursat. A busy river fishing port, **Kompong Chhnang** takes its name from the terracotta pots (*chhnang*) that are produced throughout the district, while the major cottage industry in workaday **Pursat** is marble carving. Both towns are interesting mainly for the chance to visit the remarkable **floating villages** on the Tonle Sap lake.

North of Pursat is laidback **Battambang**, Cambodia's second largest city, with a lazy riverside ambience and some of the country's finest colonial architecture. The surrounding province once had more temples than Siem Reap, although none was on the scale of Angkor Wat and most have long disappeared. The couple that remain are worth a visit, however, especially the hilltop site of **Wat Banan**, while the nearby mountain and temple complex of **Phnom Sampeu** offers a fascinating, if chilling, reminder of the atrocities of the Khmer Rouge.

In the far northwest, the unprepossessing border town of **Poipet** is the busiest crossing point into Thailand on the direct route between Phnom Penh, Siem Reap and Bangkok – and with an unfortunate but well-deserved reputation for scams and skullduggery. Most travellers arriving from Thailand plough straight on from here to Siem Reap, although it's well worth breaking your journey en route at the crossroads town of **Sisophon (Banteay Meanchey)** to explore the massive, jungle-smothered Angkorian temple of **Banteay Chhmar**.

Kompong Chhnang and around

The old colonial town of **KOMPONG CHHNANG**, 83km north of Phnom Penh on NR5, is a quiet place to stop over for a day. As its name – meaning "Pottery Port" – suggests, the area is a major centre for the production of traditional terracotta pots (*chhnang*), which are despatched countrywide via ox cart (a slow but smooth method of transport

BAMBOO RAILWAY

Highlights

❶ Floating villages Boat between the houses of the remarkable Tonle Sap floating villages near Pursat and Kompong Chhnang. **See p.109 & p.112**

❷ Battambang Cambodia's laidback second city, with the country's finest colonial architecture, a lazy riverside setting and a fledgling Western bar and restaurant scene. **See p.114**

❸ Bamboo railway Take a ride aboard one of Asia's quirkiest railways, with improvised "trains" running along a short section of track just outside Battambang. **See p.116**

❹ Phnom Sampeu Sprawling hilltop temple complex, once used as a Khmer Rouge prison, dotted with colourful shrines and vast caves. **See p.123**

❺ Wat Banan Engaging little ancient hilltop pagoda, with five crumbling towers – like a pocket-sized Angkor Wat. **See p.124**

❻ Ang Trapaeng Thmor Wonderful wetlands, home to the elegant, endangered Sarus crane. **See p.128**

❼ Banteay Chhmar The most remote and least visited of Cambodia's great ancient temple complexes, with fabulously carved ruins half enveloped in jungle. **See p.128**

HIGHLIGHTS ARE MARKED ON THE MAP ON P.108

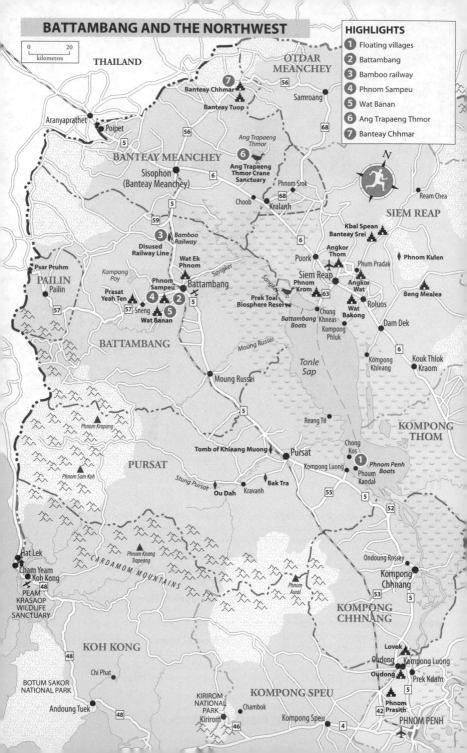

2

THE ETHNIC VIETNAMESE

The first Vietnamese settlers in Cambodia were **rice farmers**, many of whose ancestors migrated across disputed borders as long ago as the late seventeenth century; over generations they moved north along the Mekong and today mostly farm in the southeast provinces. The educated, predominantly Christian Vietnamese population of Phnom Penh has its origins in the **civil servants** brought over during Vietnamese rule and the French protectorate. Indeed, records of the time suggest Phnom Penh was more Vietnamese than Khmer. These days the majority of Cambodia's commercial fishing is accounted for by impoverished ethnic Vietnamese **fishing families**; predominantly Buddhist, they live in floating villages on the Tonle Sap and Mekong River, moving around with the annual inundation. Government estimates put the number of ethnic Vietnamese living in Cambodia at around 100,000, but given the difficulty of monitoring the large number who live in floating villages, the true figure is thought to be much higher.

Historically, Cambodians have long entertained feelings of hostility towards the Vietnamese, who are all too often referred to using the derogatory Khmer term, **Yuan**. The roots of this resentment go back to the Vietnamese annexation of the Mekong delta in the seventeenth century. Tensions were exacerbated during the brief period of Vietnamese rule over the whole country, during which time they tried to impose their language, names and mores on the Khmer. The situation was aggravated during the French protectorate, when Vietnamese clerks were installed in Cambodia's administration, and not helped when the French redrew the Cambodia–Vietnam border in favour of the Vietnamese after World War II.

You're unlikely to witness any overt racism today, despite the recent surge in anti-Vietnamese feeling stirred up by Sam Rainsy's Cambodian National Rescue Party (see p.300), who accuse the Vietnamese of taking Cambodian jobs and lands. Even so, it's as well to note that no Cambodian would be seen dead in the pointed hats worn by Vietnamese rice farmers, and that the country's current leader, Hun Sen, is often accused by his opponents of being a "Vietnamese puppet".

which reduces the risk of damage to the fragile cargo). Several **pottery-making villages** can be visited nearby.

Kompong Chhnang dates back to colonial times, and has a rather more solid and permanent air than many of Cambodia's other provincial capitals. NR5 runs right through the centre, forming a wide boulevard bounded at one end by the imposing **Independence Monument** (looking rather like a big red cake-stand) and the more modest **Vietnamese Friendship Monument** (resembling an overambitious bird table) at the other. Southeast of here stretches the sedate old **French quarter**, with rambling villas set amid spacious walled gardens, some of them still retaining old colonial touches – even the large Kompong Chhnang Prison, bang in the middle of the district, has a rustic air.

The opposite side of town, northwest from the centre and past the bustling **Psar Leu market** en route to the fishing port and Tonle Sap lake, is contrastingly lively and ramshackle. The 1.5km-long road to the lake is actually built on a causeway across the water, and although modern buildings block most views of the lake you can still see a few stilted houses with water lapping around their bases. At the end of the road the waterfront offers fine views over the lake to the pair of floating villages offshore, while the hectic **fishing harbour** is a photogenic chaos of boats, fishermen and hawkers.

The floating villages

On the Tonle Sap lake, 2km from Kompong Chhnang • Small rowing boats to explore the floating villages can be rented from the waterfront (around $6/hr); alternatively, a twice-daily ferry (1000 riel) crosses the lake, departing at around 8.30am and 11am, returning at 1pm and 4pm

The **floating villages** on the Tonle Sap lake make for a rewarding half-day excursion from Kompong Chhnang. The town is the principal fishing port for Phnom Penh,

KOMPONG CHHNANG

and throughout the year supplies of fresh fish are packed with ice and loaded daily onto a fleet of trucks to drip their way towards the city. The fishing families, primarily ethnic Vietnamese, live on the lake on **Phoum Kandal**, almost within touching distance of the shore, and **Chong Kos**, further out over the waters to the northwest – both far less touristy than the floating villages around the north end of the lake near Siem Reap (see p.157). Locals offer village tours in tiny wooden boats, rowed standing up – quoted prices can be on the high side, but, with a little persistence, can usually be bargained down.

The villages themselves are a fascinating sight, with each house floating upon its own miniature pontoon fashioned out of lashed-together bamboo trunks and other wooden flotsam. Dwellings are arranged around a neat grid of miniature "streets" busy with small fishing vessels, rowing boats and other craft, while tiny children paddle themselves, seated in large cooking pots, between the buildings. Some of the houses are little better than floating sheds; others are surprisingly luxurious, with comfortably furnished interiors complete with TVs and generators, their roofs sprouting satellite dishes and their pontoons festooned in miniature gardens of potted plants.

Phnom Santuk

3km west of the centre • Moto $5 return

Phnom Santuk is a mound of huge boulders in the grounds of the wat of the same name; climb to the top for views over rice paddies dotted with sugar-palm trees and the Tonle Sap. It's worth hiring a moto for the trip as they can weave their way across the rice paddies to the pot-making villages afterwards – a route you'd never find on your own.

Ondoung Rossey

7km northwest of Kompong Chhang • Moto $8 return; follow the Battambang road about 5km north from Kompong Chhnang and look for a small sign for the village on the left

The best-known of the pottery villages surrounding Kompong Chhnang is **ONDOUNG ROSSEY**, where locals work at preparing clay and spinning potting wheels in the shade of

THE LEGEND OF PUTHISEN AND KONG REI

Local legend has it that the hill on the far side of the Tonle Sap lake is actually the body of the lovestruck giantess **Kong Rei**, her hair flowing across the ground to the southeast, her feet to the northwest. The story (based on an apochryphal *Jataka* tale and found in various forms across Southeast Asia) tells of twelve sisters abandoned by their father in a forest and taken into the service of the giantess **Santema** and her family. Tiring of their life slaving for the giants, the sisters eventually escaped and made their way to a neighbouring kingdom, where they were married en masse to King Preah Bath Rothasith. And lived happily ever after.

Or at least might have done, had Santema not decided to pursue them. Santema began by disguising herself and charming the king into taking her as his thirteenth wife, then caused him to pluck out the eyes of the twelve sisters (save one, Neang Pov, who was permitted to retain a single eye). At Santema's command, the hapless sisters were then confined to a cave and forced to eat their own newborn children. Only one child survived, **Puthisen**, who lived in the cave with his one-eyed mother and eleven blind aunts, forced to survive by consuming the flesh of his dead cousins, and dreaming – not surprisingly – of revenge.

Years passed. Santema, increasingly fearful, plotted to destroy Puthisen, now grown to manhood, by sending him into the forest of the giants and having him killed. Unfortunately her plan backfired, and her own daughter, Kong Rei, fell in love with the wandering hero. The two were subsequently married, after which Kong Rei revealed the true nature of her mother, Santema. Unfortunately for Kong Rei, Puthisen's filial devotion proved stronger than his new conjugal ties, and he proceeded to take back the stolen eyeballs of his unfortunate mother and aunts, along with various magic potions, and make good his escape, using the potions to create a river (the Tonle Sap) between himself and his pursuing wife. The grief-stricken Kong Rei subsequently cried herself to death and transformed into the mountain you see today. Puthisen, meanwhile, returned, killed Santema and restored his mother and aunts' stolen sight, after which everyone really did live happily ever after.

In 1972 the legend was made into a classic Khmer film, *Puthisen Neang Kong Rey*, while a statue of the ill-fated couple can be seen near Kompong Chhnang's Independence Monument.

their houses (a small **Cambodian Crafts Federation** shop here sells a range of pottery). Almost every house in the village is involved in the pottery business – smaller pieces are made on a wheel spun by foot; larger items are hammered into shape with a large wooden spatula. Most are unglazed and unpainted, although some are embellished with simple etchings or appliqué designs. Items might include simple plates indented with dimples (used to bake tiny coconut cakes over charcoal fires) through to more elaborate elephant-shaped money boxes – which you'd have to break open to get at your savings.

ARRIVAL AND DEPARTURE   KOMPONG CHHNANG

Plentiful buses and shared taxis shuttle between Kompong Chhnang and Phnom Penh, with slightly less frequent services in the other direction to Pursat and Battambang (and beyond).

By bus Buses drop off and pick up passengers either at the transport stop close to the Vietnamese Friendship Monument in the centre (where you'll also find a couple of makeshift stalls selling bus tickets, including one for Phnom Penh Sorya buses) or along NR5 nearby. Leaving Kompong Chhnang, you may be able to flag down a passing bus on the main road, although it's very hit and miss.

Destinations Battambang (15 daily; 4hr); Phnom Penh (15 daily; 2hr 30min); Pursat (15 daily; 2hr).

By shared taxi Shared taxis to/from Phnom Penh use the transport stop. Taxis to/from Battambang use the stop on the road just north of Psar Leu (although it's worth checking at the transport stop as well).

Destinations Battambang (15 daily; 4hr); Phnom Penh (15 daily; 2hr 30min); Pursat (15 daily; 2hr).

GETTING AROUND

Central Kompong Chhnang is easily walkable, although you might want to catch a **moto** or **tuk-tuk** if heading down to the lake ($1–2 one way). **Bikes** ($1/day) can be rented from the *Chantea Borint Hotel*.

2

INFORMATION

Internet Try the *Sovann Phum Hotel*, who might let you use one of their machines for around $1/hr.

Money The Canadia (Visa and MasterCard) and Acleda (Visa only) banks have ATMs.

Post and phones The post office is 200m west of the transport stop; you can also make international phone calls from here.

Shop There's a well-stocked minimart at the Tela petrol station.

ACCOMMODATION

Chantea Borint Hotel (formerly Sokha's Guesthouse) Near the Independence Monument ☎012 762988. Easily the most characterful place to stay in town, with a range of spotless tiled rooms and bungalows (with hot water for an extra $2, or hot water and a/c for $7) set in a lovely courtyard garden on a leafy backstreet. Wi-fi, plus restaurant, although it's open for breakfast only. $6

Sovann Phum Hotel NR5, 200m south of the Independence Monument ☎026 989333. This sparkling modern hotel is Kompong Chnnang's most upmarket option, with immaculate a/c rooms, plus wi-fi, internet and one of the town's best restaurants. $15

EATING

Soksan Restaurant Next to the transport stop. Friendly little place (with English menu) serving tasty Khmer dishes (around $2.50), but no Western food bar a humble omelette or two. Daily 7am–8pm.

Sovann Phum Restaurant Sovann Phum Hotel, NR5, 200m south of the Independence Monument ☎026 989333. Proud home to the largest – or at least the heaviest – menu in Cambodia, featuring a range of Khmer/Chinese-style dishes, with a dash of Thai. Prices are slightly above average (mains mostly $4), although quality's good and portions are big. It's also about the only place in town where you can get a proper cup of coffee. Daily 7am–9pm.

Pursat and around

Named after a tree that used to grow along its riverbanks, the sleepy provincial capital of **PURSAT** is pretty much the quintessence of humdrum. Within Cambodia, it's famous mainly for being the nation's main **marble carving** centre, using stone quarried from the rocky outcrops of the nearby Cardamom Mountains and carved in workshops around the town and the surrounding countryside. For visitors, the main reason to come is to explore the fascinating floating village of **Kompong Luong**, and Pursat also provides a possible starting point for expeditions into the rewarding, but little explored, northern **Cardamom Mountains**. The town itself is laid out for a couple of kilometres along NR5 and bisected by the **Stung Pursat**, which flows northeast into the Tonle Sap. Most of the town's modest cluster of hotels and restaurants are close to the bridge over the river, on (or just off) the main road.

Koh Sampovmeas

500m north of the market

The main attraction in town (for what it's worth) is the faintly surreal **Koh Sampovmeas** island, in the middle of the Stung Pursat. Once an unspoilt sandbank, the island has now been encased in painted concrete walls, giving it the appearance of an enormous ship, with small shrines at prow and stern and the space between neatly paved and lawned. Come dusk, it's usually busy with games of football, shuttlecock and impromptu aerobics classes, with lines of Pursat housewives dancing energetically to the stridently amplified strains of the Cheeky Girls, or similar.

Kompong Luong floating village

35–40km east of Pursat • Motorized boat trips around the village cost $10/hr • Head east along NR5 for 30km, then turn north at Krakor to the Tonle Sap; it costs around $10–12 return from Pursat by moto, $15–20 by tuk-tuk

KOMPONG LUONG is the closest of the Tonle Sap's **floating villages** to Pursat, though

THE LEGEND OF KHLEANG MUONG

Located in the village of **Banteay Chei**, a few kilometres west of Pursat off NR5, the small, well-tended tomb of **Khleang Muong** is an attraction for locals hereabouts. The story goes that in 1605, the Khmer were losing the war against the Thais, when Khleang Muong ordered his soldiers to dig a pit and to cast their weapons into it; he then committed suicide by throwing himself into the pit. Seven days later the Khmer army defeated the Thais with help from the ghosts of Khleang Muong and his army of soldiers. The victory is marked by an offering ceremony here in April or May each year, at the start of the planting season and just before the rains. The pavilion at the tomb contains a life-size bronze statue of Khleang Muong, now a national hero, and a matching one of his wife, who, according to legend, also killed herself. The site is easily reached by moto from Pursat, but it's probably only worth a visit if you're at a completely loose end.

its precise distance from town varies, depending upon whether it's wet or dry season. Populated by a mixed community of Cham and Vietnamese families, the surprisingly large village (actually more of a floating town) is similar in design to those at Kompong Chhnang (see p.109), with buildings bobbing upon wooden pontoons and an extensive range of amenities including its own police station, temple and Catholic church.

The northern Cardamom Mountains

Pursat serves as a possible starting point for tours into the **northern Cardamom Mountains** – you can also explore the southern part of the range (see p.267) – but you'll have to arrange trips in advance through a tour operator in Phnom Penh (see p.77). Still mostly inaccessible and unexplored, the Cardamom mountain range is an area of outstanding natural beauty, its primary jungle rich in flora and fauna. A biodiversity study in 2000 established the presence of nearly four hundred different species of animal, including tigers, Asian elephants, gaur and a population of critically endangered Siamese crocodiles, previously considered extinct in the wild.

The road from Pursat up into the mountains climbs steeply through the forest, crossing tiny gorges and streams. **Ou Dah**, 56km from Pursat, is an attractive spot with rapids and a small waterfall in the jungle-clad hills. Alternatively, at **Chrok La Eing**, 73km southeast of Pursat, there's a cascade and river for a swim. Bear in mind though there's also a high risk of malaria in the mountains, so take precautions against mosquito bites.

ARRIVAL AND INFORMATION   PURSAT

By bus Buses stop in Pursat on NR5 west of the main bridge, at (or opposite) their ticket offices.
Destinations Battambang (6 daily; 2hr); Phnom Penh (6 daily; 4hr).

By shared taxi or minibus These usually arrive at/depart from the transport stop, about 1km west of the bridge on NR5. If possible, ask to be dropped by the main bridge (*spean thmor*), from where it's a just a couple of

hundred metres to the hotels and guesthouse.
Destinations Battambang (15 daily; 2hr); Kompong Chhnang (15 daily; 2hr); Phnom Penh (15 daily; 4hr).

Internet All three hotels that we review (see below) have free wi-fi; there's no other reliable source of internet access in town.

Money There are ATMs at the Canadia (Visa and MasterCard) and Acleda (Visa only) banks.

ACCOMMODATION

Phnom Pech Hotel West bank of the river, 200m north of the main bridge ☎ 052 951515. No-frills hotel offering inexpensive en-suite fan and a/c rooms (plus hot water in fan rooms for an extra $2). Fan $6; a/c $13

Pursat Century Hotel Main road, next to the Acleda Bank ☎ 017 286281, ✉ pursatcenturyhotel@gmail .com. Easily the nicest place in town – and just a fraction more expensive than its nearby rivals – offering spacious

and spotless tiled rooms with hot water and a foyer stuffed with chintzy wooden furniture and assorted pots. Free internet and on-site restaurant. Fan ~~$8~~; a/c ~~$15~~
Thmey Thansour Hotel Just north of the main road,

one block west of the river ☎012 962395. Long-running hotel with a range of fan and a/c rooms, the more expensive ones with hot water. Free wi-fi and internet. Fan ~~$7~~; a/c ~~$15~~

EATING

Lam Siveng Restaurant Main road ☎012 826948. Pretty little restaurant full of wooden furniture and cabinets packed with marble carvings. There's an English menu and a good range of mostly Chinese food (mains around $2–3), plus a few Khmer and Vietnamese options. One of the few places in town where you can get a passable

coffee (hot or iced). Daily 8am–9pm.
Tepmachha (aka The Magic Fish) Restaurant West bank of the river, 750m north of the market ☎012 921144. Friendly little place in an attractive setting right over the river, with simple Khmer and Chinese dishes (plus English menu) for $2–4. Daily 8am–9pm.

Battambang

Cambodia's second largest city, laidback **BATTAMBANG** seems to have the best of various worlds: big enough to have all the energy and bustle you'd expect of a city of around 200,000 people, but still small enough to feel like a proper slice of Cambodia, and lacking both the hyperactive traffic and crowds of Phnom Penh and the tourist crowds and wall-to-wall touts of Siem Reap. Headline attractions may be slightly lacking, but there's still plenty to fill a few days in and around town, plus an increasingly large selection of restaurants and bars fuelled by the growing number of expats who now call the city home.

The main draw in Battambang (the last syllable is usually pronounced *bong* rather than *bang*) is the city's time-warped collection of **colonial architecture**, with some interesting day-trips around town – including fun countryside rides on the quirky **bamboo railway**.

Brief history

The history of Battambang, which was founded in the eleventh century, is quite separate from the rest of Cambodia – for much of its existence the town fell under **Thai** rather than Khmer jurisdiction. In 1795, a Cambodian named **Baen** became lord governor of **Battambang province** (which at the time incorporated territory as far away as Siem Reap), paying tribute to the king in Bangkok, which effectively moved Battambang from Cambodian to Thai rule. Throughout the **nineteenth century** the province, although nominally under Thai jurisdiction, was largely left to its own affairs under a succession of all-powerful governors from the Baen family – a self-sufficient fiefdom, isolated from both Thailand and Cambodia.

The province was returned to Cambodia in 1907, at which time Battambang town was little more than a collection of wooden houses on stilts. The French moved in, modernizing the town and constructing the colonial shophouses you see today. Battambang fared relatively well during the **Khmer Rouge** years, although the Khmer Rouge launched repeated attacks throughout the province after they were driven west to Pailin, and in 1994 even briefly captured Battambang itself. Ferocious battles occurred around Wat Banan and Phnom Sampeu until the amnesty of 1996.

Psar Nat and around

Marking the centre of town is the quirky **Psar Nat** market building, a huge, rather mildewed orange pile dating from the 1930s with functional modernist lines and, at either end, a pair of white clock towers, none of whose various faces ever seem to be telling the right time.

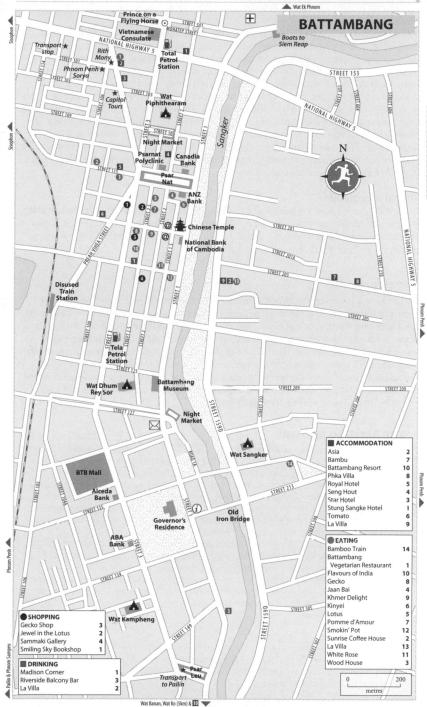

▲ Wat Ek Phnom

BATTAMBANG

Skoun ◀

Skoun ◀

Skoun ◀

Prince on a
Flying Horse ⊙

Vietnamese
Consulate

STREET 501

MOHATEP STREET

Boats to
Siem Reap

Transport ★
stop

Rith
Mony ★

NATIONAL HIGHWAY 5

Total
Petrol
Station

STREET 153

STREET 114

STREET 101

Phnom Penh ★
Sorya

STREET 103

STREET 106

STREET 109

Capitol ★
Tours

STREET 103

Wat
Piphithearam

Sangker

NATIONAL HIGHWAY 5

STREET 154

STREET 602

STREET 604

STREET 606

STREET 3

STREET 105

STREET 109

Night Market

Psarnat
Polyclinic

Canadia
Bank

STREET 113

Psar
Nat

ANZ
Bank

2

N

STREET 201

STREET 110

NATIONAL HIGHWAY 5

PREAH VIHEA STREET

Chinese Temple

National Bank
of Cambodia

STREET 201A

STREET 203

STREET 1

Disused
Train
Station

STREET 205

STREET 100

STREET 3

STREET 2.5

STREET 2

Tela
Petrol
Station

STREET 125

Wat Dhum
Rey Sor

Battambang
Museum

STREET 209

STREET 209

STREET 127

STREET 159Q

STREET 232

STREET 208

Night
Market

Phnom Penh ▶

Phnom Penh ▶

BTB Mall

Alceda
Bank

STREET 105

STREET 106A

STREET 135

Wat Sangker

ROAD 1A

STREET 213

STREET 159Q

ABA
Bank

STREET 3

Governor's
Residence

ⓘ

Old
Iron Bridge

STREET 106

STREET 136

Phnom Penh ◀

Wat Kampheng

STREET 149

STREET 159Q

STREET 305

STREET 301

Psar
Leu

Transport
to Pailin

Pailin & Phnom Sampeu ◀

Wat Banan (5km) & ◀ 10

■ **ACCOMMODATION**

Asia	2
Bambu	7
Battambang Resort	10
Phka Villa	8
Royal Hotel	5
Seng Hout	4
Star Hotel	3
Stung Sangke Hotel	1
Tomato	6
La Villa	9

● **EATING**

Bamboo Train	14
Battambang Vegetarian Restaurant	1
Flavours of India	10
Gecko	8
Jaan Bai	4
Khmer Delight	9
Kinyei	6
Lotus	5
Pomme d'Amour	7
Smokin' Pot	12
Sunrise Coffee House	2
La Villa	13
White Rose	11
Wood House	3

● **SHOPPING**

Gecko Shop	3
Jewel in the Lotus	2
Sammaki Gallery	4
Smiling Sky Bookshop	1

■ **DRINKING**

Madison Corner	1
Riverside Balcony Bar	3
La Villa	2

0 ———— 200
metres

2

The shophouses

The streets immediately south of the Psar Nat market are where you'll find most of Battambang's old **shophouses** – perhaps the finest pocket of colonial-era architecture in the country, despite the damage wreaked by modern additions, rebuildings and renovations. Most buildings follow the traditional Asian shophouse plan, with an open-fronted shop downstairs and living quarters above – the ground-floor shop is typically set back under a wide colonnaded walkway created by the overhanging upper storey, typically embellished with elaborate wrought-iron balconies. The best preserved shophouses are along the photogenic and increasingly gentrified **Street 2.5**, many of whose old buildings have now been restored and converted into touristy bars, restaurants, shops and so on. Those along **Street 1.5** are looking rather run down, while many of the facades along **streets 1, 2 and 3** have been buried beneath big plastic signs and other gimcrack modern additions.

The railway station

A short detour off Street 3 brings you to Battambang's neat little 1920s **railway station**, complete with original ticket counters. The building has been cleaned up and is now in reasonably good shape – which is more than can be said for the trio of overgrown platforms and the weed-choked tracks behind.

The riverfront

Battambang's sweeping **riverfront** with its wide grassy banks and paved walkway is a great place for a stroll. Originally the Sangker River was just 5m wide here, but when the Dambang River, south of town, was dammed by sinking a boat filled with earth across it, the Sangker gradually widened, and is now at least 30m wide (depending on water levels). In the late afternoon fruit-shake and food stalls set up near the post office while the park across the nearby bridge turns into a vast outdoor gym as the health-conscious housewives of Battambang come to exercise after work in the shadow of the eye-catching **Wat Sangker**, instantly recognizable thanks to its modern Bayon-style gateway, topped with four enormous faces.

THE BAMBOO RAILWAY

While there are currently no scheduled train services in Cambodia – for the time being at least (see p.22) – enterprising locals in Battambang have made good the deficiency with the ingenious **bamboo railway** (*norry*), running along a stretch of otherwise disused track just outside town and used to transport people, livestock and goods, as well as increasing numbers of tourists. The planned resumption of regular train services along the line has thrown the **future** of the bamboo railway into doubt, although it continues to flourish in the meantime – and indeed it's possible that even if regular trains ever resume, bamboo trains will continue to run during the gaps between scheduled services.

Currently, a dozen or so "trains" run up and down the line, each just a couple of metres long, consisting of a simple four-wheeled metal undercarriage with a detachable wooden platform placed on top. Trains were formerly propelled using long poles in the manner of an Oxbridge punt but are now powered by small motorbike or tractor engines, reaching speeds of around 40km/hr. If two trains meet en route, the one with the fewest passengers cedes right of way and is dismantled on the spot (the work of just a minute or two) and cleared from the line, allowing the other to pass.

PRACTICALITIES

The start of the line is about 7km from Battambang ($4 return by moto, $6 by tuk-tuk). The line itself runs for some 6km, with a fare of $5 per person (or $10–15 to hire an entire "train"). Trips up and down the line last around 20–30min, with trains departing as soon as sufficient passengers have climbed on board. .

> ## DAMBANG KROGNUING
>
> While you're in Battambang you may see two distinctive **statues** relating to a bizarre legend surrounding the town's name, which literally translates as "lost stick". According to the tale, a man named **Dambang Krognuing** turned black after eating rice stirred with a black stick; he then deposed the king and assumed the throne. The erstwhile king's son subsequently defeated Dambang Krognuing with the aid of a magical flying horse, despite a vain attempt by the interloper to hurl his black stick at the prince's steed. A massive statue of Dambang Krognuing decorates the traffic circle on the way out of town towards the airport, while a statue of the prince on his flying horse sits at the north end of Street 3.

2

Chinese temple
Street 1, one block south of Psar Nat

Easily missed during a walk along the riverfront is the sixteenth- or seventeenth-century **Chinese temple**, a diminutive one-storey structure (restored in 1921) wedged in tightly between the surrounding shops. The temple's dark-red doors and heavily ridged roof tiles edged with ceremonial dragons look quite incongruous amid the area's colonial architecture. Inside the temple, the rather ferocious-looking god, Kwan Tai, is worshipped at a small altar; despite his looks he's revered for his loyalty and integrity.

A few doors south of the Chinese temple, look out for the florid mansion housing the **National Bank of Cambodia** – one of Battambang's finest colonial buildings.

Battambang Museum
Street 1 • Mon–Fri 8–11am & 2–5pm • $1; no photography

The modest **Battambang Museum** comprises a gloomy hall full of statues and carvings dating from the seventh through the twentieth centuries – many are of considerable interest, despite the drab setting and lack of information. Exhibits include fine Buddhas along with various gods, nagas, yaksha (demons), lions, lingas and a number of intricate lintels, many of them featuring Indra riding his three-headed elephant Airavata, a common motif in Khmer art. Look out too for the thirteenth-century statue of a bodhisattva "tattooed" with a thousand Buddhas, and a well-worn depiction of Yama on a buffalo.

Wat Dhum Rey Sor
Street 3, behind Battambang Museum

One of the two oldest temples in Battambang, **Wat Dhum Rey Sor** has been restored several times since its construction in 1848. The "Pagoda of the White Elephant" (as its name translates) is christened after the pairs of white elephant statues flanking the eastern and western entrances to the vihara. The base of the vihara is decorated with a series of colourfully painted, low-relief carvings depicting scenes from the *Ramayana* – look out for Hanuman riding a steam engine on the east wall.

Wat Piphithearam
Street 3, one block north of Psar Nat market

One of Battambang's oldest temples, the venerable **Wat Piphithearam** is best approached from the south, where the gates are guarded by two *yeaks* (giants). The temple's monks claim that these used to sport threatening expressions, though now they wear a benign look – a strange example of the Khmer belief in metamorphosis. Many of the monks here speak English and will give you a tour of the vihara (in exchange for letting them practise their language skills), which features some elaborate modern murals illustrating the life of Buddha.

Governor's Residence

Street 1, around 1km south of the centre • No entrance to the building, but visitors are free to wander around the grounds

South of the centre, the flamboyant **Governor's Residence** adds a decidedly Gallic flourish to this part of town, with a grand entrance flanked by a pair of lions and two canons dated 1789. The pale-orange building itself could easily pass for a miniature chateau somewhere on the Loire, complete with blue-grey shuttered windows, elaborate floral stucco decoration and a big red tiled roof – only the carved elephant heads on either side of the portico spoil the otherwise perfect illusion of provincial France.

ARRIVAL AND INFORMATION   BATTAMBANG

By bus Several bus companies, including Phnom Penh Sorya, Capitol and Rith Mony, have offices in town (all clustered together north of the centre), offering fairly similar services. Arriving from Phnom Penh buses first pull into the new market about 5km out of town There's no need to get off here; stay on board until your vehicle pulls into the transport stop in the centre of town.
Destinations Kompong Chhnang (15 daily; 4hr); Pailin (1 daily; 2hr); Phnom Penh (9 daily; 6hr); Poipet (4 daily; 3hr); Pursat (15 daily; 2hr); Siem Reap (4 daily; 4hr).
By shared taxi and minibus Most vehicles arrive at/depart from the transport stop in the north of town, although shared taxis may drop you off at a hotel of your choice or at Psar Nat in the centre; transport from Pailin arrives at Psar Leu, 1km southwest of town. Private minibuses are best booked through your hotel – usually for a $1 commission, although they'll come and pick you up.
Destinations Kompong Chhnang (15 daily; 3hr 30min);

Pailin (6 daily; 1hr 30min); Phnom Penh (15 daily; 6hr); Poipet (6 daily; 2hr 30min); Pursat (15 daily; 2hr); Siem Reap (6 daily; 3hr 30min); Sisophon (6 daily; 2hr).
By boat Battambang is connected to Siem Reap by a daily thirty-seater boat (departs 7.30am; 6hr in the wet season, up to 8hr or more during the dry; $25), a rewarding trip down the Sangker River and across the Tonle Sap. It is, of course, a lot quicker and cheaper to reach Siem Reap by bus, but the journey by water is far more memorable, albeit not particularly comfortable – take food, plenty of water and a cushion. Boats arrive and depart from the pier on the east bank of the river just north of Spean Thmei, about 1km north of the centre.
Tourist office The town's tourist office is south of the centre, next to the Governor's Residence, although it's not much use and you'll do better to visit ⑩ visitbattambang .com or ask at one of the local hotels – the *Royal Hotel* is a particularly good source of information.

GETTING AROUND

By moto and tuk-tuk There are plenty of motos and tuk-tuks touting for custom. Short hops around town cost $1–2.
By bike Available at several places around town for $2/day, including the *Asia* hotel, the *Laundry Bar* (on St 2.5 just south of *Pomme d'Amour*) and *Royal Hotel*.

Soksabike also rent out bikes ($2 for 24hr) and run cycling tours (see below).
By motorbike Available from *Gecko Café* ($7/day) and the *Royal Hotel* ($7 for a manual bike, $10 for a scooter), among other places.

TOURS AND ACTIVITIES

Circus An offshoot of Siem Reap's Phare (see p.153), the Phare Ponleu Selpak circus (⑩ phareps.org) puts on shows around four times a week at 7pm at its big top on NR5 towards Sisophon. Adults $10, children $5.
Cookery classes Vannak at *Smokin' Pot* restaurant runs popular 3hr cooking classes every morning ($10/person; ☎ 012 821400).
Cycle tours Based at the *Kinyei* café, Soksabike (☎ 012 542019, ⑩ soksabike.com) runs enjoyable half- and full-day bike tours ($27/$40) through the Battambang countryside, with the chance to meet

local families and visit cottage industries.
English teaching Spend an hour, half a day or longer visiting the local Slarkram English School (⑩ brick-for -cambodia.net, ⑩ facebook.com/SlarkramEnglishSchool Cambodia), 7km south of Battambang, helping local kids with their English.
Kayaking Green Orange Kayak (☎ 017 736166, ⑩ fedacambodia.org) organize half-day kayaking trips ($12) along the Stung Sangke River between Battambang and Ksach Poy village.

ACCOMMODATION

★**Asia** North of the market ☎ 053 953523, ⑩ asrhotel .com.kh. A definite cut above most budget places, at ultra-competitive prices. There's a wide range of rooms (all en suite), nicely furnished and spotless, from bargain fan rooms

(the very cheapest lack windows) through to spacious a/c rooms with ornate wooden furniture. Bikes ($2/day) can also be rented, and the friendly staff can arrange tours and bus tickets. Fan **$6**; a/c **$13**

Bambu East of the river ☎ 053 953900, ⊛ bambuhotel .com. This neat boutique resort is the swankiest option in town, with pretty little two-storey garden villas in pseudo-Khmer village style set behind a small pool. The cool and spacious rooms come with plenty of mod cons – iPod dock, rain shower and minibar – and there's a small in-house restaurant. Rates include breakfast. $80

★**Battambang Resort** Wat Ko Village, 5km south of the centre ☎ 012 510100, ⊛ battambangresort.com. Idyllic resort a short drive south of the city, with spacious rooms set among gorgeous gardens dotted with coconut palms and mango trees. Facilities include a big pool and an attractive pavilion-style restaurant, and there's a good range of tours on offer (plus free bikes). You could also just lounge on a hammock or cruise the lake on a pedalo. Rates include breakfast. $60

Phka Villa East of the river ☎ 053 953255, ⊛ phkavilla .com. Attractive little hotel with bijou bungalows arranged around pleasant gardens and a good-sized (albeit rather shallow) pool. The ten rooms are on the small side but nicely furnished in vaguely colonial style with four-poster beds, well-appointed bathrooms and little verandas for idle lounging. Rates include breakfast. $55

Royal Hotel 100m west of Psar Nat ☎ 053 952522, ⊛ asrhotel.com.kh. Long-running travellers' favourite with a wide range of rooms, from super-cheap fan rooms with shared bath to plush en-suite doubles, all clean and good value. There's also a rooftop restaurant with town views, and it's a good place to sort out trips, tours and onward transport. Fan with shared bathroom $4; a/c $12

Seng Hout 50m north of Psar Nat ☎ 053 952900, ⊛ senghouthotel.com. Comfortable modern hotel – a slight cut above the town's other cheapies both in price and quality – with a facade festooned with flags and a lobby littered with chunky wooden furniture. Rooms (all with hot water, plus optional a/c for $5 extra) are bland but comfortable (although some lack windows), while facilities include a handy little café, a gym (weirdly, in the lobby), and a third-floor pool. $10

Star Hotel Just north of the centre ☎ 053 953522, ⊛ asrhotel.com.kh. Not quite as nice as the nearby *Asia*, but still more than adequate, with a wide range of fan and a/c rooms of various shapes, sizes and prices (the more expensive options have hot water and fridge) – you might want to look at a few before choosing. Fan $8; a/c $13

Stung Sangke Hotel North of the centre ☎ 053 953495, ⊛ stungsangkehotel.com. This big, modern 130-room hotel looks like it's been airlifted straight out of Phnom Penh or Siem Reap – not much character, but good mid-range accommodation at a very reasonable price, with spacious, nicely appointed rooms with TV, minibar, bathtub and tea-/coffee-making facilities, plus secure parking, gym and a decent-sized pool. Rates include breakfast. $30

Tomato West of Psar Nat ☎ 012 853439. The cheapest option in town, in an attractive shophouse-style building with a pretty ground-floor terrace shaded by enormous potted plants. Rooms themselves are not much more than spartan boxes but reasonably clean and quiet – and given the price you really can't complain. $3

La Villa East of the river ☎ 053 730151, ⊛ lavilla -battambang.com. Seven-room boutique retreat in a renovated 1930s merchant's house. Rooms (all a/c) have plenty of colonial ambience (albeit not much furniture) and come with TV, DVD player, and tea- and coffee-making facilities. The restaurant serves the best French food in Battambang and there's a nice little garden pool. Advance booking recommended. $65

EATING

Battambang is famed for its abundant **natural produce**, including rice, pomelos and oranges – sweet, juicy and green-skinned even when ripe. Have a look around **Psar Nat** to see what's new and fresh. There are also inexpensive **food stalls** around Psar Nat, while in late afternoons a busy **night market** sets up on the street south of Wat Piphithearam – lift the lids on the pots and see what's on offer. More stalls set up at about 4pm on the riverfront near the post office.

Bamboo Train East of the river ☎ 012 517125. Cheery little café in a shady garden pavilion under a big thatched roof. Food (mains $2.50–5) includes a good Western selection ranging from tofu burger to spag bol and Greek salad, plus cheap Khmer options. Service can be slow, but it's a nice place to linger, with a pool table to keep you entertained. Daily 6.30am–10pm.

Battambang Vegetarian Restaurant Just north of the Asia Hotel ☎ 012 642234. Simple café dishing up various Khmer/Chinese noodle, rice and soup dishes given a meat-free twist (although no Western options). Don't be put off by the quantity of "beef" on the menu – it's actually tofu and mushroom. Mains around $4.50. Daily 11am–8pm.

Flavours of India Street 2.5 ☎ 053 731553. This functional tiled café lacks any kind of atmosphere but is the only place in town to get Indian food, with a decent selection of veg and non-veg North Indian standards. Food is overpriced (mains $6–7) and strictly average, but if you're looking for something different it might do the trick. Just. Daily 10am–10.30pm.

Gecko Street 3 ☎ 017 712428, ⊛ geckocafe.net. Attractive first-floor café in a nice corner spot overlooking Street 3 – staff are recruited from underprivileged backgrounds and given the chance to train here and earn some money. The menu covers the standards – salads, sandwiches, burgers, pasta and pizza, plus assorted Asian and Mexican mains ($5–8). Daily 9am–10pm.

Jaan Bai Street 2, junction with Street 1.5

2

☎097 398 7815. Battambang's newest and most innovative restaurant (with a menu supervised by Australian Thai-food guru David Thompson) serving up top-notch Khmer, Thai and Vietnamese dishes in tapas-size portions ($3–4) using seasonal organic produce. The restaurant also helps train underprivileged young people, with profits going to the Cambodian Children's Trust. Tues–Sun 11am–9pm (last orders).

★**Khmer Delight** One block south of Psar Nat, between Street 2 & Street 2.5 ☎012 434746. One of the nicest-looking restaurants in town, with lots of cane furniture and romantic lighting after dark. Food features all the usual Khmer classics through to Western dishes such as spag bol and chicken and chips in a basket – a mite expensive (most mains around $4.50) but excellent quality, and served in big portions. Daily 7am–10pm.

Kinyei Street 1.5. Tiny café on a quiet backstreet corner serving some of the best coffee in town, plus a few breakfasts and Western light meals ($3–4). Daily 7am–7pm.

★ **Lotus** Street 2.5 ☎092 260158. Lively new bar-restaurant in a lovingly restored old Battambang shophouse given a chic urban makeover, with bright lighting and plenty of naked brick. The menu lists a short but excellent selection of Western mains (around $5) – the Lotus burger might just be the best in Cambodia – plus good coffee and a well-stocked bar. Doubles as an art gallery, so always worth having a look to see what's on show upstairs, and also hosts occasional live music and events. Tues–Sun 10am–10pm or later.

Pomme d'Amour Street 2.5 ☎053 650 2188. Upmarket little French-run restaurant on Battambang's finest colonial street – a nice place for a romantic tête-à-tête. Food is mainly classic Khmer given a French makeover – sautéed frog with Khmer pesto, for example – along with a few European dishes (mains $6.50–12). A cocktail bar is planned for next door. Daily 9am–2/3pm & 5–10pm.

Smokin' Pot Two blocks south of Psar Nat ☎012 821400. Known for its long-running cookery classes (see p.118), this simple café-restaurant serves inexpensive and authentic Khmer food, plus a decent range of Thai and Western dishes (mains $2.50–4). Or just come for a drink on the small pavement terrace and watch the world go by. Daily 7am–10pm.

Sunrise Coffee House Just west of the Royal Hotel. Old Battambang stalwart, still serving good meals (Khmer and Western) at rock-bottom prices (mains $2–3), plus the "world's best coffee cake", as it's modestly described. Mon–Sat 6.30am–8pm.

La Villa La Villa hotel, east of the river ☎012 991801, ⓦlavilla-battambang.com. Colonial-style dining (mains $6–9) in the former orangery at this characterful hotel. The French food is some of the best in town, and there's also a good Khmer selection. Or just come for a drink (see below). Daily 11am–3pm & 6–9pm.

White Rose Street 2 ☎012 536500. Travellers' favourite, with a long menu of inexpensive Khmer and Chinese dishes (mains $2–3), plus a good selection of Western breakfasts and assorted light meals and snacks. Daily 8am–10pm.

Wood House West of the market, opposite Royal Hotel ☎070 496402. Cosy little café with all the usual travellers' essentials ranging from breakfasts, salads and sandwiches to more substantial Khmer mains ($3.50–5) and an eclectic selection of Western and international ($5–6) dishes – anything from malai kofta to Wiener schnitzel. Daily 6am–10pm.

DRINKING

Madison Corner Street 2.5 ☎053 650 2189. No-frills little corner bar, always lively, with pool table, darts and a TV screening big matches and other sporting events. There's also a bit of food including a few Western and Khmer dishes, plus great ice cream and excellent crêpes. Daily 7am–midnight.

Riverside Balcony Bar Riverfront, south of the centre ☎012 437421. Atmospheric bar upstairs in an old wooden house on a curve of the river, with soft lighting, good music and moreish cocktails. Tues–Sun 4–11pm.

La Villa La Villa hotel, east of the river ⓦlavilla-battambang.com. Re-create a few French Indochina fantasies over a drink at this colonial-style hotel, with tipples including a good international wine list and a fair selection of cocktails. Daily 11am–3pm & 6–9pm.

SHOPPING

As usual, the best source of basic provisions is at one of the **minimarts** attached to the town's various petrol stations – those at the Tela (just south of the centre) and Total (north of the centre next to the Stung Sangke Hotel) stations are both well stocked – or try BB Mart, a few doors west of Madison Corner.

Gecko Shop Street 3. Downstairs from the popular Gecko café, selling a small but attractive selection of jewellery, kramas and T-shirts in colourful designs. Daily 9am–10pm.

Jewel in the Lotus Street 2.5 ☎092 260158. Possibly Cambodia's most offbeat shop, specializing in "beautiful and strange objects from around the world" and stuffed with quirky curiosities and collectibles from Cambodia,

2

SUBTERRANEAN HOMESICK BOOZE

Beer may still be the Cambodian tipple of choice, but Francophone Battambang is doing its best to diversify the range of alcoholic drinks on offer. Around 10km south of town, the **Phnom Banon Vineyard** is the country's first winery, producing a range of reds including Shiraz and Vietnamese Black Queen varieties. The results, by common consent, leave quite a lot to be desired, although with an annual production (and, presumably, consumption) of more than six thousand bottles they must be doing something right. More palatable are the various **palm wines and spirits** on offer around town (try *Pomme d'Amour* or *Madison Corner*), including assorted brews produced by the Confirel group (⚙ confirel.com). These include the feisty Jaya Palm Spirit (40 percent), tasting a bit like brandy, and Kirel Palm Wines (8–11 percent), available in ginger, pineapple and "original" flavours – the last resembling a slightly raw but very drinkable Spanish *fino*.

Vietnam, India and elsewhere – anything from Vietnamese vinyl and classic Cambodian cassettes to underground comics and Crumb cartoons. Daily noon–10pm.

Sammaki Gallery Street 2.5 ⚙ facebook.com /sammakibtb. Chic modern gallery hosting regularly changing displays of work by local artists

from Battambang and beyond. Daily 1–5pm.

Smiling Sky Bookshop Street 3, next to the Chaya hotel ☎ 099 447066. Well-stocked secondhand bookshop with plenty of fiction both pulp and literary, plus a good selection of Cambodian-related titles. Daily 8am–7pm.

DIRECTORY

Consulate The Vietnamese consulate is north of Psar Nat on Street 2 (Mon–Fri 8–11am & 2–5pm).

Health Avoid the provincial hospital near the river, where facilities are basic and conditions none too clean. You'll be better off at a private clinic – try the Phsarnat Polyclinic, north of the market, or the Polyclinique Visal Sokh (☎ 053 952401 or ☎ 012 843415), next to the Vietnamese Consulate north of the centre.

Internet Try the well-equipped World Tel on Street 2, or World Net, diagonally opposite between streets 2 and 1.5 (both daily 7am–8pm; 2000 riel/hr). Virtually all the hotels (see p.118) and restaurants (see p.119) that we review have free wi-fi.

Laundry Available at several places including the aptly named *Laundry Bar* (Street 2; near the Chinese temple $1.50/1kg of washing).

Massage Seeing Hands (massage by the blind) is available at several places around town, including next door to *Gecko* café; a few doors west of *Madison Corner*; and next to *Sunrise Coffee House*. Don't expect any frills though – you might find yourself being massaged in full view of the street.

Money There are plenty of ATMs around including at the Canadia, ANZ and ABA banks (all of which accept both Visa and MasterCard).

Phones There are cheap-rate phone booths near the market for domestic calls, and a couple of Camintel booths on the south side of the market for international calls.

Post office Street 1 in the south of town (Mon–Fri 7–11am & 2–5pm).

Swimming pools Some hotels allow non-residents to use their swimming pools for a small daily fee, including the *Stung Sangke* ($5) and *Seng Hout* ($2).

Around Battambang

Battambang makes a good base for a number of interesting ancient temples nearby, including at **Wat Banan** and **Wat Ek Phnom**, plus sobering mementoes of the Khmer Rouge era at the hilltop pagoda complex of **Phnom Sampeu** and **Kamping Poy** reservoir.

Wat Ek Phnom

12km north of Battambang on the river road • $3; ticket also valid for Phnom Sampeu (see p.123), Wat Banan (see p.124) and Kamping Poy (see p.124) • Return by moto from Battambang around $6–8, by tuk-tuk around $8–10

Surrounded by lotus ponds in the grounds of a modern pagoda, the modest ruins of the eleventh-century **Wat Ek Phnom** are relatively underwhelming, although the site and surrounding countryside are attractive enough, with fine views from the main sanctuary, with its sandstone buildings lined up in a row, joined by an enclosed walkway. The temple would originally have been reached via a couple of 2m-high terraces, though these have collapsed, and you'll now have to scramble up a small hill and through a broken section of the laterite wall surrounding the main sanctuary, or walk round to the slightly better-preserved south side, where a crumbling doorway survives, along with some carvings.

Phnom Sampeu

15km southwest of Battambang on NR57 towards Pailin • $3; ticket also valid for Wat Ek Phnom (see p.122), Wat Banan (see p.124) and Kamping Poy (see p.124) • Return from Battambang around $9 by tuk-tuk, $7 by moto (or $18/$12 combined with Wat Banan)

The craggy limestone mountain of **Phnom Sampeu** (Boat Mountain), topped with a colourful cluster of temples and shrines, makes an interesting excursion, though it's best known for its tragic associations with the Khmer Rouge, who turned the buildings here into a prison, many of whose inmates were executed.

On arrival, you'll be dropped at the foot of the **steps** leading steeply up the hill – a hard climb featuring well over five hundred steps. Alternatively walk (or catch a moto) up the **road** on your left – much less strenuous. Whichever route you take, **don't stray from clearly defined paths** as most of the hills hereabouts are thought to be mined.

The ascent

Assuming you head directly up the steps, it's a steep **climb** of twenty to thirty minutes to reach the top. The steps divide about halfway up: the left-hand fork heads directly to the top; the right-hand fork climbs more gently past a series of small shrines and temples and a large seated Buddha before reaching the road up the hill. From here you can either follow the road up to the summit, or return to the steps, which head up past two abandoned Russian-built **anti-aircraft guns**, remnants of the 1994–95 conflict, when Phnom Sampeu was at the front line of fighting between government forces and the Pailin faction of the Khmer Rouge.

The summit

The **summit** is topped with a cluster of structures, including the **Preah Jan** vihara and, next to it, an eye-catching gilded stupa (although beware the sometimes aggressive macaque monkeys who – literally – hang around up here, waiting to swipe food and other desirables from unwary tourists). During the Khmer Rouge era, the mountain-top buildings were used as a prison, interrogation centre and place of execution – it's thought that as many as ten thousand victims were pushed to their deaths over the edge of the rocks here, falling into the cave below.

From the summit, another steep staircase leads down through a rock arch into a kind of natural amphitheatre below a gigantic slab of overhanging rock from which bats dangle in a sinister manner, with a pair of stone deities keeping solemn watch. This is traditionally known as the Theatre Cave (*leahng lacaun*) on account of the theatrical performances that were once staged here, although nowadays it's more commonly referred to as the **Killing Cave** due to the number of people who fell to their deaths here, pushed over the cliff at the summit of the mountain above. Some of the bones and

---

CROCODILE TEARS

According to local legend, the hill of **Phnom Sampeu** is the broken hull of a ship, sunk by a lovestruck crocodile suffering from unrequited passion for a young girl. When the woman in question and her fiancé took to sea, the croc attacked and sunk their ship, and the lovers were drowned.

Some distance away to the northwest, another quite separate small hill, **Phnom Kropeu** (Crocodile Mountain), continues the tale: the local population, scared of the crocodile, drained all the water from the area so that he couldn't swim away, leaving the crocodile to perish, transforming into the hill you see today.

skulls of bodies found scattered across the ground have been collected and placed inside a small glass memorial, while further down the hill is a large reclining Buddha and a second memorial, with more bones of those killed here piled up inside a metal cage.

Prasat Yeah Ten

Sneng, about 25km west of Battambang (and 10km beyond Phnom Sampeu)

West of Phnom Sampeu along the road to Pailin, in the village of Sneng, are the remains of the tenth-century **Prasat Yeah Ten** temple. There's not much left of the temple itself, although three doorways have survived topped with beautifully carved lintels, one depicting the ubiquitous Churning of the Ocean of Milk (see p.169). A couple of hundred metres further down the road, in the grounds at the back of a modern wat, are three extremely old **brick sanctuaries**, perhaps also dating back to the tenth century.

Wat Banan

20km southwest of Battambang • $3; ticket also valid for Phnom Sampeu (see p.123), Kamping Poy (see below) and Wat Ek Phnom (see p.122) • Return from Battambang to Phnom Sampeu and Wat Banan around $18 by tuk-tuk or $12 by moto

Wat Banan, the best preserved of the temples around Battambang, makes a rewarding half-day trip combined with Phnom Sampeu (if you don't mind the horribly bumpy 45min ride between the two, following a backcountry dirt track through the paddy fields); you could also include Prasat Yeah Ten (see above) in the same trip. The temple was consecrated as a Buddhist shrine, although scholars are uncertain who built it or exactly when it was completed, which could have been any time between the tenth and thirteenth centuries.

From the car park at the base of the hill, it's a steep climb up some 360 steps to the temple, with five sturdy towers poking up out of the trees (which, alas, largely obscure the views). Numerous carvings survive – those on the central tower are the best – including a number of apsaras (most of them now headless), various figures bent in prayer a and couple of finely carved, if rather eroded, lintels.

Kamping Poy

Around 30km west of Battambang by road • $3; ticket also valid for Phnom Sampeu (see p.123), Wat Banan (see above) and Wat Ek Phnom (see p.122) • Take NR57 west from Battambang, then turn off north at Phnom Sampeu; return from Battambang by moto around $15–20, tuk-tuk $20–25

The prettiness of the lake at **Kamping Poy** belies the fact that it was created by the Pol Pot regime using slave labour – more than ten thousand people died of overwork, malnutrition and disease during the construction of the 8km **dam** that bounds the lake. Completed in 1977, the dam lay at the heart of an extensive irrigation system and still allows dry-season rice cultivation. At weekends and holidays the place is packed with Cambodians messing around in the water, but during the week you'll have the place to yourself. The rim of the dam is navigable by moto or on foot for several kilometres, so even at busy times you can get away for a quiet swim; there are also rowing boats ($1/hr) to rent.

Pailin

Ringed by hills near the border with Thailand, the sprawling and haphazard frontier town of **PAILIN** was once the gem-mining centre of Cambodia, although it's now a downbeat sort of place with not a lot going for it. The town is mainly interesting for its role in the later history of the **Khmer Rouge**; however, unless you've a particular

---

THE KHMER ROUGE IN PAILIN

After being ousted from power in 1979, the **Khmer Rouge** found a natural bolthole in remote Pailin, waging a disruptive guerrilla war against the government in Phnom Penh, supporting their campaigns by tapping into the area's rich natural resources including gemstones and untouched forests – it's said that gem-mining alone earned them a monthly revenue of $10 million. They held out until August 1996 when, in a move that marked the beginning of the end for the Khmer Rouge, **Ieng Sary**, the local commander, struck a deal with the Cambodian government, gaining immunity from prosecution for himself and taking three thousand defectors over to the government side – although the Khmer Rouge managed to maintain a foothold in the remote Dangkrek Escarpment on the border with Thailand right up until the death of Pol Pot in 1998. The war was vicious and the border area is still the most heavily **mined** region in the country – under no circumstances wander from clearly defined tracks.

---

obsession with the subject the main reason for coming here is to **cross the border** into Thailand, around 20km away. Other local attractions include the hill of **Phnom Yat** and a couple of **waterfalls** in the surrounding countryside, although the poorness of the roads and the ever-present danger of **land mines** doesn't really encourage you to explore.

Phnom Yat

1km or so south of the centre, on the southern edge of town • Walk, or catch a moto for around $1 or $3 return

South of Pailin centre is the small but unmistakeable hill of **Phnom Yat**, its summit dominated by mobile-telephone transmitters and a modern temple and stupa. A peaceful vantage point from which to watch the sunset, the hill was named after a Buddhist pilgrim couple who arrived in Pailin at the end of the nineteenth century. Hunting and gem-mining had already begun to destroy the countryside, and Yeah Yat and her husband set up a meditation centre on the hill where they could be close to nature and the mountain spirits. Yat began to receive messages from the spirits that there would continue to be a plentiful supply of gems in the soil as long as the miners respected the land, built temples and made appropriate offerings. As word of this prediction spread, superstitious miners did as they were told and continued to find gems; today, however, their luck is growing thin (although you might see visitors vainly scratching about in the soil around the temple). Locals say that to prevent bad luck, before you leave Pailin you should make a small offering and thank the spirits for letting you use their water and air.

Gory **tableaux** at the temple illustrate the fate that befalls those destined for hell, including a man having his tongue pulled out and another being boiled in oil. Tucked away behind the modern vihara is all that's left of the previous pagoda – wall paintings, floor tiles and a cracked stupa – after it was destroyed by the Khmer Rouge. At the bottom of the hill, the wall enclosing **Wat Ratanasaoporn** is covered in impressive bas-reliefs depicting the Churning of the Ocean of Milk (see p.169).

ARRIVAL AND INFORMATION

PAILIN

By bus or shared taxi Pailin can be reached by bus or shared taxi from Battambang, a smooth 80km trip along NR57. There's currently just one bus daily, with Paramount Angkor (2hr), continuing on to the Thai border. Shared taxis to Pailin depart from Psar Leu in the south of Battambang (6 daily; 1hr 30min), and reasonably regular shared taxis head on from Pailin to the border.

Money Although dollars and riel are both accepted in town, the Thai baht is the currency of choice. There are branches of the Canadia and Acleda banks on the main road near the traffic circle.

CROSSING TO THAILAND FROM PAILIN

Not many travellers use the border crossing into Thailand (daily 7am–8pm) between Psar Pruhm and Ban Pakard, 20km from Pailin, although it's a lot more peaceful than the

2

THE GEM MINES

Pailin has been a **gem-mining** centre for nearly a hundred years – it's said that sapphires, rubies and garnets once lay everywhere on the surface. Now much of the land is mined out, and fortune-seekers have to dig deep into the rocky ground in search of the stones, which in their raw state resemble fragments of broken glass. It's hard toil for the prospectors and, for most, hope turns to wistfulness as they sift painstakingly through mounds of red dirt, sorting earth from rocks; piles of spoil scar the landscape, creating an almost lunar scene.

Most of the claims are now abandoned, and those prospectors still at work are pretty secretive about their diggings. If you're interested ask at *Bamboo Guesthouse* for information about where the current workings are, but note that there's little to see other than a hole in the ground and a pile of earth. Typical finds today are small garnets and topazes; rubies and sapphires are now rare.

---

notorious Poipet border crossing further north (see p.130). From Pailin, the border can be reached by shared taxi (20min; $5) or moto (30min; $2.50). At the border itself there's a small market and a couple of casinos, which entertain an almost exclusively Thai clientele. Once in Thailand you can take a minibus to Chanthaburi, then another bus to Bangkok, or to Trat for Koh Chang.

ACCOMMODATION AND EATING

Pailin offers no gastronomic delights, but there are plenty of stalls in the market and cheap **restaurants** nearby. Near the top of the ridge road, the *Phkay Proek* isn't bad.

Bamboo Guesthouse 4km out of town on the road towards the border ☎012 405818. A pleasant refuge from central Pailin with a range of wooden bungalows in an attractive garden, all with hot water and a/c. The restaurant is one of the best in town, serving Khmer and Thai food, plus a few Western options. $13

Memoria Palace and Resort 5km west of Pailin ☎015 430014, ⓦmemoriapalace.com. An unexpected find in dusty Pailin, the relatively upscale *Memoria* offers attractive lodgings in an unspoilt hilltop location west of town amid the fringes of the Cardamom Mountains.

Accommodation is in a mix of spacious and very comfortable bungalows or in three extremely rustic thatched "ecolodges", and there's also a big saltwater pool and good restaurant. $25

Pailin Ruby West of the traffic circle on the main road through town ☎055 636 3603. The best and least unruly (Pailin attracts a lot of truckers) place to stay in town. Rooms are clean and pleasant enough, with en-suite bathrooms, TV and chunky wood furniture; hot water and a/c are available for an extra $5. $7

Sisophon (Banteay Meanchey)

Midway between Siem Reap and the Thai border the workaday town of **SISOPHON** has something of an identity problem. The official name is Sisophon, although it's also called Sereysophon, while locals (for reasons not entirely understood) call it Svay (mango). Just to add to the confusion, it's usually referred to (including on virtually all signs, and by bus companies) as **Banteay Meanchey**, the province of which it's capital.

Names aside, Sisophon is notable mainly for its location at the junction of the roads to Siem Reap and Battambang – with a trio of interesting sights (see p.128) that can be visited on the way to Siem Reap – and as the jumping-off point for a day-trip to the massive Angkorian temple ruins of **Banteay Chhmar**, one of the country's least visited major monuments.

ARRIVAL AND DEPARTURE   SISOPHON (BANTEAY MEANCHEY)

By bus or shared taxi Arriving by bus you'll either be dropped off at one of the bus company offices opposite the transport stop just east of the market or on the main road by the *Nasa Hotel*, where you'll be instantly pounced upon by a posse of cheery moto drivers. Leaving Sisophon, services leave from the various bus company offices, or you could try flagging down something on the main road by the *Nasa*. Shared taxis arrive/depart from the transport stop.

Destinations: by bus Battambang (6 daily; 2hr); Phnom Penh (10 daily; 7–8hr); Poipet (10 daily; 1hr); Siem Reap (10 daily; 2hr).

Destinations: by shared taxi Battambang (6 daily; 2hr); Phnom Penh (8 daily; 7hr); Poipet (10 daily; 1hr); Siem Reap (20 daily; 2hr).

GETTING AROUND

You can **walk** across pretty much the whole of Sisophon in around 15min. There are plenty of motos, though hardly any tuk-tuks. For transport to Banteay Chhmar or other destinations around town, try the *Botoum* or *Nasa* hotels.

INFORMATION

Internet Try the well-equipped Rithy VIP internet café at the Sokimex petrol station (daily 9am–8pm; 2500 riel/hr).

Money There are ATMs at the Canadia (Visa and MasterCard) and Acleda (Visa only) banks. Note that the Acleda is due to move sometime in 2014 to new premises next to the *Botoum Hotel*.

Shops There are well-stocked minimarts at the Total and Tela petrol stations.

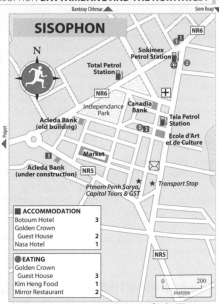

ACCOMMODATION

Botoum Hotel In the northwest of town, just off the roundabout to Poipet at the junction of NR5 & NR6 ☎012 687858, ✉botoumhotel@gmail.com. Simple hotel with friendly English-speaking owners and slightly grubby rooms with hot water and fan (plus optional a/c for $7 extra). Taller readers should beware the dangerously low-flying doors. $8

Golden Crown Guest House Town centre, just north of the market ☎011 610707. Simple, spacious tiled rooms with fan and cold water only, plus a basic restaurant downstairs (Khmer menu only). Good value, although not much English spoken. $6

Nasa Hotel Northern end of town, opposite the Sokimex petrol station ☎011 777702. Sisophon's accommodation options have lift off with the launch of this stellar new hotel, offering big, bright and spotless a/c rooms with fancy carved wooden furniture, plus TV and fridge. Prices aren't astronomical, either. $15

EATING

Food options in Sisophon are rudimentary. In the late afternoon and early evening, **stalls** selling basic Khmer food and fruit shakes open on the south side of Independence Park.

Kim Heng Food Next door to the Nasa Hotel ☎012 503847. Proud possessor of Sisophon's only English-language menu, with a short selection of inexpensive Khmer and Chinese staples (mains $2). Daily 8am–9pm.

Mirror Restaurant Opposite the Sokimex petrol station. This bright little café is Sisophon's (modest) answer to a fast-food joint, although the menu (in Khmer only) is limited to ice cream, cold coffee and *KFC*-style chicken and chips. Daily 10am–8pm.

Around Sisophon

A trio of local attractions – the stone-carving village of **Choob**, the traditional weaving village of **Phnom Sarok**, and the **Ang Trapaeng Thmor Crane sanctuary** – can be combined into an interesting day-trip from Sisophon, or visited en route between Sisophon and Siem Reap.

Choob

NR6, 30km east of Sisophon • Around $10 return by moto

You'll know when you've arrived in the small village of **CHOOB** as soon as you see the roadside lined with sandstone carvings of Buddhas and apsaras, from the tiny to the enormous. The most prized (and pricey) types of sandstone have delicate veined markings, while some of the larger pieces take months to complete, and many are commissioned by temples or government offices. For anyone prepared to lug a statue home, prices can be very reasonable after a bit of bargaining.

Phnom Srok

50km northeast of Sisophon • About $25 return by moto

Easily combined with a visit to Choob, **PHNOM SROK** is one of the few villages in the country where **sericulture** has been properly revived after the Khmer Rouge years and is also known throughout Cambodia for its thick cotton *kramas*, sold mainly in Siem Reap. Weaving looms clack away under the stilt-houses along the village's north street, and you'll see tree branches flecked with furry silkworm cocoons, looking like yellow balls. The families will be only too pleased to give you a little tour.

Ang Trapaeng Thmor Crane Sanctuary

60km northeast of Sisophon • $10 • Visits can be arranged through Sam Veasna in Siem Reap (see p.145) or from Sisophon for around $25 by moto, or around $45 by car (if you can find one)

North of Phnom Srok lies the **Ang Trapaeng Thmor** reservoir, built by forced labour during the Khmer Rouge era. The reservoir and surrounding area now serves as a dry-season refuge for the globally endangered **Sarus crane** (*kriel*), one of Cambodia's largest birds – adults can grow to up to 1.3m – and instantly recognizable thanks to their distinctive red heads. Around 350 cranes visit the reserve between around January and March and the sanctuary is also home to many other rare water birds (about two hundred species have been spotted here) including black-necked stork, greater spotted eagle and oriental plover. You might also be lucky enough to spot one of the sanctuary's Eld's deer, another highly threatened species.

Banteay Chhmar

The huge Angkorian-era temple of **Banteay Chhmar** is one of Cambodia's least-visited and most intriguing destinations, still untouched by the mass tourism that has long since enveloped the temples of Angkor and which is now (following recent road improvements) beginning to reach out even to the formerly remote and inaccessible temples of Koh Ker and Preah Vihear. Covering an area of around three square kilometres, the temple was built by Jayavarman VII as a memorial to soldiers killed while defending his son in a battle against the Chams. The temple is best known for its magnificent **carvings**, once rivalling those at the Bayon and Angkor Wat, although many of these have been looted – most notoriously in 1998 when a group of rogue soldiers removed two massive panels and trucked them across the border for sale in Bangkok. Confiscated by the Thai police and returned to Cambodia, the panels are now in the National Museum in Phnom Penh (see p.67). A massive programme run by the Global Heritage Fund and Heritage Watch is now slowly restoring the site, while efforts are also being made to have the temple listed as a UNESCO World Heritage Site.

The temple

Approaching the site you'll catch a glimpse of the temple's lotus-choked moat and laterite enclosing wall. The usual approach is via the causeway to the east and through the multiple collapsed doorways of the eastern entrance. Some of the **carvings** hereabouts are in great condition, but require a little searching to find; look out for a lintel carved with bearded musicians, one playing a harp, and another carved with dancing cranes.

The inner enclosure is surrounded by a **gallery**, mostly filled in by accumulated dust, dirt and rubble. Tiny Buddha images remain perched in some of the niches along the gallery roof, but many more have been crudely hacked out, either when the state religion switched from Buddhism back to Hinduism in the thirteenth century or as a result of looting. The **faces** of the bodhisattva Srindradeva look down from the remaining towers, while part of an eight-armed relief of Vishnu remains on the west face of the central tower, though sadly, like so many carvings here, it's missing its head.

Some of the temples finest magnificently carved **bas-reliefs** can still be seen on the western exterior of the enclosing wall including a spectacular 32-armed Avalokitesvara (there were originally eight similar carvings, although six have been removed by looters – you can still see the nearby breach in the wall from which they were taken). To the north, another section of wall illustrates tales from the *Ramayana*, with a good image of a *yeak* swallowing a horse, while on the eastern side look out for a remarkable panel showing a battle between the Chams and Khmers (not unlike the similar panel at the Bayon), with the dead below, being consumed by crocodiles.

Around the temple

Nine satellite temples survive in the vicinity of the main temple, most of them atmospherically ruined – it's best to hire a guide (see below) to explore them properly. Just south of the temple, **Prasat Ta Prohm** sports Bayon-style face towers, while west of the temple **Prasat Samnang Tasok** remains picturesquely overgrown. East of the main temple lies the temple's original *baray* (reservoir), originally more than 1.5km long but now dried up, with the remains of another temple, **Prasat Mebon** (accessible during the dry season only) at its centre.

Some 3km north of the main temple is another reservoir, the **Boeung Cheung Kru** (or "Pol Pot Baray"), built by forced labour during the Khmer Rouge era – now an important local water source and peaceful birdwatching site. Just across from the southwest corner of the moat enclosing the main temple is a French-run silk-weaving project, the **Soieries du Mékong** (⊛soieriesdumekong.com) where you can watch local women weaving silk and buy *kramas*.

Meanwhile, around 12km south of Banteay Chhmar, **Banteay Tuop** (Army Fortress) was probably constructed at the same time, and though there are fewer carvings here than at Banteay Chhmar, the towers are taller.

ARRIVAL AND INFORMATION   **BANTEAY CHHMAR**

From Sisophon It's about 60km from Sisophon to Banteay Chhmar, taking around 1hr 30min in the dry season, or up to 3hr in the wet, when the road can deteriorate dramatically. You may be able to arrange transport through the *Botoum* or *Nasa* hotels; alternatively, try the moto drivers hanging out by *Nasa* or ask around at the transport stop. The trip by moto costs roughly $25–35, by car (if you can find one) around $45–50, with prices varying according to the season.

Opening hours Daily dawn–dusk.

Admission $5 (ticket also valid for Banteay Tuop).

Guides Guides ($10) can be hired through the CBT office (see p.130) – useful for the main site, and essential if you want to properly explore the various outlying temples.

Tour packages Contact ⊛ visitbanteaychhmar.org, who arrange homestays and organize tour packages to the temple including accommodation, guide, transport and village visits (from $124 for two people for two days).

ACCOMMODATION

Homestays Banteay Chhmar village ☎012 435660, ⓦ visitbanteaychhmar.org. Although you can visit Banteay Chhmar on a day-trip from Sisophon, the local community also provides comfortable and well-run homestays in the village. It's best to arrange them in advance, although you may be able to set up something on the spot by visiting the Community Based Tourism (CBT) office just south of the temple on NR56A. **$7**

Poipet

Arriving from Bangkok at the dusty border town of **POIPET** provides the worst possible introduction to Cambodia – mainly thanks to the hassle-ridden border crossing, which has become mildly notorious thanks to the various low-grade scams practised upon new arrivals. The town itself has boomed massively in recent years thanks to the raft of **casinos** set up for Thai visitors (gambling is illegal in Thailand), and the glitzy duty-free casino zone next to the border is effectively a slice of foreign territory on Cambodian soil, with Thai the predominant language and baht the currency of choice. Away from the casinos the town remains a flyblown and faintly dismal sort of place, and one that most travellers choose to escape as rapidly as possible.

ARRIVAL AND DEPARTURE
POIPET

FROM THAILAND

The border crossing The crossing at Poipet (daily 7am–8pm) is the main transit point between Cambodia and Thailand. Coming from Thailand, try to arrive as early as possible, since onward transport dries up significantly after noon, and if you cross after 5pm you may find yourself stuck in town for the night. Crossing the border itself, be aware of various visa- and money-related scams (see box below).

POIPET BORDER SCAMS

The following are just some of the most entrenched scams – which may well have evolved into new forms by the time you read this – so have your wits about you when entering Cambodia. Keep a beady eye on your possessions, too, as petty theft and pickpocketing is common.

VISAS

Cambodian visas are issued on arrival at the border at a cost of $20 (bring one passport photo, or you may be charged an extra 100 baht in order to have your passport photo scanned; pay in dollars rather than baht, or again the fee may inflate). Ignore any touts or tuk-tuk drivers who might try to "help" you obtain your visa, no matter how legitimate they might look (including those posing as officials with fake ID badges and so on) – if pressed, just say you already have a visa. And avoid any attempts to lure you into the semi-spurious "Cambodian Consulate" on the Thai side of the border, where you'll pay double the official rate for a visa. All you actually have to do is wade your way through the various con artists, get yourself stamped out of Thailand and then walk over to the far side of the footbridge, where you can buy your visa at the official Visa Office at the clearly posted price, although even here you may be asked for an additional "processing fee", "stamping fee" or suchlike for an extra $1–3 – a bribe by any other name. A polite refusal to pay is perfectly in order, although it's probably worth coughing up the necessary lest you find that your visa is processed with unprecedented slowness. You could also purchase an **e-visa** in advance (see p.48), which generally speeds your progress through immigration – for the time being at least.

MONEY

Another regular scam involves money – you'll be told that **ATMs** in Cambodia charge inflated commission fees and/or that you should change all your baht at a spurious "government" exchange booth before crossing the border. All of which is nonsense – there are the usual ATMs in Poipet (including a commission-free Canadia Bank machine), and in any case baht are accepted throughout Poipet. That said, it's a good idea to bring some dollars with you just to be safe.

2

Poipet Transport Association Arriving in Cambodia you'll be herded into the "Free Shuttle Bus Station" run by the Poipet Transport Association. From here, shuttle buses will take you to the Poipet Tourist International Passenger Terminal, 9km down the road, from where buses and shared taxis depart to Sisophon, Siem Reap, Battambang and Phnom Penh (most services depart in the morning, although buses to Siem Reap via Sisophon continue until around 5pm). Fares on services departing from here are roughly double the usual prices on these routes, although given that it's only a question of a few dollars either way ($9 by bus to Siem Reap, for example, or $15 to Phnom Penh) it's probably not worth the hassle of trying to make your own arrangements.

Travelling independently Most onward buses from Poipet depart before noon, leaving for Siem Reap, Sisophon, Battambang and Phnom Penh. If you do decide to make your own way, you'll need to shake off the attentions of the possibly belligerent Poipet Transport Association touts (for "Association" read "mafia") and possibly even local police (who may pursue you down the road while insisting, ludicrously, that it's illegal to take a place in a local bus or shared taxi) and make your way around 2km down the road to the area in front of the market, where various bus companies including Phnom Penh Sorya, Capitol Tours and GST have offices and buses. Shared taxis can also be picked up along the roadside here.

Destinations: by bus Battambang (8 daily; 3hr); Phnom Penh (15 daily; 8hr); Siem Reap (20 daily; 3hr); Sisophon (20 daily; 1hr).

Destinations: by shared taxi Battambang (12 daily; 3hr); Phnom Penh (15 daily; 8hr); Siem Reap (25 daily; 3hr); Sisophon (20 daily; 1hr).

Pre-paid transport If you're on a pre-paid bus or minibus from Bangkok you'll have to locate your vehicle and then possibly hang around for an hour or more waiting for remaining passengers to come through, and possibly even longer if your driver decides to go hunting for further passengers to make the onward trip more lucrative.

TO THAILAND

Several companies (including Phnom Penh Sorya) run buses between Phnom Penh, Siem Reap and Bangkok. In theory this takes the headache out of arranging onward transport from the Thai side of the border, although in practice things might not work as smoothly as you'd hope thanks to cross-border bus company scams or simple inefficiency, and locating your bus on the far side of the border can sometimes turn into a major headache – meaning that it's a toss-up between buying a through ticket and trying to make your own way once over the border. If you do decide to travel independently, once across the border and into Thailand you'll need to make for Aranyaprathet – a 4km journey by tuk-tuk (around 60–80 baht) – from where buses depart regularly for Bangkok (throughout the day until around 6pm; 5hr); there are also a couple of trains, currently leaving at 6.40am and 1.55pm (you can check latest times at ⊚ thairailways.com).

INFORMATION

Money It's a good idea to arrive with some dollars to buy your visa with and as a safety net to avoid possible money-changing scams. There are ATMs (Visa and MasterCard) at the Canadia and ANZ banks in the town centre near the market. Poipet operates on no less than three currencies: Thai baht, Cambodian riel and US dollars, although baht are generally preferred to riel. Try to get up to speed with latest exchange rates as quickly as you can.

ACCOMMODATION AND EATING

Good Luck Hotel and Restaurant 200m west of the market ☎011 722408. Run by a kindly family, this is Poipet's best option, down a quiet side-street and with simple, clean en-suite rooms with a/c and TV, plus a pleasant restaurant serving tasty Thai and Khmer food. $12

Orkiday Angkor Hotel Near the traffic circle as you emerge from the immigration office ☎054 967503. In the casino zone, with functional but well-appointed a/c rooms with hot water. The neighbouring *Holiday Palace Hotel* is very similar. $15

Siem Reap and the temples of Angkor

ANGKOR WAT

Siem Reap and the temples of Angkor

The main – and for some people the only – reason to visit Cambodia is to experience at first hand the world-famous temples of Angkor, a stupendous array of ancient religious monuments virtually unrivalled anywhere in Asia (only the roughly synchronous temples of Bagan in Myanmar come close). The majestic temple of Angkor Wat, with its five iconic corncob towers rising high above the surrounding jungle, is the chief attraction, rivalled by the magical Bayon, embellished with superhuman images of the enigmatically half-smiling Avalokitesavara, and the jungle-smothered temple remains of Ta Prohm, with crumbling ruins squeezed between the roots of enormous trees and creepers. The sheer numbers of tourists descending on these sites may have eroded some of Angkor's prevailing mystery, although with judicious planning the worst of the crowds can still be avoided – and whenever you visit, the ruins will leave an indelible impression.

Headline monuments aside, Angkor has an extraordinary wealth of attractions. Literally hundreds of major temple complexes dot the countryside hereabouts, spread over an area of some four hundred square kilometres, and for many visitors it's at these lesser-known destinations that the true spirit and magic of Angkor can still be found. Even a cursory tour of the more outlying temples of **Roluos** gets you somewhat off the beaten track, while the intricately carved shrines of **Banteay Srei** are also within easy reach. Further afield the magnificent temple-citadels of **Beng Mealea** and **Koh Ker** can be conveniently combined in a single day-trip (perhaps with a visit to remote **Preah Khan** (Kompong Thom). Further north, the memorable temple of **Preah Vihear**, perched on a mountaintop overlooking Thailand, has finally re-entered the tourist mainstream after years of Khmer Rouge occupation and cross-border squabbles. It's easily combined with a visit to the border boomtown of **Anlong Veng**, famous for its

THE BAYON, ANGKOR THOM

Highlights

❶ Siem Reap Cambodia's most tourist-friendly destination, packed with bustling pavement cafés, elegant restaurants and buzzing bars, but still with a healthy slice of old-fashioned, small-town charm. **See p.138**

❷ Apsara dance Laden with symbolism, this exquisitely stylized classical dance-form was once performed exclusively for the king. **See p.154**

❸ Tonle Sap Ride a boat around the remarkable floating villages on Southeast Asia's largest freshwater lake. **See p.156**

❹ Angkor Wat Southeast Asia's most iconic building – the first glimpse of its soaring corncob

towers is something you'll never forget. **See p.165**

❺ Angkor Thom Expansive ancient walled city enclosing lavish terraces, towers and temples, including the haunting Bayon with its forest of enigmatic faces. **See p.171**

❻ Ta Prohm Atmospheric temple, now half-consumed by the jungle, its crumbling buildings held in the clutch of giant trees. **See p.180**

❼ Banteay Srei Rosy-red sandstone temple with intricate carvings of female divinities. **See p.188**

❽ Preah Vihear Imposing temple poised in a spectacular position on a ridge above the Thai border. **See p.196**

HIGHLIGHTS ARE MARKED ON THE MAP ON PP.136–137

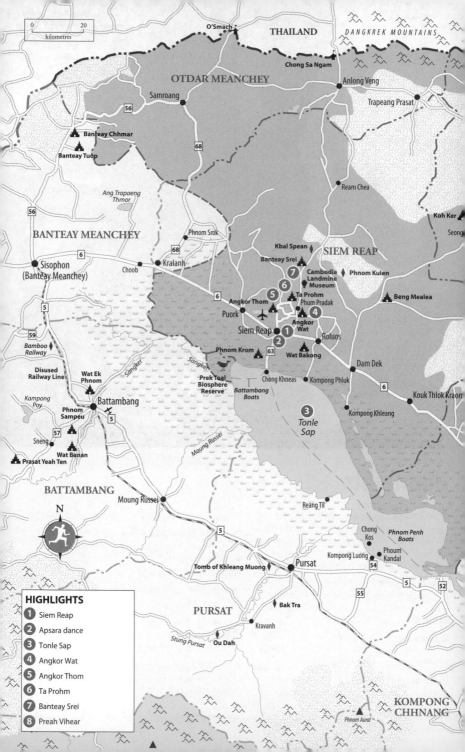

0   kilometres   20

O'Smach   **THAILAND**   *DANGREK MOUNTAINS*

Chong Sa Ngam

OTDAR MEANCHEY   Anlong Veng

Samroang   Trapeang Prasat

56

Banteay Chhmar

68

Banteay Tuóp

Ream Chea

Koh Ker

Ang Trapaeng
Thmor   Phnom Srok   Seong

BANTEAY MEANCHEY   Kbal Spean   **SIEM REAP**

Banteay Srei

6   Kralanh   ⑦   Cambodia   Phnom Kulen
Sisophon   68   Landmine
(Banteay Meanchey)   Choob   Museum   Beng Mealea

6   ⑤   Ta Prohm   ④
Angkor Thom   ⑥   Phum Pradak
Puork   Angkor
Wat

5   Siem Reap   ①
②
59   63   Roluos

Bamboo   Phnom Krom   Wat Bakong   Dam Dek
Railway

Disused   Sangker   Chong Khneas   Kompong Phluk   6   Kouk Thlok Kraom
Railway Line   Wat Ek   Prek Toal
Phnom   Biosphere   Battambang
Kampong   Reserve   Boats   Kompong Khleang
Poy   **Battambang**

Phnom   ✈
57   Sampeu   Tonle
Sneng   ③   Sap
Wat Banan
Prasat Yeah Ten

BATTAMBANG   Reang Til

Moung Russei   Chong   Phnom Penh
Kos   Boats

N   5   Kompong Luong   Phoum
Kandal
54

Tomb of Khleang Muong   Pursat
PURSAT   5   52

55

Bak Tra
PURSAT
Kravanh

Stung Pursat   Ou Dah   **KOMPONG
CHHNANG**

Phnom Aural

HIGHLIGHTS
① Siem Reap
② Apsara dance
③ Tonle Sap
④ Angkor Wat
⑤ Angkor Thom
⑥ Ta Prohm
⑦ Banteay Srei
⑧ Preah Vihear

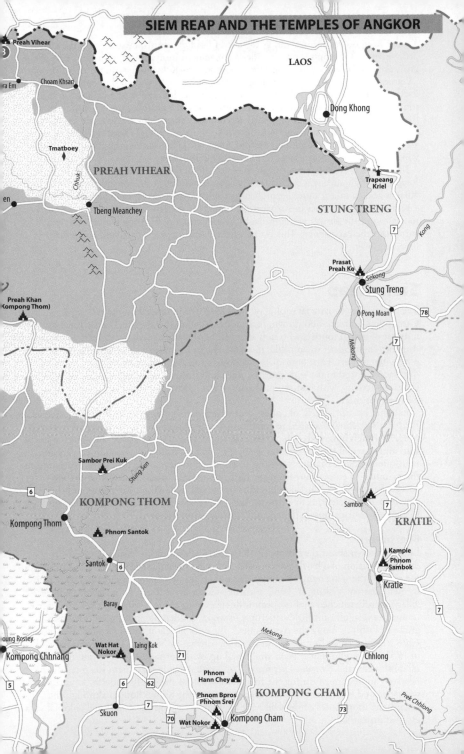

SIEM REAP AND THE TEMPLES OF ANGKOR

LAOS

Preah Vihear

ra Em

Choam Khsan

Dong Khong

Tmatboey

Cihuk

PREAH VIHEAR

Trapeang Kriel

en

Tbeng Meanchey

STUNG TRENG

Kong

Prasat Preah Ko

Sekong

Stung Treng

Preah Khan (Kompong Thom)

O Pong Moan

78

7

Mekong

Sambor Prei Kuk

Stung Sen

7

Sambor

KOMPONG THOM

KRATIE

6

Kompong Thom

Phnom Santok

Kampie

Santok

6

Phnom Sambok

Kratie

Baray

7

oung Rossey

Mekong

Kompong Chhnang

Wat Hat Nokor

Taing Kok

Chhlong

71

Phnom Hann Chey

Prek Chhlong

5

6

62

Phnom Bpros Phnom Srei

KOMPONG CHAM

73

Skuon

70

Wat Nokor

Kompong Cham

Khmer Rouge associations, and as the site of Pol Pot's death. Further east, the affable little town of **Kompong Thom** provides a convenient jumping-off point for visits to the great pre-Angkorian temple complex at **Sambor Prei Kuk**, along with other nearby sites.

Gateway to the temples is **Siem Reap**, a former backwater town that has reinvented itself as Cambodia's tourist honeypot par excellence. It's crammed with tourists and touts, but remains one of the country's most enjoyable destinations – if you don't mind the fact that it bears increasingly little resemblance to anywhere else in the country. Siem Reap is also the starting point for visits to the remarkable **floating villages** on the great Tonle Sap lake and to wild **Phnom Kulen**, at the borders of the Kulen Mountains, which divide the lush lowlands from the barren north.

Three days is enough **time** to visit most of the major sites in the vicinity of Siem Reap, although adding a day or three allows time to visit one of the nearby floating villages and to take a more leisurely approach to the Angkor archeological site itself – temple-fatigue can set in surprisingly quickly if you go at the ancient monuments too fast, and the slower you approach the vast treasury of Angkor, the more you'll gain from the experience. This is one of the world's great sights, and well worth lingering over.

3

Siem Reap

The once sleepy provincial capital of **SIEM REAP** (pronounced *See*-um *Ree*-up) is Cambodia's ultimate boomtown, its exponential growth super-fuelled by the vast number of global tourists who now descend on the place to visit the nearby **temples** of Angkor. The modern town is like nowhere else in Cambodia, packed with wall-to-wall hotels, restaurants, bars, boutiques, tour operators and massage parlours; its streets thronged day and night with tourists, touts and tuk-tuk drivers in a giddy bedlam of incessant activity, with endless quantities of hot food and cheap beer, and a nonstop party atmosphere.

It should be tourist hell, of course, but what's perhaps most surprising is that Siem Reap has somehow managed to retain much of its original small-town charm. It's easy to spend much longer here than planned, wandering the city's lively markets, colourful wats and peaceful riverside walkways by day, and exploring its restaurants, bars and boutiques by dark. Major attractions in the town itself may be thin on the ground, but there's much to enjoy apart from the obligatory temple tours. The nearby **floating villages** on the Tonle Sap lake shouldn't be missed, while there are plenty of other **activities** and attractions to keep you busy, from horseriding and quad-biking through to cookery courses, apsara dances and shadow-puppet shows.

Brief history

Little is known about the **history** of Siem Reap, said to mean "Siam defeated" in commemoration of a battle that possibly never happened. Sprawling to east and west of the river of the same name, the town has only recently grown large enough to acquire its own identity. Visiting in 1935, Geoffrey Gorer described it as "a charming little village, hardly touched by European influence, built along a winding river; the native houses are insignificant little structures in wood, hidden behind the vegetation that grows so lushly... along the river banks." The only hotels at the time were the *Grand Hotel d'Angkor*, then "a mile out of town" according to Norman Lewis, who stayed here in 1951, although it's now been swallowed up by the expanding town, and its sister establishment, the *Bungalow des Ruines*, opposite Angkor Wat. Siem Reap remained relatively undeveloped during the first **tourist rush** of the 1950s and 1960s, and much was destroyed when the town was emptied under the **Khmer Rouge**, although the *Grand*, the shophouses of the Old Market, Psar Chas, and the occasional colonial villa escaped unscathed.

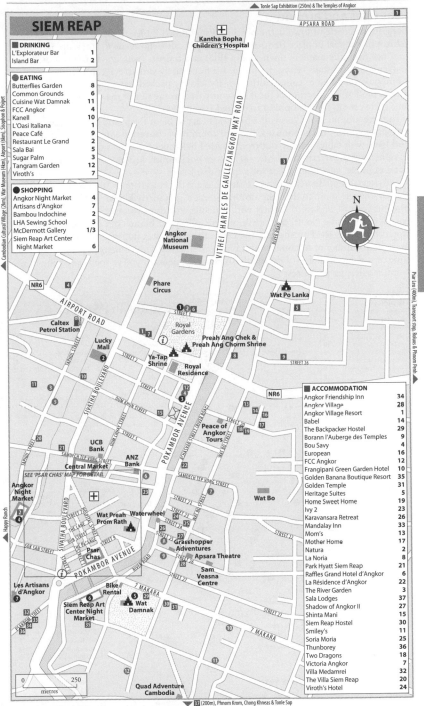

SIEM REAP

■ DRINKING
L'Explorateur Bar	1
Island Bar	2

● EATING
Butterflies Garden	8
Common Grounds	6
Cuisine Wat Damnak	11
FCC Angkor	4
Kanell	10
L'Oasi Italiana	1
Peace Café	9
Restaurant Le Grand	2
Sala Bai	5
Sugar Palm	3
Tangram Garden	12
Viroth's	7

● SHOPPING
Angkor Night Market	4
Artisans d'Angkor	7
Bambou Indochine	2
LHA Sewing School	5
McDermott Gallery	1/3
Siem Reap Art Center Night Market	6

■ ACCOMMODATION
Angkor Friendship Inn	34
Angkor Village	28
Angkor Village Resort	1
Babel	14
The Backpacker Hostel	29
Borann l'Auberge des Temples	9
Bou Savy	4
European	16
FCC Angkor	12
Frangipani Green Garden Hotel	10
Golden Banana Boutique Resort	35
Golden Temple	31
Heritage Suites	5
Home Sweet Home	19
Ivy 2	23
Karavansara Retreat	26
Mandalay Inn	33
Mom's	13
Mother Home	17
Natura	2
La Noria	8
Park Hyatt Siem Reap	21
Raffles Grand Hotel d'Angkor	6
La Résidence d'Angkor	22
The River Garden	3
Sala Lodges	37
Shadow of Angkor II	27
Shinta Mani	15
Siem Reap Hostel	30
Smiley's	11
Soria Moria	25
Thunborey	36
Two Dragons	18
Victoria Angkor	7
Villa Medamrei	32
The Villa Siem Reap	20
Viroth's Hotel	24

Tonle Sap Exhibition (250m) & The Temples of Angkor

APSARA ROAD

Kantha Bopha Children's Hospital

VITHEI CHARLES DE GAULLE/ANGKOR WAT ROAD

RIVER ROAD

Cambodian Cultural Village (2km), War Museum (4km), Airport (6km), Sisophon & Poipet

Psar Leu (400m), Transport stop, Roluos & Phnom Penh

N

3

Angkor National Museum

Phare Circus

Wat Po Lanka

NR6

AIRPORT ROAD

Caltex Petrol Station

Lucky Mall

Ya-Tap Shrine

Royal Gardens

STREET 1

Preah Ang Chek & Preah Ang Chorm Shrine

Royal Residence

STREET 26

NR6

SIVATHA BOULEVARD

OUM KHUN STREET

STREET 2

STREET 5

TAPHUL STREET

Peace of Angkor Tours

STREET 20

UCB Bank

SAMDECH TEP VONG STREET

ANZ Bank

Central Market

SEE 'PSAR CHAS' MAP FOR DETAIL

POKAMBOR AVENUE

KRAVAN STREET (RIVER ROAD)

WAT BO STREET

STREET 24

SAMDECH TEP VONG STREET

Wat Bo

Angkor Night Market

Happy Ranch

SIVATHA BOULEVARD

THE LANE

Wat Preah Prom Rath

Waterwheel

STREET 21

STREET 23

STREET 24

STREET 25

METTA STREET (WAT BO STREET)

STREET 9

THE PASSAGE

Psar Chas

POKAMBOR AVENUE

Grasshopper Adventures

Apsara Theatre

STREET 27

Sam Veasna Centre

SOK SAN STREET

Les Artisans d'Angkor

Bike Rental

Siem Reap Art Center Night Market

Wat Damnak

7 MAKARA

RIVER ROAD

STREET 22

STREET 27

7 MAKARA

Quad Adventure Cambodia

0   250
metres

37 (200m), Phnom Krom, Chong Khneas & Tonle Sap

Psar Chas and around

Bang in the centre of town is the bustling **Psar Chas** (Old Market), an enjoyably schizophrenic sort of place frequented both by locals (who come to stock up on fresh produce from the market's town-facing side) and tourists (who gravitate towards the souvenir-stacked stalls facing the river). It's not exactly your average authentic Cambodian market, of course, although the closely packed stalls and narrow alleyways offer a modest simulacrum of local life compared to the rest of the touristy city centre, and there's some good **shopping** to be had (see p.154).

The area around Psar Chas is the historic heart of Siem Reap, still boasting some original colonial-era **shophouses**, most of them now converted into vibrant restaurants and bars, with tables spilling out from shaded balconies onto the surrounding pavements – the riverfront *Shadow of Angkor* guesthouse, just east of the market, is a good example, and a nice place for a quiet drink too.

The streets immediately north of Psar Chas are the epicentre of Siem Reap's tourist scene, nowhere more so than the riotous Street 8, popularly known as **Pub Street**, for obvious reasons, and filled nightly with raucous crowds of younger tourists from every corner of the globe. South and north of here, alleyways branch out towards the parallel streets known as **The Passage** and **The Lane**, the entire area honeycombed with an incredible number of restaurants and bars and buzzing with tourists at pretty much any time of the day or night – a decidedly surreal experience if you've spent any time in the country's sleepier provinces.

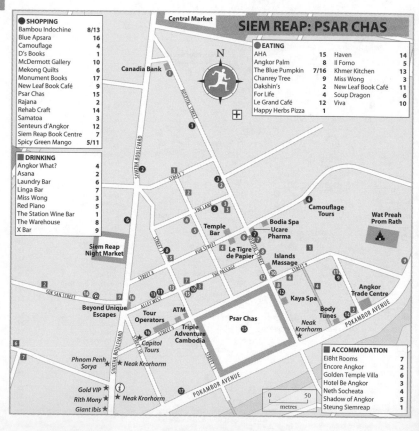

SIEM REAP: PSAR CHAS

● SHOPPING
Bambou Indochine	8/13
Blue Apsara	16
Camouflage	4
D's Books	1
McDermott Gallery	10
Mekong Quilts	6
Monument Books	17
New Leaf Book Café	9
Psar Chas	15
Rajana	2
Rehab Craft	14
Samatoa	3
Senteurs d'Angkor	12
Siem Reap Book Centre	7
Spicy Green Mango	5/11

■ DRINKING
Angkor What?	4
Asana	2
Laundry Bar	6
Linga Bar	7
Miss Wong	3
Red Piano	5
The Station Wine Bar	1
The Warehouse	8
X Bar	9

● EATING
AHA	15	Haven	14
Angkor Palm	8	Il Forno	5
The Blue Pumpkin	7/16	Khmer Kitchen	13
Chanrey Tree	9	Miss Wong	3
Dakshin's	2	New Leaf Book Café	11
For Life	4	Soup Dragon	6
Le Grand Café	12	Viva	10
Happy Herbs Pizza	1		

■ ACCOMMODATION
Ei8ht Rooms	7
Encore Angkor	2
Golden Temple Villa	6
Hotel Be Angkor	3
Neth Socheata	4
Shadow of Angkor	5
Steung Siemreap	1

MASSAGE, SPAS AND SWIMMING

You can hardly move in central Siem Reap without insistent calls of **"massage?"** following you down the street, particularly around Sihanouk Boulevard, Hospital Street and at the Angkor Night Market. While these are all bona fide establishments, the cheapest places, though usually clean, will probably give you your massage on a reclining chair or in a room with several massage couches, sometimes in full view of the street. Paying more you'll get relaxing surroundings, a robe and a private room.

Most of the cheaper places offer traditional **Khmer-style massage** – neck, head, back, full massage and so on, with or without oil, while better places (see below) offer the full range of international massages, from Thai to Swedish, along with other spa treatments. A growing number of places are offering **"Seeing Hands" massage**, given by blind masseurs, while there are around a dozen **"fish massage"** places set up on pavements where you can sit with your feet in a tank for twenty minutes while shoals of little fish nibble the dead skin off your feet.

Many hotels and guesthouses have **swimming pools**, while some allow non-guests to use theirs for a fee (or if you take drinks or a meal). Unfortunately the spectacular sunken pool at the *Raffles Grand Hotel* is out of bounds except for guests, although the lush pool at the *Victoria Angkor* runs it a close second and is sometimes open to non-guests if the hotel isn't too full ($13). The *Angkor Village Resort* is another option ($10, free if you have lunch). Cheaper pools can be found at the *Siem Reap Hostel* ($6, including $5 bar credit), *La Noria* ($3) and the *Kannell* restaurant (free with a meal). Alternatively, do as the Khmers do and head to the West Baray (see p.186) where you can swim, picnic and lounge about all day for nothing.

SPAS

Amrita Spa Raffles Grand Hotel d'Angkor ☎063 963888. Siem Reap's most upmarket spa, offering opulent massages (including Thai, Khmer, Swedish, aromatherapy and four-hand) plus facials, pedicures, manicures and herbal baths (from $60/hr).

Bodia Spa Off Hospital St ☎063 761593, ⊛bodia -spa.com. Traditional and aromatherapy massages, wraps and facials (from $25/hr).

Body Tune Spa Pokambor Ave, near Psar Chas ☎063 764141, ⊛bodytune.co.th. Highly recommended Thai spa offering affordable Thai, oil and aromatherapy massages, plus facials and scrubs (from $12/hr).

Kaya Spa Hospital St, by Senteurs d'Angkor ☎063 966736. Traditional herbal and aromatherapy massages, plus scrubs, facials and wraps (from $20/hr).

Kong Kea Spa La Résidence d'Angkor ☎063 963390. Luxurious spa at one of the city's top hotels – signature Khmer and Indochina massages, scrubs and facials (from $70/hr).

Artisans d'Angkor

West off the southern end of Sivatha Blvd • Daily 7.30am–6.30pm • Free • ☎ 063 963330, ⊛ artisansdangkor.com

A short walk west of Psar Chas, **Artisans d'Angkor** offers a fascinating snapshot of Cambodia's varied artisanal traditions collected under one roof in a single little crafts village. English-speaking guides meet visitors for a tour of the workshops, where you can see students – selected from deprived local families – following intensive studies in skills including wood and stone carving, lacquer-work, gilding and silver-working. The gorgeous end products of all this work can be bought in the upmarket boutique attached to the centre (see p.154).

The centre has also revived local silk-weaving skills, lost during the Khmer Rouge era. Silk is produced at the **Angkor Silk Farm** (daily 8am–5pm; free) at Puok, 16km west of Siem Reap off NR6, where guides explain the intricacies of silk production and weaving. Free buses run from Artisans d'Angkor to the farm daily (9.30am & 1.30pm; returning 11.30am & 3.30pm).

Wat Damnak

East of the river opposite Psar Chas and behind the Siem Reap Art Center Night Market

The sprawling **Wat Damnak** is one of the largest temples in Siem Reap. It's home to the Center for Khmer Studies – the largest library outside Phnom Penh – while at the rear of the grounds the Life & Hope Association (ⓦ lifeandhopeangkor.org) runs a women's **sewing school** where you can talk to the students and shop for ready-made or bespoke clothing (see p.155).

The riverside and Wat Preah Prom Rath

Siem Reap's nicest stroll is along the attractive **riverside walkway**, running along the west side of the Siem Reap River from Psar Chas north for 1km or so to NR6. Just north of Psar Chas you'll see the spires of the imposing **Wat Preah Prom Rath** on your left. The temple may date right back to the thirteenth century, although what you see now dates from after 1945, featuring an impressively kitsch cluster of gaudy buildings festooned with Buddhist flags, and with a central vihara guarded by a pair of quaint, snow-white bulls.

Wat Bo

Around 200m east of the river along Street 22

The eighteenth-century **Wat Bo** is the oldest and most appealing of Siem Reap's Buddhist monasteries. The interior walls of the vihara, still in good condition, were decorated in the nineteenth century with scenes from the *Reamker* incorporating quaint scenes of everyday life – a Chinese merchant puffing on an opium pipe and French colonial soldiers watching a traditional dance performance among them. The pagoda is also home to a collection of old Buddha statues.

The Royal Gardens

At the northern end of the riverside walkway are the formal **Royal Gardens**, flanked by the venerable *Grand Hotel d'Angkor* to the north and the similarly time-warped *Victoria Angkor* to the west. On the south side of the gardens, a **shrine** to the sister deities Ang Chek and Ang Chom houses figurines of the two – thought to have been Angkorian princesses – in brass and bronze. Ang Chek is the taller of the two figures, both of which extend a hand in the characteristic "Have no fear" (*abhaya*) *mudra*. The statues were originally situated in the Gallery of a Thousand Buddhas at Angkor Wat and later hidden from the eyes of invaders and treasure-hunters by successive generations of monks, being moved repeatedly before finally arriving in their current shrine in 1990. They are now heaped with offerings daily.

Just to the west, now surrounded by a traffic circle and marked by a huge tree in the middle of the road, is a shrine to **Ya Tep**, a local spirit said to bring protection and luck to the Siem Reap area. The offerings left at the shrine are sometimes quite extravagant – whole cooked chickens are not unknown.

Angkor National Museum

Vithei Charles de Gaulle/Angkor Wat Rd, 1.5km north of the centre • Daily 8.30am–6.30pm • $12, students and children under 1.2m tall $6, audioguide $3, discounts sometimes available for online reservations • ☏ 063 966601, ⓦ angkornationalmuseum.com

A visit to Siem Reap's **Angkor National Museum** is an essential adjunct to a visit to the temples themselves – the only downside is the extortionate entrance fee. Choice pieces of ancient Khmer sculpture are beautifully exhibited in vast galleries complete with explanatory signboards. Introductory and multimedia presentations provide orientation, explain the wealth of statuary on display, and give background to Cambodian history, heritage and religion. The fabulous gallery of 1000 Buddha images, in particular, should not be missed.

Kantha Bopha Children's Hospital

Vithei Charles de Gaulle/Angkor Wat Rd, 2.5km north of the centre • Concerts Thurs & Sat 7.15pm • Free • ⓦ beatocello.com • Around $2/$3 from the centre by moto/tuk-tuk

Dominated by a massive head of Jayavarman VII, the **Kantha Bopha Children's Hospital** is one of Cambodia's unsung wonders; here all treatment is free and charitable donations allow staff to be paid a living wage. Free concerts are staged twice weekly by Dr Beat Richner – usually known as "Beatocello" – the Swiss doctor and cellist who oversees the hospital. Entrance is free, although donations, either of money, blood, or both, are warmly welcomed.

Cambodian Cultural Village

3.5km west of the centre along NR6 (Airport Rd) • Daily 8am–7pm • $15 • Around $4/$5 from the centre by moto/tuk-tuk

West of the centre along the road to the airport, the **Cambodian Cultural Village** is one of those "see the whole country in an hour" theme parks that every country in Southeast Asia seems to have. As well as miniatures of many of Cambodia's temples and monuments, there are tableaux of wax figures portraying events from history. However, given the spectacularly racked-up admission price, few overseas visitors bother.

War Museum

5km from the centre (4km west along NR6/Airport Rd, then 1km along a side road north) • Daily 8am–5.30pm • $5 (including guide) • ☏ 088 848 7351, ⓦ warmuseumcambodia.com • Around $4/$5 from the centre by moto/tuk-tuk

Not far from the airport, Siem's Reap's **War Museum** provides a salutary reminder of the three decades of fighting endured by Cambodia up until 1998. The collection includes significant quantities of military hardware including a MiG jet fighter along with various tanks and plenty of guns (some of them dating back to World War II). For many visitors, though, the museum's real highlight is the chance to talk with its guides, some of them war veterans and land mine victims themselves, whose stories and reminiscences bring the Khmer Rouge era to life rather more vividly than the clunky piles of rusting weaponry.

ARRIVAL AND DEPARTURE

SIEM REAP

BY PLANE

For information about flights to Siem Reap, see Basics (see pp.19–21).

Airport transport Registered taxis ($7) and tuk-tuks ($5) for the 6km ride from the airport into town can be hired at a booth just outside the exit from the arrival lounge. Minibuses from certain hotels meet planes, so look out for them if you've booked accommodation in advance, or intend to stay at one of them.

Airlines Bangkok Airways, 571 NR6/Airport Rd (☏ 063 380191); Cambodia Angkor Air, Sivatha Blvd, near Central Market (☏ 063 969268, ⓦ cambodiaangkorair.com); Jetstar, 50 Sivatha Blvd (☏ 063 964388); Malaysia Airlines, Siem Reap Airport (☏ 063 964135); Vietnam Airlines, 342 NR6/Airport Rd (☏ 063 964488).

BY BUS

Companies Siem Reap has a plethora of bus companies (including Capitol, Neak Krorhorm, Phnom Penh Sorya, Giant Ibis and Rith Mony) servicing the popular Siem Reap–Phnom Penh route. Most also provide services to Poipet, although there are fewer services along the less-travelled routes to Battambang and Kompong Cham. Tickets can be bought through most guesthouses and hotels; alternatively, visit the bus company offices themselves, which are clustered along Sivatha Blvd west of Psar Chas.

Stations and stops Arriving in Siem Reap, buses usually call first at Chong Kov Sou bus station 3km east of town, although most continue into town (or at least to the junction of NR6 and Pokambor Ave, north of the centre, from where a tuk-tuk into town will cost $2).

Destinations Anlong Veng (2 daily; 2hr); Battambang (4 daily; 4hr); Kompong Cham (2 daily; 3hr 30min); Kompong Thom (20 daily; 2hr); Phnom Penh (20 daily; 6–8hr); Poipet (10 daily; 3hr); Sisophon (10 daily; 2hr).

BY SHARED TAXI AND MINIBUS

Arriving in Siem Reap Shared taxis stop at the transport stop 3km east of town, although most continue on into town.

Leaving Siem Reap Shared taxis to Phnom Penh and

Kompong Thom, Sisophon (for Battambang), Poipet and Anlong Veng run from the roadside at the junction of NR6 and the turning to Siem Reap's Chong Kov Sou transport stop about 2km east of town.

Destinations Anlong Veng (4 daily; 2hr); Kompong Cham (6 daily; 3hr); Kompong Thom (12 daily; 2hr); Phnom Penh (hourly; 5–6hr); Poipet (20 daily; 3hr); Sisophon (20 daily; 2hr).

BY BOAT

Arriving in Siem Reap Boats dock south of town at the port at Chong Khneas on the Tonle Sap about 15km from Siem Reap; the boat from Phnom Penh gets in between noon and early afternoon, while from Battambang it arrives mid- to late afternoon. Hotels will arrange for you to be collected from the port if you're staying with them; otherwise there's no shortage of tuk-tuks to take you into town ($4), not to mention guesthouse touts.

Leaving Siem Reap A boat leaves the Chong Khneas port daily at 7am for Phnom Penh ($35; 5–6hr) and at 8am for Battambang ($25; 6–8hr depending on water levels). You'll need to book your ticket at least a day ahead. If you buy through your guesthouse or hotel, a minibus will collect you from the door, which may mean setting out as early as 5.30am, as the vehicle will pick up passengers from various locations before heading down

to the port; if you choose to make your own way to the port, allow 30min by tuk-tuk.

TO/FROM THAILAND VIA POIPET

Arriving from Thailand Many travellers arrive overland from Thailand via Poipet (see p.130), easily done in a single day, assuming you leave early enough. If you're on a through ticket bought from one of the many travel agents on Bangkok's Khao San Road the going may be fairly slow, and you'll be dropped at one of their affiliated guesthouses in Siem Reap.

Travelling to Thailand A number of Siem Reap bus companies run buses and minibuses from Siem Reap to Bangkok via Poipet, where they link up with onward transport operated by their Thai associates – although given the various scams and delays associated with buses/minibuses going in both directions, you might be better off travelling independently. Numerous buses (3hr) run to the border at Poipet; alternatively, a shared taxi costs around $10 per seat, or $40 to hire the taxi outright. From the border at Poipet it's a further 4km to the Thai town of Aranyaprathet (around 60–80 baht by tuk-tuk). Getting to Aranyaprathet early will give you the option of choosing your onward transport in Thailand – either by bus, minibus or on the lunchtime train for the (approximately) 5hr trip to Bangkok.

INFORMATION

Tourist offices There are three tourist offices: one in the southwest corner of the Royal Gardens (in theory daily 8am–9pm), one on Sivatha Blvd near Psar Chas (daily 8am–9pm), and another on Vithei Charles de Gaulle (Angkor Wat Rd) on the way to the temples. It should be possible to hire temple guides at any of the three offices ($25/day), and also arrange a car and driver (from $30/day).

Siem Reap Angkor Visitors Guide This useful guide, published three times a year and available from some hotels, guesthouses and the tourist offices, contains detailed listings of places to stay, eat and drink; it's also available online at ⓦ canbypublications.com.

Website For up-to-the-minute listings, and a wealth of other information, check ⓦ siemreappost.com.

GETTING AROUND

By tuk-tuk or moto It's almost impossible to walk more than 10m in any direction in central Siem Reap without being offered a tuk-tuk or moto – useful if you're staying somewhere out of the centre (count on $1/2 for journeys across town). Note that although you'll see Cambodians two, three and even more upon a single moto, the government has decreed that motos can only carry one foreign passenger.

By motorbike or car Tourists are barred from renting motorbikes or driving rental cars in Siem Reap – if you see Westerners on motorcycles and scooters, they are probably

resident expats or have driven in from somewhere else.

By bike Bicycles available for rent in many places: try Camouflage (see opposite) or the useful shop on the roundabout just east of the river at the junction of 7 Makara and River Rd (just a minute's walk from Psar Chas), which has basic gearless bikes for $1/day, or fancier mountain bikes $3/$5. Alternatively, so-called white bicycles ($2/day, with profits going to local charitable causes) can be rented from a few outlets around town, including the *Rosy* guesthouse and *La Noria* hotel.

Temple transport See p.190.

TOURS AND ACTIVITIES

There are tours aplenty in Siem Reap, although many budget outfits offer identical temple or Tonle Sap itineraries, with rushed schedules and large group sizes. Rather than booking the first tour proposed by your guesthouse or hotel it's well worth checking out the **operators** below, both for general sightseeing and other activities, which frequently offer far more rewarding insights into local culture and history than you'll experience sitting on a tour bus. In addition to tours of the **floating villages** on the Tonle Sap (see p.156), specialist **activities** include hiking, camping, cycling, dirt-biking, kayaking, horseriding, quad-biking, jeep tours, boat trips, birdwatching, yoga, meditation, photography trips and more, plus cookery classes (see p.151), massage, spas and swimming (see p.141). Note that some activities (riding, quad-biking and ziplining, for example) may not be covered by your insurance policy, and you may be asked to sign a liability waiver when you sign in.

TOUR OPERATORS

Beyond Unique Escapes Cnr Alley West & Sivatha Blvd ☎077 562565, ⓦbeyonduniqueescapes.com. This excellent operator is a good first port, with quality tours at surprisingly affordable prices, with a maximum eight people per group and guaranteed departures irrespective of however many people do (or don't) turn up. Trips include a "day in the life" village tour, maybe helping with rice planting or harvesting; Tonle Sap tours to Kompong Phluk or Kompong Khleang (depending on the season); and a useful temple tour combining Beng Mealea, Banteay Srei and Bakong (plus the Landmine Museum). They also run a good, unusual, cookery class (see p.151), and can customize private tours to suit including hiking, cycling and photography trips. Full day around $35/person.

Cambodia Jeep Tours Street 9, above Father's Restaurant ☎012 908524, ⓦcambodiajeep.com. Tours in authentic American Army jeeps – you can even have a go driving one yourself. Itineraries include the usual temples, plus backcountry trips, expeditions to Phnom Kulen mountain and longer trips to Battambang and countrywide. Around $40.

Camouflage Down the road opposite the northeast end of Pub St ☎012 884909, ⓦcamouflagecambodia .com. Guided bike tours (20–65km) including temple and countryside itineraries, including a challenging Phnom Kulen itinerary. Trips $25–85.

Flight of the Gibbon Northeast cnr of Ta Keo temple in Angkor Archaeological Park ☎096 999 9101. Get a monkey's-eye view of the forest canopy from ziplines and sky bridges weaving through the treetops, connected by high-level observation platforms – needless to say, you'll need a head for heights and a reasonable level of physical fitness. $79/person.

Grasshopper Adventures Street 26 ☎012 462165, ⓦgrasshopperadventures.com. Half-, full- and multi-day cycling tours of Angkor, Beng Mealea and the local countryside. From $25/person.

The Happy Ranch ☎012 920002, ⓦthehappyranch .com. Home to more than fifty horses and ponies, and offering enjoyable horseriding trips (1–4hr; from $20/hr) through the local countryside for everyone from complete beginners to experienced equestrians, plus horse-cart rides (1–2hr). Many of the horses are rescue horses – any visiting vets who can donate some time (even a few hours) are warmly welcomed.

Hidden Cambodia Adventure Tours Off Angkor Wat Rd, near Jayavarman VII Hospital ☎012 655201, ⓦhiddencambodia.com. One of the longest-running operators in town, specializing in multi-day adventure tours by dirt bike, as well as cycling, hiking, camping and 4WD trips off the beaten track to numerous destinations, including "humanitarian" tours with the focus on sustainable tourism. They also run Tonle Sap ecotours and have their own lodge at Koh Ker. Prices vary, but the cheapest tours are around $100/person/day in group of four.

Indo Chine EX ☎092 650096, ⓦindochineex.com. Kayaking trips on the Tonle Sap, half-day hikes and bike rides through the countryside between temples and up to Phnom Kulen, and wildlife and birdwatching excursions to Prey Veng, and Ang Trapaeng Thom. Prices vary widely.

Osmose Nature Tours ⓦosmosetonlesap.net. Local NGO running ecotours to Tonle Sap and the bird sanctuary at Prek Toal (see p.159); can also organize local homestays. Prices vary.

Peace Café Street 26 ☎092 177127, ⓦpeacecafe angkor.org. Twice-daily yoga (astanga and hatha) sessions, plus private meditation classes and free "monk chat" sessions (Wed & Thurs) offering the chance to talk to an English-speaking Cambodian monk.

Peace of Angkor Tours 435 Street 20 ☎063 760475, ⓦpeaceofangkor.com. Photography tours of Angkor and elsewhere, including trips to Prek Toal sanctuary and more remote temples including Preah Vihear. From around $50/person.

Quad Adventure Cambodia Office just south of the centre near the Tangram restaurant ☎017 784727, ⓦquad-adventure-cambodia.com. Well-set-up place offering guided quad-bike excursions (from 1hr to full-day trips) through paddy fields and villages around Siem Reap, and around the little-visited Wat Athvea temple. From $30/hr.

Sam Veasna Centre Street 26 ☎063 963710, ⓦsamveasna.org. Cambodia's leading birdwatching specialist, with trips to major ornithological hotspots and exclusive access to Wildlife Conservation Society sites nationwide. Tours are well-run and led by expert guides, although probably for keen twitchers and wildlife aficionados only, given the prices. Generally well over $100/person/day.

Terre Cambodge Off Angkor Wat Rd down the side road opposite Angkor Village Resort ☎012 843401, ⓦterrecambodge.com. Trekking and mountain-bike expeditions (up to two weeks) with village accommodation or camping around Siem Reap. Around $90/person/day on longer tours.

3

Triple Adventures Cambodia Street 9, above Father's Restaurant ☎ 0888 366004, ⊕ triple-a -cambodia.com. Enjoyable day-trips combining a visit to Kompong Khleang floating village, lunch with the locals and a countryside bike ride. $39.

ACCOMMODATION

There's a super-abundance of accommodation in Siem Reap – although it always pays to **reserve in advance** if you're set on staying in a particular place, since the more popular establishments can fill up fast. At the **top end** of the scale the city offers some of Asia's most alluring accommodation, from colonial landmarks such as the *Raffles Grand Hotel d'Angkor* through to super-chic contemporary boutique resorts including *Amansara* and *La Résidence d'Angkor* and more intimate hideways *Sala Lodges* and *Angkor Village*. There's also a huge supply of comfortable, if not always particularly characterful, **mid-range hotels**, and plenty of inexpensive and often excellent **guesthouses**, though really cheap beds for under $10 a night are relatively thin on the ground, and most rooms come with a/c, whether you want it or not. Accommodation is scattered all over town. Many cheaper places can be found **around Psar Chas**, which puts you in prime position for the city's eating, drinking and nightlife, while there are further clusters of guesthouses **east of the river**, particularly in the little enclave around Street 20. Larger and more upmarket establishments (including an increasing number of big five-star international chains) tend to be located further north of the centre along **Airport** and **Angkor Wat roads**.

AROUND PSAR CHAS

Angkor Friendship Inn Psakrom St ☎ 063 965197, ⊕ angkorfriendshipinn.com; map p.139. Friendly family-run guesthouse, popular with long-stay visitors and offering spacious and excellent-value a/c rooms, all en suite with hot water. There's also a nice courtyard seating area plus small pool. Breakfast included. $16

Ei8ht Rooms Off Sivatha Blvd ☎ 063 969788, ⊕ ei8htrooms.com; map p.140. Attractive guesthouse spread over two buildings with twelve nicely furnished rooms, all with a/c and hot water, and decorated in bold colours. $16

Encore Angkor Sok San St ☎ 063 969400, ⊕ encoreangkor.com; map p.140. Intimate and soothing little hotel in a very central but relatively quiet location. Rooms (all with a/c, hot water, bathtub and safe) are attractively furnished with crisp white sheets and muslin drapes. Facilities include a restaurant and a dinky pool in its own walled garden. Breakfast included. $45

★**Golden Temple Villa** Off Sivatha Blvd ☎ 012 943459, ⊕ goldentemplevilla.com; map p.140. Hugely popular guesthouse in lush gardens with a range of bright, colourfully decorated rooms with a/c, hot water, DVD player and fridge. Complimentary tea, coffee and bananas are available throughout the day, and a free 1hr massage is included in every stay. Internet and bicycles available. Good value – and booking advised. $15

Hotel Be Angkor The Passage ☎ 063 965321, ⊕ hotelbeangkor.com; map p.140. Three exquisitely designed suites above the buzzing Passage, each uniquely styled and packed with hi-tech mod cons. There's one more, even more luxurious, suite ($250) in the adjacent *The One Hotel* (same phone, ⊕ theonehotelangkor.com). $150

Ivy 2 Just off Pokambor Ave ☎ 012 380516, ⊕ ivy -guesthouse.com; map p.139. In a rustic old ivy-clad wooden house, this is a Siem Reap guesthouse of the old school – basic, but with bags of character. Downstairs is a laidback café with bar and pool table, upstairs is a nice little veranda; accommodation is in a mix of simple fan rooms (with cold water) and slightly posher a/c rooms (with hot water). Fan $6; a/c $10

★**Mandalay Inn** Psakrom St ☎ 063 761662, ⊕ mandalayinn.com; map p.139. Long-running Siem Reap stalwart, and still the best cheapie in the city centre with a range of comfortable fan and a/c rooms (all with hot water and fridge). The super-helpful staff can arrange all kinds of tours, and there's also a rooftop gym, internet access and a good little restaurant. Fan $10; a/c $16

Neth Socheata Off Pokambor Ave ☎ 012 686171, ⊕ nethsocheatahotel.com; map p.140. Central but very peaceful mid-range hotel, on a pretty little pedestrianized alleyway just off the riverfront. Rooms (all with a/c and hot water) are nicely furnished and reasonably priced, although some are rather lacking in windows – you might want to look at a couple before checking in. $35

Shadow of Angkor Pokambor Ave ☎ 063 964774, ⊕ shadowofangkor.com; map p.140. Old-style Siem Reap guesthouse, set upstairs in a lovely old colonial shophouse by the river, with an attractive restaurant below. Rooms (all with a/c and hot water) are a bit bare and basic for the price, but for location and atmosphere it can't be beaten. $15

Steung Siemreap Street 9 ☎ 063 965169, ⊕ steungsiemreaphotel.com; map p.140. Biggish mid-range hotel on a quiet street in the heart of town, offering bright, airy rooms plus swimming pool, gym, sauna and restaurant. Quoted rates are on the high side, although big discounts are often available online (try Agoda, or similar sites). $90

Thunborey Psakrom St ☎ 063 761990, ⊕ thunborey hotel.com; map p.139. Efficiently run and good-value central hotel, with attractively furnished a/c rooms with fridge, hot water and nice bathrooms, plus a fifth-floor bar and breakfast restaurant. $18

Villa Medamrei Psakrom St ☎063 763636, ⓦvillamedamrei.com; map p.139. Attractive and very affordable little boutique hotel in a central location and with exceptionally attentive staff. It's surprisingly stylish given the modest price, with chic rooms (all with a/c, fridge and safe) clad in bright fabrics and colourful artworks covering every available surface. Breakfast included. $38

TAPHUL STREET AND AROUND
Frangipani Green Garden Hotel Formerly Green Garden Home Villa; 51 Sivatha Blvd ☎063 963342, ⓦfrangipanigreengardensiemreap.com; map p.139. Quiet little mid-range hotel in a pretty garden with swimming pool and spa. The bright, white rooms all come with a/c and hot water, while colourful Cambodian fabrics provide a welcome splash of colour. $40

Park Hyatt Siem Reap Formerly Hotel de la Paix; Sivatha Blvd ☎063 966001, ⓦsiemreap.park.hyatt .com; map p.139. Landmark downtown establishment from celebrated hotel designer Bill Bensley, with templesque portico, a skyline-dominating belvedere and serene 2m-tall apsaras welcoming you at each entrance. Recently reopened under the Park Hyatt brand following a multimillion-dollar makeover, it remains the most personable of Siem Reap's growing number of chain hotels, with suave rooms in muted whites and greys, plus a trio of restaurants and a gorgeous tree-studded pool. Rates are surprisingly low, given the quality. $200

Smiley's Taphul St ☎012 686060, ⓦsmileyguesthouse .com; map p.139. From humble beginnings this guesthouse has grown enormously, but remains one of Siem Reap's better budget options. Arranged around a quiet courtyard, rooms are clean and bright, with either fan or a/c (some with hot water), and there's a peaceful little downstairs café. Fan $8; a/c $12

The Villa Siem Reap Taphul St ☎063 761036, ⓦthevillasiemreap.com; map p.139. Good-looking boutique guesthouse with neat a/c rooms (all with hot water, minibar and safe) decorated in minimalist whites and greys, plus three bungalows in the lush gardens. Facilities include a decent-sized pool with plenty of loungers and a nice little patio restaurant. $35

THE ROYAL GARDENS AND AROUND
FCC Angkor Pokambor Ave ☎063 760280, ⓦfcccambodia.com; map p.139. This branch of the *FCC* in Phnom Penh is more modern but with just as much character, surrounded by trees in a picturesque riverfront location. Stylish rooms come with all the amenities you'd expect of a modern, boutique hotel, and there's also a terrific restaurant, bar, spa, and adjoining boutique complex. $130

★**Raffles Grand Hotel d'Angkor** Royal Gardens ☎063 963888, ⓦraffles.com/siemreap; map p.139.

Siem Reap's most famous address, providing visitors with colonial elegance since 1932. Rooms, suites and villas are furnished in luxurious period style, decorated with Khmer artefacts and provided with all mod cons. High tea and cocktails can be taken in the conservatory; there's a choice of restaurants and bars including the opulent *Restaurant Le Grand* (see p.151), bakery, swanky boutiques, business centre, gym, tennis court, the sumptuous Amrita spa (see p.141) and a vast pool. $400

The River Garden River road, north of NR6, west of the river ☎063 963400, ⓦtherivergarden.info; map p.139. Lovely little retreat, set in a verdant garden around a small pool and with a mix of contemporary and classic Asian styling. There's a wide range of accommodation of various prices and standards – the stand-alone "Khmer Cottage" is great for families. Good restaurant and bar, and also runs popular cooking classes (see p.151). Breakfast included. $47

★**Shinta Mani** Junction of Oum Khun & 14th St ⓦshintamani.com; map p.139. Idyllic, modern urban resort in a quiet side-street a short walk from the centre. A model of modern responsible tourism, the hotel is run as part of the Shinta Mani Foundation, which supports a wide range of projects, with staff recruited from their ranks and given a genuine stake in the success of the business – which accounts for the supremely friendly, attentive and efficient service found throughout the hotel. Rooms are spacious and superbly equipped, overlooking a central garden courtyard with big pool, and there's also an excellent restaurant and spa. $260

Victoria Angkor Central Park, west side of the Royal Gardens ☎063 760428, ⓦvictoriahotels-asia.com; map p.139. Rivalling the *Raffles Grand Hotel d'Angkor* for period atmosphere, and at roughly half the price. The extensive facilities include a choice of restaurants, the lovely *L'Explorateur* bar (see p.152), spa, sauna, boutique and a gorgeous pool swathed in greenery. Airport transfers and Angkor trips in the hotel's pair of vintage Citroens are also available if you fancy splashing out $250 for a day's touring around the temples. $200

EAST OF THE RIVER
SOUTH OF SAMDECH TEP VONG STREET
★**Angkor Village** Street 26, off Wat Bo St ☎063 963361, ⓦangkorvillage.com; map p.139. Idyllic "village resort", much copied, but rarely bettered. Accommodation is in Khmer-style wooden bungalows dotted around lush gardens and enveloped in greenery, like a miniature – but very luxurious – Cambodian village right in the heart of the city. Facilities include a pool and classy restaurant. $95

The Backpacker Hostel 7 Makara ☎012 313239, ⓦangkorbackpacker.com; map p.139. One of Siem Reap's cheapest sleeps, with beds on top of the five-storey

3

3

building under a rooftop awning, like a semi-outdoor dorm. It's pretty basic (and at the top of many steps) although the beds themselves are comfortable, and come with nets. Also has an average selection of spacious but rather bare rooms. Dorm $3; fan $10; a/c $15

Golden Banana Boutique Resort Phum Wat Damnak ☎063 766655, ☻goldenbanana.info/theresort; map p.139. Peaceful little hideaway (not to be confused with the adjacent *Golden Banana or Golden Banana Boutique Villa*), which is more boutique guesthouse than resort, with cool bungalows decorated in chic modern Asian style around an inviting pool. Breakfast included. $91

Golden Temple 7 Makara ☎012 756655, ☻goldentemplehotel.com; map p.139. Deservedly popular little resort hotel – not to be confused with *Golden Temple Villa* near Artisans d'Angkor – in an ersatz Khmer-style building set around attractive gardens and a good-sized pool complete with fancy fountain. The bright, colourfully furnished rooms have four-poster beds and balconies, and there's also a spa, attractive restaurant and cookery classes ($10). $80

Karavansara Retreat Street 25 ☎063 760678, ☻karavansara.com; map p.139. Attractively renovated French colonial villa with a range of well-equipped rooms: choose between the slightly austere Garden Courtyard Rooms and the fancier Colonial Heritage Suites. Facilities include a small rooftop pool, plus the upmarket *Taberu* restaurant set in a traditional Khmer wooden house in the garden. $89

★**Sala Lodges** South of the centre ☎089 321733, ☻salalodges.com; map p.139. Stunning boutique resort with accommodation in eleven genuine Khmer wooden village houses, sourced from locations around the region and then dismantled, shipped to Siem Reap and painstakingly reassembled in situ. Each has been luxuriously renovated, offering a remarkable combination of bespoke luxury and authentic Khmer atmosphere. The result is unlike anything else in the country, like some fairy-tale rural village, surrounded by attractive gardens with a lovely infinity pool at its centre. Facilities include a chic café in the soaring reception building (a work of art in its own right), and rates include airport transfer, breakfast, free bikes and tuk-tuk. Pricey, but memorable – and rates fall significantly during low season. $257

Shadow of Angkor II Wat Bo St ☎063 760363, ☻shadowofangkor.com; map p.139. Well-run and competitively priced modern hotel with pool, restaurant and spacious a/c rooms, some kitted out with traditional Khmer wood furniture. $20

Siem Reap Hostel 7 Makara ☎063 964660, ☻thesiemreaphostel.com; map p.139. Popular and well-run hostel – a lot more comfortable and stylish than your average backpacker dive, with beds in attractive dorms or well-equipped a/c rooms, plus a small spa and pool, library, pool table, yoga classes, movie screenings and

more. Basic dorms $5; deluxe dorms $6; doubles $28

Soria Moria Wat Bo St ☎063 964768, ☻thesoriamoria .com; map p.139. Siem Reap's most socially responsible hotel, established in 2007 by Norwegian expat Kristin Holdø Hansen and with majority-ownership now passed onto its staff, giving the local community a long-term stake in the success of the business. Rooms are bright and cheerful, with a hint of Scandinavian minimalist chic (superior rooms are only slightly more expensive, and significantly larger), while the attractive *Fusion Kitchen* restaurant downstairs serves a good selection of Khmer classics and international tapas – all dishes cost just $1 on Wed. Overall it's a bit expensive for what you get, but for responsible tourism in action, it can't be beaten. Breakfast included. $55

Viroth's Hotel Street 23 ☎063 761720, ☻viroth -hotel.com; map p.139. Super-cool boutique retreat sporting modern rooms with minimalist white decor and all mod cons, plus tranquil grounds with a spa and tiny swimming pool. $90

STREET 20 AND AROUND

Babel Off Street 20 ☎063 965474, ☻babelsiemreap .hostel.com; map p.139. Western-run guesthouse on a quiet backstreet. The large, clean rooms come with a/c and hot water (some also have bathtubs), and there's a nice restaurant and bar, with seating in the verdant hotel garden. Breakfast included. $20

European Off Street 20 ☎012 582237, ☻european -guesthouse.com; map p.139. Quiet and friendly and with large, spotless a/c rooms (all en suite with hot water) set around an attractive, shady garden. $18

Home Sweet Home Street 20 ☎063 760279, ☻homesweethomeangkor.com; map p.139. Family-run guesthouse. Rooms come with either fan and cold water or a/c and hot – decent value, although some of the rooms could do with a bit of TLC. Fan $10; a/c $15

Mom's Wat Bo St ☎012 630170, ☻momguesthouse .com; map p.139. Long-running place, more of a hotel now than a guesthouse, but still owned by the same friendly family. Rooms (all en suite with hot water, a/c, safe and fridge) are spacious, spotless and attractively furnished, and there's also a nice little pool. Breakfast included. $22

Mother Home Street 20 ☎063 760402, ☻mother home.motherhomeguesthouse.com; map p.139. Despite the name this is actually a hotel, with spacious, modern a/c rooms, competitively priced, and welcoming staff. Nothing out of the ordinary, but what it does it does very well. $23

★**La Résidence d'Angkor** Achasvar St ☎063 963390, ☻residencedangkor.com; map p.139. Top-notch establishment with sympathetically designed accommodation making the best use of local materials. All rooms are luxuriously appointed with teak furniture, Khmer cotton and silk furnishings, and bamboo screens to mask the massive free-form bathtubs. Facilities include restaurant, bar, spa, gym and swimming pool fed by water bubbling from a lion and a linga. **$450**

★**Two Dragons** Street 20 ☏063 965107, ⓦtwodragons-asia.com; map p.139. Well-run guesthouse, popular with local expats, and with a real home-from-home feel. The spacious and attractively furnished rooms come with a/c, hot water and cable TV, and there's a small restaurant out front serving a good range of Thai, Khmer and Western food. **$15**

NORTH OF NR6

Angkor Village Resort Apsara Rd ☏063 963361, ⓦangkorvillage.com; map p.139. Luxurious, supersized version of the *Angkor Village hotel* (see p.147), with beautifully equipped cottages scattered around luxuriant gardens and a 200m-long, river-shaped swimming pool. Deluxe **$130**; cottage **$150**

Borann l'Auberge des Temples North of NR6 ☏063 964740, ⓦborann.com; map p.139. Intimate lodge with just twenty rooms in five bungalows spread around extensive gardens stuffed with trees and shrubs. Rooms are beautifully designed with traditional Khmer styling (but no TVs – which adds to the general sense of peace), and there's a big pool and decent restaurant. **$59**

Heritage Suites Near Wat Po Lanka, 500m north of NR6 ☏063 969100, ⓦheritagesuiteshotel.com; map p.139. Secluded, luxurious Relais & Chateaux hotel with rooms and suites in a mix of colonial and contemporary styles (some with their own private gardens, including open-air shower or jacuzzi). A traditional-style wooden hall decorated with changing exhibitions houses the lounge, bar and a gallery restaurant with Western/Khmer fusion food. Swimming pool and poolside bar, spa, picnic baskets, and airport pick-up by 1962 Mercedes. **$175**

Natura Riverside Rd ☏063 763980, ⓦnaturalhotel resort.com; map p.139. Seductive little riverside boutique resort. Nature is very much to the fore (as the name suggests), with cool minimalist white buildings set around a small garden and half-swallowed by the surrounding trees. Rooms are spacious and well equipped, and there's a saltwater pool and restaurant. Rates include breakfast and airport pick-up. **$110**

La Noria River Rd ☏063 964242, ⓦlanoriaangkor .com; map p.139. Suave boutique resort, with neat

bungalows dotted around a lush garden and swimming pool. Rooms are decorated in a mix of cool minimalist whites and colourful Khmer fabrics, while regular shadow-puppet shows (see p.153) are held in the rustic garden restaurant. **$49**

★**Pavillon d'Orient** Road 60 ☏098 655738, ⓦpavillon-orient-hotel.com; map pp.160–161. Lovely place evoking the classic era of Cambodian travel in the 1920s and 1930s. Rooms are in four "mansions" scattered around a beautiful garden, decorated in a mix of colonial and Khmer style, with polished wooden floors and traditional fabrics. Facilities include two saltwater pools, spa and open-air restaurant. Rates include free use of a tuk-tuk throughout your stay. **$105**

AIRPORT ROAD

★**Bou Savy** Off Airport Rd ☏063 964967, ⓦbousavyguesthouse.com; map p.139. Excellent – despite the inconvenient location – family-run guesthouse, particularly popular with volunteers and long-staying guests thanks to its homely atmosphere. There's a mix of rooms (all en suite with hot water and fridge) spread over two buildings, so you might want to have a look at a few before you choose, and the sociable plant-strewn courtyard café is a nice place to hang. Advance bookings recommended. Breakfast included. Fan **$12**; a/c **$18**

La Maison d'Angkor 71 Airport Rd, south side ☏063 965045, ⓦlamaisondangkor.com; map pp.160–161. Relaxing boutique hotel with bungalows dotted around palm-studded gardens. Rooms are attractively decorated in smooth, modern Asian style with local fabrics, traditional artefacts and wooden furniture. Facilities include a big pool, spa, library and restaurant. The only minus is the inconvenient (unless you're arriving/leaving by plane) location. **$105**

AROUND SIEM REAP

Sojourn Treak Vilage Rd, Treak village, around 4km south of town ☏012 923437, ⓦsojournsiemreap.com; map pp.160–161. Idyllic country resort in peaceful countryside. There are just ten rooms, set in villas around a small pool and decorated in cool, modern Asian style with all mod cons (some also have outdoor showers). Facilities include the cool Origins spa and attractive open-air thatched restaurant. Rates include breakfast and transfer to airport/port/bus station. **$120**

EATING

There's an astonishing number of places to eat in Siem Reap – you could stay a year and still not devour everything the city has to offer. As you'd expect, pride of place goes to **Khmer** cuisine, ranging from inexpensive cafés serving homely versions of local classics through to numerous more upmarket places offering innovative modern takes on the national cuisine, often with a fine-dining twist. There's plenty of **Western** food too – although much of what's on offer is pretty stereotypical – as well as some good places specializing in **Chinese**, **Indian**, **Vietnamese** and **Mexican** cooking (although surprisingly little in the way of Thai food). There's also a burgeoning **coffee-house** scene, with sociable Western-style hangouts mushrooming across the city, serving up top-notch blends, and often good food as well.

PSAR CHAS AND AROUND

AHA The Passage ☎063 965501, ⓦshintamani.com; map p.140. One of the hippest restaurants in town, with urban-chic decor and excellent Khmer and contemporary Asian food with an international twist (mains $7–10). Or just come for a drink and a plate of international tapas. Daily 11.30am–9.30pm.

Angkor Palm Hospital St ☎063 761436, ⓦangkorpalm.com; map p.140. Smart-looking but budget-friendly restaurant offering an above-average selection of authentic Khmer cooking – although you'll have to get the waiters to explain what's in some of the more recondite dishes. Try the *amok* or the *samlor* curry, an explosion of lemongrass flavours in a rustic clay pot. Mains cost just $3.50–5, although rice will set you back an extra $2. Daily 9am–10.30pm.

The Blue Pumpkin Hospital St; map p.140. The original branch of this hugely popular café-cum-bakery (now with outlets all round town). Construct your own snack or picnic from a wide selection of freshly baked breads, sandwiches, cakes, shakes and ice creams – and there's even a fair selection of alcoholic beverages, served in the snowy-white "Cool Lounge" upstairs. A second branch is located nearby on Sivatha Blvd. Daily 6am–11pm.

Chanrey Tree Pokombor Ave ☎063 767997, ⓦchanreytree.com; map p.140. Suave and romantic modern riverside restaurant whose short menu of excellent and authentic Khmer dishes (mains $8–9) has a touch of fine-dining style. Choose from classic curries and stir-fries or more unusual offerings including grilled stuffed frog or fermented fish and pork. Daily 11am–2.30pm & 6–10.30pm.

Common Grounds Street 14 ☎063 965687; map p.139. Laidback and usually very peaceful coffee shop on a quiet street in the old French quarter serving good hot drinks plus fresh cakes, sandwiches and light meals ($3.50–6). Profits go to support humanitarian projects. Mon–Sat 7am–8pm.

Dakshin's Hospital St ☎012 566610; map p.140. This smooth new place is a cut above the many other slightly ropey Indian establishments around town. The menu features a good range of north Indian meat ($7–8) and veg ($5–6) classics – tandooris, birianis, kormas and so on – plus a few south Indian dishes including dosas and uttapam, all served in big portions, richly spiced. Pricey, but worth it. Daily 11am–2.30pm & 5–10.30pm.

For Life The Lane ☎012 545426, ⓦforliferestaurant .com; map p.140. A local expat favourite, slightly away from the tourist crowds and serving excellent, authentic Khmer food at very competitive prices, with almost everything for $4 (including rice) or under. Daily 11am–11pm.

Le Grand Café Cnr Hospital St & Street 9 ☎012 447316, ⓦlegrandcafe.asia; map p.140. This restored French-colonial building is full of period atmosphere, with streetside seating downstairs and an attractive open-air first floor. Food doesn't quite match the setting, sadly, with an uninspiring and rather pricey menu of Asian ($4–7) and Western ($7–10) dishes, including pizzas and pasta. Worth a visit for a coffee or an ice cream, though, for the ambience alone. Daily 7am–11pm.

Happy Herbs Pizza Hospital St ☎092 459525; map p.140. One-stop backpackers' café with a menu as long as your arm featuring good breakfasts, myriad Khmer dishes ($3.50) and some of the best pizza in town ($6.50). Daily 7.30am–9pm.

Haven Sok San St ☎078 342404, ⓦhavencambodia .com; map p.140. Peaceful Swiss-run restaurant tucked away on a quiet(ish) side street and helping to train up disadvantaged local kids. Food features well-prepared and -presented Khmer and Asian classics ($5–6) plus a small but judicious selection of Western dishes ($6–7) including good vegetarian and a couple of Swiss options. Booking is usually essential, although you might get lucky at lunch during the low season. Mon, Tues & Thurs–Sat 11.30am–2.30pm (last orders) & 5.30–9.30pm (last orders), Wed 5.30–9.30pm.

Il Forno Between The Lane & Pub St ☎078 208174, ⓦilfornorestaurantsiemreap.com; map p.140. In the buzzing heart of the Psar Chas tourist zone, this stylish modern Italian restaurant feels more like a busy corner of Milan, London or New York than anything remotely Cambodian – as do the prices. The menu features superb pizzas straight out of the Neapolitan wood-fired oven, excellent home-made pasta and top-notch mains using quality ingredients (black ink *tagliolini* with prawns and zucchini, for example, or black and white ravioli with calamari *ragù*). Pizza and pasta $4–10, mains $12–18. Daily noon–11pm.

Khmer Kitchen The Passage ☎063 966353, ⓦkhmerkitchens.com; map p.140. Inexpensive, family-run restaurant that provides great authentic Khmer home-cooking with the occasional modern twist, plus a few Thai dishes. All mains $4 (including rice). Daily 10.30am–11pm.

Miss Wong The Lane ☎092 428332, ⓦmisswong.net; map p.140. Svelte little venue, with opulent 1930s Shanghai-style decor, all moody lighting and rich-red walls. It bills itself as a cocktail bar (see p.153) but also has a short but excellent selection of classy contemporary Chinese food ($3.50–6.50), with mains including wine-flavoured chicken thigh and tea-smoked tofu pockets with mushroom stuffing, plus dumplings, hotpots, noodles and wonton. Daily 6pm–1am.

New Leaf Book Café Off Pokombor Ave ☎063 766016, ⓦnewleafbookcafe.org; map p.140. Good-looking and sociable café – one of the centre's nicest places to hang out while browsing the extensive selection of secondhand

COOKERY CLASSES

Taking a **cookery course** offers a great way to learn more about Cambodian cuisine. Classes typically last around three hours, starting with a visit to a local market to buy ingredients, after which you get into the kitchen and start cooking under the guidance of a trained chef, finishing off by eating the meal you've just prepared.

Asana Cambodian House Between St 7 & The Lane ☎ 092 987801, ⓦ asana-cambodia.com. Learn to create your own Khmer-style cocktails at the lovely little *Asana* bar (see p.152), with an introduction to the use of local herbs and spices, and to *sombai*, a classic Cambodian tipple made with infused rice wine. $15.

Beyond Unique Escapes Cnr Alley West & Sivatha Blvd ☎ 077 562565, ⓦ beyonduniqueescapes.com. Cooking classes (twice daily) with a difference, held just outside town and swapping the usual market visit for a walk through a rural village to see local food production at first hand and the chance to meet a village family and learn about Khmer cooking in a Cambodian home – after which you head to Beyond's purpose-built cooking pavilion in the village to have a go yourself. $22 half-day, $35 full day.

Cooks in Tuk-tuks The River Garden, river road, north of NR6, west of the river ☎ 063 963400, ⓦ therivergarden.info. Classes at this lovely hotel

(see p.147) start with the obligatory market visit, before cooking up a lunchtime feast with the produce you've purchased. $25.

Royal Khmer Cuisine Raffles Grand Hotel d'Angkor, Royal Gardens ☎ 063 963888, ⓦ raffles.com /siemreap. The most exclusive (and spectacularly expensive) course in town, held at this grand hotel (see p.147). After a market visit with the chef, you'll learn about ingredients and how to combine them, before cooking a number of dishes that are served at lunch with a complimentary glass of wine. A cookbook, certificate and *Raffles* apron complete the day. $100.

Le Tigre de Papier Pub St, next to Angkor What? (see p.152) ☎ 012 265811. The original Siem Reap cooking class, running since 2003 at this Pub Street restaurant. Classes include a market visit to buy ingredients for a three-course meal that you prepare and eat; proceeds help support students at nearby Sala Bai Hotel School. $14.

3

books for sale. Good coffee and drinks, including local *sombai* (rice wine infused with fruits and spices), plus the usual café food and a few Khmer and Western mains ($4–7). Try the delicious iced coffee and the simple but very satisfying Khmer chicken rice. All profits go to support local causes. Daily 7am–9.30pm.

Soup Dragon Hospital St ☎ 012 731152; map p.140. Popular restaurant spread over three floors of a street-corner building, with great views of the crowds below. The food's not bad either, with a mainly Vietnamese menu (mains $4–6) featuring classics such as *bánh xèo* (rice pancakes), *pho*, hotpots, soups, stir-fries and spicy salads, plus a few Khmer and Western dishes. Service can be excruciatingly slow. Daily 7am–11pm.

Viva Hospital St ☎ 092 209154, ⓦ ivivasiemreap.com; map p.140. Wildly popular Mexican restaurant serving tasty cover versions of all the usual Tex-Mex classics (around $5) including quesadillas, nachos, enchiladas, tacos and burritos galore. The restaurant's signature margaritas are cheap and go down fast – as do many of the punters come closing time. Daily 6am–midnight.

TAPHUL STREET

Sala Bai Taphul St ☎ 063 963329; map p.139. Hospitality school that opens to customers for training purposes; the inexpensive, daily-changing menu features a mix of Western and Khmer dishes according to what

students are learning to cook (lunch set menus $9/$11). Reservations advised, and note that the school may close during the summer. Mon–Fri 7–9am & noon–2pm.

★**Sugar Palm** Taphul St ☎ 012 818143, ⓦ thesugarpalm.com; map p.139. Attractively rustic pavilion restaurant under a huge wooden house – perfect for a romantic candlelit dinner. The menu focuses on authentic Khmer food with a short but inventive selection of dishes (mains $6–7) – frogs' legs with basil, for example, or squid with black Kampot pepper, plus flavoursome pomelo and green mango salads. Mon–Sat 11.30am–3pm & 5.30–10pm.

THE ROYAL GARDENS AND AROUND

FCC Angkor Pokambor Ave ☎ 063 760280, ⓦ fcc cambodia.com; map p.139. Siem Reap's branch of the *FCC* in Phnom Penh provides a memorable setting for top-notch Western and Asian food (mains around $8) – or just come for a drink at the attractive terrace bar. Daily 7am–midnight (bar open from 5pm).

Restaurant Le Grand Raffles Grand Hotel d'Angkor ☎ 063 963888, ⓦ raffles.com/siem-reap; map p.139. The swankiest restaurant in town, with a fine à la carte menu of Khmer and international dishes (mains around $30) backed up with a fine wine cellar and impeccable service. Booking is advised and the dress code is smart casual. Daily 6.30am–10.30pm.

3

EAST OF THE RIVER

Butterflies Garden Street 25 ☎063 761211, ⓦbutterfliesofangkor.com; map p.139. Tranquil garden café with colourful butterflies (bought from local children and released every few days) flitting between the tables. The menu features the usual Khmer ($4–5) and Western ($5–8) mains – the quality's pretty good, although service can be a bit hit-and-miss. Daily 8am–11pm.

★**Cuisine Wat Damnak** South of the centre ☎077 347762, ⓦcuisinewatdamnak.com; map p.139. Set in a romantic traditional Cambodian house and garden, this is the place to experience Khmer cuisine at its finest, using fresh, local seasonal produce given a fine-dining makeover by French head chef Joannès Rivière. The five- and six-course tasting menus ($22/$26) feature all sorts of local delicacies, memorably prepared and presented – steamed Mekong langoustine; braised pork shank with star anise and caramelized palm sugar; chocolate and holy basil ganache with rice praline; and so on. Reservations strongly advised. Tues–Sat 6.30–9.30pm (last orders).

Kanell 7 Makara ☎063 966244, ⓦkanellrestaurant.com; map p.139. Chilled-out garden restaurant, with tables set out under thatched pavilions amid lush tropical greenery and a good selection of Khmer and Western food (mains $5–8), plus a small pool (free if you spend $5 in the restaurant). Daily 9am–10pm.

L'Oasi Italiana River Rd, east of the river, 2km north of NR6 ☎092 418917, ⓦoasiitaliana.com; map p.139. A fair schlep north of town, but worth it for the excellent Italian cuisine, with handmade pasta, pizza, meats, cheeses and breads made in-house under the supervision of the resident Tuscan chef, and served in the attractive garden at tables set out under thatched pavilions. Mains $7–13. Daily 11am–11pm.

Peace Café Street 26 ☎092 177127, ⓦpeacecafeangkor.org; map p.139. Rustic garden vegetarian café serving up a good range of Western snacks, salads and light meals (around $4) plus cheaper Asian mains and various breakfasts. Also organizes regular yoga, meditation and "monk chat" sessions (see p.145). Daily 7am–9pm.

★**Tangram Garden** South of the centre ☎097 726111, ⓦtangramgarden.com; map p.139. This relaxed garden restaurant is just a short walk south of town but feels surprisingly peaceful and rural, especially after dark. The small but perfectly formed menu (mains $7–8) features a mix of good-value Western charcoal-grilled dishes (pork ribs, genuine New Zealand steaks and so on) alongside traditional Khmer dishes given a modern twist – tilapia with eggplant and tamarind cream, for instance, or shrimp kebab with aioli. Good vegetarian selection, too. Daily except Tues: mid-Oct to mid-April 11.30am–2.30pm & 5.30–10pm; mid-April to mid-Oct 5.30–10pm.

Viroth's Wat Bo St ☎012 826346; map p.139. Upmarket open-air restaurant serving inventive Asian cuisine, including lots of pork, fish and seafood dishes, plus interesting salads and soups – banana blossom salad, sour squid soup and so on. The green papaya salad and the pork with lemongrass (*laab*) both come recommended. Mains $5–6. Daily 10.30am–2pm & 5.30–10pm.

DRINKING

There's a hangover-inducing glut of **places to drink** in Siem Reap. Much of the city's drinking and nightlife is fairly down-at-heel – epitomized by the raucous, wall-to-wall drinking holes lined up along Pub Street, although more characterful and laidback bars can also be found here. Booze is cheap (and regular happy hours make things even cheaper) – draught beer (usually Angkor) is widely available at $1 a glass (sometimes even less) and cocktails usually go for just a few dollars. It's also worth trying some of the more unusual Asian-style cocktails available at places like *Asana* and *Miss Wong*, as well as *sombai* (made using rice wine infused with herbs and spices, available at *Asana*, the *New Leaf Book Café* and elsewhere).

Angkor What? Pub St ☎012 731152; map p.140. "Promoting irresponsible drinking since 1998", *Angkor What?* is the dark heart of the raucous Pub Street scene – a grungy, graffiti-covered Black Hole of Siem Reap into which crazed punters insert themselves nightly in search of cheap beer, loud music and members of the opposite sex. Daily 4pm–3am.

★**Asana** Between St 7 & The Lane ☎092 987801, ⓦasana-cambodia.com; map p.140. Occupying the last surviving wooden house in central Siem Reap, *Asana* is what a traditional Cambodian village house would look like if you put a chic urban bar inside it. Piles of rice and flour sacks double as seats upstairs, while downstairs there's a swinging hammock-bed to lounge in. Slightly above-average prices, but well worth it, particularly for the moreish *sombai* and Asian-style cocktails. Daily 11am–midnight or later.

L'Explorateur Bar Victoria Angkor hotel; map p.139. Siem Reap's most enjoyable colonial-style bar, and the perfect place for cocktails or an after-dinner coffee or *digestif*, either in the period-style a/c interior or on the sultry terrace. Not as pricey as you might expect (beers and coffee $3, cocktails $7), especially during the daily happy hour (5–7pm). Daily 7am–11.30pm.

Island Bar Angkor Night Market; map p.139. Relaxed bar at the heart of the Angkor Night Market – it feels a bit like sitting inside an enormous bamboo hat. Cheap draught beer and a pumping soundtrack tick all the right boxes – order a cocktail (just $3) and the resident mixologists might even twirl a bottle or two. Daily 4pm–midnight.

Laundry Bar Northwest of Psar Chas ☎012 301743; map p.140. The battered old brown-leather sofas aren't exactly cutting-edge chic, and the atmosphere can sometimes be sleepy going on moribund, but the long-running *Laundry* remains a nice place for a cosy quiet drink and a game of pool – while things liven up considerably during the regular live music sessions. Daily 4pm–2/3am.

Linga Bar The Passage ☎012 246912; map p.140. Pint-sized gay-friendly bar serving great cocktails and hosting Siem Reap's only drag show every Wed and Sat at 10.30. Daily 4pm–1am.

★**Miss Wong** The Lane ☎092 428332, ⓦmisswong .net; map p.140. Alluring little retro-Shanghai-style bar – one of central Siem Reap's most enjoyable places to linger of an evening. The excellent cocktails (around $5) come with a pronounced Asian twist – Singapore slings, lemongrass Collins, apricot and kaffir lime martinis and so on – and there's excellent food too (see p.150). Daily 6pm–1am.

Red Piano Pub St ☎063 964750; map p.140. One of Pub Street's more civilized drinking spots, especially if you can bag one of the coveted streetside wicker armchairs. The good drinks list includes lots of Belgian beers (Duvel, Hoegaarden, Chimay and Leffe), or try the "Tomb Raider" cocktail – still going strong after more than a decade. Daily 7am–midnight.

The Station Wine Bar Street 7 ☎097 850 4043, ⓦthestationwinebarsiemreap.com; map p.140. Chic, very gay-friendly modern wine bar offering an unrivalled selection of wines by the glass (from $3.50) and bottle, plus numerous other tipples. Also hosts regular cabaret, drag and talent shows. Daily 4pm–late.

The Warehouse Hospital St; map p.140. Relaxed two-storey bar, usually lively without being rammed (and there's plenty of space – and good street views – from upstairs if downstairs is full). Pool table and live sports on TV. Daily 9am–2pm.

X Bar Sivatha Blvd; map p.140. Grungy rooftop bar that pounds out hard rock and heavy metal until late, with live bands on Wed and Fri at around 9pm and a DJ most other nights, plus a big-screen TV showing live sports. Daily 2pm–3/4am.

NIGHTLIFE AND ENTERTAINMENT

The city is a prime place to experience traditional Cambodian arts, including **shadow puppetry** and **apsara dancing**, while the stomach-churning acrobatics performed at the intimate Phare **circus** are also well worth a look.

CULTURAL AND SHADOW PUPPET SHOWS

A number of hotels around town offer traditional dance performances as part of a cultural show (dinner included). These usually feature several different styles including apsara dance, lighthearted items depicting popular folk tales, and choreographed enacted events from the *Reamker*, with dancers opulently attired in elaborate masks and costumes heavily embroidered and embellished with tails, epaulettes and wings. You will also have the opportunity to catch shadow puppetry (see box, p.155), a Cambodian folk art dating back to Angkorian times that was all but lost during the Khmer Rouge era but has since been revived.

Acodo Orphanage 1km south of the centre along the riverside road towards Chong Khneas. Nightly performances (6.30pm) of traditional music and dance by local orphans. Free, but donations appreciated.

Apsara Terrace Raffles Grand Hotel d'Angkor, Royal Gardens ☎063 963888, ⓦraffles.com/siemreap. Pricey but memorable nightly dancing shows ($50, including pan-Asian BBQ buffet dinner) at the famous old *Raffles Grand Hotel d'Angkor* (see p.147). Mon, Wed & Fri 7pm.

Apsara Theatre Contact the Angkor Village hotel (see p.147) for information and reservations. Nightly dance performances ($25, including dinner) at the a/c Apsara Theatre, opposite the *Angkor Village* hotel.

La Noria River Rd ☎063 964242, ⓦlanoriaangkor .com. Entertaining shadow-puppet shows by street children staged over dinner at this hotel (see p.149) every Wed evening. Only a few puppets are used at each performance, changes of character being effected by dressing them in different *kramas*. $7, plus whatever food you order from the restaurant's à la carte menu.

Temple Bar Pub St ☎092 405760. Ever-popular nightly apsara dance shows held on the upstairs balcony of this long-running Pub Street bar. Around 7.30pm; free.

CIRCUS

Phare Comaille Rd (opposite Angkor Century Resort, behind the Angkor National Museum) ☎015 499480, ⓦpharecambodiancircus.org. Developed by the Phare Ponleu Selpak NGO (ⓦphareps.org) as part of their work with vulnerable Cambodian children and young adults, the Phare circus has proved a massive success both locally and internationally, with the troupe now touring regularly to destinations including Korea, Japan and India. Performances in the intimate big-top tent feature regularly changing shows and casts, comprising a mixture of slapstick narrative theatre and spectacular feats of acrobatics – performers train for thirteen years before graduating from the circus school, and to witness displays of such gymnastic virtuosity at such close quarters (with performers flipped, spun, tossed and catapulted with prodigious abandon) is a memorable, if sometimes nerve-wracking, experience. Nightly 7.30pm; $15, children 5–11 $8, under-5s free.

3

APSARA DANCE

No visit to Cambodia is complete without at least a quick glimpse of women performing the ancient art of **apsara dance**, as depicted on the walls of Angkor's temples. Wearing glittering silk tunics, sequinned tops (into which they are sewn before each performance to achieve the requisite tight fit) and elaborate golden headdresses, performers execute their movements with deftness and deliberation, knees bent in plié, heels touching the floor first at each step, coy smiles on their faces. Every position has its own particular **symbolism** – a finger pointing to the sky, for instance, indicates "today", while standing sideways to the audience with the sole of the foot facing upwards represents flying.

In the reign of Jayavarman VII there were more than three thousand apsara dancers at court – although dances were performed exclusively for the king, and so prized was their skill that when the Thais sacked Angkor in the fifteenth century, they took a troupe of dancers back home with them. Historically, the art form was taught only at the **royal court**, but so few exponents survived the ravages of the Khmer Rouge that the genre was very nearly extinguished. Subsequently, when Princess Boppha Devi – who had been a principal dancer with the royal troupe – wished to revive it, she found it helpful to study temple panels to establish the movements. It was not until 1995, a full sixteen years after the fall of the Khmer Rouge, that Cambodians once again witnessed a public performance of apsara dance, at Angkor Wat.

These days, the **Royal University of Fine Arts** in Phnom Penh takes much of the responsibility for training dancers, who are chosen not only for aptitude and youth (they start as young as 7), but for the flexibility and elegance of their hands. It takes six years for students to learn the 1500 intricate positions, and a further three to six years for them to attain the required level of artistic maturity. Also taught is the other principal Cambodian dance genre, *tontay*, in which the emphasis is on depicting folk tales and episodes from the *Reamker*. You'll be able to watch both styles of Cambodian dance in the cultural performances put on by hotels and restaurants in Siem Reap and Phnom Penh.

SHOPPING

Shopping in Siem Reap is second only to the capital for variety and quality, and in some ways it's much easier to shop here since the outlets are much closer together. The city abounds in inexpensive souvenir stalls selling all manner of goods, including T-shirts, silk tops and trousers, and traditional Khmer **sampots** in Western sizes (although note that many of the textiles here, such as the fabric used to make the cotton **sarongs** with elephant motifs, are imported from Indonesia).

MARKETS

Angkor Night Market Off Sivatha Blvd; map p.139. There's some supprisingly good shopping tucked away inside this touristy night market (once you've fought your way past Siem Reap's pushiest massage girls on the approach road). Right at the back (just to the right of the *Island Bar* by the ABA Bank ATM) an unsigned and apparently nameless shop sells a vast selection of quality handmade cotton and silk *kramas* (from $4) including many designs you won't see on factory-made pieces. Heading right around the back of the market from here brings you to the small Nabren Leather Carving Handicraft shop, selling interesting cowskin leather shadow puppets. Alternatively, head to the right around the back of the *Island Bar* to reach the Khmer Boutique (☎012 345677), selling museum-quality Buddhist and other authentic religious and other Khmer artefacts. Directly opposite there's another good *krama* shop, with demonstration loom. Most stalls 5/6–10/11pm.

Psar Chas (Old Market) By the river; map p.140. Siem Reap's main market. The town-facing side of the market is geared more towards locals (including a big fresh produce section where you can pick up inexpensive spice packets). Things become increasingly touristy as you head towards the river, where you'll find dozens of little stalls heaped with huge piles of cheap (mainly factory-made) cotton and silk *kramas*, *sampots*, pashminas and other items of clothing (including the ubiquitous elephant-motif skirts and trousers), along with stalls selling silver, paintings, carvings and fun bags made from recycled rice sacks, food packaging and so on. Daily 10am–10pm.

Siem Reap Art Center Night Market East of the river opposite Psar Chas; map p.139. Smart new market filled with handicrafts shops. Much of the stuff is similar to that found in Psar Chas and the Angkor Night Market, although there are also some more upmarket stalls selling superior carvings and jewellery.

CRAFT SHOPS AND GALLERIES

Artisans d'Angkor West off the southern end of Sivatha Blvd ☎063 963330, ⓦartisansdangkor.com;

map p.139. The retail outlet of the Artisans d'Angkor (see p.141) sells an outstanding collection of premium-quality goods, including glossy lacquer-work, exquisite carvings, stunning fabrics and garments from their silk workshops at Puok. Prices are higher than anywhere else in the city, but the quality can't be beaten. Daily 7.30am–6.30pm.

Bambou Indochine Alley West; Lucky Mall; Street 11 (near Red Piano); Siem Riep Airport; ☎063 966823, ⓦbambouindochine.com; map p.139 & p.140. Countrywide boutique selling colourful original clothing for women, men and children in a range of cotton, silk, linen and bamboo fabrics. Daily 9am–10pm.

LHA Sewing School Wat Damnak, just south of the centre ☎069 301562, ⓦlifeandhopeangkor.org; map p.139. In the grounds of Wat Damnak, this NGO sewing school offers a range of ready-made clothes and other items, and is a good place to get tailor-made garments made up. Pieces can be tailored in just a day. Bring in an existing item of clothing you want copied, ask for ideas to make something from scratch or just sketch out your own designs – staff will even take you to local markets to select fabrics. You can also have your own T-shirts individually printed in the school's silk-screen workshop. All profits go to supporting the school and other local initiatives. Mon–Fri 7am–5pm.

McDermott Gallery The Passage, Psar Chas; FCC Complex, Pokambor Ave; Raffles Grand Hotel d'Angkor; ⓦmcdermottgallery.com; map p.139 & p.140. Three upmarket galleries showcasing the spectacular Angkor photographs of acclaimed American photographer (and Siem Reap resident) John McDermott, with their magical infrared film effects. The Psar Chas gallery also shows works with an Asian theme by other leading photographers. Psar Chas: daily 9am–10pm; FCC: daily 10am–10pm; Raffles: daily 8am–10pm.

Mekong Quilts Sivatha Blvd ☎063 964498, ⓦmekong-quilts.org; map p.140. Colourful – albeit bulky – quilts, plus fun toys, bags, purses, pillowcases and so on, many in quirky, child-friendly designs. Shipping available. Daily 8am–10pm.

Rajana Sivatha Blvd ☎012 917060, ⓦrajanacrafts .org; map p.140. Fair-trade organization colourful clothes,

bags, *kramas* and wall-hangings, plus attractively packaged teas and spices. Daily 8am–11pm.

Rehab Craft Pokambor Ave ☎023 726801, ⓦrehabcraftcambodia.com; map p.140. Not-for-profit organization offering a range of crafts made by Cambodians with disabilities including attractive silk *kramas* and fun bags, wallets and pencil cases made from recycled food packaging and sacks. Daily 9am–9pm.

Samatoa Hospital St ☎012 285930, ⓦsamatoa.com; map p.140. Top-quality Cambodian silk womenswear in bright colours and contemporary designs – they also offer a tailoring service and can copy clothes if you take them in (24hr turnaround). Samatoa are also pioneering a remarkable new lotus cloth, made from fibres taken from the stems of lotus flowers: a linen-like fabric that is naturally quick drying and stain-repellent. Given that it takes around 6000 flowers to make 1m of fabric, and with individual pieces retailing for thousands of dollars, the market is likely to remain something of a niche. Visitors are welcome to watch the production process at the shop's lotus farm (ⓦlotusfarm.org) in Phnom Krom village, 8km south of town. Daily 8am–11pm.

Senteurs d'Angkor Hospital St ☎012 954815; map p.140. French chic is combined with the imaginative use of traditional Khmer materials to produce original (albeit pricey) products including carvings, candles, soaps and flavoured teas. You can also visit their workshops (free), on the south side of NR6 about 1.5km from town. Daily 7am–10.30pm.

Spicy Green Mango Branches on Alley West & The Lane ☎078 589673, ⓦspicygreenmango.com; map p.140. Affordable and attractive boutique clothing, all made in Cambodia – mainly womenswear (including funky dresses and fun T-shirts) plus a few token shirts for blokes. Daily 10am–10pm.

BOOKS

Blue Apsara Street 9 ☎012 601483; map p.140. Siem Reap's longest-running Western bookshop, with a good selection of fiction and local guides. Daily 9am–10pm.

D's Books Hospital St ☎012 262404; map p.140. Extensive range of secondhand books – mainly fiction, plus

---

SHADOW PUPPETS

Shadow puppets are made of stretched, dried cowhide, the required outline drawn freehand onto the leather and pared out, after which holes are carefully punched in designated areas to allow back light (traditionally from a burning coconut shell) to shine through onto a plain screen. Once cut and punched, the figures are painstakingly **painted** using natural black and red dyes under the strict supervision of the puppet master. Two sorts of puppet are produced: *sbaek thom* and *sbaek toich* (literally "large skin" and "small skin"). The *sbaek thom*, used to tell stories from the *Reamker*, are the larger of the two, around 1–2m tall, and lack moving parts. By contrast, *sbaek toich* puppets have moveable arms and legs, and are commonly used to tell folk tales and stories of everyday life, usually humorous and with a moral ending. Both types are manipulated from below using sticks attached to strategic points.

a smattering of travel guides. Daily 10am–10pm.

Monument Books On the riverside south of Psar Chas ☎063 966450; map p.140. One of the city's best selections of Cambodia-related titles, plus a few local newspapers and international magazines. Daily 8am–10pm.

New Leaf Book Café Off Pokambor Ave ☎063 766016, ⓦ newleafbookcafe.org; map p.140. This excellent little café (see p.150) doubles as an impromptu secondhand bookshop, its walls lined with bookshelves stuffed with assorted fiction both pulp and literary. Daily 7am–9.30pm.

Siem Reap Book Centre Hospital St (between Ucare Pharma & The Blue Pumpkin) ☎012 929298; map p.140. Excellent range of books on Cambodian history, art and architecture. Daily 8.30am–11pm.

BIKES AND CYCLING EQUIPMENT

Camouflage Down the road opposite the northeast end of Pub St ☎012 884909, ⓦcamouflagecambodia .com; map p.140. Well-equipped cycling shop with various bits of kit for sale. They also do repairs, run tours (see p.145) and have rental bikes (city bike $3, mountain bike $7, both including helmet). Daily 7am–8pm.

MINIMARKETS AND SUPERMARKETS

Minimarkets For basic provisions, there are numerous minimarkets dotted around the centre (including a cluster of places along Sivatha Blvd roughly opposite the western end of Pub St, which seem to cater exclusively to a clientele of intoxicated Western shoppers stocking up on beer and condoms).

Supermarkets There's a well-stocked supermarket in the Angkor Trade Centre on Pokambor Ave just north of Psar Chas, or try the similar Lucky Market supermarket in the Lucky Mall at the northern end of Sivatha Blvd.

DIRECTORY

Dentists Pachem Dental Clinic, Angkor Wat Rd, just north of Angkor National Museum (☎017 300300, ⓦ pachemdental.com).

Golf There's an 18-hole course designed by Nick Faldo at the Angkor Golf Resort, 5km from town south off NR6 (ⓦ www.angkor-golf.com).

Hospitals and clinics The Royal Angkor International Hospital, NR6, 2km from the airport (☎063 761888, ⓦ royalangkorhospital.com), has some of the better medical services including call-out service, 24-hour emergency care, ambulance, translation and evacuation to Bangkok. The government-run Siem Reap Provincial Hospital, 500m north of Psar Chas (☎063 963111), is basic and to be used only as a last resort.

Internet Wi-fi is almost universally available at hotels, guesthouses, restaurants and bars. If you don't have your own machine there are numerous places with internet access around town – try the huge (but nameless) place near Psar Chas between *X Bar* and the *Haven* restaurant (24hr; 3000 riel/hr).

Laundry There are laundries all over town charging $1–2/ kg of washing; some also offer quick turnaround, which includes tumble drying (essential during the rainy season) for a bit extra.

Money There are plenty of banks and ATMs throughout Siem Reap – the Canadia Bank at the junction of Sivatha Blvd and Hospital St is particularly convenient, and commission-free.

Pharmacies The best of the town's pharmacies is Ucare Pharma. Its main branch (daily 8am–midnight; ☎012 731152), with trained, English-speaking pharmacists, is on Hospital St near *The Blue Pumpkin*; branches also at the Lucky and Angkor National Museum malls. There are also plenty of pharmacies around Psar Chas and east of the river on NR6.

Phones You can make domestic calls from the booths around the markets and international calls at the main post office on Pokambor Ave (daily 7am–5.30pm). Cheap international calls can be made at Siem Reap's internet cafés. Tourist SIM cards are available from the many mobile telephone service providers, most of whom have offices on Sivatha Blvd.

Photography You'll find a handful of photographic studios along NR6, east of the river, that stock batteries, film and so on. Most of the photo shops in town can also make prints from your SD card or CD.

Police The tourist police office is opposite the main entrance to the Angkor Archaeological Park (☎012 402424). To report sex offenders (see p.37) contact the police nationwide hotline (☎023 997919) or ChildSafe (☎012 311112).

Post and couriers The post office is on Pokambor Ave (daily 8am–5pm), where you can post parcels, collect poste restante mail and make domestic and international calls. Local couriers include DHL, at 15A Sivatha Blvd near the Central Market (☎063 964949, ⓦdhl.com).

Tonle Sap lake

Temples aside, you shouldn't leave Siem Reap without exploring the fascinating string of **lakeside villages** (both floating and stilted) on the nearby **Tonle Sap**, the massive freshwater lake that dominates the map of Cambodia. The majority of these lake's inhabitants are fishermen, mostly stateless ethnic **Vietnamese** who have been here for decades, despite being widely distrusted by the Khmer. Most live in extremely basic conditions, their livelihoods increasingly threatened by the government, which has awarded large fishing concessions to wealthy businessmen at the expense of local villagers and who now have to either practise their trade illegally or rent a share from a concessionaire.

The ever-increasing numbers of tourists visiting the Tonle Sap villages has provided an important new source of revenue, although the downside (at least from the visitor's point of view) is the steady erosion of traditional local life and increasingly theme-park atmosphere, particularly at the coach-party honeypot of **Chong Khneas**, while even formerly quieter villages down the lake such as **Kompong Phluk** and **Kompong Kleang** are no longer wholly immune. For a more authentic view of the Tonle Sap, head to the floating villages near Pursat and Kompong Chnnang on the opposite side of the lake (see p.109 & p.112).

As well as the villages, twitchers are attracted to the lake to explore the **Prek Toal Biosphere Reserve**, home to numerous species of waterbird.

Phnom Krom

Access via the steep stairway that leads up from behind the petrol station in the village at the foot of the hill

If you're heading to the lake from Siem Reap, it's worth detouring up the 137m-high hill of **Phnom Krom** to the grounds of a modern pagoda on the summit, which offers commanding **views** over the Tonle Sap from the top, particularly scenic at sunset. There's also a ruined tenth-century **temple** up here, built by Yasovarman I. The three crumbling sandstone sanctuary towers, dedicated to Vishnu (north), Shiva (centre) and Brahma (south), stand in a row on a low platform; a few carvings can still be made out, including an apsara on the north face of the north tower and a *hamsa* (sacred goose) on the south tower.

Chong Khneas

Around 18km south of Siem Reap (just offshore from the Siem Reap boat dock at Phnom Penh or Battambang you'll pass the village as you pull in to the dock) • Entrance to the village plus 90min boat trip $20/person

The closest of the lakeside villages to Siem Reap (and the one that tuk-tuk drivers are talking about when they offer to take you to "the floating village"), **CHONG KHNEAS** now pulls in regular crowds of coach parties on whistlestop tours looking for a quick taste of lakeside life after a morning at the temples. It's about as authentic as a plastic dodo, increasingly dominated by tourism and with plenty of money-grabbing hassles too, although perhaps worth a look if you can't make it to any of the more peaceful villages further around the lake. In the rainy season, when the lake floods right up to

---

TOURS OF THE TONLE SAP LAKE

There are a number of options when it comes to touring the Tonle Sap lake.

TOUR OPERATORS

Beyond Unique Escapes Cnr Alley West & Sivatha Blvd ☎077 562565, ⓦbeyonduniqueescapes.com. This operator (see p.145) offers excellent value, excellent service, guaranteed departures and small groups, with tours to Kompong Phluk (or Kompong Kleang during the height of the dry season).

Osmose Nature Tours ⓦosmosetonlesap.net. Insightful lake trips run by this local NGO (see p.145) who specialize in the Prek Toal area of the Tonle.

Tara River Boat ☎092 957765, ⓦtaraboat.com. The main tour operator for the lake, offering half-day tours ($27) on their big boat around Chong Khneas, plus sunset tours ($33) with free meal and unlimited drinks. They can also arrange trips to Kompong Phluk ($60), Kompong Kleang ($72) and Prek Toal ($125) using smaller boats. Tickets for most trips can be bought from hotels and tour operators in Siem Reap (see p.145).

3

the foot of Phnom Krom, you can get a feel for the village just by walking along the causeway; during dryer parts of the year the village is moved further out onto the lake, and you'll have to get into a boat to see it properly.

Tourism nothwithstanding, Chong Khneas remains a genuine **floating village** (see box below), with houses (most of them little better than floating shacks) built on bamboo rafts, lashed together to keep them from drifting apart and arranged on an informal kind of grid-plan, with streets of water between.

GECKO exhibition centre

Daily 8.30am–5pm • Free, but donations appreciated

Chong Khneas is home to the **GECKO exhibition centre** (Greater Environment Chong Khneas Office), an NGO whose main role is to improve the environmental awareness of the local fishing population. The small centre has exhibits on the lake's flora and fauna, and on the traditional lifestyles of the fishing communities living around it, and also offers a rare opportunity to actually get inside a floating building.

Kompong Phluk

Around 35km from Siem Reap by road (turn south off the NR6 at Roluos) • Entrance to village plus boat trips $20/person

South of Chong Khneas on the lake is **KOMPONG PHLUK** – more authentic and, for now, more relaxed than Chong Khneas, although it is embracing tourism with a will. This is a **stilted** rather than a floating village (see box below), its buildings raised upon high wooden pillars, with the lake waters lapping around their bases. At the height of the **wet season** in September water levels can rise well above 10m, completely drowning the surrounding patches of forest and sometimes flooding the buildings of the village itself. During the **dry season**, lake levels fall progressively, and between March and May the waters usually vanish completely, receding around 500m from the village and leaving its houses stranded atop their huge stilts amid an expanse of mud.

For most of the year the village is marvellously photogenic, its ramshackle wooden houses and the tops of surrounding half-drowned trees rising improbably out of the waters a kilometre or so offshore. Visiting at the height of the dry season, although less obviously picture-perfect, allows you to appreciate the buildings' remarkable architecture, with houses towering 10m or so overhead atop their platforms, like some miniature bamboo Manhattan. Living conditions are as basic as you'd imagine, although the village comes equipped with its own gendarmerie and school, perched in magnificent isolation amid the waters at the entrance to the village.

Villagers offer memorable rides in sampan-style boats between the trees of the surrounding flooded forest, while a marvellous raised wooden walkway between the trees has also been constructed, which is planned to connect to a big stilted restaurant

---

FLOATS AND STILTS

The Tonle Sap villages are often generically described as the "floating villages", even though in fact not all of them are. Genuine **floating villages**, such as Chong Khneas – or those at Pursat and Kompong Chnnang (see p.109 & p.112) – are exactly that, with houses built on bamboo pontoons bobbing raftlike on the water, meaning that the entire village can be towed to a new location on the lake according to seasonally rising or falling water levels, and allowing its inhabitants convenient access to the best available supplies of fish. Conversely, other lakeside settlements, such as Kompong Phluk, are actually **stilted villages**, and float only in a metaphorical sense, their buildings being constructed on top of raised platforms perched above the water on high wooden stilts (like a supersized version of the traditional Khmer rural house). Needless to say, these villages occupy a fixed position, irrespective of prevailing water levels, and come the height of summer are generally left high and dry as the lake waters recede, stranding them amid lakeside mud.

CAMBODIA'S LARDER

The **Tonle Sap** is at once a reservoir, flood-relief system, communications route, home and larder to the people who live on and around it; even Cambodians who live nowhere near it depend on the lake as a rich food source.

At its lowest, in May, just before the rains, the lake covers an area of around 2500 square kilometres. Himalayan **meltwater** flows down the Mekong just as the monsoon rains arrive, causing the level of the river to rise so quickly that at Phnom Penh the pressure is sufficient to reverse the flow of the Tonle Sap River, which would normally drain the lake. As a result of this inflow, each year the lake inundates an area of more than **ten thousand square kilometres**, making it the largest freshwater lake in Southeast Asia. The flow of water reverts to its usual direction in late October or early November, the receding waters leaving behind fertile mud for the planting of rice, and nutrients for the fry that have spawned amid the flooded trees. February sees a bumper fish catch, much of it going to satisfy the insatiable Cambodian appetite for *prohok*.

This lake may not always be here though; its fragile ecosystem is under threat, as upstream on the Mekong the Chinese continue with the controversial building of dams.

3

further out over the lake. There are also plans to launch homestays in the village, possibly starting in 2015.

Kompong Khleang

About 50km southeast of Siem Reap by road (turn south off NR6 at Dam Dek) • Entrance to village $2 • Boats available for trips through village for around $20/hr

Around 20km further down the lake from Kompong Phluk is **KOMPONG KHLEANG**. This was a major centre of lake trade in the French colonial period and remains the most sizeable settlement hereabouts, with around sixteen thousand inhabitants living in a mixture of stilted and floating houses. It's the largest but also the least touristed of the three main Tonle Sap villages, and also remains surrounded by water year-round, making it a good alternative to Kompong Phluk when the waters there have dried up.

Prek Toal Biosphere Reserve

The Tonle Sap was designated a UNESCO Biosphere Reserve in 1997 – a status that reconciles sustainable use with conservation. One core area of the reserve, the **Prek Toal Biosphere Reserve** serves as a sanctuary for a wide range of waterbirds, including three endangered species – spot-billed pelicans, greater adjutant storks and white-winged ducks. Prek Toal lies on the northwest edge of the lake in the dry season and is easily reached from Siem Reap, though you'll have to take an organized tour – Osmose (see p.145) specialize in trips to the reserve.

The temples of Angkor: the Archaeological Park

Scattered over some four hundred square kilometres of countryside between the Tonle Sap lake and the Kulen Mountains, the **temples of Angkor** are one of the world's great architectural showpieces – an astonishing profusion of ancient monuments remarkable both for their size and number, not to mention their incredible levels of artistry. An idealized representation of the Hindu cosmos in stone, they range from great pyramidal temple-mountains of Angkor Wat and Pre Rup through to the labyrinthine monasteries of Ta Prohm and Banteay Kdei, as well as more miniature and intimate sanctuaries such as Thommanon and Preah Ko.

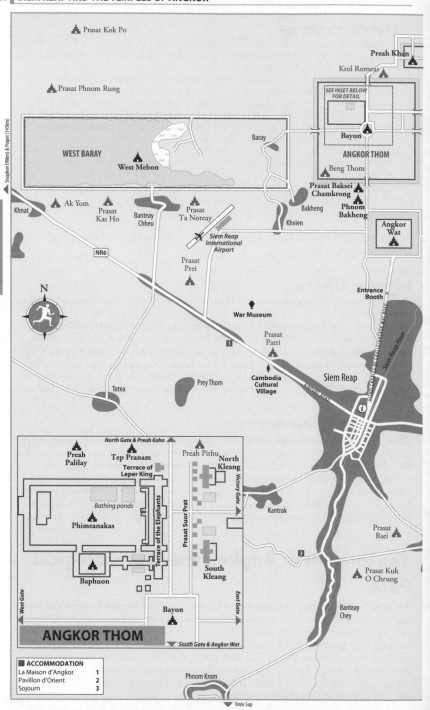

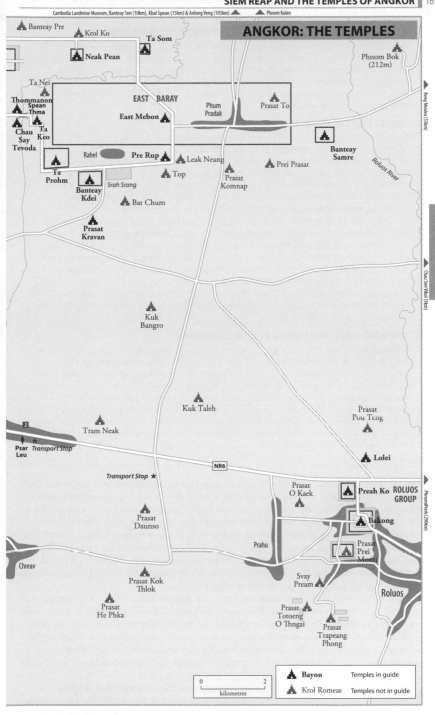

Cambodia Landmine Museum, Banteay Srei (10km), Kbal Spean (15km) & Anlong Veng (105km) ▲ ▲ Phnom Kulen

ANGKOR: THE TEMPLES

Banteay Pre
Krol Ko
Ta Som
Neak Pean
Phnom Bok (212m)

Ta Nei
Thommanon
Spean Thma
Chau Say Tevoda
Ta Keo

EAST BARAY
East Mebon
Phum Pradak
Prasat To
Banteay Samre

Ta Prohm
Rahel
Pre Rup
Leak Neang
Top
Prei Prasat
Roluos River

Banteay Kdei
Srah Srang
Prasat Komnap

Bat Chum

Prasat Kravan

Kuk Bangro

Kuk Taleh
Prasat Pou Teng

Tram Neak
Psar Leu ★ Transport Stop
Transport Stop ★
Lolei

NR6
Prasat O Kaek
Preah Ko ROLUOS GROUP

Prasat Daunso
Bakong

Prahu
Prasat Prei Monti

Chreav
Svay Pream
Roluos

Prasat Kok Thlok
Prasat Totoeng O Thngai
Prasat Trapeang Phong

Prasat He Phka

Beng Melea (55km)
Chau Srei Vibol (3km)
Phnom Penh (290km)

| ▲ **Bayon** | Temples in guide |
| ▲ Krol Romeas | Temples not in guide |

0 ——— 2
kilometres

3

THE TEMPLES OF ANGKOR: STRUCTURE AND SYMBOLISM

First encounters with the temples of Angkor can be confusing, or worse. Myriad monuments survive, in varying states of ruin or otherwise, each with its own perplexing labyrinth of towers, enclosures, shrines, galleries, causeways and moats. Diverse and disorienting as they may initially appear, however – an effect exaggerated by the ravages of time – virtually all have numerous features in common, as well as a shared underlying structure and symbolism.

MODELS OF THE UNIVERSE

Most ancient Khmer temples follow a similar pattern, serving as a miniature symbolic representation of the **mythological Hindu cosmos**. At the heart of each temple, the central sanctuary tower or towers (most commonly five of them, arranged in the characteristic "quincunx" pattern, like the five dots on a dice) represents the mythical **Mount Meru**, considered the home of the gods and the heart of the physical and spiritual universe in both Hindu and Buddhist cosmology. These towers are typically enclosed by a sequence of concentric **enclosures**, stacked within each other like a sequence of Russian dolls, symbolizing the further mountain ranges around Mount Meru, with the whole contained within a **moat**, representing the enclosing earthly ocean. **Causeways** cross these moats, often flanked by "**naga balustrades**" showing gods and demons tugging on the body of an enormous serpent, alluding to the famous legend of the Churning of the Ocean of Milk (see p.169) and perhaps providing a symbolic crossing point between the secular spaces outside the temple and the abode of the gods within.

In all but one instance, temples were designed to be approached from the **east** to catch the rays of the rising sun, symbolizing life. Angkor Wat, however, faces **west**, the direction of the setting sun – and death.

STATE TEMPLES AND THE CULT OF THE DEVARAJA

The majority of Angkor's most memorable and famous monuments – including Angkor Wat, the Bayon, Baphuon, Ta Keo, Pre Rup and Bakheng – are so-called **state temples** – great pyramidal temple-mountains rising steeply through a series of sheer-sided storeys (equivalent to the enclosures of non-royal Khmer temples) towards a tower-topped summit. Each storey corresponds to one of the universes of Hindu cosmology, leading up to the topmost towers representing Mount Meru, the abode of the gods. All state temples were constructed by a particular king for his own use. Temples built by one king were seldom used by the next, who would build in a new location – which accounts for the constantly shifting capitals of the Angkorian period. State temples were not considered as a place of public worship but as the

Magnificent to begin with, the ravages of time and nature have added immeasurably to the temples' appeal, with individual monuments now stranded romantically amid great swathes of forest, often in various states of picturesque semi-ruin – a far cry from the great days of the Angkorian empire, when each temple would have formed the centrepiece of a string of once bustling (but now entirely vanished) villages, towns and miniature cities spread across the densely inhabited countryside. Some, like Angkor Wat and the Baphuon, have been meticulously restored; others, like Ta Prohm and Beng Mealea, remain half-choked by the encroaching jungle, their buildings smothered in a photogenic tangle of creepers and strangler figs.

The most famous of the temples is the legendary **Angkor Wat**, with its five magnificent corncob towers and vast complex of bas-relief galleries. Also on everyone's itinerary is the walled city of **Angkor Thom**, where you'll find the magical **Bayon** state temple, topped with dozens of towers carved with enigmatic faces of the bodhisattva Lokesvara, one of ancient Cambodia's most iconic images. Nearby, the similarly iconic **Ta Prohm** also attracts crowds of visitors, its crumbling ruins engulfed by the surrounding jungle, with shrines and statues held in the vice-like grip of giant tree roots.

All the temples close to Siem Reap are contained within the so-called **Angkor Archaeological Park** and covered by a single entrance ticket (see p.190), as are a number private abode of each king's particular god – an aspect of the uniquely Khmer cult known as the **devaraja**, literally "god-king" (see p.302).

MONASTERIES AND SHRINES

The state temples are just one aspect of Angkorian architecture, however, and smaller temples, monasteries and other structures abound. Most famous are the sprawling **monastic** complexes of Ta Prohm, Banteay Kdei and Preah Khan. These were public rather than private shrines, serving as monasteries, universities and places of worship for the hoi polloi. Very different in effect from the soaring state temples, these "flat" temples (as they're sometimes described) nevertheless follow the same basic layout, with a cluster of central towers contained within concentric enclosures, the whole bounded by a moat.

LATERITE, BRICK AND SANDSTONE

The building materials used by the ancient Khmer changed over time. **Laterite** was the basic material, readily available and easy to quarry. This was used to construct walls and other functional structures, although its distinctively rough, pockmarked appearance made it unsuitable for fine decorative carving. Early Angkor-period temples were faced largely in **brick** (Sambor Prei Kuk and Prasat Kravan are two particularly notable examples), often carved with extraordinary finesse. Later on, the more valuable **sandstone** became the material of choice for the most important buildings, ranging from the delicate roseate sandstone used at Banteay Srei to the hard, slightly blackish stone at Ta Keo and the Baphuon. **Wooden** buildings would also have featured, although these have all long since vanished.

GODS AND GUARDIANS

Much of the beauty of Angkor can be found in the detail, with prodigious quantities of sculpture covering (in the finest temples) virtually every surface. **Doors** were the main focus, particularly **lintel** panels above entrances, often fantastically carved with gods or scenes from Hindu mythology and often featured **mythical beasts** such as the *kala* and *makara*. In addition, many doors are flanked by guardian figures, known as **dvarapalas**. Heavenly **apsaras** are another favoured motif, while walls and door jambs are often decorated in the flamboyant **floral designs** so beloved of Khmer craftsmen. The famous narrative **bas relief galleries** of the Bayon and (especially) Angkor Wat are among the most celebrated instances of Angkorian carving, although they're not found at any other temples. Perhaps most iconic of all, however, are the superhuman, enigmatic faces of the bodhisattva **Lokesvara** carved upon the towers of the Bayon, the gateways of Angkor Thom, and at various other locations around Angkor, smiling enigmatically in benign blessing over the lands beyond.

of other headline attractions slightly further afield including **Banteay Srei**, a unique micro-temple of intricately carved reddish stone, and the **Roluos Group**, home to some of Angkor's oldest temples. Several other major Angkorian monuments can be found even further from Siem Reap, outside the Archaeological Park and covered by their own tickets. These include the jungle-smothered temple of **Beng Mealea** (see p.191), the great temple-towns of **Koh Ker** (see p.192) and **Preah Khan (Kompong Thom)** (see p.194), and the stunning **Preah Vihear** (see p.196) in the far north of the country, sitting high on a mountaintop above the Thai border.

Brief history

For six hundred years from the early ninth century the area around Angkor Wat was the heart of the **Khmer Empire**. A ready supply of water and the fertility of the land meant that the area could support large populations, and successive Angkorian kings constructed their royal cities and state temples here. Despite the region's importance, there's a dearth of written records: the ancient Khmer wrote on specially treated palm trees or animal skins and none of their texts have survived. Consequently the history of Angkor had to be painstakingly pieced together through study of the temples and more than a thousand inscribed steles – mostly written in Sanskrit – found across the

EXPLORING ANGKOR: TEMPLE ITINERARIES

There are around two dozen or so major temple sites at Angkor, scattered over a considerable area. Package tours tend to follow rigid routes around the sites, although with a little ingenuity you can tweak established itineraries and enhance your experience considerably. **Time** is very much of the essence. It's horribly easy to end up rushing around breathlessly, so that one site blends seamlessly into another and you end up templed-out and forgetting almost everything you've seen. All the major temples in the environs of Siem Reap can be seen **in three days** (see our recommended itinerary), although if you can spend longer than this – taking the temples at a more leisurely pace and visiting them during quieter periods of the day – you'll be richly rewarded (for details of the **best times to visit** the major sights, see the relevant accounts). Even if you can only spare three days it's well worth making space to revisit the major sites – Angkor Wat and Angkor Thom in particular – for a second or even third look at different times of the day, as well as taking a sunrise or sunset trip to one of the major monuments.

TRADITIONAL ITINERARIES

There are two traditional temple itineraries – the Small (or "Petit") Circuit and the Grand Circuit – each sold as off-the-peg day-tours just about everywhere in town.

Small Circuit Around 30km. Starts at Angkor Wat, heads north to the Bayon and the rest of Angkor Thom before continuing east to Thommanon, Chau Say Tevoda, Ta Keo, Ta Prohm, Banteay Kdei, Srah Srang and Prasat Kravan. The Small Circuit is usually done in just one day, but really contains too many major monuments to properly appreciate in this time and is better broken up and combined with the Grand Circuit over two days (see opposite).

Grand Circuit Around 36km, or 44km if you include Banteay Samre. Starts at Srah Srang then heads east, via Pre Rup, East Mebon (from where you can extend the circuit to Banteay Samre), Ta Som, Neak Pean and Preah Khan. The Grand Circuit can easily be explored in one day (even if you include outlying Banteay Samre), leaving you with a couple of hours to spare when you could visit one or two sights on the Small Circuit.

Roluos The temples of Roluos – in a slightly outlying area west of Siem Reap – are generally covered in a separate day-trip, although they could conceivably be combined with the Grand Circuit in a single, albeit long, day.

empire. Even now, Angkorian history remains hypothetical to some degree, with the origins of many temples, the dates of their construction and even the names of kings uncertain.

Angkor's earliest monuments date from 802, when **Jayavarman II** came north from Kompong Cham to set up court at Phnom Kulen. The empire reached its apogee in the twelfth century under the leadership of **Jayavarman VII** – the greatest temple-builder of all – when it stretched from the coast of Vietnam to the Malay peninsula, to Bagan in Myanmar and north to Laos. No further stone temples were built after the reign of Jayavarman VII came to an end in 1219; either the area's resources were exhausted or the switch to Theravada Buddhism may have precluded their construction. The region's existing temples and palaces remained in use until they were sacked by the Thais in 1431; the following year, Ponhea Yat took his court south to Phnom Penh and left Angkor to the jungle. Though Angkor was never completely deserted, the local people who continued to worship at the temples were unable to maintain them.

Around 1570, **King Satha** was so enchanted when he rediscovered Angkor Thom deep in the jungle that he had the undergrowth cleared and brought his court there, though by 1594 he was back at Lovek. Another short-lived period of royal interest occurred in the middle of the seventeenth century when, according to a letter penned by a Dutch merchant to the governor-general of the Dutch East Indies, "the king [Barom Rachea VI] paid a visit to a lovely pleasant place known as Anckoor". Subsequently, despite tales of a lost city in the Cambodian jungle filtering back to the West via missionaries and traders, it wasn't until the nineteenth century that Cambodia opened up to

COMBINATIONS AND VARIATIONS

As they stand, the traditional Small and Grand circuit itineraries are far from ideal. You could, however, mix and match to come up with something far more rewarding.

Small Circuit in reverse order You might consider doing the Small Circuit in anticlockwise order, starting at Banteay Kdei and finishing at Angkor Wat. This has the great advantage of seeing the sights in ever-increasing orders of magnificence, but also runs the risk that by the time you finish up at Angkor Wat you'll be so frazzled with myriad monuments that you won't be able to properly appreciate what you're seeing.

Small Circuit/Grand Circuit combo It makes most sense to only tackle part of the Small Circuit on one day, and then mop up the remaining Small Circuit sights during a tour of the Grand Circuit on a later visit, maybe by delaying a visit to the Small Circuit temple of Ta Prohm to the beginning or end of your Grand Circuit tour (which also allows you to visit the temple when it's less crowded), or doing the same with a couple of the temples within Angkor Thom (visiting the Bayon at the end of a Grand Circuit tour, for example, which again will land you at the temple when most of the coach parties have gone).

RECOMMENDED ITINERARY

Taking into account all the points raised above, the following itinerary allows you to get the most out of three days.

Day One Tour the Grand Circuit in clockwise order, with the addition of Ta Prohm at the end (aiming to arrive at Ta Prohm after 4pm, when the worst of the crowds will have departed).

Day Two Tour the Small Circuit (minus Ta Prohm) in an anticlockwise direction, finishing at Angkor Wat (and visiting the Bayon at the end of your visit to Angkor Thom in order to avoid the crowds).

Day Three Visit the temples of Roluos, combined with a second visit to Angkor Wat (perhaps early in the morning, when the crowds are thinnest) and/or Angkor Thom and the Bayon (or, indeed, anywhere else that's caught your particular fancy).

European explorers (although, from the end of the eighteenth century, as part of Battambang province, it actually came under Thai rule – a state of affairs that lasted until 1907, when the French negotiated its return). The first proper account of Angkor Wat, published by the French missionary Charles-Emile Bouillevaux in 1858, failed to arouse wide interest, but in 1864, the diaries of botanist and explorer Henri Mouhot, who had stumbled on Angkor by accident a few years earlier, were published posthumously, and the temples gripped the world. The Briton J. Thompson published the first photographs of Angkor in 1867, and was the first to suggest a link between temple architecture and the mythical Mount Meru. Close behind him came Doudart Lagrée, who discovered Beng Mealea and Preah Khan (Kompong Thom).

Angkor Wat

However many times you've seen it on film or in photographs, nothing prepares you for the majesty of **ANGKOR WAT**. Dominated by five majestic, corncob towers, this masterpiece of Khmer architecture, consecrated in about 1150 to Vishnu, is thought to have taken around thirty years to complete. Stunning from a distance, as you approach its intricacy becomes apparent, with every surfaced covered in fine detail. If time allows, it's worth visiting at different times of day to see how the colours of the stone change with the light.

Experts have long debated whether Angkor Wat was built for worship or for funerary purposes, given that the site is approached from the west and the gallery of bas-reliefs is

3

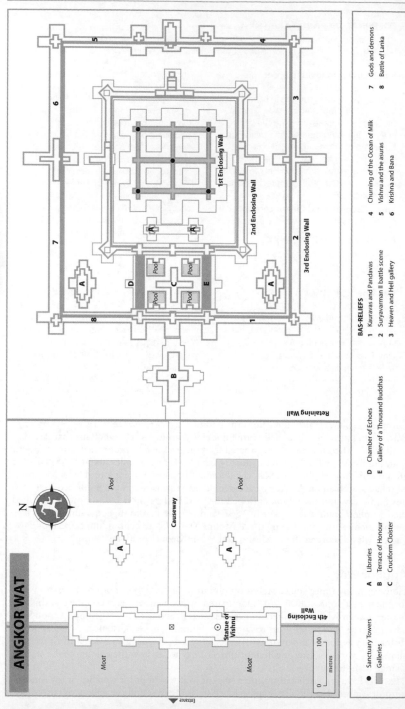

ANGKOR WAT

Entrance

Moat

Moat

Statue of Vishnu

4th Enclosing Wall

N

Causeway

Pool

Pool

A

A

B

Retaining Wall

C

D

E

Pool

Pool

Pool

Pool

A

A

1st Enclosing Wall

2nd Enclosing Wall

3rd Enclosing Wall

1

2

3

4

5

6

7

8

0   100
metres

● Sanctuary Towers

▨ Galleries

A Libraries
B Terrace of Honour
C Cruciform Cloister

D Chamber of Echoes
E Gallery of a Thousand Buddhas

BAS-RELIEFS

1 Kauravas and Pandavas
2 Suryavarman II battle scene
3 Heaven and Hell gallery

4 Churning of the Ocean of Milk
5 Vishnu and the asuras
6 Krishna and Bana

7 Gods and demons
8 Battle of Lanka

designed to be viewed anticlockwise, both of which are associated with death. Nowadays, it's generally accepted that it was used by the king for worship during his lifetime, and became his mausoleum following his death.

Moat and fourth enclosure

Entry to the complex is from the west, via an impressive laterite **causeway** built from massive blocks of stone and edged by the scant remains of a crumbling naga balustrade and with terraces guarded by lions.

The causeway crosses the 200m-wide **moat** to the western gopura of the **fourth enclosing wall**. The **western gopura** itself stretches for nearly 230m and has three towers, plus entrances large enough to allow elephants to pass through. Inside the southern section of the gopura is an eight-armed statue of **Vishnu**, more than 3m tall, while looking out from the gopura there's a panoramic view of the temple. The first of Angkor Wat's fabulous **apsaras** are carved into the sandstone on the eastern exterior of the gopura, their feet strangely foreshortened and skewed to the side.

From the gopura, a second **causeway** leads to the temple, 350m long and even more impressive than the one across the moat. The buildings partway along are libraries. In front of the temple is the cruciform-shaped **Terrace of Honour**, framed by a naga balustrade; apsara dances (see box, p.154) were once performed here and ceremonial processions received by the king. Beyond the terrace, a short flight of steps leads up to the third enclosing wall, whose western gopura is linked to a cruciform cloister and two galleries.

The third enclosure

Portraying events associated primarily with Vishnu, to whom the temple is dedicated, the famous Angkor Wat bas-reliefs, some 2m high on average, are carved into the wall of the magnificently colonnaded **gallery** that runs around the perimeter of the temple, forming the **third enclosure**. This was as far into the complex as the citizens of Angkor were allowed to get, and the scenes depicted were meant to impress them with their king's wealth and power, as well as contributing to their religious education.

Extending over 700m, the bas-reliefs are broken into sections by porches midway along each side, along with corner chambers. The older bas-reliefs are delicately carved with minute attention to detail, in contrast to the more roughly executed scenes added in the sixteenth century. In some areas you can still see evidence of the red and gold paint that once covered the reliefs, while other areas are black; one theory is that the pigments have been eroded and the stone polished by thousands of hands caressing the carvings over the years.

The account that follows assumes you progress around the gallery in an **anticlockwise** direction, in keeping with the ancient funerary practices.

West gallery: south section

The battle between the rival families of cousins, the **Kauravas** (marching from the left) and the **Pandavas** (from the right), as described in the *Mahabharata*, is in full swing in the first section of the gallery. Fighting to the death at Mount Kurukshetra, the two families are respectively backed by the supernatural powers of Kama, son of the sun god Surya, and Arjuna. Along the bottom of the panel, foot soldiers march towards the fray in the centre of the gallery; above them, generals ride in horse-drawn chariots or

---

AVOIDING THE CROWDS AT ANGKOR WAT

As Angkor's headline attraction, Angkor Wat is filled with crowds of tourists virtually every hour of the day, although fortunately there's more space here to swallow up the visiting crowds than at places like the Bayon and Ta Prohm. The **best time** to visit is early morning from around 7–9am: after the sunrise watchers have left and before the first of the coach parties arrives.

on elephants. Amid thrilling hand-to-hand combat, the Kaurava general, Bhisma, is shown shot through with arrows, while Arjuna can be seen on his chariot with Krishna serving as his charioteer.

Southwest corner

Despite erosion, some tales from the **Ramayana** (see box, p.65) and other Hindu legends can still be made out here. One panel shows Krishna holding up Mount Govardhan in one hand as a shelter for villagers against storms sent by Indra. Another depicts the duel between the monkey gods Valin and Sugriva, in which Valin dies in the arms of his wife after he is pierced by an arrow from Rama. Monkeys mourn Valin on the surrounding panels.

South gallery: west section

This gallery (running west to east on two levels) depicts a **battle scene**, beginning with a royal audience (upper level) and the palace ladies in procession (below). Further along, the Khmer commanders, mounted on elephants and shaded by parasols, muster the troops and march through the jungle. At the centre of the panel they surround Suryavarman II, who is of larger stature and has fifteen parasols around him. Beyond, the army – accompanied by musicians, standard-bearers and jesters – is joined by Cham mercenaries, identified by their moustaches and plumed headdresses. It's thought that the niches along the wall were used as hiding places for golden artefacts, though some say the chunks of stone were removed by devotees who believed they possessed magical properties.

South gallery: east section

Called the **Heaven and Hell gallery**, this panel, carved on three levels and nearly 60m long, shows the many-armed god Yama mounted on a buffalo and judging the dead. At the start of this section, a path is shown on the top level along which people ascend to heaven, while a corresponding route at the bottom leads to hell, the two paths being separated by a frieze of garudas. The people in heaven can be seen living a life of leisure in palaces, whereas sinners are pushed through a trapdoor into the underworld to have terrible punishments inflicted on them – gluttons are cut in two, vandals have their bones broken and rice stealers have red-hot irons thrust through their abdomens.

East gallery: south section

This gallery contains the most famous of Angkor Wat's bas-reliefs, depicting the **Churning of the Ocean of Milk** (see box opposite). The bas-relief picks up the story just as the churning is about to yield results; in the central band of the panel, 92 bulbous-eyed asuras with crested headdresses are shown holding the head of Vasuki and pulling from the left, while on the right, 88 devas, with almond eyes and conical headdresses, hold the tail. To the top, thousands of divine apsaras dance along the wall, and at the bottom, the ocean teems with finely detailed marine creatures.

The **chedi** just outside the east gopura was placed here in the early eighteenth century when the temple was a Buddhist monastery; its history is recorded on a wall inscription within the gopura itself.

RESTORING ANGKOR

At the time of writing, parts of Angkor Wat (and some other temples, most notably Ta Prohm and Ta Keo) are undergoing extensive **restoration**, and some towers and other buildings are covered in scaffolding and/or cordoned off. In Angkor Wat, the northwestern quarter of the second level is currently inaccessible, while various works around Cruciform Cloister mean that you might find yourself diverted when entering the main temple.

THE CHURNING OF THE OCEAN OF MILK

A popular theme in Khmer art is the **Churning of the Ocean of Milk**, a creation myth from the Hindu epic the *Bhagavata-Purana*, which describes the various incarnations of Vishnu. At the beginning of this episode, the devas (gods) and asuras (demons) are lined up on opposite sides, trying to use **Mount Mandara** to churn the ocean in order to produce *amrita*, the elixir of immortality. They tug on the serpent **Vasuki**, who is coiled around the mountain, but to no effect. **Vishnu** arrives and instructs them to pull rhythmically, but the mountain begins to sink. Things get worse when Vasuki vomits a deadly venom, which threatens to destroy the devas and asuras; Brahma asks **Shiva** to drink up the venom, which he does, but it burns his throat, which is blue thereafter. Vishnu meanwhile, in his incarnation as the tortoise **Kurma**, supports Mount Mandara, allowing the churning to continue for another thousand years, after which the *amrita* is finally produced. Unfortunately, the elixir is seized by the asuras, but Vishnu again comes to the rescue as the apparition **Maya** and regains the cup of elixir. The churning also results in the manifestation of mythical beings, including the three-headed elephant, Airavata; the goddess of beauty, Lakshmi, who becomes Vishnu's wife; and the celestial dancers, the apsaras.

3

East gallery: north section

The relief here was carved in the sixteenth century and the workmanship is rough and superficial. The scene records the asuras being defeated by Vishnu, who is shown with four heads and mounted on Garuda in the centre of the panel. The asuras approach from the south, their leaders riding chariots drawn by monsters; from the north, a group of warriors ride peacocks.

North gallery: east section

Also from the sixteenth century, the poorly rendered scenes here show the battle between **Krishna** and **Bana**, son of an asura who had come under Shiva's protection. Krishna, easily spotted with his eight arms and multiple heads, rides Garuda towards Bana, but is forced to halt by a fire surrounding a city wall, which Garuda quells with water from the Ganges. On the far west of the panel, a victorious Krishna is depicted on Mount Kailash, where Shiva entreats him to spare Bana's life. Also along this stretch of wall can be found an image of the elephant-headed god, Ganesh, his only appearance in the entire temple.

North gallery: west section

Better executed than the previous two sections, the panel here shows 21 gods from the Hindu pantheon in a terrific mêlée between **gods and demons**. Some of the easier ones to spot are (from left to right), the multi-headed and -armed Skanda, god of war, riding a peacock; Indra standing on the elephant Airavata; Vishnu mounted on Garuda and fighting with all four arms; Yama's chariot pulled by buffalo; and Shiva pulling his bow, while Brahma rides the sacred goose, Hamsa.

Northwest corner

More scenes from the **Ramayana** are to be found here, notably a depiction of Vishnu reclining on the serpent Anata. A bevy of apsaras float above him, while his wife, Lakshmi, sits near his feet. Below, a procession of gods come to ask Vishnu to return to earth.

West gallery: north section

Turning the corner, you come to the superbly carved **Battle of Lanka**. In this action-packed sequence from the *Ramayana*, Rama is shown fighting the ten-headed, twenty-armed Ravana to free his wife, Sita, from captivity; bodies of the soldiers from the monkey army, Rama's allies, fall in all directions. The two adversaries are seen in the centre of the panel, Ravana in a chariot drawn by lions, Rama standing on the monkey king, Sugriva.

First level

From the top of the steps above the Terrace of Honour, further steps head up into the **third enclosure** (which is also the **first level** of the temple pyramid), bare save for two libraries in the northwest and southwest corners.

Linking the third and second enclosures is the so-called **Cruciform Cloister**, with four deep (but dry) pools in the centre and galleries to either side. That on the west side is known as the **Gallery of a Thousand Buddhas**, which once housed a vast collection of Buddhas collected over recent centuries when Angkor Wat was a Buddhist monastery; many were taken away for safe-keeping in 1970, while those that remained were later destroyed by the Khmer Rouge, though today a few modern images have taken their place. The gallery on the opposite side is the so-called **Chamber of Echoes**. Cambodians stand here with their backs to the wall and thump their chests with their fists, thrice, to bring good fortune. Surrounding the cloister is a gallery with a frieze of apsaras above and seated ascetics carved at the bases of the columns below. Many of the columns also bear Sanskrit and Khmer inscriptions.

Second and third levels

The **second level** of the pyramid is enclosed by a gallery with windows opening on the courtyard within, whose walls are carved with a remarkable collection of more than 1500 **apsaras**, each unique. Elegantly dressed, these beautiful creatures display exotic hairstyles and enigmatic expressions; even their jewellery is lovingly sculpted. These are the earliest depictions in Angkorian art of apsaras in groups, some posed in twos or threes, arms linked and hands touching.

During the time of Suryavarman II, only the high priest and the king were allowed to visit the **third level**, but now visitors can make the ascent – although there's usually a bit of a queue to climb the steep, ladder-like staircase to the top, and you'll need a decent head for heights.

Phnom Bakheng

The first state temple to be built in the Angkor area, the temple-mountain of **PHNOM BAKHENG** was commissioned by Yasovarman I after he had moved the capital here from nearby Roluos. Dedicated in 907, it originally lay at the heart of Yasovarman's new moated city of Yasodharapura, covering an area of some four square kilometres (parts of the moat are still visible along the road from Siem Reap, 600m before Angkor Wat). The temple itself isn't the most riveting monument in Angkor, despite its historical significance, but is worth a visit if only for the magnificent **view** from its summit: west over the West Baray, southeast to Angkor Wat, south to the Tonle Sap and northeast to Phnom Kulen.

The temple **pyramid** comprises five levels, built around a natural 67m-high hill, with steps and terraces hewn into the rock and then clad in sandstone; 44 small towers are dotted around its base, with another sixty arranged around the terraces above (twelve on each level), plus five principal towers at the top arranged, for the first time in Khmer architecture, in a quincunx to symbolize the five peaks of Mount Meru. The temple was consecrated to Shiva and the central tower would have contained a linga, now lost.

PHNOM BAKHENG SUNSET ASCENT

In the late afternoon, hundreds of tourists make the trek up the steep, badly eroded rock-hewn steps of Phnom Bakheng to watch the **sun set over Angkor Wat**. You don't have to walk, however: between 3 and 5pm **elephants** wait at the foot of the hill to ferry visitors up via a roundabout track ($20); downhill trips ($15) run between 5pm and 6pm.

Prasat Baksei Chamkrong

A few hundred metres north of Phnom Bakheng is the small, often ignored **PRASAT BAKSEI CHAMKRONG**, the sole monument built by Harshavarman I. Consecrated to Shiva and his consort, the temple wasn't finished in the king's lifetime and was re-consecrated by Rajendravarman I in 948. The simple structure comprises four square tiers of decreasing size, rising to a single brick sanctuary tower with decorated sandstone lintels and columns. A Sanskrit inscription on the door frame here records that the sanctuary contained a golden image of Paramenshavara, as Jayavarman II was known posthumously. If you want to head up to the top of the temple, the northern staircase is the best of a badly worn bunch.

Angkor Thom

The wall of the city is some five miles in circumference. It has five gates each with double portals... Outside the wall stretches a great moat, across which access to the city is given by massive causeways. Flanking the causeways on each side are fifty-four divinities resembling war-lords in stone, huge and terrifying...

Zhou Daguan, visited Angkor Thom 1296–97

Still recognizable from this description by the Chinese envoy Zhou Daguan, who visited the Khmer court at the end of the thirteenth century, the ruins of the great city of **ANGKOR THOM** form the physical and architectural centrepiece of Angkor, home to a trio of state temples – **Baphuon**, **Phimeanakas** and the spectacular **Bayon** – as well as numerous other royal, religious and secular structures. The former city itself covers an area of three square kilometres, enclosed by a wide moat and an 8m-high wall reinforced by a wide earth embankment (constructed by Jayavarman VII after the city had been sacked by the Cham in 1177). Sanctuary towers stand at each corner of the walls, which are pierced by five much-photographed **entry gates** – one per cardinal direction, plus an additional eastern portal, the Victory Gate. Each gate is topped by a tower carved with four huge faces looking out in the cardinal directions and approached via a causeway lined with huge naga balustrades. Nominally, these faces are said to represent the bodhisattva Lokesvara, although they also bear a certain similarity to carved images of Jayavarman VII himself, perhaps symbolizing the far-reaching gaze of the king over his lands and subjects.

The site is most usually approached from Angkor Wat through the 23m-high **south gate** and along a 100m-long **stone causeway** flanked by a massive naga balustrade, with 54 almond-eyed gods on one side, and 54 round-eyed demons on the other holding a pair of nine-headed nagas, which are said to protect the city's wealth. Most of the heads here are replicas, the originals having been either stolen or removed for safety to the Angkor National Museum. The base of the gateway itself is decorated with sculptures of **Indra** on a three-headed elephant; the elephant's trunks hold lotus blossoms that droop to the ground, doubling as improvised columns.

The Bayon

The state temple of Jayavarman VII and his immediate successors, the **Bayon** is one of Angkor's most memorably mysterious and haunting sights, with its dozens of eroded towers carved with innumerable giant-sized images of the enigmatically half-smiling face of the bodhisattva Lokesvara. The **design** of the Bayon is unique among the state temples of Angkor. Instead of a huge central pyramid, an impression of ascending height is created by a dense cluster of towers, with the main sanctuary towers rising out of the centre of the complex like a kind of Matterhorn carved in stone – the ultimate architectural representation of the mythical Mount Meru. Approaching the temple, all you can initially see is a mass of ill-defined stone, dark and imposing, looking from a distance like some kind of bizarre natural rock formation. It's only closer up that the intricacy of the design becomes apparent and you can begin to make out the 37 towers carved with their massive faces of **Lokesvara**. It is said that there are more than two hundred in all, although no one seems to know the exact number, and exactly why they are repeated so many times remains unclear.

Built in the late twelfth and/or early thirteenth century, the Bayon was intended to embrace all the religions of the kingdom, including the Islamic beliefs of the newly conquered Cham, but was consecrated as a Buddhist temple. When the state religion reverted to Hinduism, the Buddha in the central sanctuary was torn down and cast into the well below.

Third enclosing wall bas-reliefs: east wall

Enclosing the central sanctuary is the **third enclosing wall** – actually a colonnaded gallery, though the roof has long since collapsed. Its outer walls are covered with extensive **bas-reliefs**, deeper and less fine than those at Angkor Wat (and some are unfinished). These were intended to be viewed **clockwise**, starting from the **midpoint of the eastern wall**, which is how they're described below.

Heading south along the gallery from the east approach, on the **east wall** you'll see a **military procession** depicted on three levels; bareheaded soldiers with short hair march across the uppermost level, while the level just below depicts troops with goatee beards and elaborate hairstyles. Musicians and bareback cavalry accompany them, the commanders (with parasols) seated on elephants. Close to the next door to the courtyard are the army's camp followers, their covered carts much like those used today. At the lowest level are some fascinating scenes of everyday domestic and rural life, many of them still as true now as when they were first carved.

Third enclosing wall bas-reliefs: south wall

The **southeast corner tower** is unfinished, but its carving of a boat is remarkable for continuing all the way around the corner, where you'll discover the finest of the Bayon bas-reliefs, depicting the 1177 **naval battle** between the Khmer and the Cham on the Tonle Sap lake. The victorious Khmer, led by Jayavarman VII, are shown with bare heads, whereas the Cham wear vaguely floral-looking hats. At the start, the king is seen seated in the palace directing preparations for battle, as fish swim through the trees – as in a rainy-season flood. Along the bottom are more carvings drawn from everyday life on the banks of the Tonle Sap: fishing baskets – just like those used now – hang from the ceiling, skewers of food are cooked over a charcoal fire and women are seen picking lice out of one another's hair.

A bit further along, princesses are shown amusing themselves at the palace, while around them wrestlers spar and a boar-fight takes place. Subsequently, battle commences. The Cham disembark from their boats to continue the fight on land against the Khmers – with short hair and rope tied around their bodies – who are given the appearance of giants and who are, of course, victorious. Back at the palace, **Jayavarman VII** himself looks on as the celebratory feast is prepared.

EXPLORING THE BAYON

Most coach parties descend on the Bayon from mid-morning to early afternoon, meaning that the **best time to visit** is either early in the morning (around 7–9am) or later in the afternoon. A good plan is to arrive at Angkor Thom in time for lunch, then spend the first part of the afternoon exploring the city's other sights (which will take at least a couple of hours) before heading to the Bayon at around 3/4pm, when the worst of the crowds have dispersed.

Drivers drop off passengers at various places at the beginning of visits to the Bayon and surrounding monuments. Make sure to know *exactly* where your driver is waiting to pick you up, as there's an awful lot of transport about, and several different parking areas.

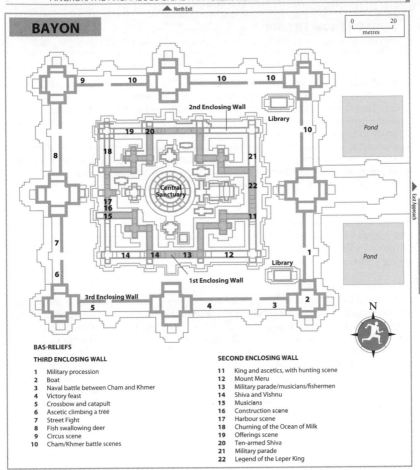

BAYON

BAS-RELIEFS

THIRD ENCLOSING WALL

1 Military procession
2 Boat
3 Naval battle between Cham and Khmer
4 Victory feast
5 Crossbow and catapult
6 Ascetic climbing a tree
7 Street Fight
8 Fish swallowing deer
9 Circus scene
10 Cham/Khmer battle scenes

SECOND ENCLOSING WALL

11 King and ascetics, with hunting scene
12 Mount Meru
13 Military parade/musicians/fishermen
14 Shiva and Vishnu
15 Musicians
16 Construction scene
17 Harbour scene
18 Churning of the Ocean of Milk
19 Offerings scene
20 Ten-armed Shiva
21 Military parade
22 Legend of the Leper King

The western side of the south wall has carvings on its lower half only, including a panel showing arms, including a **crossbow** deployed from the back of an elephant and a **catapult** on wheels.

Third enclosing wall bas-reliefs: west wall

The first portion of the **western wall** is unfinished; look out here for an **ascetic climbing a tree** to escape from a hungry tiger, near the centre of the panel. Towards the centre of the panel, before the gopura, a **street fight** is in progress: people shake their arms in anger, while above, two severed heads are shown to the crowd.

Along the northern half of the west wall, look out for the scene showing men with sticks chasing other men with round shields, passing a pond in which a **large fish swallows a small deer.**

Third enclosing wall bas-reliefs: north wall

On the western side of the **north wall**, a light-hearted **circus** scene features jugglers, acrobats and wrestlers alongside a parade of animals including rhinos, rabbits and deer. The section beyond the north gopura is badly eroded, though you can just about make

ANGKOR FROM THE AIR

An exhilarating way to see Angkor is from the air. Although over-flying of the temples is not permitted, you can still get a wonderful overview by balloon, helicopter or microlight. Angkor passes (see p.190) are not required for any of these aerial excursions.

By balloon The cheapest option is from the gondola of a tethered helium balloon ($15, children $7.50; 15min) located between the airport and Angkor Wat. Weather permitting the balloon ascends to 200m around thirty times a day, carrying up to thirty passengers at a time, offering a bird's-eye view of Angkor Wat and nearby temples.

By helicopter Thrilling 8min helicopter trips from Siem Reap's airport (from $90/person) around the Angkor Wat area run by Helistar Cambodia (☎063 966072, ⊛helistarcambodia.com) and Helicopters Cambodia (☎063 963316, ⊛helicopterscambodia .com). Longer flights can also be arranged over the Tonle Sap, Kulen hills and so on.

By microlight Most exciting of all are SkyVenture's microlight trips (⊛skyventure.org); flights start at $60/person for 15min around Roluos up to $180 for a 1hr "see it all" trip.

3

out the **fighting** between the Khmer and Cham resuming, with the Khmer running away towards the mountains. By the time you've turned the corner to the northern half of the east wall, the battle is in full swing, and even the elephants are taking part, one trying to rip out the tusk of another.

Second enclosing wall bas-reliefs

Inside the third enclosing wall, a passage on the middle of the south side of the central sanctuary leads up to the **bas-reliefs** of the **second enclosing wall**, raised up about 1.5m above the level of the third enclosure. These bas-reliefs aren't in great condition and are more difficult to follow than those of the third enclosing wall, being broken up by towers and antechambers into small panels. It is likely these were only seen by the king and his priests, unlike the scenes in the third gallery, which would have been accessible to the hoi polloi. Interestingly, although the Bayon was dedicated as a Buddhist temple, there are plenty of depictions here of **Hindu gods**. As with the bas-reliefs on the third enclosing wall, these were intended to be viewed **clockwise**, starting from the **midpoint of the eastern wall**, which is how they're described below.

In the vestibule **south of the east gopura**, a **hunt** is shown in progress, below which the king is shown tarrying in the palace, surrounded by ascetics. The wall is a bit crumbled as you turn the corner into the south gallery, but it's possible to make out **Mount Meru** rising out of the ocean – here denoted by the fish. Moving on, beyond the tower, **warriors parade** from left to right, while a band of musicians leaves the palace. Below, a dead child is being placed in a coffin; close by, a fisherman casts his net from his boat, while apsaras hover above. **Shiva and Vishnu** appear in numerous, mostly worn, scenes in the section **west of the south gopura**; towards the end of this section you'll see Shiva standing in a pool while ascetics and animals look on from the bank; in the same area people prostrate themselves around Vishnu, while a funeral is in progress.

In the **west gallery**, pop into the tower before the gopura and you'll find **musicians** playing celestial music while apsaras dance. Labourers hauling stones over rollers and lifting them into place can be seen in a curious **construction scene** (on the tiny section of gallery between the tower and the gopura) which oddly enough has had a depiction of Vishnu superimposed on it. Just before the gopura is a **harbour scene**, with chess players on board one of the boats, and a cockfight on another.

The first few sections of carvings beyond the west gopura are in poor condition, so head straight to the section of gallery **north of the tower**, where there's yet another depiction of the story of the **Churning of the Ocean of Milk** (see p.169). The reliefs around the corner in the **north gallery** are in better nick; in the first section servants are shown carrying offerings to a mountain sanctuary with elephants and other wildlife,

ANGKOR THOM BY ELEPHANT

If you want to do things in style you can make your way to the Bayon from Angkor Thom's southern gateway by **elephant** (7.30–10.30am; $10–15). The pachyderms wait at the stand by the southern causeway in the morning, although you won't find any in the afternoon, when they all head off to Phnom Bakheng (see p.170).

while boats ferry in worshippers. **Beyond the western tower**, it's worth pausing to check out the pantheon of gods: a fine **ten-armed Shiva** is flanked by Vishnu on his right and Brahma on his left, and surrounded by apsaras.

Turning the corner, you're back in the **east gallery**, where there's a **military parade** featuring musicians accompanying cavalry, and a six-wheeled chariot drawn by Hamsa, the sacred goose and mount of Brahma. The final panel of note, in the gallery just before the gopura, pertains to the legend of the **Leper King**, in which the king contracts leprosy after being spattered with the venom of a serpent he fights. As women minister to the king, a cure is sought from ascetics.

The first enclosure and central sanctuary

Besides corner towers, the second enclosing wall appears to have a further three towers per side; these are actually part of the **first enclosing wall**, which takes the form of a toothed cross, the points of which merge into the second enclosing wall. The complexity of the construction is compounded in the first enclosure, where towers bearing four faces stand closely packed, at each angle of the cross and on the small sanctuaries.

Whichever route you take into the first enclosure, you'll be presented with a veritable forest of massive, four-faced towers, each face wearing an enigmatic expression with just a glimmer of a smile. Unusually in Khmer architecture, the low platform of the central sanctuary is more or less circular, with eight linked **meditation chambers** spaced around it.

Terrace of the Elephants

Laid out in alignment with the west wall of the Bayon, the **Terrace of the Elephants** originally served as the base for a now-vanished royal reception hall and viewing platform over the surrounding area. The terrace is named for the fabulous bas-relief frieze of elephants stretching some 300m along its eastern side, with hundreds of the beasts (and their mahouts) shown hunting and fighting with tigers. Three elaborate sets of **staircases** lead up onto the terrace at its northern and southern ends and in the middle. The southern stairs are flanked with three-headed elephants, their trunks (entwined around lotus buds) forming impromptu columns. The central staircase sports lion- and garuda-head creatures, their arms upraised, as if supporting the weight of the terrace above. On top of the terrace at its northern end is a raised plaform decorated with a frieze of sacred **geese** (*hamsa*) that would formerly have supported a royal building of some kind. Close by, at the northern end of the terrace, is a striking carving of a **five-headed horse**, hidden behind a later wall that was constructed to buttress the terrace.

Terrace of the Leper King

Adjoining the Terrace of the Elephants, the **Terrace of the Leper King** is believed to have been the site of royal cremations – appropriately, the headless statue on the terrace is that of Yama, god of the underworld, although the vandalized figure is in fact a reproduction. For many years, the statue was assumed to depict Jayavarman VII himself, who several legends say contracted the disease – although there is nothing to verify this.

The base of the terrace is covered with profuse **carvings** layered in tiers. Snakes and sea creatures inhabit the lowest tier, with gods and goddesses above. On the south side at the base of the terrace a small gap leads into a narrow, trench-like walkway that loops around the terrace inside the exterior walls. Here you'll find the so-called "**hidden**

carvings", perhaps even more spectacular than those on the outside, with further elaborately bejewelled gods and goddesses arranged in tiers above multi-headed nagas. The walkway was previously filled with rubble and covered over – the theory is that the original terrace (whose outer wall this was) had begun to collapse and so a new retaining wall was built around it.

Prasat Suor Prat

Rising on the opposite side of the road from the Terrace of the Elephants are twelve distinctive laterite-and-sandstone towers, each with doors on two sides and windows on three. They're now known as the **Prasat Suor Prat**, "Towers of the Tightrope Walkers", although their original purpose isn't known – and it certainly wasn't for supporting a tightrope. According to Zhou Daguan they were places for resolving disputes: the parties concerned were kept shut up in one of the towers for between one and four days, at the end of which (it was said) unless the heavens passed judgement, after which the guilty person would inevitably be struck down by some illness or affliction, while the innocent party would emerge as healthy as at the moment they went in.

The Kleangs

Behind Prasat Suor Prat are the **Kleangs**, comprising two enormous warehouse-like buildings with 1.5m-thick walls, open at both ends – although exactly whatever they were built for remains unclear. The North Kleang is the older of the two and was erected towards the end of the tenth century, possibly by Jayavarman V or Jayaviravarman. The unfinished South Kleang is thought to have been constructed by Suryavarman I to balance the view from the royal palace.

Baphuon

Only recently reopened after fifty years of intermittent restoration (see box below), the eleventh-century **Baphuon**, the state temple of Udayadityavarman II, is one of the most brutally imposing of all Angkor's temples – a veritable mountain of stone, austere and faintly forbidding.

The principal approach is (as usual) from the east, along an impressive, 172m-long sandstone **causeway** raised on three sets of stone posts and with a ruined pavilion halfway (perhaps the base of what was originally a gopura), decorated with entertaining human and animal carvings.

BAFFLING BAPHUON

Angkor's longest-running conservation saga, the **fifty-year restoration** of the **Baphuon** temple is a dramatic illustration of the pitfalls and perils of field archeology in action. Work on the temple began in 1959 under the supervision of French architects, who decided that the only way to save Baphuon from collapse was to dismantle the vast structure piece by piece and then put it all back together again – a technique known as "anastylosis". The temple was therefore dismantled in preparation for its reconstruction, only for war to break out, after which work was abandoned in 1971.

All might have been well, even so, had the Khmer Rouge not decided, in a moment of whimsical iconoclasm, to destroy every last archeological record relating to work on the temple, including plans showing how the hundreds of thousands of stones that had been taken apart were intended to fit back together again. Meaning that when restoration work finally restarted in 1995 conservators were faced (as Pascal Royere, who oversaw the project, put it) with "a three-dimensional, 300,000-piece puzzle to which we had lost the picture".

Progress, not surprisingly, was slow, and it wasn't until 2011 that restorations were finally concluded (at a total cost of $14m) and the temple restored to something approaching its former glory. Numerous unidentified stones can still be seen laid out around the complex, even so – unplaced pieces in a great archeological jigsaw that will never entirely be solved.

At the end of the causeway rises the mighty central **pyramid** (24m high), which consists of five steep tiers divided by galleries into three enclosures (although the topmost tier remains out of bounds and steep wooden steps now replace the hopelessly eroded original stone staircases). Each gallery has elaborate **gopuras** at the four cardinal points – the outermost of the three eastern gopuras is particularly impressive, topped by a lotus-petal motif and with engaging square carvings depicting the animals of Chinese astrology. Further carvings can be found on the other gopuras, with intricate but shallow designs etched out of the blackish, hard-looking sandstone.

The outermost (third) enclosure is also where you'll find Baphuon's most memorable and unsual feature. Rising above the enclosure, the entire west-facing wall at the base of the pyramid has been moulded into the form of a gigantic **reclining Buddha**. It's a remarkable sight, although the roughness of the stones from which the Buddha is formed means that it can be surprisingly difficult to make out the shape within the stones – at least until you've seen it, when it becomes suddenly obvious, like some clever optical illusion. If you can't immediately see it, try again from a vantage point somewhere right outside the temple, since it can actually be easier to perceive from a distance.

Phimeanakas

The state temple of Suryavarman I, **Phimeanakas** originally stood in the grounds of the royal palace. Subsequently used for many purposes, it was absorbed into Angkor Thom around two hundred years later. The temple is relatively small and simple in plan, with three, steep rectangular tiers, surrounded by a small moat and all the temple buildings crammed on the topmost level. Elephants (damaged) stand at the corners of each level, while lions flank the stairs.

The temple is designed to be approached from the east; the stairs up to the top are steep and narrow and don't allow you to step off onto the first two levels. Once at the top, you can walk around the surrounding gallery, at whose centre a single cruciform sanctuary tower is raised on a platform. Zhou Daguan recorded that the sanctuary was said to be home to a spirit that took the form of a nine-headed serpent by day and a beautiful lady after dark. The king was obliged to visit her every night before seeing his wife, or else disaster would follow.

To the north of the temple are two paved **bathing ponds**, the smaller for women and the larger for men.

Tep Pranam and Preah Palilay

Tep Pranam, a couple of hundred metres northeast from the Terrace of the Leper King, dates from the ninth-century reign of Yasovarman I, although not much survives of the temple now bar an impressive, 6m-high Buddha, seated in the bhumispara (earth-witnessing) *mudra*. The Buddha actually only dates from around the sixteenth century and appears to reuse stones from the original temple, while the head may be more recent than the body on which it sits.

Further west, set in an area of quiet woodland, is **Preah Palilay**. Of the former temple only the central sandstone sanctuary – dating from the first half of the twelfth century – survives more or less intact. It too has a large seated Buddha, of modern provenance.

Thommanon

Consecrated to Vishnu, the small but florid **THOMMANON** Hindu temple was built by Suryavarman II in the early twelfth century, probably at the beginning of his reign (and therefore roughly contemporaneous with Angkor Wat). The temple follows the standard layout of the time, with a cell-like sanctuary, topped with a tower and connected to a mandapa (antechamber). Gopuras stand to the east and west, although the planned north and south gopuras were apparently never built and the wall that originally enclosed the entire complex has now almost completely vanished.

The temple was restored in 1935 and is in good condition, as are its numerous **carvings**, with finely carved devatas (female deities) in jewellery and headdresses on the exterior walls of the sanctuary, and further carvings adorning the mandapa including Vishnu on Garuda (inside on the eastern lintel) and Ravana shaking Mount Kailash (over the south doorway). Vishnu reappears on the north pediment of the eastern gopura, holding a foe by the hair, while the smaller western gopura has pretty door columns with tiny praying figures enclosed in a swirl of foliage.

Chau Say Tevoda

The sister temple to Thommanon, just over the road, **CHAU SAY TEVODA** was another creation of Suryavarman II, although dating from the end of his reign rather than the beginning. Originally even more elaborate than its sibling across the road, it's now badly eroded, and ugly lumps of grey concrete have been used to patch together the old stonework in places, with unfortunate effect.

The basic **layout** is similar to that at Thommanon, comprising a central sanctuary-plus-mandapa enclosed within a wall (now mostly disappeared) with four gopuras at the cardinal points; in addition, a pair of libraries stand either side of the mandapa. Nowadays visitors approach from the road on the north side, although originally the main approach was from the east across the impressive raised **causeway** with octagonal columns that you can still see today, although it now leads nowhere in particular.

Most of the temple's elaborate **carvings** are badly worn, although a few reasonably preserved examples survive here and there, including some rich floral decorations on the mandapa and a couple of disfigured devatas with their faces bashed off.

Spean Thma

Just 200m east of Thommanon and Chau Say Tevoda is the ancient bridge of **Spean Thma**, built using carved sandstone from nearby temples. Once spanning the Siem Reap River, the bridge is now rather stranded, the river having shifted its course. If you step off the road you'll be able to spot mismatched carvings on some of the stones, which were probably recycled from elsewhere when the bridge was rebuilt in the sixteenth century.

Ta Keo

At the western end of the East Baray reservoir stands **TA KEO**, the imposing state temple of Jayavarman V – an austere mountain of stone in the style of Baphuon and Pre Rup, topped with the usual quincunx of closely spaced towers. The temple was begun around 975 but never finished – legend has it that construction was abandoned after the temple was struck by lightning, an unlucky omen. Constructed entirely of sandstone, Ta Keo is practically undecorated; some sources say that the particular sandstone used is exceptionally hard and too difficult to carve, although fine (though weathered) floral carving around the base of the pyramid seems to contradict that.

Four sets of steep steps at the cardinal points climb up to the small **outer enclosure**, its eastern side almost completely filled by two long and narrow hallways decorated with baluster windows.

From here, further steps lead up into the slightly larger **inner enclosure**, enclosed by a narrow, cloister-like **gallery** (although only the base remains in places). This is the earliest example of what would subsequently become a recurrent feature of Khmer architecture, although unusually the gallery appears to be completely lacking in doors, suggesting that it served a purely decorative function. Two well-preserved **libraries** flank the steps on the enclosure's eastern side, their upper storeys decorated with false windows, and with a further pair of unidentified stone buildings next to them, tucked into the corners of the enclosure.

From here, you can climb one of the steep stairways that lead straight up the temple's three uppermost tiers to reach the **top of the pyramid**, more than 21m above the ground, and the five sanctuary towers, dedicated to Shiva.

Ta Prohm

The jungle-smothered ruins of **TA PROHM** are one of the most evocative of all Angkor's ancient monuments – its courtyards and terraces half-consumed by the encroaching forest, with shrines and pavilions engulfed by giant strangler figs and the massive roots of kapok trees clinging to walls, framing doorways and prising apart giant stones. The temple richly fulfils every Indiana Jones-cum-Tomb Raiderish romantic cliché you could possibly imagine – a uniquely serendipitous combination of human artifice and raw nature working together in accidental harmony, with impossibly picturesque results.

That, at least, is what the films and photographs suggest – the reality is slightly less romantic. Crowds are a serious problem, while massive ongoing restoration means that parts of the temple currently resemble an enormous building site as conservationists attempt to walk the impossible tightrope between preserving Ta Prohm's original lost-in-the-jungle atmosphere while preventing it from being obliterated entirely by the surrounding forest. It's a magical place, even so, assuming you're not expecting to be left alone to commune with nature, and especially if you can time your visit to avoid the worst of the coach parties (see box below).

Brief history

Constructed by Jayavarman VII around 1186, Ta Prohm was a **Buddhist monastery** dedicated to Prajnaparamita, and would once have housed a statue of this deity in the image of the king's mother (inscriptions say that a further 260 holy images were installed in surrounding chambers and niches). The monastery accommodated twelve thousand people, who lived and worked within its grounds, while a further eighty thousand were employed locally to service and maintain the complex. Ta Prohm also supplied provisions and medicines to the 102 hospitals that Jayavarman instituted around the kingdom.

The site

As at other temple-monasteries such as the roughly contemporaneous Banteay Kdei and Preah Khan, Ta Prohm follows the archetypal pattern of the so-called Angkorian **"flat" temple** (see box, p.163) – although myriad collapsed walls and accumulated rubble have significantly blurred the neatness of the original plan.

The majority of visitors arrive **from Ta Keo** while on the Petit Circuit, approaching from the west, but if you use the track off the road northwest of Banteay Kdei, you can enter **from the east** as was originally intended, and which is how we describe it here.

Entering the site from the east, you pass through a collapsed gopura, from where a path heads some 500m through forest to reach the temple itself to reach the main

---

CROWDS AT TA PROHM

In tourist terms, **Ta Prohm** (along with Angkor Wat and the Bayon) is one of Angkor's three big sights, and as such gets overwhelmed with visiting coach parties on a regular basis throughout most of the day. Meanwhile, the relative smallness of the site means that negotiating your way through the ruins' narrow corridors and doorways in peak hours (roughly 10am–2pm) has all the charm of a visit to a major metropolitan subway station at the height of rush hour. The whole depressing spectacle probably isn't why you came to Cambodia, and is best avoided, if possible. The **best times to visit** are in the early morning (between 7am and 9am) or in the late afternoon (after 4pm). Both early morning and late afternoon also offer the best photographic opportunities, as the light lowers and softens through the surrounding trees.

eastern gopura, decorated with fine carvings depicting the life of the Buddha. Beyond here is the impressive terrace that formerly supported the buildings of the **Hall of Dancers** (similar to that at Banteay Kdei).

The main section

Walking across the terrace beyond the eastern gopura brings you to the main section of the temple – comprising a large third enclosure within which are the more tightly packed first and second enclosures, the entire edifice topped by a baffling profusion of small towers (39 in total) in various states of photogenic decay. Some of the most photographed **trees** in the world lie further in, scattered inside the second and first enclosures – usually complete with long queues of visitors waiting for their chance to have themselves snapped posing among the roots.

The remains of richly decorated walls and various apsaras survive within the **first enclosure**, almost as if nature has compensated for the overall destruction by preserving the details. At the heart of the temple is the surprisingly tiny **central sanctuary**, now bare inside, although small holes in the walls indicate that it was once clad in wood or metal panels.

From here it's worth continuing straight ahead and out onto the western side of the temple, then retracing your way back around the northern side of the third enclosure, normally relatively peaceful even in peak hour, where further giant kapok trees can be seen hugging the temple walls, with nothing but untouched forest beyond.

Banteay Kdei

BANTEAY KDEI (Citadel of the Cells) was built by Jayavarman VII as a Buddhist monastery over the site of an earlier tenth-century temple by Rajendravarman. The overall layout is similar to Ta Prohm, although the buildings here remained in fairly continual use until the 1960s and so lack the lost-in-the-jungle atmosphere that makes Ta Prohm so memorable – and, equally, the appalling crowds. That said, ongoing habitation failed to prevent some pretty major masonry collapses, perhaps due to a combination of low-quality sandstone and poor building techniques – the most vulnerable sections are now propped up with permanent wooden struts and scaffolding.

Entrance is from the east, through the enclosing wall beneath a fine **gopura** topped with Lokesvara faces. A few minutes' walk brings you to the remains of a laterite causeway across a moat, connecting to the **Hall of the Dancers**, named for the reliefs of apsaras that decorate its pillars and exterior walls.

Immediately beyond the Hall of the Dancers is the temple proper, comprising a **central sanctuary** surrounded by two concentric **galleries** and topped by seven closely grouped **towers** – although the confusing jumble of tiny rooms and courtyards, and myriad collapsed walls, rather obscures the basic plan. Beautiful carvings survive here and there among the ruins, including elaborate leaf motifs on the walls and female divinities in niches – although many of the monastery's Buddha images have been crudely hacked out.

Srah Srang

East of Banteay Kdei, the royal bathing pool of **Srah Srang** was probably the work of Kavindramantha, an army-general-cum-architect who was also responsible for building the temples of East Mebon and Pre Rup. Excavated for Rajendravarman I, the pool once had simple earth embankments, and rules had to be issued to stop people allowing elephants to clamber over them to be bathed in the waters below. Two hundred years later, Jayavarman VII had the banks lined with sandstone and built a regal terrace offering views over the water. The remains of a paved causeway edged with naga balustrades, which once linked the pool with Banteay Kdei to the west, can also be seen here.

Prasat Kravan

South of Banteay Kdei is the simple little **PRASAT KRAVAN**, the Cardamom Sanctuary, consecrated around 921 during the reign of Harshavarman I and comprising a row of five brick towers sitting on a low platform – a 1960 restoration left them looking, if anything, a bit too neat and new, although the exceptional quality of the brickwork (precisely fitted, and held together using a kind of vegetable glue rather than mortar) might silence even the most hard-to-impress builder.

Male guardians in niches decorate the exterior of the **central tower**, although more interesting are the reliefs of Vishnu within – ones shows him mounted on Garuda; another shows his dwarf incarnation, Vamana, bestriding the universe in three giant steps; another, a rather worn rendering of Vishnu with eight arms, was probably once covered in stucco and painted. The northernmost tower is dedicated to Lakshmi, wife of Vishnu and goddess of good fortune. Inside, an intricate relief shows her bare-breasted and wearing a pleated *sampot*, flanked by two kneeling worshippers and surrounded by swags of leaves and dangling pendant motifs.

Pre Rup

One of Angkor's most impressive monuments – and the undoubted highlight of the Grand Circuit – the great state temple of **PRE RUP** (built by Rajendravarman and consecrated to Shiva in around 962) is the archetypal ancient Khmer temple-mountain. Access is from the eastern side, where five tall **brick towers** stand sentinel overlooking the road (space was left for a sixth tower, which never got built).

Entering the **first enclosure** you'll see a small stone "cistern" directly in front of you. Long assumed to be associated with cremations (the name Pre Rup means, literally, "turning the body"), it's now agreed that this probably formed the pedestal for a statue of Nandin. Flanking the cistern are a pair of brick libraries, their walls pierced with unusual slits to aid ventilation. Nearby, in the northeast corner of the enclosure a small, square, laterite building – open on all sides – once housed a stele. The rest of the enclosure is largely filled with long halls, now mostly ruined.

Stairways guarded by lions lead up all four sides of the majestic **pyramid**. Twelve small, symmetrically arranged shrines stand around the lowest level. Five quincunx **towers** stand at the summit, soaring memorably above the surrounding forest canopy. The two towers on the western side (which once housed statues of Lakshmi and Uma) feature carved reliefs of female divinities including a female consort of Brahma on the southwest tower (where you can also make out remnants of the gritty white-lime stucco that once coated the towers). Carvings of male deities adorn the central and two eastern towers, once home to statues of Vishnu and Shiva.

East Mebon

Erected in 953 for Rajendravarman, **EAST MEBON** (pronounced "*May*bon") once stood on an island surrounded by the waters of the (now dry) East Baray – the broad steps below each of the four gopuras were originally landing stages, as the temple would only have been accessible by boat. The temple was actually built by the king for his parents, although it's closer to the great state temples in style, topped by a cluster of soaring, closely spaced towers – which would doubtless have looked even more memorable when seen rising from the waters of the East Baray. Impressive from a distance, the temple is relatively disappointing close up. Much of it would originally have been colourfully plastered and painted, although the general effect now is rather bare, the general austerity relieved only by the finely carved doorways and lintels that decorate the various gopuras and towers.

Access to the temple is via the eastern gopura, which brings you into the **outer enclosure**, lined with a series of ruined meditation halls. The western gopura, on the

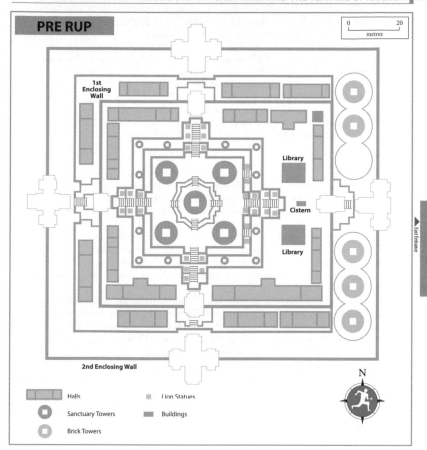

PRE RUP

0 ___ 20
metres

1st Enclosing Wall

Library

Cistern

Library

2nd Enclosing Wall

N

East Entrance

3

Halls

Lion Statues

Sanctuary Towers

Buildings

Brick Towers

opposite side of the enclosure, features a reasonably preserved lintel carving of Vishnu in his incarnation as the man-lion Narasimha, ripping apart the king of the demons.

Above rise the two tiers of the central pyramid with almost life-sized **elephant statues** positioned at each corner, serving as guardians, and so facing outwards. Four sets of steps lead up to the **inner enclosure**, each flanked with a pair of towers, their doors finely decorated with carved foliage. Five rectangular, windowless laterite buildings are arranged around the enclosure, although their original function remains unknown.

Further steps lead up to the topmost level and the five sanctuary **towers**, arranged in the customary quincunx pattern. These are made of brick but were originally covered in stucco – you can still see the numerous round holes cut into the brickwork to help the coating adhere. The **carvings** on the sandstone lintels are also worth a look: the central tower features Indra on a three-headed elephant (on its east side), Shiva on Nandin (south) and Skanda on a peacock (west).

Ta Som

The small, tumbledown Buddhist temple of **TA SOM** has been badly knocked about by time and the jungle since it was built by Jayavarman VII in the twelfth century, but still has plenty of character, feeling a little like a miniature Ta Prohm without the crowds (although recent renovations have tidied it up significantly).

The usual approach is from the road to the west of the temple, passing through a gopura with face tower, over a small moat and into the walled **central enclosure**. The sanctuary itself is nothing more than a single, crumbling cruciform tower. More interesting are the numerous niched **apsaras** decorating the wall around the enclosure. Some of these figures are quite unusual – one is nestling a bird in her hand, while a couple of others are wringing out their hair after a bath. Have a look, too, at the gopura on the eastern side of the central enclosure (next to the moat), one of whose porches has been spectacularly engulfed in a giant strangler fig.

Neak Pean

The beautiful water temple of **NEAK PEAN** (literally "entwined serpents") is quite unlike anything else at Angkor, with a single tower sitting in the centre of a large pool, connected to four subsidiary pools at the cardinal points. It's really more of a symbolic water garden than a temple, although what it all originally meant remains unclear. The most popular theory holds that it represents Anavatapa, a mythical Himalayan lake whose waters had miraculous curative powers. Zhou Daguan describes it as "having a central square tower of gold with several dozen stone rooms", suggesting that the temple may even have been a kind of spa, with pilgrims coming to take the waters.

The temple originally stood on an island in the **northern baray**, which still fills up with considerable amounts of water after rain. To reach the temple you'll have to walk over the long, raised wooden walkway that connects it with the road to the north, running through a beautiful area of forest, often flooded. Unfortunately, at present, barriers prevent you from walking around the temple itself, and you'll have to be content with a long-range view. The sanctuary tower stands directly ahead – if water levels are low enough you may be able to make out the steps, formed from coiled stone serpents, which curl round the base of the tower (hence the temple's unusual name). Emerging from the waters of the main pool on the east side of the tower is a large **statue of a horse** with people clinging to its sides; legend has it that it's Lokesvara, who once turned himself into a horse, Balaha, to rescue merchants from ogresses on an island off Sri Lanka.

Preah Khan

Built by Jayavarman VII on the site of an earlier palace, the massive complex of **PREAH KHAN** (not to be confused with the huge temple-citadel of Preah Khan in Kompong Thom province) served simultaneously as temple, monastery and university. As the last, it employed more than a thousand teachers and 97,840 ancillary staff – inscriptions found here reveal that ten tonnes of rice were delivered daily, enough to feed ten to fifteen thousand people. However, in 1191 Preah Khan was consecrated as a multi-faith temple, catering to worshippers of Buddha, Shiva and Vishnu, plus a further 282 gods, some made in the image of local dignitaries and national heroes; though the main deity was Lokesvara, made in the likeness of the king's father, and placed in the central – Buddhist – sanctuary.

> **THE SACRED SWORD**
>
> The **sacred sword**, as the name of Preah Khan translates, is said to have been a weapon ceremonially passed by Jayavarman II to his heir, and Cambodians still believe that whoever possesses this sword has the right to the country's throne – many believe a replica of the sword is kept under lock and key at the Royal Palace in Phnom Penh.

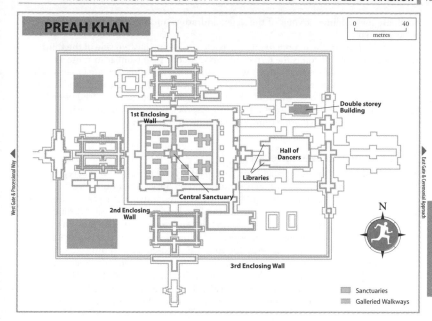

PREAH KHAN

West Gate & Processional Way

East Gate & Ceremonial Approach

1st Enclosing Wall

Double storey Building

Hall of Dancers

Libraries

Central Sanctuary

2nd Enclosing Wall

3rd Enclosing Wall

N

3

Sanctuaries

Galleried Walkways

The site

The layout of the temple is similar to that of Banteay Kdei and Ta Prohm – indeed there's a distinct touch of Ta Prohm about the site as a whole, with tumbled heaps of greenish, lichen-coated sandstone half-smothered by the surrounding trees. Large portions of the structure have collapsed. As at Banteay Kdei, this may have been the result of faulty construction – the central area, closely packed with sanctuaries and passages, was extended on numerous occasions.

Most people now approach from the west (which is how we describe it below), although you can also enter in the traditional direction from the east; or (even better) walk from one side to the other and arrange to be picked up by your driver on the opposite side to save backtracking.

The entire complex is surrounded by an enclosing wall and moat, with the usual gopuras and causeways in each cardinal direction. Approaching from the west, the first section of the path (near the car park) is lined with interesting **boundary stones**, their lower halves carved with cartoonish *kala*-like monsters – the niches at the top of each pillar once contained Buddha images, which were crudely cut out when the state religion reverted to Hinduism. Beyond here the path crosses a causeway flanked by impressive naga balustrades before reaching the main temple complex after around 250m.

Entering through the gopura here brings you into the tranquil **third enclosure** decorated with beautifully carved apsaras in niches. Beyond here lie the dense cluster of buildings within the tightly packed **second** and **first enclosures** (an intricate design further confused by large-scale masonry falls), with views of doors and windows framed within one another in receding, Escheresque perspectives. Patches of fine floral carving cover many of the walls and surfaces, as if in imitation of the natural vegetation consuming the buildings on all sides. Also dotted around here are more than twenty tiny sanctuaries that once contained holy images, while more would have been housed in the alcoves of the surrounding gallery.

At the heart of the temple, the **central sanctuary** contains a dome-shaped **stupa**, added in the sixteenth century. More tricky to find in a collapsed section to the north are two sublime carvings of the sisters **Indradevi** and **Jayadevi**, both wives of Jayavarman.

Continue through the temple to emerge back out on the **eastern side of the third enclosure**. In front of you is the terrace of the Dancers' Hall (similar to those at Banteay Kdei and Ta Prohm), dotted with columns carved with dancing apsaras, while to your left is an unusual two-storey building, its portico of round columns giving it a strangely Neoclassical look, which it's thought may have housed the **sacred sword** (see box, p.184). A photogenic scatter of towering **kapok** trees have also established themselves hereabouts, clinging onto various walls and buildings.

West Baray and West Mebon

Accessible only via the airport road from Siem Reap, Angkor's huge **West Baray** reservoir, 8km long and more than 2km wide, was excavated by Suryavarman I; it's been calculated that six thousand men would have needed more than three years to dig it out. The *baray* was restored in 1957 and, unlike the East Baray, contains water throughout the year, making it a popular local spot for **picnics and swimming**. Rest huts line the embankment at the leisure area to the south, which is also where you can rent a boat ($5) out to the island-temple, the **West Mebon**. This mid-eleventh-century temple, attributed to Udayadityavarman II, has practically disappeared; only the eastern towers, bearing small decorations of animals in square motifs, are in reasonable condition. The island on which it stands was once linked to the shore by a causeway, and surrounded by a wall with three pavilions per side and windows overlooking the *baray*.

Roluos Group

Off NR6, 12km east of Siem Reap, the temples now referred to as the **Roluos Group** – after the nearby village of that name – are spread out over the former site of the royal city of **Hariharalaya**, and encompass some of the earliest monuments of the Angkor period. Among those most easily visited are three brick-and-sandstone temples built by Indravarman I and his son, Yasovarman I, in the late ninth century, all featuring finely decorated columns and lintels. These are the **Bakong**, the first state temple of the Angkor period; **Lolei**, which has particularly fine Sanskrit inscriptions; and **Preah Ko**, which preserves some elegant carvings.

Preah Ko

PREAH KO was built by Indravarman I in 879 to honour the spirits of his ancestors, as well as one of his predecessors, Jayavarman II. The temple sits right next to the road, entered from the east through a ruined **gopura**, largely vanished bar a pair of impressive balustraded windows. Walking through the gopura you reach the temple's two inner enclosures, although the wall that originally divided them has largely disappeared. The eye-catching square brick structure (on your left as you enter) may have been a **library** or crematorium; ventilation holes have been cut into the top of the building, with eroded carvings of ascetics seated in niches between.

At the centre of the temple, on a low platform, stand six closely grouped brick-and-sandstone **towers**, arranged in two rows of three and still covered in places by the crumbling remains of the lime plaster which once covered them completely. The front three towers were dedicated to the king's paternal ancestors, watched over by a trio of sacred bulls (one headless) and with male guardians (*dvarapalas*) standing in niches at their corners. The three smaller rear towers were dedicated to maternal ancestors and have female guardians instead.

The towers are most notable for the fine **carvings** on their doorframes and lintels (a number of long inscriptions can also be seen on several doorjambs). Many feature a leering *kala* spewing out a floral arch, some with miniature horsemen galloping along the top of the arch and tiny figures riding three-headed snakes below, and with *makaras* at either end.

Opposite the temple, look out for the interesting outdoor exhibition of **miniature temple replicas** (donation appreciated) created by sculptor Dy Proeung. Meticulously executed using architectural elevations and floor plans drawn up by Proeung while working for Angkor Conservation and the École Française d'Extrême-Orient during the 1960s, the models (of Angkor Wat, Bakong, Banteay Srei, Preah Ko and Preah Vihear) give an excellent idea of what these complexes would have looked like when originally constructed.

Bakong

The undoubted highlight of the Roluos circuit, **BAKONG** is the first of the great Angkor state temples, prefiguring (if not quite rivalling) the huge temple-pyramids of Pre Rup and Baphuon. The temple was constructed by Indravarman I and consecrated to Shiva in 881, although surprisingly, the grand sanctuary **tower** at the very top wasn't added until some 250 years after the temple was first consecrated.

The entire complex is enclosed within a broad moat with a modern wat tucked into one corner – an unusually photogenic combination. From the parking area a **causeway** crosses the moat to the eastern gopura, beyond which stretches the temple's expansive **inner enclosure**, with the central pyramid rising out of its centre. Entering the enclosure the path is flanked by a pair of well-preserved hallways with ornate balustraded windows, along with two square buildings with ventilation holes in their walls, probably crematoria. Eight large brick towers in various states of decay are arranged around the base of the pyramid, two per side, their sandstone doors displaying some fine carvings,

The central **pyramid** is arranged over no less than five tiers, the overall design notably larger but less steep than later state temples. Lions flank the staircase up the pyramid, while guardian elephants stand in each corner, similar to those at East Mebon. Spaced out around the fourth tier are twelve small sandstone shrines, now empty, though they would once have housed linga.

At the summit of the pyramid stands the solitary tower – a fine structure, although it looks rather lonely up there on its own and proves how much more visually satisfying the traditional quincunx arrangement of towers at the summit of other state temples is.

Lolei

Now situated within the grounds of a modern pagoda, **LOLEI** originally stood on an artificial island in the centre of the **Indratataka Baray**, though the reservoir is now dry. Dedicated to the parents and maternal grandparents of Yasovarman I and consecrated to Shiva, the temple consists of four brick towers (six were originally planned), although one has now partially collapsed and the others are crumbling. Well-preserved Sanskrit inscriptions can be seen on the doorways of the rear towers, detailing the work rotas of temple servants, and there's also a particularly fine lintel on the rear northern tower.

Banteay Samre

Part of the Grand Circuit (although slightly remote from the other temples on that itinerary, and often omitted), **BANTEAY SAMRE** lies east of **Phum Pradak** village, 12km northeast of Siem Reap. No inscriptions have been found to date the temple, which was named after the Samres, a tribe who lived in the vicinity of Phnom Kulen. However, its style of architecture places its construction in the middle of the twelfth century, around the same time as Angkor Wat. It was superbly restored by French archeologist Maurice Glaize – one of the most notable figures in the early history of Angkor conservation – in the 1940s.

Banteay Samre is unique among the Angkor temples in having **two moats** within the complex itself. The temple, enclosed by a high laterite wall with cruciform gopuras at each of the cardinal points, is approached via a 200m-long paved causeway. Entering through the east gopura, you arrive in an open gallery whose rows of sandstone columns were once part of a roofed gallery that would have run the full perimeter of the enclosure. The paved sunken area ahead was once the first of the moats, forming the second enclosure. Tales from the *Ramayana* are depicted on various **carvings** here – the siege of Lanka is shown on the gopura pediments, the fight between Rama and Ravana on the east tower, and Rama carried by Hanuman on the north tower.

Crossing the moat, you pass through another gopura, with double vestibules to the north and south, the passages of which connect to a raised gallery separating the two moats. Rising out of the inner moat like islands are the **central sanctuary**, connected to the walkway via a gopura to the east, and two **libraries**, which would only have been reachable by boat when the moats were filled.

3

Cambodia Landmine Museum

7km south of Banteay Srei on the main road to Siem Reap • Daily 7.30am–5.30pm • $3 • ☎ 015 674163, Ⓦ cambodialandmine museum.org

South of Banteay Srei temple, the **Cambodia Landmine Museum** is the creation of Aki Ra, a self-taught de-miner who was once forced to lay mines as a Vietnamese conscript. Crammed full of rusting mines and other military paraphernalia, the museum offers a stark reminder of the ongoing devastation caused by mines both in Cambodia and elsewhere (see p.297), describing some of the historical background and human stories behind these deadly explosives. Museum profits go to support local mine victims.

Banteay Srei

Even if you're feeling pretty templed-out, you'll probably be captivated by **BANTEAY SREI**, 35km northeast of Siem Reap (and which can be conveniently combined in a single day-trip with Kbal Spean). Built of fine-grained rose-pink sandstone, it's the most elaborately decorated of all Angkor's monuments, its walls, false doors, lintels and exotic soaring pediments all richly embellished with floral motifs and *Ramayana* scenes.

Banteay Srei is also unusual in having been built not by a king, but by two local **dignitaries**: Yajnavaraha, who was a trusted guru to the monarch, and his brother. It was Rajendravarman who granted them the land and permission for a temple to be built, but although the sanctuary was consecrated in 967 to Shiva, it wasn't actually completed until the reign of Jayavarman V.

The site

The temple **layout** is relatively simple, with three enclosing walls, an inner moat and a row of three sanctuary towers at its centre. If the **eastern gopura** by which you enter the temple seems oddly stranded, that's because there was never an enclosing wall here. Note the very fine carving above the exterior of the gopura's east door, showing the god **Indra** squatting on his three-headed elephant Airavata.

From the eastern gopura, a paved **processional way** leads 75m west to the main temple complex. Around the midway point, a pavilion to the north boasts a particularly detailed engraved pediment showing Vishnu in his incarnation as the man-lion Narasimha. Just before you reach the gopura in the third enclosing wall, you'll find a carved pediment (lying upright on the ground to the right of the doorway) showing Sita swooning as she is abducted by Ravana. The **gopura** itself is one of the most dramatic at the site, with soaring finials and the carved scrolls of fine leaf decorations and floral motifs.

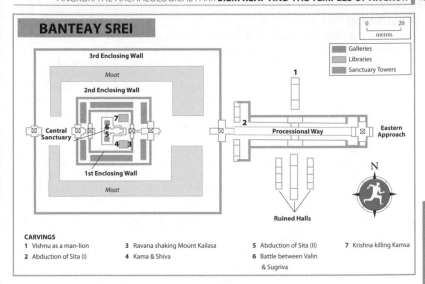

BANTEAY SREI

0   20
metres

Galleries
Libraries
Sanctuary Towers

3rd Enclosing Wall

Moat

2nd Enclosing Wall

Central
Sanctuary

1st Enclosing Wall

Moat

1

2   Processional Way   Eastern
Approach

N

Ruined Halls

CARVINGS
1 Vishnu as a man-lion   3 Ravana shaking Mount Kailasa   5 Abduction of Sita (II)   7 Krishna killing Kamsa
2 Abduction of Sita (I)   4 Kama & Shiva   6 Battle between Valin
                                                                        & Sugriva

3

In the rainy season, you'll be treated to marvellous reflections of the temple when the moat within the third enclosure fills. The narrow **second enclosure** is jammed with six long galleries, each subdivided into rooms that might have been meditation halls.

First enclosure

Virtually no surface within the **first enclosure** remains unadorned, although unfortunately you're no longer allowed inside the sanctuary towers, and the platform on which they stand is roped off to protect the carvings.

The carvings on the **sanctuary towers** are almost fussy in their profusion. The niches around the central sanctuary shelter male **guardians**, while those on the other towers house serene female **divinities**, complete with elegant *sampots* and elaborate jewellery. Crouched near the temple steps are more guardians, mythical figures with animal heads and human bodies (although these are actually reproductions, the originals having been removed, like many of the best sculptures here, during the French colonial period and taken to the Guimet museum of Asian art in Paris, where they remain, despite attempts to have them returned to Cambodia). The *Ramayana* scenes carved on the lintels of the central tower are particularly fine, featuring, to the west, another depiction of Sita being carried off by Ravana; and, to the north, the fight between the monkey gods Valin and Sugriva. The multi-tiered roofs of the towers are decorated with tiny replicas of the temple towers – meant to be homes for the temple gods.

There are more fine carvings on the east pediment of the **south library**, where Ravana is shown shaking Mount Kailash; Shiva sits on the mountain's summit with his wife Parvati, while the forest animals run away in fear. On the west pediment, Parvati can be seen asking for the aid of Kama, the god of love, after Shiva ignores her offering of a rosary; she finally wins Shiva's attention and his hand in marriage after Kama obligingly shoots him with an arrow.

The **north library** is dedicated to Vishnu, and accordingly the carvings focus on him. The close parallel streaks on the east pediment represent rain pouring down on the forest, through which Krishna – Vishnu's human incarnation – and his brother make their way, surrounded by wild animals. Krishna is seen taking revenge on his cruel uncle, King Kamsa, on the west pediment, with the palace in uproar as Krishna seizes him by the hair and prepares to kill him.

Kbal Spean

Daily 5am–3pm; allow at least 90min for the visit – it takes around 45min to climb the hill

In a magical area of jungle on the western side of the Kulen Mountains, **Kbal Spean** was used by the Khmer as a hill retreat in the mid-eleventh century, during which period they carved sacred linga and Hindu gods into the bedrock of the river – the water flowing down the river would thus be blessed by the carvings before coursing on to Angkor. The scenes depicting Vishnu are of marvellous ingenuity, not only for their skilful execution but also for the way they are tailored to the contours of the riverbed. Although looters have crudely hacked out some sections of bedrock, the scenes are almost as remarkable today as they were when first carved.

The path follows the east bank of the river and has a couple of steep stretches; you'll come to the top of the hill, a natural bridge, after about forty-five minutes' walk, which is a good place to start. Upstream lingas are carved into the riverbed, two reclining Vishnus and a carving of Uma and Shiva on the bull, Nandin. On the way down, stop to admire the veritable cobble of lingas, more reclining Vishnus and associated pantheon.

3

ARRIVAL AND DEPARTURE   TEMPLES OF ANGKOR: THE ARCHAEOLOGICAL PARK

There's no public transport to the temples, which are spread out over a fair area, so – unless you fancy **cycling** – you'll need to rent your own transport. **Tuk-tuks** are the most popular option – cheaper and more fun than a car, but more comfortable (and only slightly more expensive) than a **moto**. Note that foreign tourists are banned from riding **motorbikes** around Siem Reap and the temples, ostensibly to safeguard them from having their bikes stolen by agents of the rental companies in order to elicit a replacement fee (it's also been claimed that tourists can't safely negotiate the chaotic traffic). There are also various ways to see the temples from the air (see p.174).

By tuk-tuk or moto Siem Reap is awash with tuk-tuks and motos, although it's probably best to rent one through your guesthouse or hotel; pretty much all drivers speak at least a little English. Approximate prices are $12/$10 (tuk-tuk/moto) for the Small Circuit, $15/$12 for the Grand Circuit, $8/$6 for the Roluos Group. Add around $3/$2 if you want to start in time for sunrise. If you want to go off-menu and combine temples from the various groups (see p.164) you'll need to bargain a fare in advance.

By bike Cycling is in many ways the perfect way to experience the temples, although the distances involved are

not inconsiderable: the Small Circuit is around 30km long, and the Grand Circuit a little over 35km. This might not sound like that much in itself, but bear in mind that exploring the temples can be physically tiring on its own, even before you've started pedalling. If you do cycle, you might plan on visiting slightly fewer temples than if taking a vehicle. There are bike rental options in Siem Reap (see p.144).

By car A car and driver can be hired from most Siem Reap guesthouses and hotels, or from the tourist office (from $30). Costs are around $30/day around Angkor, $40 to Banteay Srei and $50–60 to Phnom Kulen.

INFORMATION

Opening hours All the temples within the Angkor Archaeological Park – which does not include Phnom Kulen (see opposite), Koh Ker (see p.192) and Beng Mealea (see opposite)– are open daily from 5am to 6pm.

Entry passes You must buy a pass to enter the Angkor Archaeological Park, and will need to show it at the various temples. Three categories of pass are available at the main entrance, on the Siem Reap–Angkor Wat road: one day ($20; this can also be purchased after 5pm, allowing entry for sunset on the day of purchase and all the following day); three days, valid for three days during the following week ($40); and seven days ($60), valid for one month. Children under 12 are admitted free, but you must show their passport as proof of age; children aged 12 and over are charged the full entrance fee. One-day passes only can be bought at the ticket office between the airport and Angkor Wat, at Roluos Group and at Banteay Srei. Note that payment is by cash only. There

is no need to provide a photo as these are now taken digitally at the ticket office. Separate tickets are required to visit Phnom Kulen (see opposite), Koh Ker (see p.192) and Beng Mealea (see opposite), with tickets issued at each temple.

Tour guides Highly trained, government-licensed guides to the Angkor temples can be booked through any of the various tourist offices in Siem Reap (see p.144), or sometimes at the ticket office, costing $25/day for an English-speaking guide. Note that guides do not drive tuk-tuks and tuk-tuk drivers do not guide.

Books There are several detailed and highly illustrated book-length guides to Angkor (see p.308), all widely available in Siem Reap (secondhand copies can be picked up for as little as $6 or so).

Safety If you plan to visit outlying temples we've not covered, you should seek advice from registered guides regarding the safety situation, as some sites have not been fully de-mined.

EATING AND DRINKING

There are at least a few **refreshment stalls** at most of the larger temple complexes, and restaurants at various places including Angkor Wat, the Terrace of the Leper King, Neak Pean and along the north side of Srah Srang – all sell run-of-the-mill Khmer and Chinese food at slightly inflated prices, and most have English-language menus. Alternatively, bring a picnic with you from Siem Reap; many hotels now offer a picnic basket, or you can make your own from one of the local supermarkets (see p.156) or the excellent *Blue Pumpkin* bakery (see p.150).

Phnom Kulen

50km north of Siem Reap • $20

It was at **PHNOM KULEN**, then known as Mahendrapura, that Jayavarman II had himself consecrated supreme ruler in 802 (a date that is regarded as marking the start of the Angkorian period), thereby instigating the cult of the devaraja (see p.285). Although ancient temples are scattered here and elsewhere in the Kulen Mountains, none of these can be visited due to the lack of roads and the danger of land mines. Instead, the main reason to visit Phnom Kulen, 50km north of Siem Reap, is to gawp at the massive **reclining Buddha** carved out of a huge rock in the sixteenth century – and once you're here you may find yourself very taken with the piety of the Buddhist devotees who come to worship at a chain of shrines. Unfortnately, the Angkor pass w(see opposite) isn't valid at Phnom Kulen, and the high entrance charge coupled with the cost of getting here keeps all but the most dedicated explorers from visiting. Note too that the area was heavily **mined** by the Khmer Rouge and it has yet to be fully cleared. Don't wander off to locations other than those described here unless you have an experienced local guide.

The hill

From the ticket office at the foot of the hill the road climbs steadily through forest to a sandstone plateau. On the left a track leads to a parking area from where you can walk down to the river where you may be able to make out some of the **linga** for which the river is famed, but as they're only 25cm square, they're hard to spot on the riverbed if the waters are high or turbid. It's a further 1km or so to the top of the hill, packed with stalls selling refreshments and Khmer medicine, and offering good views over the surrounding Kulen Mountains. A short climb brings you to a busy pagoda, Preah Ang Thom, which features a much-revered and impressive **reclining Buddha**, carved into a massive boulder, usually busy with Cambodians making offerings. A simple but impressive frieze of Buddha heads is carved around the base of the rock.

There are further forest **shrines** behind the pagoda – follow the locals, who come armed with huge bundles of incense to ensure they have enough to make offerings at all the shrines on the circuit. Nearly every boulder has a legend attached to it – one with holes that look like claw marks is said to be where Hanuman crash-landed. At the end of the track, Cambodians come to wash their faces in water from a **holy spring** which gushes from a boulder, believing this will give energy, good health and luck; old bottles are produced and filled to take home.

Beng Mealea

60km east of Siem Reap • $5 • Beng Mealea is connected to Siem Reap by a reasonable road, surfaced all the way (you can even get there by tuk-tuk), which continues to Koh Ker, meaning that a visit to both sites can be combined in a day-trip – it's about 1hr 30min from Siem Reap to Beng Mealea, and a further hour on to Koh Ker

Mostly hidden in rampant vegetation, the scrub-covered Hindu temple of **BENG MEALEA**, yet to be restored, gives a good idea of what the French archeologists found when they first arrived at Angkor. Locals claim that the temple was quite well preserved until being looted by the Khmer Rouge, although the pioneering French archeologist Maurice Glaize reported it being collapsed in 1944. Whichever history you believe, Beng Mealea is still relatively unexplored and atmospheric. Be aware of the possible danger of land mines, however – the site itself has been cleared, but it's best not to stray into the undergrowth.

It isn't known exactly when or why the temple was built, though stylistic features suggest that its construction probably dates from the late eleventh or early twelfth century, possibly during the reign of Suryavarman II. Just over a kilometre square, with a formidable 45m-wide moat, the site was clearly of some consequence, and it has been suggested that the temple was built as a precursor to Angkor Wat. Constructed on a single level, the temple once featured three concentric galleries and a central sanctuary tower, though the main attraction of wandering the ruins is to glimpse apsaras peering out of niches amid the jumbled stones.

3

Koh Ker

One of Cambodia's most remote Angkorian sites, 125km northeast of Siem Reap, **KOH KER** was briefly capital of the Khmer Empire in the tenth century, when Jayavarman IV – who was already ruler of his own state here when he ascended the imperial throne – decided not to relocate to Angkor, but decreed instead that the court should come to him, ordering the construction of a road linking Koh Ker and Angkor, on which the temples of Beng Mealea and Banteay Samre were later built.

Now practically engulfed by jungle, the ruins of Koh Ker have been heavily looted and badly neglected, but plenty remains, including more than forty major monuments spread across eighty square kilometres – although only a small proportion are open to visitors, and much of the area has yet to be completely de-mined. **Mines** still present a serious danger. Do not on any account stray from well-trodden paths.

Koh Ker is famous for its distinctive style of **monumental sculpture**, although most pieces have either been looted or removed for safekeeping to the country's various museums.

The site

Koh Ker's major temple complex is **Prasat Thom**, consisting of three enclosures laid out in a row (as at Preah Vihear), with the sanctuary at the centre of the final courtyard. Entrance to the complex is from the east, via the distinctive red-sandstone **Prasat Krahom** tower, part of the temple's third enclosure. Through the tower is a wide moat, crossed by a causeway with naga balustrades, giving onto a narrow second enclosure, where long thin buildings almost form a gallery. A final gopura through a sandstone wall leads into the first enclosure, where a terrace supports nine small sanctuaries in two rows, five in front and four behind, with the remains of twelve minor towers spread around the courtyard in various states of disrepair.

To the west, beyond Prasat Thom, is Koh Ker's most memorable sight, the **Prang**, a 35m-high, seven-tiered sandstone pyramid – there's a stairway up the eastern side though you may not be allowed to climb it. The Prang was meant to be Jayavarman IV's state temple but was never completed. Instead of a sanctuary tower at the top there's just a pedestal, on which a statue of Nandin would have stood.

Just as high as the Prang is the man-made hill beyond, known as **Pnoh Damrei Saw** (Tomb of the White Elephant), either the foundation of a second pyramid which never got built, or possibly the grave of Jayavarman IV himself. More sanctuaries can be found east of the **Rohal**, a 1km-long reservoir hewn out of the rock at Jayavarman IV's instigation.

FROM TOP BANTEAY SREI (P.188); APSARA DANCERS (P.154) >

From Siem Reap Improved roads mean that Koh Ker is now easy to reach, although you'll need your own transport. The temple is usually (and most easily) visited from Siem Reap, from where it's a 125km (roughly 2hr 30min) journey. It's easily combined with a trip to Beng Mealea, from where it's a 65km (1hr) drive (55km to the Seong turn-off, then 10km to Koh Ker itself). Various operators around Siem Reap offer this trip, or variants on it.

Via Tbeng Meanchey The site can also be reached from the east via Tbeng Meanchey (70km; 1hr 30min) along a decent surfaced road.

Entrance fee $10.

Preah Khan (Kompong Thom)

Some 70km north of Kompong Thom, the temple enclosure of **PREAH KHAN (KOMPONG THOM)** is the largest in Cambodia, its central sanctuary featuring the earliest example of four huge faces looking to the cardinal directions, a motif that subsequently became almost synonymous with Cambodian temple architecture. Little is known about the temple's **history**. The earliest buildings are attributed to Suryavarman I, and it's believed that Jayavarman VII spent time here before moving to Angkor – the famous carved stone image of the king displayed in the National Museum in Phnom Penh was found on the site (see p.69). In the 1870s Louis Delaporte carried off the temple's prize sculptures (they're now in the Guimet museum in Paris), while looters have also pillaged the complex in recent years, using pneumatic drills to remove statues – resulting in collapsed towers, crushed apsaras and the broken images that lie scattered on the ground.

The site

Four different temple groups and numerous prasats and buildings lie scattered around the extensive site over an area of several square kilometres. At the heart of Preah Khan, the **main temple group** dates from the twelfth century and was most likely built by Suryavarman II. Its well-preserved causeway, not dissimilar to those at Angkor Thom, is decorated with a frieze of swans (peer over the edge just before the steps up to the gopura). Making your way through the complex, via the elaborate east gopura and two sandstone galleries, you'll come to the central sanctuary, with its Bayon-style, four-faced tower.

East of the central sanctuary is the 3km-long **baray**, home to the remains of **Prasat Preah Thkol**, a cruciform sanctuary sat on an (inaccessible) island in the centre of the lake. At the west end of the *baray*, the elaborate eleventh-century **Prasat Preah Stung** boasts galleries, carvings of apsaras and a central sanctuary topped with four massive faces, the latter the hallmark of Jayavarman VII and found only in a few places outside Angkor. East of the *baray* is the small ninth-century temple, **Prasat Preah Damrei**, enclosed in a laterite wall and with its upper levels guarded by stone elephants, often draped in orange robes.

From Siem Reap Preah Khan is one of the trickiest of the major temples to get to. The route to the temple runs directly past Beng Mealea, although the last stretch of track from Beng Mealea to Preah Khan is still unsurfaced – it's generally not too bad in the dry, but can become almost impassable in the wet.

WHAT'S IN A NAME: PREAH KHAN

Note that we have followed the common practice of suffixing **Preah Khan** with the province name Kompong Thom in order to distinguish it from the temple of the same name at Angkor. It's also sometimes suffixed with the district name **Kompong Svay**, and just to add to the confusion, locals call it **Prasat Bakan**.

THE VULTURE RESTAURANT

In the depths of Preah Vihear province, **Chhep Protected Forest** is home to three critically endangered species of vulture – red-headed, slender-billed and white-rumped. Trips can be arranged through the Sam Veasna Centre (see p.145), and involve camping overnight in the forest, followed by a morning watching the vultures breakfast on a dead cow. The project is run by the Wildlife Conservation Society (⚑ wcs.org) and some of the fees collected go towards supporting livelihoods in the community.

From Kompong Thom The quickest approach is currently via Tbeng Meanchey (around 2hr 30min–3hr by car). TTAK (see p.202) in Kompong Thom can sort out transport here (perhaps in combination with Sambor Prei Kuk and/or other temples), as can various operators in Siem Reap.

Admission $5 (if there's anyone in the ticket office).

Tbeng Meanchey and around

Ongoing road improvements are steadily improving access to the formerly remote provincial capital of **TBENG MEANCHEY**, around 150km north of Kompong Thom along NR64 and 100km south of Preah Vihear temple (note that Tbeng Meanchey itself is sometimes confusingly referred to as Preah Vihear or Preah Vihear City, and the temple itself as Prasat Preah Vihear). There's not much to the town itself, which sprawls north for more than 2km from the traffic circle at its southern end, with wide, straight red-dirt roads laid out on a simple grid, although it makes a useful place for an overnight stop en route to Preah Vihear.

Weaves of Cambodia

250m east of the hospital • Mon–Sat mornings • ☎ 012 610719, ⚑ weavescambodia.com

Originally a rehabilitation centre for local disabled people, the **Weaves of Cambodia** silk-weaving co-operative is now a prosperous concern, producing high-quality silk for overseas markets. Visitors are welcome to tour the sericulture chambers and the spinning and weaving workshops, and there's a selection of silk goods to buy.

Tmatboey

30km north of Tbeng Meanchey • Visits and homestays can be arranged through Sam Veasna Centre in Siem Reap (see p.145)

Of major interest to twitchers, **Tmatboey**, one of only two nesting sites of the **giant ibis** in Asia, is 30km north of Tbeng Meanchey off the Preah Vihear road. White-shouldered ibis, greater adjutants and sarus cranes also frequent the area.

ARRIVAL AND INFORMATION	TBENG MEANCHEY AND AROUND

By shared taxi Shared taxis from Kompong Thom (5 daily; 3hr) arrive at and depart from Tbeng Meanchey's transport stop, about 1km north and two blocks west of the traffic circle.

By bus There are currently two buses daily to Tbeng Meanchey from Phnom Penh (7hr) via Kompong Thom (3hr), one with Phnom Penh Sorya, the other with Paramount Angkor.

Money There's an ATM at the Acleda Bank, 200m south of the market (Visa only).

GETTING AROUND

Motos Motos congregate around the transport stop – which is the best place to find someone who can speak a little English. Be prepared to haggle hard if you want to go to Koh Ker, Preah Khan (Kompong Thom) or Preah Vihear, as prices can be outrageous.

ACCOMMODATION

27 May Guesthouse Crossroads west of the transport stop, near the market ☎ 011 905472. Central and very cheap – albeit pretty basic – guesthouse near the market (so expect some noise). Tiny rooms with shared bathroom, plus larger en-suite rooms with optional a/c for $6 extra. $\overline{\underline{\$3}}$

Home Vattanak Guesthouse A14 St ☎ 064 636 3000 or ☎ 012 730600. Bringing a welcome splash of luxury to dusty Tbeng Meanchey, with smart, modern a/c rooms complete with flatscreen TVs and well-appointed bathrooms. $\overline{\underline{\$18}}$

Promtep Guest House Head north from the market and then east at the next block ☎ 012 964645. More of a hotel than a guesthouse, with spacious but uninspiring fan rooms (optional a/c $6 extra). $\overline{\underline{\$6}}$

Soksan Motel Off Mlou Prei St ☎ 012 564405, ⓦ soksanmotel.com. Attractive "boutique motel" with neat bungalows arranged around a pretty garden – all come with a/c, hot water, minibar and wi-fi. Decent little restaurant attached. Breakfast included. $\overline{\underline{\$19}}$

EATING

Across from the transport stop, a couple of restaurants do fried noodle and rice dishes, plus coffee. There are also **food stalls** on the west side of the market.

Dara Reas Beside the Vishnu Circle about 200m west of the traffic circle and 1km south of the market. The name may be off-putting, but this is the town's only restaurant with an English-language menu and it actually serves up pretty good soups and stir-fries. Shame about the inconvenient location.

Preah Vihear

Dedicated to Shiva in his manifestation as the mountain god Shikhareshavara, the magnificent temple of **PREAH VIHEAR** makes maximum use of its spectacular setting high up on the Dangkrek escarpment overlooking the plains of Cambodia and Thailand far below. The temple was built between the ninth and the twelfth centuries. Most of the work is attributed to Suryavarman I (r. 1011–50) who enlarged an old religious centre founded here by a son of Jayavarman II and installed one of three boundary linga defining the extent of his territory (the others were placed at Phnom Chisor and at the hitherto unidentified site of Ishanatirtha). Both Suryavarman II (r. 1113–50) and Jayavarman VII (r. 1181–1218) subsequently made further additions to the temple.

Constructed entirely of sandstone, Preah Vihear has an unusual **layout** for a Khmer temple, with four enclosures laid out in a row, rather than concentrically, as is usually the case, with each successive enclosure taking you higher and higher until you reach the summit, from where there are spectacular views along the jagged line of the **Dangkrek Mountains**.

Around 30km by road south of Preah Vihear, the formerly modest village of **SRA EM** (or Sa Em) has experienced a massive boom over the recent years as a result of military and tourist developments at Preah Vihear and now provides a useful jumping-off point for visits to the temple, with public transport, accommodation and places to eat.

The site

Note that large numbers of **land mines** (see p.37 & p.297) were laid all around Preah Vihear right up until the end of the civil war in 1998, while further mines may have been laid during the subsequent Thai–Cambodia border dispute, although both sides deny it. Do not under any circumstances stray from well-marked paths.

> #### WHAT'S IN A NAME: PRASAT PREAH VIHEAR
> Preah Vihear is often (and more precisely) referred to as **Prasat Preah Vihear** (Preah Vihear Temple) in order to distinguish it both from Preah Vihear Province and the provincial capital of Tbeng Meanchey, which is also commonly referred to as Preah Vihear, or sometimes Preah Vihear City.

The first and second gopuras

Entrance to the site is via the 162 steps of the grand entrance **stairway**, giving onto a narrow courtyard decorated with naga balustrades. The **first gopura**, in a ruinous state, is raised on a platform ahead. From here you get a terrific view along the **first avenue**, more than 200m long and boasting a monumental paved area lined with pillars originally used to support lanterns. The large bathing pool to the east, **Srah Srang**, is guarded by stone lions.

At the end of the avenue, the angle of approach and the steepness of the steps means that the only thing that can be seen of the well-preserved **second gopura** is the entrance door and the impressive triangular pediment, outlined against the sky. Above the exterior of the south gopura's door are two intricate and well-preserved **carvings** showing (on the lintel) Vishnu reclining and (on the pediment) a scene from the Churning of the Ocean of Milk (see p.169). Here Vishnu appears both as the tortoise Kurma, with the churning stick on his back, and as Krishna on the stick itself, keeping a watchful eye on the surrounding activity. The serpent Vasuki, meanwhile, coils around the stick, serving as a rope, while gods and demons pull together.

The third and fourth gopuras

Further uphill, beyond the 100m-long **second avenue**, the double vestibules of the cruciform **third gopura** form an imposing entrance to the **third avenue**. It was at this level that royal rooms were located for use by the king when he visited the temple; the two large buildings flanking the gopura were resting houses for pilgrims. The scene above the north door of the gopura is taken from the Hindu epic *Mahabharata* and depicts Shiva fighting with Arjuna, a member of the Pandava family, one of two warring clans in the tale.

The final avenue, leading to the **fourth gopura**, is flanked by ruined buildings. The ground here is thick with collapsed masonry, with some well-preserved carvings lurking in the undergrowth.

The main sanctuary

Through the fourth gopura is the **main sanctuary**, much of which has collapsed, leaving a jumbled heap of massive stones. In its day, the temple was a pioneering

Map key:
1st Enclosure
Fourth Gopura
2nd Enclosure
3RD AVENUE
Third Gopura
2ND AVENUE
3rd Enclosure
Second Gopura
Srah Srang
PROCESSIONAL AVENUE
4th Enclosure
First Gopura
Grand Stairway
N
PREAH VIHEAR
Border Area & Thailand
Army Camp
0 50 metres

1 Central Sanctuary
2 Galleries
3 Pilgrims Halls
4 Tale from the Mahabarata
5 Churning the Ocean of Milk
6 Naga balustrades

PRASAT PREAH VIHEAR: TEMPLE WARS

Much more than a simple archeological site, **Preah Vihear** has been the subject of a bitter and often bloody tug-of-war between Thailand and Cambodia, as well as the setting for several landmark moments in the Cambodian civil war – although despite the fierce fighting that has regularly erupted around it, the temple itself has, almost miraculously, escaped relatively unscathed (although you might notice a few bullet holes here and there).

The roots of the Thai – Cambodian **border conflict** date back over a century. The area was under long-term Thai control until the intervention of the French authorities in Cambodia in 1907. Attempting to ratify the border between the two countries, the French produced a map claiming the temple for Cambodia, despite an agreement that the border should run along the watershed of the Dangrek Mountains – which would have placed the temple within Thai territory. Following the withdrawal of the French from Cambodia in 1954, Thai forces reoccupied the site in an attempt to assert their rights to the temple, forcing Prime Minister Sihanouk to take the matter to the International Court of Justice in The Hague which, in a fiercely contested ruling, finally awarded the site to Cambodia in 1962.

Thanks to its almost impregnable location, the temple played a surprisingly important role during the **civil war**. In 1975, Khmer Rouge forces drove out remnants of the Khmer National Armed Forces who had taken refuge in it – the last place in Cambodia to fall to them. In 1978, Vietnamese forces recaptured the site from the Khmer Rouge – who then reoccupied the site in 1993 and continued to control it before finally surrendering in 1998; their last major stand. The temple was also the scene (in 1979) of a particularly brutal repatriation of Cambodian refugees by the Thai military government during which more than forty thousand people were driven back over the border. As many as three thousand died after being forced over the cliff on which the temple stands and driven through the minefields below.

Following the end of the civil war, the old border dispute flared up again in 2008, when Preah Vihear was awarded **UNESCO Heritage status** – which Thailand felt further reinforced Cambodian claims to sole ownership of the temple, and which they continued to dispute. Rising tensions ensued, followed by a series of increasingly violent clashes, with dozens of military and civilian casualties on both sides, culminating in 2011 in an exchange of long-range artillery fire. The case was again returned to the International Court of Justice in The Hague, who (in November 2013) once again ruled in Cambodia's favour. Peace has subsequently returned to the temple following the new ruling, with access now open from both sides of the border, although the loss of the temple continues to rankle with many Thai nationalists and offers easy political capital for Bangkok politicians seeking a popular national cause, meaning that the possibility of future clashes cannot be ruled out entirely.

project, and the vaulted galleries that surround the enclosure are some of the earliest examples of their type in Angkorian architecture. Only the north gallery has windows facing out; the windows of the other galleries look in on the enclosure. You can climb through a hole in the western wall to get out onto the mountainside and enjoy the well-earned view.

The Eastern Staircase

Offering an alternative, but much more strenuous, approach to (or descent from) the site, the **Eastern Staircase** has recently been de-mined and opened to visitors. More than two thousand steps lead through the forest using a mix of modern wooden steps and (in places) the old stone staircase itself. The bottom of the staircase is east of the ticket office, along a signposted dirt road.

ARRIVAL AND INFORMATION   PREAH VIHEAR

Access to Preah Vihear is now much easier than it was, with good new **roads** from Siem Reap (roughly 210km and 4hr away, via either Koh Ker or Anlong Veng) and from Tbeng Meanchey (from where good roads run to Kompong Thom and Stung Treng). Due to the steepness of the road up, cars, buses and tuk-tuks can't go further than the bottom of the hill below the temple, where you'll need to transfer to a moto (unless, of course, you've come on one) or possibly the back of a pick-up truck for the 5km ride up the hill ($7 return) – a 10min trip with fantastic views back over Cambodia. From the drop-off point at the

---

PREAH VIHEAR: CROSSING TO AND FROM THAILAND

Despite the conclusion of hostilities between Thailand and Cambodia, the old **border crossing** at Preah Vihear has not yet fully reopened. Approaching **from Thailand**, visitors are allowed to cross the border to visit the temple ($10 fee), but not to continue onwards into Cambodia, and no visas are issued. Meanwhile, visitors from Cambodia are allowed to cross a few hundred metres **into Thailand** to shop at the border market (10 baht fee) but no further. Rumours continue to circulate that the border will reopen fully at some point in the not too distant future.

---

top you walk further uphill to the temple; when you've finished your visit your moto/pick-up will come to collect you. Following the resolution of the border dispute (see opposite) the temple is also easily accessible from the Thai side of the border.

Tours Given the difficulties of getting here by public transport, the vast majority of visitors to Preah Vihear come on organized tours. Whistlestop day-trips from Siem Reap to the temple can now be had for as little as $30, assuming there are enough people to make it profitable. Longer tours to Preah Vihear can also be combined with other destinations en route such as Beng Mealea, Koh Ker, Anlong Veng and possibly Preah Khan (Kompong Thom) in numerous different ways – shop around tour operators in Siem Reap, or try TTAK (see p.202) in Kompong Thom.

By public transport It's tricky, but not impossible, to reach Preah Vihear by public transport. The nearby town of Sra Em has once-daily bus connections with both Siem Reap and Phnom Penh, as well as slightly more regular shared taxis to Siem Reap (3hr) and Tbeng Meanchey (2hr). From Sra Em, there are shared taxis to the foot of Preah Vihear hill, or catch a moto (around $15–20 return, including waiting time).

Opening hours Daily dawn–dusk.

Admission $5.

ACCOMMODATION AND EATING

Pkay Prek Restaurant Sra Em ☎ 012 636617. Popular open-air restaurant specializing in *phnom pleoung* ("hill of fire"; $4), a kind of DIY meal – a bit like a Korean barbecue – which you cook for yourself at your table on a miniature coal-fired volcano-shaped stove. Daily 10am–10pm.

Preah Vihear Boutique Hotel Sra Em ☎ 088 356 0501, ⓦ preahvihearhotel.com. Plush new resort-style hotel – an amazing sign of the changing times in Preah Vihear province. Accommodation is in smart rooms arranged around a big pool, there's good food in the restaurant and staff can arrange trips to the temple. It's pretty expensive, admittedly, although given the lack of local alternatives you may feel it's a price worth paying. **$100**

Tuol Monysophon Anlong Veng Rd, 500m west of Sra Em's main crossroads ☎ 099 620757. Basic lodgings with a mix of fan rooms, some with shared bathrooms, others en suite (for about $3 more). **$7.50**

Anlong Veng

Some 140km north of Siem Reap, **ANLONG VENG** is of interest as the former home and death place of Pol Pot, and also makes a convenient jumping-off point for the temple at Preah Vihear. The town itself also has a certain surreal interest thanks to its proximity to the border with Thailand (in which gambling is outlawed), which has led in the past few years to a rash of **casino** construction attracting visitors from over the border and transforming this formerly dusty little backwater into something of a miniature Thai-Las-Vegas-in-Exile.

Pol Pot cremation site

Anlong Veng is notable principally for its associations with the **Khmer Rouge**, several of whose leading figures lived here after their fall in 1979. Locals (many of whom were closely connected to the regime) remain loyal to their memory, while visiting Khmers come here in the belief that the spirit of Pol Pot will reveal winning lottery numbers, heal the sick or provide auspicious luck in some other fashion from beyond the grave.

The Khmer Rouge's fugitive leader **Pol Pot** didn't actually stay in the village itself but in a **hideout** up in the Dangkrek Mountains – a thirty-minute trip from Anlong Veng.

Some say he died from a heart attack, although it's also been claimed that he was murdered by his Khmer Rouge comrades. All that's known for certain is that Pol Pot was cremated on a pile of furniture and old tyres close to his house before anyone could verify the details. The **sites** on which the hut was located and where the hasty cremation took place are signed, though there are only a few blackened rocks to see.

Ta Mok's house

Turn left at the traffic circle and then right after a couple of hundred metres • $2

In the village itself, the late **Ta Mok**, one of the most notorious Khmer Rouge cadres, left behind a house when he died in 2006 (signed "Ta Mok House"). He is well regarded locally for creating fishing ponds and endowing a local school, but better known in the world at large as "The Butcher" for his role in ordering the murders of thousands of his compatriots. For years there were efforts to have Ta Mok stand trial for the murders, but like so many Khmer Rouge-era killers he died a natural death while Cambodia procrastinated.

ARRIVAL AND DEPARTURE   ANLONG VENG

From Siem Reap It's around a 2hr drive to Anlong Veng from Siem Reap along a good surfaced road. A couple of bus companies (GST and Paramount Angkor) run this route once daily. Otherwise, you can pick up a shared taxi from the NR6 near the transport stop in Siem Reap.

From Thailand You can also get to Anlong Veng from Thailand using either the border crossing point Chong Jom to O'Smach, or the closer Chong Sa Ngam to Anlong Veng.

The most convenient way to travel between the border and Anlong Veng, or vice versa, is to take a place in a taxi; these run throughout the day in both directions taking around 30min to make the 30km trip. Both Cambodian and Thai visas are available when you arrive at the border.

To Preah Vihear Occasional shared taxis run to the temple at Preah Vihear (1hr 30min); or you may be able to find a car for hire (around $40 return).

ACCOMMODATION

Bot Ouddom Guesthouse ☎ 011 500507. One of the most upmarket places in town, this sizeable establishment (more hotel than guesthouse) has clean and spacious rooms (all a/c, but cold water only). $15
Monorom 300m west of the traffic circle ☎ 011 884736. Smart, modern guesthouse with bright clean rooms, kitsch

furniture and a passable restaurant; more expensive rooms come with a/c and hot water. Fan $8; a/c $15
Phnom Dankrek Guesthouse ☎ 012 444067. Basic guesthouse with a mix of rooms including concrete box-style lodgings downstairs with shared bathroom, or slightly nicer en-suite rooms ($2 extra) above. $3

Kompong Thom

KOMPONG THOM, 145km from Siem Reap (and slightly further from Phnom Penh), straggles along NR6 and the Stung Sen River. The town used to be known as *kompong pos thom*, "place of the big snake" – apparently because the locals used to take offerings to a large snake that lived in a cave on the river, but this may be yet another Cambodian myth as no one now has a clue where the cave is. Most visitors stop over to visit the temples at **Sambor Prei Kuk**, 30km northeast, and the attractive **Phnom Santuk** religious complex; a couple of hours is quite enough to have a look around the town itself. Kompong Thom is also a possible jumping-off point for the remote **Preah Vihear**, two days' journey to the north, though access is now easier from Siem Reap via Sra Em (see p.196). Closer, but even more of an adventure to reach, is the massive **Preah Khan (Kompong Thom)** – go now before the tour groups do.

Central Kompong Thom

There's not a lot to central Kompong Thom, lined up along the NR6 and centred on the landmark *Arunras Hotel*, just south of the market. A pair of rattling old bridges traverse the modest **Stung Sen River**, while to the west stretches a pleasant riverfront promenade, dotted with playgrounds and fitness equipment. It's liveliest towards dusk, when the waterside becomes busy with impromptu aerobics classes and games of badminton and shuttlecock (*sey*). About 500m west of the bridge along the waterfront is the colonial **Governor's Residence**, next to a huge old tree that is home to a huge colony of **bats**. They can be seen quietly hanging upside down from the branches by day, before flying off in search of food come dusk.

KOMPONG THOM

Wat Kompong Thom (400m), Department of Arts and Culture, Siem Reap & Sambor Prei Kuk

■ **ACCOMMODATION**
Arunras Guesthouse	2
Arunras Hotel	3
Sambor Village	4
Stung Sen Royal Garden Hotel	1

●**EATING**
Arunras Hotel	3
Kompong Thom Restaurant	1
Run Amok!	2

North of town

On the main road about 500m north of the river, it's difficult to miss the gaudy **Wat Kompong Thom**, its compound crammed with exuberant pagoda buildings and stupas. Further north, Kompong Thom's modest **Department of Arts and Culture** (Mon–Fri 8–10.30am & 2.30–5pm; $1) museum houses a small collection of statuary from local archeological sites, including the original lion statues from Sambor Prei Kuk – although the inconvenient location 2km from the centre along the NR6 to Siem Reap means it's hardly worth the effort.

ARRIVAL AND DEPARTURE   KOMPONG THOM

Upon **arrival** in Kompong Thom, you'll probably be set down on the main road at the cluster of drink stalls diagonally opposite the *Arunras Hotel* – make sure your driver knows you're getting off, or you might find yourself being whisked straight through town. **Leaving** Kompong Thom is generally a swift and painless experience. Dozens of buses, minibuses and shared taxis pass through en route between Phnom Penh and Siem Reap (although few services actually begin here). Buy a ticket from the women at the drink stalls opposite the *Arunras Hotel* and they'll put you on the next available service – you shouldn't have to wait more than 15min.

By bus Buses from Phnom Penh and Kompong Cham will drop you on the main road opposite the *Arunras Hotel*; buses from Siem Reap stop outside the market.
Destinations Kompong Cham (4 daily; 2hr 30min); Phnom

Penh (every 10–15min; 4hr); Poipet (10 daily; 5hr); Siem Reap (every 10–15min; 2hr).
By minibus and shared taxi Minibuses and shared taxis stop at the transport stop just east of the main road. This is

DRUMMING UP BUSINESS

A workshop near Kompong Thom offers a rare opportunity to see **traditional drums** being produced. Look out for a small sign on the left 7km southeast of town on NR6. The small-waisted, vase-shaped *skor dae*, about 50cm tall, are carved here by hand from the heart of a jackfruit tree – the yellowish wood is valued for its resonant properties – and embellished with carved decorations; a dried snake skin is stretched across the head. The drums form part of the traditional *pinpeat* ensemble, a gamelan-style orchestra that plays at weddings and classical dance performances. Also made here are *skor sang na*, a kind of cylindrical drum, twice the height of *skor dae*, which are played slung over the shoulder during funeral processions. The welcoming family who own the workshop will encourage you to try your hand at drumming, and might give you an impromptu demonstration.

where you'll need to come if heading north to Tbeng Meanchey (though confusingly everyone refers to it as Preah Vihear, after the province of which it's capital).

Destinations Kompong Cham (6 daily; 2hr 30min); Phnom Penh (12 daily; 3hr); Siem Reap (12 daily; 2hr); Skone (12 daily; 1hr 30min); Tbeng Meanchey (3 daily; 3hr).

ACCOMMODATION

KOMPONG THOM

Arunras Guesthouse NR6 ☎012 865935. Effectively an extension of the next-door *Arunras Hotel*, under the same management, in an almost identicial (albeit smaller) building and with very similar fan rooms (plus optional a/c for $6), at fractionally lower prices. **$7**

Arunras Hotel NR6 ☎062 961294. Landmark seven-storey hotel right in the middle of town with excellent-value rooms (optional a/c $7) – although the floor-to-ceiling tiles make it feel a bit like sleeping in a public convenience and the karaoke bar on the fifth floor means rooms on floors 4 and 5 can be a bit noisy after dark. Good restaurant, too (see below). **$8**

Sambor Village 1km east of town along the river ☎062 961391, ⓦsamborvillage.com. Ildyllic little hotel, surrounded by verdant gardens and with nineteen cool and airy individually-decorated bungalows (with a/c and hot water). There's also an inviting swimming pool and a good restaurant. **$50**

Stung Sen Royal Garden Hotel NR6 ☎062 961228, ⒺStungsen_hotel@yahoo.com. A slightly more upmarket alternative to the *Arunras Hotel*, set in a shady garden overlooking the river. Quieter than you'd expect given its proximity to the main road, and with spacious, pleasantly old-fashioned rooms (all with a/c and hot water) – although they could do with an extra lightbulb or two. **$20**

AROUND KOMPONG THOM

Khmer Village Homestay Baray village, 50km southeast of Kompong Thom on NR6 to Kompong Cham ☎012 635718, ⓦkhmerhomestaybaray.com. Staying here affords the chance to get involved in village life; you can visit for just a day, or stay for longer helping with community projects. **$20**

EATING AND DRINKING

Arunras Hotel NR6 ☎062 961294. Lively hotel restaurant, busy with both locals and tourists, in a large mirror-lined dining room stuffed with wooden furniture. The menu features a large, if slightly pricey, range of excellent Chinese and Khmer dishes (mains $3–4.50), plus superb coffee – although no Western options. Daily 7am–10pm.

Kompong Thom Restaurant Riverside. Attractive modern restaurant overlooking the river. Food is relatively pricey, but features a good selection of Khmer dishes (most mains around $5.50) including some unusual offerings (try the buffalo in lemongrass sauce), plus a few more expensive Western options alongside assorted snacks, salads and sandwiches. Daily 7am–10pm.

Run Amok! Dekchaumeas, near the riverside ☎017 916219, ⓦfacebook.com/runamok.kh. Run by a Kiwi-Khmer couple, this excellent new restaurant brings an unexpected dash of culinary pizzazz to Kompong Thom, with excellent burgers (meat and veggie) and pizzas, plus mouthwatering Khmer dishes and good ice cream – try the palm sugar and peanut flavour. Mains around $3–6. Daily 5–10pm.

DIRECTORY

Internet There are a couple of (nameless) internet cafés down the road just west of the *Arunras Hotel* (2500 riel/hr), and another place on the main road one block south of the river.

Money The Canadia Bank (Visa and MasterCard) and the Acleda Bank, 500m south of the market (Visa), have ATMs.

Phones and post For international phone calls, the Camintel office is inside the post office just south of the *Arunras Hotel*.

Shops The Tela petrol station on the main road has a well-stocked minimarket.

TOURS AROUND KOMPONG THOM

First port of call if you want to arrange a tour around Kompong Thom should be the **Tourist Transportation Association Kompong Thom**, or **TTAK** (☎012 634835, ⓦcambodiattak .com), a rather grand name for a setup currently operating out of a tiny corrugated-iron shack opposite the *Stung Sen Royal Garden Hotel*. Mr Vothea and his friendly and informative team of English-speaking drivers can arrange transport to sights through the area by moto, tuk-tuk and car, ranging from local day-trips through to multi-day tours to Preah Khan (Kompong Thom), Koh Ker, Preah Vihear and elsewhere. Transport to Sambor Prei Kuk costs $8/$15/$25 by moto/tuk-tuk/car, while a trip to Phnom Santuk will set you back $6/$12/$15 – or $14/$25/$40 combined with Sambor Prei Kuk.

Sambor Prei Kuk

30km north of Kompong Thom • $3; site guides available for around $7 for 3hr; food stalls near the ticket booth • The site is easily visited from Kompong Thom (return by moto $8, tuk-tuk $15, car $25; 1hr); if you're travelling independently, 5km north of Kompong Thom turn off north along NR64 for 10km and then take the wide dirt road (clearly signed) on the right for the last 15km — it can be slow going in the rainy season

One of Cambodia's most important pre-Angkorian monuments, the Chenla-era (see p.284) capital of **SAMBOR PREI KUK** once boasted hundreds of temples, although many of them have now been lost, perhaps smothered by the encroaching forest. Sixty or so temples remain, however, dotted among beautiful woodland, some of them now restored and sporting particularly fine brick carvings and decorated sandstone lintels and columns. It's all relatively modest compared to the great Angkorian sites, admittedly, although the sylvan woodland setting and almost total lack of visitors more than compensates.

The site

The whole site is covered with the remains of towers, and carvings can be seen poking out from piles of earth or partly covered by undergrowth – exploring at random can throw up some real gems.

The temple divides into three main sections: the **north and south groups**, which date from the seventh century, and the **centre group**, a ninth-century addition. Separated from these by the access road are the ruined sanctuary tower of **Ashram Issey** and the single-towered **Prasat Bos Ram**, which has a lion's-head channel through which holy water flowed; it is now at ground level, but would originally have been more than 1m up the wall of the tower. Also just north of the entrance road is a small shrine now almost completely gobbled up by the roots of an enormous **strangler fig**, which seems to sprout from the crumbling walls as if out of some enormous pot.

North group

The **north group**, sometimes called **Prasat Sambor Prei Kuk** after its central sanctuary tower, was extended and restored during the Angkorian era. As with most Angkorian temples, the main approach is from the east and the sanctuary's five towers are arranged in a quincunx pattern. Carved into the brick on several of the towers are bas-reliefs of **"flying palaces"**, believed to be home to the local spirits who look after the temples (several similar carvings can be found in the south group and at Ashram Issey). The carved sandstone lintels and columns on some of the towers also remain in reasonably good condition — look out for cute winged horses and tiny human faces — and there's a fine image of a voluptuous Durga in the northeastern tower. Though there were once numerous other towers here, about all you'll be able to spot amid the ruins is the row of four on the west side. You'll also see a number of carved sandstone **pedestals** lying around, each about 1.5m square and designed to carry a linga.

Centre group

Of the **centre group**'s former buildings, only the main sanctuary tower, **Prasat Tao**, survives, although it's a particularly photogenic structure, with entrance steps flanked by reproduction lions and upper portions sprouting impressive quantities of weeds. The carving around a couple of the tower's doors is well preserved, including intricate foliage designs for which the Chenla period is famed.

Around 200m southwest of here, the crumbling **Prasat Trapeang Ropeak** stands almost lost in the woods, still sporting the remains of eroded friezes and an unusual triangular entrance that looks in imminent danger of collapse.

South group

The highlight of Sambor Prei Kuk is the so-called **south group**, built as the state temple of Isanavarman I and also known as Prasat Yeay Poeun (or sometimes Prasat

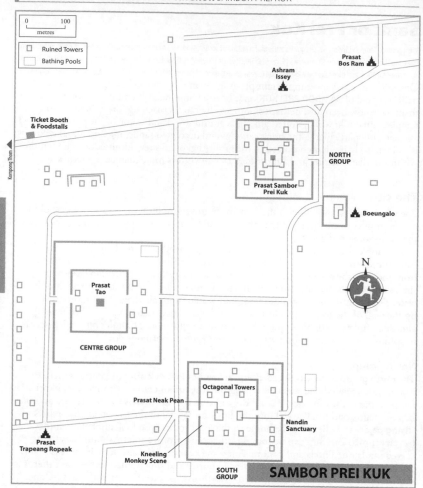

Neak Pean) after its central sanctuary tower. The main towers are located within two concentric walled enclosures: a ruined outer laterite wall plus a relatively intact inner wall built of brick. The west side of the inner wall still preseves the some elaborate but eroded **reliefs** contained in a sequence of roundels among which you can just about make out a kneeling monkey and fragments of a fighting lion – only the mane remains.

The **central sanctuary tower** itself still boasts reasonably preserved carved lintels over three of its doors, while inside a battered but delicately decorated linga base stands beneath the tower's impressively high brick vault (minus its summit). The tower was originally linked to a smaller building opposite, housing a statue of Nandin. The statue is long gone (although you can still make out some of the carvings around the pedestal on which it would have stood), and all that can be seen of the raised causeway that connected the two structures are a few pillars.

A number of unusual octagonal towers are located in the enclosure, their walls decorated with large, circular medallion-like carvings and more flying palaces.

South of Kompong Thom

There are several interesting sights south of Kompong Thom, easily combined in a day-trip with Sambor Prei Kuk and including the stone-carving village of **Santok** and the colourful hilltop temple complex at **Phnom Santok**.

Santok

15km southeast of Kompong Thom on NR6

Stretching for a couple of kilometres along NR6, the village of **SANTOK** (aka **Samnak** or **Kakaoh**) is instantly recognizable thanks to the long lines of stone carvings lined up along the roadside – ranging from huge Buddha heads fit for a temple to diminutive figurines which would fit comfortably on a small mantelpiece. Also in the village is **Santuk Silks** (Mon–Fri 7am–4pm; free; ☎012 906604), run by Vietnam veteran Bud Gibbons and his wife, where you can see silk worms munching on mulberry, watch spinners and weavers at work, and usually buy a scarf or two from the weavers (from around $20).

Phnom Santok

2km north of NR6, 17km southeast of Kompong Thom (the turn-off from NR6 is about 100m past Santuk Silks in Santok village)

An enjoyable half-day trip from Kompong Thom, the jaunty modern hilltop temple of **Phnom Santok** sits atop a 180m-high hill, conspicuous in the pancake-flat countryside. The hilltop is a popular weekend destination, but quiet during the week, when you can often have the place pretty much to yourself apart from the occasional resident monk.

From the car park at the bottom, 809 steps climb steeply up the wooded hillside (there's also a road to the top – too steep for tuk-tuks, although there might be a moto at the bottom to take you up for a dollar or two if you don't want to hike up the eight hundred-plus stairs). A pair of sweeping **naga balustrades** flank either side of the steps, with more than five hundred miniature figures on either side playing tug of war with a pair of giant snakes. The **summit** is topped with a colourful hotchpotch of mainly modern viharas, shrines and pavilions. Directly behind the central cluster of buildings, a rock overhang creates a natural shrine embellished with several small Buddhas carved into the rock face, although no one seems to know how old they are. Past here, a tiny path weaves across the hilltop past further small shrines and between large boulders (including two balanced precariously on top of one another), while to the west, a narrow path leads part of the way down the hill to a further collection of rock carvings, including an impressive reclining Buddha.

Wat Hat Nokor

2km west of the village of Taing Kok, 70km from Kompong Thom • Donation • Public transport will drop you either in the village or at the turning for the temple, from where motos are readily available ($4 return including waiting time) – if you're using public transport on to Kompong Thom, you'll need to flag down a taxi or minibus, best done at Taing Kok's small market

The small, rural **Wat Hat Nokor** is notable mainly for the eleventh-century **temple** built by Suryavarman I. The temple was never finished, and it's assumed that either the architect died or war intervened during its construction. A single gopura on the eastern side of the temple gives access to a courtyard enclosing a cruciform sanctuary, **Prasat Kuk Nokor**. The central section of the south wall has collapsed, but you can still see a chamber built into the wall, where the sick came to be cured using holy water blessed by flowing over the linga in the central sanctuary. The library in the southeast corner of the courtyard was formerly used as a prison by the Khmer Rouge.

Eastern Cambodia

MORNING MARKET, BANLUNG

Eastern Cambodia

The wide-open spaces of Cambodia's remote and sparsely populated east are a world away from the rest of the country, offering a quintessential slice of rural Khmer life largely unaffected by the modern world. Bounding the western side of the region, the mighty Mekong River forges its way south from Laos, dotted with river islands, dramatic stretches of flooded forest and the occasional floating village. Outside the main towns, much of the river remains largely off the tourist radar, although if you've got the time and energy there are myriad opportunities to explore the river and its rural hinterlands using a mix of boating, kayaking, cycling and walking.

East of the **Mekong** lie the distant highlands of **Rattanakiri** and **Mondulkiri** provinces. Rampant logging has taken a serious toll on these formerly pristine landscapes, although some jungle cover survives, providing a haven for wildlife – for the time being, at least. The highlands are also home to Cambodia's **chunchiet** population (see box, p.233) who have traditionally eked out a subsistence living cultivating crops and foraging in the jungle. This centuries-old way of life is now threatened by the encroachment of the modern world and the loss of forest on which they depend.

Gateway to the region is the laidback Mekong-side town of **Kompong Cham**, a quiet provincial capital that retains an air of faded colonial gentility. Further north along the Mekong, **Kratie** is another old French-era settlement, best known for the rare Irrawaddy dolphins that inhabit the nearby rapids at **Kampie**. There are more dolphins to be seen at **Stung Treng**, the most northerly town on Cambodia's stretch of the Mekong; this is also the starting point for rewarding tours of the beautiful surrounding countryside and for crossings into Laos. East of Stung Treng, **Banlung**, the capital of Rattanakiri province, is developing into a major centre for treks into the nearby highland jungles of **Virachey National Park** and surrounding countryside. In the southeast of the region, tranquil **Sen Monorom**, the main town of Mondulkiri province, sees fewer visitors but offers further trekking and wildlife-spotting opportunities, as well as visits to some of the spectacular waterfalls that dot the area.

GETTING AROUND

Getting around eastern Cambodia is a time-consuming business, however you approach it, although ongoing infrastructure developments are steadily improving access to the region. The major gateway to the region is **Kompong Cham**, although the construction of a new Mekong bridge near **Stung Treng**, linking up with NR64 to Tbeang Meanchey and on to Siem Reap, is already opening up an alternative approach to Rattanakiri via central Cambodia – the Stung Treng account (see p.224) has more details. Beyond Kompong Cham, most transport (and all buses) follows

YEAK LAOM

Highlights

❶ Kompong Cham Relaxed old colonial town with sweeping Mekong views and a lively selection of waterside restaurants and bars. **See p.211**

❷ Dolphin watching Take a boat trip on the Mekong for a glimpse of rare Irrawaddy dolphins slaloming through the rapids at Kampie. **See p.219**

❸ Trekking in Rattanakiri Head out from Banlung for a day's or week's trekking through the jungle-clad highlands, with rare wildlife, bamboo river-rafting and encounters with the region's indigenous chunchiet en route. **See p.231**

❹ Yeak Laom Magical lake set in the crater of an extinct volcano surrounded by jungle just outside Banlung. **See p.234**

❺ Highland waterfalls Plunging more than 30m into a forested gorge, remote Bou Sraa is Cambodia's finest cascade, although the more accessible Chha Ong, near Banlung, makes a picturesque alternative. **See p.234 & p.238**

❻ Elephant Valley Project Walk with elephants through the forests of Mondulkiri as part of this unique animal rehabilitation programme. **See p.238**

HIGHLIGHTS ARE MARKED ON THE MAP ON P.210

the good, albeit circuitous, route along National Highway 7 via **Snuol** to **Kratie**, although there's also a more direct and slightly quicker route to Kratie along the river via **Chhlong** (currently served by shared taxi only). North of Kratie the road to the memorably named village of **O Pong Moan**, just south of Stung Treng at the turn-off to Banlung, is currently in a bad way, making for a very slow and bumpy ride, although repairs may have fixed the situation by the time you read this. The road from O Pong Moan to **Banlung**, by contrast, is currently one of the best and emptiest in Cambodia. Travelling from Banlung directly **south to Sen Monorom** is currently a major off-road adventure (see box,

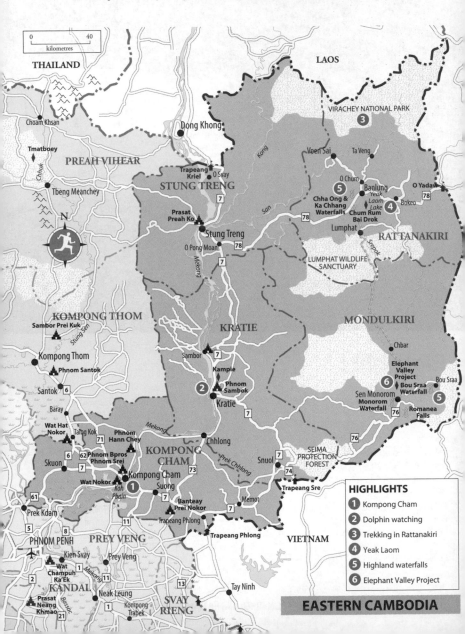

BORDER CROSSINGS IN THE EAST

Eastern Cambodia currently has four international border crossings: one with **Laos**, and three with **Vietnam**. All four are open daily from 7am to 5pm. Entering Laos and Cambodia, **visas** are issued on arrival (roughly $30–40 for a Lao visa, depending on your nationality; $20 for a Cambodian visa). Heading into Vietnam, you'll need to have acquired a visa in advance, since none are issued at the border.

TO LAOS

Trapeang Kriel–Nong Nok Khiene Popular crossing 57km north of Stung Treng. Full details are given with our Stung Treng account (see p.224).

TO VIETNAM

O Yadaw–Le Tanh The most useful of the three border crossings into Vietnam, 70km east of Banlung along a good road. Guesthouses in Banlung sell through bus tickets from Banlung to the town of Pleiku, in the central highlands of Vietnam (around a 6–7hr journey from Banlung).

Trapeang Phlong–Xa Mat Little-used (and difficult to reach) crossing around 70km east of Kompong Cham.

Trapeang Sre–Loc Ninh Around 20km southeast of Snuol. This obscure crossing isn't of much practical use given the lack of public transport on both sides of the border.

p.230), although a new road between the two towns is currently under construction, and may even have opened by the time you read this. Pending the completion of this new highway, access to Sen Monorom is via NR76, branching off the main N7 highway at Snuol.

4

Kompong Cham

Situated on the west bank of the Mekong, the mellow town of **KOMPONG CHAM** has little of the bustle that you'd expect of the biggest city in eastern Cambodia. Its small commercial port doesn't exactly hum with activity, and the riverfront, in the shadow of the massive Kizuna Bridge, is pretty quiet too since road improvements have led to the demise of most river transport. The town's attractive backwater somnolence belies its more energetic past. In the 1930s and 1940s, Kompong Cham – named after the sizeable population of local **Cham Muslims** (see box, p.215) – was a prosperous rubber and tobacco trading centre and the most cosmopolitan town in Cambodia. You can sense some evidence of its previous affluence in the wide, tree-lined streets and the faded shophouses and warehouses lining the waterfront.

Today's town has a distinct charm, and it's easy to while away a day meandering through the unhurried streets, taking in the faded colonial architecture (particularly around the market) and visiting the remains of the venerable **Wat Nokor** just outside town – as well as enjoying the convivial riverfront cafés, busy in the evenings with tourists stopping over on a slow journey through the country. In half a day you can follow the Mekong north to **Phnom Hann Chey**, a quirky hilltop temple with fabulous views of the river, while a day-trip will get you to the pre-Angkorian site of **Banteay Prei Nokor**, home to a few ruined towers surrounded by a massive earth embankment. Enjoyable **boat trips** can also be made to villages up and down the Mekong.

The riverside

Quiet by day, Kompong Cham's **riverside** really comes alive after dark, when locals come out to wander the waterside promenade and eat at the food stalls set up along its length, and the attractive string of Mekong-facing cafés fill up with crowds of tourists.

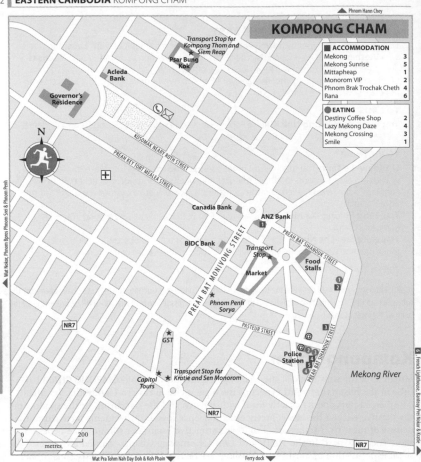

▲ Phnom Hann Chey

KOMPONG CHAM

■ **ACCOMMODATION**
Mekong	3
Mekong Sunrise	5
Mittapheap	1
Monorom VIP	2
Phnom Brak Trochak Cheth	4
Rana	6

● **EATING**
Destiny Coffee Shop	2
Lazy Mekong Daze	4
Mekong Crossing	3
Smile	1

Transport Stop for Kompong Thom and Siem Reap

Psar Bung Kok

Acleda Bank

Governor's Residence

KOSOMAK NEARY ROTH STREET

PREAH KEY TORT MEALEA STREET

Canadia Bank

ANZ Bank

PREAH BAT SIHANOUK STREET

BIDC Bank

Transport Stop

Food Stalls

PREAH BAT MONIVONG STREET

Market

Phnom Penh Sorya

NR7

PASTEUR STREET

GST

Police Station

Mekong River

Capitol Tours

Transport Stop for Kratie and Sen Monorom

NR7

0   200
metres

NR7

Wat Pra Tohm Nah Day Doh & Koh Pbain ▼   Ferry dock ▼

Dominating the riverside is the great arc of the towering bridge, built with the help of a $65m grant from Japan and known as the **Spean Kizuna** after the Khmer word for bridge (*spean*) and the Japanese word *kizuna*, signifying a bond between nations. Completed in 2001, the 1.5km-long structure was the first Cambodian bridge over the Mekong (prior to its opening, crossing the river involved an hour-long ferry ride) and offers strange contrast to the faded old warehouses and shophouses that you can still see along the waterfront.

Across the river close to the far side of the bridge is the salmon-pink French **lighthouse**, a three-tiered structure looking more like a church tower than beacon for shipping. A very steep metal staircase inside leads to the summit, although you'll need a good head for heights to make it all the way to the top.

The market

Kompong Cham's neat little **market** doesn't get especially busy, which is just as well as the stalls are jammed together so tightly inside there's hardly room to squeeze a cat, let along swing one. This is a good spot to pick up one of the **kramas** for which Kompong Cham province is famous, although you'll actually find a much wider choice of patterns and materials in Phnom Penh and Siem Reap.

> ### RIVER TRIPS AROUND KOMPONG CHAM
>
> There are several interesting places within the vicinity of Kompong Cham that can be reached by boat and make for a rewarding day out if there are a few of you to share the cost – although note that most of these sites can also be reached more cheaply by moto or tuk-tuk. Trips can be arranged through *Mekong Crossing* (see p.214), with possible destinations including **Wat Maha Leap** (about 20km south of Kompong Cham), an old wooden building with gilded teak columns; **Prei Chung Kran** village (just upstream from Maha Leap temple on the Tonle Tuok), where silk is woven on traditional hand looms; and **Wat Hann Chey**, about 20km north of Kompong Cham, where there are fantastic river views from Chenla-era ruins and a modern temple.

Wat Pra Tohm Nah Day Doh

Around 1km south of Kompong Cham centre, opposite the dry-season bamboo bridge to Koh Pbain (see p.214) • Daily • Free

Just over 1km south of the centre of Kompong Cham, **Wat Pra Tohm Nah Day Doh** is well worth a wander, though it's less than a hundred years old. In front of the complex is a huge standing Buddha, while the grounds are scattered with intriguing statues of people and animals, and a forest of miniature stupas.

ARRIVAL AND DEPARTURE

KOMPONG CHAM

By bus The majority of buses to and from Kompong Cham are run by Phnom Penh Sorya, arriving and departing from their office on Preah Bat Monivong St, the boulevard northwest of the market, a 10min walk (or less) from most of the hotels. Buses operated by other companies including Rith Mony, GST and Capitol Tours stop at their various ticket offices along NR7, just northwest of the centre. Leaving Kompong Cham there are regular buses to Phnom Penh until late afternoon, although services to other destinations are much less frequent, and generally leave in the morning only.

Destinations Banlung (1 daily; 9hr); Kompong Thom (3 daily; 2hr 30min); Kratie (5 daily; 3hr); Phnom Penh (13 daily; 3hr); Poipet (1 daily; 7–8hr); Sen Monorom (1 daily; 4hr); Siem Reap (3 daily; 5hr); Stung Treng (1 daily; 7hr).

By shared taxi and minibus Shared taxis and minibuses to/from other destinations in the east arrive and depart

from the Caltex petrol station on the roundabout just before the bridge. Services to/from Siem Reap via Kompong Thom use the Psar Bung Kok transport stop two blocks north of the post office. Transport to other destinations, including services to Phnom Penh, can be found on the northeast side of the market. Shared taxis also cover the more direct route (not covered by any buses) to Kratie via Chhlong.

Destinations Banlung (1–2 daily; 9hr); Kompong Thom (6–8 daily; 2hr); Kratie (6–8 daily; 2hr 30min); Phnom Penh (20 daily; 2hr 30min); Poipet (3–4 daily; 7hr); Prey Veng (4–6 daily; 2hr); Sen Monorom (1–2 daily; 4hr); Siem Reap (6–8 daily; 4–5hr).

By moto or tuk-tuk Taking a moto or tuk-tuk you'll pay around $3/$5 for the return trip to Wat Nokor, and $7/$10 to Phnom Bpros plus Wat Nokor.

GETTING AROUND

The three Ms – the *Mekong Crossing* and *Lazy Mekong Daze* restaurants and the *Mekong Sunrise* hotel, conveniently close to one another on the riverfront – are the best places to enquire about tours, transport and to sort out a rental bike or motorbike. They may also be able to help out with hiring a car and driver (about $40–50 per day), if required.

Motos and tuk-tuks It's easy to get around town on foot, but there are plenty of motos and tuk-tuks available.

Motorbike and bike rental Motorbikes and bicycles can be rented at *Lazy Mekong Daze* and *Mekong Crossing*

(bikes $1.50/day, motorbikes $5/day).

Boat trips *Mekong Crossing* can arrange boat trips along the Mekong (see p.214) for around $70–80/day.

ACCOMMODATION

Mekong Riverfront ☏ 042 941536. The town's longest-running hotel, and still a reasonable choice despite the slightly institutional atmosphere. Accommodation is in a mixture of fan, a/c and plusher "VIP" rooms, all with hot water and TV. Some a/c and all VIP rooms come with balconies giving great views over the Mekong. Fan $8; a/c $18

Mekong Sunrise Riverfront ☏ 088 805 7407. Popular new backpacker place in a prime riverfront location. Rooms (private bathroom $3 extra) are simple but decent value, and it's also a good place to sort out transport and tours. Tends to fill up quickly, so arrive early or reserve in advance. Fan $5; a/c $10

Mittapheap North of the market ☎ 042 941565. One of the best deals in town, this friendly and unassuming little hotel provides neat and clean tiled rooms with TV and fridge. Excellent value, if you don't mind being a few minutes' walk from the river. Fan $\overline{\$6}$; a/c $\overline{\$12}$

Monorom VIP Riverfront ☎ 092 777102, ⓦ monoromviphotel.com. The most upmarket hotel in town, and good value at current rates, with huge, minty-fresh and immaculately clean rooms, all with a/c, hot water, TV and fridge – more expensive ones also have bathtubs and tea/coffee-making facilities plus balconies with Mekong views. $\overline{\$15}$

Phnom Brak Trochak Cheth Riverfront ☎ 0884 827749. Basic family-run guesthouse right in the thick of the riverfront action and with some of the cheapest beds in town. Rooms (fan only) are poky and slightly grubby, with tiny (or no) windows, although a small communal balcony overlooking the Mekong offers compensatory views. $\overline{\$5}$

Rana 7km towards Kratie on NR7 ☎ 012 686240, ⓦ rana-ruralhomestay-cambodia.webs.com or ⓦ rana-cambodia.blogspot.co.uk. Enjoyable American-/Khmer-run homestay just outside Kratie which aims to give visitors a real insight into local rural life, with trips to nearby villages. Advance booking essential. Minimum two-night stay. Rates include all meals, tours, plus tea, coffee and bottled water. $\overline{\$50}$

EATING AND DRINKING

There's an excellent little cluster of restaurants and cafés along the waterfront. Food stalls can be found around the transport stop and market, while late in the afternoon further stalls set up along the riverfront. The tourist-oriented riverfront restaurants are usually fairly lively **after dark**, although most places usually shut up promptly at 10pm.

Destiny Coffee Shop Vithei Pasteur, just off the riverfront. This chic café is more Phnom Penh than Kompong Cham, serving up good coffee and shakes plus snacks and light meals including all-day breakfasts, salads, sandwiches and a short selection of Western and Asian mains (around $4). Mon–Sat 7am–6pm.

Lazy Mekong Daze Riverfront. Simple little backpacker café serving a decent range of Asian and (slightly pricier) Western food – a good place for breakfast or a sundowner, watching the sun dipping down into the Mekong. Pool table. Most mains $3.50–5. Daily 7.30am–10pm.

Mekong Crossing Riverfront ☎ 017 801788. Always lively, this bar-restaurant is the town's best place for a drink, either in the cosy interior or lounging on a wicker chair on the shaded terrace outside. Tipples include the biggest selection of beers in town plus a decent cocktail list, and there's the usual menu of Asian and Khmer staples (mains $2.50–3.50) plus pricier Western dishes. Daily 6am–10pm.

★ **Smile** Riverfront ☎ 017 997709. The top restaurant in town, run as training centre for orphans and vulnerable children and serving up excellent Khmer food, bursting with flavour, plus a decent range of Western dishes, salads, sandwiches and snacks. Most mains around $4. Daily 6am–10pm.

DIRECTORY

Internet and wi-fi Almost all the hotels and restaurants reviewed here have free wi-fi. There's also a trio of cheap (1500 riel/hr; roughly daily 8am–8pm) and well-equipped internet cafés around *Destiny Coffee Shop* – GreenNet, just north of the café, and Mekong Internet and Speed Up, both opposite.

Money The ATMs at the Canadia and ANZ banks both accept foreign Visa and MasterCards (although the ANZ charges a $5 commission); the ATM at the nearby BIDC accepts Visa cards.

Post and phones The post office and the Camitel office are next to each other, north of the centre. You can make domestic and international phone calls at the Camitel office, and Mekong Internet (see above) also has international phone facilities.

Around Kompong Cham

Several low-key sights dot the area around Kompong Cham. Glimpses of traditional Mekong life can be had close to town on the idyllic **Koh Pbain** river island, while it's well worth making the short trip out to the edge of town to visit **Wat Nokor**, a fine old temple with quirky modern additions, and the hilltop religious complex of **Phnom Bpros Phnom Srei**.

Koh Pbain

Around 1km southeast of Kompong Cham, the island of **Koh Pbain**, in the middle of the Mekong, is perfect for an out-of-town jaunt, especially by bicycle. During the dry

THE CHAM

Originating from the kingdom of Champa, which formerly extended from Hue to Phan Thiet on the coast of present-day Vietnam, the **Cham** are the largest minority ethnic group in Cambodia, numbering in the region of 250,000 (estimates vary) and accounting for about a third of the country's non-Khmer population. They also represent Cambodia's largest minority religion, being Sunni Muslims who converted from Hinduism some time after the fourteenth century.

Historically, the Cham were frequently at war both with the Khmer, who bordered their kingdom to the west and south, and the Vietnamese, who occupied the territory to the north. In 1177, the Cham successfully raided Angkor, only to be defeated by the intervention of Jayavarman VII in a ferocious battle on the Tonle Sap – an event depicted in the bas-reliefs at the Bayon temple (see p.171). By the end of the seventeenth century, however, the gradual whittling away of its territory by the Vietnamese meant that Champa had effectively ceased to exist, and many Cham fled to Cambodia. The **traditional Cham** – who retain many of the old beliefs and rituals, but acknowledge non-Islamic gods – make up about two-thirds of Cambodia's Cham population. They settled around the Tonle Sap, along the central rivers, and in what is now Kompong Cham province. The **orthodox Cham**, who are more similar to Muslims in other Islamic countries, settled around Oudong, Kampot and Takeo. Establishing their own villages, they took up fishing, breeding water buffalo, silver-working and weaving, activities that the vast majority still practise today. Their villages can easily be identified by the presence of a mosque and Islamic school, and by the absence of pigs.

The Cham have generally coexisted peacefully alongside the Khmer throughout their history, despite speaking their own language (Cham) and maintaining separate traditions. Only under the Khmer Rouge did they suffer significant persecution: easily picked out thanks to their Islamic dress and distinctive features (they seldom marry outsiders), many Cham were either massacred or persecuted – often by being forced to eat pork – and their mosques destroyed.

season it can be reached via a remarkable **bamboo bridge** ($1), rebuilt from scratch every year as the river waters subside. Come the rains you'll need to take the small **ferry** ($2), just big enough for a couple of motos and a few passengers.

The island itself is around 10km long, crisscrossed by tiny tracks and fringed with sand bars during the dry season – Kompong Cham's nearest equivalent to a beach. The primary crop here is tobacco – the tall, thin, mud-walled buildings are drying-houses where the leaves are hung for several days before being packed into bamboo crates. The island also has a number of **Cham villages**. The men work mainly as fishermen, while in the dry season the women weave *hol* silk and cotton *kramas*, using looms set up under the stilt houses.

Wat Nokor

2km west of Kompong Cham • $2; ticket also valid for Phnom Bpros Phnom Srei (see p.216) • Moto from Kompong Cham around $3 return, tuk-tuk $5; if you're travelling independently, head out of Kompong Cham on NR7 until you reach the roundabout with four entwined golden cobras – the temple is down the small road on the left

Located in the grounds of a modern temple on the edge of Kompong Cham, the eleventh-century **Wat Nokor** (known locally as Nokor Bachey) is one of the few significant surviving ancient temples in Cambodia's east, built towards the end of the reign of the legendary Angkorian king **Jayavarman VII** (see p.286). The original shrine is enclosed within a laterite wall (painted black during the Khmer Rouge occupation) and decorated with finely executed and well-preserved carving of apsaras, elaborate lintels and intricate panels covered in floral swirls.

The temple's main surprise is the central **sanctuary**, on top of whose eleventh-century remains a multicoloured vihara was rudely superimposed in the 1990s, complete with gaudy modern murals and fancy pillars. Notwithstanding the flagrant cultural vandalism involved, these quirky additions have proved a hit with Cambodians and ethnic Chinese. The latter closely identify with the temple's **legend**, which tells of a baby boy from Kompong Cham who was gobbled up by a large fish; the fish swam down the Mekong and on to the coast of China, where it was eventually caught and the child, still alive, discovered. The boy subsequently made his way back to Cambodia, bringing with him a retinue of Chinese, who all settled at Kompong Cham, which the locals say explains why so many Chinese live in the area, and possibly why there is a Chinese temple in the grounds.

Another modern building, just to the south of the temple complex, contains a **reclining Buddha**, decapitated during the Khmer Rouge era. The head was missing for years until a workman dreamed that it was buried close by; sure enough, the dream came true, and the head was soon dug up in the grounds and reunited with the body. Newlyweds use the temple as a backdrop for their photographs, and it's not unusual to find a group of women in the gopura helping a bride into each of her several wedding outfits.

Phnom Bpros Phnom Srei

8km west of Kompong Cham off NR7 • $2; ticket also valid for Wat Nokor (see p.215) • Moto from Kompong Cham around $7 return, tuk-tuk $10

The twin hills of **Phnom Bpros Phnom Srei** ("Man and Woman Hills") can be easily combined with a visit to Wat Nokor. The lower hill, **Phnom Bpros**, is topped by a collection of modern pagodas, the newest a grey cement structure with touches of ersatz Angkor Wat- and Banteay Srei-style decoration. It's possible to drive to the top of this hill, which is home to a colony of wild monkeys who hang around in the hope of being fed bananas sold at the refreshment stall. At the foot of the hill, on the way to Phnom Srei, is a collection of **stupas** built by relatives of the thousands of victims murdered by the Khmer Rouge in the surrounding fields; most of the remains were removed to Phnom Penh in 2000.

Phnom Srei is the higher of the two hills; leafy and less developed, it's reached by the track across fields beyond the stupas. From the base, a steep stairway goes straight to the top where, in addition to the view, you can take in the vihara's collection of Buddha statues dating back to the colonial period. The much-revered statue of Nandin in front of the altar just asks to be stroked, which is what you'll see many visitors doing.

Phnom Hann Chey

20km north of Kompong Cham • Moto from Kompong Cham around $12 return, tuk-tuk $15

For stunning views of the Mekong, **Phnom Hann Chey**, on the west bank of the Mekong, is hard to beat. The hill is also home to a modern temple complex in whose grounds you'll find a couple of Phnom Da-era brick-and-laterite prasats cheek by jowl with funky giant concrete fruits.

Kratie and around

Seventy kilometres north of Kompong Cham on the east bank of the Mekong, **KRATIE** (pronounced *Kra*-cheh) has become a popular tourist destination thanks to the rare **Irrawaddy dolphins** that inhabit the river upstream at nearby **Kampie**. Dolphin-watching trips can also be easily combined with a visit to the lovely hilltop meditation centre of **Phnom Sambok** and the temple and turtle conservation project at **Sambor**, further upriver, while the chance to explore nearby river islands, go kayaking or head off along the **Mekong Discovery Trail** (see box, p.218) may tempt you to linger longer.

Dolphins and other attractions aside, Kratie itself makes a pleasant spot to rest up for a night or two, with a decent clutch of hotels and some good restaurants lined up along the serene riverside. Parts of the town still retain vestiges of their old French colonial architecture, including the fine old **Governor's Residence**, just south of the centre (now signed as the Provincial Council Kratie).

Wat Roka Kandal

Kratie riverfront, 2km south of the town centre

Dating from the late eighteenth/early nineteenth century, the pretty little temple of **Wat Roka Kandal** is among the oldest in Kratie province. The main vihara, nondescript from the outside, conceals a beautiful interior with delicately painted, wooden hipped roof and pillars. The wat also doubles as an exhibition space, with local handicrafts sometimes displayed inside.

Koh Trong

Directly opposite Kratie in the middle of the Mekong • Ferries shuttle regularly between Kratie and the island from the boat dock in the town centre (around 5min; 1000 riel)

The small island of **Koh Trong** provides an interesting glimpse of rural river life within easy striking distance of Kratie town centre. Sights include a couple of wats, a floating Vietnamese village (located at the southwest of the island) and endangered freshwater Cantor's giant soft-shell **turtles** (*Pelochelys cantorii*) – although they're not the easiest creatures to spot, since they spend most of their time almost completely buried in sand or mud to escape predators.

The best way to explore the island is by **bike** (available for $1–2 on arrival from the village community office near the ferry landing stage, which saves you lugging a bike across from Kratie on the ferry). A complete circuit is 14km; alternatively you can hire a horse cart or tuk-tuk ($10) at the village community office for a two-hour round trip.

ACCOMMODATION
Balcony	1
Le Bungalow	2
Oudom Sambath	3
Santepheap	5
U Hong Guesthouse	4
U Hong II Guesthouse	6

EATING
Heng Heng	4
Red Sun Falling	1
Tokae	2
U Hong II Guesthouse Café	3

KRATIE

MEKONG DISCOVERY TRAIL

Covering the stretch of the Mekong between Kratie and the Laos border north of Stung Treng, the **Mekong Discovery Trail** is an initiative to get tourists off the beaten track and experience the river's rich culture, ecology and historical heritage. The so-called "trail" actually comprises ten separate itineraries using existing roads, tracks and waterways – a few signs have been set up along some of the routes, but most of the time you'll have to find your own way.

The itineraries themselves are something of a moveable feast – most can be explored using a mix of transport depending on what suits, whether on foot, by bike, or using a tuk-tuk or car. A few also include the possibility of an overnight homestay (see p.220) en route. The various routes are covered in more detail in a useful leaflet that you may be able to pick up in Kratie or from Xplore Asia (see p.226) in Stung Treng, who also arrange guided tours around parts of the trail. The following is a brief summary.

Ancient Ruins of Thala Barivat Trail 3km round-trip from Stung Treng to the ancient temple ruins at Thala Barivat.

Bamboo Sticky Rice and Bridges 9km round-trip from Stung Treng featuring Sekong views and *krolan* (sticky bamboo rice) tasting at Hang Khou Ban village.

Distant Dolphins Trail 40km by bike, or 61km by motorbike from Stung Treng to a beautiful, rarely visited stretch of the Mekong, including the dolphin pool at Damrei Phong, south of Stung Treng, and Koh Preah river island.

Dolphin and Krolan Discovery Trail 16km one way from Kratie, including the dolphin-watching site at Kampie and Phnom Sambok temple.

Koh Trong Island Trail 9km round-trip around the river island of Koh Trong, just outside Kratie.

Kratie Architecture and Alms Trail 7km round-trip tour of Kratie, including the market, Wat Roka Kandal and Wat Serey Santhor Vong.

River Life Explorer Trail 44km round-trip from Kratie, following the little-visited west bank of the Mekong from Kratie to Kampie and beyond.

Stung Treng Silk and Sunset Trail 7km round-trip from Stung Treng, including a visit to the Mekong Blue silk-weaving centre (see p.223).

Wat Sarsar Mouy and Koh Pdao Trail 35km from Kratie to Sambor, plus 15km around Koh Pdao river island.

Waterfalls, Wetland and Wildlife Trail 57km from Stung Treng to O Svay, including visits to the Sopheak Mitt falls and Anlong Cheuteal dolphin pool.

The road north from Kratie to Kampie

The road **north from Kratie** via Phnom Sambok to Kampie is one of the most magical in Cambodia, running for 15km along a seemingly endless avenue of majestic tropical trees flanked with a picture-perfect array of traditional Khmer wooden houses, raised on enormous stilts. Many are of considerable size, topped with hipped red-tiled roofs decorated with elaborate finials and linked to the road by long wooden walkways – it's particularly lovely in the rainy season when the road looks like a never-ending causeway between the encroaching waters.

Phnom Sambok

10km north of Kratie

Two-thirds of the way between Kratie and Kampie, the rustic hilltop temple complex at **Phnom Sambok** offers a tranquil slice of rural Cambodian Buddhism en route to the dolphins at Kampie. From the bottom of the hill, a steep staircase (361 steps in total), lined with life-size statues of Buddhist acolytes, leads up to the various monastic buildings scattered around the hillside above, split over three levels.

After 161 steps you reach the **first terrace**. To your left a scatter of meditation cells dot the hillside along with the living quarters of the temple's resident monks, arranged around a small **vihara**. Inside, the vihara (not always open) is decorated with cartoonish murals showing the gruesome punishments awaiting the unrighteous in the various Buddhist hells – gossips having their tongues pulled out, adulterers being impaled on a spiky tree, and so on. Some of the murals show Chinese and Japanese figures sporting bushy eyebrows and moustaches and wearing red shorts and turbans or bandanas, probably a hangover from the brief Japanese occupation during World War II.

Continuing on up, a further 73 steps bring you up to the small **second terrace** after which it's a further 127 steps to reach the topmost terrace and a small vihara decorated with murals of the Buddha's life and enlightenment, with glimpses through the trees of the Mekong far below.

Kampie

15km north of Kratie • 1hr–1hr 30min boat trips $7–9/person, or $7/person in a group of three or more • The site is easily reached by motorbike or bicycle, or there is transport from Kratie (see box, p.221)

Cambodians traditionally believe that the **Irrawaddy dolphins** (*psout*) that live around the Mekong rapids at **KAMPIE** are part human and part fish, and consequently do their best to look after them. Despite this, the dolphins' numbers have declined sharply due to the use of explosives and electric rods for fishing, and in 2004 the Irrawaddy dolphin was added to the IUCN Red List as a critically endangered species.

The **dolphin-watching site** is now run as an ecotourism project by the local community. Having purchased your ticket you'll be loaded into a boat for the trip (lasting roughly 1hr during the Nov–May dry season; closer to 1hr 30min during the wet season, when the dolphins travel further downriver). Once boats are out on the water in the vicinity of the dolphins the motor is cut and boatmen row their craft to create the minimum of disturbance. The dolphins are most active during the early morning and late afternoon, when they tend to feed, although sightings are pretty much guaranteed at any time. They're fairly easy to see (albeit almost impossible to photograph) and even easier to hear thanks to the characteristic noise they make (like the sound of someone taking a sudden deep breath through a large tube) when breaking the surface of the water to take in air.

It's also possible to see the dolphins from dry land. Continue to the stretch of open riverbank about 1km north of the centre, from where sightings are possible.

Sambor

Not much happens in the dusty riverside town of **SAMBOR**, 36km north of Kratie and accessible on various **tours** (see p.221) – for the time being, at any rate. The stretch of

---

IRRAWADDY DOLPHINS

Freshwater rivers, such as the Irrawaddy and Mekong in Southeast Asia, and the shallow tropical zones of the Indian and Pacific oceans, constitute the habitat of the **Irrawaddy dolphin** (*Orcaella brevirostris*). In the Mekong they now inhabit just a 190km stretch in the north of Cambodia, and can be spotted most easily at Kampie and north of Stung Treng near the Laos border, with occasional sightings elsewhere. In 2001, a pair were found just a few kilometres north of Phnom Penh.

Irrawaddy dolphins look more like porpoises than marine dolphins, with rounded heads and foreheads that protrude slightly over a straight mouth; noticeably, unlike their seagoing cousins, they have no beak. They're also more languid than their marine cousins, rarely leaping out of the water, chasing after boats or displaying any of the other skittish personality traits commonly identified with their species.

Irrawaddy dolphins reach maturity around the age of 5 years, when they can measure up to 2.75m in length and weigh up to 200kg. Family groups, or pods, usually consist of around six individuals, but larger groups are not unknown. In spite of good breeding rates, there is a high rate of calf mortality, which remains unexplained.

Mekong hereabouts has been earmarked for many years as the possible site of a huge dam and hydroelectric power station. This will be the largest in Cambodia, if it ever gets built, measuring up to 2km in length and forming a barrier across the entire river, although the project (along with a second, putative Mekong dam at Stung Treng) has now been mothballed until at least 2020.

Wat Tasar Moi Roi

For the time being, Sambor's most notable attraction is the modern **Wat Tasar Moi Roi** ("Pagoda of One Hundred Columns" – in fact there are actually 116 columns in total), built in 1986 with the express intention of beating the number of columns at any other wat in the country, although other pagodas have now surpassed this total. One of the columns originally belonged to a thatched temple that stood on the site and is believed to be four hundred years old. The oldest stupa in the grounds is the golden one to the north, which is claimed to house the ashes of a princess and a royal family; clearer is the tale associated with the pagoda, depicted in a series of paintings in the pavilion near the vihara. The story tells how a woman turned herself into a crocodile for fun and gave a monk a ride – unfortunately an evil fellow-crocodile tipped the monk off her back and gobbled him up. The woman was eventually caught, in her crocodile form, at Banlung and brought back to the pagoda as a trophy – or perhaps to warn other monks against cavorting with crocodiles.

Mekong Turtle Conservation Centre

Behind Wat Tasar Moi Roi • Daily 8.30am–4.30pm • $4 • ⓦ mekongturtle.com

Tucked away at the back of Wat Tasar Moi Roi is the **Mekong Turtle Conservation Centre**, established by Conservation International with the aim of boosting the local population of endangered Cantor's softshell turtles (*Pelochelys cantorii*) in the Mekong. Local hatchlings are collected and kept in tanks here for ten months before being released back into the river, significantly increasing their chances of survival. You can also see a couple of adult Cantor's turtles here, along with a few other species.

Wat Preah Gouk

Now clad in concrete, the restored **Wat Preah Gouk**, about 500m beyond Wat Tasar Moi Roi, is interesting for the old timber-framed pagoda concealed within. The magnificent tree in the courtyard, with a trunk nearly 10m in circumference, is said by locals to be seven hundred years old.

ARRIVAL AND DEPARTURE   KRATIE AND AROUND

By bus Getting to Kratie by bus involves a roundabout journey via Snuol, although a few service taxis take the more direct route from Kompong Cham via Chhlong. There are regular buses south to Kompong Cham and Phnom Penh,

---

MEKONG HOMESTAYS

Cambodian Rural Development Tours (☏ 099 834353, ⓦ crdt.org.kh) runs a number of **homestay** opportunities along the Mekong, offering one- or two-night stays at a trio of villages up and down the river and allowing visitors a rare chance to experience traditional Cambodian rural life from the inside.

Koh Pdao Just north of Sambor (and 40km north of Kratie). One- or two-night homestays on this peaceful river island, including visits to the nearby turtle conservation centre, the hundred-pillar pagoda and the dolphins at Kampie.

Koh Preah Village 35km from Stung Treng. Visits include cycling along the Mekong, the chance to sample traditional Khmer village food, a visit to the local dolphin pool and chats with village elders.

Preah Rumkel North of Stung Treng near the Laos border. Visits include kayaking, cycling and dolphin-spotting.

although travelling north bus services become rather sketchy, and you may have to catch a minibus or shared taxi instead. Buses operated by Phnom Penh Sorya Transport and Rith Mony pull up outside their respective offices on the riverfront.
Destinations Banlung (1 daily; 6hr); Kompong Cham (5 daily; 3hr); Phnom Penh (5 daily; 7hr); Stung Treng (1 daily; 3hr 30min).
By minibus Seats on so-called "express" minibuses can be booked through most guesthouses and some restaurants in Kratie – although these are really just normal minibuses by any other name, and the "express" should be taken with a

major pinch of salt. All services leave in the morning, usually at or before 7am.
Destinations Banlung (1 daily; 6hr); Kompong Cham (2 daily; 2hr 30min); Phnom Penh (4 daily; 5hr); Sen Monorom (2 daily; 5hr); Siem Reap (1 daily; 6hr); Sihanoukville (1 daily; 10hr); Stung Treng (1 daily; 3hr).
By shared taxi Shared taxis arrive/depart from Kratie's transport stop, two blocks north of the market.
Destinations Banlung (2–3 daily; 6hr); Kompong Cham (6–8 daily; 2hr 30min); Sen Monorom (1–2 daily; 4hr); Stung Treng (2–4 daily; 3hr 30min).

GETTING AROUND

Kratie town centre is compact and easily negotiated on foot, with all accommodation lying within 500m of the bus and the transport stops. For trips further afield, **bikes** ($1/day), **mountain bikes** ($2/day) and **motorbikes** ($5–7/day) can be rented at the two *U Hong* guesthouses and *Tokae* restaurant. You can also choose from a couple of tours (see below).

ACCOMMODATION

KRATIE

Balcony Riverfront, north of the centre ☎ 016 604036, ⓦ balconyguesthouse.net. Popular guesthouse with balcony restaurant and bar overlooking the river. The spacious fan rooms come with shared or (for an extra $2) private bathroom – there are just seven rooms, so it's best to book in advance. Not to be confused with the identically named restaurant and guesthouse further up the riverfront. $6
Le Bungalow Riverfront ☎ 012 660902, ⓦ rajabori -kratie.com. A cut above Kratie's other accommodation options, this boutique guesthouse has just two attractive a/c rooms furnished with bespoke artworks and antiques in an old-fashioned wooden riverfront villa. There's also a good, if pricey, French-Khmer restaurant attached. $65
Oudom Sambath Riverfront ☎ 012 965944. Large and long-established hotel, a bit worn around the edges and with hit-and-miss service and persistent resident touts.

Rooms are pretty good value, however. All are spacious and comfortably furnished (although hot water and wi-fi are erratic), and the more expensive options come with balconies and Mekong views. The large downstairs foyer doubles as a local restaurant, with a wide range of cheap Khmer dishes. Fan $7; a/c $12
Santepheap Riverfront ☎ 072 210210, ⓔ santepheap _hotel@yahoo.com. Small hotel with just seven neat but rather poky a/c rooms, all with TV, hot water, fridge and free wi-fi – a few also have river views (same price). Perfectly acceptable, although rather expensive for what you get. Rates include breakfast. $20
U Hong Guesthouse (Also signed "You Hong"); on the north side of the market ☎ 012 957003. The cheapest beds in town – although rooms (fan only) are fairly basic, and those at the front can be noisy thanks to the nearby market. There's also a pleasant downstairs restaurant and good tour and travel services. $5

4

TOURS AROUND KRATIE

Tours can be arranged through most **guesthouses** and hotels in Kratie – try either of the two *U Hong* guesthouses or the *Tokae* restaurant. The dolphin-watching trip to Kampie costs around $5 by moto, $10 by tuk-tuk (not including boat ticket); you should also be able to include a visit to Phnom Sambok as part of the same trip for an extra $1–2. Combined visits to the dolphins, Sambor and Phnom Sambok cost around $12 by moto, $20 by tuk-tuk.

TOUR OPERATORS

CRDT (Cambodian Rural Development Tours) ☎ 099 834353, ⓦ crdtours.org. Various tours and homestays (see box opposite) up and down the Mekong, with several in and around Kratie including Kampie, Sambor, Koh Trong island and tours of Kratie town itself.
Sorya Kayaking Adventures Riverfront, north of the centre ☎ 090 241148, ⓦ soryakayaking.com. The perfect way to see the Mekong without the roar of

an outboard boat engine disturbing the peace. Half-day trips include dolphin-spotting at Kampie and visits to the Mekong Island of Koh Trong, plus one- and two-day excursions on the Te River including visits to floating ethnic Vietnamese villages and the chance to paddle through beautiful stretches of flooded Mekong River forest en route. Trips start from $25/person/half-day, depending on group size.

U Hong II Guesthouse Riverfront ☎085 885168. Above the popular travellers' café (see below), this place has neat, clean fan rooms at competitive rates and is a good place to sort out travel and tours. Nicer (and quieter) – albeit slightly more expensive – than the original *U Hong* (see p.221). $7

AROUND KRATIE

Rajabori Villas Koh Trong ☎012 770150, ⊛rajabori -kratie.com. Located on Koh Trong island (see p.217), this stylish little boutique resort offers a very civilized introduction to rural Cambodian life, with accommodation in attractive wooden villas, built in traditional Khmer style and scattered around spacious grounds, plus a superb pool, all at competitive rates. $50

Relais de Chhlong Chhlong, around 20km southwest of Kratie. A very unexpected find along this largely untouristed stretch of the Mekong, set in a gorgeous old 1930s colonial house with an attractive pool and fine food. Closed for lengthy renovations at the time of writing, although very much worth a look when it eventually reopens – hopefully by the time you read this.

EATING AND DRINKING

KRATIE

Heng Heng Heng Heng Guesthouse, Riverfront ☎088 836 4758. A local alternative to the town's tourist cafés, this large hotel restaurant serves up unexpectedly good, mainly Chinese-style Asian food – much better than the prosaic menu descriptions ("Fried instant noodles with mixed vegetables", for example) would suggest. Mains $2.50–4. Daily 7am–9pm.

★**Red Sun Falling** Riverfront ☎011 465606. This cosy café is a great place to either start or end your day, with the best selection of Western breakfasts in town (carb-up with the "Super Full Monty", $6), good, very inexpensive Asian mains ($2–2.50) plus a few comforting Western favourites including chicken and chips, good salads and shakes. Cheap

beer, too, and attentive service. Daily 7am–9pm.

Tokae Street 10 ☎097 297 2118. Attractive little restaurant, romantically candlelit after dark, serving good breakfasts and an above-average range of Asian dishes at below-average prices (most mains $2–2.50), including a better than usual vegetarian selection. Free wi-fi. Daily 6.30am–10pm.

U Hong II Guesthouse Café Riverfront ☎085 885168. Bright and spacious guesthouse café dishing up inexpensive Khmer and Western travellers' staples, with beer in freshly iced glasses and a decent soundtrack – although service can be a bit erratic and it pays to check your change. Daily 6am–10pm.

DIRECTORY

Books There's a decent range of secondhand books for sale in Kratie at the *Red Sun Falling* café (see above), and a book exchange (two for one) in the *U Hong II Guesthouse* café (see above).

Internet access Virtually all Kratie's hotels and

restaurants have free wi-fi. The *U Hong II Guesthouse* restaurant also has a handful of rather aged terminals (4000 riel/hr).

Money There are ATMs at the Canadia (Visa and MasterCard) and Acleda (Visa only) banks in Kratie.

Stung Treng

Situated on the Sekong River 140km north of Kratie (and a similar distance west of Banlung), the tranquil little town of **STUNG TRENG** is a bit of a backwater. For most visitors the town is simply a staging-post en route to Laos, although the construction of a huge new Mekong bridge nearby, connecting with a new road to Tbeang Meanchey and then on to Siem Reap, may help revitalize the town's fortunes, opening up new routes between central Cambodia and the northeast, and establishing Stung Treng as an alternative gateway to the region.

There are various attractions in the countryside surrounding Stung Treng, too, many of them covered by the **Mekong Discovery Trail** (see box, p.218). It is also the jumping-off point for the splendid **river trip** along the Mekong to the Laos border, with glimpses of rare Irrawaddy dolphins and thundering waterfalls en route.

The riverfront

A statue of a *pasay* fish can be found in the patch of gardens on the **riverfront**, celebrating a prized delicacy which is caught locally in June and July near Stung Treng;

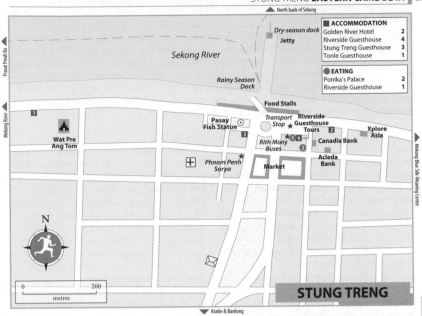

although the statue is about the size of a dolphin, the real fish is quite modest, weighing 1–1.5kg.

Further west along the riverfront is the attractive **Wat Pre Ang Tom**, reconstructed in 1992 after being destroyed by the Khmer Rouge. The central vihara, a glorious gold-and-pink confection, is so lusciously decorated it looks almost edible, while in the corner opposite stands an enormous bodhi tree, sheltering a cluster of pagoda-style shrines.

Mekong Blue silk-weaving centre

5km east of town along the river • Mon–Sat • Free • ⓦ mekongblue.com • Around $4 return by moto, $6 by tuk-tuk

One easy-to-reach destination is the **Mekong Blue silk-weaving centre**, established in 2001 and now one of a cluster of local projects run by the enterprising Stung Treng Women's Development Centre. Visitors are welcome to watch the weavers at work and visit the attached showroom, displaying some of the chic scarves, accessories, bags and bedding created here (which you can also buy online).

Prasat Preah Ko

Take the ferry (1500 riel one way) to Thala Barivat village, from where it's a 500m walk uphill from the market

Across the Mekong from Stung Treng, the riverside village of Thala Barivat is home to the ruined **Prasat Preah Ko** Chenla-era temple, built in the seventh century during the reign of Jayavarman I and comprising six ruined brick towers arranged in two lines of three. Thai robbers stripped the stone statue of Shiva's bull, Nandin, of the gems with which it was once inlaid, but even stripped of its decoration it's still a splendid object, with a fine patina and a gentle expression. A unique annual **festival** is held here in late March or early April by the Jarai (see p.233), involving much loud drumming, men parading with fishing baskets over their heads and great quantities of wine being sprayed around.

ARRIVAL AND DEPARTURE

Stung Treng is rather out on a limb when it comes to transport, all the more so given that services to and from Banlung bypass the town completely – although the construction of a massive new 1.7km-long bridge over the Mekong just west of town will significantly improve transport connections with central Cambodia, linking with the new road to **Siem Reap via Tbeang Meanchey**. Minibuses are already running along this new road to Siem Reap (with a ferry to get you across the Mekong) – significantly quicker than the bus, if you don't mind the $25 fare. Regular bus services will doubtless commence as soon as the bridge is finished (sometime in 2015, according to latest estimates). Cambodia's one and only border crossing into **Laos** is at **Trapeang Kriel**, 57km north of Stung Treng.

By bus There is currently just a single early-morning departure to Phnom Penh via Kratie and Kompong Cham operated by Phnom Penh Sorya (a second Rith Mony service had temporarily ceased operating at the time of writing, but may have resumed by the time you read this) and a second (even earlier) Phnom Penh Sorya service to Siem Reap. Buses to Banlung bypass the town, meaning that you'll have to catch a minibus or shared taxi. Phnom Penh Sorya have an office in the centre of town, while bus and minibus tickets can be booked through the *Riverside Guesthouse* and *Ponika's Palace* restaurant.

Destinations Kompong Cham (1 daily; 7hr); Kratie (3 daily; 4hr); Phnom Penh (3 daily; 10hr); Siem Reap (1 daily; 11–12hr).

By shared taxi and minibus The transport stop is in the north of town on the riverfront – given the paucity of transport, it pays to arrive early.

Destinations Banlung (4–6 daily; 2hr); Kratie (4–6 daily; 3hr 30min); Phnom Penh (4 daily; 9hr); Siem Reap via Tbeang Meanchey (1–2 daily; 7–8hr).

TO LAOS

Leaving Cambodia The road from Stung Treng to the border at Trapeang Kriel is in good condition, with the journey taking just over 1hr. The border itself is open daily 7am–5pm; Laos visas (roughly $30–40 depending on nationality) are issued on the spot if you don't have one already. Several companies run through-buses from various places in Cambodia to various destinations in Laos including Don Det (around $15) and Pakse ($17), while some minibuses also cover the same routes. Tickets for both buses and minibuses can be bought at guesthouses in Stung Treng, Banlung and elsewhere.

Entering Cambodia Visas are issued on arrival (roughly $30–40, depending on nationality). If you're not arriving on a through-bus, check out the onward transport in shared taxis and minibuses from the border to Stung Treng, and possibly further south to Kratie, Kompong Cham and even Phnom Penh depending on how early you arrive and how lucky you get, although there's a fair chance you'll end up spending the night in Stung Treng.

GETTING AROUND

Stung Treng is easily negotiated on foot; **motos** are readily available, although there aren't many **tuk-tuks** in town.

By bike and motorbike You can rent bicycles ($2/day) and motorbikes ($8–10/day) at the *Riverside Guesthouse* (see below) and *Ponika's Palace* (see p.226); the *Riverside* and *Xplore Asia* (see p.226) also have mountain bikes for $5/day and Xplore Asia offers a drop-off service whereby you can take one of their bikes for $10/day and deposit it in Kratie, Siem Reap or at their office in Phnom Penh.

ACCOMMODATION

Golden River Hotel Riverfront, just east of the transport stop ☎ 012 980678, ⊛ goldenriverhotel.com. Overlooking the Sekong River, this efficiently run hotel is the town's smartest accommodation, with neat but rather small a/c rooms. Decent value, albeit with zero character. $15

Riverside Guesthouse By the transport stop ☎ 012 439454. The epicentre of Stung Treng's very modest travellers' scene. The best of the bright, clean rooms are at the front, though they're not for light sleepers as they overlook the transport stop. There's a passable café downstairs (see p.226) with book exchange, and owner Mr T is a great source of information about local tours and onward travel. Fan $6; a/c $12

Stung Treng Guesthouse On the main road, across from the market ☎ 012 916465. Downstairs it's a furniture showroom, stuffed to the gills with huge, floridly carved sofas, beds and chairs. Upstairs is a very passable hotel, with large and nicely appointed a/c rooms with hot water and smaller but good-value fan rooms with cold water (although some lack windows). Fan $8; a/c $15

Tonle Guesthouse 500m west of town on the riverfront ☎ 092 674990. In an attractive modern villa on stilts set in a shady garden, this guesthouse serves as a vocational tourism training centre for disadvantaged local youngsters. The four simply furnished but comfortable rooms (fan only) open onto an airy communal lounge. Bathrooms are shared and meals are available but need to be pre-booked. $8

FROM TOP KA CHHANG WATERFALL (P.234); WAT NOKOR (P.215) >

TOURS AROUND STUNG TRENG

There are a number of attractions around Stung Treng: the widest range of local tours is run by Xplore Asia, but there are other options available.

TOUR OPERATORS

Riverside Guesthouse Tours By the transport stop ☎012 439454. This guesthouse is a good option for boat trips, either up the Mekong to the Laos border and back (about $70 including lunch for up to four people) or along the narrower Sekong ($15/hr).

Xplore Asia Just east of the centre on the riverfront – you're most likely to find the manager, Theara, there after 6pm ☎074 973456, ⓦxplore-cambodia.com. A good range of interesting, albeit pricey, trips, including a grand four- to five-day journey down the Mekong to Kratie that takes in parts of the Mekong Discovery Trail (see box, p.218) using a combination of

cycling, trekking and kayaking (starting from around $450 for two people). More affordable excursions include one-day trips combining kayaking, trekking and dolphin watching ($85/person), a full day's kayaking ($65/person); half-day cycling and kayaking trips ($35/person for two people); and fishing trips (the nearby section of the Mekong offers particularly good fishing even in the dry season, since the various falls across the Mekong on either side of the border prevent fish swimming upriver). They can also arrange boat trips to the Sopheak Mitt falls, dolphin watching and a spectacular stretch of flooded forest ($80/boat seating up to four people).

EATING AND DRINKING

There are no culinary frills in Stung Treng, although you won't starve, and the two places listed below do a passable selection of Khmer and Western favourites. Alternatively, head to the long line of **food stalls** along the riverfront dishing up cheap meals, beer and fruit shakes from late afternoon until after dark.

Ponika's Palace Just northeast of the market ☎012 916441. There's nothing particularly palatial about this simple little family-run, tourist-oriented café, offering economical Khmer food (mains $3–4) and more expensive Western and other dishes (not all always available) – the so-called Indian chicken masala bears a suspicious resemblance to Khmer chicken *amok*, but is very good all the same. Decent Western breakfasts too,

plus baguettes, burgers, pancakes and the like. Daily 6am–10pm.

Riverside Guesthouse Café By the transport stop ☎012 439454. Big, traveller-friendly menu featuring lots of Asian mains ($3–3.50) and Western staples – baguettes, pancakes, spaghetti and so on. The two street-side tables offer a nice perch from which to watch the world go by. Daily 6.30am–10.30pm.

DIRECTORY

Internet All the hotels and restaurants that we review (see above) have wi-fi, but there aren't many internet cafés.

Money There are ATMs at the Canadia Bank (Visa and MasterCard) and the Acleda Bank (Visa only).

North along the Mekong: Stung Treng to Laos

The stretch of Mekong between Stung Treng and the Laos border is rich in ecotourism potential, most of it still largely untapped. River islands, waterfalls, rapids and impressive stretches of flooded forest dot the waters, culminating in the thundering **Sopheak Mitt waterfalls**, which block the route on into Laos.

As at Kratie, pods of Irrawaddy dolphins are the major draw, and can be found at several spots along the river. Most visitors head for the so-called **Anlong Cheuteal dolphin pool**, just south of the Laos border. Boat trips here can be arranged at Stung Treng (see box above); alternatively, you may be able to arrange a boat (roughly $15/hr) at the nearby villages of **O Svay** and **Preah Rumkel** – homestays can also be arranged at the latter (see p.220). Dolphin numbers are smaller here than at Kampie, although there's still around a ninety percent chance of spotting them.

Rattanakiri province

Bordering Laos and Vietnam in the far northeast corner of Cambodia, the province of **Rattanakiri** used to abound in lush jungle. These days most of the region's ancient forests have been systematically logged (see box below) of their valuable hardwoods and replanted with cash-crop plantations, mainly rubber, cashew and cassava, although the vistas of misty mountains and gushing waterfalls remain, if nothing else. As befits a province whose name means "gemstone mountain", traditional gem-mining also survives amid the hills, a difficult and dangerous activity, with miners dragging soil to the surface from deep holes where it is painstakingly sifted for the gems you see in every Cambodian market.

The town of **Banlung**, located pretty much in the centre of the province, is the region's one and only tourist centre and the place to come to organize treks and tours into the surrounding countryside. Notable attractions include the magical lake of **Yeak Laom**, set in the crater of an extinct volcano just outside Banlung, along with a cluster of nearby **waterfalls**. North of Banlung, the small town of **Voen Sai** is the jumping-off point for visits to nearby Chinese, Lao and chunchiet villages and for treks into the vast **Virachey National Park**. South of Banlung, the surreal, bomb-scarred landscape at **Lumphat** offers another interestingly alternative sort of destination.

ILLEGAL LOGGING

Between 2000 and 2005 Cambodia lost nearly thirty percent of its **tropical hardwood forest** cover. Since then even more has been lost (though there are no reported figures) and if you're travelling through the provinces of Pailin, Kompong Thom, Kratie, Rattanakiri or Mondulkiri you'll now scarcely see any forest at all, with the situation not much better around Koh Kong. Most of the forest has been cleared to make way for **plantations** of rubber, cashew and cassava, a national scandal presided over by self-serving government officials, many of them close to the Prime Minister, Hun Sen.

From 1995 to 1999 multinational conglomerates were awarded logging concessions and used earth-moving equipment to extract massive hardwood trees from deep in the jungle, frequently destroying everything else in their path. This timber was generally shipped on to Thailand or Vietnam, to be turned into garden furniture and sold to Europe. The revenue from this should have swelled the treasury coffers, but instead, high-ranking officials, many military personnel, suddenly became very rich.

Despite being lobbied by environmentalists, the Cambodian government lacked the resources and the will to enforce the terms of its logging licences and it wasn't until 1999, when the aid donors insisted on independent monitoring of logging as a condition of aid provision, that the government reluctantly allowed a watchdog group, London-based **Global Witness**, to investigate the situation. But things were so bad that by 2003 Global Witness had been sacked by the Cambodian government who took exception to the frank reports that denounced it for poor management of the forests and associated corruption at the highest level. For a time the government seemed to be making some attempts to improve things; but no sooner were logging concessions terminated than they were replaced by economic land concessions, which allowed for the wholesale clearance of forest and stripped the land bare.

Monitoring, although set as a condition of aid provision by the donors themselves – who include Asian Development Bank, World Bank and International Monetary Fund – has not been reinstated and no action has been taken by the donors to limit aid that is being poured into Cambodia at a rate of $1 billion per annum. Meanwhile, the Cambodian government has hawked the rights to the country's other natural resources, including oil, minerals and even sand (with buyers including Total, Chevron and BHP Billiton), with resultant revenues lining the pockets of the country's elite.

4

GEM-MINING IN RATTANAKIRI

Gem-mining is primitive and dangerous; miners dig a circular hole about 1m in diameter and as deep as 10m, without any internal supports or reinforcement, and with only candles for light. As the miner goes deeper, the earth is hauled to the surface in a wicker basket using a variety of low-tech winches made of bamboo and rope. A series of small steps are dug in the wall so that the miner can climb out. The main gemstone found in the area is semiprecious zircon, which looks like brown glass in its raw state but turns pale blue when heated. Also found in Rattanakiri are yellowish green peridot, pale purple amethyst, clear quartz and shiny black onyx.

The sites where gems are mined in Rattanakiri province change regularly, so it's best to check in Banlung before setting out to look for them. Most activity currently centres around **Chum Rum Bai Srok**, in Bokeo district. There's not much to see – once you've seen one mining pit, you've seen them all – but the 35km trip from Banlung is interesting for the scenery, the awfulness of the track and for the sheer exhilaration of having made it. The gem-mining camp is difficult to find without a guide (around $15–20/day; ask at your guesthouse) or a good command of Khmer. South of Ka Chhang, the road soon turns into a narrow churned-up track that winds up and down valleys and forks off left and right through encroaching jungle, until it deteriorates into an even narrower rutted path. If it starts to rain, the track can become impassable and visitors have had to spend the night in the site's blue-tarpaulin-covered shacks.

Banlung

Situated 588km from Phnom Penh by road, the small provincial capital of **BANLUNG** feels a long way from the rest of Cambodia – and indeed from anywhere else. The town sprang to prominence in 1979 when it was chosen as the new provincial capital of Rattanakiri, replacing Voen Sai. Significant development followed (and continues to this day), although Banlung hasn't altogether shaken off its Wild West atmosphere. Most of the town's formerly dirt tracks have now been roughly surfaced but are so indelibly stained with red dirt and mud as to resemble outback tracks, especially after rain, while the combination of local chunchiet descending on town to visit the lively market and marauding touts attempting to flog treks to the unwary add to the place's slightly chaotic appeal. It's also notably cooler up here than down in the lowlands (for once, hot showers are more important than air conditioning), while the town also experiences significantly more rainfall than most other places in the country.

Most people come to Banlung to **trek** (see box, p.231), and there are also a number of interesting day-trips in the surrounding countryside. The town itself is pretty much devoid of attractions, bar the lively local market and the tranquil lake of Boeung Kansaing.

Banlung market

Banlung market occupies a modern concrete building south of the Independence Monument. It's most colourful in the early morning, when local chunchiet women bus or trek into town, *khapas* laden with produce, to set up shop around the outside of the market, puffing on bamboo pipes or large cigars made from tobacco rolled up in leaves. The fruit and vegetables they display neatly on the ground often include varieties you don't find in the lowlands, such as big red bananas, as well as outlandish-looking roots, herbs and flowers gathered from the forest.

WHAT'S IN A NAME?: BANLUNG AND SEN MONOROM

Note that Cambodians habitually refer to **Banlung** as Rattanakiri and **Sen Monorom** as Mondulkiri, as most provinces in Cambodia take their names from their provincial capitals.

Boeung Kansaing

1km north of the centre

Bounding the northern side of Banlung, the tranquil lake of **Boeung Kansaing** offers a complete change of pace and scenery from the slightly manic town centre. The lake is far from unspoilt, with increasing numbers of nondescript modern hotels mushrooming around its banks, but it remains a pleasant place for a wander at any time of day, particularly towards dusk, when a small cluster of food stalls set up around the lake's southern edge – a fun place to hang with the locals over a beer and watch the sun go down.

Phnom Svay

About 1km west of the airport crossroads off the Stung Treng road, from where a track runs behind Wat Eisay Patamak up to the hilltop

There are good views, especially at sunrise and sunset, from the modest hilltop at **Phnom Svay**, with panoramic vistas over the rolling countryside below and distant hills beyond. The path up heads through the pretty **Wat Eisay Patamak**, before reaching the top of the hill some 500m beyond, where an impressive reclining Buddha replaces one destroyed by the Khmer Rouge.

ARRIVAL AND DEPARTURE   BANLUNG

There's no quick way to get to Banlung – since flights stopped in 2006 the only approach is a long slog by **road** along National Routes 7 and 78. The road north of Kratie to the junction at O Pong Moan (20km south of Stung Treng) is currently in a bad way, with serious potholes and large stretches of tarmac washed away, making for a slow and rattling ride. Things

BEYOND BANLUNG: THE ROAD TO MONDULKIRI

Perhaps the major frustration of travel in eastern Cambodia is the amount of backtracking required to reach both Banlung and Sen Monorom. That's the bad news. The good news – unless you're an environmentalist – is that a road between the two is currently under construction (largely, it's said, to allow easier extraction of the region's valuable timber and other natural resources). Due to be finished by around 2015, the new **Banlung–Sen Monorom highway** will allow visitors to follow a single, far quicker, loop through Rattanakiri and Mondulkiri and save a couple of days' travel without any of the to-ing and fro-ing which getting to both of the destinations currently involves.

Pending the construction of the road, the journey is still doable in the dry season, but no picnic (and in the wet season forget it). The first 35km from Banlung is along good, recently upgraded road to **Lumphat**. Beyond here you enter thick forest, following small, confusing and badly rutted tracks for 55km before emerging from the woods at **Kaoh Nhek**, from where it's another 93km to Sen Monorom along a good graded track. Motos can be rented in Banlung and Sen Monorom to make the gruelling 8hr journey for around $80. Alternatively you could hire a 4WD for around $250, well worth the cost if you can get a group of four or five people together.

improve beyond O Pong Moan, where the wide and generally empty N78 has now been surfaced all the way to Banlung – one of the quickest and smoothest roads in the entire country.

By bus The only bus service from Banlung is the once-daily, early morning bus to Phnom Penh operated by Phnom Penh Sorya, plus a couple of local services to Voen Sai. There are no buses to Stung Treng, meaning you'll be forced to take a shared taxi or a pick-up, or cram into a minibus with the locals.
Destinations Kompong Cham (1 daily; 6hr); Kratie (1 daily; 4hr); Phnom Penh (1 daily; 8hr); Voen Sai (2 daily; 2–3hr).
By shared taxi and minibus The transport stop for taxis and minibuses is next to the market, in the centre of the traffic circle on the main road.

Destinations Kompong Cham (several daily; 6hr); Kratie (3 daily; 6hr); Phnom Penh (several daily; 8hr); Stung Treng (4 daily; 2hr 30min).
Tickets Bus and minibus tickets can be bought through *Tribal* hotel, *Tree Top Eco Lodge* and *Backpacker Pad*. Various scams continue to be reported by travellers heading by bus or minibus from Banlung to Laos. One reliable option is to book a ticket through *Tree Top Eco Lodge*, changing buses at their sister guesthouse in Stung Treng, the *Riverside* (see p.224), before proceeding to Laos.

GETTING AROUND

By moto or tuk-tuk Banlung is quite spread out. Heading between the lake and town centre you might want to hop on one of the town's plentiful motos ($1–2) or grab a tuk-tuk ($2–3), although these can be hard to find.
By bike and motorbike Bikes ($1/day) and motorbikes ($5–6/day) can be rented from various places including the *Tribal Hotel*, *Tree Top Eco Lodge* and *Backpacker Pad*. If you decide to rent a bike or motorbike and head off on your

own, bear in mind that road conditions vary dramatically in Rattanakiri; while the road to Yeak Laom lake and on the Vietnam border is now surfaced, others remain in poor shape. If you're heading out alone it's worth telling someone at your hotel or guesthouse about your route, as punctures and breakdowns do happen.
By car For car rental ($40–70/day) try the *Tribal* hotel or Parrot Tours.

ACCOMMODATION

The nicest place to stay in Banlung is around the **lake**, although most of the action (including restaurants and tour operators) are clustered together in the area about 500m east of the centre around the *Tribal* hotel – a much less attractive part of town, but with a compensatory liveliness the lakeside often lacks.

Backpacker Pad Between the town centre and Boeung Kansaing ☎092 785259, ✉banlungback packerpad@yahoo.com. On a dusty backroad between town and lake, this is Banlung's last resort for die-hard budget travellers, with super-cheap accommodation in

poky little windowless box rooms (those with private bathroom cost an extra $1) or an even cheaper dorm. Plus points include the free wi-fi and pool table, and it's also a good place to arrange trips, bus tickets and bike rental. Dorm $\overline{2}$; doubles $\overline{4}$

TOURS AND TREKKING AROUND BANLUNG

Trekking is big business in Banlung, and the reason most foreigners come here in the first place. There are at least a dozen agencies on the road leading down to the *Tribal Hotel*, although most of them give the impression of being little better than glorified bandwagon-jumpers. The treks themselves can last anything from a day to over a week – although obviously to get into the deeper part of the jungle you'll need to go on a longer visit. As well as jungle trekking, walks may include homestays in chunchiet villages, visits to chunchiet cemeteries, and river rafting on specially designed bamboo rafts. All-Inclusive rates start from around $40/person/day in a group of two, becoming steadily cheaper the larger the group you travel in. The best operators use indigenous guides wherever possible, and return part of their profits to local communities through various forms of assistance.

There are also plenty of one-day **tours** on offer should you fancy something less strenuous. The most popular excursion is the trip (around 4–5hr) combining a visit to **Yeak Laom lake** combined with the Chha Ong, Ka Chhang and Katieng waterfalls (around $15 by moto, $25 by tuk-tuk). Other possibilities include day-trips to **chunchiet villages** (around $25 by moto or $40 by tuk-tuk) and to **Lumphat** ($20 by moto, $35 by tuk-tuk).

TREKKING AND TOUR OPERATORS

DutchCo Café Alee, east of the centre (after 6pm) ☏017 571682, ⓦEcotourismCambodia.info. Banlung-based Dutch expat Rik is on a one-man mission to help preserve the forests and indigenous culture of Rattanakiri through responsible tourism, using indigenous guides wherever possible and supporting local communities. Jungle treks last 1–5 days, including a 3–5-day programme, "Giants of Virachey", trekking among giant trees in a stretch of million-year-old forest inside the national park. They also run rewarding day-trips to the chunchiet cemetery at Koah Piek ($50/person in a group of two, cheaper in larger groups) and one-day treks through Kalai forest, an impressive area of primary semi-evergreen jungle ($35/person in a group of two, cheaper in larger groups).

Gibbon Spotting Cambodia ☏+44 20 3617 8711 (UK), ⓦgibbonspottingcambodia.com. Overnight treks offering a unique opportunity to see a habituated family of rare northern yellow-cheeked gibbons in the Veun Sai–Siem Pang Conservation Area adjoining the Virachey National Park. Treks start in Voen Sai, with a maximum of six people per trek. There's a roughly eighty percent chance of spotting gibbons, and the conservation area is also rich in other wildlife. Treks run from November to mid-June only; from $200/person. Given

the limited numbers of people allowed into the area, it's recommended you book as far in advance as possible.

Parrot Tours East of the centre ☏097 837 3878, ⓦjungletrek.wix.com/parrot-tours and ⓦjungle trek.blogspot.com. One of the most switched-on operators in town, running a range of treks (one to seven nights) around Virachey National Park (including bamboo-rafting) and the chunchiet villages, and in the Lumphat Wildlife Protected Area south of Banlung. Also a good place to set up day-trips around town.

Virachey National Park Eco-tourism Office Ministry of Forest compound, north of the Gecko House restaurant (office open daily 8–11am & 2–5pm in theory, assuming there's someone around to sit behind the desk) ☏075 974013, ⓔvirachey @camintel.com. Apart from the one tour run by DutchCo (see above), this government-run outfit is the only one that actually treks inside the Virachey National Park; other operators, regardless of what they may say, only trek around the park's outskirts. Treks range from two to eight days, starting at around $90/person/day for short treks in a group of two and falling to as little as $40/person/day for week-long treks in groups of five or more. Rates include park entry fee, transport, food, indigenous guide and contributions to a community project.

4

Colonial Lake Palace Boeung Kansaing ☏0756 768444. Attractive and good-value new hotel in a shiny-bright modern building overlooking the lake. Rooms are nicely furnished (albeit not particularly "colonial") and come with flatscreen TVs and wi-fi. Fan $10; a/c $15

NorDen House Near the Tribal Monument on the road to Yeak Laom lake ☏075 690 0640, ⓦnorden houseyaklom.com. Six pleasant a/c bungalows set in a peaceful garden in an attractive rural setting slightly

outside town. Rooms come with wi-fi, flatscreen TVs and DVD players, plus solar-powered hot water, and there's a decent restaurant-cum-bar. $30

Prak Dara Guesthouse Boeung Kansaing ☏012 614608. Modern hotel set high above the lake with bright and spacious rooms. A bargain at current rates, if you don't mind the lack of English, random service and total lack of atmosphere. Fan $7; a/c $12

★**Terres Rouges Lodge** Boeung Kansaing

☎012 770650, ⌨ratanakiri-lodge.com. Luxurious guesthouse in lush gardens near the lake, offering an unexpected haven of luxury in remote Banlung. The lodge's wooden buildings look a bit like a miniature Khmer village given a chic modern makeover, with standard rooms in the main building, plus more luxurious accommodation in private bungalows arranged around a beautiful garden. Rooms (all a/c) are individually decorated with traditional fabrics and artefacts. There's also a good restaurant (see below) and a good-sized pool, plus a small spa. $52

Thy Ath Lodge Boeung Kansaing ☎097 315 5559, ✉thy.ath.lodge@gmail.com. Friendly family guesthouse in a sparkling new building close to the lake. Rooms (all a/c) are spacious, spotless and very comfortable, while those upstairs ($5 extra) have good lake views too. $20

★**Tree Top Eco Lodge** ☎012 490333, ⌨treetop-ecolodge.com. Banlung's most original place to stay, with accommodation in bungalows scattered across a thickly wooded hillside and connected by a picturesque network of raised walkways – you'll feel a bit like Tarzan just getting

to reception. The bungalows themselves (all en suite, fan only) are fairly basic, although the stone-pebbled bathrooms are a nice touch. More expensive ones have hot water, and some also have nice balconies with hammocks to loll in. There's also a restaurant and free wi-fi, and staff can arrange tours and onward travel. $7

Tribal East of the centre ☎075 650 8555. Long-running Banlung institution, although now somewhat past its best. The wood-panelled rooms are spacious but a bit gloomy (and could be cleaner), although perfectly OK for the price. The attractive attached restaurant (see below) is a major plus, and staff can also sort out transport and tours. Fan $7; a/c $12

Yaklom Hill Lodge 6km east of town, beyond the Hill Tribe Monument ☎011 790510, ⌨yaklom.blogspot.co.uk. For real isolation this eco-resort is hard to beat, with fifteen stilted wooden bungalows dotted amid jungly grounds featuring sunset- and sunrise-viewing platforms, linked by a nature trail amid the trees. Rooms (fan only) are simply but nicely furnished, although there are communal showers only, and the electricity goes off nightly at 9pm. Rates include breakfast. $15

EATING, DRINKING AND NIGHTLIFE

A'Dam East of the centre ☎012 411115. This pavilion restaurant is generally quiet (sometimes bordering on comatose), but the food more than compensates, with a good selection of fresh and flavoursome Chinese dishes, plus a few Thai and Khmer options (mains $2.50–3). Daily 8am–10pm.

Café Alee East of the centre. The newest kid on the Banlung block, with a telephone directory-sized menu stuffed with all the usual Western and Khmer favourites (mains $2.50–4) along with a truckload of other home-from-home comforts – anything from cookies and fruit bread to pancakes and popcorn, plus an interesting selection of local coffees. Doubles as the office of DutchCo (see p.231) in the evenings. Daily 7am until late.

Coconut Shake Boeung Kansaing ☎077 912021. Simple little Khmer restaurant in a pleasant lakeside setting. All the usual Khmer standards (mains $2.50–4), plus a few baguettes and a smattering of more expensive Western options including that old sailor's favourite, "Fish & Ship". The signature coconut shake itself ($1, when available) gets mixed reviews. Daily 7am–9pm.

Gecko House East of the centre ☎012 422228. In a vaguely jungly-looking thatched construction, *Gecko* is usually the liveliest place in town, and can get a bit of a party atmosphere if there are enough trekkers around. The big menu features plenty of Thai, Khmer and Chinese options (mains $4–5.50), plus a good Western selection, although the slighty above-average prices aren't always reflected in the quality of the food. Daily 8am–11pm.

Terres Rouges Lodge Boeung Kansaing ☎012 770650. The place to go for a special meal by sultry lamplight with a good range of Asian dishes ($4.50–6) plus various pastas and a few French options ($11–12) including meltingly tender *coq au vin*. Reservations recommended. Daily 11.30am–2pm & 6–9.30pm.

Tribal Restaurant Tribal hotel, east of the centre ☎075 650 8555. Attractive pavilion restaurant serving up nicely presented Khmer (mains $3–4) and more expensive Western food. A good place for breakfast or lunch (including tip-top baguettes), with cheap beer and a well-stocked bar come sundown – or indeed earlier if you fancy. Daily 6am–10.30pm.

DIRECTORY

Internet Most of the hotels and restaurants that we review (see above) have free wi-fi. Alternatively try Srey Mon Internet Café, near the *Tribal* hotel, or the well-equipped GreenNet close by on the side road just before *A'Dam* restaurant. Both charge $1/hr and are open from around 9am to 9pm.

Money There are ATMs at the Canadia Bank (Visa and MasterCard) and Acleda Bank (Visa only) in the centre of town.

Phones and post office The post office, on the main road 500m east of the Independence Monument (Mon–Fri 8–11am & 2–5pm) has facilities for international phone

THE CHUNCHIET

Cambodia's **chunchiet** (literally "nationality") or **Khmer Loeu** ("upland Khmer") are one of the ethnic minority groups found scattered throughout the hinterlands of Cambodia, Burma, Thailand, Laos, Vietnam and parts of southeastern China. The chunchiet live primarily in the remote villages of Rattanakiri and Mondulkiri provinces, although small communities also inhabit parts of Stung Treng and Kratie provinces, and a few live in the mountains of southwest Cambodia, near Koh Kong. It's estimated that the chunchiet make up one percent of Cambodia's population, although in the highlands of the east and northeast they have always been the majority, at least until the recent influx of Khmer from the rest of the country.

The chunchiet, like the Khmer, are regarded as **indigenous** inhabitants of the country. Smaller in stature and darker-skinned than the Khmer, they divide into more than thirty distinct tribes, ranging from comparatively large groups such as the Tampoun, Kreung-Brou, Jarai, Stieng and Phnong, all of which number in the thousands, to much smaller tribes, including the Kavat, Lun, Peahr and Meul, which are believed to number fewer than a hundred each. Every group has its own **language**, each with several dialects; additionally, none of the chunchiet tongues has a written form. Traditional garments are used only on ceremonial occasions, from which strangers are normally excluded. Indeed, relatively little is known about chunchiet rituals and ceremonies, though it is known that **animism** and **ancestor worship** are central to the chunchiet belief system.

Unfortunately, the traditional way of life is now nearly extinct. Repeated attempts have been made to bring the tribes round to the Khmer way of life. The French recruited them to work in the rubber plantations and on road-building projects, while the Sihanouk government tried to restrict them to farming fixed plots. In the mid-1960s, government troops seeking the guerrilla Khmer Rouge – who had fled to the jungles of Rattanakiri – burned down chunchiet villages. Indeed, bombed by the US in the early 1970s and continually harassed by Lon Nol soldiers, the chunchiet were ripe for recruitment by the Khmer Rouge, although those who did join them were most likely siding with them against a common enemy rather than sharing their ideology.

Today, in theory, chunchiet lands are state-owned and cannot be sold to private Cambodians, but since 2001 tribal lands have been sold, sometimes by village headmen, to savvy Khmer who have cleared the land for farms. Latterly, the government has allowed economic land concessions (ELCs), which permit ground to be **cleared** for plantations. According to Cambodian law, ELCs can only be used to clear non-forested land, but regardless of this, vast swathes of forest have now been cleared to make way for plantations of rubber and cashew; according to a report by Global Witness (see p.227) this is a way of flouting the rules regarding illegal logging. The consequence for the chunchiet is that the forest on which they have long relied for their livelihood has been largely destroyed. Appeals for the return of their land has been to no avail. Some still manage to eke a living out of the land, others have found work locally in tourism, while some have been forced to abandon their traditional way of life entirely.

Although many villagers have become accustomed to foreign visitors, they remain shy and modest – some may even see your presence as voyeuristic, so it's always better to visit in the company of a local guide. It's also worth noting that the chunchiet do not like having their pictures taken and are embarrassed by shows of public affection and by exposed flesh (bare legs, arms and so on).

4

---

calls; you can also call abroad using VoIP at the internet shops. Domestic calls can be made at the cheap-rate booths near the market.

Police Just north of the Independence Monument (☎ 012 308988).

Shopping A few dealers in and around the market sell cut and polished local gemstones (see p.228), which you can get made up into jewellery for around $15–20; you'll also find a few rings and pendants. The gemstones here are hardly world-class, but there's no evidence of fakes being passed off as genuine. Even so, it's not wise to pay a lot of money for a stone you like unless you have some knowledge of gemology and know what any particular stone is worth.

Swimming Non-residents can use the pool at *Terres Rouges* for $5/day.

Yeak Laom lake

5km east of Banlung • Daily dawn–dusk • 6000 riel • Head east out of Banlung and turn south at the Hill Tribe Monument roundabout; dropping down the hill you reach the lake after 1.5km; the return trip by moto costs around $5, including waiting time

Surrounded by unspoilt forest, the clear turquoise waters of **Yeak Laom lake**, 800m across and up to 50m deep, are warm and inviting. There are wooden platforms for bathing, and the 3km track around the lake perimeter makes for a tranquil little hike. The setting is mesmerizing: stands of bamboo rim the lake, lush ferns sprout from fallen trees, the reflections of clouds skim across the lake's surface, and in the late afternoon an ethereal mist can be seen rising off the water. Watch out for your stuff though – there have been thefts from bags left on the bank while visitors are swimming.

The area is regarded as sacred by the Tampoun, who manage it for the benefit of their community. Chunchiet culture is showcased at the small and rather ramshackle **Cultural and Environment Centre** (300 riel), around 300m anticlockwise round the lake from the entrance steps, with a few dusty displays of chunchiet artefacts. The small craft stall next door sells locally produced textiles, the money from sales going directly to the community.

Waterfalls around Banlung

Entry to each waterfall costs 2000 riel • For Chha Ong head 2km west of Banlung along NR78 to reach the crossroads at the Lina petrol station – turn right immediately past the petrol station (bearing left at the fork after about 1km and continuing through the small village of Chha Ong); for Katieng turn left at the Lina petrol station, following the sign to Swift Rubber Factory/Rattanakiri Rubber Plantations, and take a right turn immediately past the factory (unsigned, although the track is clear); for Ka Chhang continue straight on along the road past the rubber factory

There are a few modest but picturesque **waterfalls** within easy reach of Banlung, easily combined into a half-day trip along with a visit to Yeak Laom lake. The falls at **Chha Ong**, around 8km northwest of Banlung, are the largest, the river flowing through lush jungle before plunging 30m into a gorge. The pool at the base is deep enough to swim in, and daring souls can climb onto a ledge behind the curtain of water.

Southwest of Banlung, hidden in a bamboo-clad valley, are the **Ka Chhang** falls, just 10m high, but impressive after rain and with a pool for taking a dip. Nearby are the small and similar **Katieng** falls. You can hop on an elephant ride here ($10/hr) for a trip around the falls, although the animals are often overworked.

Voen Sai

Stretching along the south side of the pretty **San River**, the former provincial capital of **VOEN SAI**, 35km northwest of Banlung and accessible by bus, is the largest village in the vicinity of Virachey National Park. From the centre of the village a **ferry** (1000 riel) runs to the far bank of the river, on which there are some Chinese and Lao villages, notably different in appearance to others in the area. The Chinese village a couple of kilometres to the west has a tidy school and a general store; the main street is flanked by neat bright-blue houses planted firmly on the ground rather than on stilts. **Boats** can be rented along the river for trips upstream to Kreung and Kraval villages (1hr; around $15 return) and further on to the Tampoun chunchiet cemetery (3hr; $50 return).

If you have your own transport you can make an interesting little diversion en route to Voen Sai at **Veal Rum Plan**, an ancient lava field of huge flat stones. To reach the lava field, head east at the O Chum crossroads, about 10km north of Banlung, and then continue straight down the road for around 4km.

Virachey National Park

Daily • $5/day • Treks into the park must be arranged through the Virachey National Park Eco-tourism Office in Banlung (see box, p.231), apart from one tour offered by DutchCo (see p.231)

Spreading north of Voen Sai, the **Virachey National Park** covers more than three thousand square kilometres of remote, mountainous countryside running north to the Laos border and east to Vietnam, comprising a mix of landscapes from dense jungle lowlands through to montane forests and rolling upland savannahs. It's also the largest "protected" area in Cambodia, although exactly what kind of protection it's currently receiving is a moot point – local reports suggest that as much as sixty percent of the park has already been earmarked for future logging.

Virachey's outstandingly rich **wildlife** is yet to be fully explored or understood. The world's largest population of rare northern yellow-cheeked **gibbons** in the **Veun Sai–Siem Pang Conservation Area** adjoining the park weren't discovered until as recently as 2010, while a couple of other entirely new species – the iridescent short-legged lizard and Walston's tube-nosed bat – have also recently been unearthed for the first time. Other forest inhabitants include elephants, pig-tailed macaques, douc langurs, sun bears, the rare giant ibis and clouded leopards. Rumours of tigers and Javan rhinos living deep inside the forest also occasionally surface, although the alleged sightings may contain rather more fiction than fact.

Visiting the park (see p.231), the most challenging and rewarding expedition is the week-long trek to the remote grassland wilderness of **Phnom Veal Thom**, with spectacular views over the mountainous hinterlands bordering Laos and Vietnam. Shorter treks include the overnight trek to Yark Koung Kreav mountain and the three-night trek to Yark Kea waterfall.

Lumphat

There's not much left of **LUMPHAT**, 35km south of Banlung. Capital of Rattanakiri until 1975, when the Khmer Rouge moved it to Voen Sai, the town sustained heavy bombing during the 1970s and still has a faintly postapocalyptic air, with a few ruined shells of concrete buildings all that survives of its days as provincial capital, along with patches of cratered wasteland caused by American B-52 bombing runs. There are no land mines here, but **unexploded ordnance** may still be a risk.

Lumphat is also the jumping-off point for trips into the **Lumphat Wildlife Sanctuary**. Some tour operators in Banlung (see box, p.231) offer treks into the sanctuary, although as at Virachey National Park rampant logging is taking a steady toll on the natural environment – a process which is likely to proceed with even more unseemly haste once the new road through to Sen Monorom (see box, p.230) is finally completed.

Mondulkiri province

The country's largest but most sparsely populated province, mountainous **Mondulkiri** sees fewer travellers in a year than Rattanakiri does in a month, although improved access is gradually bringing Cambodia's "Wild East" into the tourist mainstream. As in neighbouring Rattanakiri, Mondulkiri's once wild landscape has suffered greatly from indiscriminate logging and other forms of development, including the creation of Chinese and Australian gold mines, although areas of impenetrable jungle survive, home to rare and endangered wildlife including elephants, Asian dogs and green peafowl. The compact provincial capital, **Sen Monorom**, makes a good base for local treks and visits to surrounding attractions, including the mighty **Bou Sraa** waterfall and the innovative **Elephant Valley Project**.

4

Mondulkiri's main indigenous group are the **Bunong** (also known as the Phnong), who made up nearly eighty percent of the province's population until the 1990s, when they were joined by an influx of impoverished Khmer returning from the refugee camps in Thailand. The Khmer are still coming, though nowadays it's rich ones who are buying land cheaply then clearing it for farms and plantations.

Sen Monorom

SEN MONOROM is still little more than a large village set amid a landscape of rolling grass-covered hills – more reminiscent of England than Cambodia – dotted with copses of pine planted in the late 1960s at the king's behest. The two **lakes** close to town are pleasant for an early morning or late afternoon stroll, while 2km northeast from town is the sacred mountain **Phnom Dosh Kramom** (known as Youk Srosh Phlom to the Bunong), a small hill with a meditation pagoda, from which there are splendid views.

ARRIVAL AND DEPARTURE

SEN MONOROM

Despite recent road improvements, transport to Mondulkiri remains sketchy, with just a couple of buses (run by Phnom Penh Sorya and Rith Mony) daily from **Phnom Penh** via **Kompong Cham**. There are also a couple of early-morning minibuses and shared taxis from these places, and also from **Kratie**. It's possible to catch a bus, minibus or shared taxi to **Snuol** on the main road north and try to pick up onward transport to Sen Monorom from there, although you might end up waiting a long time – or even conceivably getting stuck overnight. There is also a challenging off-road route from **Banlung** (see box, p.230).

By bus Buses run by Rith Mony and Phnom Penh Sorya stop at their respective offices on the main road next to the market right in the middle of town.
Destinations Kompong Cham (2 daily; 4hr 30min); Phnom Penh (2 daily; 8hr).
By shared taxi and minibus Taxis and minibuses arrive and leave from the transport stop in the north of town, just uphill from the market; the driver will usually drop you off at a guesthouse of your choice.
Destinations Kompong Cham (2–3 daily; 4hr); Kratie (2–4 daily; 4hr 30min); Phnom Penh (1–2 daily; 6–7hr); Snuol (3–4 daily; 2hr).

GETTING AROUND

You won't need a vehicle to get around the diminutive town centre, although there are plenty of motos available (around $20–25/day) for trips into the surrounding countryside, and you can also rent **bikes** ($1–2/day), **mountain bikes** ($5/day), **motorbikes** ($8) and **trail bikes** ($15) from several guesthouses around town including *The Green House*, as well as the Bunong Centre.

ACCOMMODATION

Long Vibol 1km from town towards Bou Sraa waterfall ☎012 944647. Country resort-style place with a selection of bungalows (fan only) spread around attractively lush gardens. The cheapest rooms are rather lacking in frills; more expensive ones come with balcony, hot water and TV. $8

Mondulkiri Off NR76 around 500m south of the market on the back road between the hospital and the wat ☎012 777057, ⓦmondulkiri-hotel.com. Large, identikit modern hotel with smart a/c rooms well equipped with hot water, satelite TV and fridge. There's also a pool, massage and a decent restaurant overlooking the river. $15

Nature Lodge 2km north of town ☎012 230272, ⓦnaturelodgecambodia.com. Idyllic little ecolodge, tucked away in a valley north of town, with accommodation in wooden cabins (fan and hot water) dotted amid the trees, plus a rustic little restaurant, bar and library. $10

Phanyro 500m from town ☎017 770867. Attractive guesthouse with accommodation in a cluster of neat bungalows (with fan and hot water) lined up on a hill just outside town. Popular with visiting NGOs, so it's worth booking ahead. $7

★**Pich Kiri** On the uphill stretch on the way into town just east of the market ☎012 932102. Sen Monorom's longest-running guesthouse; the cheapest rooms are slightly musty with fan and cold water only; plusher rooms in the classy new block come with a/c and hot water. There's also a great restaurant and leafy garden. Fan $6; a/c $15

Sum Dy 1.5km from town ☎092 285721. Good-value

TREKKING AND ELEPHANT RIDES AROUND SEN MONOROM

Trekking in Sen Monorom, although not yet as big as in Banlung, is becoming increasingly popular, with a variety of routes lasting from a day to a week. The best operators use Bunong guides, who intimately know the forests through which you'll be walking. Treks generally include a mix of cultural and scenic attractions, with visits to Bunong villages and waterfalls along with jungle hiking and wild swimming.

Also popular are the ubiquitous **elephant rides** touted in just about every guesthouse in town – although none rivals the experience you'll get at the **Elephant Valley Project** (see p.238). Treks start either from the village of Phulung, about 8km north of town, or from Potang, 8km to the south; a half- or full day rolling around on an elephant costs $15/$30, including transport to the village, a Phnong-speaking guide and lunch if you're out for the full day. Overnight camping treks are also possible, but for most the novelty wears off after a few hours of bumping about.

TREKKING AND TOUR OPERATORS

The Bunong Place On the main road just south of the market. The Bunong staff here can also arrange visits to local villages and elephant rides.

Green House Tours On the main road near the market ☎017 905659, ⊛greenhouse-tour.blogspot.co.uk. Owner Sam is a good source of information and arranges a range of treks and excursions, including tours by mountain bike into the hills.

Mondulkiri Tour Guide ☎088 593 5588, ⊛mondulkiritourguide.com. Authentic off-the-beaten-track treks – not cheap, but well run, with licensed English-speaking guides and everything provided.

4

lodgings in large bungalows, nicely furnished and with hot water, fans and hill views from their private balconies.

Good value, although it's 1.5km to town and there's no restaurant or bar. **$12**

EATING AND DRINKING

★**Banana's** 500m down the hill west of the market ☎092 412680. This Dutch-owned place is the classiest of Sen Monorom's modest selection of restaurants, set in a mini-jungle by the river and serving up good Western food ranging from *Schnitzels* to *coq au vin*. The food isn't cheap (mains around $7) but servings are generous and the quality's high. Daily 9am–10pm.

The Green House On the main road near the market ☎017 905659. A long-running travellers' stalwart, serving up the usual selection of Khmer and Western staples (mains $2–4). Also a popular place for an after-dark drink, with a decent beer and cocktail selection. Daily 7am–10pm.

Khmer Kitchen Just east of the market. Tourist-friendly local café (with English menu) dishing up good, inexpensive Khmer and Chinese-style food (plus a few less convincing Western dishes), with mains around $3. Daily 8am–9pm.

Mondulkiri Pizza Behind the hospital ☎0975 222219. Newish restaurant in a cute little bamboo building with a lively atmosphere and the best pizza (around $5) you could reasonably expect in the wilds of Mondulkiri. Daily 10am–9pm.

Sovannkiri NR76 ☎097 474 4528. Australian-Khmer-run place with a great selection of local and Western dishes including good burgers and steaks, plus cheap beer. Mains $2–6. Daily 8am–10pm.

DIRECTORY

Internet Try *The Green House* café/bar (see above); most guesthouses in town now have free wi-fi.

Money There's an ATM at the Acleda Bank (Visa only)

opposite *The Green House*.

Shopping The minimart at the Total petrol station is handy for basic provisions.

Phnom Bai Chuw and the Sea Forest

7km northeast of Sen Monorom, along the road past Phnom Dosh Kramom

Northeast of Sen Monorom, an observation platform atop the grassy hill of **Phnom Bai Chuw** offers one of Mondulkiri's classic views, looking down over miles of jungle canopy as it sweeps and rolls over the hills below – the so-called **"Sea Forest"**, as it's popularly known. Squint a little, and you really can almost believe you're looking at the supersized waves of some gigantic green ocean.

The Elephant Valley Project

10km northwest of Sen Monorom • Day-visit $70, or $40 including a half-day's volunteer work; longer visits (including seven-day volunteer programmes) are also available (see the website for details); overnight stays $20 (dorm), $50 (private bungalow with half-board) • ☎ 099 696041, Ⓦ elephantvalleyproject.org

A place where "Elephants get to be elephants again", the innovative **Elephant Valley Project** was set up to create a haven for Cambodia's increasingly threatened pachyderm population. The project is the complete antithesis of the usual tourist theme-park, with all the animal exploitation it inevitably entails. There are no elephant rides here (something the project actively discourages). Instead, visitors get the chance to shadow the project's two resident elephant families, walking with them through the jungle and observing them at leisure in their natural environment, while learning about them from their Khmer mahouts.

The project is part of the Elephant Livelihood Initiative Environment NGO or **ELIE**, for short, which works to improve the welfare of domestic elephants in Mondulkiri, many of whom suffer overwork, malnutrition and abuse. ELIE runs several projects locally, including an elephant research and monitoring programme and a mobile vet service.

Waterfalls around Sen Monorom

To get to Bou Sraa or Romanea you'll need to rent a motorbike (see p.236) or rent a moto (about $25 for the return trip to both falls) – the road to Bou Sraa ($2 toll) is only so-so at best, and can be tortuous in the rainy season (expect the journey to take at least 90min); for Romanea take the main road back from Bou Sraa towards Snuol for about 10km, and then fork left and left again; Monorom waterfall can be easily reached by moto (around $3 return) or on foot

Cambodia's most dramatic cascade, **Bou Sraa** waterfall is a fabulous two-tiered cascade some 35km from Sen Monorom, towards the Vietnamese border. The setting alone makes the falls worth visiting, the river dropping over 30m into a jungle gorge. Getting there is something of an expedition, however, making it easy to see why the locals get around by elephant. Not nearly as dramatic as Bou Sraa, but a whole lot easier to get to (though the road is unsurfaced and can be tricky after rain), are the three-tier **Romanea falls**.

Just 4km northwest of Sen Monorom is the 10m-high **Monorom waterfall** (also known as the Sihanouk falls). Along the way you'll pass the ruins of the (rarely used) royal residence, after which you should follow the left fork to the falls. You can swim in the pool at the base of the falls, even in the dry season.

Seima Protection Forest

Southwest of Sen Monorom, flanking the road to Snuol, is the **Seima Protection Forest (SPF)**. Established in 2009, the SPF is home to some of Cambodia's most spectacular wildlife, although the forest's daunting size and lack of infrastructure means that ecotourism here is still very much in its infancy. Resident animals include elephants, tigers, banteng and gaur, along with more than 300 species of bird and some 2500 yellow-cheeked crested gibbons. The forest is also home to the world's largest population of **black-shanked douc langurs**, with an estimated 42,000 of these engaging blue-faced monkeys living here. Remarkably, their presence in the forest went completely unrecorded until a few years back – prior to their discovery the world's largest reported group of black-shanked doucs (in Vietnam) was a mere six hundred. Access to the forest is strictly limited at present, although visits can be arranged through Green House Tours (see p.237), who currently offer treks into the forest lasting between one and three days.

Mondulkiri Protected Forest

Beyond Sen Monorom, a great swath of trees blankets the northern reaches of Mondulkiri province and onwards into Rattanakiri. Some of the most pristine forest can be found in the remote **Mondulkiri Protected Forest**, near the border with Vietnam, only now opening up (slowly) to tourists. The forest is home to a superb range of endangered wildlife including elephant, tiger, banteng, gaur and wild buffalo. Birds are also plentiful, including rare Sarus cranes, giant ibis, and lesser adjutant. Visits and homestays can be arranged through the WWF-supported **Dei Ey Forest Experience** (Ⓦmondulkiritourism.org). The project works with indigenous Bunong communities living within the forest, and visitor activities include collecting wild honey, walking with elephants and working with villagers in the fields.

4

Sihanoukville and the south

BEACH BAR, KOH RONG

5

Sihanoukville and the south

Cambodia's southern provinces offer ravishing contrasts – a near-iridescent green quilt of rice paddies, the looming crags of the Cardamom and Elephant mountain ranges and a palm-fringed coastline stretching for more than 440km. The relative inaccessibility of much of the southwest, thanks to heavy forest cover, the presence of the mountains and the lack of roads, only adds to its charm, although encroaching development – even within the region's pristine national parks – is a constant threat. Numerous islands dot the azure Andaman Sea, and although many are also earmarked for resort development (with some already under way), a castaway ambience still prevails.

Southeastern Cambodia – roughly comprising **Kampot** and **Takeo provinces** – is dotted with craggy karst formations that project starkly from the plains. This is one of the country's most productive agricultural regions: parts of Kampot province are like one vast market garden, producing durian, watermelon and coconuts, while in Takeo province rice paddies dominate. Salt, and more importantly, **pepper**, are also key products. The former is extracted from the saltpans of the coast and plays an important part in the manufacture of the country's *prohok* (salted fermented fish paste); the latter is cultivated almost like hops, with regimented vines clinging to cords, and was once *the* condiment of the colonial occupiers – at the time, no Parisian table worth its salt was without Kampot pepper.

Most visitors come to the south to hit the beach at **Sihanoukville** or use the town as a jumping-off point to the **islands**, their white sands washed by warm, shallow waters. Sihanoukville sits on a peninsula jutting into the Gulf of Thailand, its coastline scalloped with gently shelving, tree-fringed white-sand beaches, and hazy islands looming enticingly out at sea. But don't expect atoll-like isolation: the town is attracting increasing numbers of party-animals keen to live it up in the clubs by night and in the **Ochheuteal Beach** bars by day. That said, a short moto-ride along the coast in either direction uncovers stretches of less developed, peaceful beach, particularly during the week.

Sihanoukville is also the base for another area of outstanding natural beauty, **Ream National Park**, with mangrove forest and fine sandy beaches. East of town, **Bokor National Park** remains worth visiting for an eerie walk around the abandoned hill station amid its jungle-clad slopes, although private development is starting to diminish some, if not all, of its unearthly appeal. It's most easily reached from the charming riverside town of **Kampot**, as is **Kep**, a sleepy seaside destination famed for its fresh crab.

East of Kep, you'll find the down-at-heel remains of the Funan-era city of **Angkor Borei**, home to a fascinating museum of early statuary and interesting records of the archeological digs of the ancient city scattered around the town; close by, the hilltop

VILLAGE JETTY, REAM NATIONAL PARK

Highlights

❶ Kirirom and Ream national parks From the cool jungle-clad hills and waterfalls of Kirirom to the stunning coastal scenery of Ream, the region's natural beauty begs to be explored. **See p.245 & p.261**

❷ Sihanoukville Cambodia's premier coastal town, mixing wild nightlife with a relaxed beach vibe. **See p.247**

❸ Island hopping Swap the mainland crowds for tranquil, pristine beaches, on the south coast's palm-fringed islands. **See p.258 & p.262**

❹ Chi Phat A well-run, community-based ecotourism initiative where you can sleep in a homestay and hike or mountain-bike through the pristine southern Cardamoms. **See p.267**

❺ Kampot A charming riverside town with a rich colonial history that makes an ideal base for exploring the surrounding area's caves, waterfalls and islands. **See p.267**

❻ Kep Enjoy crab feasts at the beachside market or sip a sundowner in sumptuous luxury at this 1960s seaside resort, now being restored to its former elegance. **See p.273**

HIGHLIGHTS ARE MARKED ON THE MAP ON P.244

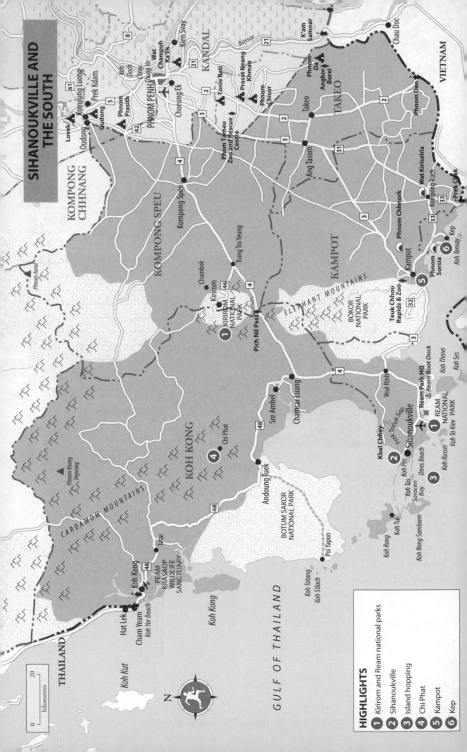

temple of **Phnom Da** is easily visited by boat from **Takeo**, a shabby little town that still feels far removed from the tourist trail, despite its proximity to Phnom Penh.

In **southwestern Cambodia**, meanwhile, the **Cardamom Mountains**, a lush expanse of forested valleys and peaks rising towards 1830m, are accessible from the community village of **Chi Phat** where you can go trekking and experience a Cambodian **homestay**. You can also access the Cardamoms on foot from the sleepy border town of **Koh Kong**, an emerging ecotourism destination, whose engaging hinterland attractions include waterfalls, isolated beaches and a mangrove sanctuary.

Kirirom National Park

From Phnom Penh NR4 makes its way through a typical Cambodian landscape of rice fields and sugar palms before the distant blue peaks of the Cardamom Mountains to the north and the Elephant Mountains to the south begin to loom on the horizon. After 100km, a detour takes you to the pine-clad hills of **Kirirom National Park**, an important wildlife sanctuary often ignored by travellers, but worth the effort of reaching for its almost alpine scenery and crisp mountain air.

The rolling hills of the park are zigzagged with well-trodden trails and dotted with waterfalls, lakes and abundant wild plants. These slopes are home, despite illegal logging, to **forests** of *Pinus merkusii*, a pine tree not found anywhere else in Cambodia. Although poaching has taken its toll, species of deer, wild ox (gaur and banteng), elephant and leopard still inhabit the depths of the park. In a 1995 survey, tiger tracks were found, but the lack of subsequent sightings gives little hope that tigers survive here today.

In the 1940s a road was cut through the forest, and, following a visit from King Norodom, who named the area Kirirom – "Happiness Mountain" – work began on building a **hill station**. Construction was hindered by the Khmer Issarak guerrilla troops who prowled the forests until the 1960s, and the completed resort was abandoned during the Khmer Rouge years. In the mid-1990s it became accessible again as an attractive holiday destination, including two royal residences. Nowadays, it's well worth staying a few days. Kirirom begs to be explored on foot – and the area has been entirely cleared of land mines.

Exploring the park

From the entrance, the road climbs steadily for 16km to a rolling forested **plateau**, where you'll find the majority of the park's attractions and its few facilities. About halfway up the hill, a signpost points down a narrow path to **Outasek waterfall**, a series of cascades just a short hike off the main road. There's usually water for splashing about in here, except during the very driest part of the year.

As you arrive on the plateau, a side road leads to a cluster of derelict buildings, including the newer of the two **royal residences**, a fairly well preserved, whitish building with a red roof. Further on, you can scramble through the overgrown garden of the older royal residence for views over the forest and out to a magical lake, **Sras Srorng**, which can be reached by heading downhill along a rough track from the palace. Back on the main road, and about 1km further on, is the **park office**. After another 500m or so you reach the only major road **junction** in the park, from where signs point towards various sights. The most appealing option (particularly in the rainy season) is the track north to a series of three **waterfalls**, I, II and III, numbered according to increasing size, and located roughly every 2km.

ARRIVAL AND DEPARTURE   **KIRIROM NATIONAL PARK**

By public transport The park can be reached by public transport, though with some difficulty, as it's a 24km trip from the turn-off from NR4 to the upland plateau and Chambok. Take a Sihanoukville bus from Phnom Penh, ask

5

CAMBODIA'S CONSERVATION MUDDLE

With proper, sustainable management, Cambodia's **forests** could represent a valuable source of income, not just in terms of providing timber, but also as a focus for ecotourism. Regrettably, the last few decades have seen the country's forest cover decline dramatically – a 2005 survey by the UN Food and Agriculture Organization (FAO) suggested that it has decreased by 2.5 million hectares since 1990. Initially the deforestation was due to logging, mainly illegally for timber, but more recently they have been cleared in vast swathes to make way for plantations, such as rubber in Kompong Cham province, and more worryingly, for the illegal production of the drug MDMA, better known as Ecstasy, in the Cardamom Mountains.

In 2001, the Cambodian government (forced by the World Bank) began to take action to reduce some of the most glaring environmental abuses. However, the government soon fell out with **Global Witness** (w globalwitness.org), the environmental watchdog appointed by the Bank to monitor Cambodia's forests, when its findings were not to its liking. In June 2007, a damning report issued by Global Witness naming a number of high-ranking government officials as using the country's resources for personal gain was met with derision; the government responded by calling for heads to roll at Global Witness. In the meantime, more than a decade after a cessation in logging was announced, little has really happened and the country's natural resources continue to diminish at an alarming rate.

Cambodia's forests are home to a vast, diverse **wildlife** population, including globally threatened species including the tiger. Ironically, the improvements in infrastructure that followed the establishment of the country's national parks in 1993 have sometimes made it easier for poachers to capture wild animals, which are either sold in local markets for the pot or used to produce medicines and charms. Until a government clampdown in 2001 it was possible to buy **game** taken from the Kirirom park, particularly venison, along NR4 nearby, while **restaurants** specializing in rare meats such as pangolin were easy to find in Phnom Penh. Nowadays, this appears to have mostly stopped and you'll see anti-hunting posters along NR4 instead, although poachers still sell their bounty on the black market.

Despite its official stance on logging and poaching, Cambodia appears to lack the will to implement sound conservation policies. Most recently, concessions have been granted to international companies to explore for oil and gas offshore, and – after a nifty change in the law – for bauxite, gold and copper in a protected area of Mondulkiri. Though it could be that the government simply doesn't recognize the long-term implications of the present shambles, ecological organizations claim that exploiting the country's natural resources offers just too many tempting opportunities for personal profit – witness the current situations at Bokor (see box, p.272) and Botum Sakor (see p.263) national parks.

to alight at Trang Tro Yeung and then ask one of the moto drivers around the market to take you to the park (about $12 return). Make it clear where you wish to alight before you set off.

By motorbike or car The park is an easy day-trip from Phnom Penh or Sihanoukville; hire a car and driver (around $60) or rent your own motorbike. The road to the top is sealed (if badly potholed), so access is possible all year round. If you're staying at the top for the night, you can arrange for your driver to return the next day to take you back to Trang Tro Yeung; otherwise you'll need to beg a lift with the accommodation's supply truck.

INFORMATION

Entry fee To enter the park (daily 8am–5pm), you'll need to pay an admission fee ($5/person for foreigners) at the small shack at the park entrance opposite the *Kirirom Hillside Resort*, 10km from the main road.

Park office The park office has no information for visitors, although a nearby noticeboard has a useful map and shots of various park locations, as well as photos of dead animals illegally caught here.

Temperature The temperature up on the plateau averages 25°C by day, dropping by 5–10°C at night, making long trousers and warm clothing essential after dark.

ACCOMMODATION AND EATING

At weekends, Kirirom tends to get overrun with trippers from the city, though few of these stay overnight. The most economical way to stay is with a **homestay**; if you have no luck with that, try the resort within the park itself, which also has a restaurant. The only other places to get **food** are the stalls beyond the park office (lunch only).

5

> ## YEAH MAO: THE BLACK GRANDMOTHER
>
> There are regular traffic jams on NR4 south of Kirirom at the **Pich Nil pass**. This is due to Cambodian motorists breaking their journey to make offerings at the shrine of **Yeah Mao**, or **Black Grandmother**, who is believed to protect travellers and fishermen – the most popular story has it that she perished in the waves after setting out to find her husband who had left to fight at sea.
>
> To pick out her shrine, follow the eye-watering haze of incense – a smoke-dimmed image of her can be found within it. The rows of spirit houses are recent additions and are a bit of a scam by local stallholders, but most Khmer would prefer to make an offering rather than risk offending the spirits.

Chambok Eco Tourism Site ☎ 012 500142, ✉ info @ccben.org, ⓦ chambok.org. Community-based homestay project established in 2001, with 37 homes enrolled. Meals cost $3–$4. Sadly the programme has been in decline in recent years and getting in touch can be a trial. Per person $̶4̶

Kirirom Hillside Resort Opposite the park entrance at the foot of the hill ☎ 016 590999, ⓦ kiriromresort.com.

A/c rooms and smart bungalows scattered around landscaped gardens, plus a few tents for rent. The dinosaur sculptures and piped birdsong in the restaurant may not be to everyone's taste, but the *Paradise* café is good for a sundowner, and the resort (non-residents $5) offers an impressive range of activities, from canoeing and fishing to tennis and horseriding, as well as a small zoo. Tent $̶3̶5̶; double $̶5̶0̶

Sihanoukville and the beaches

Cambodia's primary coastal party town, **SIHANOUKVILLE** occupies a hilly headland rising above island-speckled waters and six gently shelving white-sand beaches. The sprawling, workaday town centre, also known as "**Downtown**" sits a little way inland, and offers few attractions – though this is where you'll find the banks, internet cafés, markets and supermarkets, and it does at least have the relaxed atmosphere you'd expect of a seaside resort.

The main hub of activity is on and around **Ochheuteal Beach**, roughly 4km south of Downtown, and the southern end of **Serendipity Beach Road**, off which you'll find the majority of the bars, restaurants and guesthouses. In recent years, development on **Otres**, the town's furthest-flung beach, has mushroomed, yet still poses a mellower alternative to the inner town strands. The sixty off-shore **islands** dotting the Gulf of Thailand offer further escapism; a handful are easily accessible from town (see p.258). There are also a couple of inland **waterfalls** to visit north of Sihanoukville.

Psar Leu

Psar Leu is a huge market that was given a facelift after being devastated by a fire in 2008. You can stock up here on everything from fishing lines to fruit and vegetables before heading out to the islands, and it's a great place to meander, especially the fish section with its sea urchins, octopus, huge coloured crabs and mighty sea creatures with fierce eyes and bristling whiskers.

Wat Leu and around

Wat Leu, on the summit of Phnom Sihanoukville, is one of five pagodas in town. Accessed by a track behind the Cambrew Brewery, the temple atop this 132m hill – otherwise known as the "Upper Wat" – is the highest point in town and worth a visit for the panoramic views. It's easily visited in conjunction with **Wat Krom**, set on a boulder-strewn hillside off Santepheap Street, which is home to a sanctuary commemorating **Yeah Mao**, the "Black Grandmother" (see above).

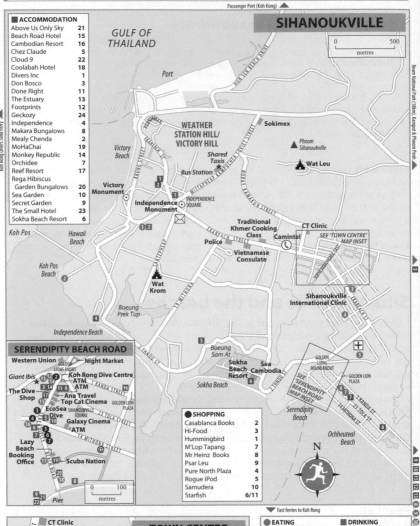

SIHANOUKVILLE

Passenger Port (Koh Kong) ▲

GULF OF THAILAND

■ ACCOMMODATION	
Above Us Only Sky	21
Beach Road Hotel	15
Cambodian Resort	16
Chez Claude	5
Cloud 9	22
Coolabah Hotel	18
Divers Inc	1
Don Bosco	3
Done Right	11
The Estuary	13
Footprints	12
Geckozy	24
Independence	4
Makara Bungalows	8
Mealy Chenda	2
MoHaChai	19
Monkey Republic	14
Orchidee	7
Reef Resort	17
Rega Hibiscus Garden Bungalows	20
Sea Garden	10
Secret Garden	9
The Small Hotel	23
Sokha Beach Resort	6

Koh Rong Divers Slow Ferry

Ream National Park (18km), Kampot & Phnom Penh

Port

WEATHER STATION HILL/ VICTORY HILL

Victory Beach

Sokimex

Phnom Sihanoukville

Wat Leu

Shared Taxis

Bus Station

Victory Monument

Independence Monument

INDEPENDENCE SQUARE

Traditional Khmer Cooking Class

CT Clinic

Camintel

Police

Vietnamese Consulate

SEE 'TOWN CENTRE' MAP INSET

Koh Pos

Hawaii Beach

Koh Pos Beach

Wat Krom

Sihanoukville International Clinic

Boeung Prek Tup

Independence Beach

Boeung Sam At

Sokha Beach Resort

Sea Cambodia

GOLDEN LIONS ROUNDABOUT

SEE 'SERENDIPITY BEACH ROAD' MAP INSET

GOLDEN LIONS PLAZA

GOLDEN LION PLAZA

Sokha Beach

Serendipity Beach

Ochheuteal Beach

SERENDIPITY BEACH ROAD

Western Union

Night Market

Giant Ibis

GOLDEN LIONS RNDBT

Koh Rong Dive Centre

ATM

The Dive Shop

ATM

Ana Travel

Top Cat Cinema

GOLDEN LION PLAZA

EcoSea Dive

SIHANOUKVILLE SQUARE

Galaxy Cinema

ATM

Lazy Beach Booking Office

Scuba Nation

Pier

● SHOPPING	
Casablanca Books	2
Hi-Food	3
Hummingbird	1
M'Lop Tapang	7
Mr Heinz Books	8
Psar Leu	9
Pure North Plaza	4
Rogue iPod	5
Samudera	10
Starfish	6/11

N

Fast ferries to Koh Rong

Otres Beach (3km), FlyBoarding Cambodia, Hurricane & Otres Nautica

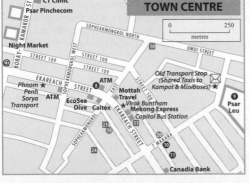

TOWN CENTRE

CT Clinic

Psar Pinchecom

KAMAKOR ST

SOPHEAKMONGKOL NORTH

OMUI STREET

Night Market

STREET 109

STREET 108

STREET 109

STREET 108

STREET 109

Phnom Penh Sorya Transport

EKAREACH STREET

ATM

EAST STREET

Old Transport Stop (Shared Taxis to Kampot & Minibuses)

ATM

EcoSea Dive

Caltex

Mottah Travel

Virak Buntham

Mekong Express

Capitol Bus Station

Psar Leu

Canadia Bank

● EATING	
Beach Club Resort	6
Café Mango	17
Carpe Diem	9
Chamka Chek	5
Delicious	16
Gelato Italiano	20
Happa	15
Happy Herb Pizza	7
Holy Cow	3
Ku-Kai	4
Marco Polo	13
Mick and Craig's	14
Papa Pippo	10
Sandan	12
The Small Hotel	19
Snake House	1
So	18
Sunshine Café	8
Tamu	11
Treasure Island Seafood	2

■ DRINKING AND NIGHTLIFE	
Above Us Only Sky	9
Beach Road Hotel	4
The Beer House	2
Dolphin Shack	8
The Emerald	10
G'Day Mate	11
Led Zephyr	6
Maybe Later	7
Mojo's	1
Monkey Republic	3
utopia	5

Ochheuteal Beach

South of the town centre, **Ochheuteal Beach**, the town's longest and busiest strand, is a 3km stretch of fine sand lined with bars and restaurants. The roads behind have a good selection of hotels and guesthouses, while the sand itself is lined by near-identical beach bars, prevented from encroaching too far onto the beach by a tiled pedestrian walkway. That said, their respective beach umbrellas, deck chairs and tables still stretch to the water. Freshwater showers and toilets cater for the pretty much 24-hour activity. During the day it's packed with Cambodian families and sun-soaking tourists; by night, the BBQs are fired up and the cocktails start flowing into the early hours.

Serendipity Beach

At the north end of Ochheuteal Beach, the area known as **Serendipity Beach** is lined with bungalows that wind up the hill. There is no public sand here; the thin sliver, encased by rocks and boulders, is reserved for patrons of the bungalows. Fortunately most of these have bars on the rocks just above beach level that make great spots for a sundowner.

Otres Beach

A 6km moto or tuk-tuk ride southeast from the town centre will bring you to **Otres Beach**, which boasts the whitest and widest stretch of casuarina-shaded sand. This is still the best bet if you want to escape the crowds and bustle of the beaches in town, although the number of rustic cabanas, restaurants and bars is mushrooming at an alarming pace.

In 2010, Otres Beach was split into two when 2.5km of beachfront was purged of resorts for a private development, although at the time of writing, this had yet to commence. As a general rule, the furthest, easterly strip of sand (**Otres 2**) tends to be quieter and more intimate than **Otres 1**, a noisier, more backpacker-orientated stretch.

In the absence of beach land, more options have recently begun springing up along the river estuary, 1km inland of Otres, home to a few chilled-out guesthouses and a **Saturday night market** – an arts space with stalls that hosts live music and parties that push on until dawn.

Victory Beach and around

Before 2012, when the action shifted to Ochheuteal and then Otres Beach, **Weather Station Hill** (also known as **Victory Hill**) was prime backpacker territory, densely packed with sunset-facing guesthouses and late-night hostess bars. The hill itself has an

---

SIHANOUKVILLE BEACH LIFE

For the Khmer, a visit to Sihanoukville is an excuse for an eating and drinking binge, with a dip in the sea as a fringe benefit. Their **conservative** nature, coupled with a concern – verging on paranoia for the women – about maintaining whiteness, means that **shade** is everything. Accordingly, the most popular beaches have a plethora of beach parasols and deck chairs for rent at a nominal sum, and men, women and even young people take to the sea fully clothed. Consequently, many will stare in amazement at foreigners stripped off and baking in the blazing sun. For women, bikinis are just about acceptable, but going topless is a definite no-no.

You may find yourself almost bullied into buying **massages**, manicures and leg-hair threading from the women who patrol Ochheuteal Beach, telling you that your nails are dreadful and must be tended to – men are targeted just as much as women and it takes nerves of steel not to buckle under their relentless attention. A $5 massage is not bad value, and usually turns out to be a relaxing experience, but buying bracelets and trinkets from the **children** only encourages them to stay out of school or work late into the evening, so maintain a firm resolve if you can.

CRIME AND SAFETY IN SIHANOUKVILLE

As Sihanoukville flourishes, so does petty **crime**. It is rarely serious, and mostly opportunistic, and certainly not something that should put you off visiting, but it's a good idea to make the most of hotel safety-deposit boxes and keep an eye on your belongings when on the beach. Bag snatching, even from motos and tuk-tuks, is on the rise. As a rule, don't carry anything with you that you can't afford to lose.

Personal **safety** is another issue altogether; there have been several incidents of assault at Weather Station Hill/Victory Hill and along the dark unlit road to Otres Beach late at night, and drunken brawls are not uncommon, so it is safer to travel home by tuk-tuk rather than on foot or by moto, even around the main beaches.

Although none of this is anything to be paranoid about, it's as well to ask your guesthouse when you arrive if there have been any recent incidents. Ultimately, the fun happens in the well-lit parts of town, so it shouldn't be too hard to stick to them.

insalubrious reputation after dark, but the nearby **Victory Beach** is a family-friendly stretch, more relaxing than Ochheuteal, with a small row of beach bars (and a casino) along the northern tip.

Independence Beach

Independence Beach, more than 1km long, is rather narrow, and best visited at low tide. Much of it is closed for development, but you can chill out at the northern end – *The Small Hotel* (see p.254), runs a good (daytime) restaurant-bar here beyond which the pier marks the section of beach reserved for guests of the *Independence Hotel*.

Sokha Beach

Just 200m of pretty **Sokha Beach** is fully accessible to the public. The rest is reserved for residents of the *Sokha Beach Resort*. It is OK for foreigners (but not Cambodians) to walk along the full length of the beach, but if you want to linger you'll have to pay (Mon–Fri $5, Sat, Sun & public holidays $7), which includes use of the hotel's swimming pools. Rocky headlands at both ends of Sokha Beach draw small fish and make for great snorkelling, and it's a wonderful place at sunset when the islands of Koh Tre and Koh Dah Ghiel are thrown into silhouette.

Kbal Chhay waterfalls

Picnic platforms 5000 riel/day • Head east out of Sihanoukville on NR4, turning left after about 7km at a sign for the falls, then continuing another 8km north; moto/tuk-tuk return trips should cost $8/$15

Popular with Khmer families, the **Kbal Chhay waterfalls**, a series of cascades fed by the Prek Toeuk Sap, gained recognition after appearing in Cambodia's post-civil war movie *Pos Keng Kong* (The Giant Snake); impressive in the rainy season, the falls aren't worth the trip in the dry.

ARRIVAL AND DEPARTURE   SIHANOUKVILLE AND THE BEACHES

BY BUS

Bus station The new bus station is off Mittheap Kampuchea Soviet St, in the Weather Station/Victory Hill area, northeast of Independence Square. It's less than 10min in a moto or tuk-tuk to Ochheuteal and Serendipity beaches, 5min to Downtown. Phnom Penh Sorya has its own bus terminus on Ekareach St. A few buses pick up (and drop off) passengers along Serendipity Beach Rd, especially

at night. Note that the principal guesthouses will send transport to meet buses.

Companies and routes Phnom Penh Sorya, Mekong Express, GST, Virak Buntham and others have outlets at the station (and offices along Ekareach St) from where they run efficient express buses to Phnom Penh, with numerous departures from early morning to early afternoon. The best service is run by Giant Ibis (☎ 089 999 818, ⦿ giantibis.com) whose office is on the road to Sokha Beach. You'll seldom have a problem getting a seat on any of these services except on public holidays, when it's best to book. Virak Buntham operates a daily bus to Koh Kong at 8.15am (☎ 016 754358), which continues across the Thai border (change of bus) and on to Bangkok. Phnom Penh Sorya has the most widespread services, including to Vientiane in Laos, Bangkok and HCMC (all via Phnom Penh). Others travel to Vietnam, including Mekong Express which makes for HCMC and Siem Reap via Phnom Penh. Capitol Tours (Ekareach St; ☎ 034 934042) runs buses to Phnom Penh via Kampot.

Destinations Bangkok (2 daily; 12hr); HCMC (6 daily; 10hr); Kampot (8 daily; 2hr 30min); Koh Kong (2 daily; 4–5hr); Phnom Penh (12 daily; 3hr 30min); Siem Reap (10 daily; 10hr).

BY SHARED TAXI AND MINIBUS

Shared taxis and minibuses depart throughout the day from the bus station for Phnom Penh and destinations en route

(25,000–35,000 riel); for Koh Kong, there are intermittent shared taxis (40,000 riel) while for Poi Yapon (for the Koh S'dach archipelago) you'll first need to take a shared taxi to Veal Rinh, 45min north of the city, to catch the town's 7am daily minibus. Shared taxis to Kampot also depart from opposite Psar Leu. Minibuses to Kep ($10) and the Ha Tien border in Vietnam ($16) are also offered by a few local companies, including Kampot Tours and Mekong Tours, their first morning service connecting with Phu Quoc island.

Destinations Ha Tien (5 daily; 5hr); Kampot (5 daily; 2hr); Kep (5 daily; 3hr); Koh Kong (4 daily; 4hr); Phnom Penh (20 daily; 3hr 30min); Veal Rinh (12 daily; 45min).

BY PLANE

Sihanoukville International Airport Off NR4, 23km from town; to get here, a private taxi costs $20, a tuk-tuk $15 and a bus $6. Cambodia Angkor Air (☎ 023 222360, ⓦ cambodiaangkorair.com) is the only carrier, connecting to Siem Reap (daily; 1hr).

INFORMATION AND TOURS

Tourist office The tourist office on Ochheuteal Beach is friendly enough, but has no real information (Mon–Fri 8–11am & 2–5pm).

Visitor guides Two booklets, the *Sihanoukville Visitors Guide* and *The Sihanoukville Advertiser*, keep abreast of new places to sleep, eat and drink. Both are available free in bars, restaurants and guesthouses.

Travel agents Ana Travel, Serendipity Beach Rd, next to *Beach Road Hotel* (8am–9pm; ☎ 012 915301, ⓦ anatravelandtours.com), and Mottah Travel, 193 Ekareach St, Downtown (☎ 012 996604, ⓦ mottah.com), can arrange visas/extensions, boat tickets, bus tickets, car rental, local tours, and both domestic and international flights.

GETTING AROUND

The main areas of interest are quite spread out, and as Sihanoukville is a little hilly, getting around on foot can be hard work. If travelling to Otres, you'll definitely need transport.

By moto and tuk-tuk Motos and tuk-tuks are readily available, especially along Serendipity Beach Rd, Downtown and at Ochheuteal Beach, and motos hang around most other tourist spots. Prices are fixed to the Serendipity Beach area: $3 for a moto, $6 for a tuk-tuk.

When picking up a moto or tuk-tuk on arrival, bear in mind that many drivers get commission from guesthouses, so be firm if there's somewhere particular you want to stay (you may be regaled with stories about how your chosen hotel has closed or is full of prostitutes).

ON THE ROAD: SURVIVAL TIPS

While there is no more exhilarating way to explore Sihanoukville's coastline than on the back of your own rented motorbike, you need to be on your guard for prowling policemen looking for a **bribe**. There is currently no legal requirement for tourists to hold a license but the police have come up with a few reasons to pull you over and take your money. There are some measures you can take to keep them at bay.

The first, and one that we would recommend regardless of police interference, is to wear a **helmet**; it's every one for themselves on the road, so safety should be your number-one priority. Riding without a shirt is enough to have you pulled over and, bizarrely, driving with your lights on during the day is unacceptable; allegedly, it's the privilege of travelling dignitaries only.

Being stopped for any of these offences will result in you being asked to hand over a fistful of dollars (up to $100). However, in almost every case you can barter this down to one or two. If you know you haven't done anything wrong, insisting on handling the situation down at the station is a big deterrent, as the police are not actually charging you with anything.

5

Motorbike rental Renting a motorbike is a brilliant way to explore the coastline and it's no longer illegal for tourists to ride, though you may be stopped by the police (see p.251). Guesthouses rent bikes from $8/day.

Car/driver hire Hotels, guesthouses and tour operators can help you hire a car and driver for the day (from $30). Alternatively, head to the transport hub by the market and negotiate with the drivers directly.

ACTIVITIES

Cookery courses Traditional Khmer cookery classes are offered at 335 Ekareach St, near the Independence Monument ($15/half-day, $25/day; ☎092 738615, ⓦcambodiancookeryclass.com).

Flyboarding Cambodia Queenco Palm Beach Resort, Otres 1 ☎0888 301150, ⓦflyboardingcambodia.com. Offers a new way to get high on Otres Beach for $50/15min.

Hurricane Queenco Palm Beach Resort, Otres 1 ☎017 471604, ⓦwindsurf-cambodia.com. Western-run outfit, with good equipment, tuition for windsurfing ($25/hr), surfing ($19/hr) and stand-up paddleboarding ($15/hr), plus gear rental. Also rents kayaks ($15/5hr) for jaunts to nearby Koh Kreah Island.

Massage and spas Blind and sight-impaired masseurs work at Seeing Hands 3, 95 Ekareach St, near the *Holy Cow* restaurant (daily 8am–9pm; $6/hr; ☎012 799016). More

exclusive is the Jasmine Spa at the *Sokha Beach Resort* (from $50; ☎034 935999).

Otres Nautica Otres 1 ☎092 230065. Established sailing club that rents sit-on-top kayaks for $8/half-day and Hobies from $30/half-day. Also offers trips to the closest, uninhabited islands.

Sea Cambodia Sokha Beach Resort ⓦseacambodia .com. World-class watersports facility with jet skis, wakeboards, kneeboards, water skis, tubes, kayaks and wakesleds, plus regular fishing excursions.

Swimming pools You can pay to use the swimming pool and other facilities as a day-visitor at the *Beach Road Hotel* ($5) and at the *Sokha Beach Resort* ($5/day Mon–Fri, $7/ day Sat, Sun & public holidays).

Tennis There are floodlit tennis courts ($5/hr) at *Sokha Beach Resort*.

ACCOMMODATION

From $4 bunks to $400 suites, Sihanoukville caters to all budgets. Hotels and guesthouses can get incredibly busy during public holidays and festivals, when it's as well to **book** if you want to stay at a particular place, though you're unlikely to be completely stuck for anywhere to sleep. During peak season (Nov–March) and major holidays (particularly Khmer New Year), hotels may hike their prices up by 25–30 percent. It's worth trying to negotiate a discount if you plan to stay for a

---

SIHANOUKVILLE DIVING

Diving Cambodia's uncharted waters is a colourful experience, all the better for the lack of other divers. In places **visibility** reaches up to 20m, and, with a wealth of islands to choose from, operators can offer itineraries ranging from reefs encased in coral to an almost overabundance of marine life, including barracuda, puffer fish, moray eels, giant mussels and parrot fish. Closest to Sihanoukville at just two hours away, **Koh Rong Samloem** (see p.260) is the most popular day-excursion; trips include a couple of dives, a lazy lunch and a spot of beachcombing on its gloriously white sands. You could also stay overnight. Further afield, more experienced divers might prefer overnight trips to Koh Tang and Koh Prins (each a 5–7hr boat ride away), with reefs, coral bommies, a wreck or two and better visibility in their deeper waters.

DIVING OPERATORS

The Dive Shop Serendipity Beach Rd ☎034 933664, ⓔdiveshopcambodia.com. Friendly German-owned PADI five-star dive centre – HQ is at *Robinson's Bungalows* on Koh Rong Samloem. Offers two-dive day packages ($80), two-night liveaboard trips ($295) and three-day Open Water courses ($320) with free dorm accommodation on the island, plus a number of speciality courses.

EcoSea Dive Between the Golden Lions roundabout and Serendipity Beach ☎034 934631, ⓦecoseadive.com. Another experienced outfit

running PADI courses, fun dives, day-trips and overnights including accommodation in dorms, tents or bungalows, from their base on Koh Rong Samloem.

Scuba Nation MoHaChai guesthouse, Serendipity Beach Rd ☎012 604680, ⓦdivecambodia.com. Fully insured five-star PADI outfit with highly qualified instructors and some of the most advanced courses in Cambodia; options include four-day Open Water courses ($445), day-trips ($85) and overnighters ($220–325) – including night dives – on their tailor-made boat; the pricier trips make for Koh Tang.

week or more, or if you arrive during the week, even during the peak season. Pretty much all accommodation now offers free wi-fi and most can make bus and tour bookings.

THE BEACHES

Many people arriving in Sihanoukville head straight to Ochheuteal and Serendipity beaches. This is where you'll find the best range of budget and mid-range accommodation, with easy access to the bars, shops and restaurants along Serendipity Beach Rd. Just north of Ochheuteal and Serendipity, both Sokha Beach and Independence Beach are immaculate, but have been virtually requisitioned for the exclusive use of residents at their respective namesake resorts. Otres Beach, south of Ochheuteal, features a growing number of bungalow resorts.

SERENDIPITY BEACH ROAD

Beach Road Hotel ✆017 827677, ⊛beachroad-hotel .com. Despite its proximity to the wildest bars, and particularly its own popular sports bar out front, the a/c rooms and pool area are impressively quiet and refined. Non-residents can lounge by the pool for $5. $24

★Coolabah Hotel 14 Mithona St ✆017 678218, ⊛coolabah-hotel.com. A range of stylish a/c rooms with good mattresses and blackout curtains, the more expensive with nice tiled terraces. There's also a pool with spa jets, mouthwatering food (their Sunday roasts are renowned; $6) and impeccable service. $41

MoHaChai ✆034 933586, ⊛mohachai.com. Options range from budget fan rooms from $5 in the low season, to more comfortable a/c rooms with private terraces and TVs, all with private bathrooms. Rooms are well presented and the guesthouse prides itself on its affordable restaurant and top security. Fan $6; a/c $20

★Monkey Republic ✆012 490290, ⊛monkeyrepublic.info. The latest incarnation of this popular backpackers' – a fire burned the building to the ground (and those of its neighbours) in March 2013 – is a slick enterprise with a range of sparkling en-suite fan rooms (for up to four), plus newer a/c rooms with hot water, and an inviting pub-style restaurant with well-stocked bar. No advance bookings. Fan $8

Reef Resort ✆034 934281 or ✆012 315338, ⊛reefresort.com.kh. This classy boutique hotel right in the thick of the action has fashionable a/c rooms, with plenty of white linen and rattan furniture, set in blocks around the swimming pool. The restaurant serves classic American dishes, and there's a cocktail bar and pool table. Rates drop by up to a third in the low season. Breakfast included. $40

Rega Hibiscus Garden Bungalows ✆012 219505, ⊛rega-guesthouse.com. Just 30m from the beach, rooms here, set around lovely, secluded gardens, are simple but attractive, in muted shades with some period

furnishings. Some have a/c and hot water. There's also a restaurant. Fan $8; a/c $15

SERENDIPITY BEACH

★Above Us Only Sky ✆089 822318, ⊛aboveus onlysky.net. These cute bungalows are a firm favourite for their spectacular, uninterrupted sea views and the excellent sunset cocktail bar that sits at their base (see p.256). Booking is essential to ensure one of the four tastefully decorated a/c cabins, each with its own veranda. Prices vary dramatically depending on the season. $50

Cloud 9 ✆098 215166, ⊛cloud9bungalows.com. At the furthest reaches of Serendipity, these seven wooden fan-cooled bungalows – some with stunning sea views – sit dotted among the trees behind a beachfront restaurant-bar (7am–10pm), justifiably famed for its delectable Thai green curry ($6). $45

OCHHEUTEAL BEACH

Cambodian Resort Polowai St ✆034 934657, ⊛cambodianresort.com. A popular, clean and friendly option, 200m from the beach. Each smart, well-appointed a/c room looks out over the lavish pool and bar area. Service is taken very seriously. $66

Makara Bungalows 1 Kanda St ✆034 933449, ⊛makarabungalows.com. At the more peaceful, southern end of the beach, these clean, well-furnished a/c bungalows are always busy. There's a swimming pool, restaurant and all tourist services, including motorbike rental. $30

Orchidee 23 Tola St ✆034 933639, ⊛orchidee -guesthouse.com. Colourful orchids hang everywhere in the shady courtyard of this deceptively large hotel. Rooms are light and airy, with TV and a/c; bathrooms have hot water. There's a swimming pool, plus a quiet balcony sitting area. $20

INDEPENDENCE AND SOKHA BEACHES

Chez Claude 2 Thnou Beach Rd, on the hill between Independence and Sokha beaches ✆034 900105, ⊛claudecambodge.com. En-suite accommodation in individually designed wooden bungalows on an extremely steep hill in an out-of-the-way location overlooking Sokha Beach, with private balconies looking out to sea. The hotel also has a French restaurant, and can arrange diving trips. Fan $30; a/c $40

Independence Independence Beach ✆034 934300, ⊛independencehotel.net. Sympathetically restored to its former glory, this impressive hotel towers above the north end of Independence Beach. Known locally as

5

Bprahm-bpel Jawn (Seven Storeys), it was once a glamorous venue attracting celebrities such as Jacqueline Kennedy, after whom the finest suite is now named. At the onset of war, it was abandoned, and from 1975 to 1979 housed high-ranking Khmer Rouge officials. Today it oozes luxury, with a spa and a glass elevator down to a private beach. $180

Sokha Beach Resort Sokha Beach ☎034 935999, ⓦsokhahotels.com. This luxury hotel has some four hundred rooms and over-water chalets in a huge complex occupying almost the whole of Sokha Beach. Rooms have all the amenities you'd expect and there's also a spa, fitness centre, tennis courts, swimming pools, watersports centre and a choice of restaurants and bars. Free shuttle to town and other beaches. $150

OTRES BEACH

Done Right Otres 2 ☎034 630 1100, ⓦdoneright.se. Set back from the beach, with "geos" – domed cement fan-cooled bungalows that wouldn't look out of place in Hobbiton – and some tiny loft rooms (also with fan) above the restaurant (the walls are thin, so it can get noisy), including a few singles. $6

The Estuary Otres Village ☎097 763 0149. Beside a tranquil river, 600m from the beach, the vibe here is super-laidback, with accommodation in spacious thatched fan-cooled bungalows. Activities include fishing and kayaking, or you could jump into the river for a swim. The en-suite rooms are worth the extra $5. $10

Footprints Otres 2 ☎097 262 1598, ⓦotresfootprints .tk. A hostel on Otres' quieter eastern beach with wood-panelled dorms of various sizes, and whitewashed double and triple rooms (all with fans), 10m back from the beach. There's a communal TV lounge on the ground floor and safe parking for motorbikes. Dorms $6; doubles $15

Sea Garden Otres 1 ☎096 253 8131, ⓦsea-garden.se. This laidback option is one of the best places to stay, or just hang out, in Otres. The fan-cooled bungalows (those on stilts are slightly more breezy) share clean bathrooms and are mere footsteps from the ocean. The restaurant – dotted with cushioned satellite chairs – is lovely (chicken with ginger $3.75), and there are private cooking classes. Minimum two nights. $14

Secret Garden Otres 2 ☎097 649 5131, ⓦsecret gardenotres.com. At the far end of Otres' eastern beach, these pretty wooden single, double and family a/c bungalows, set in flower-filled gardens with a freeform pool, each come with their own bathrooms, some with open-to-the-sky jungle showers. $99

WEATHER STATION HILL/VICTORY HILL

Once the backpackers' area, Weather Station Hill (aka Victory Hill) is now full of late-night girlie bars, and many guesthouses have closed down; those that remain are pleasant and do their best to minimize the effect of late-night bars on their visitors. By day the area is better, with a more Cambodian vibe than the main Westernized beaches and it's just a short walk from peaceful, family-friendly Victory Beach.

Divers Inc Krong Preah Sihanouk (next to Golden Rooster) ☎034 641 9000, ⓦdiversinchotel.com. You don't have to be a diver to stay here (although they will make all arrangements for you as they work with local dive shops), and the staff are more than welcoming. The a/c rooms are clean, bright and great value (some have balconies), and beds are all warmly topped with duvets. $12

Mealy Chenda ☎034 933472, ⓔmealychenda @gmail.com. A massive guesthouse occupying three buildings. Rooms in the newest block are better – bright, cheerful and en suite, some with a/c with sea views from the balconies. The cheaper, somewhat scruffy rooms, have shared bathrooms. Fan $10; a/c $15

DOWNTOWN

Downtown has a mix of budget and mid-range accommodation. Several of the area's sports bars (many of doubtful repute) also have rooms, although are best avoided by single women travellers or anyone who wants peace and quiet.

Geckozy Two blocks southeast of Caltex off Ekareach St ☎012 495825, ⓦgeckozy-guesthouse.com. In an area of town still very much belonging to the local Cambodians, this little guesthouse ticks all the boxes with bright, well-equipped fan rooms and great communal hangout areas. The only downside is that there's no food. $7

★**The Small Hotel** One block southeast of Caltex off Ekareach St ☎034 630 6161, ⓦthesmallhotel .info. A small place with a big reputation, thanks to the Swedish-Khmer owners who are authorities on the local area and run the guesthouse brilliantly. Rooms, with a/c, TVs, DVD players and safes, are superb value and there's an excellent library and a small restaurant-bar famed for its meatballs (they also have a little restaurant on Independence Beach). Rents out motos; booking essential in high season. $20

OUT OF TOWN

Don Bosco 3km east of town ☎034 933765, ⓦdonboscohotelschool.com. This hotel provides its staff, young adults from poor backgrounds, with the skills necessary to work in the tourist industry. Rooms (a/c) are large, smart, bright and slightly more luxurious than you'd expect in this price range. Wins major points for its garden, swimming pool and attentive service. $20

EATING

Don't leave town without savouring the local **seafood**, priced by the kilogram and cheaper than anywhere else in the country. If you prefer something informal, flop in a deck chair on the beach and order what you fancy from passing hawkers, and the fabulous (and fabulously cheap) evening seafood **barbecues** on Ochheuteal Beach ($3.50). For cheap eats in the centre, the **night market** opens up south of Ekareach St near the Golden Lions roundabout in late afternoon, and there are dozens of street vendors around Psar Leu. You'll find a good range of **Western-oriented** places on the streets behind Ochheuteal and Serendipity, serving everything from fish and chips to wood-fired pizza and falafel. Most of the restaurants on Otres double up as bars.

THE BEACHES

SERENDIPITY BEACH ROAD AND AROUND

Café Mango ☎ 013 440075. Small, easy-to-miss Italian café that serves home-made linguini, spaghetti, lasagne, gnocchi and ravioli, as well as pizza. Breakfast is good, too (muesli and yoghurt $2.50). Daily 9am–3pm & 5–10pm.

Chamka Chek Near the public hospital ☎ 012 660477. You'd hardly know this popular local restaurant, tucked down a side street, existed. Carved wooden screens separate tables and the menu includes a tasty bistro-style garlic-stuffed beef fillet (20,000 riel) and a zesty papaya and mango salad (20,000 riel). Beer costs $1. Staff barely speak English, but are helpful. Daily noon–2am.

Delicious North Plaza ☎ 012 574603. This tiny café, just off Serendipity Beach Rd, feels like an extension of the charming owner's house with just one long table down the middle. The food is great, and cheap – try the *roti canai* ($1.50). Other offerings include pizzas (from $3), *amok* ($2) and a breakfast eggburger ($1). Daily 6.30am–midnight.

Happa ☎ 034 934380. Cosy place where you grill your own food on a teppanyaki hot-plate, to eat with a choice of tasty and tangy sauces. Tapas-size portions of fresh fish, meat and tofu at $4–6/plate. Daily 5–10pm.

Marco Polo Sokha Beach Rd, just west of the Golden Lions roundabout ☎ 092 920866. The town's best stone-baked pizza (from $4) and big portions of typical Italian food (*penne siciliana* $6) at this friendly restaurant. There's a secluded garden at the back. Daily 5–10pm.

Mick and Craig's ☎ 034 934845, ✎ mickandcraigs.com. Look out for the special themed nights at this popular restaurant next to *Monkey Republic* (see p.253), including slap-up Sunday roasts and BBQs (Thurs & Fri, $6), which are as popular as the rooms in their excellent guesthouse. Daily 7am–11pm.

Sandan Sokha Beach Rd, 100m west of the Golden Lions roundabout ☎ 032 452 4000. Allied with *Friends Restaurant* in Phnom Penh (see p.84), this restaurant is staffed by youths enrolled in M'Lop Tapang's vocational training programmes, which help get kids off the streets. Creative Cambodian food (crispy crickets $3) is served to tables on a leafy pillared terrace, and there's a play area for the kids. Mon–Sat 5–9pm.

★**So** New Sea View Villa ☎ 017 918966, ✎ sihanoukville-hotel.com. Set in a beautiful, candlelit courtyard, this is the perfect place to treat yourself without breaking the bank.

The menu, largely fish with some European dishes, ranges from a tequila-and-lime-marinated swordfish carpaccio starter ($2.50) to a perfectly grilled surf-and-turf ($7). Two-course early-bird dinner specials for two cost just $10 (5–7pm). Also runs a decent guesthouse. Daily 7am–9pm.

OCHHEUTEAL BEACH

Beach Club Resort 23 Tola St ☎ 034 933634. A favourite with expats who come here for the daily all-you-can-eat buffet breakfast ($5.50; 6.45–10am). For lunch and dinner, refuel on burgers, sandwiches, steak, seafood and pasta. They also have decent rooms and a pool. Daily 6.45am–10pm.

Happy Herb Pizza 23 Tola St ☎ 088 440333. Reliable pizzas, pasta dishes and salads from $4.50 in a branch of the popular Phnom Penh pizzeria, as well as all-day breakfasts and barbecues. Daily happy hour 4–8pm. Sun–Thurs 7am–11pm, Fri & Sat 7am–midnight.

OTRES BEACH

Carpe Diem Otres Village, 400m back from Otres 2 ☎ 097 701 1262. The Italian couple who run this charming guesthouse with three bungalows ($25) also have a teeny restaurant and do their own cooking; try the *penne puttanesca* ($7). Worth the trek from the beach. Daily 7am–9.30pm.

Papa Pippo Eastern end of Otres 1 ☎ 010 359725. Tasty home-made pasta, gnocchi and pizza and home-baked cakes, pastries and yummy tiramisu. Service is friendly and pretty efficient, and they also have some decent bungalows. Daily 7am–10pm.

Sunshine Café Otres 1 ☎ 012 828432. Unassuming place that serves up good Khmer food, plus a few Polish specialities; try *banh chhaev* (Cambodian pancake) with seafood in Khmer spices ($3). Daily 9am–11pm.

Tamu Otres 2 ☎ 088 901 7451. Currently Otres' most upscale dining option, where you can eat Asian and European dishes including salads and grilled fish, while still feeling the sand beneath your toes. Also offers uber-stylish rooms in a new building behind. Daily 7.30am–9.30pm.

BETWEEN WEATHER STATION HILL/ VICTORY HILL AND HAWAII BEACH

Snake House Off Soviet St ☎ 012 673805. International and Russian food (beef stroganoff $7) is served at this unique location, where you'll find rare and exotic snakes in glass cases around the shady garden and occasionally

5

under the glass-topped tables (but not, fortunately, on the menu). Diners get to visit its crocodile farm for free (non-diners pay $3). Daily 8am–11pm.

Treasure Island Seafood South of Hawaii Beach, Independence headland ☎012 830505. Head down the steps behind the decrepit *Koh Pos Hotel* to reach this beachside Chinese restaurant, specializing in fish and seafood – the grilled squid is delicious ($5), and there's a lovely little beach to laze on afterwards. Best to go at lunchtime as the road to reach it is pitch black at night. Daily 9am–9pm.

DOWNTOWN

Gelato Italiano 11–13A Phum 2 ☎034 699 9900. Restaurant and ice-cream parlour dishing out delicious Italian-style ices (3000 riel) made by students at the *Don*

Bosco hotel school (see p.254); seasonal flavours, such as mango or jackfruit, are exceptional. Daily 7am–9.30pm.

Holy Cow Ekareach St ☎012 478510, ⓦholycowcambodia.com. Inexpensive Khmer and Western food (jacket potato with beef and beans $4.75) served in a traditional wooden house set back from the main road; laidback atmosphere, eclectic music and *Cambodia Daily* on hand. Daily 7am–9.30pm.

★**Ku Kai** Makara St, off Ekareach St ☎097 697 1327. Dining in this intimate Japanese restaurant feels like you're a guest in someone's home. The food is authentic, and the nightly sashimi (a steal at $3) sells out early. Other hits include the lightly seared beef ($2.75) or the fried pork with ginger sauce ($4.74). It's hugely popular, so book ahead. Tues–Sun 5–9pm.

DRINKING AND NIGHTLIFE

Sihanoukville has some of the best **nightlife** in the country. With so many bars, with new favourites popping up and others closing almost weekly, it's worth asking at your guesthouse or looking in the *Sihanoukville Visitors Guide* for the latest hangouts; *utopia* and *Monkey Republic* are usually packed each night.

THE BEACHES
SERENDIPITY BEACH ROAD

Beach Road Hotel ☎017 827677, ⓦbeachroad-hotel .com. A good place if you want to watch Western sports, mix with the local expats and have a few beers without being deafened or propositioned. Happy hour 5–10pm. Daily 7am–11pm.

Led Zephyr Cnr Serendipity Beach Rd & 14 Mithona St ☎034 698 2121, ⓦtheledzephyr.com. Live music nightly (6–9pm) and a large guitar-shaped bar. Their fishbowls $3.50 (great for sharing) get you in the party mood. Daily 7am–2am.

★**Maybe Later** ☎097 869 5264. A brilliant place for cocktails (try the creamy Bad Panda); or soak up the tequilas and rums by grazing on the excellent menu of quesadillas, tacos ($3.50) and burritos ($5) right up until they close. Daily 5pm–2am.

Monkey Republic ☎012 490290. A popular spot in the thick of the action, with a pool table and plenty of deals on shooters, spirits and beers (happy hour 6–9pm). It's also one of the few places you can get sloshed on Jagermeister. Very acceptable food, too. Daily 8am–midnight.

utopia Cnr Serendipity Beach Rd & 14 Mithona St ☎034 934319. Possibly the busiest Western bar in town, with draught beer for 50c (9–10pm), $2.50 cocktails, fire dancers around the pool, a 25-person hot tub and parties every night from 10pm. Also serves cheap food. Daily 10am–late.

SERENDIPITY AND OCHHUTEAL BEACHES

Above Us Only Sky Serendipity Beach ☎089 822318. Stunning sea views (especially at sunset) and the best cocktails in town, which can be enjoyed from

scarlet-cushioned loungers atop the timber terrace. Happy hour 4–8pm with all cocktails $2.50 and draught beer 75c. Daily 7am–11pm.

Dolphin Shack Ochhuteal Beach ⓦdolphinshack.com. A popular open-all-hours beach bar with nightly DJs, fireshows and the odd mud-wrestling competition. Get the party started with a $4 vodka bucket. Also runs booze cruises and full-moon parties. Daily 24hr.

WEATHER STATION HILL/VICTORY HILL

The Beer House Snake House, southwest of Independence Monument ☎012 673805. Sports bar with 2m screen, pool tables and plenty of female (and reptilian) company. Daily 8pm until late.

Mojo's Victory Hill ☎016 397704. This long-running, French-owned, heavily muralled music-bar along Victory Hill's "drinking street" has parties every Mon night. Daily 11am–dawn.

DOWNTOWN

The Emerald Cnr Sopheakmongkol & Omuli streets ☎012 249525. There's plenty of atmosphere in this Scottish-owned Irish pub, filled to the brim with priceless memorabilia from the Emerald Isle. They brew their own cider, serve ice-cold Guinness and have a huge selection of whiskey (from $2). There's also a pool table, good, cheap food (Irish strew $4.50) and a couple of basic rooms (from $8). Daily noon–2am.

G'day Mate 163 Ekareach St. Expat bar and restaurant, with the usual Western and Asian dishes, plus a pool table and big-screen TV showing live sports including rugby, motor sports and Aussie rules football. Daily 24hr.

FROM TOP CHI PHAT (P.267); OTRES BEACH (P.249) >

SHOPPING

Western groceries, toiletries and wines can be bought at a number of **supermarkets** and minimarts around the town centre and on 14 Mithona St and Serendipity Beach Rd, which is also lined by **boutiques** selling beach attire and souvenirs.

Casablanca Books Near the Golden Lions roundabout. Sell, buy or swap your used books here, and check out their new ones. Daily 7am–11pm.

Hi-Food Serendipity Beach Road, near utopia. Handy minimarket selling snacks, cold drinks, sandwiches and alcohol. Daily 24hr.

Hummingbird Otres 1, next to Blame Canada ☎ 088 518 6318. Unique unisex beachwear and clothing. There's a sister stall (Little House of Narnia) at Otres Market (Sat 4pm–late). Daily noon–sunset.

M'Lop Tapang Serendipity Beach Road & Sandan restaurant ⓦ mloptapang.org. NGO-supported gift shops selling bags, scarves, iPod covers and T-shirts produced by parents of former street children. Daily 10am–8pm.

Mr Heinz Books 219 Ekareach St. Secondhand books to buy, sell or swap and a selection of new international titles. Daily 9am–6pm.

Psar Leu 7 Makara St. This local market is great for picking up fresh fruit and simple snacks, not to mention

cheap clothes and flip-flops. Daily 8am–5pm.

Pure North Plaza Serendipity Beach Rd. The varied shops around this little plaza are good for stocking up on tourist gear, and there's even a North Face outlet. Hours vary.

Rogue iPod Serendipity Beach Rd ⓦ roguecambodia .com. A massive selection of tracks, TV series and films (75c each) for iPod and MP3; their catalogues are in many of the bars and restaurants. Daily 8.30am–9.30pm.

Samudera 7 Makara St, near Psar Leu. The oldest supermarket in town, very well stocked with meats, cheeses, drinks, canned goods, sweets and snacks, and popular with expats. Daily 6am–midnight.

Starfish Behind Samudera supermarket, Downtown; Serendipity Beach Rd ☎ 012 952011. These gift shops – the Downtown branch is attached to a nice little café – sell silks, recycled bags and clothing, plus Kampot pepper, Cambodian coffee and tea; sales help to support impoverished local families. Daily 8am–8pm.

DIRECTORY

Cinemas Galaxy Cinema (near Serendipity Beach; $2.50) has a VIP Room (four people) and a big room (from six people). Top Cat (Serendipity Beach Rd; $4.50) is similarly set up with, a library of more than six thousand movies and TV series.

Consulate The Vietnamese consulate is on Ekareach St, west of the town centre (☎ 034 934039). Vietnamese visas cost $60 and take two days; there is no longer a same-day service.

Hospital Sihanoukville International Clinic, on Ekareach St (☎ 012 738803), has 24hr emergency service. CT Clinic, on Borei-Kamakor Rd, on the edge of Downtown (☎ 034 936666), offers more complete medical services, accepts credit cards and has English-speaking doctors available (or on call) 24hr. Alternatively, call International SOS Medical Clinic in Phnom Penh (☎ 012 816911).

Money ANZ Royal, Canadia and Union Commercial banks all have branches on Ekareach St, where you can change

travellers' cheques and get cash advances on cards; Ana Travel offer the same service (see p.251), and there's an ATM out front. Canadia Bank is the only one not to charge a $4 fee for withdrawals. ANZ Royal and Western Union both have ATMs at the Golden Lions end of Serendipity Beach Rd. You can change dollars to riel at Acleda Bank, also on Ekareach St, or at the exchange booths and telephone shops in or around the market.

Newspapers The *Cambodia Daily* and the *Phnom Penh Post* are sold at stands in front of the Psar Leu market.

Photography Most of the town's many internet cafés have the capacity to burn digital photos to CD or DVD.

Police The main police station is on Ekareach St (☎ 011 683307); to contact the tourist police call ☎ 093 666260-1.

Post office The main post office, on Ekareach St near the Independence Monument, has all the usual services, including poste restante (Mon–Sat 7.30am–noon & 2–5.30pm).

Islands near Sihanoukville

Cambodia's coastal waters are peppered with tens of tropical **offshore islands,** many of them an easy trip from Sihanoukville and a couple of which lie within Ream (see p.261). Peaceful and idyllic – for now (see box opposite) – lapped by clear seas and graced with **white-sand beaches,** they're great places to hole up in for a few days, and offer a smattering of **rustic accommodation**. Snorkelling, sunbathing, gentle walks and lounging are positively encouraged; all of these improve the further you travel offshore (particularly the snorkelling). They are also superb destinations for **diving** (see box, p.252).

TROUBLE IN PARADISE

Although change doesn't happen too quickly in Cambodia, many of the idyllic islands around Sihanoukville do have a shelf life. Since 2006 the government has leased numerous islands (possibly as many as 22) to international companies for the development of **luxury hotels** and **golf courses** destined to wipe out the fragile communities of wooden bungalows. So far, around fourteen five-star resorts and a staggering **eighteen golf courses** have been mooted, and a Russian company, which has leased both Hawaii Beach and its off-island, Koh Pos (Snake Island), has already built a **bridge** between the two, juxtaposing grimly against the crystalline waters and the lush jungle on either side.

On the upside, these developments will provide much-needed **employment** for Cambodians, but it would seem that the downsides are greater, with the money spent by tourists going directly to the overseas corporations, and the resorts adding a further **drain on resources** such as water, which is already severely limited (in summer it's not unknown for Sihanoukville to run out of water for several weeks).

For now, plenty of stalwart bungalows and huts are weathering the developers' storm, but time is of the essence if you want to visit the islands before their humble tranquillity is obliterated entirely.

Koh Russei

Koh Russei (or Bamboo Island) is a common stop on island-hopping day-trips due to its close proximity (less than 1hr) to Sihanoukville. The last resort was cleared from the island in 2013 to make way for a large new resort development, which for the moment appears to have stalled.

Koh Tas

Koh Tas (1hr from Sihanoukville by boat), a popular island-hopping stopoff, has sandy, gently shelving beaches, great snorkelling and a good chance, if you take fishing tackle, of hooking a fish for the barbecue.

Koh Rong

Offering the quintessential island experience, **Koh Rong** is Cambodia's second largest island, boasting 43km of dazzling white casuarina-fringed beaches and a hilly, forested interior home to wildlife and birds. A new fast ferry service from Sihanoukville, started in 2013, has reduced travel time from over two hours to just 45 minutes. Except in its southeast, Koh Rong is largely undeveloped so, with a little effort – or none at all, if you choose to stay in one of the isolated resorts – it's easy to find a blissfully secluded bay to yourself; westerly **Long Set Beach**, backed by cashew nut groves, is one of the most beautiful. The turquoise seas teem with marine life and there's decent snorkelling and diving to be had offshore.

KOH TUI, also known as Koh Touch, the largest village on the island, is a favourite of young backpackers, with tiny-roomed guesthouses crammed shoulder-to-shoulder beside a 300m stretch of beach, along with cafés, bars and a nightly diet of firedancers, starlit barbecues and late-night music. It's easy enough to escape if this isn't your thing; other bays across the island offer more peace and quiet. The lush, hilly interior is ripe for trekking; you'll find no better guide than Gil (4–5hr jungle treks $20 for two; ☏088 3796528; ask for him at *Paradise Bungalows*).

Koh Rong's future is uncertain, however. The island was leased in 2006 to the Royal Group who have plans to transform it into a luxurious eco-resort complete with hotels, houses, a beach club, marina, restaurants, reservoirs and golf course, as well as an airport. To check up on their progress, see ⓦkohrong.com.kh.

5

Koh Rong Samloem

Koh Rong Samloem, two and a half hours from Sihanoukville (or less than an hour's sail from neighbouring Koh Rong), has eight beaches and a rocky reef with good diving (see p.252). Low-key bungalow resorts are scattered all around the island, including at the beautiful, blinding white sands of **Lazy Beach** to the south, shallow **Saracen Bay** to the east where the largest concentration of bungalows can be found, and in the fishing village of **M'Pai Bay** (Village 23) on the northernmost tip. The network of French roads on the island have long since been swallowed up by jungle, although you can trek through the forested interior to the lighthouse on the southern tip and across the island from east to west; **wildlife** on the island includes kingfishers, great hornbills and ospreys as well as macaques, black squirrels, lizards and snakes.

Koh Ta Kiev

The white-sand beaches of **Koh Ta Kiev** (quieter on the western side) and sprinkling of rustic thatched bungalows make this one of the most idyllic of Sihanoukville's islands, a real castaway experience. There are a handful of beaches to explore, trails to trek and decent **snorkelling offshore** with giant mussels to look out for to the north of the island. Sadly, the island has been leased to developers and a new eco-resort is already under construction, so it's anybody's guess as to how long the current businesses (and mellow vibe) will be allowed to remain.

Koh Tang and around

If you're a **diver** or have plenty of time, get out to deeper waters, such as those around **Koh Tang** and **Koh Prins** – between five and seven hours from Sihanoukville. Koh Tang's claim to fame is that it was the site of a major battle to free the *Mayaguez*, an American-owned container ship captured by the Khmer Rouge on May 13, 1975, in the early days of their regime. The US Navy and Air Force launched a mission to liberate the ship but met heavy resistance, and Ream naval base and Sihanoukville's industrial areas were bombed during the battle. Divers (see p.252) can check out two shipwrecks 40m down, northwest of Koh Prins.

ARRIVAL AND DEPARTURE   ISLANDS NEAR SIHANOUKVILLE

In addition to ferries, many of the Sihanoukville resorts arrange boat transfers to inhabited islands. You can also make your own arrangements with a local fisherman on Ochheuteal or Otres beaches, take an organized island-hopping or snorkelling excursion (from $10) with a Sihanoukville guesthouse, or try a tour operator such as Ana Travel (see p.251).

By ferry Sea Cambodia's zippy fast ferries to Koh Rong depart from Serendipity Beach pier (9am, 11am, 1pm & 3pm; return 10am, noon, 2pm & 4pm; $13 one way; 40min; book online at ⓦseacambodia.com). The Koh Rong Dive Center (ⓦkohrong-divecenter.com) has a similar service to Koh Rong (3 daily; $15 one way; 40min), and to Saracen Bay on Koh Rong Samloem ($15 one way; 35min). They also have a cheaper slow boat to Koh Rong (2 daily; $20 return; 2hr 30min), and a daily ferry that connects the two islands ($5; 30min).

Tours Sun Tours (ⓦsuntours-cambodia.com) offer a great day-tour to Koh Rong Samloem (10am–5pm; $25/person),

including buffet lunch and a snorkelling stop at Koh Tas. Romney Travel and Tours (☎016 861459, ⓔromneytour @yahoo.com) has been going forever; offerings include a day-trip to Koh Rong via Koh Tas ($20), and an island-hopping tour that drops in on Koh Cha Lush, Koh Russei and Koh Tres ($15).

Interisland travel At the time of writing, aside from Koh Rong Dive Center's daily service between Koh Rong and Koh Rong Samloem, interisland ferries were nonexistent. To reach other islands independently, the only (expensive) option is to hire a longtail boat.

ACCOMMODATION AND EATING

There is no mains **electricity**; some bungalows use solar-charged batteries or generators for power at night (usually just for lights; fans are rare) – generally between sunset and 10pm only. With the exception of Koh Tui on Koh Rong and Saracen

5

Bay on Koh Rong Samloem, where there are a number of guesthouses and bungalow resorts, it's advisable to book ahead. All the bungalows will have a **restaurant** of some description.

KOH RONG

Most of the island's accommodation is squeezed into a small 300m stretch close to the main pier, known as Koh Tui Village. Guesthouses here are much of a muchness; rooms and dorms are small, and walls paper-thin. With such a concentration of places, many with their own bars, don't expect a quiet night's sleep.

Lonely Beach ☎081 343457, ⓦlonely-beach.com. Escapism doesn't get much better than at *Lonely Beach*, set on the far northern tip of the island. Bungalows enjoy sea views, there's an open-sided dorm and you can fish, trek or beachcomb to your heart's content. Boat transfers cost $20. Dorm $10; doubles $35

Monkey Island ☎081 830991, ⓦmonkeyisland -kohrong.com. Bungalows, set back from the white sands, just 50m from the action on Koh Tui beach, are basic but comfortable. Also home to a lively restaurant-bar that's open late. Booking office at *Monkey Republic* in Sihanoukville (see p.253). $20

Paradise Bungalows ☎092 548883, ⓦparadise -bungalows.com. The smartest place to stay within earshot (just) of the village; nine types of spacious, comfortable fan-cooled bungalow are scattered near the beach and up the hillside and there's 24hr electricity, hot showers and wi-fi. The stilted restaurant has fab sea views, and serves some of the best food on the island (chicken wrapped in bacon $6). $35

Pura Vita ☎015 700083, ⓦpuravitaresort.com. Its show-stopping location on Koh Rong's best brilliant-white beach accounts for the higher than average rates – the six timber bungalows (and one room) are perfectly adequate, plus there's snorkelling to enjoy nearby. Free pick-up from the pier. $45

White Rose Guesthouse ☎010 758767, ⓔmengly007 @gmail.com. One of the nicer and better-run guesthouses in the village, well located for the pier. Rooms are clean and there's a cool hammock-strung deck for chilling out. Nice views from the upper floor. Dorm $5; doubles $10

KOH RONG SAMLOEM

Accommodation is scattered all around the island, with the largest concentration (around seven resorts, and rising) at the idyllic 3km-long eastern curve of Saracen Bay, where most of the (day) tour boats disembark.

The Fishing Hook M'Pai Village ☎081 332718. Susan and Pacaday offer just four bunk-beds in their cute, unassuming over-water home, prettily furnished with driftwood furniture, in the heart of the village. They support the local community and have a tiny café-bar (daily 8.30am–10pm) that spills onto the neighbour's deck. Drop in for delicious fried crab with black pepper ($5), pancakes or an ice-cold beer. $5

Huba-Huba Robinson's Beach ☎088 554 5619, ⓦhuba -hubacambodia.com. Four individual bungalows with lovely pebbled cold-water bathrooms (some open-air) and sunset views beside an idyllic white-sand beach. The charming owners cook delicious Swiss-French food and batteries provide power (for lights) overnight. The Dive Shop, just 100m away, provides the transfers ($20). $30

★Lazy Beach Lazy Beach ☎016 214211, ⓦlazybeachcambodia.com. Your money goes a long way here; en-suite bungalows with comfy beds set along stretches of sand so fine it squeaks and there's an atmospheric restaurant-bar. Booking office on Serendipity Beach Rd in Sihanoukville. Transfers $20. $50

Sun Island Eco Village Saracen Bay ☎077 765069, ⓦsun-island-eco-village.com. These tidy bungalows (private or shared bathrooms) and coconut-roofed tents (nicely furnished, with front porches) all enjoy 24hr solar power. The big stilted restaurant-bar has a pool table and serves good portions of tasty food (daily 7am–9pm); try the fried prawn in green pepper ($7.50). $20

KOH TA KIEV

★Crusoe Island ☎097 253 9082, ⓦcrusoeisland .asia. Pick your own beachfront campsite (equipment provided), bag a hammock or stay in one of four bungalows. Facilities are shared, there's a communal restaurant-bar (meals $2–12), and activities include guided walks, fishing, archery and spear-gun workshops. Transfers from Otres $10 return. Hammocks $3.50; campsite $6; bungalows $15

Ten103 Treehouse Bay ☎097 943 7587, ⓦten103 cambodia.com. Accommodation is in a hammock, a dorm or a treehouse, perched a few metres above ground, while the Mediterranean-inspired food is the talk of the island – unusually, they also offer home-brewed absinthe. Return transfers to the resort from Otres $13. Hammocks $7; dorm $8; treehouse $25

Ream National Park

Some 18km to the east of Sihanoukville, **Ream National Park** (also known as the Preah Sihanouk National Park) is unique in Cambodia, covering 210 square kilometres of both terrestrial and marine habitat, including stunning coastal scenery, mangrove swamps,

5

lowland evergreen forest and the **islands** of **Koh Thmei** and Koh Ses. At least 155 species of **bird** have been recorded in the park, and for resident and visiting waders, the mangrove-lined **Prek Toeuk Sap** River is an important habitat. Besides supporting a large population of fishing eagles, the river is also home to milky and adjutant storks, and kingfishers, which are regularly spotted on the river trips – and dolphins often put in an appearance between December and April. The list of **mammals** includes deer, wild pig and fishing cats, though these are all elusive and you're more likely to see monkeys.

ARRIVAL AND INFORMATION · REAM NATIONAL PARK

DAY-TRIPS

Most visitors to the park go on an all-day trip arranged through cafés and guesthouses in Sihanoukville, on tours with outfits including Romney Travel and Tours (see p.260), or through travel agents such as Ana Travel (see p.251). Costing from $20/person, trips include a boat trip down the Prek Toeuk Sap, a guided walk through the jungle either from or to Thmor Tom (a small village in the park), and swimming and a barbecue at the stunning white-sand beach of Koh Sam Pouch.

TRAVELLING INDEPENDENTLY

Park headquarters The park headquarters (daily 7.30–11am & 2–5pm; ☎016 767686) is in a green wooden building just beyond the entrance to Sihanoukville International Airport (see p.251) – turn up early or phone

the day before to book a boat or guide from here.

By moto/tuk-tuk A moto/tuk-tuk from Sihanoukville to the park entrance will cost about $10/$15; if you're coming for the boat trips, ask your driver to drop you at the ranger station from where the boats leave.

Boat trips Boat trips on the Prek Toeuk Sap cost about $35 for up to five people ($8/person thereafter) for a 2hr voyage to Mangrove Island or $50/boat for a 4–5hr trip that continues on to Thmor Tom village and Koh Sam Pouch beach. Arrange via the park headquarters or at the ranger station next to the bridge over the Prek Toeuk Sap, on NR4, 25km towards Phnom Penh, which is where the boats depart. You'll need to take food, water and sun protection.

Guided walks Treks – which you arrange at the park headquarters – cost from $8/person for a 2hr wander along forested nature trails.

ACCOMMODATION AND EATING

Koh Thmei Resort ☎097 737 0400, ⌨koh-thmei-resort.com. A very secluded island resort (the only one) within Ream, with back-to-basics bungalows with newish

bathrooms, and a simple restaurant. Pass the time in a hammock, or take one of the rubber tubes and go floating in the sea. **$25**

Koh S'dach and the outlying islands

Lying in clear blue waters roughly halfway between Sihanoukville and Koh Kong, just off the coast of Koh Kong province, the small rocky island of **Koh S'dach** (King's Island) gets its name from the legend surrounding the **royal spring** behind the port, which is said to have gushed forth miraculously when the king and his army were desperate for drinking water as they battled invaders here. Supporting a population of a couple of thousand, Koh S'dach may not look too exciting at first glance, but is refreshingly authentic, has wonderful snorkelling and fishing (even quite close to shore, though you'll need your own equipment) and is a good base from which to explore little-visited, and still largely undeveloped outlying islands. It is also, by fishing village standards anyway, quite a prosperous little community due to the village's ice factory, which supports the fishing fleet.

Koh S'dach is just a couple of kilometres long, and 1km wide. There's a rocky **beach** on its seaward side, reached by a path through the compound of the simple pagoda, **Wat Koy Koh**. The beach isn't brilliant, but vivid coral and shoals of fish found close to shore compensate.

The best of the nearby islands is **Koh S'mach**, just 1km away, home to a small fishing community and with some sandy beaches. Tiny **Koh Totang**, 2km off Koh S'dach, has a population of just seven (plus a few dogs) that almost doubles during the dry season when the owners of *Nomad's Land*, the island's only accommodation option, return to set up shop. Aside from this it's completely undeveloped and you can wander through the wooded interior to seek out hidden beaches.

5

> ### KOH S'DACH BOAT TRIPS AND DIVING
>
> To get to neighbouring islands or go fishing from Koh S'dach, you'll need to **hire a boat**; agree a schedule with the boatman beforehand and expect to pay upwards of $30/day. Meanwhile, **Koh Kong Divers** (☎011 384545, ⓦ kohkongdiving.com), based at Shallow Waters HQ (a professional British NGO involved in marine conservation), on Koh S'dach, run snorkelling and diving trips ($65 a dive), and are currently the only PADI-certified dive outfit in the area (Open Water $350). You can volunteer here as a research assistant (ⓦ shallow-waters .org) or kip down in their dorm (see below).

ARRIVAL AND DEPARTURE KOH S'DACH AND THE OUTLYING ISLANDS

The easiest way to reach Koh S'dach, Koh S'mach and Koh Totang used to be via the now-redundant express ferry that ran between Sihanoukville, Koh Kong and Thailand. Nowadays, minibuses and motos ply the new red-dirt four-lane highway to Poi Yapon, access point for the islands, which leads off the paved NR48, a few kilometres west of the village of Andoung Tuek. Sadly, this new road (which will eventually be paved) cuts a wide swathe through **Botum Sakor**, a supposedly protected national park, and is just phase one of a $5 billion, seven-resort, Chinese development due to open in 2025.

By bus and moto From Sihanoukville take a Koh Kong-bound bus (or minibus) to Andoung Tuek, where you can take a minibus (until 1pm; $7.50) or a moto ($15) through Botum Sakor National Park to Poi Yapon. From here, small speedboats whizz you to the islands ($5). If you take the first Koh Kong bus (around 8am), you should arrive at the islands by 3pm.

By cargo boat A rare choice these days, but cargo boats depart Sihanoukville for Koh S'dach between noon and 2pm daily (5–6hr); bring a hammock as there are no seats.

ACCOMMODATION AND EATING

KOH S'DACH

Local food is the norm and you can fill up anywhere along the main drag. The grocery shop is well stocked with water, drinks, biscuits and general products, but expect to pay more than you would on the mainland.

★**Belinda Beach** The end of the peninsula ☎017 517517, ⓦ belindabeach.com. Pure isolated luxury, *Belinda* has a handful of a/c bungalows, an infinity pool with jacuzzi, gorgeous gardens and breathtaking views of the mainland across azure seas. It also has its own little beach and a volleyball net, a good fusion restaurant and a well-stocked bar. $150

Mean Chay Guesthouse On the west of the island ☎011 983806; no English spoken. Clean, concrete bungalows offering superb sea views and no-frills comforts – private bathrooms and fans or a/c for a few dollars more. *Yvonne's*, a great little Italian restaurant (the island's best), is here too. Fan $10

Shallow Waters Near the pier ☎011 384545, ⓦ kohkongdiving.com or ⓦ shallow-waters.org. British NGO, carrying out marine research in the region, where snorkelling and diving trips (see above) can be arranged. It's possible to bunk down with the volunteers in their timber-clad over-water dorms if a bed's available, but you must book in advance. Rates include three meals. $15

KOH TOTANG

★**Nomad's Land** ☎011 916171, ⓦ nomadsland cambodia.com. The five individual bungalows here fit in gently with their glorious natural surroundings and have shared outdoor showers and compost lavatories. There's good snorkelling and diving from the beach and the vibe couldn't be more laidback; the excellent home-cooked meals (included) are shared (usually in the form of a buffet) around the large table in the communal area. Book ahead. $65

Koh Kong and around

The provincial town of **KOH KONG**, once a prosperous little logging town, has now lapsed into a quiet backwater. Laid out on a simple grid on the east bank of the Kah Bpow River, the town is dotted with wooden houses whose style owes more to neighbouring Thailand than Cambodia; there's no colonial architecture at all. Sights, such as they are, are low-key.

Outside town and across the province, stretching down as far as the northern tip of Sihanoukville, is a fantastic destination for nature lovers and outdoor enthusiasts. The majestic **Cardamom mountain range**, more than 1800m at its highest elevation, is still

5

CHAM YEAM: THE BORDER WITH THAILAND

To get from Koh Kong to the border at **Cham Yeam** (daily 7am–8pm), a 20min trip, it's easiest to take a moto or tuk-tuk ($4/$10; note that prices *from* the border into Koh Kong are significantly higher). Taxis for Cham Yeam leave from the transport stop 2km west of Koh Kong, beyond the disused warehouse. Once across the border take a minibus (20m beyond immigration, on the right-hand side; departs every 40min 7am–5pm approx; 120 baht) to Trat where good a/c buses leave regularly for Bangkok (270 baht; 6hr) and other major destinations across Thailand.

There are a couple of scams to watch out for – the attempt to charge 1000 baht (around $30) or more for a visa when entering Cambodia, with the excuse that "This is a land crossing, it's different". No it isn't! A Cambodian visa is $20 regardless of where or how you enter the country. If this happens to you, ask for a receipt; record the time, date and the name of the border official (or jot down the number on his shoulder) and report it, as soon as you get the opportunity, to the Ministry of Tourism (☎023 884974, ✉info@tourismcambodia.org) and the Immigration Department (☎017 812763, ✉immigration@gov.kh). Other scams include a bogus "quarantine station" beyond Thai immigration (you do not need any health forms to get your visa) and touts offering to "facilitate" the visa process by filling your forms in for a fee (anything from 100–300 baht); politely refuse as this is nothing you can't do yourself. You can avoid all these hassles by buying your visa online.

---

home to some of the rarest species on the planet, including the Asian elephant, the clouded leopard, the Siamese crocodile and the Indochinese tiger (although there have been no official sightings of the last since the 1990s). Meanwhile, Irrawaddy dolphins are often seen playing in the saline waters of the extensive mangrove network along the coast, explorable in the **Peam Krasaop Wildlife Sanctuary**, 6km from town.

Many people come to Koh Kong just for the **border crossing** with Thailand at **Cham Yeam**, though eco-outfits in town are doing their best to change that. The Cardamoms' virgin forests and secluded waterfalls are accessible on day-treks, while longer, multi-day adventures take you deep into the remote Areng Valley (see box, p.265). Boat trips depart for **Koh Kong island**, a surprisingly large and attractive place, with seven pristine stretches of sand on its seaward side.

Wat Neang Kok

On the western bank of the river (across the bridge) • A moto/tuk-tuk from Koh Kong should cost $2/$5

On the western banks of the river, **Wat Neang Kok** is a Buddhist pagoda with dramatic rock paintings portraying scenes of torture in hell, mixed up with what appear to be scenes of Khmer Rouge atrocities – the latter presumably painted recently, as this was Khmer Rouge territory until around 1997.

Koh Yor Beach

7km west of town • A moto/tuk-tuk from Koh Kong centre should cost $7/$15

Dotted with seafood shacks, **Koh Yor Beach** is worth the short trip from town if you fancy a few hours of solitude (although the weekends can get busy). The soft white sand is good for shell collecting, and the best time to visit is in late afternoon when you can sip a beer and feast on local fish and crab while watching the sun sink beneath the horizon.

Peam Krasaop Wildlife Sanctuary (PKWS)

6km south of Koh Kong • Daily 6.30am–6pm • 5000 riel • A moto/tuk-tuk from Koh Kong should cost $5/$10

Koh Kong province has the country's largest area of mangrove forest, forming a vast and intricate network of "islands" which are the foundations of a rich and varied saltwater ecosystem. From Koh Kong you can make an enjoyable excursion to the **Peam Krasaop Wildlife Sanctuary (PKWS)**, a 250-square-kilometre area of stunning mangrove forest that was designated as a protected area in 1997. Ten thousand people, mainly fishermen, live in floating hamlets and make their livings from the abundant marine life.

From the entrance, a 600m concrete walkway takes you through the eerie mangrove forest towards a rickety bridge and a 15m-high observation tower. Across the bridge (and at the sanctuary entrance) you can hire a motorboat to take you through the waterways, past mangrove islands and into authentic local fishing villages.

ARRIVAL AND DEPARTURE

KOH KONG AND AROUND

By bus Buses drop off at the new bus stop, east of town, near Acleda Bank, from where it's a $1–2 moto ride into town. If you're buying a bus ticket for onward travel, it's worth shopping around (or asking at Ritthy Eco Adventure Tours) as guesthouses often add a few dollars surcharge. A few companies offer morning services to Phnom Penh (between 7am and 8am) and Sihanoukville (8am, 11.45am & 2pm) from their offices in town. Note that for Sihanoukville, only Virak Bunthan offers a "direct" service; other companies may claim to send you direct, but you usually have to alight at Sre Ambal and board a smaller minibus (same company) the rest of the way.

Destinations Phnom Penh (5 daily; 6hr); Sihanoukville (3 daily; 4hr).

By minibus and shared taxi Minibuses and shared taxis are becoming less popular now that there are big a/c buses and better roads. However, minibuses (30,000 riel) and shared taxis (40,000 riel) run to Phnom Penh direct from Koh Kong, bypassing Sihanoukville, and Sihanoukville-bound shared taxis (40,000 riel) leave from the transport stop at the market. A couple of minibuses (departing between 8am and 9am) travel to Kampot and Kep for $10/person.

Destinations Kampot (2 daily; 6hr); Kep (2 daily; 7hr); Phnom Penh (6 daily; 6hr); Sihanoukville (4 daily; 4hr).

GETTING AROUND

Bike and motorbike rental Most guesthouses can sort you out with a motorbike for around $5–6/day or a bicycle for $1.50/24hr.

Motos There are plenty of motos around; Mr Han (☎097 280 0232) is reliable.

ACCOMMODATION

Most accommodation is within walking distance of the jetty. If staying in the town doesn't appeal, try one of the growing number of excellent options beside the **Tatai River**, around 20km east of town (a moto or tuk-tuk to the bridge at Tatai should cost $6/$15).

KOH KONG TOURS AND ACTIVITIES

A few companies (and guesthouses such as *Blue Moon*) offer excursions to **waterfalls** upstream or the **beaches** on nearby **Koh Kong island**. The boat ride there takes about an hour (although the choppy seas shouldn't be crossed between June and October). Guided treks into the hinterland are also easily arranged.

TOUR OPERATORS

Neptune Tatai, 18km east of town ⓦneptuneadventure-cambodia.com. Experienced outfit with a tranquil riverside guesthouse and all sorts of river tours on offer, including kayaking and boat trips to the waterfall and nearby mangroves.

Ritthy Koh Kong Eco Adventure Tours Waterfront, close to Bob's Ice Cream (look for the orange sign) ☎012 707719, ⓦkohkongeco adventure.com. The town's longest-running operator, offering a range of excursions that includes day-trips to waterfalls and to Koh Kong island, as well as kayaking

and multi-day treks in the Cardamom Mountains.

Wild KK Project ☎097 989 7999, ⓦwildkkproject .com. Working with nature, a grassroots movement and local communities, these adventurous ecology- and culture-focused small group tours to the Areng Valley – a pristine region deep in the Cardamoms threatened by a proposed hydroelectric dam, and home to rare Siamese crocs – run for a minimum of four days. You'll sleep in hammocks and eat local food while activities include trekking, kayaking and cycling. Expect plenty of interaction with local communities.

5

KOH KONG

Asian Hotel Waterfront ☎035 936667, ⓦasiankohkong.com. Great value and abundantly staffed, this hotel has fresh and clean well-furnished en-suite a/c rooms with TVs and minibars. The more expensive have partial river views. The good *Baan Peakmai* restaurant is on site (see below). $15

Kaing Kaing Guesthouse Riverfront, near the old boat dock ☎035 674 7111. One of many good-value Khmer-run guesthouses in town, right on the riverfront. The fan rooms – most with furnitureless balconies and river views – are tidy and well furnished. The friendly staff don't speak English. $10

Koh Kong City Hotel Riverfront, just north of the boat dock ☎035 936777, ⓦkkcthotel.netkhmer.com. Comfortable modern hotel with business-class a/c rooms and a riverside restaurant-bar. The more expensive rooms come with a river view. Great value. $20

★**Oasis** 2km north of town ☎016 331556, ⓦoasisresort.netkhmer.com. This friendly resort has five simple, roomy, family bungalows with a/c, TVs, DVD players and mini fridges in an idyllic garden. There's also a nice pool (non-residents $3), restaurant and great mountain views. $25

Otto's Signposted 50m down a small road from the old boat dock ☎012 924249. Located in a traditional stilt-house, this original backpacker guesthouse is still the cheapest in town. Rooms (fan only) are small and rather dingy with shared bathrooms, but there's a good, inexpensive restaurant and bar. $5

AROUND KOH KONG

4 Rivers Ecolodge Tatai village, 20km out of town on the road to Phnom Penh ☎023 217358, ⓦecolodges .asia. In a magnificent location on the river, this resort offers luxury to the point of decadence in fan-cooled floating tents containing four-poster beds, DVD players and all other mod cons, while also trying to neutralize its carbon footprint with sustainable building materials and solar electricity, among other measures. River- and land-based tours, including trips up to the thundering Tatai rapids, are available. $200

★**The Rainbow Lodge** Tatai River, 20km towards Phnom Penh ☎012 160 2585, ⓦrainbow lodgecambodia.com. Secluded ecolodge with seven stilted bungalows (with fans) set in verdant scrubland with river views; eco initiatives include solar power and rainwater collection. Rates include breakfast, lunch and three-course dinners (menu choices available), and use of kayaks. They can organize treks to the Cardamom Mountains and boat trips to the waterfalls. Cash only. $80

★**Thmorda Garden Riverside Resort** 169 Neuk Kok Village, 6km northwest of town ☎035 690 0324, ⓦthmordagarden.com. On the far side of the river, the en-suite a/c rooms here are small but well furnished and cosy. Their adjacent over-water *Crab Restaurant* is surprisingly stylish, with good food, nice cocktails and free kayaks. A good option en route to Thailand if you wish to bypass town. They offer free pick-ups from the border and Koh Kong bus station, if you book ahead. $25

EATING

KOH KONG

Baan Peakmai Waterfront ☎035 936667, ⓦasiankohkong.com. This smart a/c restaurant serves a delicious selection of Thai food, including many vegetarian dishes, all at reasonable prices. The Thai green curry comes highly recommended ($5). Daily 6.30–9.30am, 11am–2pm & 5–10pm.

Café Laurent Riverfront, just north of the old boat dock ☎012 373737, ⓦcafelaurent.asia. A sumptuous plant-festooned restaurant-bar on stilts over the river with a huge menu of Khmer, Thai and Western dishes (grilled sea bass $9.50), plus wicked desserts and

home-made ice cream. Daily 7am–midnight.

Crab Chack Koh Yor Beach. For a good local feed (or sunset beer), this simple, family-run shack on the beach at Koh Yor is pretty much unbeatable; prices are cheap although curiously they're not shown on the menu (barbecue fish and fried crab with black pepper both cost 20,000 riel). Daily 8am–8pm.

Fat Sam's High Street, near the roundabout ☎097 737 0707. The expansive Welsh owner, Sam, is well known and liked around town, and not only for his hearty English breakfasts ($5). Popular with expats; has a pool table and rents motorbikes. Mon–Sat 9am–10pm, Sun 4–10pm.

DIRECTORY

Health The Sen Sok Clinic on Street 3 (24hr) has English-speaking doctors and the hospital is 500m north of the market, but you may be better off going across the border to the better-equipped one at Trat.

Internet and phone calls International phone calls can be made from one of the internet cafés along the high street (internet around 3000 riel/hr).

Money Baht, riel and dollars are all accepted in town. Baht can be exchanged at the reliable Ratha Exchange (7am–5pm) on Street 2. There are a couple of ATMs in town, including Acleda (near the bus station, Visa only) and Canadia (no charge).

Post office North of the hospital, on the same road (Mon–Fri 8–10.30am & 2–4.40pm).

Chi Phat

A shining example of the success of Cambodia's community-based ecotourism projects, **CHI PHAT** is a remote riverside settlement nestled in the southern valleys of the Cardamom Mountains, accessible by moto or by long-tail boat from Andoung Tuek some 20km away, up the Preak Piphot River. Thanks to its isolation, Chi Phat is a good hike off the tourist trail and provides an excellent opportunity to enjoy the forest surroundings while supporting the local community. Established by the Wildlife Alliance in 2008 in an effort to protect the forests from illegal logging and poaching, the Chi Phat Community-based Ecotourism project (**CBET**), set in a four-village commune home to around 550 families, was designed to empower villagers to pursue sustainable forms of income. Its members – many, former poachers – are trained in nature awareness, earning their keep by guiding and opening up their homes to visitors.

There are scores of **guided activities** on offer; trips cost around $35/day, including guide (some with decent English), packed lunch and water. An overnight stay is enough to get a flavour of Chi Phat, although a few days or even a week is better if you want to explore the huge network of **jungle trails**, either on foot or **mountain bike**, visiting waterfalls in secluded clearings, bat caves and ancient jar burial sites. There are also sunrise **birdwatching** excursions (the silver oriole, the yellow-bellied warbler and great hornbill are highlights) and peaceful **river cruises** in traditional rowing boats.

ARRIVAL AND DEPARTURE
CHI PHAT

To get to Chi Phat, you'll need to first make for the village of **Andoung Tuek** from where you can either take a **moto** ($7; 45min) or a boat upriver. **CBET boats** ($10; 2hr) wait for the arrival of the Virak Buntham Phnom Penh–Koh Kong bus (it passes through around noon–1pm); however it's advisable to book your place on the boat in advance (☎ 035 675 6444, ⓦ chi-phat.org). If you're coming on a morning bus from Sihanoukville (2hr 30min) or Koh Kong (2hr), you'll be there in plenty of time. From the bridge dock it's also easy to charter a **motorboat**, which costs significantly more ($30). Watch out for rogue motorboat owners claiming there's no scheduled boat. This is not the case, although if you miss the lunchtime boat it's a 24hr wait for the next one.

ACCOMMODATION AND EATING

Chi Phat **accommodation** can be booked with the CBET Visitor Centre when you arrive or, better still, in advance (☎ 035 6756444, ⓦ chi-phat.org). **Homestays** are available, along with **guesthouses** and more upmarket **bungalows** on Butterfly Island. Most, but not all, have electricity from at least sunset to 10pm; some, overnight. If you're heading off on one of the multi-day treks, a hammock or tent, plus basic bedding, will be provided. You can buy cheap noodle dishes for less than $1 at the market, and there are two **restaurants**.

Butterfly Island A 20min walk from the CBET office. The most upmarket accommodation, in fan-cooled bungalows, with evening electricity only. $15
CBET restaurant The small CBET restaurant serves substantial, nourishing meals made from local produce ($2.50 breakfast, $3.50 lunch/dinner). Daily 6–8.30am, 11am–1pm & 6–7.30pm.
Guesthouses Chi Phat has fourteen basic, homely guesthouses. $6
Homestays There are eleven homestays available.

Your hosts will speak limited English, if at all, but are wonderfully hospitable. Expect to live as they do; although they will have gone to great trouble to make your quarters spotless, be prepared for outdoor loos, scoop showers and close proximity to farm animals. Rates include dinner. One person $5; two people $7
Mama's Next door to the CBET restaurant. Drop in here for a change from the CBET restaurant. Hours vary.

Kampot

Charming, compact **KAMPOT**, on the north bank of the Teuk Chhou River (aka Kampong Bay River), enjoys one of the nicest settings in Cambodia, and has become a popular destination for weekending Khmer and expats from Phnom Penh, as well as

5

for foreign tourists. Once a bustling trading port, Kampot still boasts a Chinese population, their single-storey houses, built without stilts, contrasting with the Khmer stilt-houses and colonial shophouses that grace the town's streets behind the sun-kissed, tree-lined **riverfront**. The town makes an excellent base for exploring the many attractions in the surrounding **province**.

The riverfront

Southwest of Kampot's central roundabout is the colourful **French quarter**, where shophouses line the streets down to the **river** and flowers planted in cans and pots give the place an almost Mediterranean aura. Getting to the riverfront with a camera for the **sunset** as the night fishermen head out to sea in their brightly coloured boats is a must.

The elongated **old market** – abandoned some years ago when a new market building was constructed – was restored in 2011 and is now home to a burgeoning collection of boutiques, bookshops and cafés. Further along are the government offices, the post office and, at the end of the road, the Governor's Residence, which has been restored to its original grandeur.

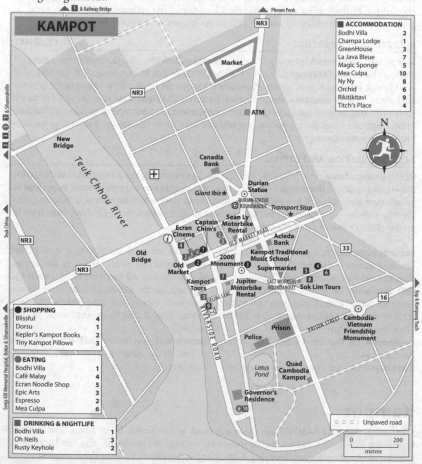

KAMPOT

ACCOMMODATION

Bodhi Villa	2
Champa Lodge	1
GreenHouse	3
La Java Bleue	7
Magic Sponge	5
Mea Culpa	10
Ny Ny	8
Orchid	6
Rikitikitavi	9
Titch's Place	4

SHOPPING

Blissful	4
Dorsu	1
Kepler's Kampot Books	2
Tiny Kampot Pillows	3

EATING

Bodhi Villa	1
Café Malay	4
Ecran Noodle Shop	5
Epic Arts	3
Espresso	2
Mea Culpa	6

DRINKING & NIGHTLIFE

Bodhi Villa	1
Oh Neils	3
Rusty Keyhole	2

= = = : Unpaved road

0 ——— 200

metres

THE CHINESE IN CAMBODIA

There has been a **Chinese presence** in Cambodia since the very earliest times – indeed, accounts written by Chinese traders and envoys from the third century onwards have played a major part in chronicling the country's history – but it was only after the fifteenth century that the Chinese began to settle in significant numbers. Marrying into rich Khmer families and assuming positions as tax collectors, bankers, gold dealers and restaurateurs, ethnic Chinese soon established themselves as arguably the most influential minority in the country.

A flood of new immigrants arrived as a result of China's economic crisis in the 1930s. In the main, the Chinese community continued to prosper until the 1970s, when they were **persecuted** first by the Lon Nol government – which resented their success – and then by the Khmer Rouge, who wanted them eliminated. Things became more complicated in 1979 when the Vietnamese liberation of Cambodia was followed by a short-lived Chinese invasion of Vietnam. This resulted in many Cambodian Chinese fleeing to Thailand; those Chinese who remained were subsequently permitted to resume limited business activities, but it wasn't until after the 1993 elections that they were properly able to reassert their influence on business – which they did wholeheartedly, capitalizing on their access to investment capital through their extensive overseas networks. Nowadays, the number of Chinese-owned businesses is clear to see from the Chinese signage on streets in any Cambodian town.

Cambodia's Chinese have managed to retain their own culture and language (most are **bilingual**) while at the same time integrating very well into Cambodian society. In towns such as Voen Sai and Kampot they are more visible by virtue of maintaining their own Chinese-language **schools**. And in Phnom Penh, although Chinese New Year is not an official holiday, it assumes a festive importance akin to the Khmer New Year, with energetic dragon dances performed in the streets.

For a pleasant stroll, follow the river from the old road bridge to the disused railway bridge in the north. There you can cross the river on the rusty, pockmarked walkway, and return to town along the other bank.

Kampot Traditional Music School

On the edge of the park northeast of the old market • Mon–Fri 6–9pm • Free, but a donation is appreciated

Kampot Traditional Music School teaches traditional and folk music and dance to orphaned and disabled children. Visitors are welcome to come and watch the classes and a timetable is displayed outside. There are regular **performances**, too.

ARRIVAL AND DEPARTURE   KAMPOT

Arriving by bus from Phnom Penh, you can either get dropped by the (new) market, north of the centre, or 700m further on at the transport stop, between the Durian statue and Total petrol station, where shared taxis and minibuses also arrive.

By bus Phnom Penh Sorya Transport and Hua Lian have booking desks next to the transport stop; they run big buses (5hr) to Phnom Penh via Kep. Paramount, Capitol and Rith Mony also offer direct buses to Phnom Penh (4hr), while Giant Ibis is faster still.
Destinations Kep (10 daily; 1hr); Phnom Penh (12 daily; 2hr 30min–5hr).
By shared taxi and minibus Shared transport departs from opposite the bus terminus; Champa Mekong run an afternoon service to Sihanoukville. Kampot Tours' buses serve

Sihanoukville ($5), Kep ($3) and Koh Kong ($10), as well as Ha Tien ($8), for Vietnam, with uncomfortable services (involving a change of vehicle at the border) to HCMC ($18) and Bangkok ($35). Giant Ibis operates comfortable twelve-seater express nonstop minibuses direct to Phnom Penh directly ($8). Shared taxis also travel to Takeo ($3).
Destinations Bangkok (daily; 12hr); Ha Tien (daily; 2hr); HCMC (daily; 10hr); Kep (3 daily; 1hr); Koh Kong (daily; 5hr); Phnom Penh (12 daily; 3hr–3hr 30min); Sihanoukville (10 daily; 2hr 30min); Takeo (8–12 daily; 2hr).

GETTING AROUND

Built on a grid system, Kampot is bordered on the west by the Teuk Chhou/Kampong Bay River, spanned in the south by a rustic old bridge for local traffic. To the north, NR3 runs along a modern concrete bridge. The **town centre** is at the Durian

5

statue roundabout, where roads converge from all directions. The streets are quiet and most things you need are easily reached on foot.

Car rental Cars with driver can be hired through hotels and guesthouses for around $50/day; or try English-speaking Mr Panya (☎ 010 503053, ✉ pagnia2007@yahoo.com). You can rent a car through Kampot Car Rental for $20/day (☎ 088 5102702, ✉ info@kampotcarrental.com); rates don't include insurance.

Motorbike rental Motorbikes are available for rent at many of the guesthouses as well as Sean Ly (daily 7am–9pm; ☎ 012 944687), south of the Durian statue roundabout, near the old theatre. A 125cc runabout costs $5/day, a smart 250cc off-road bike is $12. Jupiter (daily 8am–6pm; ☎ 095 984079), west of the 2000 Monument, rents Endure 200cc and 250cc trail bikes for $15/day, including full-face helmet and gloves.

INFORMATION

Tourist information centre You can get good advice about the local area from Mr Pov and his team at the new information centre on the waterfront near the old bridge (7am–7pm; ☎ 012 655 5541, ✉ kampottourismoffice @gmail.com). They can also arrange visas, make bus and taxi bookings and book tours.

TOURS AND ACTIVITIES

Bart the (Belgian) Boatman ☎ 092 174280. The best boat trips in town (private charters only; 3–4hr; $40/boat).

Climbodia ☎ 095 581951, ⓦ climbodia.com. Belgian-run rock climbing in and around Kampot's caves using high-quality gear; programmes include beginner's half-day courses and full-day Via Ferratas and abseiling.

Massage Seeing Hands Massage, near *Bokor Mountain Lodge* on Riverside Rd (7am–11pm; $4/hr). You can also get a massage, as well as a scrub, mani or wax from Jolie Jolie, 20m north of *Captain Chim's* (☎ 092 936867).

Quad Cambodia Kampot South of town, near the Salt Workers roundabout ☎ 033 699 1010. ATV countryside

tours to isolated villages, salt flats and rice fields (a 1hr 15min Easy Ride costs $40 for two).

Sightseeing tours The main guesthouses, the tourist office, *Captain Chim's* (opposite the old market), Sok Lim Tours, next to *Ny Ny*, and many outlets across town can arrange sightseeing trips, including to Bokor (from $12) and the surrounding countryside, which take in salt and pepper plantations, nearby caves, Kep and, often, Rabbit Island too ($15–20). Also on offer are boat trips upriver or to the islands, plus sunset ($5) and firefly cruises ($7).

Swimming The *Borey Bokor* hotel, east of the hospital, has a swimming pool ($5).

ACCOMMODATION

There's a pleasant selection of **places to stay** in Kampot, including some of the cheapest backpacker accommodation in the south. Some of the nicer options are found a few kilometres out of town, dotted along the banks of the **Kampot River**.

★**Bodhi Villa** 2km north of town ☎ 012 728884, ⓦ bodhivilla.com. Set in a veritable jungle of garden on the river this blissful guesthouse, one of a few side-by-side backpacker options, offers accommodation for all budgets, from a mattress and mosquito net on the balcony to comfortable open-fronted fan-cooled bungalows and an idyllic floating room – try and stick around for one of the owner's Friday-night live music sessions. Good restaurant, too (see opposite). Mattress $2; doubles $5

★**Champa Lodge** Riverside Rd, 4km north of town ☎ 092 525835, ⓦ champalodge.com. Idyllic family-run riverside retreat – one of Cambodia's best – home to five charming fan-cooled rooms within three original stilted Khmer houses, renovated to include luxe bathrooms, plus a convivial restaurant-bar serving top-notch home-cooked food and Belgian beers. The friendly owners are a mine of information about the area, and have kayaks for exploring hidden loops of the river. The spacious Boat Lodge ($50) is well worth the splurge for its panoramic private balcony

and unrivalled river views. $35

GreenHouse 6km west of town, off the Teuk Chhou Rd ☎ 088 886 3071, ⓦ greenhousekampot.com. The original green timber structure here was formerly home to *Snowy's*, a bar stilted over the Tonle Sap near Phnom Penh, before it was transplanted in 2012 to the banks of the Kampot River. It continues to serve as a restaurant and bar, and shares a lush garden with a variety of straw-roofed bungalows with fans (the cheapest with shared bathrooms), many stilted and with ace river views. $10

La Java Bleue Road 27, 100m west of the 2000 Monument ☎ 033 667 6679, ⓦ lajava-bleue.biz. A French-Aussie-run colonial boutique hotel with three well-appointed themed rooms in the main building (the top-floor Chinese room has a private balcony), plus two en-suite bedrooms (ideal for a family) in a building nearby, all a/c. Delicious food, including a popular nightly barbecue (from 6pm). $50

Magic Sponge 100m east of the Salt Workers roundabout ☎ 017 946428, ⓦ magicspongecambodia .com. Backpacker guesthouse with bright, cheap and clean fan-cooled rooms and a six-bed "penthouse" dorm – beds have reading lights and there's a nice balcony – in a refurbished villa with a mini-golf course in the grounds. The restaurant serves good Western and Indian food (veg thali $5). Live music on Wed. Dorm $3; fan $9; a/c $14

Mea Culpa A block back from the river, behind the Governor's Residence ☎ 012 504769, ⓦ meaculpa kampot.com. Clean and comfortable, out-of-the-way guesthouse with bright bedrooms and all mod cons including cable TV, fridges and a/c. Good on-site restaurant (see below). $25

Ny Ny Opposite Magic Sponge ☎ 033 932460, ⓔ nyny hotel@yahoo.com. More a hotel than a guesthouse, this orange high-rise has clean, great-value en-suite rooms (a/c rooms are larger and double the price), just 5min from the bus stop and riverside. Wi-fi is a little patchy. $6

Orchid 120m east of the Salt Workers roundabout ☎ 092 226996, ⓔ orchidguesthousekampot@yahoo .com. A range of well-priced fan and more comfortable a/c rooms, plus charming bungalows with their own tiny balconies in a garden. Restaurant, tours and pleasant owners combine to make this a good choice. Fan $7; a/c $15

Rikitikitavi Riverside Rd, south of the old bridge ☎ 012 235102, ⓦ rikitikitavi-kampot.com. Booking is essential to secure one of the six comfortable, stylish a/c rooms. The first-floor restaurant-bar is a fabulous spot to watch the sunset, and their food is some of the best in town. $43

Titch's Place Riverside Rd, near the old bridge ☎ 033 650 1631, ⓦ tictchsplaceguesthouse.webs.com. Backpacker-friendly riverfront digs with sizeable dorms (including a girls-only dorm) with ceiling fans, bunks, reading lights and balconies, as well as communal timber lockers and a nice rooftop. $4

EATING, DRINKING AND NIGHTLIFE

Kampot has plenty of **eating** options. In addition to the restaurants listed below, there are the usual rice and noodle shops around the market, by the transport stop and along the road from the roundabout to the old bridge (where you'll find stalls selling fruit shakes and desserts in the evening). Metaheap supermarket is on the northern side of the Salt Workers roundabout. **Nightlife** in Kampot is low-key, with a couple of Western bars.

Bodhi Villa 2km north of town ☎ 012 728884, ⓦ bodhivilla.com. Even if you're not staying, it's worth the trip here for the superb food, ranging from Cambodian and Thai to Western classics, with a heavenly beef *lok lak*. Angkor-battered fish and chips $3. The Friday-night parties are the talk of the town. Daily 7am–10pm.

Café Malay Old Market St, opposite the old market ☎ 097 993 8641. Small, friendly café, decorated with hanging teapots, serving top food, and particularly great breakfasts (big brekkie $3.75), some including beer. Free wi-fi. Daily 9am–9.45pm.

Ecran Noodle Shop Old Market St, opposite the old market. A concise menu of hand-pulled Chinese noodles and dumplings in this friendly café attached to the Ecran Cinema, where the chef cooks right by the street (noodle and dumpling soup $2.50). The owner is a mine of information on the area. Wed–Mon 11am–9pm.

Epic Arts Old Market St, northeast of the old market ⓦ epicarts.org.uk. Run by a group of deaf people, this tiny café serves home-made cakes, teas and coffee. Instructions in the menu help you sign your order. Breakfast bruschetta $3; nut and banana brioche $3. Daily 7am–4pm.

Espresso 30m north of Epic Arts ☎ 092 388736. You'll get the best coffee (from $1.50) in town at this friendly muralled café, which is also a hot spot for breakfast (eggs Benedict $4). Tues–Sun 8am–5pm.

Mea Culpa A block back from the river, behind the Governor's Residence ☎ 012 504769, ⓦ meaculpakampot.com. Open-air restaurant serving excellent food. The stone-baked pizzas (9-inch Margherita $5.50) are delicious, as are the ingredients available for "build your own" sandwiches – perfect to take away if you're off on an excursion. Daily 7–9.30am & noon–9pm.

Oh Neils Riverside Rd, near Kipling Lane ☎ 015 207790, ⓦ ohneils.com. A favourite haunt of local expats, this small Irish bar spills onto the street and gets livelier as the night goes on. Brunty's $2. Daily 5pm–3am.

Rusty Keyhole Cnr Riverside Rd & Old Market Rd ☎ 012 679607. This iconic bar and restaurant has a prime position on the riverfront, near the old market. It's a top spot to relax over a beer or two while your spare ribs are barbecued; one portion will fill two. Also runs a sports bar next to the 2000 Monument. Daily 11.30am–10pm.

SHOPPING

Dorsu Old Market Rd, opposite the old market ☎ 012 960225, ⓔ dorsucambodia@gmail.com, ⓦ dorsu.org/store. Pretty dresses, *kramas* and other accessories produced by local women as part of a social-enterprise system with an impressive ethical focus. Creative types can volunteer here, helping to increase their product range and improve store operation. Daily 9am–5pm.

5

Kepler's Kampot Books Old Market, Old Market Rd. A great selection of new and secondhand books, with a good range on Cambodia. Daily 8am–8pm.

Tiny Kampot Pillows East side of the 2000 Monument junction ☎097 766 6094, ⊛tinykampotpillows.com. Silk *kramas*, cushions and pillows handmade locally, as well as bags, place mats, photos and prints. Daily 10am–7pm.

DIRECTORY

Books In addition to Kepler's Kampot Books, *Blissful* guesthouse, east of *Magic Sponge*, has a book exchange and sells used books.

Cinema The Ecran Cinema and Movie House, Old Market Rd (☎093 249411), has two intimate a/c movie rooms showing Cambodian films at 4pm and Hollywood flicks at 7.30pm ($3.50). You can also rent the smallest screen and watch your own preferred film (Wed–Mon 11am–10pm).

Hospital Riverside Rd, between the new and old bridges.

The new Sonja Kill Memorial Hospital (⊛skmh.org), 7km west of town, is staffed by highly qualified Khmer- and English-speaking doctors.

Money The Canadia Bank, north of the Durian statue roundabout, can change travellers' cheques and has an ATM. There are moneychangers in the market; there's also an Acleda Bank in town (with ATM – Visa only) near the Kampot Music School, a block north of the Salt Workers roundabout.

Post office Riverside Rd, south of the old bridge.

Around Kampot

Kampot province is one of Cambodia's most picturesque, its landscape ranging from the cloud-topped mountains of the **Bokor National Park**, an extraordinary deserted hill station that's fallen into the hands of developers, to salt flats and misty, uninhabited offshore **islands**. Kampot town is ideally located for visiting a wealth of nature-based attractions, including **wild rapids**, a zoo and a smattering of **temple caves** as well as some of the region's famed **pepper plantations**.

Teuk Chhou Zoo

8km northeast of Kampot, on the west bank of the Teuk Chhou River • Daily 7am–5.30pm • $4 • Moto from Kampot $3

Set among gardens and fruit plantations at the foot of the Elephant Mountains, **Teuk Chhou Zoo** is home to a wide range of animals, including tigers, a pair of playful young elephants, lemurs and gibbons, spread across a wide area permeated by incongruous piped music. The zoo relies on donations, and as in most zoos, the animals look none too happy.

BOKOR NATIONAL PARK

The story of **Bokor National Park** is a fascinating but sad one. Wandering through the crumbling, chilling remnants of the 1920s **French colonial hill station**, often swathed in thick fog, was once a huge tourist attraction, until, in 2007 Hun Sen's government effectively sold the mountain in its entirety to the Sokimex Group (owner of the Sokha Resorts and Sokimex Oil among others) for $100m. The Chinese conglomerate now owns a 99-year lease and has begun an extravagant development project that will see the refurbishment of the dilapidated hill station (which was also the scene of a dramatic showdown between the Khmer Rouge and the Vietnamese in 1979) and the construction of hotels (they've finished one already, as well as a neighbouring casino), numerous villas, golf courses, a cable car and water parks. Plans extend to the coast, where a major port is being built with a view to landing cruise ships before helicoptering guests to the plateau.

A new 32km toll road carving a thick ribbon of tarmac into the steep hillside has been finished and development across the mountain is gaining pace (though is usually easy to avoid). To explore the mountain's old relics and two waterfalls, you could hire a moto (the road is too steep for tuk-tuks) or better still, go with a local tour operator (see p.270). However, depending on the developer's rate of progress and their attitude towards them, tours may soon be a thing of the past.

Teuk Chhou Rapids

8km northeast of Kampot, on the west bank of the Teuk Chhou River • $2 for foreigners; 6000 riel to cross the bridge • Moto from Kampot $3

A couple of hundred metres further upstream from Teuk Chhou Zoo, the river becomes more scenic, racing down the valley and bubbling over the rocks in a series of gurgling **rapids** (although a new Chinese-built hydroelectric dam 5km upstream has tamed the flow somewhat).

Phnom Chhnork

12km east of Kampot • 4000 riel for foreigners • Hiring a moto/tuk-tuk from Kampot to take you here and to Phnom Sorsia (see below) will cost $8/$10; you can also rent your own motorbike ($4–6) – turn left off the road to Kep about 6km from Kampot, signposted through a portico, and then head out along a well-made but unsurfaced road to the hill (about another 6km)

Phnom Chhnork is the closest cave system to Kampot. The entrance to the hill is through a wat, where you can leave your motorbike with a local boy for a few hundred riel. From here it's a walk of 1km or so through fields of well-tended vegetable plots to the foot of the hill. Intrepid types can explore a couple of poky holes at the foot of the hill before venturing up the rickety steps, passing a collection of pagoda buildings, to the main caves. If you look carefully, through the gloom you will see a brick-built **pre-Angkor prasat**; the rock seems to be trying to claim the ruin, which is slowly being coated with limestone as water drips from the roof. Child guides don't have much information, but for a dollar they can help you negotiate the paths within the caves. There are no facilities – wear stout shoes and take a torch.

Phnom Sorsia

16km southeast of Kampot • Hiring a moto/tuk-tuk from Kampot to take you here and to Phnom Chhnork (see above) will cost $8/$10; you can also rent your own motorbike ($4–6) – take NR33 towards Kep for around 14km before turning left (signposted in blue and white) through another grand portico onto a dirt track that leads after 1km to the foot of the hill

The **Phnom Sorsia** caves sit within a hillside Buddhist complex; from the summit of the hill, panoramic views stretch across the province and the ocean towards the Vietnamese island of Phu Quoc.

From the pagoda, take the staircase and at the top, turn left and follow the rocky path for 50m to reach **Ruhng Dhumrey Saw** (White Elephant Cave). Just inside the entrance is a seated Buddha statue, from where rickety steps head down into the cave proper; here you can see the large cream-and-grey rock formation, vaguely resembling an elephant's head, which gives the cave its name. Back at the main steps, take the path to the right, which leads after about 150m to the far side of the hill and **Leahng Bpodjioh** (Bat Cave), filled with the ear-splitting sound of squeaking bats. The stench of ammonia is overpowering, and watch you don't get guano in the eye if you look up. The cave is smaller and darker than Ruhng Dhumrey Saw, although a few shafts of light penetrate the gloom, highlighting the tree roots that poke down spookily from the roof of the chamber. Back outside, you may be lucky enough to see the monkeys that live in the woods on the hillside, while from the top of the hill there's a good view over the rice paddies along the coast. Be sure to wear stout shoes and carry a torch.

Kep

Back in the 1960s, when Sihanoukville was just a fishing village, **KEP**, 25km from Kampot, was already an affluent seaside resort. Subsequent events were unkind to the town, but today, though now eclipsed by Sihanoukville, it is making a spirited comeback as a day-trip destination from Phnom Penh. It's not the beach (narrow, dark brown) that brings people here, however. Cambodians largely come for the **food** –

5

particularly the offerings at the **crab market** – while foreigners linger to enjoy Kep's mellow atmosphere, excellent accommodation options, and the possibility of trips to offshore **islands** and into the beautiful surrounding countryside.

Traces of the town's sombre past remain. The region is dotted with the gutted shells of **colonial villas** – tragic evidence of the Khmer Rouge's destruction. Until recently, most were smothered by prolific tropical vegetation and home to squatters; now some have been restored, with more likely to follow, although the difficulty of establishing ownership means this will be a slow process.

Colonial villas

Between the Yeah Mao statue and the Rabbit Island pier, you can still see **colonial villas** that were deliberately wrecked by the Khmer Rouge and left to be swallowed up by the jungle. Dating back to Kep's golden era of the 1960s, many of these modern gems were inspired by the French contemporary architect Le Corbusier. You'll also see plenty of ostentatious government buildings, a vast mansion on the hill belonging to a government minister and another colonial construction near *Breezes* restaurant, known as the **Queen's Palace**, that King Norodom Sihanouk built but never stayed in.

Kep National Park

On the hill behind Kep, you can get away from it all and enjoy fantastic views over the province and bay by following an 8km track through **Kep National Park** ($1; access is behind *Veranda Natural Resort*); the hike to the mountain top will take about an hour and a half, or you can go around the mountain in two to three hours. Viewpoints and benches scatter the trail. The *Led Zed Café*, 300m inside the park, makes a useful refreshment stop; you can pick up a park map from here and get good information on other local trails, including a hike to 182m Sunset Rock.

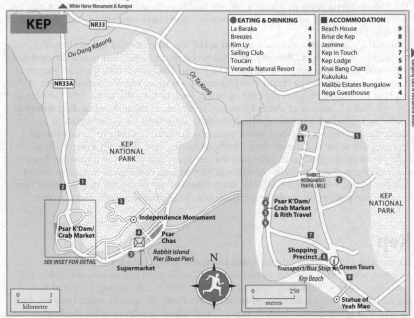

KEP

▲ White Horse Monument & Kampot

NR33
Ou Dang Kdaong
NR33A
O Ta Kong

KEP NATIONAL PARK

Psar K'Dam/ Crab Market
SEE INSET FOR DETAIL

Independence Monument

Psar Chas

Rabbit Island Pier (Boat Pier)

Supermarket

N

● EATING & DRINKING		■ ACCOMMODATION	
La Baraka	4	Beach House	9
Breezes	1	Brise de Kep	8
Kim Ly	6	Jasmine	3
Sailing Club	2	Kep in Touch	7
Toucan	5	Kep Lodge	5
Veranda Natural Resort	3	Knai Bang Chatt	6
		Kukuluku	2
		Malibu Estates Bungalow	1
		Rega Guesthouse	4

Kampong Trach & Vietnamese Border

KEP NATIONAL PARK

MARKET ROUNDABOUT/ TRAFFIC CIRCLE

Psar K'Dam/ Crab Market & Rith Travel

Shopping Precinct

Transport/Bus Stop

Green Tours

Kep Beach

Statue of Yeah Mao

0   1
kilometre

0   250
metres

KEP ORIENTATION

Kep is a sprawling place. The road for town branches away from NR33 at the prominent **White Horse Monument**, from where it's 5 or 6km to the right turn to **Psar K'Dam**, the famous crab market. From here the road runs along the seafront for 1km or so to **Kep Beach**, where the narrow, dark-sand beach broadens out fractionally. Set back in a circular precinct is the transport stop, as well as a couple of hotels, some local stores and several of the ubiquitous huts furnished with mats and hammocks that Cambodians love to rent out for a day's relaxing (it gets busy here at weekends). Getting back from here to the **crab market**, the one-way system dictates that you head north away from the beach and take the first left at the roundabout. East of Kep, the paved road runs to the **Vietnamese border**, and the crossing at Prek Chak (for Ha Tien and Phu Quoc).

ARRIVAL AND DEPARTURE   KEP

By moto/tuk-tuk A moto/tuk-tuk to Kampot costs $10/$15, or to the Vietnam border, $12/$18.

By bus Phnom Penh Sorya, Hua Lin and Capitol buses stop en route between Kampot and Phnom Penh, dropping off by the tourist office on the beachfront near the showers in Kep Thmei. There are plenty of motos to take you to your guesthouse ($3–5).

Destinations Kampot (5 daily; 1hr); Phnom Penh (5 daily; 3hr).

By minibus and shared taxi Kampot Tours, has minibuses between Kampot and Kep ($2), Sihanoukville and Ha Tien. You can also get a shared taxi to Phnom Penh. Rith Travel (☎016 789994, ✉rithtravel@hotmail.com), in the crab market, runs minibuses to Kampot, Sihanoukville and the Vietnam border.

Destinations Ha Tien (daily; 2hr); Kampot (5 daily; 1hr); Phnom Penh (8 daily; 3hr); Sihanoukville (3 daily; 3hr); Takeo (daily; 2hr).

INFORMATION AND TOURS

Tourist office On the beachfront near the showers in Kep Thmei, though it has little to offer. The free information booklet *Coastal* is the most up-to-date info source on the town.

Travel and tour operators A string of small tour operators cluster around the tourist office, including

Green Tours (☎036 630 3666, ✉greentours2010@yahoo .com) who offer countryside and Rabbit Island tours and fishing/snorkelling trips to Rabbit Island and Koh Poh as well as Phu Quoc and the Vietnam border (tours $14–25). Rith Travel (see above) can also assist with Vietnamese and Laos visas.

ACCOMMODATION

Kep **accommodation** ranges from stunning converted villas to rustic guesthouses; the very best are sumptuous and stylish while the cheaper places are generally basic, but clean. Options are spread widely, with possibilities at Kep Thmei, on the road east of town, towards the national park and near the Rabbit Island pier.

Beach House Centre of Kep near the beach ☎012 712750, ⊕thebeachhousekep.com. Smart, modern a/c rooms, some with sea views, at a newish hotel on the hillside; swimming pool with jacuzzi, spa and terrace café. $40

Brise de Kep Opposite the transport stop in the shopping precinct ☎012 301017, ⊕brisedekep.com. Well located by shops, the beach and the transport stop, offering decent fan rooms with attention to detail, and good management. The first-floor restaurant isn't bad, either. There's a more upmarket sister branch, *Brise de Kep Boutique*, with lovely sea-facing a/c rooms near the Rabbit Island pier ($28). $15

★**Jasmine** Jasmine Valley, at the base of Kep National Park ☎097 791 7635, ⊕jasminevalley.com. Gorgeous ecolodge, tucked away, with dense forest views on one side (with the chance of spotting nesting great hornbills) and the ocean on the other. The mud-brick or open-sided timber bungalows, some built at dizzying heights, are

tastefully decorated with personal touches (no fans or a/c). It's working towards total self-sufficiency, with fruit and vegetables in the elaborate gardens and fish in the ponds; they even brew their own starfruit cider. Family friendly, and a great place to meet other travellers. $28

Kep in Touch Street of the Old King ☎092 877193, ✉kepintouchbedandbreakfast.com. Charming French-owned Khmer-style timber guesthouse with its own boat for fishing and island-hopping trips. Just three cosy fan rooms share a bathroom, and there's a nice communal area with games such as backgammon, chess and carom. Fri night is movie night, and they offer good home-cooked food and lovely milkshakes. $8

Kep Lodge 1km north of market roundabout, signposted on the right with Treetop Bungalows ☎092 435330, ⊕keplodge.com. Each of these hillside bungalows, decorated with original watercolours on the walls, is named after the plant that grows in its own patch

5

of garden; non-guests can use the pool for $5. The bar has great sunset views. Fan **$33**; a/c **$42**

Knai Bang Chatt On the coast down a track near the one-way system ☏078 888556, ⊛knaibangchatt.com. Exclusive resort with eleven boutique rooms, beautifully furnished in cool linen and polished stone. The grounds stretch down to the sea where a slender beach has been created – complete with muslin-shaded day-beds. Plus swimming pool, sailing, bar and lovely sunset views. Booking essential. **$180**

Kukuluku 1.5km north of the crab market on the main road ☏036 630 0150, ⊛kukuluku-beachclub .com. The fan-cooled dorm at this French-run guesthouse boasts lovely views over Bokor, particularly at sunset. There's also a sliver of beach, a teeny swimming pool, a lively restaurant-bar (crêpes are a speciality) and frequent

parties – it's a popular backpacker hangout. Dorm **$6**; doubles **$15**

Malibu Estates Bungalows 500m off the main road, turning opposite Kukuluku ☏097 389 9201, ⊛malibuestatesbungalows.com. Centred around a beautiful pool area looking up and beyond into the jungle, this French-run place has a range of a/c bungalows and rooms decorated to an impressive standard, plus a decent French and Khmer restaurant. An idyllic, relaxing spot. **$30**

Rega Guesthouse A block south of the main road, close to the Rabbit Island pier ☏097 383 9064, ⊛keprega.com. This new guesthouse is a bit off the beaten track but staff can book motos, and the rooms are well built, centred around a jungle garden with a nice restaurant. A/c supplement $5. **$15**

EATING AND DRINKING

There's nothing to do in Kep after about 11pm, but there are some excellent restaurants; **crab** is the local speciality. Cheap eats are a little hard to find, but the **market** is a good place to pick up barbecued seafood, and there's a supermarket by the Rabbit Island pier. The crab market is flanked to the south by dozens of overpriced seafood restaurants that form the bulk of Kep's low-key **nightlife**.

La Baraka Northern end of crab-market strip ☏097 461 2543. A little blue-lit respite from seafood, with good pizza (Neapolitana 25,000 riel) and other Western food in a nicely decorated restaurant overlooking Bokor; it turns into a decent little bar later in the evening. Daily 8am–10pm.

★**Breezes** Along the coast road towards the Rabbit Island pier, signposted beyond the Provincial Hall ☏012 251454. Beachside elegance. The good Western-orientated menu (pork in caramel $4.75) includes oysters, a rare treat in these parts, and the owner offers free tuk-tuks home after dinner (for spends of more than $20). There's also an excellent wine list. Daily 9am–10pm.

Kim Ly Southern end of crab-market strip. This famous waterfront seafood restaurant is often packed; try the crab with Kampot pepper ($7.25). Its popularity has pushed prices up in recent years; most of the restaurants at the crab market are of a similar quality (try good-value *Sre Mao*). Daily 9am–10pm.

Sailing Club Next to Knai Bang Chatt ☏078 333685.

The best place to enjoy a sunset happy-hour cocktail (5–7pm), the *Sailing Club* has a stunning location gently lapped by the waves. The food (largely seafood) is expensive but good value; feast on the Saturday-night seafood BBQ ($15) or Sunday brunch ($13). By day, you can rent Hobie cats or waterski with a boat captain. Daily 7am–10pm.

Toucan In the centre of the crab market ☏097 853 1057. Pool table, classic rock, cheap beers, late-night snacks and tapas: this is the closest Kep gets to a party bar (cocktails $3.50). Daily 9am–3am.

Veranda Natural Resort Kep Mountain Hillside Resort ☏033 399035, ⊛veranda-resort.com. The restaurant at this smart resort is a must-visit, even if you just pop in for a beer and stunning views over wild jungle fauna, dilapidated colonial villas and across the sea to Bokor. The food's good (prawn with green pepper $8.50) and the hotel itself is fine (rooms $70). Non-guests can use the lovely pool for $7. Daily 7am–9pm.

DIRECTORY

Money There are no banks or reliable ATMs, but you can change dollars to riel at the market and *Kep Lodge* offers cashback on credit cards for a charge.

Post office On the way to Psar Chas, opposite the Rabbit Island pier.

Kep's offshore islands

The beaches in Kep aren't up to much: slim stretches of dark sand that don't lend themselves to lounging. Luckily, a number of trips to the offshore islands are on offer. Closest is **Koh Tonsay** (Rabbit Island), with three nice beaches. Further out, **Koh Poh**

5

(Coral Island) has clean white sands, turquoise water, coral reefs and great snorkelling. The huge island that dominates the horizon is **Phu Quoc**, in Vietnamese waters; locals still call it Koh Kut, dating back to when it belonged to Cambodia.

Koh Tonsay

A thirty-minute journey from the mainland, **Koh Tonsay**, or **Rabbit Island**, as it is better known, is – for now at least – a peaceful paradise of pale sand, clear waters, lofty palms and a few very basic bungalows. Just 8km in circumference, it boasts stretches of beach around the southwestern side that take you even further from the sparse crowds that arrive daily. It makes a good day out, but by far the best time to be here is at 4.15pm when the final day-tripper boat has disappeared behind the peninsula, in the direction of the mainland, and you are left behind with a few other shipwrecked souls, a cold beer and the sun heading gently for the horizon.

ARRIVAL AND INFORMATION   KEP'S OFFSHORE ISLANDS

Boats can be arranged to Koh Tonsay and Koh Poh through Kep's guesthouses, or you can charter long-tailed boats on the beach – ask at the food stalls or at the Rabbit Island pier.

To Koh Tonsay The boat to Koh Tonsay (30min) should cost you no more than $8. Some operators will offer lunch, guided walks and snorkelling for a few dollars more, but this is not recommended – too many travellers tell of errant guides and hungry stomachs. The snorkelling isn't up to much anyway and it's easy enough to explore the island along the rocky path that circumnavigates it.

To Koh Poh The 2hr trip to Koh Poh costs $50, though it shouldn't be considered in stormy weather.

ACCOMMODATION
Bungalows Five small businesses on Koh Tonsay run basic bungalows, most of them with squat toilets. $5

Kompong Trach

East of Kep, amid stunning karst landscapes, lies the friendly town of **KOMPONG TRACH**, 30km east of Kampot and 15km from Kep on NR33. The main reason to head out here is to visit **Wat Kirisehla**, 5km outside town, which is home to a reclining Buddha set in a substantial natural cavity in the limestone hills.

Wat Kirisehla

$1 • From Kompong Trach take the turning north off the main road, about 100m east of the market; the road passes the hospital before leaving town and heading off into the rice fields, where you'll soon see a large craggy hill ahead

Before you even reach the Buddhist cave temple of **Wat Kirisehla** you will most likely be approached by smiling children offering to give you a guided tour. Ask them how much and they'll say "up to you", but $1 is really the minimum. They don't have any real knowledge of the history, but the good ones have torches and can show you such dubious relics as the blood of Buddha on the cave floor. Exploring alone, it's an idea to take your own torch as the 100m-long tunnel to the centre of the hill is rather dark. Many of the formations in the cave have names; look out for the **elephant** at the entrance and a **tortoise** just beyond it. The centre of the hill is an almost circular cavity around 50m in diameter, ringed by high cliffs whose walls are eroded into caves. The large **reclining Buddha** here is a recent replacement for one destroyed by the Khmer Rouge, who holed up here for years without being rumbled.

ACCOMMODATION AND EATING   KOMPONG TRACH

You can get **food and drink** at the market and a couple of restaurants, all of which are opposite the main pagoda in the middle of town.

Vine Retreat Phnom Voar ☎036 633 3383, ⓦ thevineretreat.com. This excellent resort doubles up as an organic farm, with breathtaking views of the countryside stretching out to the Gulf of Thailand. Great food (including a raw menu), community-led trekking and tours, yoga weekends and a restaurant with raw food menu. It's a 5km hike off NR33 between Kep and Phnom Penh; call for directions. **$25**

Takeo province

Much of **Takeo province** disappears in an annual inundation by the waters of the Mekong and Bassac rivers, leaving **Takeo town** isolated on the shore of a vast inland sea, and outlying villages transformed into islands. As the waters recede, an ancient network of canals, which once linked the area to the trading port of Oc Eo (now a ruined site across the border in Vietnam), is revealed. These continue to be vital for local communication and trade, and getting around the area is still easiest by boat – indeed, for much of the year there is no alternative.

Takeo town

A key port on the trading route with Vietnam, the town of **TAKEO** (pronounced *ta-kow*) consists of two separate hives of activity: to the south, a dusty (or muddy, depending on the season) market and transport stop on NR2 – which has little to recommend it unless you want to visit one of the karaoke parlours – and to the north, a more picturesque area around the **Rokha Khnong Lake**, canal and port. Takeo makes a good base from which to visit the only **Funanese** sites so far identified in Cambodia, **Angkor Borei** and the nearby **Phnom Da**, which can be combined on a boat trip from town; an informative museum at Angkor Borei displays artefacts and statues unearthed at both sites. Since Takeo is only two hours from Phnom Penh, it's possible to visit these sights on a day-trip.

Rokha Khnong Lake

Southwest of the canal, a park with views over the marshy, lily-covered **Rokha Khnong Lake** makes a pleasant spot for an early morning or sunset stroll. Taking up a beautiful spot in the middle of the lake, the home of former Khmer Rouge chief of staff, **Ta Mok** – nicknamed "The Butcher" – was built for seclusion and protection in 1976 and until recently was used as a police training facility. Although you can't enter the building, you can cross the bridge to stroll in the grounds.

The port

You could while away a little time at Takeo's **port**, watching large wooden boats arriving from Vietnam laden with cheap terracotta tiles destined for Phnom Penh; the vessels are easily identified by the protective all-seeing eye painted on their bows. Takeo's colonial past is evident in the crumbling square behind the waterfront, and there's a small market, **Psar Nat**, which is busy in the early morning and late afternoon with local farmers and fisherfolk. The town's shophouses are sadly neglected, but still retain a discernible sense of French style.

ARRIVAL AND INFORMATION   TAKEO TOWN

By bus and shared taxi Takeo is straightforward to reach by bus (Phnom Penh Sorya) or shared taxi along NR2 from Phnom Penh (10,000 riel), both of which will drop you in front of Psar Thmei. To get to Kampot or Kep, shared taxis leave from Angk Tasaom, 13km west of town ($2/$5 by moto/tuk-tuk). As you enter the town on NR2, the road forks; the left branch takes you past the lake and out to the port, while the right fork (NR2) continues 1km to the Independence Monument traffic roundabout and then a further 1km to the market and transport stop. Here you'll also be able to get onward transport for the 30km trip to Phnom Den (for Tinh Bien in Vietnam; border open daily 7am–8pm, Vietnamese visas not available), usually via Kirivong.

5

Destinations (bus) Phnom Penh (10 daily; 2hr).
Internet There are several internet cafés ($1/hr) around town.
Money There's an Acleda Bank by the Independence Monument, a Canadia Bank with an ATM, and moneychangers at the market. There's nowhere in town to cash travellers' cheques.
Tourist office Set back a couple of blocks from the boat jetty – it's not particularly helpful (Mon–Fri 8–11am & 2.30–5.30pm; ☎032 931323).

ACCOMMODATION

Boeng Takeo Guesthouse Near the lakeside ☎032 210345. Reasonable en-suite rooms with cable TV and fan or a/c, and a nice first-floor balcony with views towards Ta Mok's house across the water. Fan $\overline{5}$; a/c $\overline{\$10}$
Meas Family Homestay Prey Theat, 2km from Ang Ta Som Market (intersection of NR3 & NR33) ☎011 925428, ⓦcambodianhomestay.com. Absorb Takeo's rural ambience with a hands-on experience at this family-run homestay on the outskirts of town. Set amid paddy fields and fruit trees, accommodation is in cosy fan-cooled bungalows or timber-panelled rooms in the main house, and all meals are included. Wonderfully welcoming owners Siphean and Mach encourage guests to help on the farm

(paddy harvest June–Dec), or perhaps teach English in the nearby school. Per person $\overline{\$17}$
Mittapheap Guesthouse By the Independence Monument roundabout ☎032 931205, ⓔmaochanna99@yahoo.com. Friendly English-speaking guesthouse with acceptable fan rooms, some with optional a/c. Small charge for hot water ($1–2). Inexpensive food stalls nearby. Fan $\overline{\$6}$; a/c $\overline{\$10}$
Nita Guesthouse On the canal near the boat dock ☎012 955526. Bare, spacious en-suite fan rooms, some with optional a/c in probably the town's most modern guesthouse. A little English is spoken. Free wi-fi. Fan $\overline{5}$; a/c $\overline{\$10}$

EATING

Other than the few restaurants along the lakeside promenade, which produce some elegant **seafood** dishes, including local freshwater lobster (Aug–Nov), eating options are limited. The **market** is a good bet for breakfast, with stalls selling sweet doughnuts, fried bananas, bread and coffee.

Delikes Restaurant Near the market ☎032 454 0345. Dishes range from beef *lok lak* ($2) to spaghetti bolognaise ($3.50) and the only Western breakfast in town. Daily 6am–8pm.
Steung Takeo Street 9 ☎016 404929. This stilted (the

area floods in the rainy season) Khmer restaurant is one of the more atmospheric in Takeo, and serves fish, meat and lobster in various guises (from $4). Also a good place for a beer overlooking the floodplains. The menu's in English. Daily 9am–9pm.

Angkor Borei and around

The pleasantly leafy town of **ANGKOR BOREI**, some 25km from Takeo, sits on the banks of the Prek Angkor, a tributary of the Bassac. It's well known to scholars as where the earliest known example of written Khmer was discovered, and archeological excavations have identified many features of the **pre-Angkorian town**, including a moat 22m wide, a section of high brick wall and numerous extensive water tanks. Unfortunately, there is now little to see of the site apart from the finds in the fine local **museum**.

Angkor Borei can be reached year-round by boat, 20km up a canal and river, an interesting journey through **wetlands** that are home to a variety of waterbirds, with all types of boats coming and going. The museum is the main draw, but you can also explore the excavated Funan-era archeological sites here and at nearby **Phnom Da**.

Angkor Borei museum

Daily 8am–4.30pm; closed in the rainy season • $1
Boats pull up on the riverside near the bridge, just downstream from which, on the same side of the river, a white colonial building surrounded by a large garden houses the well-managed **Angkor Borei museum**, with a diverse collection of ceramics, beads, stone statues, carved pediments from the Funanese era and a photographic exhibition of the excavations. Some stylish sculptures of Vishnu and Shiva line the walls, but the eight-armed Vishnu surrounded by an arc is a reproduction. One highlight is a pediment removed from Phnom Da showing Vishnu reclining on a dragon. Aerial

photos show the extent of the old settlement and identify many of the features being excavated.

Phnom Da
$2

Ironically for a site that has given its name to a style of sculpture, the remains of the temple of **Phnom Da** are now rather bare; everything of value has been removed to the museums in Phnom Penh and Angkor Borei. The ruins remain pretty imposing, however, constructed on top of two 40m-high mounds built to protect the temple from rising waters. Experts differ on the temple's vintage, some believing that it was built in the early sixth century by Rudravarman, others that it dates from later.

Boats moor at the small village at the foot of Phnom Da, where local children will offer to show you up meandering paths to the top of the hill, passing at least three of the site's five caves on the way. On the higher of the two mounds the ancient **Prasat Phnom Da** comprises a single laterite tower, visible from way off and dominating the landscape. The tower's four doorways boast ornate sandstone columns and pediments of carved naga heads, though all but the eastern entrance are false.

On the lower hill, to the west, is a unique Hindu temple, **Ashram Maha Russei**, dedicated to Vishnu and built of grey laterite. Dating from the seventh century, the structure is a temple in miniature, the enclosing walls so close together that there's barely room to squeeze between them. On the outside, a spout can still be seen poking through the wall, through which water that had been blessed by flowing over the temple's linga would once have poured.

ARRIVAL AND DEPARTURE	ANGKOR BOREI AND AROUND

Allow a full day if you want to do justice to both sites, though a half-day trip is sufficient to get a feel for them.

By boat The easiest way to get to both Angkor Borei and Phnom Da is to hire a boat from Takeo's jetty (about $50; 40min; seats up to four). The boat from Angkor Borei to Phnom Da takes about 15min.
By moto In the dry season you can also usually reach Phnom Da by moto from Takeo ($4 return).

CARVED AND PAINTED PANEL, WAT PHNOM, PHNOM PENH

Contexts

History

The study of Cambodia's history is hampered by a lack of records. During the time of Angkor, the texts that filled temple libraries were written on tanned skins or palm leaves, but unfortunately these were not copied by successive generations and none has survived; inscribed stone steles at temple sites usually recorded only aspects of temple life, and even this information ceased to be compiled with the demise of Angkor. But the steles, coupled with accounts by Chinese traders and envoys, have at least allowed historians to piece together something of Cambodia's story up until the late thirteenth century.

Though foreign traders and Western missionaries in Cambodia wrote various accounts after the sixteenth century, these leave substantial periods unaccounted for. More recently, the French documented their protectorate in some detail, but these records were largely destroyed by the Khmer Rouge. What is known of Cambodia's history is thus something of a hotchpotch, and though much has been deduced, even more remains obscure and will probably never be fully known.

Beginnings

The **earliest settlements** so far uncovered in Cambodia date from 6800 BC and were situated along the coast, where the risk of annual flooding was minor and there was a ready supply of food. Hunter-gatherers were living in the caves at Leang Spean, northwest of Battambang, by 4300 BC, cultivating dry-season rice and producing ceramics, which are similar in shape and decoration to those in use today. **Neolithic** settlements uncovered at **Samrong Sen**, in central Cambodia, indicate that by 2000 BC animals had been domesticated and slash-and-burn agriculture developed. Five hundred years later, Cambodia entered the **Bronze Age** when the art of smelting copper and tin was mastered, the ores probably originating from present-day Thailand. By 500 BC, a prosperous **Iron Age** civilization was in full swing: farming, implements and weapons were produced, and skills for working with ceramics, metal and glass were being refined. The population slowly divided: highland dwellers continued growing only rainy-season rice, while lowland settlers farmed the river valleys and coastal strips, where they learned to make use of the floods, conserving water for dry-season irrigation and prospering from the fertile soils deposited.

Funan

The origins of the state of modern Cambodia date back to the first century AD and the emergence of the state of **Funan**, on the Gulf of Thailand, centred on the Mekong delta and spreading across modern-day Vietnam and Cambodia (and, at its apogee, into

6800 BC	2000 BC	1st century AD
Earliest recorded evidence of human settlement in Cambodia	Neolithic settlements at Samrong Sen show evidence of primitive agriculture and domesticated livestock	Origins of the kingdom of Funan, on the Gulf of Thailand, one of Southeast Asia's earliest large-scale civilizations

Thailand and Burma) – an area populated by a mixture of **Mon** and **Khmer** peoples, the latter a dark-skinned tribe who had migrated from the north along the Mekong, and from whom Cambodians today trace their origins.

Virtually all that's known about ancient Funan is what can be gleaned from the scant writings of Chinese merchants and travellers. The state is first mentioned in Chinese chronicles of the third century, and it's known that the Funanese were an affluent, Indian-influenced society, living in wooden stilt-houses thatched with palm, speaking Khmer but writing in Sanskrit. Using engineering skills learned from Indian traders, they dug canals and developed the inland port of Angkor Borei (near present-day Takeo in southern Cambodia); drainage and irrigation channels were cut to allow wet-rice cultivation and provide fresh water. The Funanese also exploited their location on trade routes between India and China: ships had to pay dues to berth and take on fresh water, while warehouses were built to store high-value cargoes – animal hides, rhinoceros horn, spices and gold.

Accompanying the traders arriving from India were Brahmans (Hindu priests), who converted many Funanese to Hinduism. Rich Funanese gained merit by financing temples, while the poor earned theirs by contributing the labour to build them. By the fifth century, shrines had been built on Funan hilltops and kings began to add the Indian suffix *-varman* to their name, meaning "protector".

Funan was partly the architect of its own downfall when, in the late fifth or early sixth century, assuming its position to be unassailable, it increased already steep shipping tariffs. New ports along the coast began to compete, feuds sprang up, and the state fragmented and declined.

Chenla

In the late sixth century, **Chenla**, previously a northern dependency of Funan, gained its independence. Details of the Chenla period are particularly sparse, and (again) such information as there is comes from Chinese sources (the name name "Chenla" is itself of Chinese rather than Khmer origin).

By the seventh century, all references to Funan had ceased and the kingdom of Chenla had established itself, covering an area roughly contiguous with that of present-day Cambodia (and also including parts of Vietnam). Around this time **Bhavavarman I** founded a capital at **Sambor Prei Kuk**, in central Cambodia. He was succeeded by **Ishanavarman I** (reigned 610–625), who founded Ishanapura (named in accordance with the Indian-derived custom of naming a capital by suffixing the king's name with *-pura* – the Sanskrit word for town) and whose state-temple at Sambor Prei Kuk became the largest in Southeast Asia. Although already elderly when he became king, Ishanavarman seems to have succeeded in annexing many smaller states. He was succeeded by his son, **Bhavavarman II**, about whom nothing is known.

The capital tended to change location with each new king. **Jayavarman I** (great-grandson of Ishanavarman; reigned 635–681) ruled over an area extending at least from Battambang to Prey Veng. Although many sanctuaries were consecrated during his reign, none can be specifically attributed to him, and his capital has so far not been identified. Inscriptions indicate that he was an able soldier who succeeded in extending his territory, though he was ultimately killed by invaders, probably from Java, after which the

2nd–3rd century	Late 6th century
Increasing influence of Indian culture and religion on Funan, with many of the region's native Khmer converted to Hinduism. First temples built	The Khmer kingdom of Chenla asserts its independence from Funan. Bhavavarman establishes a new capital at Sambor Prei Kuk

succession passed first to his son-in-law and then to his daughter, **Jayadevi**, one of only a handful of queens in Cambodian history, despite the fact that women were regarded as equals, and inheritance of property, slaves and lands passed through the female line.

The Angkor empire

By the eighth century, Chenla had **divided** into two states, Land (or Upper) Chenla and Water (or Lower) Chenla. In the late eighth century, **Jayavarman II** – generally regarded as the founder of the Angkor empire – appeared on the scene and in 795 declared himself ruler of a kingdom called Kambujadesa, having himself proclaimed a **devaraja**, or "god king" (a tradition followed by subsequent Angkorian monarchs for the next five centuries) in an elaborate ceremony at Phnom Kulen, where he appears to have resided for a period. He also established a new capital at **Hariharalaya** (in the area of present-day Roluos), the first city in the region which would later be known as **Angkor**.

The empire in the ascendant

Jayavarman II was succeeded by his son, **Jayavarman III** (850–877), and then by **Indravarman I** (877–889), who established a pattern of three-fold building work that most subsequent Angkorian kings would emulate. First, he honoured the water gods by creating the Indratataka *baray* (lake) at Roluos; secondly, he built a temple to his ancestors at Preah Ko; thirdly, he erected the Bakong state-temple. Indravarman's son, **Yasovarman I** (889–900) had to fight his brothers to assume the throne, and his reign seems to have carried on in a military vein. After completing the temple of Lolei at Roluos he moved northwest, where he constructed the first state-temple in the Angkor area proper, on the hill of Phnom Bakheng. He followed this by excavating the massive East Baray, more than 7km long and almost 2km wide. He was succeeded by his two sons, **Harshavarman I** (900–922), and **Ishanavarman II** (922–927). Their uncle, **Jayavarman IV** (928–941), became the only Angkorian king to rule from a distance. He ascended the throne when he was already ruling his own state from Koh Ker (see p.192).

After the death of Jayavarman IV, his son **Harshavarman II** (941–944) lasted just a short time before he was ousted by his cousin, **Rajendravarman I** (944–968) who went on to commission the temples of East Mebon and Pre Rup. He also granted land to his guru, Yajnavaraha, to build the beautiful shrine at Banteay Srei. Rajendravarman waged war against the Cham, hailing from the state of **Champa** on the coast of Vietnam, and annexed neighbouring states, making them provinces of the Khmer empire. Rajendravarman I was succeeded by his son **Jayavarman V** (968–1001) who at some point was successful in extending his territory into what is now northeast Thailand.

In 1002, two rivals, Jayaviravarman (1002–10) and Suryavarman I were both proclaimed king. **Jayaviravarman** was subsequently overthrown by **Suryavarman I** (1011–50), during whose long reign further territory was added to the kingdom, with provinces as far away as Lopburi in present-day Thailand paying allegiance to him. Suryavarman I left a substantial legacy including the temple of Preah Vihear; he also built the massive West Baray reservoir, which is still in use to this day. His successor, **Udayadityavarman II** (1050–66), had his work cut out warding off rival claimants to the throne, but still found time to build the huge Baphuon temple. He was succeeded by his brother, **Harshavarman III** (1066–80) and then by **Jayavarman VI** (1080–1107).

Early 7th century	795
Ishanavarman I (reigned 610–625) builds numerous temples at Sambor Prei Kuk, which develops into the greatest of Cambodia's pre-Angkorian capitals	Jayavarman II declares himself devaraja ("god king") and has himself consecrated in an elaborate ceremony at his new capital at Phnom Kulen

Angkor at its apogee

Dharanindravarman I (1107–13), the brother of Jayavarman VI, was soon overthrown by his nephew, **Suryavarman II** (1113–50), possibly the best known of Angkor's kings, thanks to his state-temple, Angkor Wat. A few minor ups and downs apart, his reign marked the beginning of a golden period for Angkor; the empire was at its height, stretching from Champa (in present-day central and southern Vietnam) in the east to Bagan (in present-day Myanmar).

Uncertainty surrounds his supposed successor, **Dharanindravarman II** (1150–60); some writers doubt that he actually ascended the throne, suggesting that he merely ruled over an independent kingdom in the area. He was the **first Buddhist king** of the Khmer, but did not attempt to convert his subjects. He is credited with building Preah Palilay and (with less certainty) the addition of Buddhist carvings to Banteay Samre and Beng Mealea. After him came **Yasovarman II** (1160–65) and then **Tribhuvanadityavarman** (1165–77), who was killed during a Cham invasion of 1177, during which Angkor Thom was sacked and a Cham prince briefly put on the Khmer throne.

Following a brief spell when Angkor was ruled by the Cham, the status quo was restored by **Jayavarman VII** (1181–1218), son of Dharanindravarman II, who won a huge naval battle against the Cham on the Tonle Sap – his success is commemorated in the bas-reliefs of the Bayon. By 1181 had rebuilt Angkor Thom and reunited the country sufficiently to have himself consecrated as devaraja. As well as managing his vast empire, which rivalled that of Suryavarman II, the king is remembered as perhaps the most prolific of all the Angkorian temple-builders, completing Ta Som, Preah Khan, Banteay Chhmar and Neak Pean, as well as a state-temple, the Bayon, consecrated to Mahayana Buddhism.

The decline of Angkor

After Jayavarman VII's death the Khmer empire began to fragment, probably due at least in part to his massive building programme, which had heavily depleted the kingdom's resources. Little is known about the following two kings, **Indravarman II** (1219–43) and **Jayavarman VIII** (1243–95). The Mongols arrived in Southeast Asia during the latter's reign, and he seems to have been prudent enough to send tribute to Kublai Khan. A zealous Hindu, Jayavarman VIII was also responsible for destroying many of Cambodia's Buddhist images.

Legend tells that Jayavarman's beloved daughter took the sacred sword, Preah Khan, and gave it to her husband, causing Jayavarman VIII to abdicate. The tale is mentioned in the writings of the Chinese envoy Zhou Daguan, who spent a year at Angkor in 1296 and left a colourful account of the court. But notwithstanding Zhou's glowing account, the kingdom was dramatically reduced in size by the middle of the thirteenth century, by which time the Thais had ousted the Khmer from Sukhothai, and Lopburi had claimed independence. By the early fourteenth century, the Cham had also reclaimed their independence, leaving what was left of the Khmer kingdom exposed and unable to summon much resistance to Thai invasions.

When the Thais next sacked Angkor in 1432, **King Ponhea Yat** left Angkor, and taking his court with him, set up a new capital in **Phnom Penh**, where he created a number of Buddhist monasteries which still exist today.

Late 9th century	Early 11th century
At Roluos, Indratataka Lake and the Preah Ko and Bakong temples are created during the reign of Indravarman I (877–889). His son Yasovarman I (889–900) builds Phnom Bakheng temple and the great East Baray reservoir	Suryavarman I (1011–50) further consolidates the territory of the Angkor empire, which now stretches as far as Lopburi in present-day Thailand. He also builds Preah Vihear and the West Baray reservoir

Lovek and Oudong

Thai records suggest that the capital may have returned briefly to Angkor around 1467, but by the early sixteenth century **Ang Chan** (1505/1516–56) had set up court at **Lovek**. While the Thais were busy fending off advances from invading Burmese, Ang Chan gathered an army and made a successful attack on the Thais, managing to regain control of towns such as Pursat and Battambang, which had been lost when Angkor was abandoned.

The sixteenth century saw the arrival of the first **Western** missionaries and explorers in Cambodia; though the former were utterly unsuccessful in gaining converts, some of the latter became influential within the Khmer establishment, such as the Spanish adventurers Blas Ruiz and Diego Veloso, whose knowledge of firearms would eventually earn them marriages with Cambodian princesses and provincial governorships under **King Satha** (1575–94). Accounts of the time, by Spanish and Portuguese colonials from the Philippines and Malacca respectively, report multicultural trading settlements at Lovek and Phnom Penh, with quarters for Chinese, Arabs, Japanese, Spanish and Portuguese; the area around these two towns was the most prosperous in the country, trading in gold, animal skins and ivory, silk and precious stones.

The Khmer court continued to face threats from the **Thais**, however, forcing King Satha to ask the Spanish in the Philippines for help, although this aid never materialized and Satha fled to Laos (where he subsequently died), while Lovek was sacked by the Thais in 1594. The succession subsequently passed rapidly to a number of kings, including **Chey Chettha**, who established a new capital at **Oudong**, between Lovek and Phnom Penh, where it would remain for some two hundred years.

Towards the end of the seventeenth century, the **Vietnamese** began to move south into Champa and, before long, into the Mekong delta. Cambodia was now squeezed between two powerful neighbours, and over the next century the royal family aggravated matters by splitting into pro-Vietnamese and pro-Thai factions, the crown changing hands frequently. The populace, without a strong king to look to, paid scant regard to what was said in Oudong, which further aggravated the king's inability to resist invasions.

Events took a turn for the worse in 1767 when a Thai prince sought refuge in Cambodia, intending to set up a government in exile. This incensed the Thai general, Taksin, who launched an invasion, destroyed Phnom Penh and assumed control of Cambodia for several decades. The Thais put a 7-year-old prince, **Ang Eng** (1779–97), on the throne under a Thai regent, and then reinforced their influence by taking him to Bangkok, where he stayed for four years. On his return, he installed himself at Oudong, where he died in 1797, leaving four sons and a lineage that lasts to this day.

The run-up to the French protectorate

Worsening to-ing and fro-ing between the Thais and Vietnamese ultimately led to the Cambodians appealing to France for protection. Ang Eng's eldest son and heir, **Ang Chan**, was only 6 at the time of his father's death and didn't assume the throne for nine years. Meanwhile, the Thais annexed the province of Battambang, which then stretched as far as Siem Reap, and which remained under Thai rule until 1907. By the time he was crowned monarch, Ang Chan (1806–34) had become fervently anti-Thai and

Early to mid-12th century	1177	Late 12th–early 13th century
Suryavarman II (1113–50) commissions the building of Angkor Wat, along with numerous other works. The empire of Angkor now stretches from Burma to Vietnam	Cham invade Angkor and sack Angkor Thom	Jayavarman VII (1181–1218) defeats Cham in a great naval battle on Tonle Sap, rebuilds Angkor Thom and embarks on a spree of construction works including Ta Prohm and the Bayon

requested help from the Vietnamese – who then promptly annexed the whole of the Mekong delta and took effective control of large parts of Cambodia, with the king reduced to a puppet ruler. In 1812, Ang Chan relocated the court to Phnom Penh, from where he proceeded to send secret emissaries to Bangkok, assuring them of his continued allegiance.

The Thai king, Rama III, decided in the early 1830s to re-exert his influence on Cambodia and, seizing upon the opportunity provided by the death of the Vietnamese viceroy in 1832, sent in an army to oust the Vietnamese – who had already left by the time Thai troops arrived, taking Ang Chan with them. The Thais sought to install as king one of Ang Chan's two brothers who had been living in exile in Bangkok, but later abandoned the idea, unable to gain any popular support for either. The Vietnamese, keeping Ang Chan under close supervision, returned to Phnom Penh a couple of years later; he died shortly afterwards, leaving no male heir. They duly installed Chan's second daughter, **Mei**, as queen (1835–41), thinking she would be malleable, and set about imposing Vietnamese culture and customs on the Cambodians. Their disregard for Theravada Buddhism and their attempts to enforce the use of the Vietnamese language sowed deep resentment, and anti-Vietnamese riots flared repeatedly from 1836.

Losing their patience, the Vietnamese blamed Queen Mei for their own failure to install a disciplined Vietnamese-style administration, and arrested her in 1840; though the Cambodians had not liked being forced to accept a Vietnamese-appointed queen, they now resented her detention and rioted again. Thai troops poised on the border marched in and forced the Vietnamese out, and despite sporadic skirmishes the Vietnamese never regained control. They withdrew from Cambodia in 1847; the following year, Chan's brother, **Duang** (1848–59), was crowned king at Oudong with full Buddhist ceremony.

Meanwhile, the **French** had arrived in Southeast Asia, but were rebuffed in their attempt to establish trading arrangements with Vietnam. On the pretext that French missionaries were being persecuted, they invaded the Mekong delta, annexing the southern provinces of Vietnam. In Cambodia, Duang feared another Vietnamese invasion and asked the French for help; they eventually sent a diplomatic mission but it was turned back before it could reach him at Oudong and Duang died before any discussions could be held, leaving it to **Norodom** (1859–1904) to agree a treaty with the French in 1863.

The French protectorate

Norodom's **treaty** with France afforded Cambodia French protection in exchange for wide-ranging mineral and timber rights, along with freedom for the French to preach Christianity and to move around the country. Having signed the treaty, however, Norodom continued the double-dealing of his predecessors, and continued secretly to reassure the Thais of his loyalty to Bangkok.

With riots flaring in the provinces against Norodom and his French allegiances, the French pressed for a new treaty allowing them to install administrative **residents** in all provincial centres – effectively taking over the day-to-day running of the country. Rebellion sprang up across the nation, which the French, even with the assistance of Vietnamese troops, had difficulty in quelling. Despite this resistance a new treaty was

13th century	1432
Gradual decline of Angkor under Jayavarman VII's successors. Hinduism is once again in the ascendancy, with many Buddha images defaced or destroyed. Thai forces regain large swathes of territory formerly ruled from Angkor	Thai forces sack Angkor. King Ponhea Yat abandons the ancient city and establishes a new capital at Phnom Penh

signed in 1886, eroding much of Norodom's power and allowing the French to collect taxes and to have residents installed in ten provincial towns.

Towards the end of the century Norodom, already an **opium addict**, became ill, and the French *résident supérieur* was granted permission from Paris to assume executive authority. By the time Norodom died in 1904, France was effectively ruling Cambodia. Norodom's compliant half-brother **Sisowath** (ruled 1904–27) was installed on the throne, the French having passed over Monivong, Norodom's son and natural heir. Sisowath, a figurehead, had little impact on affairs during his reign.

By the early part of the twentieth century, the French were disillusioned with the Cambodians, whom they regarded as indolent and corrupt. Consequently, they did little to develop Cambodia's human resources (the most tangible legacy of their ninety-year rule is arguably the country's communications network, including more than 5000km of roads and a railway line from Phnom Penh to the Thai border). Instead, the French filled key clerical positions with Vietnamese, who also ran many of the small businesses and took labouring jobs. Meanwhile, the ethnic Chinese, who had been established in Cambodia for centuries, continued their lucrative trades as bankers and merchants.

This neglect of the Khmer, and the crippling taxes levied by the French, bred resentment to which the French, in their complacency, remained oblivious. They were shocked when revolts against taxation broke out in 1916, and doubly horrified when Felix Bardez – the French resident in Kompong Chhnang – was **beaten to death** by locals in 1925 while investigating resistance to tax payments in a provincial village.

World War II

The **Japanese invasion** of Southeast Asia in 1941–42 brought little change to the status quo in Indochina, where the Japanese allowed the (now Vichy) French to continue administering the day-to-day running of the country. The Thais, who were allies of the Japanese and who sensed a degree of vulnerability in the French position, took the opportunity to launch attacks across the border into Cambodia, with the aim of recovering the provinces of Battambang and Siem Reap, reluctantly given up to Cambodia earlier in the century. The French roundly defeated the Thai navy, however, forcing the Japanese to save Thai face by compelling the French administration to hand over the provinces for a nominal sum. **King Sisowath Monivong** blamed the French for this loss of territory and refused to deal with them again – although in fact this wasn't to be for long, since he died shortly afterwards. The Japanese allowed the next king to be chosen by the French who, seeking a compliant successor, passed over Monivong's son in favour of his youthful and inexperienced grandson, **Norodom Sihanouk**, who was crowned in September 1941.

Despite their hands-off approach in Indochina, the Japanese were supportive of anti-colonial feeling, partly to gain support for their own presence. The effect of these sentiments would become manifest after the Japanese surrender in August 1945, by which time they had dissolved the French administration.

Towards independence

Though the French had reinstated their officials by the end of 1945, the prewar status quo was never quite restored. The Thai government were now funding anti-Japanese

---

Early 16th century	1594	1767
Ang Chan (ruled 1505/1516–56) establishes new court and capital at Lovek	Continuing Thai incursions culminate in the sack of Lovek. King Chey Chettha establishes a new capital at Oudong	Thai general Taksin invades Cambodia, ransacks Phnom Penh and assumes control of the country

and anti-French causes, and anti-royalist Cambodian groups in exile began to gather along the Thai border. A year later these factions had banded together to form the essentially left-wing **Khmer Issarak**, a band of fledgling idealists that grew into a powerful armed guerrilla movement that waged something approaching a war of independence against the French; between 1947 and 1950, the Khmer Issarak actually controlled fifty percent of the country.

The seeds of the movement had been sown back in the 1930s with the opening of Cambodia's first high school, the **Lycée Sisowath** in Phnom Penh, whose students soon began to question the standing of educated Khmer in a country where Vietnamese dominated the middle levels of the administration. When the first Khmer-language **newspaper**, *Nagara Vatta*, was launched (Khmer had hitherto been used only for the publication of religious texts), it was aimed at these newly educated Cambodians, propounding Khmer nationalist views. The editors were allied to the *sangka* (the Buddhist clergy), led by Phnom Penh's **Institut Bouddhique**, the backbone of Buddhism in Cambodia, which had taken responsibility for most education until the opening of the *lycée*.

When Sihanouk requested Cambodia's independence late in 1945, the French (afraid of losing their grip on Indochina) reluctantly agreed to allow elections and the formation of a National Assembly, but refused to contemplate full independence. Thus, for the first time in Cambodian history, political parties were created, **elections** held (in 1946) and a new government formed. The election was resoundingly won by the democratic (and anti-royalist) party, Krom Pracheathipodei, which adopted a constitution along the lines of that of republican France; Sihanouk, although he retained his throne, was left virtually powerless. Late in 1949, Cambodia was granted **partial independence**, though the French continued to control the judiciary, customs and excise and foreign policy, and retained the right to maintain military bases in the country.

Frustrated by his lack of political power and the residual French grip on the country, in June 1952 Sihanouk staged a **coup**, dismissing the cabinet, suspending the constitution and appointing himself prime minister; in the early months of 1953 he declared martial law and dissolved the National Assembly. Sihanouk then took the first of what was to become a habitual series of trips abroad "for his health" – in reality to lobby the French in Paris to withdraw and grant Cambodia full independence. With France fighting a losing battle in Vietnam against the communist Viet Minh, the French government eventually did an about-face, and on **November 9, 1953**, Cambodia duly celebrated full independence.

The Sihanouk era

Cambodians were ecstatic at achieving **independence**, and Sihanouk was feted as a national hero. The following year, accords were signed in Geneva laying down the terms of French withdrawal from Indochina. Key points included the disbanding of the Khmer Issarak, Cambodian **neutrality** and the **partition of Vietnam** at the seventeenth parallel into what would become communist North Vietnam and the non-communist South Vietnam.

Early on, it was clear that Sihanouk, though politically adept, would change sides at the drop of a hat to achieve his ends, driven by an unassailable belief that, having won

1779	Early 19th century	1812
Ang Eng (1779–97) is installed as king under Thai patronage, establishing a royal lineage which endures to this day	Thai forces seize Battambang, while the Vietnamese annexe the Mekong delta, leaving the Cambodian monarch, Ang Chan (ruled 1806–34), increasingly helpless	Ang Chan moves the royal court to Phnom Penh

independence for Cambodia, he should be the one to run it. He needed the adulation of his public and took to making trips to the countryside, where he made lengthy orations, believing that his "children", as he referred to the people, supported his policies. However, for impoverished farmers, who formed the majority of the population, independence had made no change to their subsistence lifestyles.

When Sihanouk's efforts to manipulate the constitution to gain power for the monarchy failed, he surprised everyone by **abdicating** in 1955 in favour of his father Norodom Suramarit, taking once again the title of prince. Gambling on the continuation of massive popular support for himself in the wake of the independence struggle, he set up his own political party, **Sangkum Reastr Niyum**, the Popular Socialist Community (Sangkum for short). The party managed to win all the seats in the National Assembly in the heavily rigged 1955 elections, and Sihanouk's dirty tactics ensured that Sangkum remained unchallenged at the next elections two years later. The monarchy was effectively dissolved in 1960 when King Suramarit died, whereupon Sihanouk became head of state once again – although he continued to be referred to as "Prince Sihanouk", rather than king. Sihanouk was both hard-working and creative – he even found time to produce a number of films that drew upon traditional Cambodian cultures and values – but his conceit and bullying made him difficult to work with. Many right-wing intellectuals, whom the prince perceived as competition, mysteriously disappeared; meanwhile, he toyed with socialism and often favoured the left.

At the same time, in the schools and colleges left-wing teachers such as **Saloth Sar** (later known as Pol Pot) and **Ieng Sary** (so-called Brother Number Three in the Khmer Rouge hierarchy) had become senior Communist Party figures by the early 1960s and were recruiting further members. Another future senior figure in the Khmer Rouge, **Khieu Samphan**, meanwhile hid his communist leanings and joined Sangkum.

In 1963, in yet another of Sihanouk's policy shifts, a government purge of known communists saw Saloth Sar flee Phnom Penh to take up the life of a full-time revolutionary. Along with many others in the Cambodian communist movement, he spent time in Vietnam and China, where he was trained and groomed by communist forces.

The slide towards war

In the late 1950s, with the knowledge of the United States, plots had been hatched against Sihanouk by a paramilitary, right-wing, anti-Sihanouk group, the **Khmer Serei** (led by a former editor of *Nagara Vatta*), who were recruited and supported by the Thai and South Vietnamese governments. Although these events compounded his distrust of the pro-American Thais and South Vietnamese, Sihanouk continued to court the US and accept American military aid – while at the same time forming an alliance with China, who were anxious to prevent US dominance in the area. Subsequently, in another abrupt change of direction, in mid-1963 Sihanouk accused the US of supplying arms to the Khmer Serei, and later that year ordered all US aid stopped. The same year, Sihanouk nationalized banking, insurance and all import-export trade.

The economy was soon destabilized by the combination of Sihanouk's policies and the spillover into Cambodia of the conflict between North and South Vietnam.

1832	Mid-19th century	1863
Thai monarch Rama III sends an army into Cambodia to expel Vietnamese forces – who flee in advance of the invasion, taking Ang Chan with them	French forces invade the Mekong delta and annexe southern Vietnam	King Norodom (1859–1904) signs first treaty with French, securing French protection in return for wide-ranging concessions

POL POT

The contemptible Pot was a lovely child.

Loth Suong, Pol Pot's older brother

The factors that turned **Pol Pot** from a sweet-natured child into a paranoid mass-murderer will probably never be fully understood. He was born **Saloth Sar** in 1928 at Prek Sbaur, near Kompong Thom, where his father was a prosperous farmer. Sent to live with his brother, Loth Suong, in Phnom Penh, at the age of 6, he had a relatively privileged upbringing – the family was well connected through a cousin, who was a ballet dancer at the royal court. Academically, Saloth Sar was unremarkable, and it was probably thanks to the influence of his cousin rather than through aptitude that he was chosen to attend the newly opened Collège Norodom Sihanouk in Kompong Cham in 1942 – Sar subsequently left without passing a single exam. He went on to study at the Lycée Sisowath in Phnom Penh, and his academic performance must, at some point, have improved as, in 1949, he was among a hundred students chosen to study in France.

In Paris, Sar joined the French Communist Party (along with his friends Ieng Sary and Khieu Samphan) and was exposed to radical new ideas; he also met Khieu Ponnery, a highly educated Cambodian woman who was to become his first wife. Returning to Cambodia in 1952, Saloth Sar joined the Vietnamese-run Indochina Communist Party and set about campaigning for the socialist cause in Cambodia. Imperceptibly, he began veiling himself in secrecy, isolating himself from his family, keeping a low profile and beginning to use an alias, "Pol". An ardent member of the newly created **Cambodian Communist Party**, he appeared content to work in the lower ranks, giving seminars and recruiting for the cause through his job as a teacher. Those who met him at this time remarked that he was a kind-hearted and mild-mannered – albeit enigmatic – figure. Without ever seeming to promote himself, he rose steadily through the party ranks, from lowly assistant to Party Secretary.

By 1963, Sihanouk's support for the socialists had turned to persecution, and Saloth Sar, along with other key party members, was forced to flee the capital and seek refuge on the border with Vietnam. Moving frequently, the Cambodian communists were supported first by their North Vietnamese comrades, and later by the Chinese – whom "Pol" visited on several occasions and held in great esteem for the "success" of their Cultural Revolution. Isolated in the northeast by the escalating Vietnam War, "Pol" had ample time to develop his own plan for a better state, run on Marxist-Leninist principles. Living simply in the jungle he developed great admiration for the peasant's life, and by the time the revolutionaries – now dubbed the **Khmer Rouge** – had gained control of Cambodia in 1975, he was probably reasonably certain of his formula for returning to a basic agrarian society and the implementation of his (ultimately disastrous) "Four Year Plan".

Sihanouk was forced into a delicate **balancing act** to preserve some semblance of neutrality and avoid Cambodia being drawn into the Vietnamese conflict. In 1963, he broke off relations with South Vietnam, (which was receiving financial and military support from the US), though US planes were allowed to fly over Cambodia in the mid-1960s on their way to bomb North Vietnam Meanwhile Sihanouk had been unable to prevent North Vietnam sending men and arms via Cambodian territory to the communist **Viet Cong** guerrillas in South Vietnam, leaving him little option but to sign a secret agreement with the North Vietnamese in 1966, allowing them safe passage.

1904	Early 20th century
Death of King Norodom. The French install his half-brother Sisowath (ruled 1904–27), although the monarchy is increasingly reduced to a ceremonial figurehead	Crippling taxes imposed by the French and widespread Vietnamese immigration and influence lead to disillusionment

Ever secretive, the Khmer Rouge leaders, rather than expose themselves as individuals, now hid behind a collective name, the mysterious **"Angkar"** – the central committee of the "Organization", as the leaders now referred to the party. This committee comprised thirteen members (eleven men and two women), its unchallenged head being Pol Pot, as Saloth Sar was by now known (it isn't known why he chose this pseudonym, which has no meaning in Cambodian). He was also known as "Brother Pol" and, after his appointment as prime minister of Democratic Kampuchea (1976), as **Brother Number One**. Other leading members of Angkar were Pol Pot's long-standing comrade and second in command, Nuon Chea (Brother Number Two); and Pol Pot's friends from his student days, Ieng Sary (Brother Number Three) and Khieu Samphan, the party frontman.

Increasingly suspicious, the cadre were convinced that they were surrounded by traitors. The party was subsequently **purged** of "enemies", with around twenty thousand comrades and their families interrogated and murdered at the Toul Sleng torture prison (interrogation at Toul Sleng was reserved for those who were close to the leadership – in fact, most were loyal party members). While it's not clear whether Pol Pot directly ordered the interrogations and killings, it is certain that he was fully aware of, and probably supported, them. Whether or not he ever felt remorse isn't known, but he certainly refused to acknowledge responsibility – instead, when the atrocities were exposed by liberating Vietnamese forces in 1979, he accused the Vietnamese of being the perpetrators. Choosing to flee rather than face the Vietnamese army, he escaped to Thailand. He never doubted that the path he had chosen for Cambodia was the right one, believing instead that he had been betrayed by those whom he had trusted.

Sentenced to death by a Cambodian tribunal in absentia, Pol Pot lay low and remained at liberty in Thailand. In the mid-1980s, Khieu Ponnery went insane; Pol Pot divorced her in 1987 and married again, fathering his only child, a daughter called Malee. At some point, probably around 1993, Pol Pot crossed back into northern Cambodia where, surrounded by loyal supporters in the relative security of a Khmer Rouge enclave in the vicinity of Anlong Veng, he organized guerrilla attacks against the newly elected Cambodian government. Meanwhile, Ieng Sary, who had been waging a disruptive guerrilla war against the government from Pailin, defected in 1996. This must have come as a blow to Pol Pot, and signalled the end of the Khmer Rouge. Just a year later, an increasingly paranoid Pol Pot ordered the murder of his long-standing friend, Sun Sen and his family; for this murder, he was tried by his own people and sentenced to life imprisonment. Eleven months later he was dead – apparently in his sleep from natural causes – his body was cremated a few days later on a pile of rubbish and old tyres.

Bizarrely, Pol Pot has something of a cult status among Cambodians, and the site of his cremation near Anlong Veng is now a tourist attraction.

Meanwhile, in the northeast of the country, the CPK (Communist Party of Kampuchea) – or the **Khmer Rouge**, as Sihanouk dubbed them – comprising Cambodian communists who had been sheltering in North Vietnam, began a campaign of insurgency. Ironically, the Khmer Rouge probably owed their eventual victory to the US, who launched a vast, covert bombing programme, code-named **Operation Menu**, over supposedly neutral Cambodia, aimed at destroying communist bases and supply lines in the southern provinces of Cambodia along the border with Vietnam. All in all, more than half a million tonnes of ordnance were dropped on the country in three thousand raids between March 1969 and January

1925	1945
Felix Bardez, the French resident in Kompong Chhnang, is beaten to death by locals infuriated by French rule	End of World War II and Japanese surrender. The French attempt to reimpose their rule, but agree to allow national elections and the formation of a national assembly

1973, which had the effect of forcing communist Vietnamese deeper into Cambodian territory and thus alienating provincial Cambodians, causing them to side with the CPK.

Lon Nol takes charge

Elected prime minister in 1966, **General Lon Nol** had been regarded as Sihanouk's man but began to shift his position in response to unrest among a military upset by a lack of equipment and supplies, and a middle class dissatisfied with the prince's economic policies. Plots continued to be hatched against Sihanouk, and in 1970, while he was out of the country, Lon Nol headed a coup, removing the prince as chief of state, abolishing the monarchy and renaming the country the **Khmer Republic**. Sihanouk broadcast an impassioned plea from Beijing, begging his supporters to fight Lon Nol, but the Chinese persuaded him to join with the communists whom he had forced into exile in 1963 to form an alternative government.

At home, details of Sihanouk's secret treaty with the North Vietnamese surfaced, and the elimination of their supply trail from Cambodian soil became a national preoccupation. Thousands of Cambodians joined the army to help, but they were poorly trained and ill equipped (despite renewed US financial support, which served only to feed widespread corruption). In the event, the Cambodians were no match for the battle-hardened Vietnamese, and after tens of thousands of Cambodians died in fighting, Lon Nol called a halt to the offensive in 1971.

The **Khmer Rouge** meanwhile were battling towards Phnom Penh. In 1970 they already controlled an estimated twenty percent of Cambodia, primarily in the northeast and northwest; by the end of 1972, all but Phnom Penh and a few provincial capitals were under their control. Although heavy US bombing brought a momentary halt to their advance in 1973, they pushed steadily forward; refugees fled to Phnom Penh ahead of their advance, bringing with them tales of whole villages being slaughtered. The stories were dismissed by the capital's inhabitants as unfounded, and all blame was laid at the door of the Vietnamese. By early 1975, Phnom Penh was surrounded, access to the rest of Cambodia was cut off and the US was flying in supplies to the besieged city. Endemic corruption and constant warfare had taken its toll on the people, and when the communists walked into Phnom Penh on April 17, 1975 they were greeted with relief. On April 30, the last Americans withdrew from Saigon, just ahead of North Vietnamese forces, and US military involvement in Indochina came to an end.

It's believed that **more than 300,000 Cambodians** were killed as a result of the four years of fighting against the Vietnamese and the Khmer Rouge, coupled with indiscriminate bombing by the US. Sihanouk's worst fears had been realized, but this was nothing compared to what was to come.

The Khmer Rouge era

The Khmer Rouge had its roots in the Khmer People's Revolutionary Party (**KPRP**), formed in the early 1950s. As well as appealing to anti-monarchist elements, the KPRP attracted young Cambodians who had been exposed to communist ideals while studying in France. Three of these rose to powerful positions in the Khmer Rouge: Saloth Sar – later known as **Pol Pot** – who rose to the exalted rank of "Brother Number

1946	1947–50
The first elections in Cambodian history lead to the formation of a new government under Krom Pracheathipodei	The left-wing Khmer Issarak guerrilla movement launches attacks against French forces and gains control of large swathes of Cambodian territory

One"; his contemporary, **Ieng Sary**, subsequently foreign minister of Democratic Kampuchea; and **Khieu Samphan**, the future party chairman.

When the Khmer Rouge arrived in Phnom Penh, they set out to achieve their ideal: a nation of **peasants** working in an agrarian society where family, wealth and status were irrelevant. Family groups were broken up, money was abolished and everyday life – down to the smallest detail – was dictated by **Angkar**, the secretive revolutionary organization behind the Khmer Rouge. Within hours of entering Phnom Penh, the Khmer Rouge had begun to clear the city; within a week the capital was deserted. In other towns around Cambodia (now renamed **Democratic Kampuchea**) the scenario was repeated, and practically the whole population of the country was displaced. **Forced labour** was deployed in the fields or on specific building projects supervised by party cadres. The regime was harsh and nutrition inadequate; hundreds of thousands perished in the fields, dying of simple illnesses and starvation. Almost immediately after seizing power, the Khmer Rouge began a programme of **mass execution**, though the twisted logic that lay behind this has never been made clear. Senior military commanders were among the first to die, but before long it was the turn of monks, the elite, the educated, those who spoke a foreign language, even those who wore glasses.

Prince Sihanouk, his wife and family had returned to Phnom Penh from exile in Beijing in mid-1975; they lived out the rest of the Khmer Rouge years under virtual house arrest.

As time went on, the regime became increasingly paranoid and began to look inward, murdering its own cadres. It's estimated that between one and two million people, around **twenty percent of the population**, died under the Khmer Rouge. Those who could escape fled to refugee camps in Thailand or to Vietnam, but the majority had no option but to endure the three years, eight months and twenty days – as any older Cambodian will still say today – of Khmer Rouge rule, and to which they still refer as *samai a-pot*, the Pol Pot era.

The Khmer Rouge's eventual **downfall** was orchestrated by their original mentors, the Vietnamese. Frequent border skirmishes initiated by the Khmer Rouge irritated the Vietnamese, who sent troops into Cambodia in 1977, though this incursion lasted just a few months. The final straw for the Vietnamese came when the Khmer Rouge massacred Vietnamese villagers along the border in early 1978. This caused Vietnam to begin supporting anti-Khmer Rouge factions, a shift that led to the formation of the Khmer National United Front for National Salvation, or **KNUFNS**. On December 22, 1978, a Vietnamese invasion force of more than 100,000 entered Cambodia, and just seventeen days later they had taken Phnom Penh. The leaders of the Khmer Rouge made their escape just ahead of the invading forces, Pol Pot by helicopter to Thailand, the rest crowded onto the train north to Battambang. Following their leaders, Khmer Rouge troops and villagers loyal to them retreated to the jungles along the northwest border.

The Vietnamese era

Although opinions about the **Vietnamese era** are divided between those who call them liberators and those who call them occupiers, no one disputes that they were widely

1952	1953	1963
King Sihanouk stages a coup, dismissing the government and appointing himself prime minister	Cambodia achieves full independence from the French, now embroiled in fighting in Vietnam	Government-led communist purges lead to Saloth Sar and several other future Khmer Rouge leaders fleeing Phnom Penh to become full-time revolutionaries

welcomed, their arrival saving countless Cambodian lives. The Vietnamese found the country starving and devastated, the infrastructure shattered. Cambodia now became the **People's Republic of Kampuchea** (**PRK**), as the Vietnamese formed an interim government in Phnom Penh made up of members of the KNUFNS; the president was Heng Samrin, an ex-Khmer Rouge divisional commander, and its foreign minister another ex-Khmer Rouge member (and future Cambodian prime minister), **Hun Sen**, who had fled to Vietnam in 1977.

Under the PRK, markets, schools, freedom of movement and private farming were re-established immediately, and by the following year, the use of money and religious practice on a limited scale were reintroduced. Nevertheless, the formation of the PRK caused many educated Cambodians, who had no intention of suffering more communist rule, to flee to Thailand, where they swelled the already bursting refugee camps; by 1981, 630,000 refugees had descended on Thailand (many of them Khmer Rouge) and a further 150,000 were living in Vietnam.

Although coverage of Cambodia's plight brought limited aid from the West, the havoc wrought by the Khmer Rouge was in general disregarded by the major powers, who deemed Cambodia to be occupied under the Vietnamese and consequently **ostracized** the PRK (the USSR and India were notable exceptions). Safe in Thailand, Pol Pot was supported by the Thai, Chinese and US governments, all ardently against the communist Vietnamese, as the prime minister of the legitimate government. As news of the Khmer Rouge atrocities surfaced, his supporters preferred to continue to punish Vietnam; bizarrely, the Thais and Chinese fed, clothed, trained and even rearmed Khmer Rouge soldiers, while UN agencies were allowed to look after Khmer Rouge in their camps, but were prevented from helping the decimated population of Cambodia.

As a counterweight to the PRK, the **Coalition Government of Democratic Kampuchea** (**CGDK**) was created as a government-in-exile in Thailand in 1982. It comprised Prince Sihanouk, persuaded to join by the Chinese, and his FUNCINPEC party; Son Sann, a previous prime minister of Cambodia and leader of the Khmer People's National Liberation Front (KPNLF); and members of the Khmer Rouge. Although the CGDK shared a common aim to rid Cambodia of the Vietnamese, they had no mechanism for achieving it. The Khmer Rouge had the superior military forces and sent frequent sorties across the border into Cambodia where they were repelled by the Vietnamese and PRK. After particularly harsh fighting in 1983–85, the PRK went on a mine-laying spree along the border with Thailand in an attempt to prevent these forays – the start of the **land-mine scourge** which still plagues Cambodia today.

The Vietnamese withdrawal and its aftermath

Vietnam had never considered the occupation of Cambodia to be a long-term goal, and while in charge had trained the Cambodian army in preparation for its own withdrawal. With the crisis in Eastern Europe building up, the USSR drastically reduced aid to the PRK government, making the occupation too expensive for the Vietnamese to sustain, and by the end of September 1989 they had withdrawn completely; shortly afterwards, the PRK government renamed the country the **State of Cambodia (SOC)**. Meanwhile, the government had altered the constitution to institute Buddhism as the state religion and allowed people the right to own, trade

1966	1969–73
Sihanouk signs secret agreement with Viet Cong guerrillas in South Vietnam allowing them access to Cambodian territory	The US launches massive, covert bombing raids over Cambodia in attempt to target Viet Cong, with huge civilian casualties. At the same time, the emerging Khmer Rouge begins a campaign of insurgency

LAND-MINE LEGACY

Land mines are supposed to maim rather than kill, but more than a quarter of Cambodians injured by mines die of shock and blood-loss before reaching hospital. For those who survive – more than forty thousand Cambodians have become **amputees** as a direct result of land-mine injuries – the impact of an injury on their families is financially devastating, emotional consequences aside. To meet the costs of treatment, their families usually have to sell what few possessions they have, reducing them to an extreme poverty from which they seldom recover. For **young female** mine victims, the stigma is often unbearable: being disabled means that they are frequently unable to find a husband and have to remain with their families, where they may be reduced to the status of slaves. The more fortunate amputees have access to a **prosthetics** workshop where, once their injury has healed sufficiently, they can receive a false limb. However, even if they are subsequently able to get a place at a skills or crafts training centre, there's no guarantee of employment once they've completed their training, and without the capital to set up on their own, land-mine victims all too often find their prospects little improved.

In Cambodia, international and domestic **NGOs** are undertaking the delicate, painstaking task of mine clearance. Trained crews of Cambodians (many of whom are the widows of land-mine victims) work hard to inform rural communities in heavily contaminated areas of the **dangers** of mines, which are more subtle than might appear: during the rainy season, mines which are buried too deep to go off can move towards the surface as the land floods, rendering previously "safe" territory risky.

The actual process of mine clearance is slow and expensive. As yet no mechanical system is available that is reliable enough to allow land to be declared as cleared. So, once a minefield has been identified, the site is sealed off and divided into lanes for trained **personnel**, lying on their stomachs, to **probe** systematically every centimetre of ground for buried objects, using a thin blade. The mines thus detected are carefully uncovered and destroyed, usually by blowing them up in situ. Given that as many as six million land mines (according to some estimates) have still to be removed, the scale of the problem is easily appreciated.

and inherit property. This was all very well, but the country was virtually bankrupt; practically no aid was being received, electricity and fuel were in short supply, and even basic needs such as health care couldn't be provided. Corruption, although not on the scale of earlier regimes, was still rife: the nouveaux riches built spacious villas, drove smart cars and ate out in restaurants, while the majority of Cambodians could barely afford rice. On the borders, a black economy thrived, with gems and timber flowing out, and consumer goods – which commanded a premium price on the home market – coming in.

Meanwhile, the Khmer Rouge was stepping up guerrilla activities, capturing Pailin in 1989. During 1990 they consolidated their position along the Thai border and regularly encroached further into Cambodia, destroying bridges, mining roads and raiding villages; by the end of that year they controlled the jungle areas to the northwest and southwest, going so far as to threaten Sihanoukville and Kampot. In the middle of that year, however, first the US, then China, **withdrew support** from the Khmer Rouge, which was to prove something of a turning point: a ceasefire was declared in July 1991, and in October a conference was held in **Paris** to discuss the country's future.

1970	1975	1975–78
Prime Minister Lon Nol stages coup against Sihanouk. Sihanouk forms a government-in-exile in Beijing	The Khmer Rouge capture Phnom Penh and drive the capital's population out into the countryside	Khmer Rouge rule in Cambodia. Millions are executed or die as the result of starvation or disease

To the millennium

Thirteen years of war should have come to an end with the Paris conference, at which a number of agreements were reached. The central idea was to establish an interim coalition government for Cambodia, the **Supreme National Council**, pending United Nations-supervised elections. But the Khmer Rouge had other ideas and, still supported by Thailand, continued to create insurgency around the country, unsettling an already shaky peace.

UNTAC

The United Nations Transitional Authority in Cambodia, **UNTAC**, was created to stabilize the country and supervise the promised elections, though its forces didn't arrive in Cambodia until March 1992, and even then they were deployed slowly, allowing the Khmer Rouge to expand the area under its control. Refusing to lay down arms or be monitored, the Khmer Rouge continued with disruptive attacks, mining roads and railways, intimidating villagers and murdering ethnic Vietnamese; they also refused to stand in the elections. The return of refugees proceeded relatively peacefully, at least.

Costing $2 billion, the UNTAC mission (numbering 22,000 military and civilian staff) was, at the time, the most expensive operation ever launched by the UN, though it's debatable just how successful it really was. The international forces (from around a dozen countries, including Indonesia, India, Ghana, Uruguay, Pakistan and Bangladesh) were ill prepared for their role as peacekeepers – many were only trained for combat. Often criticized for insensitivity, many of the UNTAC forces – unaccustomed to the high salaries they were being paid – led high-rolling lifestyles, paying well over the odds for even basic services. At the time, business boomed, only to collapse when UNTAC withdrew; a fledgling tourist industry started up (albeit limited by the guerrilla tactics of the Khmer Rouge); and prostitution mushroomed – UNTAC did not test staff for HIV and, rightly or wrongly, is widely blamed for the AIDS epidemic now affecting Cambodia. Today, Cambodians' feelings about UNTAC remain ambivalent. Some say that it failed to restore peace – and created more problems than it solved. Others suggest that without UNTAC the country might well have fallen again into Khmer Rouge hands.

The return of constitutional monarchy

The elections of July 1993 saw a turnout of nearly ninety percent, despite being marred by intimidation and political killings. However, even though the **FUNCINPEC** party – headed by Sihanouk's son **Prince Ranariddh** – emerged with a majority, the interim government, now led by former Khmer Rouge battalion commander **Hun Sen**, refused to cede the authority they had held since 1979. In the event, a government was formed which had two prime ministers, Prince Ranariddh and Hun Sen. A **constitutional monarchy** was reinstated, and Prince Sihanouk persuaded to resume the throne he had abdicated in 1955, although without being given any direct say in government.

Political infighting soon led to the government being dominated by the **Cambodian People's Party** (**CPP**) of Hun Sen, which had retained control of police, defence and provincial governments, and Prince Ranariddh became little more than a figurehead. The tensions between the two prime ministers grew until mid-1997, when fighting

1978	Early 1980s
Vietnamese forces invade Cambodia, driving out the Khmer Rouge. Former Khmer Rouge cadre Hun Sen assumes leadership under Vietnamese patronage	Pol Pot takes refuge in Thailand, while enjoying the support of the US and Chinese governments suspicious of Communist Vietnam's intentions

broke out on the streets of Phnom Penh, resulting in many deaths, and Prince Ranariddh, who had just left the country, was ousted by Hun Sen in the **coup of July 1997**. Foreseeing a bloody struggle, many foreign workers fled the country and investors hurriedly pulled out, leaving projects half-completed, bills unpaid and thousands out of work; the Asian financial crisis of the time only exacerbated matters.

The **1998 elections** were the first to be self-administered post-Khmer Rouge. In addition to the CPP and FUNCINPEC, the elections were contested by the **Sam Rainsy Party**, a breakaway association of ex-FUNCINPEC members (for all the proliferation of parties, there remains little real ideological difference between them, although FUNCINPEC is generally regarded as royalist, the CPP as "communist", and Sam Rainsy as "democratic"). The CPP won the majority of the seats in the Assembly, but failed to achieve the required two-thirds of the vote to form a government, and a tense few months ensued until another coalition was formed, with Hun Sen as prime minister and Prince Ranariddh as speaker of parliament.

The end of the Khmer Rouge

Outlawed in 1994, the Khmer Rouge started to suffer **defections** to the government almost immediately. Nevertheless, they retained control of the north and northwest of the country, where their leaders remained in hiding, amassing immense wealth from the proceeds of illegal logging and gem mining. Their guerrillas continued to stage random attacks, kidnapping and murdering foreigners and Cambodians, while their presence prevented access to many parts of Cambodia and deterred tourists and investors alike.

The ultimate demise of the Khmer Rouge came a step closer in 1996 when, after striking a deal of immunity from prosecution, **Ieng Sary**, erstwhile Brother Number Three, and two thousand of his troops defected to the government side, leaving a last rebel enclave, led by Ta Mok and Pol Pot, isolated in the north around Anlong Veng and Preah Vihear. An internal feud led to Pol Pot being tried by a court of his comrades in July 1997 for the apparent attempted murder of a cadre. Some nine months later he was dead, though it remains unclear if this was due to natural causes or whether he was murdered; whatever the truth, he was hastily cremated in Anlong Veng. Late in 1998, **Khieu Samphan**, who had been the public face of the Khmer Rouge and president of Democratic Kampuchea, and **Nuon Chea**, Brother Number Two, gave themselves up to the authorities. Anlong Veng was effectively returned to Cambodian jurisdiction the following year. **Ta Mok**, "The Butcher", was arrested attempting to cross to Thailand in March 1999, and finally, in May the same year, Kang Kek Leu, alias **Duch**, the notorious commandant of Toul Sleng torture prison, was tracked down and arrested.

The new millennium

The **elections** of 2003 were acknowledged as having been the most successful to date. Although they were won, unsurprisingly, by the CPP, opposition parties were well represented, with the Sam Rainsy Party (SRP) – the nearest the country had to a liberal party – and FUNCINPEC polling enough votes between them to stop the CPP forming a government. The resulting stalemate lasted the best part of a year, and it wasn't until June 2004 that Hun Sen and Prince Ranariddh agreed to form a coalition.

1989	1990	1993
Vietnamese forces withdraw from Cambodia. The Khmer Rouge retake Pailin and establish themselves in areas around the Thai border	China and the US withdraw support for the Khmer Rouge	Sihanouk's son Prince Ranariddh wins national elections – but is forced into a coalition with Hun Sen

A new king

In October 2004, just days before his 82nd birthday, Norodom Sihanouk surprised the country by abdicating on the grounds of age and ill-health. Prince Ranariddh had already ruled himself out of the succession (which is not hereditary in Cambodia) and the hurriedly assembled Throne Council quickly selected the sole surviving son of Norodom Sihanouk and his wife, Monineath, **Norodom Sihamoni** – an uncontroversial choice.

National **elections** were held again in 2008. As expected, Hun Sen's CPP retained power with almost 60 percent of the vote, while Sam Rainsy finished in second place with just under 22 percent – most would say it did as well as could be expected. Observers claimed that the elections were free(ish) and that there was less violence than in any of the previous elections.

Tensions with Thailand resurfaced in later 2008 as both countries moved troops into the disputed regions around **Preah Vihear** temple (see box, p.198), with soldiers on both sides being killed in exchanges of cross-border fire – while relations soured still further in early 2009 when Cambodia refused to extradite former Thai prime minister Thaksin Shinawatra, appointing him a government economic advisor instead. At the same time the notorious governor of Toul Sleng prison, **Duch**, the first of five prominent Khmer Rouge leaders arrested in 2007 (see box opposite), went on trial for war crimes.

The year **2012** was something of a watershed for Cambodia. In July, Thailand and Cambodia agreed to withdraw troops from around Preah Vihear, paving the way for a resolution of the conflict and the return of peace to this troubled area. More or less simultaneously, the three last surviving members of the Khmer Rouge hierarchy finally went on trial for war crimes, while in October Cambodia's self-proclaimed "King Father", Norodom Sihanouk, died in Beijing of a heart attack, just a few days before his 90th birthday, marking the end of an era in modern Cambodia.

The 2013 elections and after

The sense of a new chapter was reinforced by the **elections of July 2013** – the fifth and most controversial in the country's recent history. Results showed a massive swing against Hun Sen's ruling CPP, although they still secured a slender victory with 68 seats compared to runner-up Sam Rainsy, whose Cambodian National Rescue Party (CNRP) won all remaining 55 seats. Widespread voting irregularities had been reported even before the elections were held, however, and given the closeness of the poll (48 versus 44 percent of the vote) Rainsy declared that he and his party were unable to accept the results. Hun Sen's CPP government, meanwhile, refused calls by both the CNRP and international community to address reports of electoral malpractice.

Mass demonstrations were held in September and December 2013 in Phnom Penh and elsewhere protesting the election results and other social concerns – a kind of Cambodian Spring in which a long-suffering populace finally rose up against a long-serving and increasingly dictatorial and self-serving leader. Protests have continued sporadically through to the time of writing, with several demonstrators being killed in clashes with police in early 2014. Rainsy's promise of a rise in the government minimum wage has struck a chord with impoverished voters, becoming a major issue in the ongoing protests, while his tub-thumping anti-Vietnamese rhetoric has also played well with the local electorate – although less well with Cambodian

1996	1997	1998
Leading Khmer Rouge commander Ieng Sary defects to the government side, taking two thousand cadres with him	Hun Sen launches a coup against Prince Ranariddh; riots on the streets of Phnom Penh	Death of Pol Pot in Anlong Veng, in mysterious circumstances

THE KHMER ROUGE ON TRIAL

In 2001, after considerable procrastination, the Cambodian government reluctantly formed a tribunal to investigate former Khmer Rouge leaders for **war crimes** and **crimes against humanity**. Five of the regime's former supremos were eventually arrested in 2007, charged and held in detention pending trial. (A sixth leading Khmer Rouge potentate, **Ta Mok**, popularly known as "The Butcher", had already died, with exemplary timing, in 2006.)

Justice has been excessively slow in coming, however, and of the five arrested only **Duch**, former head of the notorious Toul Sleng prison (see p.71), has so far been convicted. Duch's trial began in March 2009 and lasted more than a year before he was found guilty and sentenced to 35 years (commuted to 19 years) imprisonment – subsequently extended in 2012 to life, following an ill-fated appeal.

The long-awaited trial of the other defendants finally got under way in mid-2012. Of the four remaining accused, **Ieng Sary**, Pol Pot's brother-in-law, died in March 2013 before the end of the trial (his wife and fellow defendant **Ieng Thirith** had already been ruled mentally unfit to stand trial due to progressive Alzheimer's and released in 2011). The trial of the two remaining commanders, **Nuon Chea**, Brother Number Two, and **Khieu Samphan**, the public face of the Khmer Rouge, finally concluded in October 2013, with a verdict being expected in early 2014 – if either is still alive (they are now aged 87 and 82 respectively). Both Chea and Samphan have expressed regret over the atrocities committed during the Khmer Rouge period, but both continue to staunchly protest their innocence and lack of personal involvement in the crimes of which they stand charged.

Vietnamese, who have found themselves threatened and their properties attacked at the hands of mobs inflamed by Rainsy's nationalist posturing. Whether the authoritarian rule of Hun Sen (now in office for almost thirty years) and his grip on power will be weakened, and the CPP forced into concessions and reforms, is still unclear.

Modern Cambodia faces many challenges. In spite of being supported by hundreds of millions of dollars of aid every year, improvements in basic living conditions have been slow in coming. Essentially an **agricultural** nation, Cambodia has never had much of a manufacturing base, although investors tempted by a plentiful supply of cheap labour have set up garment and shoe factories in Phnom Penh, Sihanoukville and Bavet. Some city-dwellers may have seen a modest improvement in their standard of living, but the majority of rural Cambodians still lack clean water, electricity, and adequate health care, while **land mines** and unexploded ordnance continue to maim hundreds of villagers each year. Endemic **corruption** remains a fact of life, while the systematic destruction of the environment and uncontrolled **logging** (with proceeds going directly to the ruling elite) have already transformed large swathes of formerly beautiful and biodiverse countryside into a sterile monoculture of cash-crop plantations. Aid donors repeatedly try to get tough, but their warnings are consistently ignored. The country's ever-expanding **tourism** industry remains one beacon of hope, offering increasing numbers of Cambodians the possibility of advancement, education and economic security thanks to the work of numerous socially enlightened hotels, restaurants, tour operators and NGOs. Such schemes are, necessarily, only a small solution to a wider problem, and to what extent the embattled government of Hun Sen and his cronies (or their possible successors) can succeed in providing a decent quality of life for Cambodia's long-suffering populace remains to be seen.

2007	2009–11	October 2013
Several Khmer Rouge supremos including Ieng Sary, Duch, Ta Mok and Khieu Samphan arrested, pending trial	Repeated clashes with Thailand in and around the disputed temple of Preah Vihear	Conclusion of Khmer Rouge trials, although of the original defendants only Nuon Chea and Khieu Samphan now survive

Religion and beliefs

Buddhism influences practically every aspect of Cambodian life, as is evident from the daily gifts of food made to barefoot, saffron-robed monks, and the dedication to preparing for major festivals, when pagodas take on a carnival air. However, it was Hinduism that predominated among the Khmer from the first until the early fourteenth century, and much temple art and architecture is influenced by the Hindu cosmology.

Islam is the most widespread of Cambodia's minority faiths, being practised by the Cham community. **Christianity**, introduced by missionary groups, has failed to make much impact. **Buddhism** in Cambodia is noticeably less dogmatic and formal than in Thailand or Myanmar/Burma, and the age-old traditions of paying respects to **spirits** and deceased **ancestors** survive, so woven into the fabric of Cambodian life that at times there is no clear line between them and local Buddhist practice.

Hinduism's historical role

Hinduism was introduced to the area by the Brahman priests who accompanied Indian traders to Funan around the first century, and was adopted by the majority of the pre-Angkorian and Angkorian kings. Even today, **Hindu influences** play an important cultural role in Cambodia: two Hindu epics, the *Ramayana* and (to a lesser extent) the *Mahabharata*, form the basis for classical dance and shadow-puppet performances and a subject for contemporary artists.

The Hindu creed is diverse, encompassing a belief in **reincarnation**, the notion of **karma** (the idea that deeds in one life can influence status in subsequent reincarnations), a colourful **cosmology** – including a vast pantheon of gods. The three principal deities are **Brahma**, the creator and lord of all gods; **Vishnu**, the benevolent preserver who regulates fate; and **Shiva**, the destroyer, who is responsible for both death and rebirth. Shiva was especially worshipped in the form of a **linga**, a phallic stone pillar. Frequently these linga were carved in three sections, the square base representing Brahma, the octagonal middle corresponding to Vishnu, and the circular top symbolizing Shiva. Just as linga were frequently a melding of the triad of gods, so the **Harihara**, a popular deity of the pre-Angkorian era, melded the characteristics of both Shiva (on the right-hand side of Harihara images) and Vishnu (on the left).

In the ninth century, Cambodian Hinduism was pervaded by the **devaraja cult** introduced by Jayavarman II. The idea was that, on ascending the throne, the king created an image (consecrated to Shiva or Vishnu) that was installed in the main sanctuary of his state-temple. On his death the king was believed to become one with the god and to be able to protect his kingdom from beyond the grave.

Buddhism

Buddhism has its origins in India, developing out of Hinduism around the sixth century BC, when the teachings of prince-turned-ascetic **Siddhartha Gautama** became popular. Born to a royal family in Lumbini, in present-day Nepal, around 560 BC, Gautama was protected from the sufferings of the outside world and knew nothing other than the comfortable life of the court, where he married and fathered a son. When he reached the age of 29, however, curiosity caused him to venture out of the palace, where he encountered an old man, a sick person, a funeral procession and a monk begging for alms.

Horrified by what he had seen, Gautama undertook to give up his life as a prince, leaving the palace and taking up the simple life to see if he could discover a way to end suffering. Having sought out different religious instructors to no avail, he eventually adopted a programme of self-denial, fasting almost to the point of death, until he finally understood that this austerity only perpetuated the suffering he was trying to resolve. On three successive nights, while meditating under a bodhi tree, he received revelations leading to his **enlightenment**: on the first night he saw his former lives pass before him; on the second night he understood the cycle of life, death and rebirth; on the third, the four holy truths of suffering were shown to him.

Rather than passing straight to **nirvana** – a state free of suffering – as was his right as one who had attained Buddhahood, he remained on earth to spread the **dharma**, the doctrine of the **Middle Way**, encompassing the Four Noble Truths (see below) and avoiding both the extremes of self-indulgence and self-denial. He preached his first sermon at Sarnath, near Varanasi in northern India, and spent the rest of his life travelling and teaching.

Mahayana and Theravada

Soon after the Buddha's death at the age of 80, his followers met to agree a consensus on his teachings, which were passed on by word of mouth. By the time another meeting of this type was called a hundred years later, variations had crept in (indeed Buddhist teachings weren't written down until around 100 BC), leading to a schism: two schools of Buddhism developed, Theravada and Mahayana. **Mahayana Buddhism** propounds that nirvana is accessible to everyone, and not confined only to a few ascetics. It also holds that nirvana can be attained with the help of **bodhisattvas** (literally "enlightened beings"), future Buddhas who, rather than entering nirvana, have chosen to remain in one of the various Buddhist heavens in order to assist other beings along the road to enlightenment. Such bodhisattvas are worshipped in their own right as compassionate deities. One example is Lokesvara (the local name for Avalokitesvara, as he's usually known), whose image appears on the towers of the Bayon and elsewhere.

In contrast, **Theravada Buddhism** (the dominant form of the religion in modern Cambodia) does not accept the concept of the bodhisattva and holds that enlightenment can only be attained by following a lengthy path of meditation, making nirvana practically unattainable even for monks, let alone lay people. Ancient Theravada Buddhist texts tell that seven Buddhas have already been to earth, the most important of whom was Gautama, with one left to come, though later texts say that nearly thirty Buddhas would appear (but only one per historic period). Among Buddhist countries, it is only in Myanmar/Burma, Cambodia, Laos, Sri Lanka and Thailand that Theravada Buddhism dominates.

Doctrine

Buddhism aims to release individuals from the endless cycle of birth, death and rebirth. Each life is affected by the actions of the previous life, and it is possible to be reborn at a higher or lower status depending on earlier actions. By right thoughts and deeds, individuals accrue **karma**, or merit, in this life towards the next world and the next reincarnation.

At the heart of Buddhist teachings are the **Four Noble Truths**, revealed to the Buddha under the bodhi tree. The first is that all of human life is suffering. The second, that suffering results from desire (the need for possessions, company, food, even for rebirth) or ignorance (doing the right things, but in the wrong way). The third states that suffering can cease and that the cycle of reincarnation can be broken.

The fourth truth lays down the path by which suffering is removed, namely the **Eightfold Path**, comprising right knowledge (an understanding of the Four Noble Truths); right attitude (a quiet mind free from desire, envy and greed); right speech (truthful, thoughtful words); right action (good moral conduct); right occupation (one's way of life must not harm others); right effort (good actions develop good thoughts and deeds); right mindfulness (carefully considered actions, speech and mental attitude); and right composure (concentration and focus). The Eightfold Path fosters morality, spirituality and insight without austerity or indulgence; much store is set by meditation, putting away the dramas of everyday life to achieve a calm, untroubled mind.

Buddhism in Cambodia

In Cambodia, Mahayana Buddhism survived side by side with Hinduism from the days of Funan, both creeds having been brought by Indian traders. Buddhism was not, however, widely adopted until the twelfth century when, under Jayavarman VII, it briefly replaced Hinduism as the state religion. With the passing of Jayavarman VII, Hinduism experienced a brief resurgence in the early thirteenth century, but thereafter it was **Theravada Buddhism** that gripped the population, though the reasons for the change are unclear. **Monasteries** were founded, acting as schools and libraries, and serving as guardians of the national religion, language and moral code. They also provided other social services such as care for the elderly and sick.

In 1975, the Khmer Rouge banned all religion, destroying or desecrating temples, texts and statues, and persecuting Buddhist monks – fewer than three thousand out of an estimated 65,000 monks survived the regime. Buddhism was tolerated, if not encouraged, during the Vietnamese occupation, and reinstated as the national religion in 1989. Today, Buddhism is practised by some 95 percent of the country's population.

The sangha

Monks play an important role in Cambodian life, and it's not uncommon for Cambodian men to enter the **sangha**, or monkhood, for a period in their lives, often between the ages of 13 and 15 or upon the death of a parent (in the not so distant past this was seen as a right of passage, making men fit for marriage and raising a family). This ordination can be for quite short periods, perhaps a couple of months, or (reflecting modern times) even just a day. Novices are ordained in the rainy season, when their heads are shaved and they receive their saffron robes, comprising the *sampot ngout*, the undergarment; a *sbang*, covering the lower body; a *hang sac*, a garment with

---

WATS

A **wat** (often, if confusingly, described in English as a "pagoda") is essentially a temple-monastery, although the term is frequently used loosely to refer to any religious structure. Most wats are enclosed by four walls with entrances on each side. At its heart is the **vihara**, the main sanctuary, which contains the most important Buddha images. The vihara is used solely by the monks for their religious ceremonies, and is often kept locked. Separate buildings elsewhere in the wat will house the monks' living quarters and a hall in which meals and religious classes are taken and ceremonies for the laity performed. Also commonly found within pagodas are **crematoria**, reflecting the prevalence of cremation rather than burial, and numerous miniature **chedi** (stupas) containing the ashes of the deceased. Buildings (especially the main vihara) are often colourfully decorated with **murals and carvings** showing scenes from the life of the Buddha or from the various *Jataka* tales, a collection of stories recording the previous lives of the Buddha. Many are donated by rich Cambodians to earn religious merit.

There's no fixed programme of **worship** for Buddhist Cambodians, although many will visit on offering days or as and when they feel the need. Buddhists pay their respects to (rather than worship) images of the Buddha, placing their palms together in front of the chin and then raising them to the forehead while bowing slightly, an action which is repeated three times. It's also usual to light three sticks of incense; if asking for divine assistance, lotus buds are placed in vases near the altar. It is customary for worshippers to leave a donation of a few thousand riel.

many pockets worn over one shoulder; and the *chipor*, a shawl that covers the upper body and is thrown across the shoulders (inside the pagoda, the right shoulder is left uncovered). **Women** are never ordained but can become lay nuns, undertaking various tasks around the pagoda, including looking after the senior monks; often this is a way for older women and widows with no family to be looked after.

Besides practising meditation and chanting, monks have to follow 227 precepts, and undertake daily study of Buddhist scriptures and philosophy. Life in the wat is governed by ten basic injunctions, including not eating after noon, abstaining from alcohol and sexual relations, not partaking of entertainment (television is thus not permitted, though, in Cambodia at least, having a mobile phone and using a computer seem to be allowed), not wearing personal adornments or sleeping on a luxurious bed. The most evident aspect of the monkhood in Cambodia is the daily need to go out into the community to ask for **alms**. Begging monks go barefoot, signifying the simplicity of their lives (the donor should also have bare feet). Donations of money go to support the wat or to pay for transport, while food is collected in bowls or bags, to be shared among all the monks. In return, the donors receive a simple blessing, helping them to gain merit for the next life.

Though monks are not allowed to marry, they are often asked to bless couples who are to be married, and they also officiate at funerals, presiding over the cremation of the body and storage of the ashes at the pagoda. Monks also play a major role in the private religious ceremonies for reasons ranging from alleviation of bad luck to acquiring merit for the next life. These events can involve anything from a blessing at the wat, with elaborate offerings and chanting monks, to making a small offering of fruit or the purchase and release of a small bird from a cage.

Islam and Christianity

Islam arrived with the **Cham**, who fled to Cambodia from Vietnam around the beginning of the eighteenth century; today, the Cham (see p.215) account for some two percent of the population. The most striking thing about Islam in Cambodia is the mixing of the precepts of the faith (the monotheistic worship of Allah, the requirement to pray five times a day and make the pilgrimage to Mecca, and so on) with elements of traditional animist worship – some Cambodian Muslims use charms to ward off evil spirits or consult sorcerers for magical cures. The Cham suffered badly at the hands of the Khmer Rouge: mosques were destroyed or desecrated, and forty thousand Muslims murdered in Kompong Cham alone. After the Khmer Rouge, the Cham were able to resume their religious practices, and Muslim numbers now exceed that of pre-1975. The country's **main mosque**, built with Saudi money in 1994, is in the Boeung Kak area of Phnom Penh and has space for five hundred worshippers.

In spite of the efforts of missionaries and a lengthy period under French rule, **Christianity** is followed by less than one percent of the population. Phnom Penh once had a Catholic cathedral but it was razed to the ground by the Khmer Rouge. More than a hundred Christian NGO and missionary groups operate in Cambodia today, providing services in the fields of education (in particular English-language lessons), health care and rural development. A few years ago, however, the government curtailed their freedom, and now groups have to seek approval before building churches and are banned from proselytizing as a result of reports of children being coerced with sweets and gifts into becoming Christian.

Animism, ancestor worship and superstitions

According to **animist** belief, all things in nature possess an inherent spiritual essence, and offerings of incense, fruit, flowers and water are traditionally made at **spirit houses** to keep the spirits of the natural world happy, and to request good luck or give thanks, particularly before the rice harvest. Spirit houses can be found all over Cambodia (and often in the grounds of Buddhist wats), consisting of anything from simple wooden trays with a tin can filled with incense sticks through to elaborate, wooden or stone affairs resembling miniature temples. Offerings may also be seen laid out at particular trees, rocks and so forth which are considered particularly auspicious either for their beauty or their supposed magical or medicinal properties.

Respect for the **ancestors** is important to most Cambodians. In **chunchiet** culture small wooden funerary figurines are placed on graves to protect the dead. **Buddhists** celebrate their ancestors in the three-day festival of **Bonn Pchum Ben**, in September or October, when offerings are taken to as many as seven pagodas and family picnics are held around the chedi. The homes of ethnic **Chinese** often have two spirit houses, one dedicated to the house spirit, the other to the ancestors; incense is burnt daily to assure good fortune.

Cambodians are highly **superstitious**, regularly consulting fortune-tellers, astrologers and psychics, and even making use of sacred **tattoos** for self-protection. Fortune-tellers are often found at the pagoda, where they give readings from numbered sticks drawn at random or a book of fortunes. Astrologers are key to arranging a marriage and are normally consulted early on to ensure that couples are compatible and to determine the best day for a wedding. The Cambodians also practise a form of *feng shui*, and practitioners are consulted particularly to assess land before purchase and advise on the removal of trees and construction of property.

Books

Until fairly recently books about Cambodia fell into two categories: dry, factual tomes about the temples of Angkor, and harrowing Khmer Rouge-era autobiographies. Coverage of culture and the rest of Cambodia's history was relatively sparse, and novels hardly existed. Now, however, there's an ample choice of contemporary books, but it's still worth seeking out older titles if you are interested in pre-Khmer Rouge history. Titles marked ★ are particularly recommended.

NOVELS, TRAVEL AND CULTURE

Liz Anderson *Red Lights and Green Lizards*. Moving account of early 1990s Cambodia through the eyes of a British doctor who volunteered in the riverside brothels of Phnom Penh and set up the city's first-ever clinic for prostitutes.

★**Robert Casey** *Four Faces of Siva*. Eminently readable 1920s travelogue, in which the author weaves fact and fantasy into his personal discovery of Cambodia's hidden cities. The compelling description of the author's foolhardy trek to explore the remote Preah Khan in Kompong Thom province still resonates today.

★**Karen J. Coates** *Cambodia Now: Life in the Wake of War*. Insightful, anecdotal tales from the time the author spent in Cambodia as a journalist on the *Cambodia Daily*, portraying the lives of ordinary Cambodians and showing how they survive in often distressing circumstances.

Amit Gilboa *Off the Rails in Phnom Penh*. Self-styled, voyeuristic "guns, girls and ganja" foray into the seedy side of Phnom Penh in the mid-1990s.

Gillian Green *Traditional Textiles of Cambodia: Cultural Threads and Material Heritage*. Full-colour study of Cambodian textiles; comprehensively researched and containing a wealth of information on why and how textiles are produced.

Christopher J. Koch *Highways to a War*. This novel embraces the war in both Cambodia and Vietnam; the conflict is given a human touch through the experiences of its intrepid, war-photographer hero.

Norman Lewis *A Dragon Apparent: Travels in Cambodia, Laos and Vietnam*. Though light on Cambodia content, what there is gives a fascinating, all-too-rare glimpse of the country around the time of independence; best of all are the observations of the people and everyday events.

Carol Livingstone *Gecko Tails: Journey Through Cambodia*. Lighthearted account of the life of a would-be foreign correspondent during Cambodia's free-rolling UNTAC era; a bit of politics, some history and a lot of human interest wrapped up in a sensitively told yarn.

Jeff Long *The Reckoning*. Novel with a supernatural bent: a missing-in-action team search the Cambodian countryside for lost comrades; while deep in the jungle a deserted temple gradually gives up the secrets of a disappeared GI patrol, but not without wreaking revenge on those who dare to venture there.

Walter Mason *Destination Cambodia: Adventures in the Kingdom*. Entertaining and insightful travelogue, set mainly in Phnom Penh and featuring an eclectic cast, from Vietnamese transsexuals to monks with dark pasts. A lot better than its lame title would suggest.

★**Henri Mouhot** *Travels in the Central Parts of Indo-China (Siam), Cambodia and Laos*. The first Cambodian travelogue, Mouhot's diary contains a fascinating account of the "discovery" of Angkor Wat in 1856 and was responsible for sparking off Cambodia-fever in nineteenth-century Europe.

Toni Samantha Phim and Ashley Thompson *Dance in Cambodia*. This compact guide crams in information on the history and styles of Cambodian dance, along with a pictorial glossary of traditional musical instruments.

Colin Poole and Eleanor Briggs *Tonle Sap: Heart of Cambodia's Natural Heritage*. Superb photographic record of life, people and nature on the Tonle Sap lake.

★**Geoff Ryman** *The King's Last Song*. Page-turner of a novel about the discovery of an ancient diary etched in gold. The story cleverly interweaves the intrigue of the twelfth-century Angkorian court with the lives of its present-day heroes, an ex-Khmer Rouge soldier and a young moto driver.

Lucretia Stewart *Tiger Balm: Travels in Laos, Vietnam and Cambodia*. A sizeable chunk of this book is taken up with a visit to the poverty-stricken and oppressed Cambodia of 1989, when only the bravest of travellers ventured there; the characters the author meets along the way make this a good read.

Jon Swain *River of Time*. Part love affair with Indochina and part eyewitness account of the fall of Phnom Penh, written by a respected war correspondent.

Connor Wall and Hans Kemp *Carrying Cambodia*.

Delightful photographs of Cambodia's transport system in all its amusing and colourful guises.

Camron Wright *The Rent Collector*. Unexpectedly life-affirming novel about Cambodia's urban poor, set in the vast Stung Meanchey municipal waste dump on the southern edge of Phnom Penh.

HISTORY AND POLITICS

Joel Brinkley *Cambodia's Curse*. Pulitzer Prize-winning journalist Brinkley's damning assessment of the present state of the Cambodian nation under the government of Hun Sen.

★**David Chandler** *A History of Cambodia*. Now in its fourth edition, this is a readable, concise history of Cambodia from prehistoric times to the early twenty-first century by a pre-eminent author on Cambodia.

David Chandler *Voices from S-21*. This thought-provoking book delves into archive material from the interrogation and torture centre at Toul Sleng to attempt an explanation of why such atrocities happened – often neither captive nor interrogator knew what crime had supposedly been committed.

★**Chou Ta-Kuan** *The Customs of Cambodia* (o/p). The sole surviving record of thirteenth-century Cambodia, written by a visiting Chinese envoy Chou Ta-Kuan (Zhou Daguan), with graphic accounts of the customs of the time, the buildings and ceremonies at court.

Ian Harris *Cambodian Buddhism: History and Practice*. A readable, if slightly dry, account of the history and practice of Buddhism in Cambodia to the present day.

Eva Mysliwiec *Punishing the Poor: The International Isolation of Kampuchea* (o/p). Dated but valuable chronicle of how the West ostracized Cambodia after the Vietnamese invasion.

William Shawcross *Sideshow: Kissinger, Nixon and the Destruction of Cambodia*. Starting with a single mission to destroy a North Vietnamese command base believed to be located in Cambodia, this book traces the unfolding of the United States' horrendous clandestine bombing campaign against the country and its subsequent cover-up – compulsive reading.

John Tully *A Short History of Cambodia: From Empire to Survival*. Straightforward – though not as short as the title suggests – history of Cambodia.

ANGKOR

Bruno Dagens *Angkor, Heart of an Asian Empire*. The story of the rediscovery of Angkor Wat and the explorers who brought the magnificent temple to the attention of the Western world, illustrated with old photographs and detailed sketches.

Maurice Glaize *The Monuments of the Angkor Group* (o/p). Classic guide to the temples originally published in 1944, with detailed maps and photographs; read it online or download in full from ⦵ theangkorguide.com.

Geoffrey Gorer *Bali and Angkor: A 1930s Pleasure Trip Looking at Life and Death*. The acidic, condescending comments on everything from transport to temples make it hard to see why Gorer bothered to visit Angkor at all, but his off-the-wall interpretations of the rationale behind Khmer art certainly make for an alternative view to the accepted texts.

★**Claude Jacques and Michael Freeman** *Ancient Angkor*. Superbly illustrated and well-written guide to the monuments of Angkor.

Claude Jacques and Michael Freeman *Angkor: Cities and Temples*. Stunning coffee-table volume featuring fabulous photographs and evocative descriptions of the temples.

Steve McCurry *Sanctuary: The Temples of Angkor*. Magical images of the temples from this renowned photographer.

Christopher Pym *The Ancient Civilization of Angkor* (o/p). Fascinating wander through the life and times of the ancient Khmer, exploring everything from how kingfishers were caught to the techniques used to move massive stone blocks for the building of temples.

Dawn Rooney *Angkor: Cambodia's Wondrous Khmer Temples*. Easy-to-use guide, with good background information and plans for each of the principal temples. Recently republished in a new and considerably expanded sixth edition.

Vittorio Roveda *Sacred Angkor: The Carved Reliefs of Angkor Wat* (o/p). Perfect for temple buffs, this is a detailed study of the reliefs, offering alternative suggestions for their interpretation.

BIOGRAPHY AND MEMOIR

François Bizot *The Gate*. Gripping first-person account of being kidnapped by the Khmer Rouge for three months in 1971; the author's release was attributable to the rapport he built up with the notorious Duch, one of the regime's most murderous henchmen.

David Chandler *Brother Number One: A Political Biography of Pol Pot*. The original work on Pol Pot, this meticulously researched book reconstructs the life of this reclusive subject. The rather scant actual information about him is bolstered by juicy details about other Khmer Rouge leaders.

Nic Dunlop *The Lost Executioner: A Story of the Khmer Rouge*. Duch, the infamous commandant of the Khmer Rouge torture prison S-21, was found living in a remote area of Cambodia. This easy-to-read book reveals details of his life and ponders the rise of the Khmer Rouge, comparing their philosophy to those of Stalin and of the French Revolution.

Adam Fifield *A Blessing Over Ashes*. The author's candid account of growing up in 1980s America with Soeuth, his adopted Cambodian brother, seen from both sides of the cultural gap. Especially touching is the visit to Cambodia, where Soeuth discovers that his Khmer family is still alive.

Bree Lafreniere *Music through the Dark*. Musician Daran Kravanh only survived imprisonment by the Khmer Rouge because the cadre took a liking to his music, often calling him to play his accordion after a day toiling in the fields.

Harish C. Mehta and Julie B. Mehta *Hun Sen, Strongman of Cambodia*. Based on interviews with Hun Sen himself, his family and colleagues, this provides a frank portrait of the man, though the authors have undoubtedly chosen their words carefully.

Vann Nath *A Cambodian Prison Portrait: One Year in the Khmer Rouge's S-21*. A survivor's account of Toul Sleng; Nath, a trained artist, has since used his skills to create a pictorial document of the appalling practices once visited on inmates in the Toul Sleng Genocide Museum.

Haing S. Ngor and Roger Warner *Survival in the Killing Fields*. Harrowing account by a doctor who survived torture by the Khmer Rouge, but was unable to save his wife, who died in childbirth. Fleeing Cambodia, the author eventually reached America, where he won an Oscar for his role as Dith Pran in the film *The Killing Fields*. He was murdered in 1996 by muggers, eight years after this book was written.

Milton Osborne *Sihanouk, Prince of Light, Prince of Darkness*. No-nonsense behind-the-scenes look at the contradictory King-Father. He comes across as a likeable, all-too-human character, if often petulant and egotistical.

★**U Sam Oeur** *Crossing Three Wildernesses*. Poet, scholar, engineer and politician, Oeur not only recounts his enthralling life story in this memoir, but also packs it with details of everyday Cambodian life, historic fact and political intrigue.

Philip Short *Pol Pot: The History of a Nightmare*. Drawing on such first-hand accounts as there are for an in-depth analysis of Pol Pot and the circumstances that allowed the Khmer Rouge to come to power.

★**Loung Ung** *First They Killed My Father*. The author pulls no punches in this heart-rending personal narrative of the destruction of her family under the Khmer Rouge. A sequel, *After They Killed Our Father: A Refugee from the Killing Fields Reunites with the Sister She Left Behind* completes the story.

Khmer

Belonging to the Austro-Asiatic family of languages, Khmer is the national language of Cambodia, and is also spoken in the Mekong delta and pockets of northeast Thailand, as well as forming the basis of the language used at the Thai royal court. Many Khmer words have their origins in two old Indian languages – Sanskrit (which was introduced along with Hinduism during the Funan era) and Pali – while Malay, Chinese, Vietnamese, Thai, French and English have all added to the language's development.

Although in the major towns and tourist centres English is increasingly spoken (particularly by the younger generation who learn it at school and often take private lessons to develop this sought-after skill), learning even a few words of Khmer will go a long way to endearing you to Cambodians; off the beaten track you'll find it especially helpful to know some basic Khmer phrases. Fortunately, it is a relatively easy language to get to grips with, being **non-tonal** and relatively simple in its grammar. Sentences follow the subject–verb–object pattern of English, although, as in French, adjectives are added after the noun. Khmer verbs don't conjugate, and tenses are indicated by the addition before the verb of a word indicating the time frame; *nung*, for instance, indicates an action taking place in the future. Articles and plurals aren't used in Khmer (quantity is indicated by stating the number or using general terms for "some" or "many").

Khmer **script** is an artistic mix of loops and swirls, comprising **33 consonants** and **23 vowels**; the vowels are written above and below the consonants and to either side. Capital forms of the letters exist, but are seldom used. In writing, words run left to right with no spaces in between; sentences end with a little symbol that looks a bit like the numeral "7", playing the role of a full stop. **Transliteration** into the Roman alphabet is not straightforward, and differences in approach account for many of the variations on maps and restaurant menus. The rudiments of a system were developed during the French protectorate, though this is rarely employed nowadays.

Pronunciation

If you are trying out your language skills, the Cambodians will do their best to understand you and will patiently repeat words for you to copy. **Regional dialects** present a challenge, as many words are quite different from the formally correct words spoken in Phnom Penh. Another problem is that Cambodians often abbreviate their sentences, missing out many words, chopping them short and changing words and

---

LANGUAGE PRIMERS

The most widely available primer is the long-running *Colloquial Cambodian*, with book plus CD; alternatively, the interactive *Talk Now! Learn Khmer* CD-ROM is another good resource. The *Foreign Service Method Khmer Basic Course* (available at ⓦ multilingualbooks.com) is for those wishing to delve deeper. In Phnom Penh, at Psar Thmei and Psar Toul Tom Poung, you can buy the excellent *Seam & Blake's English–Khmer* pocket dictionary, which lists words in Khmer script and in Roman transliteration.

A free **iPhone app** (also available as an iPod-compatible MP3 download) with a fifteen-minute Khmer language lesson and fifty introductory phrases is available at ⓦ journals .worldnomads.com/language-guides. It's also worth searching for "learn Khmer" on **YouTube**.

phrases around – and that some sounds in Khmer have no English equivalent. Cambodians use intonation for emphasis, but while you're learning Khmer it's best to keep your speech somewhat monotonous in order to avoid causing misunderstanding.

CONSONANTS

Most consonants in our transliteration scheme are pronounced as they would be in English, though note that consecutive consonants are pronounced individually. The following combinations should also be noted:

bp sharp sound, between the English "b" and "p".

dt sharp sound between the English "d" and "t".

gk guttural sound between the English "g" and "k".

ng as in sing; often found at the beginning of words.

ny as in canyon.

VOWELS

a as in ago.

aa as in bar.

ai as in tie.

ao or **ou** as in cow.

ay as in pay.

e as in let.

ea as in ear.

ee as in see.

eu is similar to the French fleur.

i as in fin.

o as in long.

oa as in moan.

ohs as in pot (the **hs** is practically silent).

oo as in shoot.

OO as in look.

ow as in toe.

oy as in toy.

u as in fun.

Useful words and phrases

The polite **form of address** for men is "*loak*", for women "*loak srei*"; in a formal situation Cambodians will often introduce themselves with one of these two terms, then give their full name with the family name first. Although you will be asked your name a lot as you travel around, Cambodians do not really use names in everyday situations, preferring to use a range of respectful forms of address. These terms can be either polite or familiar depending on the situation, and are used even when meeting someone for the first time. The choice of term depends not only on whether the person being spoken to is male or female, but also on whether they are older or younger than the speaker. An older person is often (both politely and familiarly) addressed as either *yeah* or *dah* (grandmother or grandfather), or *ming* or *boh* (auntie or uncle), depending on just how much older they are than the speaker. When speaking to someone younger, *kmoouy bprohs* or *kmoouy srei* (nephew or niece) can be used, or more familiarly, *bpohn bprohs* or *bpohn srei* (younger brother or sister). Take your lead from the Cambodians and listen to how they address you or other people.

GREETINGS AND CIVILITIES

hello (formal/informal)	chum ree-eu-bp soo-a/ soo-a s'day	(formal/informal) see you later	haowee chewubp kynear t'ngai keraowee
welcome	swah-ghOOm		
how are you?	nee'ak sok sa bai gee-ar dtey?	please if you please	som unchurn
I'm well/fine	k'nyom sok sa bai	thank you	or-kOOn
goodbye	chum ree-eu-bp lear/lear	excuse me/sorry	som dtohs

BASIC TERMS AND PHRASES

yes (spoken by a male/female)	baht/jahs	large or big little or small	tom toight
no	dtay	come/go	mow/dhow

to have (also used for "there is/are")	mee-un	I don't have any children	k'nyom ot towan mee-un
sleep	gayn	I have one child/two children	k'nyom mee-un gk'cone moi/bpee
take	daea	where are you staying?	nee'ak s'nak now ai nar?
what is your...?	nee'ak...ai?	can you speak English/ Cambodian?	nee'ak jehs nit-yaiy pia -sar onglai/k'mair roo dtay?
...name	ch-moo-ah		
...nationality	jon-jee-ut		
where do you come from?	nee'ak mau bpe pro-teh nar?	I know (can speak) a little	k'nyom jehs tick-tick
I am from...	k'nyom mau bpe pro-teh...	I don't understand	k'nyom s'dabp men baan/k'nyom ot yull
Britain	onglais	how old are you?	a'yup bpon-maan chnam?
Ireland	ear-lond	not yet	ot toe-un
US	amei-rik	I don't know	k'nyom ot dung
Canada	kana-daa	there aren't.../we don't have...	ot mee-un...
Australia	orstra-lee		
New Zealand	nyew seelend	none left/finished	ohs haowee
are you married?	nee'ak riep-ghar hauwee roo now?	it can't be done	ot baarn
		no problem	ot banyaha
how many children do you have?	nee'ak mee-un gk'cone bpon maan nee'ak?	just a minute/please wait a minute	som jam bon tick

GETTING AROUND

where are you going? (also used as a general greeting)	dtow nar?	west	dteu khang leh'j
		bus	laan tom
		cyclo	see-klo
I am going to a/an/the...	k'nyom dtow...	minibus	laan dubp-bpee gonlaing
I want to go to a/an/the...	k'nyom chong dtow...	motorbike taxi	motodubp/moto
where is the...?	...now ai nar?	pick-up	laan nee-san/laan ch'noo-ul laan gk'bah
airport	jom nort yoo-un hohs/ drang yoo-unhohs	taxi	dtak-see
bus station	seta-nee laan kerong	express boat	karnowt lou-en
taxi stand	seta-nee laan dtak-see	slow boat	karnowt
train station	seta-nee roteh pleung	small boat	dtook
jetty	gkumpong bpai	where do I buy a ticket?	k'nyom trouw ting sambort now ai nar?
bank	t'nee-a-geer		
embassy (Thai/Lao/ Vietnamese)	sa-tarn-toot (tai/lao/ vietnam)	how much to go to...?	dtow...bpon maan?
		will you go for...?	dtow...baan tday?
guesthouse	pteah sumnat	...per person	...moi nee'ak
hotel	sontdakee-a/owhtel	does this...go to?	laan neeh mee-an dtow...dtay?
market	psar		
money changer	gonlaing dt'loi	when does the... depart?	...neeh je-ny dtow maung bpon maan?
museum	sarat montee		
pharmacy	farmasee	how long does it take to get to...?	doll...o'h bpon maan maung?
police station	bpohs bpoli		
post office	bprey-sa-nee	is the...far away?	...che-ngai dtay?
restaurant	porjarnee-a tarn/restoran	it's (not) a long way	(ot) che-ngai
shop	harng	how much to hire... outright?	ch'noo-el teeyeng oughs...nee'ak yor bpon maan?
go straight	dtow dtrong		
please stop here	som choap tee neeh		
(turn) left/right	(bot) ch'wayng/s'dam	don't pick up any other passengers	kgom to-tooel nee'ak dhum-now tee-et dtoh
north	dteu khang jeung		
east	dteu khang kea-et	do you agree to the price?	dumlai neeh baan dtay?
south	dteu khang tb'ohng		

is this seat vacant?	gonlaing neeh dohs dtey roo dtay?	what's wrong with the vehicle?	laan neeh koit dtay?
it's vacant	dohs dtey	I need to stop to go to the toilet	k'nyom som choap bot cheung
it's taken	mee-un nee'ak		

ACCOMMODATION

do you have any rooms?	nee'ak mee-un bontobp roo dtay?	a mosquito net	moohng
		a telephone	toora-saap
do you have a single room	bontobp sum-rab moi nee-ak	the room key	souw bontobp leik
room with two beds	bontobp graiy bpee	toilet paper	gro-dahs
with...	mee-un...	a towel	gkon-saing
air conditioning	maa-sin dtro-chey-at	how many nights will you stay?	nee'ak s'nak now tee neeh bpon maan yoobp?
bathroom	bontobp dtuek	can you clean the room?	som sum-art bontobp neeh baan dtay?
fan	dong harl		
hot water	dtuek g'daow	can I move to another room?	k'nyom som doa bon-tobp?
toilet	bong-kgun		
window	bong-ooit	this room is...	bontobp neeh...
how much is it per night?	moi yoobp bpon-maan?	full of mosquitos	mee-un moohs che-raan
can I see the room?	som merl baan dtay?	too noisy	telong payk
can you discount the price?	johs bon-tick baan dtay?	do you have a laundry service?	mee-un bauk cao-aow?
can I have...?	k'nyom som...?	do you have a bicycle/ motorbike for rent?	mee-un kong/moto sum-rabp ch'ooel?
a blanket	bphooey		

SHOPPING AND CHANGING MONEY

where do they sell...?	gay mee-unloo-uk ...now ai nar?	toothpaste	t'nam doh t'meny
		washing powder	saa-bo bowk cao-aow
do you have...?	nee'ak mee-un...?	what do you call this?	neeh how awaiy?
candles	dtien	how much does it cost?	telai bpon maan?
cigarettes	baar rai	very expensive!	telai nahs!
clothes	cao-aow	what is your best price?	dait bpon maan?
medicine	t'nam	can you go down a bit?	johs bon tick baan dtay?
mosquito coils	took dot	I only have riel/dollars	k'nyom mee-un dtai riel/ dol-lar
silk	soort		
soap	saa-boo	I want to change money	k'nyom chong dow loi
souvenirs	kgar-dow/soo-ven-neer		

EMERGENCIES AND HEALTH MATTERS

help!	choo-ee	I need a doctor	k'nyom trauv ghar gkroo pay-et
thief	jowl		
my passport has been stolen	brum-dain/pa'hport rebohs k'nyom gai lou'it	I have...	k'nyom mee-un...
		a fever	gkrun
I have lost my...	k'nyom bat lik-khet ch'long...	diarrhoea	rey'ak
		pain	choohs
my pack/suitcase is missing	gkar-borb/val-lee trauv bat	where is the toilet?	mee-un bong-khun now ai nar?
there's been an accident	mee-un kroo-ah t'nak	are there any land mines here?	gon-laing neeh mee-un min dtay?
please take me to hospital	som june k'nyom dtow mon-tee pey-et	I'm lost	k'nyom vung-veing plaow
please call an ambulance	som hao laan pay-et		
I am not well	k'nyom men se-rooel kloo-un dtay		

NUMBERS

zero	sohn	forty	si-sep
one	moi	fifty	hahs-sep
two	bpee	sixty	hohk-sep
three	bpai	seventy	jet-sep
four	bpoun	eighty	bpaet-sep
five	bphrahm	ninety	cow-sep
six	bphrahm-moi	one hundred, two hundred, etc	moi-roi, bpee-roi
seven	bphrahm-bpee/bpel		
eight	bphrahm-bpai	one hundred and one	moi-roi moi
nine	bphrahm-bpoun	one thousand, two thousand, etc	moi-bpouhn, bpee-bpouhn
ten	dhop		
eleven, twelve, etc	dhop-moi, dhop-bpee	ten thousand	moi-meun
twenty	m'pay	one hundred thousand	dhop-meun
twenty-one, twenty-two, etc	m'pay-moi, m'pay-bpee	one million	moi-leuhn
		first, second, etc	dte-moi, dte-bpee
thirty	sam-sep		

TIMES AND DATES

The time is generally expressed by stating the word for hour, then the hour itself, then the number of minutes past the hour and the word for minute; thus 5.05 is rendered *maung bprahm, bprahm nee-ar tee*. Morning, afternoon or night are added to confirm the right time. In business the 24-hour clock is usually used, and months are referred to by number – thus October is *kai dhop*.

what's the time?	maung bpon maan?	Wednesday	t'ngai bot
hour	maung	Thursday	t'ngai brou-hohs
minute	nee-ar tee	Friday	t'ngai sok
morning	bpel p'ruk	Saturday	t'ngai sou
noon	t'ngai terong	Sunday	t'ngai ah-tet
afternoon	bpel rohsiel	last/next/this...	...mun/k'raowee/neeh
evening	bpel l'ngeit	week	ah tet
night	bpel yob	month	kai
day	t'ngai	year	chnam
today	t'ngai neeh	now	ailouw neeh
tomorrow	t'ngai sa-ait	later	bpel k'raowee
yesterday	m'sell-mine	not yet	ot t'w-an
Monday	t'ngai jarn	just now	a-bany mainy
Tuesday	t'ngai ong-keeya	already	hauwee

A food and drink glossary

As most Khmer dishes are ordered simply by stating what type of food you want to eat and how you'd like it prepared (thus stir-fried pork with ginger is *sait jerook cha khyay*), we've listed Khmer terms for various ingredients and standard cooking methods; a few specific dishes are also listed by name. To specify that a particular ingredient should *not* be added to your food, prefix the item in question with *ot dak* (without) – thus if you don't want sugar in your drink, say *ot dak skar*.

COOKING METHODS AND GENERAL TERMS

...cha	stir-fried...	...dot	roasted...
...cha knyay	stir-fried...with ginger	ma-horb	food (prepared)
...jew aim	sweet-and-sour...	nOOm-bpang	bread
...ang	grilled...	pong	egg

pong mowan	hen's egg	skar	sugar
pong dteer	duck's egg	bong ai'm	dessert
be jaing/msow sobp	monosodium glutamate (MSG)	k'nyom poo ahs	I'm vegetarian
		ot bpah'aim	not sweet (useful when
m'rik	pepper		ordering drinks)
um-beul	salt		

MEAT, POULTRY AND FISH

g'dam	crab	sait jerook	pork
kongaib	frog	sait mowan	chicken
ot yoh kroeng knong	offal, intestine or gizzard	trei	fish
sait dteer	duck	trei muk	squid
sait gow	beef		

VEGETABLES (BON LAI)

bpenh pohs	tomato	pgar katnar	cauliflower
bpowrt sngaow	sweet corn	pset	mushroom
draw sok	cucumber	sal-lat	lettuce
dumlong barang	potato	spei	cabbage
gee	herbs	sun dike	beans
k'tum barang	onion	sun dike bon dohs	bean sprouts
k'tum	garlic	sundike day	peanuts
karot	carrot	tro-ab	aubergine/eggplant
mteahs	chilli	trokooen morning	glory
mteahs plouwk	capsicum		

SOUPS (SOMLAR/SOP), STEWS (KOR) AND CURRIES (KA-REE)

amok trei	mild fish curry cooked in banana leaves		can be made with chicken),
kaar	stew made with pig's trotters		complemented by pineapple, tomato
sop chhnang day	fondue-like dish, cooked in a clay pot at the table		and lotus flower stems, sometimes with
somlar mjew gruoeng	slightly spicy soup made with beef, deer or		added egg
	chicken, along with	somlar ngam ngouw	lemon broth
	lemon grass, turmeric	somlar khtiss jerooet	clear chicken or fish soup
	and galangal	somlar troyoung jayk sait mowan	chicken with banana-flower soup (variations
somlar mjew vietnam	Vietnamese sour soup, usually based on fish (it		use fish or duck in place of chicken)

NOODLES (MEE) AND RICE (BAI) DISHES

bai sait mowan/sait jeruk	rice topped with fried chicken/pork	loat chat	fried macaroni-like noodle
borbor	rice porridge	mee ganychop	instant noodles made up
borbor sawr	unseasoned rice porridge		from a packet
geautieuv	rice noodles	mee kilo	yellow noodles
geautieuv sop (sait...)	rice noodle in soup (with...)	nom bany jowk	flat white noodle served cold with a curry sauce

SOME COMMON MEAT AND VEGETABLE DISHES

cha bon lai cropmok	fried mixed vegetables	chhnang phnom pleung	thin slices of beef barbecued at the table
cha katnar chia moi pset	fried pak choy with mushrooms		over a charcoal burner

dumlong barang	French fries	jay yior	spring rolls
gee-yan		mowan dort	baked chicken

FRUIT (PELAI CHER)

dum pay-yang bai jew	grape	pelai bporm	apples
jayk	banana	pelai burr	avocado
koulen	lychee	pelai seyree	pear
kroit chhmar	lime	pelai sroegar ne-yak	dragon fruit
kroit pursat	orange	sow maow	rambutan
kroit telong	pomelo	svai	mango
le-mot	sapodilla	tee-ab barang	soursop
lehong	papaya	tee-ab swut	custard apple
manoahs	pineapple	tooren	durian
meeyan	longan	troubike	guava
morkgoot	mangosteen	umpbel	tamarind
ohluck	watermelon		

SNACKS (JUM NEIGH AREHAR), CAKES (NOAM) AND ACCOMPANIMENTS

banh chhaev	savoury pancake stuffed with bean sprouts, pork and shrimp	noam gdam	croissant (literally, crab cake)
		noam pang patey	sandwich made with pâté
bok lehong/som tam	papaya salad	noam pong teeya/	cupcake
chook	lotus seed	noam barang	
grolan	sticky rice in bamboo	noam srooey	cookie
jayk ang	grilled bananas	pong dteer braiy	"thousand-year egg", a
jeruik	pickles		duck's egg preserved in
noam bpaow	dumplings		salt
noam downg dot	coconut cake	pong dteer gowne	duck's egg containing
noam eclair	éclair		unhatched duckling
noam ensaum jayk	sticky rice cakes with banana	prohok	fermented fish paste
		sait kreyuam	dried meat slices
noam gachiey	chive burger		

DRINKS (PAY-SEJEYAT)

coca	Coca-Cola	kumpong	can
dorbp	bottle	siro s	yrup
dtai gdouw	hot lemon tea	sraa bier	beer
kroit chhmar		tuk dhowng	juice of green coconut
dtai grolab	strong local tea	tuk duh	milk
dtai	tea	tuk kork	ice
dtai tuk kork	iced tea with lemon	tuk krolok dak kropmok	mixed fruit shake
kroit chhmar		tuk krolok	fruit shake
ka-fei	coffee	tuk sot	drinking water
kafei kmaow (tuk kork)	black (iced) coffee	tuk sun dike	soya milk
kafei tuk duh gow	white (iced) coffee	tuk tnaowt jew	sugar-palm beer
(tuk kork)		tuk umpow	sugar-cane juice

Glossary

Achar Learned lay-person at a pagoda.

Agni Hindu god of fire.

Amrita Elixir of immortality produced during the Churning of the Ocean of Milk.

APSARA Authority for the Protection and Manage-ment of Angkor and the Region of Siem Reap.

Apsara Celestial dancer of Hindu mythology, born of the Churning of the Ocean of Milk.

ASEAN Association of Southeast Asian Nations.

Asura Demon (from Hindu mythology).

Avalokitesvara See "Lokesvara".

Avatar Incarnation of a Hindu deity.

Banteay Citadel or fortified enclosure.

Barang Slang term meaning French, and often applied to foreigners in general.

Baray Reservoir or Lake.

Bodhisattva One who has attained enlightenment but forgoes nirvana to help others.

Boeung lake.

Brahma Hindu god, often referred to as the Creator.

Brahman Hindu priest.

Buddha One who has achieved enlightenment.

Cham Major ethnic group living in Cambodia and Vietnam, and forming the majority of Muslims in both these countries.

Chedi Structure in which cremated ashes are interred; also called a stupa.

Chunchiet Generic term for the minority hill-tribe groups.

CPP Cambodian People's Party.

Cyclo Three-wheeled bicycle rickshaw.

Deva Male deity.

Devaraja Literally "god who would be king"; the Khmer king, according to the devaraja cult, would fuse with a deity upon his death.

Devata Female deity.

Dvarapala Temple guardians – usually carved figures found flanking entrances to shrines.

FUNCINPEC Front Uni National pour un Cambodge Indépendant, Neutre, Pacifique et Coopératif – the royalist political party.

Ganesh Elephant-headed Hindu god of good fortune and success.

Garuda Mythical creature associated with Vishnu, having the body of a man with the head and feet of a bird.

Gopura Entry pavilion/gatehouse to the sacred area of a temple.

Hamsa Sacred goose associated with Brahma.

Hanuman Monkey god and right-hand man (or, rather, monkey) to Krishna in the *Ramayana*.

Harihara God created from the union of Shiva and Vishnu.

Heng Mythical bird.

Hol Method of weaving; pattern of silk fabric.

Indochina Cambodia, Laos and Vietnam.

Indra Hindu god of the sky.

Jataka Tales recounting the past lives of the Buddha.

Kala Mythical creature with bulbous eyes, claws and no lower jaw.

Khapa Chunchiet basket with shoulder straps, worn on the back.

Khmer The principal indigenous people of Cambodia – the term is often used interchangeably with Cambodian – and also the name of their language.

Koh Island.

Kompong Village on a river or lake.

Krama Cambodian checked scarf.

Krishna The eighth incarnation (avatar) of Vishnu. Often shown playing a flute.

Kurma Second incarnation (avatar) of Vishnu, when he appeared as a giant turtle to support Mount Mandara during the Churning of the Ocean of Milk.

Lakshmi Wife of Vishnu, and the goddess of good fortune and beauty.

Laterite Soft, porous rock that hardens in the sun to a hard, resilient stone.

Leahng Cave.

Linga Phallic-shaped stone representing Shiva.

Lokesvara Cambodian name for the bodhisattva Avalokitesvara, often called "the compassionate".

Mahabharata Hindu epic dealing with the rivalry between the Kaurava and Pandava families.

Mahayana One of the two principal schools of Buddhism, along with Theravada Buddhism.

Makara Mythical sea monster with the body of a crocodile and the trunk of an elephant.

Mandapa Antechamber attached to the central sanctuary tower of a Hindu temple.

Matsya The first incarnation (avatar) of Vishnu, during which he appeared as a giant fish.

Mount Meru Mountain home of the gods, at the centre of the universe in Hindu cosmology.

Mudra Traditional Buddhist poses, widely depicted in Buddhist art, and also in Cambodian classical dancing.

Naga Sacred multi-headed snake, seen as a protector and often depicted along staircases or across causeways.

Nandin Sacred bull, and mount of Shiva.

Narasimha Fourth incarnation (avatar) of Vishnu, as half man-half lion.

Nirvana A state in which desire ends and the cycle of birth, death and rebirth is broken.

NRP Norodom Ranariddh Party.

Pagoda Cambodian wat/temple.

Parvati Hindu goddess and wife of Shiva.

Phnom Mountain or hill.

Phum Village.

Pinpeat Cambodian "orchestra", usually comprising around ten instruments, mainly wind and percussion.

Prasat Sanctuary tower.

Preah A title of spiritual respect, used for gods and holy men; also means "sacred".

Psar Market.

Quincunx Arrangement of five objects with one at the centre and the others at each corner of a rectangle – like the five dots on the face of a die. Used to describe the placing of sanctuary towers in Cambodian architecture.

Rahu Demon with a monster's head and no body, usually depicted swallowing the sun and moon.

Rama Seventh avatar of Vishnu, hero of the *Ramayana*.

Ramayana Hindu epic tale describing the battle between Rama and the demon Ravana.

Ravana The great demon king of Lanka and Rama's principal antagonist in the *Ramayana*.

Reamker Cambodian version of the *Ramayana*.

Remorque Alternative name for Cambodian tuk-tuk.

Sampot Wraparound skirt; by extension, a length of fabric sufficient to make a skirt.

Shiva One of the three principal Hindu gods, often referred to as the Destroyer.

Sita Wife of Rama, who was kidnapped in the *Ramayana*.

Sompeyar Traditional Cambodian gesture of greeting, with hands placed together in a prayer-like gesture.

Spean Bridge.

Srah Pond, lake or reservoir.

SRP Sam Rainsy Party.

State-temple Principal temple built to house the god with whom the devaraja king was associated; a temple-mountain.

Stele Upright stone block inscribed with writing.

Stucco A type of plaster made with lime, and used for decoration, particularly of brick buildings.

Stung Medium-sized river, smaller than a tonle.

Stupa See chedi.

Surya Hindu god of the sun.

Temple In the context of Cambodia, an ancient building or collection of buildings, built by kings to honour ancestors, or to house the devaraja god.

Temple-mountain Temple constructed as a representation of Mount Meru.

Theravada One of the two main schools of Buddhism (along with Mahayana Buddhism) and the dominant form of the religion in Cambodia today.

Tonle Major river.

Toul Low mound.

Tuk-tuk Motorbike-drawn passenger carriage; sometimes called remorque.

UNESCO United Nations Educational, Scientific and Cultural Organization.

UNTAC United Nations Transitional Authority for Cambodia.

UXO Unexploded ordnance.

Valin Monkey king, killed by Rama in the *Ramayana*.

Vasuki The giant naga used to churn the Ocean of Milk.

Vihara Main sanctuary of a wat.

Vishnu One of three principal Hindu gods, the Preserver.

Wat Buddhist monastery and associated religious buildings; often translated into English as "pagoda".

Yaksha Male spirit, depicted with bulging eyes, fangs and a leer; serves as a temple guardian.

Yama God of the Underworld.

Yeak Giant.

Small print and index

Rough Guide credits

Editor: Samantha Cook
Layout: Anita Singh
Cartography: Katie Bennett and Ed Wright
Picture editor: Marta Bescos
Proofreader: Diane Margolis
Managing editor: Keith Drew
Assistant editor: Dipika Dasgupta

Production: Charlotte Cade
Cover design: Nicole Newman, Jess Carter, Anita Singh
Editorial assistant: Rebecca Hallett
Senior pre-press designer: Dan May
Programme manager: Helen Blount
Publisher: Joanna Kirby

Publishing information

This fifth edition published September 2014
Rough Guides Ltd,
80 Strand, London WC2R 0RL
11, Community Centre, Panchsheel Park,
New Delhi 110017, India
Distributed by Penguin Random House
Penguin Books Ltd,
80 Strand, London WC2R 0RL
Penguin Group (USA)
345 Hudson Street, NY 10014, USA
Penguin Group (Australia)
250 Camberwell Road, Camberwell,
Victoria 3124, Australia
Penguin Group (NZ)
67 Apollo Drive, Mairangi Bay, Auckland 1310,
New Zealand
Penguin Group (South Africa)
Block D, Rosebank Office Park, 181 Jan Smuts Avenue,
Parktown North, Gauteng, South Africa 2193
Rough Guides is represented in Canada by Tourmaline
Editions Inc. 662 King Street West, Suite 304, Toronto,
Ontario M5V 1M7
Printed in Malaysia by Vivar Printing Sdn.Bhd

© Rough Guides 2014
Maps © Rough Guides
No part of this book may be reproduced in any form
without permission from the publisher except for the
quotation of brief passages in reviews.
328pp includes index
A catalogue record for this book is available from the
British Library
ISBN: 978-1-40934-881-8
The publishers and authors have done their best to ensure
the accuracy and currency of all the information in **The
Rough Guide to Cambodia**, however, they can accept
no responsibility for any loss, injury, or inconvenience
sustained by any traveller as a result of information or
advice contained in the guide.
1 3 5 7 9 8 6 4 2

```
FSC
www.fsc.org

MIX
Paper from
responsible sources
FSC™ C018179
```

Help us update

We've gone to a lot of effort to ensure that the fifth edition
of **The Rough Guide to Cambodia** is accurate and up-to-
date. However, things change – places get "discovered",
opening hours are notoriously fickle, restaurants and
rooms raise prices or lower standards. If you feel we've got
it wrong or left something out, we'd like to know, and if
you can remember the address, the price, the hours, the
phone number, so much the better.

Please send your comments with the subject line
"**Rough Guide Cambodia Update**" to ⊜mail
@uk.roughguides.com. We'll credit all contributions and
send a copy of the next edition (or any other Rough Guide
if you prefer) for the very best emails.
Find more travel information, connect with fellow
travellers and plan your trip on ⓦroughguides.com

ABOUT THE AUTHORS

Emma Boyle is a Sri Lanka-based travel writer, author and foodie. In addition to the *Rough Guide to Cambodia* she has contributed to the Rough Guides to Australia, India and Southeast Asia on a Budget, researching Borneo, Hong Kong and Macau, Rajasthan and Queensland.

Gavin Thomas has spent much of his life trying to be somewhere else. A regular Rough Guide author and editor for over fifteen years, he has written and contributed to numerous titles including the Rough Guides to Sri Lanka, Dubai, Oman, Rajasthan, India and the forthcoming *Rough Guide to Myanmar*.

Acknowledgements

Emma Boyle: Many thanks to Jake Corke and to Jack Bartholomew at Khiri Travel for sound Cambodia advice. In Phnom Penh, big thanks to Alexis de Suremain and Adi Jaya for assistance; to Ducky for foodie advice; to Stéphane and Dara for helping me fill in the gaps; and to Jo Crisp at Urban Adventures. In Kampot, big shout outs to Stephane and Yan for company and insights, and also to (another) Stephane of Coastal. In Sihanoukville, cheers to The Dive Shop for helping me island hop and to Ana, Mick and the team for travel advice. My appreciation to Owen, Sarah and Luca at Shallow Waters; to the very helpful Martin Leighfield at Chi Phat; and also to Jason Webb in Koh Kong for up-to-date info. Finally, thanks to Rosie and Ian for insightful updates on Phnom Penh's dining scene!

Gavin Thomas: Thanks to everyone in Siem Reap for making my stay in the city so enjoyable, particularly Christian de Boer and Dean McLachlan, and to all the lovely folk at the *Mandalay Inn* and *Shinta Mani*. Thanks also to Darren Swallow in Battambang; Rik in Banlung; Mr T in Stung Treng; Chin Vothea and team in Kompong Thom; and all the many other people of Cambodia who made my journey such a pleasure. At Rough Guides, thanks to my fellow author Emma Boyle for sharing insights and info; to Katie Bennett and Ed Wright for consummate cartography; and especially to my editor Sam Cook, for making enjoyably light work of a very heavy update. And finally to Allison, Laura and Jamie, for sharing Cambodia in spirit, and eating many imaginary spiders along the way.

Readers' updates

Thanks to all the readers who have taken the time to write in with comments and suggestions (and apologies if we've inadvertently omitted or misspelt anyone's name):

Boris Tierno Becerra; Nathalie Brun; Tommy Buehner; Andy Conner; Andrea Decker; John Garratt; Monica Mackaness; Lionel Maitrepierre; James Molony; Mimosa Nguyen; Mo Nguyen; Lena Oruszczak; Eilish Russell Smith; Sandy Schagen; Andrea Zobel.

Photo credits

All photos © Rough Guides except the following:
(Key: t-top; c-centre; b-bottom; l-left; r-right)

p.1 Getty Images: Flickr Open
p.2 4Corners: Günter Gräfenhain
p.4 Alamy Images: Hemis (l); 4Corners: Ben Pipe (r)
p.6 Alamy Images: Nick Rains
p.7 Emma Boyle (t); Getty Images: Michael Toh (c); Latitude: LOOK (b)
p.9 AWL Images: Nigel Pavitt/John Warburton-Lee Photography Ltd
p.10 AWL Images: Ian Trower
p.11 Alamy Images: Tom Vater (tl); 123RF.com: Luciano Mortula (c); Getty Images: Fairfax Media (b)
p.12 Corbis: CHOR SOKUNTHEA/X01072/Reuters (tl); Wendy Kay (tr); Alamy Images: GFC Collection (b)
p.13 Dreamstime.com: Toby Williams (t)
p.14 Alamy Images: Pawel Bienkowski (t); Getty Images: Jeff Hutchens (c); Kraig Lieb (b)
p.15 Dreamstime.com: Donyanedomam (tl); Alamy Images: Hemis (bl)
p.16 Emma Boyle
pp.50–51 Getty Images: Pietro Scozzari
p.73 123RF.com: jackmalipan (tl); AWL Images: Travel Pix Collection (b)

p.93 Dreamstime.com: Kelvintt (t); AWL Images: Travel Pix Collection (b)
p.107 Alamy Images: Neil Setchfield
p.121 Alamy Images: age fotostock (tr); Nick Ledger (b)
p.175 Alamy Images: Steve Vidler (t); AWL Images: Shaun Egan (b)
p.225 Corbis: Kevin R. Morris (t); Alamy Images: John Brown (b)
p.240–241 Alamy Images: Jack Malipan Travel Photography
p.243 Dreamstime.com: Donyanedomam
p.257 Alamy Images: Pawel Bienkowski (t); Mike Finn-Kelcey (b)
p.277 Alamy Images: Jack Malipan Travel Photography (t); Emma Boyle (b)
p.282 Latitude: TTL

Front cover Banteay Srei © SuperStock: imagebroker.net
Back cover Angkor Wat © AWL Images: Nigel Pavitt (t); Ochheuteal Beach, Sihanoukville © AWL Images: Ian Trower (bl); Local crafts near Banlung © Rough Guides: Tim Draper (br)

Index

Maps are marked in grey

Map symbols

The symbols below are used on maps throughout the book

✈	International airport	⊠	Gate/gopura	🐦	Nature reserve/biosphere	▪	Building
✗	Domestic airport	∴	Ruins	🕊	Border crossing	▢	Market
★	Transport stop	⊙	Statue/monument	⌂	Park HQ	◯	Stadium
♦	Point of interest	⌃	Mountain range	⚓	Dock	▦	Park
@	Internet access	▲	Mountain peak		Road	▢	Beach
ⓘ	Tourist information	◠	Cave		Unpaved road	▦	Swamp/ seasonally flooded area
✉	Post office	🌊	Waterfall		Railway		
🕐	Telephone office	▲	Temple		Disused railway		
⊞	Hospital	🏯	Chinese temple		Ferry route		
♟	Museum	♦	National Park		Footpath		

Listings key

- ▪ Accommodation
- ● Eating
- ▪ Drinking and nightlife
- ● Shopping

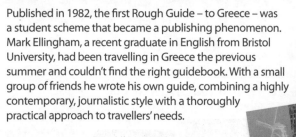